DEAFNESS
AND
COMMUNICATION

ASSESSMENT AND TRAINING

DEAFNESS AND COMMUNICATION

ASSESSMENT AND TRAINING

Edited by

Donald G. Sims, Ph.D.
Research Associate
Department of Communication Research

Gerard G. Walter, Ed.D.
Chairperson
Department of Communication Assessment and Advising

Robert L. Whitehead, Ph.D.
Chairperson
Department of Communication Research

NATIONAL TECHNICAL INSTITUTE FOR THE DEAF
ROCHESTER INSTITUTE OF TECHNOLOGY
ROCHESTER, NEW YORK

WILLIAMS & WILKINS
Baltimore/London

Made in the United States of America

Library of Congress Cataloging in Publication Data

Main entry under title:

Deafness and communication.

    Includes index.
    1. Deaf—Means of communication. 2. Deafness. I. Sims, Donald G. II. Walter, Gerard G. III. Whitehead, Robert L.
HV2471.D4   362.4′283   81-14686
ISBN 0-683-07755-4   AACR2

Composed and printed at the
Waverly Press, Inc.
Mt. Royal and Guilford Aves.
Baltimore, MD 21202, U.S.A.

FOREWORD

Severe hearing impairment, particularly when present at birth or soon thereafter, threatens ready communication within family, workplace, and community. This has always been the case.

- What families do, how families live, and what families say have changed and continue to change.
- Where people work, the nature of work, and the communication requirements of the workplace have changed and continue to change.
- Where people live, how people relate to immediate and distant communities, and extent of participation have changed and continue to change.

The foregoing conditions, in constant flux, differentially influence hearing-impaired individuals and at the same time present special challenges to those significant others who intervene on their behalf.

Verbal communication, whether in spoken, written, fingerspelled, or signed form, is exclusively humankind. Its acquisition and continuous refinement, naturally achieved in people with intact hearing, come only with special assistance in severely hearing-impaired individuals.

Existing literature is replete with ingenious techniques and procedures aimed at minimizing and/or eliminating primary communication effects and secondary socioeducational consequences of auditory disabilities. With notable exceptions, these attempts have been largely intuitive, anecdotal in form, and cross-sectional (one-time efforts) in character. Early severe hearing impairment clearly has not responded to the "quick fix."

The reality of the National Technical Institute for the Deaf (NTID) provides the platform for the current effort. Its clinical and research scientists recognize the need for sustained organized inquiry into the many facets of human communication and its importance to severely hearing-impaired people. Editors Sims, Walter, and Whitehead have been successful in pulling together results of systematic research studies in communication conducted at NTID and have incorporated correlated work of others from institutions having an abiding interest in the problem.

These efforts take advantage of state-of-the-art measurement devices and techniques used in varied disciplines, such as speech science, audiology, physics, experimental psychology, linguistics, education, speech pathology, and neurophysiology. Each study represents advance in our understanding. As a group these studies

- Add scientific rigor to a literature rich in inventiveness and intuition.
- Represent, as a result of the existence of NTID, an emergence of continuity and systematic scientific inquiry into the multidimensional communication problems confronting severely hearing-impaired people.

Apropos of this noteworthy publication, "He has half the deed done, who has made a beginning"; and this indeed augurs well for improvements in the assessment and treatment of children, youth, and adults beset with severe hearing impairment.

Robert Frisina, Ph.D.
Vice-President
Rochester Institute of Technology
Rochester, New York

PREFACE

The motivating factors for producing a text can be the result of personal, collegial, financial, or intellectual needs. This present volume originated because of a collegial relationship among the editors and a professional need to have a text that addresses the communicative handicapping effects of severe to profound hearing impairment. It has only been during the past decade that the disciplines associated with hearing impairment have begun to address communication problems in an integrated manner. As a result, we have attempted to synthesize into the structure of this book the disciplines of linguistics, speech, audiology, and education. It is our feeling that each of these disciplines provides unique insights into remediating the handicapping effects of severe to profound hearing impairment. But instruction and development of communicative competence is the bottom line, and good instruction, while it must be scientific, is also largely still an art.

As a result there is a broad range of tones to the chapters in this book, from the more formal research review chapters to those which emphasize application of assessment and instruction to the hearing-impaired population. We have tried, in each of the discipline areas, to provide for a balance between review of research and application. In order to accomplish this, the book contains chapters that review current practice in each of the areas and chapters which offer strategies for diagnosing and instructing. In addition, we believe it important, because of Public Law 94–142, to provide special discussions of this legislation as it applies to communication skill training and the providing of support services in integrated educational settings. As such, the providing of support services in integrated settings focuses on providing for the hearing-impaired person not being able to receive and produce an intelligible signal through the usual channels of communication used by hearing persons.

It is probably this belief in the need to bring together in one place "state-of-the-art" information about communication of the severely to profoundly hearing-impaired, coupled with the emphasis on mainstreaming, that has been the strongest motivator for producing the book. As a result, we intend that the primary user of the text will be those individuals schooled in one of the disciplines commonly associated with hearing impairment but who need upgrading in order to carry on responsibilities defined by a student's individual educational program. Thus, the book is for the speech therapist, English teacher, or audiologist who has responsibility for severely hearing-impaired students in terms of their communication training. This text should provide a good overview of the relevant literature and practices in coping with the special problems offered by this population of handicapped individuals.

Donald Sims
Gerard Walter
Robert Whitehead

ACKNOWLEDGMENTS —————

The editors express their sincere gratitude to the National Technical Institute for the Deaf (NTID) at the Rochester Institute of Technology, which promotes and encourages multidisciplinary interaction among professionals and which thus initiated this book and provided many of the resources necessary for the satisfactory completion of it. Appreciation is given to Dr. Kathleen Crandall, Associate Dean and Director of the Communication Program, NTID, for her continual support of this entire effort, as well as for her own contributed chapter. To all the authors who, for the most part, diligently met the editorial timelines and who devoted substantial time and effort to the completion of their manuscripts, grateful appreciation is also given. Recognition is made of the valuable contributions by Dr. Nancy S. McGarr of Haskins Laboratories, New Haven, Connecticut, and by Mrs. Brenda Whitehead of NTID, and of the advice and assistance of Dr. Mary Jo Osberger and Dr. Noel Matkin. A special thanks goes to the NTID Word Processing Center, without whose efforts the manuscript would never have been typed and to the NTID Media Department whose talents and perseverance resulted in the successful completion of the artwork. Sincere gratitude is given to the government of the United States of America, who, through approval of Public Law 89-36, has provided for the establishment and maintenance of the National Technical Institute for the Deaf.

D.G.S.
G.G.W.
R.L.W.

CONTRIBUTORS ──────────────

Richard L. Baldwin, Ed.D.
Special Education Consultant
State of Michigan, Department of Education
Lansing, Michigan
Chapter 13

Sidney M. Barefoot, M.S.
Chairperson, Communication Instruction
   Department III
National Technical Institute for the Deaf
Rochester Institute of Technology
Rochester, New York
Chapter 14

Joseph H. Bochner, M.A.
Coordinator of Test Development
Department of Communication Assessment
   and Advising
National Technical Institute for the Deaf
Rochester Institute of Technology
Rochester, New York
Chapter 7

Judith L. Braeges, M.S.
Speech Pathologist
Center for Communication Research
Rochester, New York
Chapter 15

Mary E. Campbell, Ph.D.
Supervisor
Monroe County Program for Hearing-
   Impaired Children
Ida, Michigan
Chapters 13 and 26

Kathleen Eilers Crandall, Ph.D.
Associate Dean
Division of Communication Programs
National Technical Institute of Technology
Rochester, New York
Chapter 23

Carol L. De Filippo, Ph.D.
Research Associate
Department of Communication Research
National Technical Institute for the Deaf
Rochester Institute of Technology
Rochester, New York
Chapter 3

Richard Dirst, M.S.
Executive Director
Registry of Interpreters for the Deaf

Silver Spring, Maryland
Chapter 24

Alinda M. Drury, Ph.D.
Reading Laboratory Specialist
Communication Instruction Department I
National Technical Institute for the Deaf
Rochester Institute of Technology
Rochester, New York
Chapter 22

Richard P. Durity, M.A.
Audiologist
Communication Instruction Department I
National Technical Institute for the Deaf
Rochester Institute of Technology
Rochester, New York
Chapter 19

Susan D. Fischer, Ph.D.
Research Associate
Department of Communication Research
National Technical Institue for the Deaf
Rochester Institute of Technology
Rochester, New York
Chapters 1 and 6

Jaclyn Gauger, M.A.
Coordinator of Assessment
Department of Communication Assessment
   and Advising
National Technical Institute for the Deaf
Rochester Institute of Technology
Rochester, New York
Chapter 20

Nancy Hatfield, Ph.D.
Experimental Education Unit
University of Washington
Seattle, Washington
Chapter 12

Robert Hoffmeister, Ph.D.
Associate Professor
Division of Reading and Language
   Development
Boston University
Boston, Massachusetts
Chapter 22

Robert A. Houde, Ph.D.
Director
Center for Communications Research
Rochester, New York
Chapters 15 and 21

Marjorie Adamson Jacobs
Consultant, Communication Programs
National Technical Institute for the Deaf
Rochester Institute for the Deaf
Rochester, New York
Chapter 18

Ann K. Lieberth, M.A.
Assistant Professor
Department of Speech and Theatre Arts
Nazareth College
Rochester, New York
Chapter 16

James J. Mahshie, Ph.D.
Assistant Professor
Department of Audiology
Gallaudet College
Washington, D.C.
Chapter 5

Dale E. Metz, Ph.D.
Research Associate
Department of Communication Research
National Technical Institute for the Deaf
Rochester Institute of Technology
Rochester, New York
Chapter 5

Mary Pat Moeller, M.S.
Coordinator of Aural Rehabilitation
The Boys Town Institute for Communication
   Disorders in Children
Omaha, Nebraska
Chapter 8

Ila Parasnis, Ph.D.
Research Associate
Department of Communication Research
National Technical Institute for the Deaf
Rochester Institute of Technology
Rochester, New York
Chapter 4

Charles W. Parkins, Ph.D.
Associate Professor, Otolaryngology
University of Rochester, Medical Center
Rochester, New York
Chapter 21

Marietta M. Paterson, M.Sc.
University Lecturer
School of Human Communication Disorders
McGill University

Montreal, Canada
Chapter 17

James M. Pickett, Ph.D.
Director, Sensory Communication Research
   Laboratory
Gallaudet College
Washington, D.C.
Chapter 2

Sally G. Revoile, Ph.D.
Research Associate
Sensory Communication Research
   Laboratory
Gallaudet College
Washington, D.C.
Chapter 2

Roberta Moreau Robbins, M.A.
Audiologist
Deer Valley School District
Phoenix, Arizona
Chapter 20

Vincent J. Samar, Ph.D.
Research Associate
Department of Communication Research
National Technical Institute for the Deaf
Rochester Institute of Technology
Rochester, New York
Chapter 4

Donald G. Sims, Ph.D.
Research Associate
Department of Communication Research
National Technical Institute for the Deaf
Rochester Institute of Technology
Rochester, New York
Chapter 9

Joanne D. Subtelny, Ph.D.
Professor, Communication Programs
National Technical Institute for the Deaf
Rochester Institute of Technology
Rochester, New York
Chapter 10

Gerard G. Walter, Ed.D.
Chairperson
Department of Communication Assessment
   and Advising
National Technical Institute for the Deaf
Rochester Institute of Technology
Rochester, New York
Chapter 11

Robert L. Whitehead, Ph.D.
Chairperson, Department of Communication
  Research
National Technical Institute for the Deaf
Rochester Institute of Technology
Rochester, New York
Chapter 5

Jimmie Joan Wilson, M.A.
Coordinator, Tutor/Notetaker Training
National Technical Institute for the Deaf
Rochester Institute of Technology
Rochester, New York
Chapter 25

Anna Witter-Merithew
6639 Barcliff Drive
Charlotte, North Carolina
Chapter 24

CONTENTS

How Do You Dance without Music?

SHANNY MOW
National Theatre of the Deaf
Waterford, Connecticut

My name is Sam. Sometimes I'm called Silent Sam, a tag I loathe out of prejudice—both mine and the bestower's. Besides it is misleading, since I make more noise sipping my soup than the guy at the next table, who is not deaf but wishes he were every time I take a particularly enthusiastic spoonful.

This is my story, of how I live through a day and the problems I face as a deaf human being, as told to and written by another deaf human being who is fortunate to have the words I do not.

I would be presumptuous to claim that my problems are typical of all deaf persons, or that I qualify as a "typical deaf person," whatever that is. There are prelingually and postlingually deaf individuals. There are the college-educated and the illiterate. The hard of hearing and the deaf. There are those with deafness plus other handicaps. You may say each is a breed apart. Each has problems of his own.

In a style that belies my blue-collar job, my recorder has set down what I think, what I believe, and what I go through.

I can dance better than I can write. Seeing me on the dance floor, hearing people always ask, "How do you dance without music?" "Actually I don't, I dance to vibrations," I tell them. One night I realized I had been giving an incomplete answer to this question. Now I tell them, ". . . the vibrations of life."

* * *

"But you can't see a thing from the driver's side," the Volkswagen dealer explains. Sam reads the hurried scribbling, and for a minute fingers his new driver's license. Under RE-STRICTIONS, it reads LEFT AND RIGHT REAR VIEW MIRRORS.

Ten dollars goodbye for a right rear view mirror that doesn't give you the view you don't need. Since when did the bureaucrats at the Motor Vehicles decide deafness is a luxury? Be grateful that they let you drive at all?

Wearily he takes the pad and writes, "Install it anyway. I'll be back."

In the noon sun he squints but still can make out the drug store two blocks away. Carefully he looks left, then right and left again and crosses the street. Midway he pauses to look right again.

A lot can happen in two blocks. A lost motorist yelling for directions. A nervous smoker asking for a match. A friendly stranger with sinister motives wanting to talk. A policeman blowing his whistle and suspecting you for a fugitive when you walk on. A dog biting from behind. A runaway grocery cart hitting from the blind side. You grow weary and wary of such people who, at the sight of you pointing to your ear, always seem to forget suddenly their purpose for approaching you. As for whistle-blowing policemen, biting dogs and runaway carts, you develop your own brand of oriental fatalism.

Inside the drug store Sam asks for a package of Salem cigarettes, pronouncing the brand name as distinctly as he can. The clerk gives him an odd look, then reaches down the counter. Her hand reappears with the Salems. He breathes easier.

You feel like a poker player who is also a compulsive bluffer. Mervin Garretson has explained why he switched brands, rather than fight. As long as you pronounce something safe like Salem, not Chesterfield, there is little danger of receiving cough syrup instead. You can never relax when you cannot hear what you speak. Not even if you've been up to your ears in speech training. Maybe you can, in front of a trained ear, someone who is familiar with the "deaf accent," but unfortunately is not always around.

Sam also selects a Chap Stick and a roll of Life Savers. The clerk says something which he can at best only guess. His pocket feels heavy with change, but he reaches for his wallet, takes out a dollar bill and hands it to her.

The tension is even worse when you attempt to lip-read. The name of this game is "Figure Out the Fingerprint." Like the whorls on his fingertips, each person's lips are different and moved in a peculiar way of their own. When young, you build confidence as you guess correctly "ball," "fish," "top," and "shoe" on your teacher's lips. This confidence doesn't last. As soon as you discover there are more than four words in the dictionary, it evaporates. Seventy percent of the words when appearing on the lips are no more than blurs. Lipreading is a precious and cruel art which rewards a few who have mastered it and tortures the many who have tried and failed.

The lunch hour is almost over. Sam drives back to the plant, ignoring the new chrome outside his Volkswagen. Several workers nod or wave at him as he makes his way to his workbench. He waves back, but today he feels no desire to join them for the usual banter that precedes the job at hand.

These are good guys. We get along. They like you, even respect you. You laugh at their jokes and fake punches to their jaws. Yet there remains an invisible, insurmountable wall between us. No man can become completely a part of another man's world. He is never more eloquently reminded of this impossibility than when there is no way he can talk with the other man.

Without a word, the foreman nods. Sam scribbles down another question. The foreman nods again. Still another question. More nodding, this time with marked annoyance. Sam then knows it is pointless to continue.

Communication is the father of human relationships. From infancy a person learns to speak at a rate closely synchronized with his thinking processes. Deviation from this timing between thinking and speaking upsets his natural flow of thought. He loses his tongue or forces out words which sound so artificial that they disgust him. As a deaf person, you sympathize with this mental block in the hearing person who tries to speak to you. In fact, you expect it. For this reason, just or not, you always wonder why he takes the trouble to speak to you.

You feel no less helpless in your search for meaningful communication. When the hearing person does not know, as he usually does not, sign language, the only recourse lies with the pencil and pad. Here your language defeats you before you begin. You have been deprived of the natural process of learning language, i.e., through hearing. English is a language so complicated and inconsistent that its mastery is for you as elusive as the pot of gold at the end of the rainbow. Gamely you pick up the pencil only to find the hearing person hung-up in his own way: poor penmanship, bad spelling, or some other reasons known only to him. Inhibition reduces communication to a superficial level, a most unsatisfactory relationship to both parties. Speech and lipreading? Try discussing Kazantzakis, or any subject, limiting yourself to the thirty percent of the words that can be lip-read with no guarantee that there would be none of the words you have not seen before.

Tired as he is, Sam cannot go home yet. He remembers he has a couple of errands to perform. He surveys the traffic. It is getting bad. He tries but cannot think of a short cut to the other side of town where Paul lives. He shifts the gears, passing one roadside booth after another, each displaying the familiar Bell symbol.

His finger is tiring. From pressing continuously the door button that is rigged to a light bulb inside. He searches through a window, then another. No sign of life except for the parakeet. Refraining from kicking the door, he hastily writes down the message, inserts it in a crack in the door, and returns to his car. Sweat streaks down his forehead and he wipes it away. Hopefully he eyes the door once more.

How soon will you get Paul's reply? Will the note still be there when he comes home? When will he come home? He could not know you were driving down. You took your chance and lost. An alternate to this external courtship with chance is to plan ahead. Carry out, no wavering. Build a reputation as a man of his word. Your word determines the kind of relationship you will enjoy with your fellowmen. It does not have the freedom and flexibility made possible by the telephone with its sanctuary of distance, so dear to the hearing person at the eleventh hour. When you have committed yourself, by mail or in a previous visit, to come to a party, you come. Even if you are feeling particularly misanthropic that night. You may excuse yourself with a few days advance notice, again by mail or in person, but you have to be mighty convincing when you explain to the host that Jeane Dixon has divulged the future to you—that on the night of the party you would feel terribly antisocial; therefore, it would be wise if you stay away.

"Your number is 48," the girl behind the counter smiles sweetly and turns to the next customer. Sam hesitates, then shrugs and finds a seat close to the TAKE-OUT counter.

Bright kid, this girl. She reacted as if there were nothing out of the ordinary when a customer grabs the order pad and places his own order. No doubt she is also a great believer in miracles, that somehow your deafness will disappear before your pizza is ready and the number, whatever it is, announced on the loudspeaker.

The pizza tastes cold but good. Sam settles back and watches with affection as Brian and Brenda finish their portions. He waits until Jane returns with the coffee before waving for the family's attention. "Want to go to the lake next week?" he more announces, then asks with his hands and fingers. Shrieks of delight answer him, unheard.

In group discussions where you alone are deaf, you do not exist. Because you cannot present your ideas through a medium everyone is accustomed to, you are not expected, much less asked, to contribute them. Because you are deaf, they turn deaf. Just do what your parents, friends, fellow workers—who can hear—tell you; you will know soon enough as we go along. Yours is not to reason why; yours is to do and die, silently. Does no one realize that security comes from knowing what you will be doing next, knowing what to expect? Does no one agree that much of the joy of performing an activity stems from the realization that you had a hand in planning it?

"Yes, you may bring Barb and Jo along," Sam smiles as Brenda hugs the dolls and skips happily out of the room. To his seven-year-old son, he says, "Brian, tell me, what can we do at the lake?"

You never forget that frightening experience. When you were Brian's age. You were left out of the dinner table conversation. It is called mental isolation. While everyone is talking or laughing, you are as far away as a lone Arab on a desert that stretches to every horizon. Everyone and everything are a mirage; you see them but you cannot touch or become a part of them. You thirst for connection. You suffocate inside but you cannot tell anyone of this horrible feeling. You do not know how to. You get the impression nobody

understands or cares. You have no one to share your childish enthusiasm and curiosity, no sympathetic listener who can give meaning to your world and the desert around you. You are not granted even the illusion of participation. You are expected to spend fifteen years in the straitjacket of speech training and lipreading. You learn not how to communicate, only how to parrot words, never to speak your own. Meantime your parents never bother to put in an hour a day to learn the sign language or some part of it. One hour out of twenty-four that can change a lifetime for you. Instead, the most natural form of expression for you is dismissed as vulgar. It has never occurred to them that communication is more than method or talk. That it is a sense of belonging, an exchange of understanding, a mutual respect for the other's humanity.

The kids have been put in bed. Sam pours a third cup of coffee for himself. Jane is doing the dishes, and he decides to get his pipe from the living room. He cannot find it and returns to the kitchen.

Your eyes are your contact with the world, but there is only so much you can see. Seeing is waiting. From the living room you cannot ask Jane about the pipe. In the kitchen you cannot ask while she is washing the carving knife. She cannot answer until the knife is safely put down. You must stop with half of the shaving lather still on your face to answer how you want your eggs done. Then Jane must hurry back to the kitchen before the waffle burns. You always have laryngitis when you call Brian and Brenda to supper. It is rude to notice the fly in your pie while Jane is talking. You must walk across the room and touch her shoulder if you want her attention. Or stamp on the floor and probably ruin her mood or concentration for the next half hour.

The man on the tube looks as if he has a goldfish flipping inside his mouth. He refuses to leave; another joins him, mouthing likewise. Sam sighs and reaches for the channel dial. In a split second the Shakespeare Special is replaced by an undersea scene.

A big fish approaches the diver. Barracuda? It is going to attack the diver, or is it? Why does it hesitate, then swim off? What did the diver do that was not visibly obvious? Would he be attacked had he acted otherwise? But is the damn fish some kind of shark? The commentator supplies all the answers, but they pass through you as if you were a sieve. Desperately you grab for what you can, but you cannot see what you cannot hear. A wealth of information, both practical and exotic, escapes you daily. Television, movies and the stage hold limited meaning for you. Radio, phonographs, tape recorders, and loudspeakers have none. Then to what do you turn for information? The nearby human being is too unreliable. So you have only books. You read twice, thrice, four times, as much as the average person to know just as much. Slowly you close the cultural gap that is widening even faster by the incredible speed and ease of modern media.

Sam is alone is the living room, illuminated by a single lamp. Jane has long since retired, but he himself feels no urgency for sleep. From the coffee table he picks up Remarque's *All Quiet on the Western Front*. Hardly has he opened the book before he reaches for the dictionary.

What are haricot beans? Messtin? Dollop? Voracity? Already four words out of your vocabulary, all from the first paragraph on the first page! You read this classic as an adult while others read it in their teens. You are lucky you can recognize the words as English. For some deaf adults they might well be reading the original version in German. Others with a little more reading ability plod through page by page, this laborious effort dimming the brilliant power of the message and the brutal grace of the story. In addition, there are unfamiliar idioms, colloquialisms, and expressions. The difficult language which you have never mastered makes for difficult reading. As if it is not enough, you lack the background information necessary for comprehension of the subject. Scratch out another—or your last—reliable source of information.

Finishing a chapter, he puts the book down and closes the edge-torn dictionary. He rubs his eyes and stretches his arms. The *Tribune* comes in his field of vision, and he opens it to the classified ads section.

Maybe there's something you overlooked earlier tonight. . . . Yes, here's a possibility. . . . Damn it, no address, just a lousy phone number. . . . Have you enough of the job at the plant! Eight years of brain-numbing drudgery. Is one such a coward not to quit? When you contemplate a job change, you are not half as concerned about the new location, working conditions, fringe benefits, school for your children, new friends, etc., as you are about basic survival and a decent income that will permit your family to live in relative comfort. You don't move on because you itch for a change of scenery or because your boss doesn't like the length of your hair. You do not doubt your ability to change jobs, to perform the job or to keep the job, only whether you would be given a chance to prove this ability, to convince the prospective but skeptical employer that ability is all that counts. You can't write or read well. You can't speak. How do you sell yourself, by drawing pictures? All things being equal, the job goes to the applicant whose ears do not just hold up his eyeglasses.

Against the vast black nothingness, a fleck of light winks here and there, like a distant planet greeting a lost traveler. Watching through the window, Sam suddenly realizes how much he loves the city.

In one city you dare not hope for many job openings, any kind, where the deafness of a worker is treated as irrelevant or routine. You may have to cross a dozen city limits, perhaps half a continent, before you find one. Then the lesser factors take on new importance. Such as Brian and Brenda's new playmates. The slow and often painful acceptance. The children are still learning to live with their and your handicap. Then there is the search for housing in want ads which seem to conspire against you, listing only phone numbers for the most desirable and reasonably priced units. And the orientation of local merchants and new neighbors to your deafness. And the deaf population in the new city which may turn out to consist entirely of your family. You are well settled here. Need you push your luck?

Slowly he folds the paper and gets up. He switches the lamp off and walks cautiously down the dark hall. His hands move along the wall, keeping in contact for balance which was affected when he became deaf. At the door of his bedroom he pauses. As his eyes adjust to the darkness, he can make out the features of Jane's face.

Sam, do you love her or are you merely fond of her? You married her because she was available, the best of a limited lot. Probably she had said "Yes" for the same reason. It has always been this way: You don't have a ghost of a choice. Education, ambition, job, wife, friends, recreation, and sometimes religion. For you, choice is a limited word. You are the novelist's delight, the lonely, soul-searching character who has never found what he seeks in life. Unlike the perennial wanderer, you know which road you want to travel, but you keep running into one roadblock or another. The day you lost your hearing your universe shrank many times over; your power of choice in a world of sound is drastically reduced. Thrown in the storm of silence, you seek refuge among your own kind and become a part of a microcosm which you are not sure you want. It is a closed society whose bond among members is founded not on mutual interests or intellectual equality but on a common desire for escape from the "cruel outside world," for communication although this communication frequently turns out to be an illusion. It breeds dependence, stagnation, pettiness, and finally boredom. It is a microcosm that unmercifully tries your individuality. You either surrender to tribal conformity or return to the other world. Or live on the fringes of both worlds, never to fully accept one and never to be fully accepted by the other.

He tosses in the bed. Unable to sleep, he stares at the far corner of the room. Jane stirs but is still again. He moves his hands to the back of his head and folds them.

Are you indulging in excessive self-pity? Brood and brood until there is no objectivity left in you? Is that why psychologists analyze you as being self-centered, immature, suspicious and narrowminded, always self-conscious and defensive about your inability to hear? An unhealthy mental attitude? Or shall we call it inevitable? This outlook is not a product of deafness per se but of a general public attitude to, or ignorance of, the nature of deafness and the problems it creates.

Imagine yourself in a living room full of people who all know what is going on. Except you, who inquire and are answered with a polite smile which only underlines your helplessness. Everyone seems relaxed, enjoying himself. Except you, who are uneasily waiting for something to happen which makes sense to you. Everyone chats congenially with one another. Except you, who receive more polite smiles and furtive glances. Everyone tells something hilarious and laughs. Except you, who

debate with yourself whether you would appear less ridiculous going along and laughing at God-knows-what or remaining stoic, thus making your deafness even more conspicuous in an atmosphere already made uneasy by your presence.

Leaving the room means crawling back into your "deaf shell" from which you seek escape in the first place. A triumph of futility. So you stay on, making the best of your dilemma, waiting, hoping for the breakthrough when someone will realize you are indeed human. And tolerance may yet become acceptance.

You find it difficult to forget for a moment you are deaf when you are continuously reminded by an unwitting public. You are daily subjected to this public's unpredictable reaction and to the necessity of proving yourself. A lifetime of unending strain. After all this, can you kid yourself about not becoming oversensitive in your human relationships?

You know you are getting a raw deal, but you do not know whom to blame. Public ignorance is a faceless enemy against whom you have no weapon, only your battle-weary ingenuity. How do you get a society to accept you when it is ruled by this enemy? It can be educated to show understanding, compassion, but it does not always listen. Sometimes you wonder why it seems to be afraid of you.

People are, however, not your *raison d'être*. Each unpleasant episode with them is an unavoidable skirmish. They represent only obstacles in your battle. The objective of the battle is a life in which you can sing between dejections, laugh between tears, and dream between nightmares. Breathe between repressions, love between prejudices, and grow between defeats. And, by God, you are making it.

Peace settles over Sam. He falls asleep with his arms around Jane.

Part I
Introduction

An Orientation to Language

SUSAN D. FISCHER, PH.D.

This chapter is designed to introduce you to what a linguist does and, in particular, to what language, speech, and communication have to do with each other. I shall begin with some basic definitions of terms and then discuss examples from various forms of communication; I shall include languages you may not know, as well as languages you may already know.

This chapter is written from the point of view of a *linguist*, someone who deals with the analysis of language. Linguists do many different things, and I shall touch on some of them in this chapter. Basically, linguists are concerned with language as a phenomenon of the human mind. The way they go about their work may seem a bit strange at first, but their methods can be applied to many different areas of analysis, not just language (Jackendoff and Lehrdahl, 1980; Hymes, 1968). A linguist is *not* necessarily someone who knows a lot of different languages, though to be a good linguist, it helps to be aware of the structure of many different languages. Rather, a linguist is someone who analyzes language; perhaps s/he will analyze a particular language in detail in order to elucidate language structure in general.

LANGUAGE AND COMMUNICATION

How can we define language? A first approximation might be that language is communication. This is an inadequate definition at best. We can clarify this inadequacy by looking at various forms of communication and comparing them to language in order to see what language has that other forms of communication may lack.

"Well, then," the Cat went on, "you see a dog growls when it's angry, and wags its tail when it's pleased. Now *I* growl when I'm pleased, and wag my tail when I'm angry...."

Lewis Carroll
Alice in Wonderland

The Cheshire Cat has pointed out a few interesting facts about language and communication in this passage. First, we see that when a cat or dog wags its tail, it is communicating with whoever is watching and can interpret its action; in the case of a dog, it is communicating that it is happy; in the case of the cat, it is communicating that it is angry. Is that language? The tail-wagging does have one thing in common with language, in that the same behavior can mean something different depending on who is doing it. This is similar to the idea that the same grouping of sounds in two spoken languages can have very different meanings; e.g., the sounds which we write in English as "bye-bye" mean something like marketing in Japanese. But why is the tail-wagging not a language?

One thing that makes tail-wagging different from language is that it is not *intentional*; i.e., the dog or cat is wagging its tail on an automatic basis. Another difference between tail-wagging and language is that the dog or cat could not, for example, combine different sorts of tail-wagging to produce a different or more highly structured meaning. Further, the dog or cat could not use its tail-wagging to talk about having felt happy or angry the previous day; i.e., the tail-wagging cannot refer to something that is not physically present, either in space or in time. Tail-wagging is limited; the dog or cat cannot say anything else. It is also situation-bound; one has to be there in order to know what the cat or dog is "saying."

Another example of something that is a kind of communication but is not language is discussed in van Lawick-Goodall (1971). She found that when a female chimpanzee enters her fertile period, her genital opening swells up and turns a bright pink. This serves as a signal to the male chimpanzee that she is physically ready for copulation. Obviously, something is being communicated, but we certainly would not call that language. Like the tail-wagging, it is not intentional; a female chimpanzee's genitalia may turn pink but she refuses the advances of the male. Another difference between this form of communication and language is that it is not learned; without any exposure to other chimpanzees, a female chimp will still start turning pink on a regular basis when she reaches sexual maturity. As with the tail-wagging, the female chimp wouldn't be able to combine two different shades of pink to get a new message.

Combining two existing elements to make a new message is exactly what we do when we communicate using language. We can take old words, which we may have used before individually but not together, and make a new idea. Almost no animal can do that. If I utter a sentence like (1),

(1) Yesterday I saw a green giraffe with the measles.

I assure you that before writing (1), I had never used it before. Yet you understood exactly what I meant. It may not relate to the real world, but something in your head makes it possible to understand a novel sentence like (1), where by *novel* I mean something that has never been uttered before—a sentence could be mundane and still novel. When you think about it, it's rather an amazing feat that humans can do what even the smartest computer cannot. It is even more amazing when you think that if, say, English is your first language, nobody ever sat down and taught it to you, except for a few rules of politeness ("Say 'thank you' to the nice lady"). You could not learn language by memorizing sentences, since there is an infinite number of them.

Before we return to the human realm permanently, let us look at one more example of animal communication which is some respects is language-like. Karl von Frisch studied the behavior of bees, and he found that bees were able to communicate to other bees the direction, distance, and quality of a source of nectar, by performing a complicated "dance." The language-like elements of the bee dance are that first, there is an infinite number of messages. Second, the bees are able to "talk" about things that are not immediately present physically and temporally. However, important as these elements are, the bee dance is still not language. Why? First, the bees can only discourse on one topic: the source of nectar; they could not, for example, say "Gee, it's such a nice day, why don't we go have a picnic instead of going out for the nectar." In addition, bees are incapable of lying—one wouldn't find a bee misleading the other bees in order to get more nectar for itself. By contrast, we can use language to talk about *anything*, including language itself. Furthermore, we can use language to talk about things in a variety of ways. As Chomsky (1959) has pointed out, if I show you a pencil and ask you to say something, you might respond in any of the following ways:

(2) That's a pencil.
(3) Oh, I forgot to bring my pencil.
(4) That reminds me, my mother (who is very very skinny) is coming to visit today, and I had better clean up the bathroom before she arrives.

And so forth. Unlike animal communication, language is not situation-bound, as (2)–(4) show. Except for certain social rituals, we can never expect the exact response to a question or a situation, and although we may be able to control the subject matter to a certain extent, the form and the content of the response are, potentially, infinitely variable. As users of language, we can invent, we can lie, and we can do many things with language that we cannot do with other kinds of communication.

Language has an infinite capacity for expression and comprehension. One of the key reasons why this is so is that unlike many forms of communication, language is *systematic*. To a linguist, the most amazing fact about language is that we are able to both produce and understand sentences that we have never heard or seen before. With a potentially infinite variety of sentences, we have to deal with them with a brain whose capacity, though large, is still finite; it is thus necessary to, as Wilhelm von Humboldt put it over 100 years ago, make infinite use of finite means. Linguists account for this ability to make infinite use of finite means by positing a model of our linguistic knowledge which we call a *grammar*. Linguists say that inside our heads there must be something that acts like this grammar or model of linguistic knowledge. This sort of grammar is very different from the kind of grammar you may have studied in school. A linguist's grammar is a model of your intuitions and knowledge about your language. Linguists write rules to *describe* that knowledge and intuitive ability. They are not at all concerned with *pre*scribing or *pro*scribing, with telling you what you are supposed to say or not supposed to say; they are concerned with accounting for the regularities of what you actually say. These are rules that nobody ever

taught you. For example, what is wrong with utterance (5)?

(5) * I want that you leave.
(Linguists use an asterisk (*) to indicate that an utterance is ungrammatical.)

If you are a native speaker, you know that there is something strange about (5), even if you might have trouble articulating what is wrong. Nobody ever told you not to say things like (5). You learned on your own that it is much better to say something like (6):

(6) I want you to leave.

Notice that you have no trouble understanding the intended meaning of (5); you simply recognize it as incorrect. The rule for English is that verbs like *want* require that sentences subordinated to them be in the infinitive. This is not the case for all languages. For example, in French, the translation of (5) is grammatical, while the translation of (6) is ungrammatical, exactly the opposite:

(7) Je veux que tu partes.
(8) * Je te veux partir.

To summarize, then, we can say that language is a systematic form of communication which enables its users to talk about anything anywhere according to a system of grammatical rules which are learned and internalized without being inculcated. Someone with language can imagine, invent, lie, or persuade and can communicate anything without difficulty with anyone who shares the same language.

This is the ideal situation. But many "unideal" factors can intervene. For example, a description of our knowledge of a language would permit us to form sentences which exceed our memory capacity. Further, the "rules" of language that a linguist posits are in no way literally followed by a human being actually producing and understanding utterances in real time. Even when we *know* what we are supposed to say, we make mistakes (we also make mistakes when we perceive language) due to external factors, such as fatigue, noise, or preoccupation with other matters. The study of linguistic performance (i.e., what we really *do* when we produce and understand utterances) as opposed to linguistic competence (what we know about our language) is called *psycholinguistics*. In terms of the language spoken in the environment, hearing-impaired people have difficulties in both competence *and* performance; i.e., many hearing-impaired people will have a knowledge of English that differs a great deal from the knowledge that a native, hearing speaker would have. Most hearing-impaired people also have some difficulty producing and understanding spoken English—this may be due to an interaction between difficulties in competence and difficulties in performance. These issues will be elaborated in later chapters.

LANGUAGE AND CHANNEL

We have clarified the distinction between *language* and *communication*. Now we must draw another very important distinction: that between *language* and *channel* or modality. It is possible to have one language, e.g., English, communicated in many different channels. For example, we could communicate English through speech, through writing, through drums (as people do in Africa with African languages), through a teletype, or through signing. Signing is not a language; it is a modality, or channel, through which many possible languages could be communicated. It is possible to sign English, Swedish, or Japanese, as well as American Sign Language (ASL), Swedish Sign Language, or Japanese Sign Language. So here we have one channel, signing, that could be used for many different languages, or we could have one language, say English, that could be communicated through many different modalities.

One more distinction needs to be clarified before we look at language analysis in detail; namely, the distinction between LANGUAGE and *A* LANGUAGE in particular. It is very common for educators to talk about LANGUAGE (or language arts) as if it were synonymous with English. One may hear a person comment, "That child has very bad [deficient] language." Such an individual is being imprecise. First, the child's language may be just fine; s/he may simply lack, if s/he is bilingual, for example, the English to convey a concept s/he is capable of expressing in some other language. Alternatively, s/he may have an internally consistent linguistic system which simply does not match the linguistic system known as Standard English, as in speakers of nonstandard dialects. You may also come across people who say that a child has bad language, when what they really mean is that the child has faulty speech. The internal system could be intact, so that the child might be able to express a particular language, e.g., English, in writing, but the modality of speech could be difficult for that child to master without hindering the child's mastery of English in particular or of language in general. We shall see below that languages and dialects differ from each other on many levels but that they also have many commonalities in terms of basic structure.

STRUCTURAL ASPECTS OF LANGUAGE

Let us focus in on what linguists do when they analyze a particular language. When a linguist analyzes a language, s/he looks at different levels of structure within that language. Starting at the smallest unit, s/he looks at the *phonological* or *sublexical* level, i.e., the level of analysis smaller than the word. Although *phonological* originally referred only to spoken languages, we will see that the analogy to signed languages is equally valid; i.e., there is a sublexical structure for sign languages just as there is for spoken languages, so for this chapter (and book) we will use the term *phonology* to refer to sublexical structure, whether that structure is composed of sounds or visual signals. The field of phonology is, for spoken language, the study of the sound system of a particular language, or the regularities of sound systems for all languages. In the case of a sign language, when we study its phonology, we are studying the system of subwords that are used to put words together. That is, we are studying the level of analysis that is well below the level of the word.

Another level of analysis is *morphology*, i.e., how words are structured (some examples are given below). *Syntax* is the analysis of the formation of sentences, and *semantics* is the analysis of the structure of meaning. What linguists are ultimately interested in are, first, what language as a phenomenon can tell us about the human mind, and second, what relation exists between meaning and its ultimate expression, be that sound or sign or Morse code. To put it another way, linguists are interested in the relationship between the signal and its meaning; a linguist's grammar is an attempt to make that relationship explicit.

Sublexical Structures

PHONETIC ASPECTS

A language will have an inventory of sounds, if that language is spoken, or of individual handshapes, locations, orientations, and movements, if that language is signed. Thus, English has a certain inventory of sounds that it uses which another language may not. By the same token, some other language may have sounds that English does not use. For example, French has two sounds that do not occur in English: the uvular "r," usually symbolized as [R], and the sound symbolized in the International Phonetic Alphabet (IPA) as [y]. The uvular "r" sound does not occur at all in English as a linguistic entity; we come very close to it when we gargle, but it is not part of English sound structure at all. The [y] sound is made by saying [i:] (in traditional orthography, "ee") while rounding the lips; it is a phonological rule of English (remember, this describes what we know about our language) that all rounded vowels are made at the back of the mouth. Since [i:] is made at the front of the mouth, the [y] sound cannot be part of the inventory of sounds in English (this sound may occur nondistinctively in some southwestern dialects of English as a variant of the [u:] sound, however). By the same token, the American [r] is not part of the inventory of sounds of French.

Another example of a sound in another language which English does not have, at least linguistically, is the whole class of "click" sounds. A click is an ingressive stop which may be aspirated, and can be made in a variety of locations within the mouth. We use clicks nonlinguistically in English to kiss (a bilabial or, sometimes, quadrilabial click), to urge on a horse (a lateral click), or to express mild disapproval (an alveolar click), but it is very difficult for a speaker of English to use a click within a word. Clicks are thus not a part of the inventory of sounds of English. But there are many distinctive clicks in Bantu languages, such as Xhosa (which has a click even in its name) or Hottentot.

Sign languages as well have their own particular inventories of elements. For example, just as there are no clicks in English, American Sign Language (ASL) does not have any signs made in the armpit.

PHONEMIC ASPECTS

Another kind of thing that may differ from language to language is what classes of signals (auditory or visual) count as the same. This is a very important distinction to make. In traditional linguistics, a class of sounds that count as the same for a particular language is called a *phoneme*. The notion of phonemic representation is thus language-particular; it must be defined relative to a particular language. This is in contrast to *phonetic* representation which is not language-specific.

Let us look at examples of the contrast between phonetic and phonemic representation. In linguistics, we enclose a phonetic representation in square brackets, e.g., [pʰɪt], and we use slashes to enclose phonemic representation (e.g., /pɪt/). One of the examples we cited before was the French /y/ sound which, we noted, occurs nondistinctively in some southwestern dialects of English. The key word here is nondistinctive. Someone from Dallas might say [rym]; another person from Dallas will hear this as referring to "room." If a difference in sound does not affect meaning, we say that the two sounds are phonetically distinct but phonemically the same, i.e., both sounds, or phones, are members of the same phoneme class for that language. In French, for example, the sounds [y] and [u] are members of separate phoneme classes, for they cannot be substituted for each other without altering meaning; the sequence [syʀ] means "certain," while the sequence [suʀ] means "deaf."

Let us consider a slightly different example. In many languages spoken in India, the following are all distinct *phonemes*, i.e., they count as different from each other: [t], [d], [tʰ], [dʰ]. The "h" in these representations refers to aspiration, a little puff of air that occurs following the release of the stop. Of these four sounds, [dʰ] never occurs in English; the other three occur as two English phonemes, namely, /t/ and /d/. The phoneme class /t/ contains, for English, both [t] and [tʰ]; similarly, the phoneme class /p/ contains both [p] and [pʰ], and the phoneme class /k/ contains both [k] and [kʰ]. The members of each class count as the same for English, though as we have seen, not for Hindi. Unless you are trained as a phonetician, in fact, you may not be able to hear the difference between these two kinds of sounds. Another of those rules of English that you know but don't know that you know covers voiceless stops (such as /p/, /t/, /k/, which in English are aspirated at the beginning of a word but unaspirated after the sound [s]). If you hold a lighted match in front of your mouth and say "spit" ([spɪt]), the match will not go out. If you say "pit" ([pʰɪt]), it *will*; the aspiration makes the difference, but it may still be very difficult to hear.

To summarize, we have both [p] and [pʰ] in the inventory of sounds for English, but they count as the same for English, while they might not count as the same for some other language.

In the case of a sign language, there are similar groupings of elements into "phonemes." For example, in American Sign Language (ASL), except for finger spelling, which may violate many aspects of the phonological system of ASL, the handshapes for "A" and "S", as well as for "T", all count as the same. Just as we found for aspirated and unaspirated consonants in English, there are predictable environments in ASL where "A" and "S" will occur. Stokoe, 1960, coined the term "chereme" (based on the Greek root meaning handy) instead of "phoneme" for talking about sign language. However, I shall continue to use the term "phoneme" for talking about a class of elements in any language that counts as the same, irrespective of the modality of communication.

PHONOTACTICS

Phonology is concerned with more than just the inventory of elements or classes of elements. It is also concerned with the allowable combinations of elements. In English, if we have three consonant sounds at the beginning of a word, the first one has to be [s], and the third one has to be [l], [r], [w], or

[y]. So the sequences in (6) are all right in English, but those in (7) are not.

(6) [skyuw] "skew"   (7) *[skmuw]
   [sklɔrɔtɪk] "sclerotic"   *[skpərɔtɪk]
   [sprɛd] "spread"   *[nprɛd]
   [skwer] "square"   *[spter]

Similarly, if in English we have two consonant sounds at the beginning of a word, either the first must be [s] (or [ʃ] in some marginal cases), or the second must be a sonorant, such as [m], [n], [l], [r], [y], or [w]. The sequence in (8) is thus unacceptable for English but is, in fact, the German word for "horse".

(8) [pfert] (the German word for horse is spelled "pferd" but in isolation is pronounced [pfert])

By contrast, while English allows both [s] and [ʃ] before [p] word-initially, German allows only [ʃ]. Another example of such combinations is that the [ŋ] sound which can end words in English cannot begin them, while the [h] sound that can begin words in English cannot end them. These constraints are not universal to all languages; Vietnamese, for example, permits initial engma, while Arabic and Hindi permit word-final [h].

Sign languages have analogous rules for combination. For example, the "F" hand can touch or be touched only near the thumb and forefinger, not on the other fingers. However, the Hong Kong sign for "name" requires the last three fingers of a "f" hand to touch the palm of the other hand. This sign would be just as unacceptable for ASL as "pferd" is unacceptable for English.

Another aspect of sublexical structure in which linguists are interested is how one sublexical element influences another in the environment. For example, the English word "input" is almost never pronounced as [inpʊt]; rather, the presence of [p] influences the pronunciation of the nasal /n/, and the end result is [impʊt]. This is a process called *assimilation*, which is common to all languages, including sign languages. An example from fingerspelling is that the actual realization of the letter "E" changes, depending on the environment; if the previous or following letter uses only two fingers, the E is done with those two fingers as well instead of four. Other examples are given in Chapter 6.

To summarize, then, the sublexical or phonological structure of a language considers the inventory of elements, the classes of elements the language contains, the rules of combination of those elements, and the ways in which elements affect each other. These processes operate analogously, regardless of the channel in which the language is being communicated.

Meaning

We can think of the meaning of a word as analyzable into subelements of meaning just as the sound of a word may be analyzable into subelements. A particular word in a particular language may cover a slightly different set of subelements from its translation into another language. Languages differ a great deal in terms of what their individual words may refer to, what we call the semantic extension of those words. The most obvious example of this is the case of color words. Different languages have different numbers of color words, which generally covers the spectrum. For example, the English word "brown" covers a specific range of colors. The French word *marron*, however, covers some of the things that "brown" covers but not others; in particular, French would never use the word *marron* to refer to brown hair— that is always *brun*. Furthermore, for some reason known only to the French, brown shoes are called *jaune*, which is usually translated as "yellow." To look at a less obvious example, the word "be" in English will be translated differently into Spanish, depending on whether it is referring to existence or equation. Similarly, the verb "to know" will be translated differently into Romance languages, depending on whether one is talking about knowledge or acquaintance. The verb "run" translates differently into ASL, depending on what or who is running and with what. I would like to emphasize here that any time we translate from one language into another language, there will be some overlap and some nonoverlap. This does not make one language better than another; it especially does not make one language more "concep-

tual" than another, as has been suggested for ASL. The problem of translation exists between any two languages. Furthermore, the many-one or one-many translation problem is usually reciprocal: Many words in French have several English translations, and vice versa, just as many words in ASL also have several English translations, and vice versa.

Perhaps it is appropriate here to talk about the relationship between language and thought. It has been remarked that the Eskimo language has 20 different words for snow, and ASL, 100 different words for looking. Does this mean that Eskimos can see more distinctions than non-Eskimos? No. Eskimos are around snow a lot; it is important to their culture and life, so they formally notice distinctions that we might overlook but could see if we felt like it, as we do when skiing. Americans similarly have many words for cars. When a culture acquires a new concept, that culture will either develop a word within the language or borrow a word from another language to label that concept. Similarly, when a language is used in new contexts, it may need to enrich its vocabulary accordingly. This it does again either by coining words within the language or by borrowing words from another language.

Any language can express any concept; however, there is always a trade-off between effficiency of expressing a particular kind of concept and ease of comprehension. Some things will be expressed grammatically in one language but in separate words in another.

Morphology

Languages differ in terms of the kinds of things that can be incorporated into word structure and different ways to make new words. For example, English has two major ways to make new words: One is by compounding existing words from English, as in input, killjoy, ripoff, etc; another way is by borrowing *morphemes* (minimal units of meaning) from Greek or Latin and putting them together, as in the case of automobile, television, or hydrogen. Other languages may do similar things. For example, Japanese uses Chinese the same way that English makes use of Greek and Latin. Thus, the Japanese word for automobile, borrowed from Chinese, translates as self-moving cart, totally analogous to the English "automobile."

There are two kinds of morphology: inflectional morphology, in which one changes the word to make it fit into the sentence, such as the addition of -ing, -s, or -ed in English; and derivational morphology, in which one usually changes the part of speech, as in adding -ment to a verb to make it a noun in English.

INFLECTIONAL MORPHOLOGY

I shall use some examples to show how much languages can differ in terms of the kinds of things for which they inflect. Table 1.1 consists of data from Swahili, which can inflect the verb for tense (as, say, English does) but also can inflect the verb for case (unlike English); i.e., the verb shows a relic of the nouns that take part in grammatical relations, such as subject and object. We note also that the verb in various languages can inflect by adding things to the beginning of a word as well as to the end, and can even inflect by putting things in the middle. The minimal unit in a language that can convey meaning is called a morpheme.

Table 1.2 presents another example from Pangasinan, which is spoken in the Philippines. Here we have another kind of inflection, known as reduplication. In the case of Pangasinan, the first syllable of a word is repeated to make a plural. We shall see in the case of ASL (Chapter 6) that reduplication can also be used in other languages for showing various forms of verbal aspect as well as pluralization.

ASL also has a kind of reduplication used for similar purposes, which will be discussed in Chapter 6. This kind of reduplication is totally analogous to the kind of reduplication we find in Pangasinan and many other languages.

Table 1.1
Some Verb Inflections in Swahili[1,2]

nilikimbia	I ran away	walitukata	they cut us
ulikimbia	you (sg.) ran away	walituita	they called us
utakimbia	you (sg.) will run away	tulimita	we called {him / her}
nitakuambia	I will tell you (sg.)	atamita	s/he will call {him / her}
nitakukata	I will cut you (sg.)	utamita	you (sg.) will call {him / her}
nitamkata	I will cut {him / her}	nilimita	I called {him / her}
walimkata	they cut {him / her}	niliwaita	I called {them / you (pl.)}
watakukata	they will cut you (sg.)	mliwaita	you (pl.) called them
alitukata	s/he cut you (sg.)	tuliwaita	we called {them / you (pl.)}
atamkata	s/he will cut {him / her}	tutakuita	we will call you (sg.)
atanikata	s/he will cut me	utanikata	you (sg.) will cut me

[1] References: Driever, 1976; Polome, 1967.
[2] sg., singular; pl., plural.

Table 1.2
Reduplication in Pangasinan[1]

kanáyon	relative	kakanáyon	relatives
nióg	coconut	niniók	coconuts
láta	can	laláta	cans
lópot	rag	lólopot	rags
kán	eat	mañgakán	is eating
táwagen	be called	tatáwagen	is being called

[1] Reference: Benton, 1971.

DERIVATIONAL MORPHOLOGY

Derivational morphology refers to word construction, the making of new words out of old words and/or old words and affixes. An *affix* is a morpheme which cannot be a word by itself but which is used to build other words—another term for this is *bound morpheme*. A *free morpheme* is a morpheme that could be a word all by itself but may also be used to build other words. An English word like *perceive* consists of two bound morphemes, while a word like *killjoy* consists of two free morphemes. The word *sexuality* consists of one free morpheme with two bound morphemes, *-al* (or *-ual*), which changes the noun to an adjective, and *-ity*, which changes the adjective back to a noun, but this time to an abstract noun.

Derivational morphology is currently one of the areas in research in ASL that is receiving the most attention. One of the first explicit discussions of derivational morphology in ASL is in Supalla and Newport (1978). They talk about the derivation of nouns from verbs in ASL. They found a systematic relationship between pairs of signs like FLY versus AIRPLANE, and SIT versus CHAIR. Other aspects of derivational morphology in sign language are discussed in Chapter 6.

Syntax

Syntax examines how languages differ in their sentence structure. For a language like Latin, and in fact for ASL, who does what to whom can be shown by using endings or affixes on either nouns or verbs. In Latin, a sentence like "the boy sees the girl" could be translated as any of the following:

(14) Puer   videt   puellam.
     boy   see   girl
     (nominative) (third singular) (accusative)

(15) Puellam videt puer.
(16) Videt puellam puer.

In fact, any of the other three permutations of these three words is grammatical Latin, and the meaning remains constant. Similarly, in ASL, with the use of directional verbs, some flexibility in word order is permitted. By contrast, English must rely on word order; if the order of "the girl sees the boy" is given, the meaning changes from the original. ASL also has word order restrictions, as in fact does Latin, but there are interactions with semantic plausibility and syntactic complexity. Also, changes in word order do change subtle differences in meaning, such as topic.

Even if a language has a fixed word order, that may vary from language to language. Thus English has the order subject-verb-object. Many Philippine languages have the order verb-subject-object. Languages like Japanese have the order subject-object-verb.

In addition to differences in word order, languages also vary syntactically in terms of what they *must* express grammatically. It is important to reiterate here that all languages can express virtually any idea; but some ideas are more *grammaticized*. Some examples of these differences are given in sentences (17)–(20). In addition, languages can differ in terms of what they can express grammatically. Let us consider these sentences from Japanese.

(17) If it rains, I don't want to go for a walk.
     ame ga   fur-eba sampo shi-ta-ku
     rain subject fall-if, stroll do-want-adverb
       -na-i
       -not (adjective) present

(18) The rain that was falling during the summer was warm.
     natsu   ni fut -te   i-ta   ame
     summer in fall participle be past rain
       wa   atataka -katta
       topic warm   past (for adjective)

(19) I bought pencil(s).
     enpitsu o   kat -ta
     pencil   object buy past

(20) I bought two pencils.
     enpitsu o   ni hon   kat -ta
     pencil   object 2 stick-shape buy past

Looking first at (17), we see that rain is only a noun and that the idea of "if" is conveyed not as a separate word but as an inflection on the verb. Similarly, "want" is also an inflection on the verb instead of a separate word, and the negative in Japanese is an adjective instead of an adverb, as in English.

In (18), we find other contrasts with English. Japanese doesn't have prepositions; rather, it has *post*positions, such as *ni* (in, on, at). Relative clauses (such as *natsu ni futte ita*) occur before, instead of after, the nouns that they modify, and adjectives as well as verbs are inflected for tense. (English, because it cannot inflect adjectives, uses the verb *to be* to carry the tense.)

If we look at (19) and (20), we see another contrast with English in terms of what *must* be expressed versus what *can* be expressed. Japanese has no regular plural marker that is attached to nouns or verbs, as English does. Also, like many other languages, Japanese does not require all sentences to have overt subjects. In particular, without any other context, the subject "I" is assumed or inferred in a declarative sentence, while "you" is understood in interrogative sentences. However, the number marking system for Japanese is much more complicated than that for English. It is not enough to just say TWO; rather, "two" is inflected for certain semantic properties of what is being counted. Other examples of this are given in (21) and (22). Notice the different inflections and, in the case of people, even a different root; a competent speaker of Japanese will know dozens of different numerical classifiers, as these inflections are called, depending on various semantic categories.

(21) I bought two books.
    Hon o   ni-satsu kat -ta
    book object 2-volume buy past
(22) I saw two teachers.
    Sensei o   futa -ri   mi -ta
    teacher object two human see past

We shall see in Chapter 6 that ASL has a system of classifiers attached to verbs which categorize the world in a fashion similar to Japanese.

To reiterate, the above examples have been cited to elucidate several points. First, different languages have different things that they

must specify in order for a sentence to be grammatical. Second, when they do specify something, languages will use a variety of means to express that function. For example, to express who does what to whom, English uses word order, Latin uses case marking on nouns plus verb agreement, and ASL uses a form of case marking on verbs, along with such things as eye gaze. Languages such as Finnish use case marking instead of the prepositions or postpositions used by other languages.

No language is "simpler" or more primitive than any other. Rather, there will usually be a trade-off between simplicity in one part of the grammar of a language and complexity in another. For example, English has a simple, i.e., practically no, system of case marking or verb inflection but a complex system of prepositions and a very complex lexicon, as well as a rather complex phonology. Latin has complex systems for inflecting nouns and verbs but no grammatical markers for definiteness. Japanese has no plural marker, but a very rich system for counting specific kinds of semantic categories. ASL, as we shall see later, has very rich systems of aspect markers and noun classifiers but no grammatical way of marking time. It does not use tense, but rather adverbs of time, to convey this concept.

We should also reemphasize here that just as no language is simpler than any other, all languages have equal capacity to express any concept or collection of concepts. If all that is needed is a word, a new one can be borrowed or coined. If something like plurality or size and shape must be expressed, the grammar, the lexicon, or the syntax can be used to express it. Languages will naturally vary in terms of what is expressed with a systematic grammatical device and what is expressed in a less systematic fashion. If any language tried to make grammatically explicit *everything* that language made explicit, it would be extremely unwieldy. There are options, and languages may well opt differently, depending on historical circumstances.

It is perfectly natural, however, for the speaker of one language to be surprised and even frustrated at what another language "leaves out" or "puts in." It is important to realize, though, that the converse will be equally true. For example, English will look just as strange to a speaker of Xhosa as Xhosa looks (or sounds) to a speaker of English.

SOCIAL ASPECTS OF LANGUAGE

Language does not exist in a vacuum; it occurs in a social, and often a political, context. It is important to know about social and political aspects of language use when dealing with *any* population. it is imperative when dealing with the hearing-impaired population: first, because the socialization to language can vary dramatically within the hearing-impaired population, since even the amount of language acquired—be it English, ASL, or some other language—may be restricted in use for different social settings; and second, because at least some elements of the hearing-impaired population function as a minority, with many of the same concerns as other minority groups embedded in the context of a majority culture. These social and political factors can, in turn, have consequences for language structure, a topic to which we shall return in some detail in Chapter 6. The study of the interaction of language and society is called *sociolinguistics*.

Language use reflects social structure; at the same time, language differences can help to perpetrate social differences. This may be most striking within a language at the level of phonology. George Bernard Shaw's *Pygmalion* (popularized as *My Fair Lady*) is sensitive to this issue, as Shaw himself was: "The moment an Englishman speaks he makes some other Englishman despise him!" The woman who cannot put the "H" in its proper place in a sentence like "in Hertford, Hereford, and Hampshire, hurricanes hardly ever happen" cannot get a job in a flower shop.

We notice class differences reflected in language structure at other levels as well. A user of so-called Standard English will be able to make a pretty good guess about the social origins of someone who says something like (23):

(23) Us guys ain't going nowhere.

One of the things that helps to perpetrate social differences is the use of different varieties or *registers* of a language in complementary settings. Most speakers of a language have at their command a wide range of registers used in these settings; one doesn't talk the same way in a bar as one does in a university lecture. Someone who doesn't know that whole range may be limited socially. Most commonly, someone who knows a more casual register, as exemplified in (23), may not know the more formal register, as exemplified in (24):

(24) We fellows are not going anywhere.

However, the opposite can occur, i.e., a person may know the more formal register but lack the more colloquial register; this is often true of second-language learners (who "speak like a book") and of some hearing-impaired people as well. We should stress again that in some informal settings, (23) would be *more* appropriate than (24), just as in more formal settings (24) would clearly be more appropriate. For example, if we consider sentences like (25) or (26),

(25) The Yanks are gonna win the pennant for sure
(26) It is practically certain that the Yankees will secure the championship,

it is clear that someone who utters (26) in a bar will be hooted down, just as someone who *writes* (25) in a front-page newspaper article will probably be called in for a heart-to-heart chat with the editor.

Other languages have social reflections of language functions even more striking than English. Japanese, for example, has different lexical and grammatical rules, depending on the relative position of speaker, addressee, and subject of conversation, both in terms of social status and degree of intimacy. Romance languages, such as French or Spanish, as well as most Indo-European languages in general, have different grammatical forms for "you," depending on considerations of some combination of degree of intimacy and relative social status. (English used to have this distinction; "thou," "thee," and "thine" are the relics of an archaic intimate form.)

It is one thing to recognize the variation that occurs naturally in language. After all, there can be regional as well as socially conditioned variation. It is quite another thing to judge that one variety is more acceptable than, or superior to, another or that one language is better than another; this is where political considerations enter in. Most cultures have either explicitly or implicitly adopted a "standard" language or language variety. That variety of language is officially sanctioned in schools, used in newspapers, and generally preferred in formal situations by educated persons often in the upper strata of society.

Since most of the world is multilingual, many governments must, for practical reasons, make very hard decisions about the position of minority languages or dialects. For example, in developing island countries, such as Indonesia or New Guinea, it is not uncommon for there to be several *hundred* languages in use. A developing country cannot afford to produce, say, educational materials in 250 different languages—it is often a strain on the economy to produce those materials in only one or two. In this situation a decision must be made. If wisely made, the decision for the planning of language can be a unifying influence for the country. If, however, the planning does not take into account the appropriate political and social factors, it can be divisive instead of unifying. For example, until recent years, monolingual speakers of French in Canada tended to be in the lower strata of society though in the numerical majority in the province of Quebec. Monolingual English speakers were perceived as maintaining this balance of power by requiring official business to be conducted in English. Recent changes in policy in Quebec, emphasizing bilingualism, have helped somewhat to ease the tensions between Anglophones and Francophones (speakers of English and French, respectively). Canada as a whole, however, is not yet totally bilingual; thus, there are continued tensions within the population, especially since in Canada French is associated with low prestige not only among English speakers but even among French speakers (see, for example, the work of Lambert and his colleagues).

We have suggested that political factors enter into the success or failure of language planning. Another way in which political considerations affect language, and one's perception of it, is in the definition of language itself. We might think that the decision as to whether two entities constitute dialects of one language versus distinct languages was purely a matter of some objectively definable linguistic distance. For example, we might say that if a speaker of X can understand a speaker of Y, X and Y are dialects, whereas if speakers of X and Y cannot understand each other, X and Y must be distinct languages. Often, however, the definition of language versus dialect is a political one, though social and even religious factors can become relevant. For example, linguists talk about one of the major languages of India as Hindi-Urdu, but because "Hindi" and "Urdu" are used by different religious groups (Hindu and Moslem, respectively) and use different writing systems (Devanagari and Arabic script, respectively), they are felt to be two different languages. (In fact, there is some divergence in vocabulary, but the grammars are the same.) Dutch and German, at least in some dialects, are mutually intelligible; yet speakers of both insist that the two are separate languages, due to the traditional political antagonisms that exist between the two nations. On the other hand, Mandarin and Cantonese are NOT mutually intelligible, but they are officially as well as popularly perceived as dialects rather than as separate languages because they are all within China and are both written in Chinese characters.

Another problem of a definition occurs when one "language" has the lexical base of another but a distinct grammar or structure, as in the case of creoles. Such an entity may in some cases be classified as a dialect of the language from which the lexical base is drawn, but in others it may be defined as a separate language. Further, the distinction can shift as the politics shift without the linguistic realities changing at all. Often monolingual (or monodialectal) speakers of a creole cannot understand speakers of the prestige "standard" language, and vice versa, so that by the purely linguistic definition they would count as two languages, but because speakers of a creole are generally exposed to the standard language in school, and because of the shared lexical base, as well as the frequent perception of monolingual creole speakers as socially inferior to standard speakers, a creole is often regarded simply as an "inferior" or "ungrammatical" dialect of the standard language. A nonstandard dialect of *any* language may violate the rules of the standard dialect, but it is just as internally consistent. By the same token, the standard dialect does not follow the grammar of the nonstandard dialect any more than English follows the rules of Latin. Defining one dialect or language as standard and another as nonstandard depends more on such nonlinguistic factors as the social prestige associated with users of a particular dialect than on even the number of people who use it. However, while a prestige dialect can be imposed from the top down, such as in the schools, a great deal of work in the field of sociolinguistics (especially that of Labov) suggests that it is the less prestigious dialects that lead the vanguard of linguistic change; e.g., despite the efforts of several generations of English teachers, the use of "whom" as an object pronoun is rapidly disappearing from even "standard" American English (a fact already noted by the linguist Sapir nearly 60 years ago). We will return to some of these issues in Chapter 6.

In traditional linguistics, languages are spoken of as being *genetically* related. In this sort of model, English is closely related to Dutch, since both are in the *Germanic* subfamily; Rumanian and Spanish are both *Romance* languages, and in turn, Germanic, Romance, and Slavic languages are subgroups of the *Indo-European* family. One can draw branching family trees to show other families, such as Athabascan, a family that includes Navajo, the Dravidian family which includes Tamil, or the Finno-Ugric family that includes Hungarian. However, when two language communities abut on each other geographically, or when one language group colonizes or migrates into another, even if the two language groups are unrelated, one language can influence another, or two languages can have a mutual influence, at many levels of the grammar: phonology, syntax, and (usually the leading edge) the lexicon.

An an example, in the Southwest United States, existing Spanish-speaking communities have been colonized by English speakers. Spanish speakers constantly exposed to English may begin sprinkling their Spanish sentences with English words. Bilingual Spanish-English speakers may even speak an amalgam of the two languages, known colloquially as Spanglish, which has its own norms and grammatical rules (Haugen (1977)). Is it English or Spanish??? It is often difficult, and perhaps pointless, to decide.

We can find similar phenomena if we look at the difference between Old English and Middle English. Old English and Middle English are separated by a political event: the Norman Conquest of 1066. This resulted in a massive infusion of French vocabulary into Old English (interestingly enough, Norman French in turn was a dialect of French with quite a bit of exposure to, and influence from, Germanic languages). This influx led to a change in English phonology, which ultimately had an effect on morphology, which in turn ended up affecting sentence structure.

We can see from these examples that language does not exist in a vacuum; it is responsive to many kinds of forces: social, political, geographical, and historical. The phenomenon of language cannot be fully understood unless we take all of these forces into account. There is, however, a great deal of information about language to be gained by looking at it in isolation from complicating factors. Most of the following chapters will try to clarify the phenomenon of language not only by looking at language as distinct from complicating factors in the real world but also by looking at aspects of language, such as speech, auditory comprehension, and signing, as if they were also separate from each other and sometimes from language itself. Of course, we know that all of these factors are really related, but since we cannot look at everything at once, we may choose to narrow our focus; one has to start somewhere, so let us begin.

References

Benton, R.A. *Pangasinan Reference Grammar*. Honolulu: University of Hawaii Press, 1971.

Chomsky, N. Review of Skinner: Verbal behavior. *Language*, 1959, *35*, 26–58.

Driever, D. *Aspects of a Case Grammer of Mombasa Swahili*. Hamburg: Helmut Buske Verlag, 1976.

Gleason, H.A. *Workbook in Descriptive Linguistics*. New York: Holt, Rinehart & Winston, 1955.

Haugen, E. Norm and deviation in bilingual communities. In P. Hornby (ed.), *Bilingualism: Psychological, Social, and Educational Implications*. New York: Academic Press, 1977, 91–102.

Hymes, D. The ethnography of speaking. In J. Fishman (ed.), *Readings in the Sociology of Language*. The Hague: Mouton, 1968, 99–138.

Jackendoff, R., and Lerdahl, F. Generative music theory and its relation to psychology. Bloomington, Indiana: Indiana University Linguistics Circle, 1980.

van Lawick-Goodall, J. *In the Shadow of Man*. New York: Houghton-Mifflin, 1971.

Polome, E.C. *Swahili Language Handbook*. Washington, D.C.: Center for Applied Linguistics, 1967.

Stokoe, W. *Sign Language Structure*. Silver Spring, Maryland: Linstock Press, 1960.

Supalla, T., and E. Newport. How many seats in a chair? The derivation of nouns and verbs in American sign language. In P. Siple (ed.), *Understanding Language through Sign Language Research*. New York: Academic Press, 1978, 91–132.

Recommended Reading

It is impossible to provide thorough coverage of linguistics in a short chapter. If you are interested in learning more, see the books recommended below.

Falk, J. *Linguistics and Language*, ed. 2. New York: John Wiley & Sons, 1978.

Foss, D., and Hakes, D. *Psycholinguistics: An Introduction to the Psychology of Language*. Englewood Cliffs, New Jersey: Prentice-Hall, 1978.

Hornby, P. *Bilingualism: Psychological, Social, and Educational Implications*. New York: Academic Press, 1977.

Labov, W. *Language in the Inner City*. Philadelphia: University of Pennsylvania Press, 1972.

Lambert, W., and Tucker R. *Bilingual Education of Children: The St. Lambert Experiment*. Rowley, Massachusetts: Newbury House, 1972.

Part II

Perception

Chapter 2

Speech Perception by the Severely Hearing-Impaired

SALLY G. REVOILE, PH.D.
JAMES M. PICKETT, PH.D.

Essential information for auditory rehabilitation is knowledge of the hearing-impaired person's speech perception abilities. A complete evaluation of impaired speech understanding should include measures of specific auditory abilities as well as higher-level linguistic capabilities. Since linguistic characteristics of the severely hearing-impaired are considered in other chapters, we will limit our discussions of impaired speech perception to the linguistic level of the phoneme. We review below some of the literature on perception of consonants and vowels by hearing-impaired listeners. We describe impaired speech perception in relation to consonant articulatory features that have been developed in the phonetic literature. Further, we discuss impaired reception for some of the acoustic patterns associated with consonant identification.

We note incidentally that the traditional index of an individual's overall speech perception—a score representing the percentage of words correctly identified on a word recognition (speech discrimination) test—is not of great importance for purposes of auditory rehabilitation. Such scores may not differentiate very well among various degrees of hearing loss (Bess and Townsend, 1977). However, responses to individual items on word recognition tests may provide more-useful information for auditory training. Error responses are of particular interest, since they indicate the phoneme confusions of the hearing-impaired person.

Error responses on word recognition tests can be examined most systematically, using multiple-choice or closed-response formats for which the listener marks or writes the word heard from among a printed group of words that include the test word. When such formats are used to test consonant perception, the words in each group typically differ only for either initial or final phonemes, as in the following examples from the Modified Rhyme Test (MRT) (Kreul et al., 1968):

Teal	Tear	Kith	Kid
Tease	Teak	Kill	Kiss
Team	Teach	King	Kick

Differences in word familiarity are minimized, since the possible responses are apparent in the closed set. The examples show that the words used may be uncommon. In some tests, all of the items are nonsense syllables.

The results of such tests can be tabled in a confusion matrix to examine the phonemes tested versus the phonemes perceived. In analyzing the underlying nature of phoneme confusions, the acoustical differences or cues among speech sounds should be considered. Reduced reception for particular acoustic cues could explain phoneme confusions. Knowledge of the impaired listener's reception for acoustic cues of speech may be useful information for aural rehabilitation. For example, if it can be determined that auditory reception is better for durational cues than spectral cues of speech, auditory training and hearing-aid fitting could be carried out relative to such information. Acoustic speech cue reception by the hearing-impaired has been investigated in several studies that are described below in the literature review.

The acoustic patterns of speech are the basis for some of the categories used in the feature systems developed in linguistics for describing phonemes (Wickelgren, 1966; Miller and Nicely, 1955). These feature systems sometimes employ both articulatory and acoustic descriptors to characterize phonemes. Some of the more general articulatory feature classes that have been developed for differentiating the consonant phonemes are place of articulation, voicing, and manner of articulation. For each of these features any consonant phoneme can be categorized according to its "value" on the feature; e.g., the consonant /b/ has labial place, is voiced, and is produced with a plosive manner of articulation; the consonant /f/ has labiodental place, is voiceless, and is produced with a fricative manner of articulation; the consonant /n/ has dental-alveolar place, is voiced, and is produced with nasal manner of artic-

ulation. In some feature systems the articulatory and acoustic descriptors for speech sound classification are more detailed than in others. For example, categorizations of specific locations or shapes of articulation may be employed, such as high-anterior, coronal, palatalized; also, categories may be concerned with the general shape of the sound spectrum, such as being compact or diffuse, and as rising or falling over the entire frequency scale.

Studies of normal speech perception have shown that in identifying phonemes, listeners seem to use features as a primary perceptual framework. That is, in the initial stages of processing, listeners appear to classify phonemes on the basis of pattern characteristics represented by the features of each phoneme. For example, under conditions in which the middle and high frequencies of speech are lacking, listeners tend to confuse places of articulation but correctly perceive voicing and nasal manner (Miller and Nicely, 1955). This kind of information tells us how to design vocabularies for such a situation or, conversely, what words in a required vocabulary would be better perceived if we could arrange for transmission of the deficient frequency range. For the hearing-impaired similar insights and benefits relative to their speech perception could be obtained through the speech feature approach. For example, since it is known that many hearing-impaired listeners have major difficulty with place features, tests of place reception should be the most efficient in selecting a hearing aid for such persons. Also, since the acoustic cues to phonemic place features are known to be certain patterns in the middle and high frequencies, hearing aids may be especially designed to enhance these patterns.

In the following literature review we first describe some of the feature-oriented research on hearing-impaired listeners. Our discussions are not limited exclusively to the severely hearing-impaired adults, primarily because available information on speech perception by such persons is fairly limited. Thus, in our review we indicate the degrees of hearing impairment reported in the various studies described and extrapolate to the severely impaired whenever necessary.

REVIEW OF RESEARCH

Feature Descriptions of Impaired Speech Perception

Feature use in consonant perception by the hearing-impaired has been studied with word recognition tasks and/or judgments of consonant similarities. With the severely hearing-impaired, generally only word or syllable recognition tests have been employed.

FEATURE ANALYSIS FROM CONSONANT IDENTIFICATION IN WORD RECOGNITION TASKS

An early application of feature analysis for consonant perception by severely impaired listeners was that of Cox (1969). Initial consonant identification in monosyllabic words was tested for 20 Gallaudet undergraduate students with average tone thresholds at 500, 1000, and 2000 Hz (3FA), ranging from 45- to 80-dB hearing level (HL) (mean, 70 dB). Three closed-response, word recognition tests were administered, each using a different vowel: either /i/, /ɑ/, or /u/. The tests were presented at each listener's most comfortable listening level (MCL), either unfiltered, or filtered with various amounts of middle and high frequencies eliminated (low-pass filtering). Responses over all listeners were examined for the consonants grouped according to the features of voicing, manner, and place of articulation. Place errors occurred the most, manner errors somewhat less, and voicing errors generally the least. When the low-pass cutoff frequency was decreased from 2000 to 1000 to 500 Hz, manner and place errors increased more than voicing errors. Among the vowels there were more errors of place and of manner for consonants with the [i], which has a high-frequency second formant (F2), than with [ɑ] and [u]. These findings indicate that the higher frequencies in speech are more important for reception of place and manner features than for reception of voicing features, by hearing-impaired listeners. Miller and Nicely (1955) reported a similar effect for normal-hearing listeners who discriminated consonants in nonsense syllables presented with low-pass filtering.

A study that examined consonant perception for a relatively large number of severely hearing-impaired listeners was that of Pickett et al. (1972). A modified version of the MRT was administered to 99 Gallaudet students. Perception was tested for 20 initial consonants, 20 final consonants, and 10 vowels, which occurred in 50 monosyllabic words used in a closed-response format. The words were presented monaurally (better ear) at each listener's most comfortable listening level plus 6 dB. The results were described on the basis of percent correct perception for three features: voicing, place of articulation, and low continuant—the presence of strong low-frequency energy in nasals, liquids, and glides, as contrasted to stops and fricatives, which have less low-frequency energy. Responses that occurred in the appropriate feature category were considered correct, regardless of the accuracy of consonant recognition. To examine feature perception for different levels of performance among the 99 listeners, the distribution of percent word recognition scores for the MRT was divided into quartiles. Among the quartiles (Q) the listeners' mean consonant perception and mean 3FAs were, respectively: Q_1, 80% and 67 dB; Q_2, 61% and 73 dB; Q_3, 43% and 82 dB; Q_4, 27% and 88 dB. Thus, the more severe the hearing impairment among the quartile groups, the poorer the consonant perception. For all groups, perception of place of articulation for the consonants was poorer than perception of voicing or low continuant. The group with the best hearing showed near-perfect feature perception for voicing and low continuant, but reduced perception for place of articulation. For some of the listeners in the group with the most severe impairments, perception for all three features was incorrect for more than 80% of their responses. Among all listeners the features in initial consonants tended to be perceived somewhat better than in the final consonants. An important finding in this study was that some listeners with very severe hearing impairments showed difficulty distinguishing consonant voicing and also discriminating consonants on the basis of low-frequency energy.

In some subsequent studies of impaired speech perception that have employed feature analyses, an additional aim was to examine listeners' patterns of speech feature perception in comparison to their audiometric contours. Bilger and Wang (1976) grouped listeners according to similarities in feature perception and examined the pure tone threshold contours within each listener group. Consonant identification was tested in nonsense syllables presented 40 dB above listeners' speech reception thresholds (SRT). Confusion matrices were constructed and compared among listeners for homogeneity in feature patterns. The matrices were analyzed to differentiate features on the basis of the relative amounts of information they contributed for consonant perception. Features that contributed more information were considered well-perceived. For one group of listeners, sibilance, nasality, and high-anterior or back were well-perceived, and for some tests, frication and voicing were well-perceived. In this group, nearly all of the six listeners had either normal hearing or mild losses with flat contours. In a second listener group, features well-perceived were, in order, sibilance, duration, voicing, and high-anterior or place; nasality was not easily perceived. Generally, these seven listeners had moderate to severe losses with either flat, sloping, or somewhat-rising audiograms. The third group of 10 listeners showed good feature perception for nasality and/or voicing; other features were perceived as in the first group above, except that sibilance was poorly perceived. These listeners tended to have rather precipitous sloping losses, with various degrees of impairment. For three listeners from the second and third groups, who had 3FAs from 70- to 73-dB HL, the voicing feature was generally perceived best. Other features affecting perception were consistent with these listeners' groupings for feature patterns.

To corroborate their findings, Bilger and Wang (1976) examined feature perception for another sample of 12 listeners (studied first by Reed (1975)) after assigning them to the groups above, based on audiogram similarity. Feature perception for the new listeners tended to correspond to that shown within the groups to which they were assigned. Thus, it was found that hearing-impaired listeners who have certain similarities in pure tone threshold contours may also show similar feature perception.

The patterns of consonant confusions found by Bilger and Wang for groups of the hearing-impaired listeners were compared in a subsequent study to the patterns of consonant confusions of normal-hearing listeners presented the same nonsense syllables originally used, with and without filtering (Wang et al., 1978). The normal-hearing listeners received the syllables with various degrees of high-frequency or low-frequency filtering in order to examine whether such filtering might yield consonant confusion patterns similar to the hearing-impaired listeners, according to the configuration of their losses. Of most interest for our purposes here are certain of the low-pass filtering conditions, which might be representative of severe, sloping losses. When the frequency range between 80 and 500 or 710 Hz was presented, the features well-perceived were voicing, in particular, and nasality; frication and continuant were also important, while sibilance was poorly perceived. Generally, these effects were seen as well for the 80–1000-Hz range. Hence, normal-hearing listeners who were presented the syllables with high frequencies removed showed feature patterns similar to those found earlier by Bilger and Wang (1976) for hearing-impaired listeners with precipitous, sloping losses (group 3 above).

The use of filtered speech with normals, to simulate impaired-hearing characteristics, has been employed by other investigators in studies of feature perception. Walden et al. (1981) examined speech feature perception between the impaired and normal ears for each of eight adults with unilateral losses. The listeners' impairments ranged from 18- to 71-dB HL (3FA), and their audiometric contours were generally sloping. Perception was tested for 20 initial consonants with [ɑ] (closed-response format), using listening levels in each subject's normal ear that simulated the levels used in the impaired ear. In addition, six normal-hearing adults with unilateral losses that were artificially induced via filtering, were tested with the nonsense syllables, using listening levels in the normal ear, simulating those in the artificially impaired ear. For simulating the listening levels in the impaired ear, each subject used filters in a spectrum shaper to adjust the level of tones in the normal ear to be equal in loudness to tones of a constant SPL heard in the impaired ear.

For subjects with unilateral losses, the nonsense syllables were presented to the impaired ear without filtering and to the normal ear with the spectrum shaper simulating the listening levels of the impaired ear. For the normal-hearing subjects, filtered syllables were presented to both ears: to one ear through filters that artificially induced a hearing loss and to the other ear through the spectrum shaper simulating the listening levels of the contralateral ear.

Most of the listeners with unilateral losses showed poorer consonant identification in the impaired ear than in the normal ear, which used listening levels simulating those of the impaired ear. In contrast, for individual normal-hearing listeners, consonant identification scores were quite similar between ears, both of which received the stimuli through filtering. However, in both groups, individual listeners showed feature patterns of consonant recognition that were similar between ears. The features that tended to be best-perceived by the impaired listeners were, in order, nasal, unvoiced stops, sonorance, and place. The two listeners with more-severe unilateral losses (3FA, 65- and 71-dB HL) obtained the poorest impaired-ear consonant identification scores, and one showed the lowest relation between ears for identification of individual consonants.

The finding by Walden et al. (1981) of differences between the normal ear and impaired ear in overall consonant identification for listeners with unilateral losses suggests that general speech perception ability may not be adequately simulated for normal listeners by filtering of speech. On the other hand, Sher and Owens (1972) found similar consonant identification scores between a group of 35 listeners with high-frequency losses above 2000 Hz and a group of 28 normal listeners tested under filtering to simulate a high-frequency loss. Perception was tested for stop, fricative, and affricate consonants in the initial and/or final position among 100 monosyllabic words in closed-response sets. For initial consonants, nearly all errors were in place of articulation, while for final consonants, errors in place and manner were seen. No voicing errors occurred.

In the studies above, we examined results especially for severely hearing-impaired listeners. Among those listeners generally the voicing feature was less susceptible to deterioration than other features, although for some listeners with more severe impairments, perception was reduced for voicing as well as for other features. Place perception tended to be reduced more than manner. Some features were more easily perceived than others; e.g., nasal was perceived more easily than sibilance. The similarities in feature patterns seen between impaired listeners and normal listeners presented speech through filters simulating an impairment suggest that reduced speech perception for some hearing-impaired listeners may merely be an effect of reduced audibility for speech acoustic cues. Further investigations of this filtering technique are needed, using larger groups of impaired listeners carefully matched for degree and contour of hearing loss. It might be interesting to explore distortions added to filtering to try to equate the normal to the impaired ear.

FEATURE ANALYSES FROM CONSONANT SIMILARITY JUDGMENTS

Consonant similarity judgments have been used experimentally to examine feature use in speech perception by the hearing-impaired. Similarity judgments are obtained by having a listener rate the similarity of two consonants. Generally, a 7-point rating scale is used, with one end of the scale representing a judgment of "very similar" and the other end representing a judgment of "very dissimilar." Comparisons of similarity are made for two consonants at a time, each spoken with the same vowel in a consonant-vowel (CV) syllable, e.g., /ba, sa/. For each pair of consonants the CV syllables are presented about 1 second apart, with the listener receiving the syllables at a comfortable level. The listener is instructed merely to rate the similarity of the consonants in each pair, using the 7-point scale. In this manner, similarity ratings are obtained for each consonant paired with every other consonant.

Similarity ratings have been analyzed by using multidimensional scaling techniques that yield dimensions along which consonants are found to cluster, according to the perceptual qualities represented by each dimension. The consonant clusters that emerge generally have enabled differentiation of dimensions on the basis of features of speech, thus indicating that the analysis techniques yield dimensions consistent with the acoustics of speech production.

Judgments of consonant similarities and multidimensional scaling were used by Walden and Montgomery (1975) to study the perceptual dimensions of consonants for normal listeners and for impaired listeners with either flat or sloping losses. Similarity ratings were obtained for all possible pairs of 20 consonants spoken in the initial position before the vowel [ɑ] by a male talker. The listeners' consonant similarity ratings were analyzed by using INDSCAL, a multidimensional scaling procedure. The procedure scales the value of each consonant on several dimensions. Three perceptual dimensions of the consonants emerged. The dimensions were interpretable according to the features: sibilant/nonsibilant, continuant/stop, and sonorant/nonsonorant. Along each dimension, listeners' individual weighting values were provided by the scaling procedure, thus indicating the degree to which a listener used each dimension in judging consonant similarity. This enabled comparisons among listeners along each dimension.

The hearing-impaired listeners with sloping losses were more sensitive to sonorance in their similarity ratings than were the listeners with flat losses who tended to be influenced more by sibilance in their ratings. Interestingly, these two groups were quite similar in word recognition scores. In contrast to the impaired groups, the group of normal listeners did not show dependence on particular features in making consonant similarity judgments.

Lawarre and Danhauer (1976) also examined consonant similarity ratings for hearing-impaired listeners in a study like that of Walden and Montgomery (1975). Between the studies, some findings were comparable; e.g., voicing did not emerge as a strong dimension in the consonant similarity judgments. The effective dimensions for the hearing-impaired were sibilant, plosive, and nasal/liquid-glide. Feature dominance was not differentiated among listeners according to audiometric contour, in contrast to the Walden and Montgomery findings.

Walden et al. (1980) later compared, for individual listeners, consonant similarity ratings to identification of those consonants in syllable recognition tests. In addition, consonant similarity ratings were examined between auditory and visual stimulus presentations, as one means of studying whether the listeners processed the consonants by labeling them. Twenty consonants each preceding [a] were combined in all possible pairs for the similarity ratings. Visual presentation of the pairs was via closed-circuit TV. After the similarity rating of each pair presented auditorily, the listeners wrote the consonants heard, in order. The listeners were five normal-hearing adults and two groups of five impaired adults: one group showing average moderate losses that were acquired, and the other, average severe losses that were congenital.

The comparison of the similarity ratings versus the identification of the consonants indicated that consonants found to be highly confusable were not those judged to be the most similar. Various analyses indicated that the listeners did apply phonemic labels to the consonants in judging their similarity.

For each group of listeners the similarity ratings seemed to be dominated by the manner of articulation of the consonants. For example, /d/ and /k/, both stops, would be rated more similar than /d/ and /s/, which have the same place of articulation but have stop versus fricative manner. However, for either group of impaired listeners, manner of articulation was important in the similarity judgments only when correctly perceived consonants were considered, as opposed to the consonants actually presented. For example, if the pair /ba, fa/ was presented, but the listener heard /ba, ta/, the similarity rating of the /b-t/ pair would explain the responses rather than the /b, f/ pair. Between the groups of listeners with acquired versus congenital impairments, the consonant similarity ratings were not consistently different.

In summary, consonant similarity judgments, although a novel research technique, seem to offer little promise for convenient assessment of speech perception errors preliminary to auditory training. The use of similarity judgments for predicting consonant confusions is complicated by the necessity to determine consonant misperceptions, thus obviating the similarity ratings.

Acoustic Cues Used for Consonant Perception

Acoustic cue use in speech perception by normal-hearing listeners has been studied rather extensively (Borden and Harris, 1980; Pickett, 1980). In comparison, research has been limited on speech acoustic cues used by the hearing-impaired. Below we describe some recent studies on acoustic cue use in speech perception by hearing-impaired listeners.

ACOUSTIC CUES IN VOICING PERCEPTION

Several studies have examined voicing perception for stop consonants. Bennett and Ling (1973) studied initial stop consonants in recorded CV stimuli that contained systematic variations in voice onset time (VOT). VOT is the interval following the release of the initial stop, prior to the onset of the following vowel; this interval is brief for voiced stops and longer for voiceless stops. VOT was varied by a male talker during articulation of the CVs. Ten normal-hearing children and 10 hearing-impaired children (better ear, 3FA > 73-dB HL) listened binaurally at comfort levels to the CV stimuli and marked which of the six stops was heard after each stimulus presentation. For the normal-hearing children, perceptual distinction between the voiced and voiceless stops occurred at VOTs between 20 and 40 msec, similar to those seen for normal-hearing adults. In contrast, the hearing-impaired children generally showed inconsistent voicing distinctions of the stops, for the various VOTs. Furthermore, among the impaired children there was a tendency to identify more voiceless stops than voiced stops for VOTs of 60 msec or greater. The hearing-impaired children made markedly more errors in place perception among the stops than the normal-hearing children.

Parady et al. (1981) also studied the effects of different VOTs on voicing perception for initial stop consonants but used synthetic [dɑ]-[tɑ] stimuli. VOT was the duration during which a synthetic noise excited the F2 and F3 regions of the stimuli, prior to the onset of periodic excitation for F1, F2, and F3. Two tasks were used in studying perception of the stimuli. In an identification task, listeners indicated whether /dɑ/ or /tɑ/ was heard following each stimulus presentation. In a discrimination task, two stimuli with the same or different VOTs were presented consecutively, and the listener responded "same" or "different." The stimuli were presented to 21 hearing-impaired and 10 normal-hearing children at about 25 dB above the 3FA for each listener's better ear. The results indicated that identification along the VOT continuum was similar to that seen for normal-hearing adults for: the normal-hearing children, the moderately impaired (3FA, 42–68-dB HL), and one half of the severely impaired children and also for one profoundly impaired child. Generally, stimuli with a VOT of about 30 msec or more were heard as /tɑ/. However, for the other severely (N, 5) and profoundly impaired (N, 2) children, longer-than-normal VOTs were needed for them to identify /tɑ/. In the discrimination task, only one profoundly impaired and two severely impaired children were unable to discriminate VOT, and they also could not identify /tɑ/ consistently for the longest VOT.

Thus, in comparison to those with moderate impairments, children with severe or profound hearing impairments were more likely to require longer-than-normal VOTs for identifying /tɑ/. Three characteristics that occurred among some of the impaired children who required longer VOTs in identifying /tɑ/ were: a lower sensation level used for stimulus presentation, a later age for first hearing-aid use, or an earlier age at onset of loss.

In general, at least half of the severely or profoundly impaired children (3FA > 70-dB HL) studied by Parady et al., and the group of severely and profoundly impaired children studied by Bennett and Ling (3FA > 73-dB HL) showed reduced ability to differentiate voicing for initial stops, at the VOT boundaries used by normal-hearing listeners in stop voicing perception for synthetic stimuli. Thus,

VOT seemed to be of limited use for those hearing-impaired children in perceiving voicing for initial stops.

Revoile et al. (1981) studied voicing perception by altering acoustic cues for initial stops in monosyllables. Ten tokens of each test stimulus were recorded by a male talker. The syllables were presented at comfortable levels to the better ear of each listener—normal or severely hearing-impaired students at Gallaudet College. For the natural unaltered syllables, voicing perception was generally 100% for the normal-hearing listeners and between 70 and 100% among the hearing-impaired listeners. In one test condition of the VOT cue, the release burst (transient plus aspiration) for the voiced and for the voiceless stops was deleted prior to the vowel onset. This adjustment yielded syllables of different lengths and possibly with quantitatively different spectral information, since the voiceless stop burst was about 50 msec longer than the voiced burst. (Among all syllables the vowel durations were similar.) Consequently, in another condition the bursts of the syllables with initial voiced stops were cut back by the same amount as the syllables with initial voiceless bursts. The syllables with burst deleted for the initial stops yielded reduced voiceless stop perception for the majority of listeners, while fewer listeners showed reduced performance for the voiced stops. However, voiced stop perception was degraded for the majority of the listeners when the syllables with initial voiced stops were cut back according to the duration of the voiceless stop burst. Thus for some hearing-impaired (3FA, 30–84-dB HL) and normal-hearing students, VOT appears to be an important cue for initial stop voicing perception, especially for voiceless stops.

In another study at Gallaudet, acoustic cues to *final* stop voicing were examined (Revoile et al., in review). Impaired and normal-hearing listeners identified numerous /dɑC/ syllables, with C being either [p], [t], [k], [b], [d], or [g]. Responses were scored according to the correctness of stop voicing perception, regardless of consonant place errors. Among different test conditions, various acoustic cues to final stop voicing were altered in the syllables.

Perception for final voiced stops was reduced for over a third of the impaired listeners when vowel duration was made similar between syllables with voiced versus voiceless consonants. For the normal listeners, perception was minimally affected by this adjustment to vowel duration. Voiced stop perception was also reduced for some hearing-impaired listeners when, in addition to the adjustment of vowel duration, the voiced murmur was deleted between the vowel and the release burst of the final stop. For this condition the normal listeners again performed well.

Voicing perception for the voiceless stops among conditions of cue adjustments showed generally similar patterns of performance between the groups of normal and impaired hearing listeners, although performance was generally better for the normal group. When the vowels were made similar between the syllables with voiced and voiceless stops, nearly one half of the hearing-impaired and the normal listeners showed reduced voicing perception for the final voiceless stops. Perception was decreased for more than half of the listeners for the voiceless stops, when the final bursts were removed from the syllables. When the off-going transitions of the vowels were interchanged between syllable pairs of opposite stop voicing, the level of voicing perception seen for many of the impaired-hearing listeners and all of the normal-hearing listeners indicated that the vowel transitions were an important additional source of cues to final stop voicing perception.

ACOUSTIC CUES IN PLACE PERCEPTION

For certain consonants, differences in place of articulation can be distinguished on the basis of the rate of transition frequency change in formants of the preceding and/or following vowels. Differences in the rate of transition frequency change were used by Godfrey and Millay (1978) to study identification of /bɛ/ and /wɛ/ synthetic stimuli by mildly and moderately hearing-impaired listeners and normal-hearing listeners. Twelve 2-formant stimuli were used that differed only in transition duration, which varied from 10 to 120 msec, in 10-msec steps among the 12 stimuli. The stimuli with transitions of 40 msec or less were identified as /bɛ/, and those with transitions of 80 msec or more were identified as /wɛ/ by the normal-hearing listeners. Nine of the 15 hearing-impaired listeners identified /bɛ/ and /wɛ/ normally. In comparison, the other six hearing-impaired listeners showed abnormal patterns of responses along the continuum of transition durations. The response patterns varied among listeners and for individual listeners, depending on the presentation level of the stimuli. For example, some individual response patterns showed all transition durations identified as either /bɛ/ or /wɛ/; other patterns showed almost random labeling between /bɛ/ and /wɛ/ across the continuum of transition durations. The results of additional experiments with other normal-hearing listeners suggested that the abnormal response patterns for some of the hearing-impaired listeners were not due to their age or to the possibility of reduced hearing sensitivity in the F2 frequency region. Hence, these findings showed that some hearing-impaired listeners with only mild or moderate losses were unable to use rate of transition change normally, for identifying synthetic /bɛ/ and /wɛ/ stimuli.

Additional studies are needed of acoustic cue use in speech perception by the hearing-impaired. Thus far, the results suggest that differences in speech perception among hearing-impaired listeners are related to differences in acoustic cue reception. In addition, different acoustic cues may be used among impaired listeners for perception of given phonemes. In our future work we plan to study the effects of acoustic cue enhancement on reduced phoneme perception.

Vowel Perception

Hearing-impaired listeners generally show considerably better perception for vowels than for consonants. Below, we review several studies that reported the types of vowel misperceptions that may occur among severely impaired listeners.

Pickett et al. (1972) showed percent correct responses and confusions among the vowels /i, u, ɪ, oʊ, ʌ, ɔ, æ/ for 99 Gallaudet students who were divided into four groups based on their word recognition scores from a special version of the MRT (see above for more procedural information). The approximate

mean HL (3FA) for each group was 67 dB, 73 dB, 82 dB, and 88 dB, and the groups' corresponding correct overall vowel recognition scores were 91%, 76%, 62%, and 48%. The group with the lowest 3FA (67 dB) and the best word recognition showed minimal vowel confusions. In the second and third groups (73- and 82-dB HL), most of the vowel confusions occurred between vowels having F1 in similar frequency regions. For example, vowels with F1 in the low frequencies tended to be confused more with each other than with vowels having F1 at higher frequencies. In the group of listeners with the poorest hearing (3FA, 88-dB HL), there was also some tendency for the confusions to occur between vowels having F1 in the same frequency region, especially for vowels with F1 in the low frequencies. However, in this group the vowel confusions tended to occur more randomly across the vowels, regardless of the F1 frequency region.

Risberg (1976) summarized the ability of listeners (ages 10–21) to differentiate vowels on the basis of formant frequencies above and below 1500 Hz. (Some of the findings had been reported earlier by Martony (1974).) The vowels were in monosyllabic Swedish words presented individually, with the listener circling which of two printed words, each with a test vowel, was heard. To examine reception for formant frequencies below 1500 Hz, the vowels /u/, /o/, and /ɑ/ were tested. Those vowels differ in frequency for F1 and F2 but are similar in frequency for F3 and F4. Reception for formant frequency above 1500 Hz was tested between the vowels /u/ and /i/ and between /ɑ/ and /æ/. Within each pair the first formant frequencies are similar, but the second formant frequencies differ. The results were presented for the listeners grouped according to decades of hearing levels for their pure tone thresholds, either 3FA or at 2000 Hz.

Vowel recognition was best for listeners with losses between 60 and 69 dB, although they showed some confusion for vowels differing in formant frequency above 1500 Hz. For listeners with losses from 70 and 79 dB, mean recognition was near 90% for the vowels with different formant information below 1500 Hz, while mean recognition was reduced to about 70% for the vowels that differed above 1500 Hz. The loss group from 80 to 89 dB showed mean recognition of about 70% for the vowels with different formant frequencies below 1500 Hz; for the vowels with F2 differing above 1500 Hz, mean recognition dropped to about 40% when corrected for guessing. It is important to note that for discriminating the vowels /u/, /o/, and /ɑ/, the listeners may also have been using intensity cues; in Swedish these vowels are rather different in intensity.

These results suggest that for listeners with less severe losses, confusions may occur only for vowels that are distinguished on the basis of high-frequency formants. In contrast, listeners with more severe losses may confuse vowels regardless of differences in vowel formant frequencies.

RECOMMENDED METHODS

In a program of communication training for a hearing-impaired person, the training objectives and strategies determine the types of information needed relative to the person's speech perception. The methods suggested below for measuring speech perception assume that one training strategy will involve work on deficient phoneme perception. Consequently, speech perception measurements are recommended that will enable examination of the listener's phoneme confusions.

Phoneme confusions can be examined conveniently from the results of word recognition (speech discrimination) tests with closed-response formats, i.e., the response choices are restricted to a given set of words or syllables. Tests with closed-response sets probably have greater validity for identifying phoneme confusions than tests with free responses, such as the Central Institute for the Deaf (CID) W-22 word lists. In a free-response test, the true phoneme confusions may not be identifiable from the error responses. For example, the error response may differ from the test word in several phonemes (Owens and Schubert, 1968). When this occurs, one might question whether each of the substituted phonemes represents an actual confusion, or whether the response used was chosen because it was a more familiar word, or to avoid an emotionally loaded word or a nonsense utterance. For listeners who are linguistically impover-

ished, errors on free-response tests may be limited by a reduced vocabulary. As a possibility for eliminating lexical concerns, tests of nonsense syllables in free-response formats have been examined (Edgerton and Danhauer, 1979). Confusions under this method would be subject to phoneme frequency effects. Further, correct scoring depends on the accuracy with which a listener's responses are perceived by the tester. Scoring accuracy may be particularly difficult to ensure for a hearing-impaired listener with deficient speech production.

The drawbacks of closed-response formats are related to guessing—a possibility, since listeners are forced to respond. For example, although a test word may be misperceived, by chance the listener might guess the correct response. The chances of guessing correctly are lessened as more foils are included in the response set. Guessing could also occur for error responses, resulting in misrepresentation of the listener's phoneme confusions (Owens and Schubert, 1977). Due to the possibility of guessing, a speech perception test with a closed-response format should be administered more than once to enhance reliability in assessing a listener's phoneme confusions. For retesting, typically the presentation order of the stimuli is changed, and the foils are rearranged in each response set.

In test-retests for phoneme confusions, it is understood that a given recording of speech materials will be used. Unrecorded lists of words, as such, should not be thought of as test material (Kreul et al., 1969). Hood and Poole (1980) showed that recordings by different speakers of the same monosyllabic words yielded speech test materials that differed considerably in difficulty. In fact, it has been found that re-recordings of speech material by the same speaker can effect differences in test results (Owens and Schubert, 1977). Thus, where a listener's phoneme confusions are compared for recordings by different speakers, confusions may be speaker-dependent. Nevertheless, consistency in the findings of studies described above indicate that certain types of errors are likely to occur for severely hearing-impaired listeners. This information should be considered in the selection of material for testing phoneme confusions of the severely impaired.

Our literature review indicates that vowel and especially consonant perception may be reduced for severely impaired listeners. Among consonants, those produced in the same manner tend to show the most confusions, especially sibilants. On the other hand, nasals seem to be well-perceived. Consonants with the same place of articulation may also be confused. To a lesser degree, some confusions may occur between voiced and voiceless consonants, an effect that may be seen mostly for those with the same place and manner of articulation.

Some recently developed, closed-response, speech perception tests contain stimuli that will assess many of the types of errors seen among the severely hearing-impaired. For example, the California Consonant Test is being developed specifically for use with impaired listeners (Owens and Schubert, 1977). The 100 CVC words (male speaker) that currently comprise the test were selected from a larger pool of items presented in various combinations among several pilot experiments to different groups of hearing-impaired listeners with reduced W-22 scores (Owens and Schubert, 1968). Each closed-response set includes a test item and three foils (Schubert and Owens, 1971). Within sets, perception is tested for consonants in either the initial or final position and for consonants that differ in place and/or manner of articulation. Comparisons of certain phonemes are not included among the items, generally on the basis that pilot testing of those comparisons yielded minimal information. One aspect of the test that may be a limitation for some severely hearing-impaired listeners is that confusions are not tested for consonants differing in voicing.

In the development of the California Consonant Test, closed response items for testing vowel confusions were also studied (Owens et al., 1968). Based on results for listeners with impairments due to either Meniére's disease, presbyacusis, or noise exposure, most of the items were deemed too easy for inclusion as part of a speech discrimination test (Owens et al., 1971). However, recent use of this material with some students at the National Technical Institute for the Deaf (Webster and O'Shea, 1980) suggests that it may provide information on vowel confusions for severely hearing-impaired listeners.

A closed-response, nonsense syllable test was developed by Resnick to examine the phoneme confusions of moderately to severely hearing-impaired listeners using amplification (Levitt and Resnick, 1978). The test, recorded by both male and female speakers, consists of seven subtests, each of which employs a closed set of seven, eight, or nine nonsense syllables, containing different consonants with a common vowel, e.g., [iʃ], [if], [it], [ik], [is], [iθ], [ip], which differs among the subtests. More stop and fricative consonants are included than nasals, liquids, and glides. Within each subtest, consonant confusions for manner and place are possible, but not for voicing. For use with listeners having greater hearing impairments, Levitt and Resnick suggest testing fewer voiceless and more voiced consonants. Also of interest would be tests for voiced versus voiceless consonant confusions.

Prior to any test for assessing phoneme confusions, but particularly for one using nonsense syllables, it is important to examine the listener's orthographic versus auditory percepts for the stimuli. That is, does the listener correctly know the speech sounds associated with the printed stimuli? When reading the stimuli aloud, a listener's errors may merely reflect faulty speech production. On the other hand, some errors could represent inaccurate knowledge of the speech sounds associated with a printed stimulus. Our experience, experimentally, indicates that inaccurate orthographic-auditory associations usually persist in perceptual tasks, even after the listener is informed of the error and correctly reads aloud the stimulus. The effect of these inaccuracies is to confound analyses of phoneme confusions.

For examining phoneme confusions from a speech perception test, the phonemes perceived can be plotted against the phonemes presented, to generate a confusion matrix. Table 2.1 shows a confusion matrix for some results for a severely hearing-impaired listener on the six subtests of the MRT. Each quantity in a cell is the proportion of responses, obtained by dividing the number of times a particular phoneme was perceived, by the total number of presentations for a phoneme.

Table 2.1
Confusion Matrix for Results of Six Subtests of the MRT Presented to a Severely Hearing-impaired Listener[1]

Phonemes Presented	Phonemes Perceived																						Total Number of Presentations per Phoneme
	p	t	k	f	θ	s	ʃ	tʃ	h	b	d	g	v	ð	z	dʒ	w	r	l	m	n	ŋ	
p	.64	.09	.14		.04												.04			.04			22
t	.11	.63	.07	.04		.04					.04								.04		.04		27
k	.08	.20	.60	.04					.04			.04											25
f	.13			.53		.13			.07	.13													15
θ		.16			.66	.17																	6
s	.08					.92																	26
ʃ							1.00																3
tʃ						.25		.75															4
h	.08	.08							.83														12
b	.10	.05							.05	.60	.05	.10						.05	.05				20
d	.10	.10								.10	.57	.13											21
g			.06							.06	.13	.75											16
v	.17					.17							.50										6
ð	.50										.50												2
z															1.00								3
dʒ																.75		.25					4
w			.14														.71	.14					7
r																	.23	.77					13
l																			1.00				18
m													.07										15
n	.04	.04									.04							.04		.20	.60	.04	25
ŋ																						1.00	4

[1] Proportions are approximate.

Many of this listener's confusions were among the voiceless stop consonants and among the nasals, in word-initial and word-final positions. For the phonemes confused, the acoustic cue differences represent the types of acoustic speech information that was imperceptible for the listener. In differentiating initial voiceless stops, for example, we know that normal-hearing listeners use acoustical information or cues in the release bursts of the consonants and in the beginning (transitional portion) of the following vowel (Stevens and Blumstein, 1978). (Additional information on acoustic cues normally used for speech sound discrimination can be found in Borden and Harris (1980) and in Pickett (1980).) Thus, this impaired listener apparently did not make use of these acoustical cues in some instances when tested with the voiceless stops; the cues may have been inaudible or distorted for the listener, or possibly audible but simply never learned.

Tests are needed that directly assess reception for acoustic cues. We briefly discuss such tests in the next section.

FUTURE DIRECTIONS

The knowledge of acoustic cues in speech perception and the technology of sound processing are both advancing rapidly. This new information and technology can be used to develop improved tests of speech perception for auditory habilitation.

For diagnostic testing it is now feasible to use automated speech tests that could provide a speech feature profile for subsequent guidance in a listener's hearing-aid fitting and auditory training. Tests might be developed for producing feature perception profiles, using for adults stimuli similar to that of Resnick's (Levitt and Resnick, 1978) and, for children, material like that of Merklein (1981). Several small sets of rhyming words could be used as test stimuli, with the responses scored for correct feature perception. For example, identification responses to a test with the stimulus set *bad, mad, pad, dad, nad, tad* might be scored separately for place, nasal, and voicing. Similarly, the set *die, nigh, lie, by, my, why* may be scored for place, nasal, and glide perception. Other sets could be designed and scored along similar lines

with some final and intervocalic consonants tested as well. A test would be comprised of about 10 independent tokens of each stimulus syllable spoken by a single speaker. The syllables would be presented automatically from flexible digital storage by a digital testing system, which would include capability for recording and tallying a listener's responses from an answer box. Thus, the system could accumulate a confusion matrix display showing the responses and the percent correct perception for the features tested.

This automated procedure might also lend itself to auditory training. For example, feedback could be given after each response. Special pools of test words could be available from the digital store that could be used to develop generalized ability to perceive the speech features for different speakers. It is possible that compensation for different speakers is especially difficult for the prelingually impaired. The training procedure could be used to test and train this ability.

Research is now underway to investigate the use of acoustic cues in speech perception by the hearing-impaired. Reduced reception for specific cues may be found as a contributing cause for many of the difficulties in speech perception experienced by hearing-impaired listeners. This could lead to the development of clinical tests to assess acoustic cue reception. Such tests might involve psychoacoustic measures requiring discrimination of acoustical differences in complex stimuli patterned after speech acoustic cues (Danaher and Pickett, 1975; Revoile et al., 1982). Or, cue reception might be examined indirectly in a phoneme identification task, using synthetic speech stimuli that vary along a physical continuum that represents a particular cue (Fourcin, 1980; Godfrey and Millay, 1978; Parady et al., 1981). Additionally, real-speech stimuli with individual acoustic cues neutralized might enable assessment of cue use in word or syllable identification tasks (Revoile et al., 1981 and in review).

There are cues in speech perception that are patterned over larger units than the phoneme, namely, the prosodic cues of intonation contours, syllable rhythm and durational patterns, and vowel quality differences depending on syllable stress. It is possible that many severely prelingually impaired persons can discriminate these prosodic cues fairly well but do not use them properly in decoding speech. Systems need to be developed for testing prosodic decoding and for retraining in the use of prosodic cues. These procedures should be designed for use in conjunction with feature tests of the acoustic cues to phonemes because the two sets of cues would be expected to interact with each other in speech production and perception. Some materials are under development for assessing reception for certain prosodic cues (Levitt and Resnick, 1978; Fourcin, 1980).

In summary, when speech perception by the severely hearing-impaired is examined according to phoneme identification, vowels and especially consonants may be found to be misperceived. Impaired vowel perception seems to depend on the frequency location and proximity of the first and second formants. Vowels that are difficult to perceive tend to be those with higher frequency formants. Among consonants, those produced with the same manner of articulation are often the most easily confused. Some confusions are seen also for consonants with the same place of articulation. In comparison, fewer misperceptions occur between voiced and voiceless consonants. Phoneme confusions can be examined systematically through the use of recorded, word recognition tests that employ closed-response formats.

References

Bennett, C., and Ling, D. Discrimination of the voiced-voiceless distinction by severely hearing-impaired children. *J. Aud. Res.*, 1973, *13*, 271–279.

Bess, J.H., and Townsend, T.H. Word discrimination for listeners with flat sensorineural hearing losses. *J. Speech Hear. Disord.*, 1977, *42*, 232–237.

Bilger, R., and Wang, M. Consonant confusions in patients with sensorineural loss. *J. Speech Hear. Res.*, 1976, *19*, 718–748.

Borden, G., and Harris, K. *Speech Science Primer*. Baltimore: Williams & Wilkins, 1980.

Cox, B.P. The identification of unfiltered and filtered consonant-vowel-consonant stimuli by sensorineural hearing-impaired persons. Doctoral dissertation, University of Pittsburgh, 1969.

Danaher, E.M., and Pickett, J.M. Some masking effects produced by low-frequency vowel formants in persons with sensorineural loss. *J. Speech Hear. Res.*, 1975, *18*, 79–89.

Edgerton, B., and Danhauer, J. *Clinical Implications of Speech Discrimination Testing Using Nonsense Stimuli.*

Baltimore: University Park Press, 1979.

Fourcin, A.J. Speech pattern audiometry. In H.A. Beagley (ed.), *Auditory Investigation: The Scientific and Technological Basis.* Oxford: Clarendon Press, 1980.

Godfrey, J., and Millay, K. Perception of rapid spectral change in speech by listeners with mild and moderate sensorineural hearing loss. *J. Am. Audiol. Soc.*, 1978, *3*, 200–208 (now *Ear Hear.*).

Hood, J.D., and Poole, J.P. Influence of the speaker and other factors affecting speech intelligibility. *Audiology*, 1980, *19*, 434–455.

Kreul, E.J., Bell, D., and Nixon, J. Factors affecting speech discrimination test difficulty. *J. Speech Hear. Res.*, 1969, *12*, 281–287.

Kreul, E.J., Nixon, J., Kryter, K., Bell, D., Lang, J., and Schubert, E. A proposed clinical test of speech discrimination. *J. Speech Hear. Res.*, 1968, *11*, 536–552.

Lawarre, R., and Danhauer, J. Perceptual features of normally hearing and hearing-impaired subjects revisited. Paper presented at the Spring Meeting, Acoustical Society of America, Washington, D.C., April 1976.

Levitt, H., and Resnick, S. Speech reception by the hearing impaired: Methods of testing and the development of new tests. *Scand. Audiol.*, 1978, Suppl. 6, 107–130.

Mártony, J. On a rhyme test. In *Quarterly Progress and Status Report 2–3.* Stockholm: Speech Transmission Laboratory, 1974, 57–71.

Merklein, R.A. A short speech perception test for severely and profoundly deaf children. *Volta Rev*, 1981, *83*, 36–45.

Miller, G., and Nicely, P. An analysis of perceptual confusions among some English consonants. *J. Acoust. Soc. Am.*, 1955, 338–352.

Owens, E., Benedict, M., and Schubert, E. Further investigation of vowel items in multiple-choice speech discrimination testing. *J. Speech Hear. Res.*, 1971, *14*, 841–847.

Owens, E., and Schubert, E. The development of constant items for speech discrimination testing. *J. Speech Hear. Res.*, 1968, *11*, 656–667.

Owens, E., and Schubert, E. Development of the California consonant test. *J. Speech Hear. Res.*, 1977, *20*, 463–474.

Owens, E., Talbott, C., and Schubert, E. Vowel discrimination of hearing-impaired listeners. *J. Speech Hear. Res.*, 1968, *11*, 648–655.

Parady, S., Dorman, M., Whaley, P., and Raphael, L. Identification and discrimination of a synthesized voicing contrast by normal and sensorineural hearing-impaired children. *J. Acoust. Soc. Am.*, 1981, *69*, 783–790.

Pickett, J.M. *The Sounds of Speech Communication.* Baltimore: University Park Press, 1980.

Pickett, J.M., Martin, E., Johnson, D., Smith, S., Daniel, Z., Willis, D., and Otis, W. On patterns of speech feature reception by deaf listeners. In G. Fant (ed.), *Proceedings. International Symposium on Speech Communication Ability and Profound Deafness.* White Plains, New York: Phiebig, 1972.

Reed, C. Identification and discrimination of vowel-consonant syllables in listeners with sensorineural hearing loss. *J. Speech Hear. Res.*, 1975, *18*, 773–794.

Revoile, S., Pickett, J.M., Holden, L., and Talkin, D.

Initial stop voicing perception for cue-adjusted syllables for impaired- and normal-hearing listners. *J.
Acoust. Soc. Am.,* 1981, *70* (Suppl. 1, S34).

Revoile, S., Pickett, J.M., Holden, L., and Talkin, D.
Acoustic cues to final stop voicing for impaired- and
normal-hearing listeners. *J. Acoust. Soc. Am.,* (in review).

Revoile, S., Pickett, J.M., and Wilson, M.P. Masking of
noise bursts by an adjacent vowel for hearing-impaired
listeners. *J. Speech Hear. Res.,* 1982, *24,* 27–30.

Risberg, A. A diagnostic rhyme test for speech audiometry with severely hard of hearing and profoundly deaf
children. In *Quarterly Progress and Status Report 2–3.*
Stockholm: Speech Transmission Laboratory, 1976,
40–58.

Schubert, E., and Owens, E. CVC words as test items. *J.
Aud. Res.,* 1971, *11,* 88–100.

Sher, A., and Owens, E. Consonant confusions associated
with hearing loss above 2000 Hz. *J. Speech Hear. Res.,*
1974, *17,* 669–681.

Stevens, K., and Blumstein, S. Invariant cues for place
of articulation in stop consonants. *J. Acoust. Soc. Am.,*
1978, *64,* 1358–1368.

Walden, B., and Montgomery, A. Dimensions of consonant perception in normal and hearing-impaired listeners. *J. Speech Hear. Res.,* 1975, *18,* 444–455.

Walden, B., Montgomery, A., Prosek, R., and Schwartz,
D. Consonant similarity judgments by normal and
hearing-impaired listeners. *J. Speech Hear. Res.,* 1980,
23, 162–184.

Walden, B., Schwartz, D., Montgomery, A., and Prosek,
R. A comparison of the effects of hearing impairment
and acoustic filtering on consonant recognition. *J.
Speech Hear. Res.,* 1981, *46,* 32–43.

Wang, M.D., Reed, C.M., and Bilger, R.C. Comparison
of the effects of filtering and sensorineural hearing
loss on patterns of consonant confusions. *J. Speech
Hear. Res.,* 1978, *21,* 5–36.

Webster, J., and O'Shea, N. Current developments in
auditory speech discrimination tests for the profoundly
deaf at NTID. *Am. Ann. Deaf,* 1980, *125,* 350–359.

Wickelgren, W. Distinctive features and errors in short-
term memory for English consonants. *J. Acoust. Soc.
Am.,* 1966, *39,* 388–398.

Tactile Perception[1]

CAROL LEE DE FILIPPO, PH.D.

By what means does a hearing-impaired person engage in speech communication? The majority are capable of perceiving speech—their own and that of others—auditorily alone. Some, whom we will define as severely hearing-impaired, must supplement auditory perceptions with visual information, primarily through lipreading. For this group we still cannot specify what sensory images are used to monitor speech production (Erber, 1980b). A third, smaller group—the profoundly hearing-impaired—perform as though speech is predominantly an optical

[1] This work was supported in part by Program Project Grant NS 03856 from the National Institute of Neurological and Communicative Disorders and Stroke to the Central Institute for the Deaf, St. Louis, Missouri.

signal for them. Some in this group use the tactile sense to aid their understanding and production of speech.

TACTILE SENSE IN HEARING-IMPAIRED PERSONS

Rationale for Tactile Training

By definition, the *profoundly* hearing-impaired communicator does not have the sensory capacity to experience sound auditorily (Erber, 1979b; Risberg, 1977). This is the child who demonstrates thresholds for sound at his ears at levels similar to tactile thresholds (Ericson and Risberg, 1977; Nober, 1967). Also, his ears are no better at resolving small differences in frequency than is his skin (DiCarlo, 1962; Risberg, 1976; Risberg et al., 1975). Thus, when lipreading speech, he derives a relatively small amount of benefit when we add either "auditory" or tactile cues, and his audiovisual speech perception performance is similar to his tactile-visual performance (Hudgins, 1954; Gault, 1928; Erber, 1972a and b and 1978). In some cases, there may be no increment in lipreading scores when sound is added, or there may even be a decrement (Hudgins, 1954). Because of the similarities between audiovisual and tactile-visual performance, we assume that the stimulation provided by high-power hearing aids is tactile. Simple tests are now available to distinguish tactile perceivers from true hearers (Erber, 1980a; Risberg, 1976; Merklein, 1981).

If a hearing aid has performed as a tactile stimulator for many profoundly hearing-impaired children, why place any emphasis on special tactile devices and training? There are several disadvantages of conventional auditory amplification when used for tactile stimulation. First, high levels of sound are needed to vibrate the case of a hearing-aid receiver adequately. Also, the skin of the outer/middle ear may not have the same sensitivity to vibration as other parts of the body. Thus, the profoundly hearing-impaired child may detect only the high-intensity, low-frequency components of speech through a vibrating hearing-aid receiver, coupled to an earmold,

without our increasing the sound intensity to harmful levels (Ericson and Risberg, 1977). Through other means we may be able to stimulate the skin (at some ideal site) more efficiently and thus may provide a wider range between detectability and discomfort. Also, with other devices we may enhance frequency and time resolution through the skin by preprocessing the speech signal.

Occasionally, a *severely* hearing-impaired student also will benefit from training in tactile perception to help him to learn how to attend to minimal auditory cues. Transfer to auditory stimulation would be the primary goal. The tactile stimulus would be a tool to be discarded or faded out as quickly as possible.

Tactile Sense for Speech Perception

Receptors in the skin are sensitive to several forms of energy, including acoustic energy (Sherrick, 1975). The skin sense, the sense of touch, or the tactile system refers to a complex of structures and functions. For the purpose of speech perception, investigators have generally restricted themselves to the skin's ability to detect a touch (movement perpendicular to the skin), a stroke (movement parallel to the skin), vibration (a series of rapid touches), and electrical stimulation. Until the age of electronics, the skin was a near-field receptor, unlike the eye and the ear which can receive stimulation from energy sources at relatively long distances.

The most common application of direct tactile stimulation has been in the classroom for hearing-impaired children. The teacher places the child's hand on her head, cheek, nose, throat, or chest, and then on his own body, to match the sensations. In the Tadoma method of speech reception, the deaf-blind pupil arranges the fingers of his hand(s) on the talker's face so as to feel nasal, buccal, and throat vibration, the air stream from the nose and mouth, the shape of the lips, and muscle tension in the cheeks, lips, and throat (Norton et al., 1977).

Since scientists have advanced in methods of electronic signal transmission, teachers no longer depend on feeling the direct effect of articulation through hands-on contact. Now, the speech of a talker can be delivered via a microphone, accelerometer, or electrode. It can be processed to derive selected aspects of speech that are thought to be important for perception. These can then be transformed into signals that are meant to match the skin's sensory capabilities.

The skin is not ideally organized for receiving acoustic speech energy as it is normally presented to the ear. The skin is much more limited than the ear in its resolving power for time, intensity, and frequency of acoustic stimulation (Geldard, 1961). We are most sensitive to low-frequency energy, about 100–500 Hz (Goff, 1967). Despite any inherent insufficiencies in the tactile sense, there are some users who have derived considerable information through the skin (Gault, 1926a; Norton et al., 1977; Reed et al., 1978; Craig, 1977). This suggests that the limiting factors are our ingenuity in presenting speech information to the skin, and our understanding of how to train attention to the relevant sensations.

Design Goals for Tactile Devices

In this chapter we will not pursue the applications of direct "hands-on" transmission of speech through touch, as in the Tadoma method, or as an occasional adjunct to speech instruction (Ling, 1976; Calvert and Silverman, 1975) but will consider electromechanical means to tactile speech perception. At present, there is no tactile device which has conveyed enough information about speech to rival the auditory device that is the normal ear. A sensory *substitution* device, one which can take the place of the ear, is a design goal for the future (Bach-y-Rita, 1980). Instead, most engineers have designed devices as sensory *aids*, specifically as aids to lipreading. With a sensory aid, the child needs to acquire information from several sensory channels, no one of which transmits all of the spoken message.

One logical approach to designing a lipreading aid is to analyze what information is available through lipreading and to provide the missing information through another channel (Erber, 1974). This is essentially how the severely hearing-impaired person seems to comprehend speech (Erber, 1972a). His (impaired) auditory system provides infor-

mation on voicing and nasality, for example, which is not reliably available in the optical signal.

The profoundly hearing-impaired child cannot perceive such articulatory manner information through his impaired ears as can the severely hearing-impaired child. He can, however, use his unimpaired tactile sense to receive the information via an appropriate skin code. The two senses would complement each other and result in accurate acoustic speech perception, at least as good as that realized by the severely hearing-impaired.

A system of exclusively *complementary* cues may not be ideal, however. Even the normal-hearing listener depends on *redundant* cues to facilitate accurate speech perception. We also know that the profoundly hearing-impaired lipreader usually benefits from wearing a hearing aid in his ear, even though much of this information is redundant with lipread cues (Erber, 1979b). We conclude, then, that redundant information also may be helpful if provided through a tactile aid to lipreading (Weichbrodt, 1932).

REVIEW OF RESEARCH

A comprehensive review of tactile speech perception with use of ordinary amplification equipment has been published by Erber (1978, and 1979b). Much of the early work was pioneered by Gault (1926a). We have learned that a lipreader can benefit from receiving information about any of several aspects of a spoken message. Various kinds of information, from simple codes to complex signals, have been transmitted through tactile devices. These are summarized below.

Categories of Tactile Information

PRESENCE/ABSENCE/LEVEL OF SOUND

The most basic kind of information is whether sound is on or off. Most devices provide this information, including the conventional hearing aid, whether connected to earphones or a vibrator (Plant, 1979; Schulte, 1975). Their utility, however, depends on the threshold of detection of the wearer. Some profoundly hearing-impaired children require such high levels of sound input that only some vowel sounds, spoken close to the hearing-aid microphone, will be detected at their ears. The use of a vibrator increases the range of sounds that is detectable, but still requires that the talker be close to the microphone.

Voice detection is useful to the *lipreader* to draw his attention to the fact that someone has begun to speak, so that he may quickly search for the talker (Erber and Hirsh, 1978). In addition, a detection aid can help the lipreader to distinguish purposeful speech movements from nonspeech movements. For example, some movements of the mouth are preparatory to speaking but are not accompanied by sound (such as the opening of the lips before articulating the bilabial in, "Please"). This information is especially helpful in initial training of young hearing-impaired children (Goldstein and Stark, 1976).

A detection aid also is helpful to the hearing-impaired *talker* so that he can monitor use of his voice and avoid trailing off into voicelessness at the ends of sentences, for example (Summers and Martin, 1980). With devices like the hearing aid, which do not process the speech signal beyond amplification and filtering, most profoundly hearing-impaired children are aware of only two levels of sound—on or off. With a device which categorized level, the deaf talker would know how loud his voice is (Sparks et al., 1978).

Sound detection is useful not only for speech perception and production but also for relaying messages of warning. One device which uses a radiofrequency transmitter presents an electrotactile stimulus that the sender can pulse on and off (Sparks, 1977). It was evaluated as a tactile Morse code transmitter, but each user can establish any dit-dot code for the messages that are meaningful to him.

VOICE PITCH

Use of a normal pitch range, and use of pitch to serve a language function, usually are difficult tasks for the profoundly hearing-impaired talker. With tactile displays of pitch, hearing-impaired talkers can perceive the fundamental frequency of their voice. Students modify their typical pitch pattern by matching their memory of the tactile sensation produced by a teacher's model (Stratton, 1974; Willemain and Lee, 1971). This memory constraint is unique to auditory and tactile displays because the model is not stationary, as in an optical display.

Pitch information (fundamental frequency) also may benefit the lipreader (Ardell et al., 1979; Risberg, 1974). Changes in pitch—sentence intonation—aid intelligibility as well as awareness of emotional intent. On the skin, perception of fundamental frequency depends on how the signal is coded by the tactile device. With a single vibrator and no special processing of the signal, subjects could not distinguish between "You are going to the store" and "You are going to the store?" (Hawes, 1978).

If we expand the single-vibrator display into a row of vibrators, we can make each vibrator respond to a unique range of pitches (Rothenberg, 1978). By assigning each pitch range to a different location on the skin, we create a *spatial* code. Or, we can create a code of *qualitative* differences by activating a single vibrator with signals of different frequency or wave shape (optimally selected for the skin) and making the frequency of stimulation analogous to the pitch of the input (Rothenberg et al., 1977; Scott and De Filippo, 1977). In theory, those frequencies in the range of maximal tactile sensitivity should provide sufficient information to identify about eight different emotional intents (Ross et al., 1973). When this frequency range was presented to the skin, however, recognition of emotion from the unprocessed signal was difficult (Erber, 1978).

In a *spatiotemporal* display, the code is based on the pattern of stimulation over an area rather than at one location. On one such spatiotemporal display, the fundamental frequency contour moved across the contactors like the letters of the news on the Times Square display. It used a surface of 6 × 24 vibrating points and did aid sentence lipreading (Spens, 1975).

SPEECH PATTERNS

Early research demonstrated that, even with a single stimulator, a student could indicate number of words and syllables in a sentence, marking relative duration and stress and location of pauses (Gault, 1926b). One of the first vocoders, the Gault Teletactor, allowed students to achieve similar results by presenting different frequency bands of energy to different locations on the hand (Carhart, 1935). Later experiments also demonstrated the possibility of identifying sentence stress (e.g., "*John* was a good boy" *versus* "John was a *good* boy") by feeling speech through a single vibrator (Hawes, 1978). A student can apply this ability in identifying a specific message (sentence) if it is presented as one of a known set of distinctively patterned sentences (Erber and Cramer, 1974; Gault, 1926a).

FREQUENCY BAND ANALYSIS

Spectral coding, as in a tactile vocoder, is based on sampling the frequency spectra that represent speech, and presenting information about the energy in several selected bands at each point in time. The several vocoders that have been designed differ in number of channels (i.e., frequency range, bandwidth size, and spacing of center frequencies of the bands), in amount of preprocessing or "shaping" of the speech input (e.g., including the effect of the outer ear canal resonance), and in the method of matching the output of the band analysis to the frequency response of the skin (e.g., through frequency dividing or modulation techniques) (Gault, 1928; Gault and Crane, 1928; Weichbrodt, 1932; Guelke and Huyssen, 1959; Pickett, 1963; Pickett and Pickett, 1963; Kringlebotn, 1968; Saunders et al., 1976; Yeni-Komshian and Goldstein, 1977; Sparks et al., 1978, Sparks et al., 1979).

In many vocoders, most of the important frequency range for speech is represented. For this reason, one might expect the vocoder to be a sensory substitution device. To date, however, vocoders have been used more successfully as lipreading aids. Speech perception scores through vocoders alone have not been promising except with restricted message sets.

SOUND "LABELS"

Specific sound "labeling" is a goal of certain devices which signal the presence of sounds outside of the frequency range of tactile sensitivity. One example is a fricative detector consisting of a vibrator that produces an 800-Hz buzz whenever it receives input energy above 5000 Hz (Ling and Sofin, 1975). Another produces electrical stimulation in response to energy above 4000 Hz (De Filippo and Scott, 1978).

An alternative to simple sound labeling is selective sound analysis in which a group of sounds is represented by a *pattern* of stimulation. The student must identify the pattern before he can assign meaning to it. Designers of these sensory aids often select vowel energy as an important signal to code. Although an experienced observer can identify vowel quality in the unprocessed speech signal (Crane, 1927–28), there have been efforts to improve the ease and accuracy of recognition by isolating vowel information. In one device, the student feels the pattern of a line drawing that is like a two-formant spectrogram moving across his fingers (Kirman, 1974). In another, the quality of the tactile sensation (roughness or smoothness determined by the frequency of stimulation) is related to vowel first formant (Scott and De Filippo, 1977). Consonant information also has been provided through a graded intensity and frequency display on a single vibrator (Traunmüller, 1977).

LINGUISTIC FEATURES

Sound analysis also can be used to derive linguistic, primarily phonetic, features of speech. The display does not present the student merely with a spectral breakdown of the sound, but signals whether it is voiced or voiceless (Mártony et al., 1974), or nasal (Miller et al., 1974). Information on the manner of articulation often is selected because of the lack of manner cues in the optical (lipread) stimulus. The success of linguistic feature coding depends on the readiness with which the adult or child can learn the appropriate labels. For example, when he sees closed lips and feels the nasality and voicing indicators, he must recall that this combination is labeled "m"; a similar combination, but without the nasality indicator, might be "b." Some work we have done with older deaf adults indicates that this may be a difficult concept.

METHODS

Guidelines

AIMS

The hearing-impaired communicator has two needs which can be served by special devices. He needs to understand the speech of others and to produce speech that sounds intelligible (Erber, in press). Devices have been built to aid either perception or production, but often both aspects of communication are involved. The student who successfully uses a speech *production* aid obviously engages some perceptual process while attending to the feedback sensation. The student who wears a speech *perception* aid *may* use it as a speech production aid. He can learn sensory cues for evaluating his own speech if his voice is fed back through the same system as his teacher's voice and if he is given frequent communication experiences. Typically, however, tactile speech production aids are for *remediation* rather than communication, to correct or monitor articulation. In contrast, tactile speech perception aids are primarily "real-time" devices for use in *communication*.

A distinction of practical importance is whether a device is used to assist language *acquisition* or is applied to later *development* (refinement) of speech communication performance. Two programs that have routinely provided tactile stimulation for young profoundly hearing-impaired children are examples of sensory aid use for language acquisition. The first, instruction using verbotonal procedures, maximizes awareness of acoustic cues through low-frequency amplification provided by special speech-filtering equipment (Guberina, 1964; Craig et al., 1972). Children wear earphones as well as a vibrator during movement, speech, and language activities. The second, the Fonator system, is a set of German-made devices which also provide amplified speech through earphones and a special vibrator. German investigators have announced a project to develop a wireless version of the Fonator in order to extend tactile speech stimulation to infants (Gerzymisch, 1978).

Tactile stimulation should play the same role as early auditory stimulation in language acquisition. A child who is introduced to a sensory aid at a later time may need to recode vocabulary into tactile (or tactile-plus-visual) features before the device can become useful. The aided *infant* has an opportunity to organize perceptual/cognitive relations as they are learned, and to establish a permanent set of intersensory relations (Myklebust, 1964). For him, tactile sensations will become a necessary part of successful speech communication.

To make early tactile stimulation a widespread reality, American educators need to make a commitment to nonexperimental use of tactile devices, as they have done historically with auditory amplification (Plouer, 1934). The vibrator is a practical, readily available means for tactile stimulation. As experimental devices become commercially available, they can then substitute for the single vibrator.

Educators now recognize the need for early amplification. Audiologists now have improved test methods for differentiating between severely and profoundly hearing-impaired children. We now easily can adapt the conventional hearing aid as a tactile aid. Given the acknowledgment of the need, the diagnostic tests to identify the appropriate children, and the necessary equipment, we lack only the implementation in schools, parent-infant programs, and clinics.

MODALITY

The teacher must decide which mode(s) to stimulate during communication training (Erber, in press). Some teachers prefer unisensory training because it draws attention to the cues specific to that modality. Others choose bisensory or multisensory stimulation so that the child learns how different sensory cues are interrelated. They also emphasize that aided lipreading is the child's typical form of communication in daily living and for other classroom instruction. When learning sensory cues, however, the child may be distracted by a dominant stimulus (usually the optical, or lipread, stimulus) that is received through a normal or less-impaired channel (vision) (Erber, 1979a).

We cannot be sure that the cues we attend to when they reach us through a single modality (as in unaided lipreading) are the same as those we notice when the cues are multimodal (as in aided lipreading). The teacher, therefore, may choose to set aside time for practice with tactile stimulation alone while offering most instruction through tactile-plus-visual means, depending on the child's success (Erber, in press). The teacher will have to adapt to individual differences in the ability to integrate visual and tactile input (Erber and De Filippo, 1978).

One method that combines unisensory and bisensory stimulation is a fading technique. The signal to the dominant sense (vision) is degraded, so the lipreader is guided to the tactile signal (Erber, 1979a). Various levels of visual "noise" are introduced by spacing a sheet of rough-surfaced Plexiglas between the talker and the lipreader, by adding wide-band noise to a closed-circuit television picture, or by defocusing the image on a video tape monitor. The teacher can program a graduated sequence of fluctuating noise levels to bring the lipreader to truly bisensory perception under normal lipreading conditions. In this way, we might call attention to the complementary or redundant information provided by the aid without resorting to practice with the tactile signal in isolation, which can be a frustrating and less meaningful task. Montgomery (1977), also, has devised a method of differentially attenuating the vowel and consonant portions of an audiovisual message so that one portion is presented through both modes, and the other portion through only one mode.

A fading technique also may be useful in transferring from tactile perception, through a hand-held vibrator, to tactile/auditory perception at the ear. Some profoundly hearing-impaired children might learn to perform just as well with a conventional hearing aid as with a vibrator. Some severely hearing-impaired children might need help in perceiving auditory cues. For both types of children, the teacher may attach the vibrator to the hearing-aid receiver at the ear, simultaneously providing sound through earphone and vibrator. The next step is gradually to attenuate the signal at the vibrator. Tests of this sort also allow the teacher to verify the need for tactile training and to modify recommendations for particular children as necessary (Erber, 1979c). Those who respond to acoustic cues at their ears may have appeared to be profoundly hearing-impaired at an initial audiological assessment but later demonstrate that they can benefit from auditory rather than tactile training.

TYPES OF SKILL

Erber (1979b) defined two kinds of perceptual training: closed-set drills, and exercises to build generalizable skills. Often, the cues that we teach in identification and discrimination drills (Erber and Hirsh, 1978) are valid for the material we select for the drills, but disappear or change in connected speech. An example might be a pause cue to mark clause boundaries, or the prevoicing cue for the voiced bilabial (in a carefully articulated /b/, the voicing can be felt on a vibrator just prior to the opening of the lips). Closed-set drills are helpful to train the student to perceive differences in tactile qualities (such as frequency of the signal, which makes the sensation feel "rough" or "smooth"), timing (duration; rate of syllable onsets, offsets, or transitions), or patterning (changes over time or location of stimulation). However, discrimination/identification of such distinctions is not sufficient for *comprehending* speech. The teacher must add exercises to highlight broader concepts of tactile cues that apply across talkers and message sets.

The teacher also will need to select exercises that reflect the age of the child, i.e., his language and sensory experiences. For older students, the teacher may try to develop conscious strategies by talking about the tactile sensations. Younger children may need repeated, systematic, perceptual/language experiences from which they gradually can induce relations between sensation and meaning (Moog, 1975). The teacher may carefully select the language, for work in special exercises, which optimizes this learning. We know that certain words, syllable groups, and sentences are more easily identified than others, both visually (Argila, 1978) and through tactile stimulation (Erber, 1978). The idea of language engineering is a familiar one for facilitating language acquisition but also may be beneficial if applied to sensory learning.

UNDERSTANDING THE PROCESS

It is likely that the child using a tactile device will not always experience success.

The teacher will need to know the source of the problem in order to correct it. For example, the same error can result if the child attends to either the visual or the tactile input and does not combine the information; if the child responds to the wrong aspect of a stimulus, such as its intensity rather than its frequency; if the teacher assumes a tactile cue that is not, in fact, present in the given speech sample; or if the equipment malfunctions (Zeiser and Erber, 1977).

To explain the child's performance, the teacher might try the same tasks with the tactile device, while wearing earplugs and listening to masking noise. Experience with a simulated profound hearing impairment is invaluable for learning about perceptual "errors" (Erber and Zeiser, 1974). In addition, the teacher will want to experiment with the tactile device, while wearing it, to understand the effects of changes in voice level, precision of articulation, syllable rate, location of stimulators, and pressure of application, for example. In an ideal situation, the teacher always wears the same apparatus as the child, in order to be aware constantly of the sensations created by voice, environmental noise, or machine malfunction.

In some instances, additional instructional aids are helpful to inform the child about the tactile code. Schematic diagrams were used early as mnemonic devices for adult subjects (Gault, 1926a). With school-age children the teacher may discover two benefits of instructional aids: the child may learn what aspects of the sensations to attend to, and he may acquire some means of communicating with the teacher about his experience (Goldstein, 1939; Stratton, 1974; Erber, 1976). The idea of a syllable, for example, is primarily an auditory concept for the normal-hearing person. For profoundly hearing-impaired children using a tactile device, a word-sorting task can be devised (Erber, 1976) that teaches a tactile concept of the syllable. By associating spoken/written labels (or pictures of ideal examples) with the tactile stimulus, the teacher can define a metalanguage for talking about the tactile and visual codes the child is learning. Concepts such as pitch, duration, and pause patterns also can be developed in this way. In addition to the audio tapecard machine described by Erber (1976), teachers

have used the oscilloscope as a visual aid to create optical analogs to the tactile signal (Erber, 1978). "Seeing" the stimulus sometimes helps in understanding the perception.

Examples

TRAINING FOR HEARING-IMPAIRED CHILDREN

Investigators at the Oregon Research Institute developed a vocoder that was first tested with a small number of hearing and hearing-impaired persons (Engelmann and Rosov, 1975) and then applied to a broader study in classrooms of hearing-impaired children (Engelmann and Skillman, 1977). The vocoder analyzed speech into 24 bands and displayed the energy in each band on one of 24 vibrators arranged in two banks on each thigh.

The proposed training program, to be carried out in 1.5-hour sessions/day, was based on an integration of production, perception, and language activities. Engelmann and Skillman developed a systematic plan to build skills sequentially with isolated sounds, then words, followed by phrases and sentences. As production of each unit was mastered with tactile-plus-visual cues, the teacher presented that unit in a tactile perception task (closed-set identification). The same vocabulary was used in developing language concepts. The program listed specific stepwise procedures, including criteria for when to present a model utterance, number of trials at task, and a schedule of reinforcement. Results of this program have not yet been reported.

TRAINING FOR HEARING-IMPAIRED ADULTS

Plant (1979) and Connors and McPherson (1978) reported results of short-term rehabilitation programs, using tactile stimulation with three adventitiously deafened persons. None of the three could tolerate a hearing aid due to discomfort, distortion, or loss of sensation following even brief periods of stimulation. In both projects, the clients were given high-power body hearing aids which delivered amplified sound to a bone conduction vibrator held in the hand or the fingers. Training consisted of two parts: tactile-plus-visual stimulation, and tactile stimulation alone. The teachers presented sounds, syllables, words, and sentences in tasks requiring discrimination and identification.

Plant reported exercises also with fast/slow, loud/soft, and short/long sound patterns, environmental sounds, and telephone codes. After four weeks (54 hours) of training, Plant's client made measurable gains in aided lipreading performance, primarily with sentence material, but not with words or syllables. This is to be expected, since a single vibrator is a good display of the time-intensity pattern of speech.

Only one of the young adults tested by Connors and McPherson demonstrated gains with her tactile aid. On a sentence test, she scored higher when lipreading with the tactile aid than without it. The second student improved in lipreading, but the training did not affect his use of tactile cues.

LABORATORY PROCEDURES

A novel training procedure was used in two laboratory series with normal-hearing adults. Sparks et al. (1979) tested a 36-band vocoder modeled after some frequency-processing characteristics of the cochlea. Within each band, intensity was graded over eight steps. The display was an 8×36 matrix of electrodes worn on a belt around the abdomen. Scott and De Filippo (1977) developed a three-channel tactile lipreading aid. The first formant of vowels was coded by frequency of stimulation, felt as a gradient of tactile roughness or smoothness. Mid- and high-frequency sibilants controlled breadth of stimulation. Voicing and voicelessness were displayed as a periodic (buzz) or aperiodic (noise) signal. Two versions of the aid were built: one combined electrical and vibratory stimulation; another delivered all tactile cues through three vibrators.

The training procedure used by both research groups was "tracking" (De Filippo and Scott, 1978). Tracking is a method in which a talker must communicate a passage of speech verbatim to a receiver. The talker reads a short portion of text (a phrase or sentence), and the receiver repeats it back. If an error is made, the talker must select and apply some vocal/verbal strategy to correct the error, such as repetition, emphasis of an articulatory cue, shortening the selection to a word or sequence of single sounds, or re-phrasing (De Filippo and Scott, 1978). After the receiver is guided to a verbatim repetition of the talker's first chunk of text, the talker speaks the next phrase or sentence of the text, and the receiver again attempts to repeat it back. Tracking is continued for a predetermined timed interval. After 10 minutes, for example, the talker stops and counts the number of words in the passage read thus far. The receiver is then given a score in terms of words per minute, which reflects the efficiency of the communication situation.

Subjects participated in two conditions: lipreading with no added cues, and lipreading while wearing the tactile device. With both types of tactile aid described above, most subjects improved their tracking rate over 4–20 hours of experience. These gains are difficult to evaluate, however, because some subjects also made comparable gains in rate of tracking without the tactile aid. Nonetheless, it is clear that the procedure does effect learning—learning of *communication* strategies on the part of both talker and receiver, and learning of *perceptual* strategies by the receiver. With tracking, a teacher can provide practice on many levels of stimulus complexity, from the isolated sound to the sentence. Compared to drills with sets of unrelated syllables, words, or sentences, tracking more closely approximates the perceptual requirements of real communication situations. Teachers must still experiment with the method, however, to learn how to modify it for children with limited language knowledge and poor speech intelligibility. Part of this problem can be solved by using teacher-made stories as text.

FUTURE DIRECTIONS

Needs in Education

Despite a long history of interest, and advances in technology, tactile aids are far from commonplace in American schools for the deaf. Investigators have developed experimental models of a number of devices. Many have remained experimental despite some demonstrated utility, perhaps because they are not wearable or practical for daylong use, like a hearing aid. In addition, they have yet to provide greater overall benefit than the one aid that is readily wearable, the high-power body hearing aid with a vibrator output. Since we now have sufficient evidence that we can improve the speech perception performance of a profoundly hearing-impaired child without special equipment, we hope we can look forward to widespread use of at least the simple vibrator hearing aid.

Success with tactile aids depends, however, not only on their availability. We also need to extend their use to *younger* children. And, we must provide some format for *training*, or opportunities for guided sensory experience with speech. The methods described by Erber (in press) are recommended for integrating a logical approach to training into regular classroom instruction for hearing-impaired children.

Teachers are now being invited to assist researchers in evaluating tactile aids. Some investigators have determined that they cannot assess an aid's value until it has been worn over some period of training provided in a teaching situation. It may not be realistic to expect maximum performance to occur instantly, although many aids have been evaluated after only minimal practice.

Research Needs

Basic research will undoubtedly continue to implement concepts in sensory *substitution* devices. In addition, we need further testing of the ideas embodied in the many devices, primarily communication *aids*, that have already been assembled (Spens, 1980; De Filippo, 1978). For example, how well can the skin "read" a spectrogram in real time? Is spectral information more valuable to the lipreader than the same information coded into phonetic features? Under what conditions is perception improved by presenting fundamental frequency? The answers to such questions may depend on three separate areas of investigation: the lipreader, the speech signal, and the tactile mode of perception.

First, we need to study the profoundly hearing-impaired lipreader who may view speech—and organize the optical images he receives—differently than the typical normal-hearing laboratory subject. At the same time, we must beware of automatically drawing conclusions about unaided visual speech perception from results of bisensory speech perception performance. Second, we may benefit from developing experimental systems that present error-free information on any of several aspects of speech. These might be presented systematically and in combination to the profoundly hearing-impaired lipreader. If, for example, information on syllable boundaries is to be evaluated, the researcher may insert a signal by hand onto the sound track of a video tape to coincide with every dictionary-defined syllable in the talker's speech. Thus, he need not rely on a less-than-perfect electronic analysis of syllable location. The added signals might then be presented as light flashes or vibratory pulses to the lipreader. A similar arrangement may be helpful to assess the contribution of perfect vowel labeling or accurate nasality and voicing cues. Of course, work will continue on ways to procure this same information from the acoustic speech signal (Hirsh, 1978). Third, basic work is ongoing in exploring new dimensions, or types, of sensation in tactile perception (Geldard, 1961; Kirman, 1973; Sherrick and Cholewiak, 1977; Pickett, 1978; Rothenberg, 1978).

The final thrust, of course, required for successful use of any sensory communication device may have to be in the direction of a wearable, cosmetically acceptable package, preferably on the head or even all-in-the-ear. Further, it must be shown to the profoundly hearing-impaired lipreader that he communicates more efficiently when he wears the special device than when he feels the speech of his teacher on an ordinary vibrator.

References

Ardell, L.H., Kuhl, P.K., Sparks, D.W., and Grant, K.W. The contribution of synthetic low-frequency speech information to speechreaders. *J. Acoust. Soc. Am.*, 1979, *66*, (S1), S88 (A).

Argila, C.A. A Computer Simulation of Lip-Reading. Doctoral Dissertation, University of Santo Tomas, 1978.

Bach-y-Rita, P. Sensory substitution in rehabilitation. *Sens. World*, 1980, No. 39, 12–19.

Calvert, D.R., and Silverman, S.R. *Speech and Deafness: A Text for Learning and Teaching*. Washington, D.C.: A.G. Bell Association for the Deaf, 1975.

Carhart, R. A method of using the Gault-Teletactor to teach speech rhythms. *Am. Ann. Deaf*, 1935, *80*, 260–263.

Connors, S., and McPherson, D. A vibrotactile training program for the deaf using a single vibrator. In D.

McPherson (ed.), *Advances in Prosthetic Devices for the Deaf: A Technical Workshop*. Rochester, New York: NTID, 1978, 208–217.

Craig, J.C. Vibrotactile pattern perception: Extraordinary observers. *Science*, 1977, *196*, 450–452.

Craig, W.N., Craig, H.B., and DiJohnson, A. Preschool verbotonal instruction for deaf children. *Volta Rev.*, 1972, *74*, 236–246.

Crane, G.W. The tactual qualities of spoken vowels and diphthongs. *J. Abnorm. Soc. Psychol.*, 1927–28, *22*, 473–479.

De Filippo, C.L. Tactile aids for the deaf: Design and evaluation strategies. In D. McPherson, *Advances in Prosthetic Devices for the Deaf: A Technical Workshop*. Rochester, New York: NTID, 1978, 189–197.

De Filippo, C.L., and Scott, B.L. A method for training and evaluating the reception of ongoing speech. *J. Acoust. Soc. Am.*, 1978, *63*, 1186–1192.

DiCarlo, L.M. Some relations between frequency discrimination and speech reception performance. *J. Aud. Res.*, 1962, *2*, 37–49.

Engelmann, S., and Rosov, R. Tactual hearing experiment with deaf and hearing subjects. *Except. Child.*, 1975, *41*, 243–253.

Engelmann, S., and Skillman, L. Developing a tactual hearing program for deaf children. Research Conference on Speech Processing Aids for the Deaf, Gallaudet College, 1977.

Erber, N.P. Auditory, visual, and auditory-visual recognition of consonants by children with normal and impaired hearing. *J. Speech Hear. Res.*, 1972a, *15*, 413–422.

Erber, N.P. Speech-envelope cues as an acoustic aid to lipreading for profoundly deaf children. *J. Acoust. Soc. Am.*, 1972b, *51*, 1224–1227.

Erber, N.P. Visual perception of speech by deaf children: Recent developments and continuing needs. *J. Speech Hear. Disord.*, 1974, *39*, 178–185.

Erber, N.P. The use of audio-tape cards in auditory training for hearing-impaired children. *Volta Rev.*, 1976, *78*, 209–218.

Erber, N.P. Vibratory perception by deaf children. *Int. J. Rehabil. Res.*, 1978, *1*, 27–37.

Erber, N.P. Auditory-visual perception of speech with reduced optical clarity. *J. Speech Hear. Res.*, 1979a, *22*, 212–223.

Erber, N.P. Speech perception by profoundly hearing-impaired children. *J. Speech Hear. Disord.*, 1979b, *44*, 255–270.

Erber, N.P. An approach to evaluating auditory speech perception ability. *Volta Rev.*, 1979c, *81*, 16–24.

Erber, N.P. Use of the Auditory Numbers Test to evaluate speech perception abilities of hearing-impaired children. *J. Speech Hear. Disord.*, 1980a, *45*, 527–532.

Erber, N.P. Speech correction through the use of acoustic models. In J.D. Subtelny (ed.), *Speech Assessment and Speech Improvement for the Hearing Impaired*. Washington, D.C.: A.G. Bell Association for the Deaf, 1980b, 222–241.

Erber, N.P. *Auditory Training*. Washington, D.C.: A.G. Bell Association for the Deaf (in press).

Erber, N.P., and Cramer, K.D. Vibrotactile recognition of sentences. *Am. Ann. Deaf*, 1974, *119*, 716–720.

Erber, N.P., and De Filippo, C.L. Voice/mouth synthesis and tactual/visual perception of /pa, ba, ma/. *J. Acoust. Soc. Am.*, 1978, *64*, 1015–1019.

Erber, N.P., and Hirsh, I.J. Auditory training. In H. Davis and S.R. Silverman (eds.), *Hearing and Deafness*, ed. 4. New York: Holt, Rinehart & Winston, 1978, 358–374.

Erber, N.P., and Zeiser, M.L. Classroom observation under conditions of simulated profound deafness. *Volta Rev.*, 1974, *76*, 352–360.

Ericson, L., and Risberg, A. Threshold of hearing, vibration, and discomfort in a group of severely hard of hearing and profoundly deaf students. In *Quarterly Progress and Status Report 4*. Stockholm: Speech Transmission Laboratory, 1977, 22–28.

Gault, R.H. On the interpretation of speech sounds by means of their tactual correlates. *Ann. Otol.*, 1926a, *35*, 1050–1063.

Gault, R.H. The interpretation of speech by tactual and visual impression. *Arch. Otolaryngol.*, 1926b, *3*, 228–239.

Gault, R.H. Interpretation of spoken language when the feel of speech supplements vision of the speaking face. *Volta Rev.*, 1928, *30*, 379–386.

Gault, R.H., and Crane, G.W. Tactual patterns of certain vowel qualities instrumentally communicated from a speaker to a subject's fingers. *J. Gen. Psychol.*, 1928, *1*, 353–359.

Geldard, F.A. Cutaneous channels of communication. In W. Rosenblith (ed.), *Sensory Communication*. MIT Press, 1961, 73–87.

Gerzymisch, H. The Mini-Fonator. In D. McPherson (ed.), *Advances in Prosthetic Devices for the Deaf: A Technical Workshop*. Rochester, New York: NTID, 1978, 243–244.

Goff, G.D. Differential discrimination of frequency of cutaneous mechanical vibration. *J. Exp. Psychol.*, 1967, *74*, 294–299.

Goldstein, M.A. *The Acoustic Method for the Training of the Deaf and Hard-of-Hearing Child*. St. Louis, Laryngoscope Press, 1939.

Goldstein, M.H., and Stark, R.E. Modification of vocalizations of preschool deaf children by vibrotactile and visual displays. *J. Acoust. Soc. Am.*, 1976, *59*, 1477–1481.

Guberina, P. Verbotonal method and its application to the rehabilitation of the deaf. In *Report of the Proceedings of the International Congress of Educators of the Deaf, 41st Mtg. CAID*. Washington, D.C.: Government Printing Offices, 1964, 279–293.

Guelke, R.W., and Huyssen, R.M.J. Development of apparatus for the analysis of sound by the sense of touch. *J. Acoust. Soc. Am.*, 1959, *31*, 799–809.

Hawes, M.D. Tactile perception of stress and intonation. *J. Aud. Res.*, 1978, *18*, 141–145.

Hirsh, I.J. Compensatory electroacoustic processing of speech. In. M. Ross and T. Giolas (eds.), *Auditory Management of Hearing-Impaired Children*. Baltimore: University Park Press, 1978, 239–254.

Hudgins, C.V. Auditory training: Its possibilities and limitations. *Volta Rev.*, 1954, *56*, 339–349.

Kirman, J.H. Tactile communication of speech: A review and an analysis. *Psychol. Bull.*, 1973, *80*, 54–74.

Kirman, J.H. Tactile perception of computer-derived formant patterns from voiced speech. *J. Acoust. Soc.*

Am., 1974, *55*, 163–169.

Kringlebotn, M. Experiments with some visual and vibrotactile aids for the deaf. *Am. Ann. Deaf*, 1968, *113*, 311–317.

Ling, D. *Speech and the Hearing-Impaired Child: Theory and Practice.* Washington, D.C.: A.G. Bell Association for the Deaf, 1976.

Ling, D., and Sofin, B. Discrimination of fricatives by hearing impaired children using a vibrotactile cue. *Br. J. Audiol.*, 1975, *9*, 14–18.

Mártony, J., Agelfors, E., Blomberg, M., Boberg, G., Elenius, K., Risberg, A., Spens, K.-E., and Öster, A.M. Experiments with electronic lipreading aids. Speech Communication Seminar, Stockholm, 1974.

Merklein, R.A. A short speech perception test for severely and profoundly deaf children. *Volta Rev.*, 1981, *83*, 36–45.

Miller, J.D., Engebretson, A.M., and De Filippo, C.L. Preliminary research with a three-channel vibrotactile speech-reception aid for the deaf. Speech Communication Seminar, Stockholm, 1974.

Montgomery, A.A. Assessment of a new auditory-visual integration training technique. Paper presented at the Convention of ASHA, Chicago, 1977.

Moog, J.S. Language instruction determined by diagnostic observation. *Volta Rev.*, 1975, *77*, 561–570.

Myklebust, H.R. *The Psychology of Deafness: Sensory Deprivation, Learning, and Adjustment.* New York: Grune & Stratton, 1964.

Nober, E.H. Vibrotactile sensitivity of deaf children to high intensity sound. *Laryngoscope*, 1967, *77*, 2128–2146.

Norton, S.J., Schultz, M.C., Reed, C.M., Braida, L.D., Durlach, N.I., Rabinowitz, W.M., and Chomsky, C. Analytic study of the Tadoma method: Background and preliminary results. *J. Speech Hear. Res.*, 1977, *20*, 574–595.

Pickett, J.M. Tactile communication of speech sounds to the deaf: Comparison with lipreading. *J. Speech Hear. Res.*, 1963, *28*, 315–330.

Pickett, J.M. On somesthetic transforms of speech for deaf persons. In D. McPherson (ed.), *Advances in Prosthetic Devices for the Deaf: A Technical Workshop.* Rochester, New York: NTID, 1978, 184–188.

Pickett, J.M., and Pickett, B.H. Communication of speech sounds by tactual vocoder. *J. Speech Hear. Res.*, 1963, *6*, 207–222.

Plant, G.L. The use of tactile supplements in the rehabilitation of the deafened: A case study. *Aust. J. Audiol.*, 1979, *1*, 76–82.

Plouer, A.N. The Gault Teletactor at the Illinois school. *Volta Rev.*, 1934, *36*, 83–84, 116.

Reed, C.M., Rubin, S.I., Braida, L.D., and Durlach, N.I. Analytic study of the Tadoma method: Discrimination ability of untrained observers. *J. Speech Hear. Res.*, 1978, *21*, 625–637.

Risberg, A. The importance of prosodic speech elements for the lipreader. *Scand. Audiol.* [*Suppl. 4*], 1974, 153–164.

Risberg, A. Diagnostic rhyme test for speech audiometry with severely hard of hearing and profoundly deaf children. In *Quarterly Progress and Status Report 2-3.* Stockholm: Speech Transmission Laboratory, 1976, 40–58.

Risberg, A. Hearing loss and auditory capacity. Research Conference on Speech-Processing Aids for the Deaf, Gallaudet College, 1977.

Risberg, A., Agelfors, E., and Boberg, G. Measurements of frequency-discrimination ability of severely and profoundly hearing-impaired children. In *Quarterly Progress and Status Report 2-3.* Stockholm: Speech Transmission Laboratory, 1975, 40–48.

Ross, M., Duffy, R.J., Cooker, H.S., and Sargeant, R.L. Contribution of the lower audible frequencies to the recognition of emotions. *Am. Ann. Deaf*, 1973, *118*, 37–42.

Rothenberg, M. Optimizing sensory substitution. In D. McPherson (ed.), *Advances in Prosthetic Devices for the Deaf: A Technical Workshop.* Rochester, New York: NTID, 1978, 232–237.

Rothenberg, M., Verrillo, R.T., Zahorian, S.A., Brachman, M.E., and Bolanowski, S.J. Vibrotactile frequency for encoding a speech parameter. *J. Acoust. Soc. Am.*, 1977, *62*, 1003–1012.

Saunders, F.A., Hill, W.A., and Simpson, C.A. *Speech Perception Via the Tactile Mode: Progress Report.* San Francisco: Smith-Kettlewell Institute of Visual Sciences, 1976.

Schulte, K. Speech production—the capacity of communication-systems structuring speech for the deaf. Proceedings of the International Congress on Education of the Deaf, Tokyo, 1975, 76–83.

Scott, B.L., and De Filippo, C.L. Progress in the development of a tactile aid for the deaf. *J. Acoust. Soc. Am.*, 1977, *62*, (S1), S76 (A).

Sherrick, C.E. The art of tactile communication. *Am. Psychologist*, 1975, *30*, 353–360.

Sherrick, C.E., and Cholewiak, R.W. Matching speech to vision and touch. Research Conference on Speech-Processing Aids for the Deaf, Gallaudet College, 1977.

Sparks, D.W. A remotely activated tactual communication aid for the hearing impaired. *J. Speech Hear. Disord.*, 1977, *42*, 416–421.

Sparks, D.W., Ardell, L.A., Bourgeois, M., Wiedmer, B., and Kuhl, P.K. Investigating the MESA (Multipoint Electrotactile Speech Aid): The transmission of connected discourse. *J. Acoust. Soc. Am.*, 1979, *65*, 810–815.

Sparks, D.W., Kuhl, P.K., Edmonds, A.E., and Gray, G.P. Investigating the MESA (Multipoint Electrotactile Speech Aid): The transmission of segmental features of speech. *J. Acoust. Soc. Am.*, 1978, *63*, 246–257.

Spens, K.E. Pitch information displayed on a vibrator matrix as a speech reading aid. Some preliminary results. In *Quarterly Progress and Status Report 2-3.* Stockholm: Speech Transmission Laboratory, 1975, 34–39.

Spens, K.E. Tactile speech communication aids for the deaf: A comparison. In *Quarterly Progress and Status Report 4.* Stockholm: Speech Transmission Laboratory, 1980, 23–39.

Stratton, W.D. Intonation feedback through a tactile display. *Volta Rev.*, 1974, *76*, 26–35.

Summers, I.R., and Martin, M.C. A tactile sound level monitor for the profoundly deaf. *Br. J. Audiol.*, 1980, *14*, 30–33.

Traunmüller, H. The Sentiphone: A tactual speech communication aid. Research Conference on Speech-Processing Aids for the Deaf, Gallaudet College, 1977.

Weichbrodt, M. Tactual compared with visual discrimination of consonantal qualities. *J. Gen. Psychol.*, 1932, *7*, 203–206.

Willemain, T.R., and Lee, F.F. Tactile pitch feedback for deaf speakers. *Volta Rev.*, 1971, *73*, 541–553.

Yeni-Komshian, G.H., and Goldstein, M.H. Identification of speech sounds displayed on a vibrotactile vocoder. *J. Acoust. Soc. Am.*, 1977, *62*, 194–198.

Zeiser, M.L., and Erber, N.P. Auditory/vibratory perception of syllabic structure in words by profoundly hearing-impaired children. *J. Speech Hear. Res.*, 1977, *20*, 430–436.

Chapter 4

Visual Perception of Verbal Information by Deaf People

ILA PARASNIS, PH.D.
VINCENT J. SAMAR, PH.D.

A major consequence of profound deafness is that vision becomes the primary modality for the acquisition and processing of language. As such, it is important to understand the capabilities of the visual system and the nature of perceptual and attentional strategies to appreciate fully how verbal information presented on the hands, on the lips, or in print is processed by deaf people. Current research in experimental psychology indicates that each sensory system actively selects and transforms sensory information rather than passively transduces it from physical stimulus to percept. Furthermore, the research indicates that we have a limited capacity to attend to and process sensory information, and thus there is a continual selection of sensory information to receive further processing in the conceptual/memory system (see Massaro, 1975, for an overview). One important implication of this research is that language acquisition and processing by deaf people may be uniquely constrained by the characteristics of the visual system. It cannot be taken for granted that there is a qualitative identity between the visual and auditory processing of linguistic stimuli. Furthermore, it is possible that deafness may place demands on the visual system which may alter both the functioning of the visual system and the selection and processing of information in the conceptual/memory system. It is, therefore, important to understand how the visual modality is utilized by deaf people and what constraints are placed on the processing of verbal information by the utilization of the visual modality. Such an understanding may lead to informed decisions concerning optimal methods of presenting verbal information and to the development of programs or techniques to teach deaf people effective strategies to process verbal information.

Unfortunately, very little valid information is available from previous research with deaf people. Historically, visual perceptual research on deafness was mainly conducted to make inferences about the intelligence or cognitive abilities of deaf people. Some studies have examined the relationship between visual perceptual skills and language skills, but it is difficult to generalize from these studies, since they focused mainly on the English language and generally have many methodological problems (Furth, 1964 and 1971; Farwell, 1976; Hoemann, 1978). However, there is a growing awareness in the field that systematic investigation of the visual perception of verbal information is needed (Hoemann, 1978; Nickerson, 1978). The goal of this chapter is to heighten this awareness by providing relevant information from general research about the visual system and perceptual processes and by showing how this information can provide a framework for the study of verbal information processing by deaf people. We will use the term "verbal information" to refer to all linguistic representations, natural or invented, including sign, print, finger alphabets, and lip movements during speech.

VISUAL PERCEPTION

As a Constructive Process

We rely on our senses to provide information about the world around us. We seldom question the veracity of that information except in philosophical discussions about reality. Practically, what we perceive also exists in the physical world, and our senses seem to give us quite an accurate copy of it. Visual perception, however, is a complex process requiring the brain to impose a structure on sensory information which does not necessarily exist in that particular physical scene. When we say that perception is constructive, we are referring to this imposition of structure or organization on sensory data.

BOTTOM-UP AND TOP-DOWN PROCESSES

The act of perception involves both "bottom-up" and "top-down" processes (see Norman, 1976, for discussion). A "bottom-up" process consists of a series of successive processing steps in which the output of each step serves as the input for the step that follows it. A "top-down" process, on the other hand, is a process in which the output of a lower mechanism is influenced by the activity of a higher one. In our discussion, bottom-up processing refers to the way information is coded and transmitted from the eye to the cortex through increasingly more sophisticated levels of analyses. A relatively fixed set of properties of the visual system, such as the optics of the eye, and the structure of the retina and its neural mechanisms determines the bottom-up processing of information. Top-down processing of information refers to the way higher level general knowledge and expectations affect the interpretation of the sensory information encoded by bottom-up processes. Both processes interact in the visual perception of verbal information. In a way, what we perceive most of the time is a kind of perceptual sculpture, true in principle to what was presented but possessing features which have been highlighted or in some cases altered to conform both to the peculiarities of visual coding mechanisms and to expectations.

The interaction of bottom-up and top-down processes in perception of verbal information may be illustrated by the following example. In reading a book, the level of light in the room, the typeface, and the contrast of the print against the page affect how well we perceive the words. Bottom-up processes are responsive to these physical conditions, and more or less faithfully code them. Our previous knowledge of the topic, the context of what we have read, and our facility with language also affect our perception. These top-down processes facilitate the perception of the information provided by bottom-up processes. The dynamic interaction of these two processing mechanisms is reflected in the common experience of misreading a word. Generally, we have a perceptually clear image of the misread word. In fact, we know we misread it only when we go back to check it. Generally, the mistake is due to subtle spelling deviations which, when misperceived, give an entirely different meaning to the sentence. We seldom mistakenly perceive a word with radically different orthography from the actual printed word. Thus, both bottom-up and top-down processes influence the final perceptual experience.

As a Selective Process

The selective nature of perception is an important aspect of its constructive nature. By selection we mean the active choice of certain components of the presented visual information for further processing and the rejection or suppression of other presented information. Phenomenally, we have the common experience that all the information in the world around us is present and in focus, and that we are viewing the world continuously. This is an illusion; it can be shown that we constantly select certain aspects of stimuli over others, and we sample the visual scene only a few times a second rather than continuously. The illusion of continuity in the world we view is a constructive perceptual act.

Selection operates during sensory processing as well as during processing in the conceptual/memory system. When the stimulus is within fixation, certain stimulus features like color and movement are automatically selected and coded in the visual system. The neural coding mechanisms which accomplish this are not under voluntary control and are not modified by or accessible to manipulation by cognitive variables. Selection of information also occurs through eye movements by which we sample the visual scene, and this process can be under voluntary or involuntary control. We can voluntarily move our eyes to look at a certain part of the scene. Our eyes will also move involuntarily and fixate on a part of the scene if there is a sudden movement in the "corner of our eye," which draws them there. This is an alerting function which serves to inform us of a situation which may require further attention.

At the level of the conceptual/memory system, selection is under some voluntary control. We can decide which perceptual information to attend to and which to ignore; in other words, we can make a conscious decision about it. However, not all selection is under conscious control. As we mentioned before, we have a limited capacity to process information, and thus the amount of information we attend to, are aware of, or are conscious of at any given moment is limited. (For the purposes of this discussion we are using the terms attention, consciousness, and awareness interchangeably). There is ample evidence that selection of meaningful information can occur at early stages of processing. This selective process may be automatic, may involve both bottom-up and top-down processes, and is an intricate component of the attentional mechanism (see Glass et al., 1979, and Posner, 1978, for an overview).

Generally, the direction of gaze and the deployment of attention are closely linked. That is, if we want to direct our attention to a certain part of the field, we direct our eyes to fixate on it. Conversely, if our eyes are looking at something, we generally attend to that information. However, attention and gaze can be dissociated. It is possible to allocate attention to information falling on the retina some distance from the center of the gaze (Bashinski and Bacharach, 1980; Posner et al., 1978). This fact, as we will see, has some implications for the processing of verbal information when it is presented more peripherally in the visual scene.

In the sections that follow, we will briefly consider how verbal information is coded by the visual and the conceptual/memory systems. We will consider in some detail how selection and construction processes at the level of sensory coding and at the level of cognitive processing influence perceptual recognition of verbal information. Finally, we will discuss how these factors should be taken into consideration in understanding visual perception of verbal information by deaf people.

PROCESSING WITHIN THE VISUAL SYSTEM

Let us begin by briefly considering how information is coded by the visual system and how the selection process is influenced by the organization and properties of the system.

Coding and Selection at the Retina

Figure 4.1 schematizes the structure of the human eye. Light rays from an object pass through the cornea, aqueous humor, lens, and the vitreous humor and fall on the retina. At first glance, the eye appears to be like a camera. The cornea and the lens are primarily responsible for refracting the rays in such a way that an upside-down image of the object is focused on the retina. The pupillary opening, which varies in diameter according to the level of illumination, controls the amount of light that enters the eye. The retina contains photosensitive receptors which absorb the light and transmit the information to the brain. However, the eye is not nearly as good an optical system as a camera. The image that falls on the retina is blurred, and a significant amount of light never reaches the receptors because it is diffracted, scattered, or absorbed in the eye. In spite of this degraded optical image, the percept is sharp partly because the visual system is organized to code information from the visual scene by enhancing lines and edges. That is, lines and edges are selected automatically for enhancement. This enhancement is an aspect of the constructive nature of perception.

Let us look at the retina more closely. The retina covers about 200° of the inner surface of the eyeball. That is, if it were not for the nose, each eye could "see" more than a full hemisphere of the visual world about the observer. The retina contains two classes of receptors, called rods and cones, and several layers of interconnected nerve cells that code,

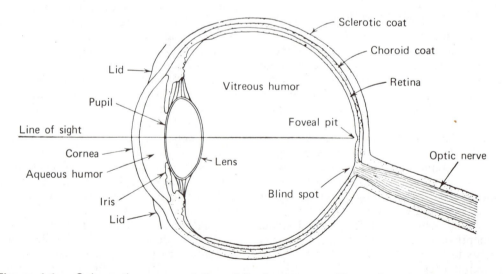

Figure 4.1. Schematic representation of the human eye. (Reproduced with permission from D.B. Judd, *Color in Business, Science, and Industry.* New York: John Wiley & Sons, 1952.)

reduce, and transmit information from the receptors to the brain. The small indentation in the retina is called the fovea, which points directly at the center of the visual scene. The fovea, which is about 1–2° wide, contains only cones. The region 15–20° medial from the fovea is called the optic disk or blind spot. This region, about 3° in diameter, is the spot where all the fibers from the retinal neural network exit into the optic nerve. Although it is totally devoid of receptors, we are unaware of this "hole" in our vision partly because the information falling across the blind spot is interpolated by the brain, another instance of perceptual construction.

Rods and cones are specialized for different types of information processing. Cones operate at high levels of illumination and thus are heavily involved in normal daytime vision. Cones are primarily responsible for pattern perception because the neural network they feed into is organized to maintain nearly a one-to-one connection of cones to neuron channels projecting to the brain, and therefore to preserve the fine spatial details of the visual scene. They also mediate color vision because they normally come in three types, each type maximally sensitive to either red, green, or blue light. Rods, on the other hand, operate at low levels of illumination and are primarily involved in night vision. They are not sensitive to color information. They do not contribute much to fine pattern analysis, since their neural network is organized in such a way that the millions of rods distributed across the retina feed into far fewer neural channels. Any of several rods distributed over a wide area of the retina may detect light and signal the event to the brain over a single nerve fiber, but the brain has little way of knowing which of these rods signaled the message. Thus, rods are good at signaling the occurrence of an event, but they do not preserve information about spatial detail.

The density distribution of rods and cones across the retina is shown in Figure 4.2. Cones are maximally concentrated in the fovea, and their number per area drops off rapidly as the distance from the fovea increases. As the figure shows, there are significantly fewer cones in the retina beyond 20°, and their density beyond that point stays fairly constant. Rods, on the other hand, are not present in the fovea. Their density starts increasing as the distance from the fovea increases. They are maximally dense at about 20° from the fovea. They are also present in large numbers in the periphery.

The distribution of rods and cones in the retina is directly related to visual acuity or the spatial resolving power of the eye across the visual field. Visual acuity is maximum at the fovea and decreases dramatically as distance from the fovea increases. Pattern acuity drops 50% when the distance away from the center of the fovea is only 1°, and when the distance increases to 80° from the center, it is only 15% of the maximum (Riggs, 1965). A direct consequence of these facts is that in processing verbal information we have a very limited field of view for discriminating the finer features of words, lip movements, or signs. The periphery can signal movement, sudden presence or absence of a stimulus, and can detect stimuli under low levels of light; however, it cannot be used for identification and recognition of information which requires fine, detailed analysis.

Of course, most of the visual system lies beyond the receptors, in the retinal neural network and in the brain. There is considerable evidence for the existence of feature extraction mechanisms or detectors at various subcortical and cortical levels. The visual system codes color and brightness, lines and edges, orientation, angular relationships, and movement at higher and higher levels of the nervous system. Thus, selection of information continually occurs in the visual system. It is possible to modify the properties of the visual system at different levels by surgically altering the system at birth or by manipulating the visual input during early development (see Hirsch and Leventhal, 1978, and Movshon and Van Sluyters, 1981, for reviews). Such modifications can change the organization of the feature analysis processes. However, once the visual system has developed normally, selection of stimulus features by these processes is a fixed property of the system.

Selective Attention

Our discussion, so far, suggests that the properties of coding mechanisms in the visual system constrain the processing of informa-

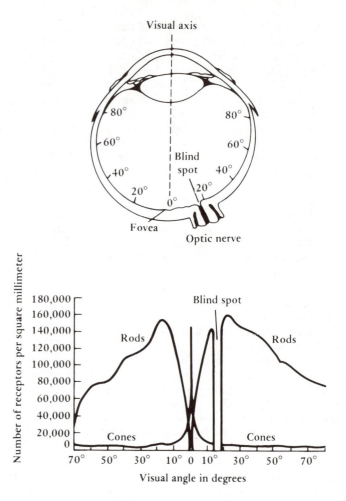

Figure 4.2. Density of rods and cones across the retinal surface. (Reproduced with permission from R. Haber and M. Hershenson, *The Psychology of Visual Perception*, 1980.)

tion by automatically selecting aspects of the stimulus for further processing. But this is not the whole story. Another factor that influences perception of information is the way a viewer selectively attends to that information. A viewer can control and direct attention to properties of stimuli or features within stimuli if s/he has prior knowledge of what to look for. This perceptual set, or deliberate tuning of attention to expected stimulus characteristics, has been shown to facilitate processing of attended information at the expense of unattended information (Posner, 1978). Attention can also be allocated, selectively, to different parts of the visual field even within a fixation. That is, perceptual set can be established not only for stimulus meaning or conceptual category but also for the location in space of expected events. Processing of the

stimuli occurring in the attended part of the field is facilitated, while that in the nonattended parts is inhibited (Bashinski and Bacharach, 1980; Posner et al., 1978).

A special case of the selective distribution of attention over visual space is represented in the phenomenon of the "effective visual field." The effective visual field (Harris and MacFarlane, 1974; Rayner et al., 1980), also called the useful field of view (Mackworth, 1976), is the area around the point of fixation, which can be used effectively to process visual information. Although the distribution of cones around fixation is an important determinant of the boundaries of this field, it is not the sole determinant. The size of this field varies according to task demands. It has been shown that as the informational load on the fovea increases, the diameter of the effective visual field constricts (Ikeda and Takeuchi, 1975). It has also been shown that if the information load in the periphery is increased while foveal information is being processed, the diameter of the effective visual field still constricts, presumably to prevent overloading the processing system. Mackworth (1965) has termed this phenomenon "tunnel vision." Thus, task demands can alter the allocation of attention across the visual field, and do so in such a way that there is a functional priority given to processing of foveal information. However, as we saw above, attention can also be shifted away from the fovea upon instruction. How peripheral information is processed thus depends on where attention is allocated, which in turn is influenced by the nature of task demands. Thus, the efficiency of processing peripheral information is not entirely predicted by the visual acuity function.

The size of the useful field of view can also be larger than that defined by the acuity function when a reader's task is to read familiar meaningful material. When a reader can make predictions about what s/he will see in the periphery, based upon previous knowledge of language and context, s/he can process more information from the periphery than the visual acuity function alone would predict (Haber and Hershenson, 1980).

Role of Eye Movements in Selection

So far we have discussed how information within a glance is processed. Normally, a visual scene requires several glances to process the information in it. Furthermore, it is usually the case that objects move, or the body and head move, in relation to objects in the visual scene. Let us briefly consider how we process information from a continually changing visual environment.

We sample the visual scene by making eye movements. Eye movements allow us to fixate on a near or distant target with both eyes, maintain fixation when the body or the head moves, keep a moving target in fixation, and sample different parts of the scene. Here, we will only consider those eye movements that allow us to sample different parts of the scene, since they are the most important in processing verbal information. Rapid jumps called saccadic eye movements occur when we de-

cide to change fixations or when an object is suddenly displaced in the field. Thus, they can be considered as voluntary or involuntary. Saccadic eye movements are ballistic in nature; once they are programmed, the direction, velocity, and distance of the eye movement cannot be changed. The typical latency to program an eye movement is about 125–250 msec. This means that once the eye has landed on a fixation, it may dwell there for up to 250 msec before another eye movement can take place. Once initiated, the eye movement can be very fast, as fast as 830° per second (Alpern, 1971). Generally, in reading, it takes about 25–30 msec to move the distance of 8–9 character spaces (Rayner, 1978). During this eye movement, the coding of new information is suppressed (Latour, 1962; Volkmann et al., 1968), perhaps to defeat the disruptive effects of the blur of information across the retinae as the eyes bolt from one position to another (Volkmann, 1978). The implications of these facts are that we sample chunks of information only a few times a second rather than continually monitor the entire scene, and we process most of that information during the fixation periods. Thus, our subjective impression of smoothly moving our eyes to scan a scene is a result of the constructive nature of perception.

Eye Movement in Reading

The reading process is a special and, for our purposes, important case of visual scene sampling. Research on reading shows that readers move their eyes generally from left to right in the case of reading English. There are also some regressions, which are saccadic eye movements that occur in the direction opposite to the normal direction of reading. In the case of English, this is from right to left. These regressions occur when the reader misunderstands the text or does not fully process the information obtained from the fixation prior to the regression. They may also occur to correct a prior saccade which caused the eyes to overshoot the intended fixation. In skilled readers, the average length of a saccade is about 8–9 character spaces (or about 2° of visual angle), and saccades consume about 10% of the reading time. Regressions comprise approximately 10–20% of reading time, and fixations, with an average duration of 200–250 msec, consume the remaining time (Rayner, 1978).

Eye movement patterns have been shown to differentiate good and poor readers as groups. The difference mostly involves the length of the saccades and the number of regressions made (Haber and Hershenson, 1980). There are also differences in eye movement patterns between normal and disabled readers (see Pirozzolo and Rayner, 1978, for review). Furthermore, there are individual differences in eye movements during reading, and the difficulty of the text influences eye movement patterns within the same reader (Carpenter and Just, 1977; Rothkopf, 1978). These general findings indicate that eye movement patterns during reading provide valuable information about the nature of text processing and individual differences among readers. No attention has been given to the study of eye movements during reading in the deaf population. However, eye movement studies clearly hold potential for the systematic study of reading processes in deaf people, since eye movements reflect the fine structure of central processing operations (Just and Carpenter, 1976; Rayner, 1978) and, in particular, reflect the progressive structure of the cognitive selection process. Furthermore, a sophisticated technology now exists to monitor eye movements (Young and Sheena, 1975) and relate the results to student characteristics and task demands. Many cognitive factors influence the nature of eye movements during reading. We will describe these factors in some detail in the following section.

In conclusion, the organization and properties of the visual system govern the selection and abstraction of visual information. Our limited capacity to allocate attention to information further influences the selection of information to be processed. There are, therefore, limits imposed on verbal information processing by the nature of the sensory modality and the nature of the attentional mechanism.

PROCESSING IN THE CONCEPTUAL/MEMORY SYSTEM

Let us briefly consider how verbal information is coded and processed by the conceptual/memory system and how selection and construction processes operate in this system.

Initial Representation of Visual Information

There is evidence that all the information that is coded by the visual system is available for processing during its initial representation in the memory system, even though people can rarely report more than 7 ± 2 unrelated items from what they have seen. The duration of this initial representation generally matches the stimulus duration but is at least about 250 msec if the stimulus duration is shorter than that (Sperling, 1960). That is, if the stimulus duration is only 50 msec, the perceiver continues to "see" the entire display for 250 msec if it is not interrupted by other stimuli. If a subject is briefly shown (<250-msec presentation) three rows of letters containing 5 letters each and is asked to report all 15 letters, the person usually is only able to report 5–7 of them. However, if a visual or auditory cue which identifies a selected part of the visual display is presented immediately following stimulus presentation, the subject is able to report the information which was cued, regardless of where it is in the display, or how much other information is present. If the cue is delayed more than 250 msec after stimulus presentation, the subject will begin to make errors in reporting the cued information (Sperling, 1960). These data demonstrate that no matter how complex a visual display is, all the information in the display is coded by the visual system and is available for further processing for about 250 msec. After that, only selected pieces of information will continue to be processed, through the operation of a recoding mechanism or chunking strategy, which is usually either visual or speech-based in nature. Whether the 250-msec persistence is due to continued retinal activity or due to the nature of the central memory process is controversial (Sakitt, 1976). Nevertheless, its existence demonstrates that selection must occur after initial coding but still at a very early stage of information processing.

Representation in Short-Term and Long-Term Memory

In normal-hearing people, when verbal stimuli are presented in print, it has been shown that people generally tend to recode those stimuli in a speech-based code in short-term memory. This has been demonstrated by analyzing the types of errors people make in remembering what they have just read. Shortly after reading, people tend to confuse words that sound alike rather than look alike (Conrad, 1964). After longer intervals, people tend to confuse words that are similar in meaning, and thus the nature of coding in long-term memory seems to be semantic (Baddeley, 1966).

Recent research has, however, shown that visual coding of verbal stimuli can occur in short-term memory (Kroll et al., 1970) and that some visual aspects of verbal information, like the type case in which the words are printed, are retained at the long-term memory (Hintzman and Summers, 1973). This evidence shows that the memory system is capable of coding information in visual/spatial as well as speech-based codes. Primarily, however, hearing people tend to encode printed verbal information in a speech-based code in short-term memory and in a semantic code in long-term memory.

Role of Cognitive Factors in Selection

Let us now consider some of the important variables that influence top-down processing and thereby perception of verbal information. Familiarity, which is a function of how frequently we have come across certain information, significantly influences perception of verbal information. It has been shown that familiar information is encoded in conceptual memory faster than unfamiliar information (Mewhort et al., 1969). Familiarity with the material also influences the reading of connected discourse. It is easier to read and remember familiar material than unfamiliar material (Haber and Hershenson, 1980).

The meaningfulness of verbal information also facilitates its perception. By meaningfulness we mean the degree to which verbal items will invoke associations or the degree to which they are integrated in the conceptual/memory network. Within one fixation, more meaningful stimuli are seen more accurately than nonsense strings (Eichelman, 1970; Reicher, 1969). Context set by meaningful stimuli also helps considerably in guiding fixations when reading text. For ex-

ample, it has been shown that reading speed is greater when the material is meaningful than when it is not (Morton, 1964).

Verbal information also tends to be redundant. The term redundancy refers to an intrinsic predictability in textual materials, which results from the existence of lawful constraints on the combination of linguistic units. For example, at the orthographic level in English, certain letter combinations cannot exist; if we see the letter "q," the probability that it will be followed by a "u" is very high, while the probability that it will be followed by an "x" is nil, if we are reading normally occurring linguistic material. Similarly, if we are reading a sentence, we can use syntactic rules to predict word order and word class to some extent. These rules and decision processes may not be available to introspection. However, they are normally used in making linguistic decisions (see Haber and Hershenson, 1980, for general discussion).

Another important factor is the world knowledge we bring to the situation. It is now known that in processing verbal information, we depend heavily on our general world knowledge. That is, we use previous knowledge to integrate new information into our general knowledge base. It can be demonstrated easily that previous knowledge about a topic dramatically influences reading comprehension. For example, read the following passage from Bransford and Johnson (1972) with the intention to remember it:

"The procedure is quite simple. First you arrange things into different groups. Of course, one pile may be sufficient depending on how much there is to do. If you have to go somewhere else due to the lack of facilities, that is the next step, otherwise you are pretty well set. It is important not to overdo things. That is, it is better to do too few things at once than too many. . . . At first, the whole procedure will seem complicated. Soon, however, it will become just another facet of life. . . . After the procedure is completed, one arranges the material into different groups again. Then they can be put into their appropriate places."

Although you will be able to use knowledge of English to understand the passage, you will probably find it difficult to remember because it seems to contain arbitrarily related sentences. But, suppose you knew beforehand that the passage would describe the chore of doing the laundry. Would you find it difficult to remember then? Go back and read the passage again, and you will find that the sentences make much more sense and are meaningfully related to each other. It was empirically demonstrated by Bransford and Johnson (1972) that prior knowledge of the topic of passages facilitates memory for passages in normal-hearing college students.

Reading is usually defined as extraction of meaning from a text (Gibson and Levin, 1975). It has been suggested that a reader engages in active hypothesis-testing behavior in search for meaning (Smith, 1971). The formation of hypotheses is influenced by the cognitive variables that we discussed above. The reader tests an hypothesis, corrects it if necessary, and moves on. Thus, top-down processes are intricately involved in processing print.

The reader's ability to control and direct attention to relevant parts of the text also plays a part in effective reading, since it aids in the selection and abstraction of information and therefore in hypothesis testing. Changes in the viewing conditions and, therefore, in the capability of the visual system to code information also influence reading performance. However, even when the optimum sensory conditions for bottom-up processing are met, there are large individual differences in reading skill which are due to differences in the world knowledge and linguistic knowledge that individuals bring to the situation.

PROCESSING OF VERBAL INFORMATION BY DEAF PEOPLE

The principles of perception and information processing developed in the previous section can be directly applied to an understanding of the way deaf people process verbal information. We will now consider the constraints imposed by the use of the visual modality and the role of top-down processes in processing information presented in signs, in print, or on the lips.

Processing of Signed Information

Although manual communication is a widely used form of communication among deaf people, its use in educational settings has been a subject of controversy for many years. The controversy stems from a long-standing history of speculation and untested convictions about the nature of sign language vis-à-vis *language*, and the implications of the use of sign language for the acquisition of English skills. It has often been assumed by educators that sign language is gestural and concrete, an impoverished sublanguage form of communication which imprecisely conveys meaning through pantomime. Therefore, the use of sign language has been viewed by many educators as an impediment to cognitive and linguistic development.

These prejudices have been significantly eroded in recent years by the systematic efforts of linguists and psycholinguists to formally describe and understand the structure and evolution of American sign language (ASL), one of the several sign languages in existence throughout the world. ASL, like all natural languages, has been shown to possess a systematic phonology characterized by the use of linguistic features. These features are, naturally, visual/spatial, rather than acoustic, and involve handshape configuration, location in space with respect to the body, configuration of movement, and hand orientation (Battison, 1974; Stokoe et al., 1965). In other words, the features conform to (are constrained by) the properties of the visual modality. ASL possesses a complex morphology and syntax, displays fundamentally arbitrary symbol-meaning assignment in the lexicon, and is capable of expressing abstract ideas. It is not our purpose to describe the linguistics of ASL or the developmental studies on the use of manual communication (see Siple, 1978a, and Liben, 1978, for overviews). Rather, we are interested in a related issue: given the increasing recognition of the linguistic complexity of ASL, the increasing interest in other forms of manual communication, such as the various forms of signed English, and current emphasis on simultaneous communication in educational settings, how is a visual language processed in the perceptual/memory system, and how might this knowledge be exploited in the educational setting? We will briefly consider what little is known about the processing of signed information in memory and then turn our attention to perceptual issues.

REPRESENTATION OF SIGNS IN MEMORY

The visual/spatial nature of ASL raises several questions about its representation at different levels of the memory system. For example, how is a visual/spatial language coded and organized in memory? Are there differences in the way material presented in a visual/spatial language and an oral language is retrieved? A few studies have examined how signs are coded in short-term and long-term memory by fluent signers. They indicate that at the short-term memory level, signs seem to be coded in a visual/spatial code, since the intrusion errors in immediate recall of signs are based on the similarities in formational properties of signs (Bellugi et al., 1975; Bellugi and Siple, 1974). The finding contrasts with the general finding that words are in a speech-based code in short-term memory. Thus, although signs and words are both linguistic symbols, their coding in short-term memory is different in that it is modality-dependent. At the level of long-term memory, signs seem to be organized semantically, just as words are. Siple et al. (1977) showed that in fluent signers, errors in recognition memory for signs were based on semantic rather than formational similarities. Liben et al. (1978) showed that there was a spontaneous semantic clustering of signs in free recall of fluent signers. These findings clearly indicate that ASL possesses both modality-dependent and modality-independent properties and imply that the acoustical coding characteristic of short-term memory for aural languages is, in fact, a modality-dependent process, not a universal characteristic of language.

Can the visual/spatial aspects of sign facilitate coding and retrieval of information from memory? The data of Siple et al. also indicated that there may be a facilitation of recognition memory for signs. They found that information presented in signs was recognized better than information presented in words. However, since they tested memory for signs and words only in deaf native ASL users, it is not certain whether this facilitation occurred because sign was a dominant language for their signers or because the visual/spatial nature of signs, per se, aided the recognition process. Parasnis (1980) tested 40 deaf and 40 hearing fluent signers to compare how signs and words are processed and retrieved from memory. Four conditions in the experiment were created by varying the mode of presentation with the mode of retrieval of information. Thus, the presentation of the list was in either words or signs, and it was retrieved in either words or signs. Deaf and hearing signers were randomly assigned to these four different conditions. The deaf groups were matched for amount of hearing loss, English language skill, manual language skill, and visual/spatial skill. All subjects were congenitally deaf college students who had learned to sign before age 5. The hearing groups were matched with each other for their age, education, years of experience in signing, and knowledge of ASL. Subjects were tested individually, and each subject was asked to retrieve the information first in a free recall task which was followed by a recognition task.

Analysis of the recall data showed that the mode of presentation or retrieval did not significantly affect the number of items recalled by either deaf or hearing fluent signers. Analysis of the recognition data, however, showed that information presented in signs is recognized better than information presented in words by both deaf and hearing fluent signers. All hearing signers were native speakers of English and learned to sign later in life, except for eight who learned English and ASL from birth. Thus, the facilitatory effect of the sign mode cannot be attributed to sign being a dominant language, as Siple et al. had suggested. This result indicates that although words and signs are both linguistic symbols, the richer visual/spatial nature of signs may still facilitate their retrieval in a recognition task.

PERCEPTUAL PROCESSES IN SIGN RECEPTION

We turn our attention now to perceptual factors in sign processing. Factors that affect the spatial/temporal resolving power of the eye will also affect the processing of signed information, since signs generally require fine spatial/temporal analysis. The level of illumination in the room and the contrast of the hands against the background will influence the functioning of cones and hence the processing of signs. Furthermore, the location of a sign on the retina will also affect its processing, since the spatial and temporal resolving power of the eye is greatest at the fovea and falls rapidly in the periphery. Thus, it is clear that where people look and how they change fixations during signing will change the quality of the processing of signs from moment to moment, since signs at and near the fovea will be discriminated better than signs in the periphery.

Where do people look, then, when they are receiving a signed communication? It has been argued that viewers tend to fixate the signer's face during ASL communication (Siple, 1978b). This argument requires empirical documentation before it can be assumed to be true. It is possible to do so by monitoring the eye movement patterns of the viewer as s/he processes signed communication. If the observation is correct, the viewer will spend most of the viewing time looking at the face, and the shifts in gaze due to eye movements will be small, will be overlapping, and will tend to have the signer's face in the center of fixation regardless of the nature of signs.

Let us examine this issue in more detail. If proficient signers do tend to look at the face, it is possible that this tendency develops as a person becomes more proficient in processing signs. It may be efficient to look at the face in sign processing for several reasons. First, since the sign space extends around the signer, resting the gaze in the middle of the sign space may maximize the chance that signs made anywhere in the field are noticed and initially processed to some extent. The viewer can then decide if an eye movement is needed to fixate on them for further detailed processing. Second, apart from being a mere reference point, the face may give important syntactic and semantic cues for the decoding of signed sentences (Baker and Padden, 1978). Furthermore, the face and the eyes of the signer may provide important cues to the viewer about when to shift the gaze away from the face and to the hands. If the face does provide important information to the receiver, it makes sense that the face may become the usual target of fixation, simply because facial movement would require the finely detailed spatial-temporal resolving

power of the fovea. By monitoring the eye movements of people who have varying degrees of sign skills, or by testing people longitudinally as they develop sign skills, we can determine if and how a strategy to look at the face develops.

The facial cues we are discussing may serve to facilitate the tracking of a signed communication by providing information to the receiver about upcoming events, or by disambiguating components of the information presented at other locations in the sign space. Thus, facial cues may provide a means of engaging top-down processes involved in hypothesis testing during sign reception. It is necessary to understand the nature of these cues, and the extent to which people rely upon them to process signed information, in order to develop fully effective educational materials which employ signed information. This is especially important when mixed communication forms are used, such as manually coded English. These forms have been invented for educational purposes. They have not evolved naturally but rather are abstractions of preexisting natural sign languages which have been modified to conform to English syntax and word order. To the extent that facial cues are an integral part of lexical and supralexical structures, the borrowing of hand configurations and their arrangement in a nonnatural order may involve a nonobvious, submaximal utilization of visual redundancy and processing cues. Eye movement studies, therefore, can provide information which may lead to improved forms of manually coded English and improved visual instruction materials.

ATTENTIONAL PROCESSES IN SIGN RECEPTION

Another issue relevant to the perceptual processing of manually presented information is the nature of attentional demands. For example, the useful visual field may be closely dependent upon the visual acuity function across the retina; however, visual acuity is not the sole determinant of the boundaries of the useful visual field. As we saw, task demands and top-down processes can contract or expand the field described by the acuity function. This implies that the complexity of the presented material may interact with the physical properties of media presentation—size of signing space, luminance, contrast, rate of presentation, etc.—to differentially affect the discriminability of peripheral components of the display and therefore to alter comprehension of the material. Similarly, degree of proficiency in signed communication, which involves individual differences in the automaticity of sign processing and the management of attention, may further interact with these factors. The influence of the attentional factor on the effective visual field must be understood before it can be taken into account in the development of visual communication materials. Exploratory studies are needed which specifically address the influence of the interaction of task demands, language proficiency, and physical parameters of sign presentation on the processing and comprehension of visually presented verbal information.

The nature of simultaneous communication creates an intriguing problem with respect to the effect of attention upon message processing, a problem which does not exist for conventional language processing. The problem is that in the simultaneous communication situation, the receiver is presented with several interacting sequential/simultaneous sources of information about the same message, each having different physical representations. These include auditory input, lip movement, fingerspelling, and signing, all of which must vie for attention from moment to moment within the constraints of the receiver's limited processing capacity. These components each have somewhat different sensory/perceptual processing requirements. Furthermore, the complexity of the message encoded by each component will vary from situation to situation. Therefore, we must ask the nontrivial question, how precisely does the allocation of attention among the coded components of simultaneously communicated messages occur, and what is the effect upon message comprehension?

We do not have the data to provide a satisfactory answer to this question at present. However, we can suggest some reasonable research questions. For example, does the lipreading component put such high demands upon detailed foveal processing that the effective visual field of the viewer constricts significantly, therefore reducing the efficiency of processing signs in the periphery? Does increasing the overall complexity of the message cause a redistribution of attention across the components of coding, thereby drawing more attention to one component at the expense of another (e.g., away from the lips to the hands)? How do student characteristics, such as proficiency in lipreading or signing, further affect the partitioning of attention among the component codes of simultaneously communicated messages? These questions may be addressed experimentally by monitoring eye movements in properly controlled simultaneous communication situations. The eye movement data will provide information about the relative extent to which viewers direct their attention to the coding components under different task demands and may reveal meaningful relationships between student characteristics or the structure of visual displays and attentional allocation. These data may affect decisions concerning the matching of communication methods or visual display parameters with student characteristics to optimize communication and instruction. For example, simultaneous communication may not be the method of choice for all instructional purposes or for all students. It may be optimal in some situations and not in others. This is essentially an empirical question, and it appears that the issue of attention may very well be at the root of the question.

Processing of Printed Information

Very few deaf people, unless they are postlingually deaf, are as proficient in English as an average hearing adult. Historically, both oralists and manualists have recognized the importance of teaching English to deaf children; and teaching reading, in particular, has been a standard part of the curriculum in deaf education, regardless of general educational philosophy. Notwithstanding the history of interest and good intention, very little research has been conducted to determine how deaf people process printed English and how to improve the reading process.

Nickerson (1978) comments that " . . . the lack of research aimed at finding more effective ways of teaching reading, specifically to deaf persons, suggests that there must be a consensus among researchers that the problem is not different in any significant respects from that of teaching reading to hearing persons."

However, it is obvious that there are important differences in the way deaf and hearing children acquire reading skill and the way they process information in memory. Generally, hearing children acquire reading skill after they have developed basic language skills through spoken communication. Very few deaf children develop basic competence in English before they are taught to read. For hearing children, then, the major task is to learn a written symbolic system for the language they can use and understand in spoken form, while for many deaf children, as Furth (1973) notes, learning to read is tantamount to learning a language per se. This fundamental difference in the knowledge of language that deaf and hearing children bring to the reading task may significantly affect their acquisition of reading skill.

RECODING OF PRINTED INFORMATION IN SHORT-TERM MEMORY

What are the limitations imposed by deafness on the reading process? One possibility, for which some research support is available, is that deaf people may lack useful reading strategies which allow the reader to maintain an efficient working memory of the text being read. Generally, hearing people tend to recode printed information into a speech-based code in short-term memory. This ability depends upon prior knowledge of the phonological structure of English, which is naturally obtained as a result of having heard English spoken. While there is evidence that phonological recoding is not absolutely necessary for the identification of word meaning (Colthart, 1978), there is also evidence that the availability of phonological codes facilitates reading (Kleiman, 1975). Conrad (1979) reported that reading skill correlated positively with a measure of the tendency to recode printed information phonologically in deaf children, even when IQ and hearing loss were controlled. There is some evidence that deaf people may develop alternative visual or kinesthetic coding strategies for printed information (Locke and Locke, 1971). However, it is not known what the relative efficiency of

each coding strategy is or if and how each affects reading skill. It is also not known if coding strategies can be taught. These are questions for future research.

TOP-DOWN PROCESSES IN READING

In general, in any research on reading with the deaf population, the utilization of top-down processing must be taken into account. As we noted earlier, knowledge of language, familiarity with context, and prior knowledge about the topic can affect reading performance by facilitating perception, processing, and comprehension of the material. Since many deaf people have a low level of English language competence to begin with, they will have difficulty in understanding the syntactic structure and the vocabulary used in printed English. This difficulty will, in turn, affect their future development of familiarity with the structure of English and the material available in print.

Can deaf people use context and prior knowledge in reading as well as hearing people if the passage is within the level of their linguistic competence? There are no empirical data on this issue. However, Furth (1973) has suggested that auditory impairment may lead to limited world knowledge, since many deaf children will not have the normal social interactions and experiences of hearing children. If this is so, the reading performance of deaf people, as a group, will tend to remain impaired even if they possess or are trained in the comprehension of the grammatical structures of English sentences. This is because, as we saw before, existing general knowledge in memory significantly influences the interpretation of printed information. If a deaf person does not have previous knowledge of the event or experience s/he is reading about, the encoding and subsequent memory for that passage will not be as good as that of a person who possesses such knowledge. If Furth is correct, it will be important to differentiate between the linguistic knowledge and the world knowledge that a deaf person brings to the reading situation, in order to understand that person's reading performance.

It should now be clear that reading skill is influenced by many perceptual and cognitive factors and that individual differences among deaf people and differences between deaf and hearing people in reading skill may be due to any one or a combination of these factors. To find optimal ways to present information and to teach effective reading strategies, we have to understand and be sensitive to the complexity of the top-down processes that operate in a reading situation. Again, basic and applied research with such a perspective needs to be undertaken to further our understanding of the reading process in deaf people.

Some researchers have begun to study reading with such a perspective. Geoffrion (1981) recently suggested that deaf children can benefit from a specific training which would allow them to identify words from their spelling patterns, as they may not have an adequate phonological coding strategy available to them. His pilot data showed that deaf third graders improved in their reading and spelling vocabularies after being trained for eight weeks to attend to the visual structure of words when identifying them. One area of research in which we are directly engaged is the study of the eye movement patterns of deaf adults during reading. In general, the reading skills of deaf people have been measured by standard reading comprehension tests. Such tests confound the ability to read with the ability to remember and retrieve what is read at a later time. Thus, performance on these tests do not directly indicate how deaf people employ top-down processes *during* reading. Currently, we are conducting eye movement studies addressed to the following issues: What is the useful field of view available to deaf people when they read? How well can they utilize peripheral information while reading? What is the temporal structure and distribution of fixations, saccades, and regressions in readers at different levels of linguistic skill? What is the effect of textual complexity on eye movement patterns during reading? As we saw in the previous section, these questions have been asked with hearing people, and the studies have continued to increase our insight into the role of top-down processes in reading. It is our belief that eye movement research with deaf people will similarly increase our understanding and will help us identify some fundamental characteristics of good and poor readers within the deaf population.

Speechreading

Speechreading generally refers to the ability to comprehend a spoken message presented visually on the lips and face, with or without the aid of simultaneous auditory information. Historically, training deaf children in speechreading has been defended and emphasized by oralists. Several different training methods have been developed, and many deaf children are routinely trained in speechreading as a part of their educational program. Unfortunately, these programs generally suffer from two limitations. First, their design has been motivated more by clinical observations or untested assumptions about the essential prerequisites for good speechreading ability than by empirical studies of the factors contributing to the skill. Indeed, very little research on this topic exists. Second, despite their wide use in educational settings, there has been little systematic effort to validate the effectiveness of various speechreading programs. The research that does exist either suffers from methodological problems or is limited in the scope of its query. Consequently, little knowledge is available about how speechreading skill is acquired and what factors are fundamental to its expression (see Farwell, 1976, and Jeffers and Barley, 1971, for reviews).

BOTTOM-UP AND TOP-DOWN PROCESSES IN SPEECHREADING

It is quite clear that visual information can be used to understand spoken messages. Many researchers have shown that when the acoustic speech signal is degraded, hearing subjects utilize visual cues from lips to understand speech (see Erber, 1975, for review). It is also well known that many deaf people have good speechreading skills, although they have very impoverished hearing. What is not well understood is what factors affect speechreading skill and contribute to the effectiveness of training programs.

Clearly, visual acuity is a fundamental contributing factor. Degradation of optical clarity has been shown to impair speechreading performance in deaf and hearing people (Erber, 1974; Hardick and Oyer, 1970; Romano and Berlow, 1976). This is quite understandable, since the processing of lip, jaw, and facial movements requires fine spatial and temporal analysis. The presence of simultaneous auditory information improves speechreading performance to a degree inversely related to the observer's hearing loss. Severely deaf people show a performance improvement considerably greater than profoundly deaf people (Erber, 1979). This demonstrates that if deaf people can use their residual hearing, they will do so in the speechreading situation. Erber also found that for both severely deaf and hearing people, when the visual display is systematically degraded by blurring in a visual/auditory condition, the decrement in speechreading performance drops slowly and asymptotes at about 45–50% at maximum blur. The same degradation manipulation in a vision-only condition produces a more sharply dropping performance curve which reaches chance levels far before maximum blur is attained. These data argue that auditory and visual information cooperate in aiding the perception of speech, with audition, alone, even in severely hearing-impaired people, contributing to speechreading as much as 50%.

It is still unclear from this research how the two sources of input cooperate. It is conceivable that they provide nonoverlapping information about the speech signal. However, a more interesting hypothesis is that vision and audition cooperate to disambiguate information from both modalities. In line with the writings of Risberg and Agelfors (1978), we suggest that the information from both modalities is integrated during the perceptual process, under the control of top-down processes, which bring expectations and knowledge to bear upon the coordinated results of the two sources of bottom-up analysis. This implies a degree of construction in the perceptual process, which occurs across modalities. It also implies that individual differences in linguistic knowledge and the conceptual/memory network, i.e., in the factors affecting top-down processing, will contribute to the expression of speechreading ability.

The existence of a constructive process concerned with intermodality integration is suggested by the work of McGurk and MacDonald (1976). Their normal-hearing subjects received simultaneous, conflicting auditory and visual syllabic information and attempted to identify the presented speech. The syllables pa-pa presented auditorily with the syllables ka-ka presented simultaneously on the lips resulted in 81% of the subjects identifying the utterances as ta-ta. Similarly, ga-ga presented with ba-ba was perceived by 54% of subjects as gabga, bagba, baga, or gaba. Clearly, most subjects did not simply ignore a modality, nor did they recognize the conflict. Rather, the information was integrated into a plausible percept. Thus, the inclusion of auditory input may have important perceptual consequences for the processing of visually presented information, and vice versa.

INFORMATION PROCESSING APPROACH TO SPEECHREADING

Apart from Erber's psychophysical work, we have little direct experimental information on the factors contributing to speechreading skill or its acquisition. Previous research has concentrated on correlating speechreading scores on various tests with intelligence, visual speed, visual closure, and synthetic skills, and various tests of language skills. Without exception, this literature documents moderate correlations at best (Jeffers and Barley, 1971). Despite the variety of tests used, and the motivating assumption in various studies that speechreading may depend generally upon one or another category of skills, there has been no attempt to demonstrate within a single experiment the separate contributions of several skill factors. To be more explicit, it seems reasonable to expect that speechreading ability is a weighted function of sensory, visual/perceptual, memory, attentional, and linguistic processes. In the context of the perceptual perspective presented here, speechreading performance is a product of both bottom-up and top-down processes. If so, one would not expect high correlations with single skill measures but rather would expect high multiple correlations of speechreading with general sensory, perceptual, memory, attentional, and linguistic variables.

A major reason why our understanding of speechreading has not progressed far beyond single variable studies is that research questions have not been formulated within the context of a general theory of information processing. A notable exception is the work of Risberg and Agelfors (1978), who have proposed an information processing model for audiovisual speech perception, which includes both top-down and bottom-up processes as contributing factors. By administering a battery of tests designed to selectively engage various sensory, perceptual, and cognitive processes assumed within the model, they were able to show that speechreading clearly depends upon two general aspects of processing: the ability to recognize minimal information-bearing elements in the message, such as articulatory units associated with the syllables, and the ability to process the recognized information through memory contact. It is clear that the first of these skills depends critically on sensory processes, while the second depends closely on conceptual/memory processes. What is required, then, in the future study of speechreading is a factor analysis approach guided by a theoretical information-processing framework. It is necessary to define and develop a battery of tests which will uniquely measure individual differences in general categories of information processing and then incorporate those tests into multifactor studies.

Samar and Sims (in press) have made some recent progress in defining a physiological measure of individual differences in speechreading, based on the initial work of Shepherd et al. (1977). Shepherd et al. reported that the latency of the negative peak occurring at about 130 msec in the visual-evoked response (VER) to flashes of light correlated highly ($-.9$) with speechreading skill in a group of normal-hearing subjects. The relationship was such that quicker latencies were associated with better speechreading performance on the Utley Speech Reading Test (Utley, 1946). Shepherd et al. suggested that the latency measure reflected the speed of visual-neural firing and, as such, individuals with visual systems which processed sensory information quicker were better speechreaders. Samar and Sims (in press) have replicated the procedures of Shepherd et al. and the fundamental latency relationship, but found a considerably weaker correlation ($-.58$). However, a factor analysis of the VER data revealed three statistically independent electrophysiological components related to

speechreading, one of which was completely independent of the latency measure and correlated $-.60$ with speechreading scores. The other two correlated with the latency measure and combined with the first to strongly predict speechreading scores ($R = .84$). The most interesting property of the first component is that it reflected individual differences in the VER to flashes of light which occur very early, at about 16 msec after the stimulus is presented, and continue to affect the VER waveform to 50 msec. Samar and Sims have named this component VF16.

The very early latency of VF16 suggests either that it is a correlate of individual differences in fixed properties of visual-neural organization or that it reflects individual differences in the moment-to-moment allocation of attention to external perceptual space. Its correlation with speechreading can be explained under either hypothesis. The first hypothesis implies that VF16 reflects the efficiency of sensory neural mechanisms which are responsible for bottom-up analyses of sensory data, e.g., speechreading stimuli, and, as such, should correlate with speechreading performance. The second hypothesis implies that VF16 reflects the operation of a top-down process: the deployment of attention to the visual channel at the time of stimulus presentation. Individual differences in a subject's tendency to selectively attend to the visual modality may be quite general, i.e., consistent over different tasks for that individual. Therefore, one would expect a correlation between a measure of attentional allocation in the light flash condition and speechreading scores, to the extent that the same tendency for each individual to allocate attention is occurring in the speechreading task.

Samar and Sims are currently engaged in a series of studies to define the nature of the information reflected by VF16 in deaf and hearing people. Once its nature is known, VF16 may be useful in a variety of research and clinical contexts. For example, individuals may be poor speech readers for different reasons. Some may be limited by inadequate knowledge of language, some by inappropriate allocation of attention, and some by inefficient sensory processing. If VF16 reflects structural aspects of sensory neural organization, which are likely to be resistant to clinical intervention, it will be useful in distinguishing students who are fundamentally limited in speechreading skill from those who are merely circumstantially limited by a lack of more basic, trainable skills. However, if VF16 reflects self-consistent tendencies to allocate attention to visual stimuli, it may be useful in identifying students who would benefit from a training program specifically designed to optimize perceptual preparation in the speechreading situation.

In general, we recommend that future researchers consider speechreading skill to be the product of the application of general principles of human information processing to a specific type of sensory/linguistic data. Studies designed within the context of contemporary models of information processing, which take into account the multiplicity of factors which can affect the processing of visually presented language, will provide data which can properly motivate the design and assessment of future speechreading training programs.

References

Alpern, M. Effector mechanisms in vision. In J. Kling and L. Riggs (eds.), *Woodworth and Schosberg's Experimental Psychology*, ed. 3. New York: Holt, Rinehart and Winston, 1971.

Baddeley, A. The influence of acoustic and semantic similarity on long-term memory for word sequences. *Q. J. Exp. Psychol.*, 1966, *18*, 302–309.

Baker, C., and Padden, C. Focussing on the non-manual components of American sign language. In P. Siple (ed.), *Understanding Language through Sign Language Research*. New York: Academic Press, 1978.

Bashinski, H., and Bacharach, V. Enhancement of perceptual sensitivity as the result of selectively attending to spatial locations. *Percept. Psychophys.*, 1980, *28*(3), 241–248.

Battison, R. Phonological deletion in American sign language. *Sign Lang. Stud.*, 1974, *5*, 1–19.

Bellugi, U., Klima, E., and Siple, P. Remembering in signs. *Cognition*, 1975, *3*, 93–125.

Bellugi, U., and Siple, P. Remembering with and without words. In *Current Problems in Psycholinguistics*. Paris: Centre National de la Recherche Scientifique, 1974.

Bransford, J., and Johnson, M. Contextual prerequisites for understanding: Some investigations of comprehension and recall. *J. Verb. Learn. Verb. Behav.*, 1972, *11*, 717–721.

Carpenter, P., and Just, M. Reading comprehension as eyes see it. In M. Just and P. Carpenter (eds.), *Cognitive Processes in Comprehension*. Hillsdale, New Jersey: Lawrence Erlbaum Associates, 1977.

Colthart, M. Lexical access in simple reading tasks. In G. Underwood (ed.), *Strategies of Information Processing*. New York: Academic Press, 1978.

Conrad, R. Acoustic confusions in immediate memory. *Br. J. Psychol.*, 1964, *55*, 75–84.

Conrad, R. *The Deaf School Child*. London: Harper & Row, 1979.

Eichelman, W. Familiarity effects in the simultaneous matching task. *J. Exp. Psychol.*, 1970, *86*, 275–282.

Erber, N. Effects of angle, distance, and illumination on visual reception of speech by profoundly deaf children. *J. Speech Hear. Res.*, 1974, *17*, 99–112.

Erber, N. Auditory-visual perception of speech. *J. Speech Hear. Idsord.*, 1975, *40*, 481–492.

Erber, N. Auditory-visual perception of speech with reduced optical clarity. *J. Speech Hear. Res.*, 1979, *22*, 212–223.

Farwell, R. Speech reading: A research review. *Am. Ann. Deaf*, 1976, *121*, 19–30.

Furth, H. Research with the deaf: Implications for language and cognition. *Psychol. Bull.*, 1964, *62*, 145–164.

Furth, H. Linguistic deficiency and thinking: Research with deaf subjects. *Psychol. Bull.*, 1971, *76*, 58–72.

Furth, H. *Deafness and Learning: A Psychological Approach*. Belmont, California: Wadsworth Publishing, 1973.

Geoffrion, L. Developing word-identification skills within a total communication program. *Am. Ann. Deaf*, 1981, *126*, 49–56.

Gibson, E., and Levin, H. *The Psychology of Reading*. Cambridge, Massachusetts: MIT Press, 1975.

Glass, A., Holyoak, K., and Santa, J. *Cognition*. Reading, Massachusetts: Addison-Wesley, 1979.

Haber, R., and Hershenson, M. *The Psychology of Visual Perception*. New York: Holt, Rinehart & Winston, 1980.

Hardick, E., and Oyer, H. Lipreading performance as related to measurement of vision. *J. Speech Hear. Res.*, 1970, *13*, 92–100.

Harris, P., and MacFarlane, A. The growth of the effective visual field from birth to seven weeks. *J. Exp. Child Psychol.*, 1974, *18*, 340–348.

Hintzman, D., and Summers, J. Long-term visual traces of visually presented words. *Bull. Psychon. Soc.*, 1973, *1*, 325–327.

Hirsch, I., and Leventhal, A. Functional modification of the developing visual system. In J. Jacobson (ed.), *Handbook of Sensory Physiology*, vol. 9, *Development of Sensory Systems*. New York: Springer, 1978.

Hoemann, H. Perception by the deaf. In E. Carterette and M. Freidman (eds.), *Handbook of Perception*, vol. 10, *Perceptual Ecology*. New York: Academic Press, 1978.

Ikeda, M., and Takeuchi, T. Influence of foveal load on functional visual field. *Percept. Psychophys.*, 1975, *18*(4), 255–260.

Jeffers, J., and Barley, M. *Speechreading (Lipreading)*. Springfield, Illinois: Charles C Thomas, Publishers, 1971.

Just, M., and Carpenter, P. The role of eye fixation research in cognitive psychology. *Behav. Res. Methods Instrum.*, 1976, *8*, 139–143.

Kleiman, G. Speech recoding in reading. *J. Verb. Learn. Verb. Behav.*, 1975, *14*, 323–329.

Kroll, N., Parks, T., Parkinson, S., Bieber, S., and Johnson, A. Short-term memory while shadowing: Recall of visually and aurally presented letters. *J. Exp. Psychol.*, 1970, *85,* 220–224.

Latour, P. Visual threshold during eye movements. *Vision Res.*, 1962, *2,* 261–262.

Liben, L. *Deaf children: Developmental Perspectives.* New York: Academic Press, 1978.

Liben, L., Nowell, R., and Posnansky, C. Semantic and formational clustering in deaf and hearing subjects' free recall of signs. *Memory Cognit.*, 1978, *6,* 599–606.

Locke, J., and Locke, V. Deaf children's phonetic, visual and dactylic coding in a grapheme recall task. *J. Exp. Psychol.*, 1971, *89,* 142–146.

Mackworth, N. Visual noise causes tunnel vision. *Psychon. Sci.*, 1965, *3,* 67–68.

Mackworth, N. Stimulus diversity limits the useful field of view. In R. Monty and J. Senders, (eds.), *Eye Movements and Psychological Processes.* Hillsdale, New Jersey: Lawrence Erlbaum Associates, 1976.

Massaro, D. *Experimental Psychology and Information Processing.* Chicago: Rand McNally, 1975.

McGurk, M., and MacDonald, J. Hearing lips and seeing voices. *Nature,* 1976, *264,* 746–748.

Mewhort, D., Merikle, P., and Bryden, M. On the transfer from iconic to short-term memory. *J. Exp. Psychol.*, 1969, *81,* 89–94.

Morton, J. The effects of content upon speed of reading, eye movements and eye-voice span. *Q. J. Exp. Psychol.*, 1964, *16,* 340–355.

Movshon, J., and Van Sluyters, R. Visual neural development. *Ann. Rev. Psychol.*, 1981, *32,* 477–522.

Nickerson, R. On the role of vision in language acquisition by deaf children. In L. Liben (ed.), *Deaf Children: Developmental Perspectives.* New York: Academic Press, 1978.

Norman, D. *Memory and Attention.* New York: John Wiley & Sons, 1976.

Parasnis, I. The effect of imagery on memory for signs and words. Unpublished doctoral dissertation, University of Rochester, 1980.

Pirozzolo, F., and Rayner, K. The neural control of eye movements in acquired and developmental reading disorders. In H. Avakian-Whitaker and M. Whitaker (eds.), *Advances in Neurolinguistics and Psycholinguistics.* New York: Academic Press, 1978.

Posner, M. *Chronometric Explorations of Mind.* New Jersey: Lawrence Erlbaum Associates, 1978.

Posner, M., Nissen, M., and Ogden, W. Attended and unattended processing modes: The role of set for spatial location. In H. Pick, Jr., and E. Saltzman (eds.), *Modes of Perceiving and Processing Information.* Hillsdale, New Jersey: Lawrence Erlbaum Associates, 1978.

Rayner, K. Eye movements in reading and information processing. *Psychol. Bull.*, 1978, *85,* 1–50.

Rayner, K., Well, A., and Pollatsek, A. A symmetry of the effective visual field in reading. *Percept. Psychophys.*, 1980, *27*(6), 537–544.

Reicher, G. Perceptual recognition as a function of meaningfulness of stimulus material. *J. Exp. Psychol.*, 1969, *81,* 275–280.

Riggs, L. Visual acuity. In C.H. Graham (ed.), *Vision and Visual Perception.* New York: John Wiley & Sons, 1965, 321–349.

Risberg, A., and Agelfors, E. Information extraction and information processing in speechreading. *Quarterly Progress and Status Report 2–3.* Stockholm: Speech Transmission Laboratory, 1978.

Romano, P., and Berlow, S. Visual requirements for lipreading. *Am. Ann. Deaf,* 1976, *119,* 383–386.

Rothkopf, E. Analyzing eye movements to infer processing styles during learning from text. In J. Senders, D. Fisher, and R. Monty (eds.), *Eye Movements and the Higher Psychological Functions.* Hillsdale, New Jersey: Lawrence Erlbaum Associates, 1978.

Sakitt, B. Iconic memory. *Psychol. Rev.*, 1976, *83,* 257–276.

Samar, V., and Sims, D. Visual evoked response correlates of speech reading ability in normal-hearing adults: A replication and factor analytic extension. *J. Speech Hear. Res.* (in press).

Shepherd, D., DeLavergne, R., Freuh, F., and Clobridge, C. Visual-neural correlate of speechreading ability in normal hearing adults. *J. Speech Hear. Res.*, 1977, *20,* 752–765.

Siple, P. *Understanding Language through Sign Language.* New York: Academic Press, 1978a.

Siple, P. Visual constraints for sign language communication. *Sign Lang. Stud.*, 1978b, *19,* 95–110.

Siple, P., Fischer, S., and Bellugi, U. Memory for nonsemantic attributes of American sign language signs and English words. *J. Verb. Learn. Verb. Behav.*, 1977, *16,* 561–574.

Smith, F. *Understanding Reading.* New York: Holt, Rinehart & Winston, 1971.

Sperling, G. The information available in brief visual presentations. *Psychol. Monogr.*, 1960, *74,* 1–29.

Stokoe, W., Casterline, D., and Croneberg, G. *A Dictionary of American Sign Language on Linguistic Principles.* Washington, D.C.: Gallaudet College Press, 1965.

Utley, J. A test of lip reading activity. *J. Speech Hear. Disord.*, 1946, *11,* 109–116.

Volkmann, F. Saccadic suppression: A brief review. In R. Monty and J. Senders (eds.), *Eye Movements and Psychological Processes.* Hillsdale, New Jersey: Lawrence Erlbaum Associates, 1978.

Volksmann, F., Schick, A., and Riggs, L. Time course of visual inhibition during voluntary saccades. *J. Opt. Soc. Am.*, 1968, *58,* 562–569.

Young, L., and Sheena, D. Survey of eye movement recording methods. *Behav. Res. Methods Instrum.*, 1975, *1,* 397–429.

Part III

Production and Expression

Chapter 5

Physiological Correlates of the Speech of the Deaf: A Preliminary View

DALE E. METZ, PH.D.
ROBERT L. WHITEHEAD, PH.D.
JAMES J. MAHSHIE, PH.D.

RESPIRATORY KINEMATICS AND AERODYNAMIC ASPECTS
NORMAL SPEECH BREATHING
SPEECH BREATHING PATTERNS OF THE DEAF

LARYNGEAL ASPECTS
PHONATORY PARAMETERS
LARYNGEAL ARTICULATORY PARAMETERS

ARTICULATORY ASPECTS

One of the most recognized but probably least understood concomitants of deafness is a deficit of oral communication skills. The speech produced by many deaf persons is frequently unintelligible to even experienced listeners. Moreover, it is frequently difficult to determine the exact nature of speech errors that reduce the deaf's speech intelligibility. The deaf's speech errors can be related to abnormal respiratory, laryngeal, and articulatory activities. By virtue of this physiological complexity, accurate surface level descriptions of the deaf's speech errors are frequently precluded. As such, perceptual and/or acoustical analysis procedures may not provide sufficient detail regarding the underlying nature of the deaf's unintelligible speech. Without a clear understanding of the underlying nature of the deaf's unintelligible speech, the development of effective clinical strategies is limited. Recently, Zimmermann and Rettaliata (1981) suggested that the development of effective remedial strategies could be enhanced by analyzing normal and deviant speech production from a physiological perspective. In this regard, the study of speech physiology may provide important insights regarding the basic nature of deaf speech.

Speech physiology is the discipline concerned with the neuromuscular, biomechanical, and aerodynamic events that support speech production. These physiological processes are considered to be the most basic properties of speech production, and there is a close relationship between these processes and acoustic output. Through detailed physiological analysis, one can determine how certain (ab)normal physiological events affect the speech signal. From a physiological perspective, intelligible speech is viewed as the determined product of temporally coordinated neuromuscular, biomechanical, and aerodynamic events. Conversely, unintelligible speech is viewed as the mismanagement of these events. The basic principles of the study of speech physiology are succinctly stated by Moll et al. (1977). These researchers (Moll et al., 1977, p. 119) suggest that speech production behavior should be studied by

"...determining the fundamental properties of the system, analyzing the timing relationships of movements, and studying the relationships between the detailed characteristics of motor unit activity and the parameters of movement. Such an approach will change our focus from questions about why the system fails to operate in accord with our preconceived constructs to questions about why the system operates as it does."

A reasonable extension of the position of Moll et al. (1977) is to suggest that our understanding of the deaf person's speech would be increased by knowledge of the fundamental physiological properties that directly underlie the unintelligible speech produced by the deaf. A clear understanding of the physiological nature of "deaf speech" could lead to a better appreciation of how deafness affects the control of speech production and to the development of more effective clinical strategies. These strategies would be designed to alter aberrant physiological behaviors that directly underlie the deaf's unintelligible speech.

As Abbs and Watkin (1976) point out, it has only been within the last 10 years that the study of speech physiology has become sufficiently sophisticated to take a permanent position alongside more traditional avenues of speech science investigation. By virtue of the above and the fact that the techniques used to study speech physiology have only recently been applied to the deaf, data are limited. The precise relationships between aberrant physiological activity and the resultant oral communication problems of the deaf are not fully understood. The research discussed in this chapter does, however, illustrate that important and exciting inroads are being made toward an understanding of the physiological underpinnings of the deaf's unintelligible speech. Space is devoted in each section of this chapter to normal aspects of speech production to provide the reader with a template for comparison purposes. Measurement techniques are briefly discussed to illustrate how the data have been derived.

RESPIRATORY KINEMATICS AND AERODYNAMIC ASPECTS

The primary purpose of respiration is to maintain life, but respiratory processes also provide the driving energy for speech production. Speech breathing processes are complex, but out understanding of the biomechanics of speech breathing has been greatly facilitated by the recent work of Hixon et al. (1973 and 1976). These researchers have investigated the biomechanical events associated with air volume displacements during speech breathing, and their theoretical formulations and measurement procedures form the cornerstone for much of the recent research regarding speech breathing patterns for the deaf. As such, it is worthwhile to survey briefly the theoretical basis for their measurement technique.

The chest wall (all extrapulmonary parts of the body that share changes in the volume of the lungs) is considered as a mechanism which displaces volume as it moves. Functionally, the chest wall is comprised of two parts, the rib cage and abdomen. When the respiratory pathways have an open communication with the atmosphere, changes in lung volume can be accomplished by independent displacements of the rib cage or abdomen or any combination of relative displacements of the two parts.

Relative volume displacemetns can be determined by measuring changes in the anteroposterior diameters of the rib cage and abdomen because volumes displaced by the body surface are equal to those displaced by pulmonary structures. Hixon et al. (1973) used electromagnetic transducers (magnetometers) to detect anteroposterior diameter changes of the rib cage and abdomen of normal hearing speakers during a variety of speech tasks. The principle behind determining relative volume displacements with magnetometers is as follows: A magnetic field is developed by small generator coils positioned at the midline of the anterior surface of the rib cage and abdomen. Sensor coils are positioned at the midline of the posterior surface of the rib cage and abdomen at the same axial level as its generator mate. The anteroposterior diameters of the rib cage and abdomen increase and decrease as volumes of air are inhaled and exhaled, resulting in increases and decreases in the strength of the magnetic fields between the generator and sensor coils. Voltages induced in the sensor coil associated with the strength of the magnetic field are inversely proportional to the distance between the two coil mates. With appropriate calibrations and data displays, one can determine the independent and collective volume displacements of the rib cage and abdomen and at what relative lung volume these displacements are occurring.

Normal Speech Breathing

Normal speech breathing patterns are highly individualistic and task-dependent (Hixon et al., 1973), but there are certain respiratory adjustments that are fairly consistent across speakers during discourse-type utterances. During normally intense discourse-type utterances, speaking is restricted to the midrange of vital capacity. Utterances are generally initiated from levels above the end-inspiratory level (the level achieved at the termination of a quiet inspiration) and are rarely extended beyond the functional reserve capacity (FRC) (the volume of air remaining in the lungs at the termination of a quiet expiration when all respiratory muscles are relaxed). Hixon et al. (1973) suggest that speaking within the midvolume range is mechanically efficient because it is the least demanding portion of the vital capacity range with respect to the muscular cost required against the elastic recoil properties of the respiratory apparatus. Speaking outside the midvolume range of vital capacity requires greater expenditures of muscular energy because the respiratory apparatus is less compliant.

Linguistic factors appear to play a major role in normal speech breathing, and the normal speaker appears to possess highly developed regulatory patterns that strongly influence when a breath will be taken during speech. As Hixon (1973) states, the respiratory system's task in sustained utterances is to provide a relatively continuous expiration, halted occasionally for inspiratory refills or breath holdings at sentence or phrase boundaries or other appropriate linguistic points.

One final point regarding normal speech breathing patterns needs to be taken into consideration: the relative volume displacements of the rib cage and abdomen during speaking. Individual subjects appear to perform very differently with respect to relative volume displacements of the rib cage and abdomen during speech, which probably relates to how the individual learned to use his muscular system against the passive mechanical properties of his respiratory apparatus (Hixon et al., 1973). Typically, however, the rib cage and abdomen work in synchrony.

Speech Breathing Patterns of the Deaf

In the previous section we briefly discussed three general aspects of normal speech breathing: (1) relative lung volumes used during speaking, (2) linguistic influences on speech breathing, and (3) the relative contribution of the rib cage and abdomen in volume displacements for speech breathing.

Forner and Hixon (1977), employing magnetometers, investigated the speech breathing patterns of 10 profoundly hearing-impaired speakers. Their findings indicated that, in similar fashion to normally hearing speakers, the majority of their deaf subjects spoke within the midvolume range of vital capacity. Also, the majority of their subjects initiated speech from lung volume levels above the functional reserve capacity (FRC). Three of their subjects, however, consistently initiated speech at or below FRC. Similar findings have been reported by Whitehead (in press).

Whitehead investigated respiratory kinematics of five normal-hearing speakers, five intelligible hearing-impaired speakers, and five semi-intelligible hearing-impaired speakers. Whitehead's results indicate that the normal-hearing and the intelligible deaf adults typically initiated speech between 700 and 800 cc above FRC (Fig. 5.1). The semi-intelligible deaf speakers, however, tended to initiate speech at substantially lower lung volumes (average, 125 cc above FRC). Perhaps more importantly, the semi-intelligible hearing-impaired speakers demonstrated a consistent tendency to continue speaking at lung volumes well below FRC in direct contrast to the normal-hearing and intelligible hearing-

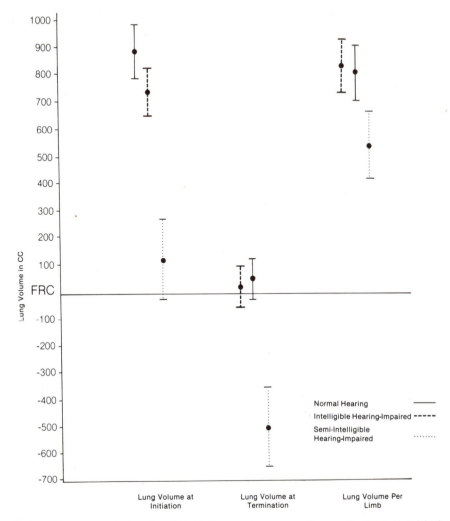

Figure 5.1. Means and standard deviations of average lung volumes at initiation and termination of speech phrases, and average lung volume expenditure per speech phrase for 5 normally hearing, 5 intelligible hearing-impaired, and 15 semi-intelligible hearing-impaired speakers.

impaired subjects who rarely spoke at levels below FRC.

Forner and Hixon (1977) further observed that the average air expenditure per syllable of their deaf subjects was on the order of 100 cc, which is severalfold greater than the average air expenditure per syllable observed in normal-hearing speakers. This excessive air expenditure per syllable probably accounts for Forner and Hixon's finding that their deaf subjects only produced 4.5 syllables/breath (expiratory limb) in contrast to 13.5 syllables/

expiratory limb produced by a comparison group of 10 normal-hearing individuals. Whitehead (in press) also observed that his normally hearing speakers and intelligible hearing-impaired speakers averaged 14 and 10 syllables/expiratory limb, respectively, but the semi-intelligible deaf speakers averaged only 3 syllables/expiratory limb.

The deaf speakers tendency to waste air during speech production appears to be further complicated by many "unnecessary and seemingly unlawful interruptions for breaths and holdings at points other than those known to be linguistically appropriate ... [Forner and Hixon, 1977, p. 395]." These abnormal haltings occurred between syllables within a single expiratory limb.

With respect to relative volume displacements of the rib cage and abdomen, Forner and Hixon (1977) found that their subjects fell within the range of observations previously made on normally hearing individuals (Hixon et al., 1973 and 1976). One subject did demonstrate rib cage-abdomen synchronization problems, but this finding was not considered to be characteristic of deaf speakers in general. Whitehead (in press) arrived at a similar conclusion regarding rib cage-abdomen synchronization problems of the deaf.

The findings of both Forner and Hixon (1977) and Whitehead (in press) strongly suggest that deaf individuals have difficulty regulating the respiratory apparatus in a coordinated efficient fashion for speech production. Moreover, difficulties regulating speech breathing processes appear to be complicated by inefficient valving of the air stream at the level of the larynx and in the upper airways as demonstrated by the high syllabic air volume expenditures some deaf persons exhibit. These kinematic data also suggest that abnormal mechanical adjustments of the respiratory system could interfere with the realization of certain linguistic parameters. For example, speaking at lung volumes below FRC is considered to be an abnormal mechanical adjustment of the respiratory system. Such an abnormal mechanical adjustment, coupled with atypical valving of the air stream, could disturb requisite air pressure and flow events associated with normal contrastive stress and the production of consonants that require a steady constant breath pressure. This assertion is supported by recent aerodynamic research findings that indicate certain aspects of breath stream dynamics are disturbed in the speech of the deaf.

Aerodynamics is a branch of physics that deals with the forces (resistances, pressures, etc.) exerted by air on other gases. In speech research the term aerodynamics is usually associated with measurement of air flow and pressure changes attendant with laryngeal and upper articulator valving of the air

stream during speech. Aerodynamic measures of changes in air flow and pressures thus reflect considerably on underlying physiological processes and have provided researchers with information about voicing characteristics, manners of production, and many other parameters of speech production. (For an excellent discussion of measurement procedures and air flow and pressure events during normal speech production see Warren (1976).)

As stated above, air flow and pressure events associated with the speech of the deaf are frequently abnormal (Gilbert, 1974; Hutchinson and Smith, 1976). For example, voiceless consonants are normally characterized by greater peak air flow rates than voiced consonants by virtue of the high degree of glottal resistance to air flow associated with voicing. In many deaf speakers, however, the peak air flow rates for voiced and voiceless consonants is approximately equal, suggesting inappropriate laryngeal adductory behavior during voiceless consonant production.

Whitehead and Barefoot (1980, and in review) investigated aerodynamic patterns associated with plosive and fricative consonant production of normal-hearing speakers, intelligible hearing-impaired speakers, and semi-intelligible hearing-impaired speakers. Figures 5.2 and 5.3 present the general findings for plosive and fricative consonant productions, respectively. As these figures depict, the semi-intelligible subjects distinguished themselves from the other two groups with reduced and/or nondifferentiated air flow patterns. These findings suggest that inefficient and/or inaccurate modulation of the air stream may be a pivotal dimension of reduced speech intelligibility for deaf speakers.

It is reasonable to suggest that the aberrant air flow patterns exhibited by the semi-intelligible deaf speakers relates to both abnormal respiratory activity and abnormal upper airway activity. The correlational relationship between disturbed air flow patterns and reduced speech intelligiblity strongly suggests the need to determine how abnormal respiratory, laryngeal, and articulatory activities affect breath stream dynamics of the deaf. Such research is especially critical when one considers that disturbed air flow patterns are a manifestation of abnormal biomechanical

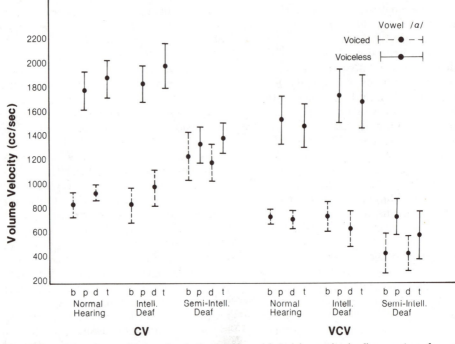

Figure 5.2. Means and standard deviations of peak oral air flow rates for plosive consonants in CV and VCV environments with the vowel /a/ produced by 10 normally hearing, 10 intelligible hearing-impaired, and 10 semi-intelligible hearing-impaired speakers.

events somewhere in the vocal tract which could directly relate to reduced speech intelligibility. Continued aerodynamic research can resolve some of these issues, but additional research techniques will need to be employed to determine the exact nature of laryngeal and upper articulator contributions to reduced speech intelligiblity of the deaf.

LARYNGEAL ASPECTS

The human larynx is an efficient, versatile, and intricate piece of machinery that has important biological functions and serves as the major source of acoustic energy for speech (Fink, 1975). In addition to providing the acoustic energy for speech, the laryngeal mechanism plays an integral role in varying intonation and stress patterns (phonatory parameters) and differentiating the voicing status of certain segments (articulatory parameters). Our discussion of laryngeal aspects

will reflect the functional dichotomy between phonatory and articulatory parameters.

Phonatory Parameters

Since the formalization of the myoelastic-aerodynamic theory of vocal fold vibration (van den Berg, 1956), it has been generally accepted that vocal fold vibration is the result of an interaction of the myoelastic forces of the vocal folds with the air flow through the glottis. Control over these myoelastic and aerodynamic forces normally permits the speaker to maintain a fairly constant fundamental frequency (F_o) and systematically vary F_o to signal changes in intonation and stress patterns associated with spoken utterances. The relative contribution of myoelastic versus aerodynamic forces to control F_o is not fully understood (cf. Titze, 1980). However, recent electromyographic data (Shipp and McGlone, 1971) and computer simulations of vocal fold vibration (Titze and Talkin, 1979) indicate that the primary determinant of F_o

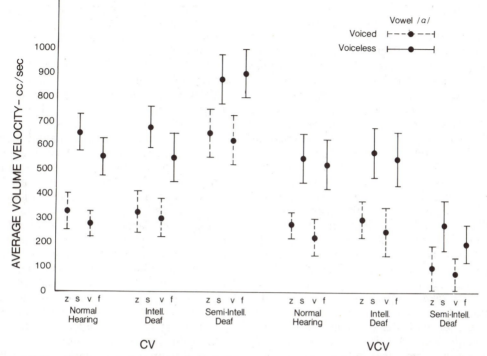

Figure 5.3. Means and standard deviations of average oral air flow rates for fricative consonants in CV and VCV environments with the vowel /a/ produced by 10 normally hearing, 10 intelligible hearing-impaired, and 10 semi-intelligible hearing-impaired speakers.

is the degree of longitudinal tension on the vocal folds, which is a function of fold length and stiffness. Additionally, marked changes in intonation, like the rise in F_o frequently associated with the termination of interrogative phrases, appear to be a function of laryngeal muscle activity that effects vocal fold tension. Contrastive stress may require systematic alterations in the aerodynamic forces operating on the larynx. In addition to increased F_o, stressed syllables may be of greater intensity (a function of increased subglottic pressure) and longer duration than adjacent syllables. As Monsen et al. (1979) point out, however, increased F_o appears to be most important in making a syllable more prominent than adjacent syllables.

Deaf individuals frequently exhibit difficulty controlling laryngeal function for speech purposes, resulting in abnormal voice qualities and failures to instantiate appropriate intonation and stress patterns. Some data regarding the physiological underpinnings of

such abnormal laryngeal functioning among deaf speakers comes from indirect laryngeal assessments via reflectionless tube procedures (Sondhi, 1975; Monsen et al., 1978 and 1979). Briefly, this procedure requires a subject to phonate a neutral vowel into an acoustically reflectionless tube which acts as a pseudoinfinite termination of the vocal tract. Because the tube is reflectionless, vocal tract resonances are damped. A microphone positioned inside the tube records a pressure waveform which is considered to be an approximation of the glottal volume velocity waveform (actual air flow through the glottis). Appropriate analysis of variations in the frequency and relative intensity of this glottal waveform can yield important insights regarding certain aspects of laryngeal functioning during speech. For example, it is generally agreed, *ceteris paribus*, that increases in vocal fold tension will produce attendant changes in vocal F_o and that increases in subglottic pressure (primarily a respiratory function) will produce attendant changes in vocal intensity. Thus, from the variations in the frequency and intensity of the pressure waveform, collected from within the reflectionless tube, inferences can be made regarding the physiological mechanism(s) underlying the variations.

Monsen et al. (1979) employed a reflectionless tube procedure to study laryngeal control problems of 20 deaf adolescents. Data collected from the deaf adolescents were compared to a group of normally hearing adolescents. Analysis of the glottal waveforms indicated that the average speaking F_o of the deaf subjects, although slightly higher, fell within the F_o range of the normal-hearing subjects. Variability of F_o (average period-to-period frequency variation, or jitter) of the deaf subjects, however, was frequently found to be greater than that of their normally hearing counterparts. Similarly, variations in intensity (average period-to-period intensity variability, or shimmer) for some of the deaf subjects doubled the shimmer values of the normally hearing subjects. These findings suggest that some deaf individuals have difficulty maintaining an appropriate tension balance between the two vocal folds, which may be related to the rough/harsh voice quality frequently exhibited by deaf speakers.

One of the more interesting findings of Monsen et al. (1979) relates to how deaf individuals control glottal activity within and between syllables. Subjects were instructed to phonate a sequence of trisyllable words that are normally produced with stress on the second syllable. The stressed syllables produced by the normally hearing subjects always had a higher F_o and usually were of greater intensity than the adjacent syllables in the word. Nine of the 20 deaf subjects produced the stimulus words with patterns of frequency and intensity change similar to the normal-hearing subjects. Eleven of the deaf subjects, however, produced stressed syllables characterized by lower F_os and intensities than those of the unstressed syllables. Monsen et al. (1979) suggest that the most serious laryngeal control problem exhibited by the deaf subjects was their inability to control F_o within a syllable. This lack of control was characterized by inappropriate increases and decreases in F_o in both the first and third (unstressed) syllables. In some instances,

these inappropriate fluctuations of F_o resulted in certain portions of the unstressed syllables having a considerably higher F_o than that of the stressed syllable.

The aberrant F_o and intensity patterns observed by Monsen et al. (1979) suggest that deaf individuals have difficulty making appropriate adjustments in vocal fold tension to appropriately vary F_o. Their results also suggest that some deaf individuals have difficulty coordinating respiratory and laryngeal activity to vary intensity appropriately. Laryngeal control problems of this nature probably find their expression in abnormal intonation and stress patterns.

High-speed laryngeal filming procedures have recently suggested another dimension to the problems deaf persons exhibit controlling laryngeal functioning for speech. Metz and Whitehead (1980) filmed (at 4000 frames/sec) laryngeal activity of one normal-hearing and four profoundly deaf adult subjects. The experimental task required each subject to produce on /ihi/ syllable from a quiet breathing position on experimenter command. This protocol permitted observation of phonation onset and the laryngeal devoicing gesture associated with the /h/ segment.

Phonation onsets of the normally hearing subject were typically characterized by a coordinated adductory movement of the arytenoid cartilages, which resulted in vocal fold adduction. Generally, the folds did not make contact during this prephonatory period. Approximately 100 msec after the initial adductory gesture, small oscillations of the vocal folds were observed (vocal fold response to the egressive air flow from the lungs). The magnitude of these oscillations gradually increased until a stable vibratory pattern had been achieved, involving the entire length of the vocal folds.

Two of the deaf subjects consistently exhibited phonation onsets that were substantively different from the normal-hearing subject. Both these deaf subjects initiated phonation by positioning the vocal folds in contact with one another (vocal fold contact prior to phonation onset is not necessarily abnormal). The prephonatory periods of both subjects frequently exceeded 350 msec, and when vocal fold vibration began, only the anterior one third of the vocal folds particpated. Apparently, these subjects exerted an abnormally high degree of medial compression on the aryteroid cartilages, which prohibited vibration of the posterior two thirds of the vocal folds. This abnormal vibratory mode frequently continued for over 200 msec, roughly half the duration of the initial /i/ vowel in the /ihi/ syllable. Not surprisingly, the F_o associated with this abnormal vibratory mode was considerably higher than the F_o attained once the vocal folds assumed a more normal vibratory mode. It is reasonable to speculate that such abnormal laryngeal postures figure centrally in the deafs' frequent inability to control F_o and intensity when they begin to speak. Additional findings from this study will be discussed later.

Laryngeal Articulatory Parameters

As mentioned earlier, the larynx plays an important role in normal speech production, differentiating certain segments from one another along the voicing dimension. It is well established that normally hearing speakers use unique laryngeal gestures for production of voiced, compared to voiceless, consonants (cf. Sawashima et al., 1970, Kim, 1970, Hirose et al., 1972, Lindqvist, 1972, and Benguerel et al., 1978). More specifically, it has been shown that normally hearing speakers produce voiceless obstruent consonants with an opening-closing gesture of the vocal folds, while voiced consonants are typically produced with no such vocal fold gesture. Thus, while certain voicing characteristics like F_o are primarily determined by laryngeal tension/mass adjustments, the contrastive presence or absence of voicing is chiefly determined in normally hearing speakers by abductory/adductory laryngeal adjustments (Hirose et al., 1973; Benguerel et al., 1978) which have been properly timed relative to oral articulatory gestures (Rothenberg, 1968). In fact, it has been suggested that voice onset time (VOT) distinctions can be regarded as "symptoms of the state of the glottis" during productions of voiced and voiceless consonants (Kim; 1970; Catford, 1977; Lisker, 1978).

Voicing errors are prevalent in the speech of the deaf (cf. Hudgins and Numbers, 1942, and Smith, 1973). Aerodynamic and acoustic measures of deaf speech suggest that deaf persons may use inappropriate laryngeal gestures and inaccurately timed laryngeal gestures with articulatory gestures during certain sound productions (Calvert, 1961; Millin, 1971; Monsen, 1976; Rothman, 1977; Whitehead and Barefoot, 1980). Based on these aerodynamic and acoustic research findings, it is reasonable to suggest that the deaf speakers' frequent failure to produce correct VOT distinctions may be related to atypical laryngeal adjustments during consonantal production.

To test this notion, Mahshie (1980) recorded the laryngeal adjustments of four normal-hearing and four deaf adults during their productions of voiced and voiceless consonants with a fiberscopic nasolaryngoscope (fiberscope). The fiberscope is a small-diameter flexible tube containing fiberoptic bundles. Small light-conducting fiberoptics are arranged in concentric circles around a larger single fiberoptic. Light energy from an external source is directed through the small fiberoptics to illuminate an area in question. Images from the illuminated area are transmitted back through the large fiberoptic which can be connected to a camera or video tape deck. Mahshie's procedure involved passing the fiberscope through the nasal passage, over the velum, and down through the oropharynx behind the tongue such that the fiberscope was positioned immediately superior to the larynx. This procedure permits the subject to speak freely with a minimum of discomfort.

The results of Mahshie's (1980) study indicate that the deaf speakers' abductory/adductory vocal fold adjustment during consonantal production differed noticeably from those of normal-hearing speakers as well as from each other. In contrast to the normally hearing speakers, who distinguish their voiced and voiceless consonants by producing them with adducted and opening-closing laryngeal gestures, respectively, the deaf speakers typically failed to distinguish their voiced and voiceless consonants by means of unique vocal fold gestures. In addition, listener-perceived errors in voicing during a deaf speaker's consonantal productions were consistently related to the speaker's use of an abductory/adductory laryngeal adjustment that was inappropriate (as compared to normal-hearing speakers) for the sound being produced (e.g., segments produced with adducted vocal folds were typically perceived as voiced consonants, regardless of the intended voicing status of that production).

These findings suggest that while deaf speakers demonstrate varying abilities to alter laryngeal adjustment during consonantal production, they commonly use inappropriate laryngeal adjustments for a particular voicing class of speech sound segments. It appears that the deaf speaker's voiced and voiceless consonant production is often accomplished with similar vocal fold gestures, resulting in acoustically similar speech signals which cause listeners to perceive similar voicing characteristics for intended voiced and voiceless consonants.

The failure of some deaf speakers to employ appropriate abductory/adductory gestures to contrast certain segments may be further complicated by the direction and magnitude of the gesture. Compare *A*, *B*, and *C* of Figure 5.4. Figure 5.4*A* depicts the glottal configuration assumed by a normal-hearing speaker during production of the /h/ segment in an /ihi/ syllable. Note that the vocal folds are in a semiadducted posture in the medial glottal plane. Although the vocal folds may continue to oscillate, they do not contact one another during /h/ production.

Figure 5.4*B* depicts the glottal configuration assumed by a deaf female during production of the /h/ segment in an /ihi/ syllable. Note the extremely wide separation of the vocal folds during /h/ production. The vocal folds are not in the medial glottal plane and probably not positioned appropriately to make a smooth transition to the terminal /i/ segment. This notion is supported by aerodynamic and perceptual data that indicated this subject exhibited excessively high air flow rates associated with /h/ production and discontinuities between the individual segments of the syllable (Whitehead and Metz, 1980). It is almost as though this subject treated each segment of the /ihi/ syllable as an independent element without regard for the adjacent segments. It is suggested that this glottal configuration is an abnormal abductory posture (Metz and Whitehead, 1980).

Observe the glottal configuration (Fig. 5.4*C*) assumed by a deaf male during /h/ production in an /ihi/ syllable. This subject

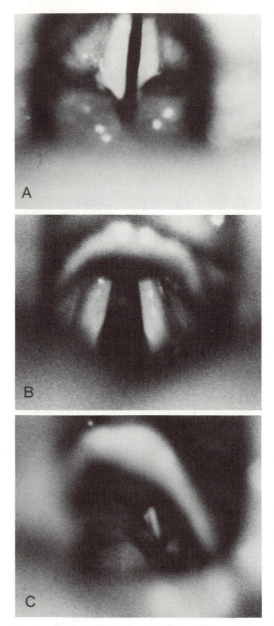

Figure 5.4. Glottal configurations assumed by a normal hearing female (*A*), a deaf female (*B*), and a deaf male (*C*) during /h/ production in the /ihi/ syllable. Each frame was excised from films that were exposed at 4000 frames/sec.

devoiced the /h/ segment with an adductory gesture of the true vocal folds and the ventricular folds. Air flow measurements of this subject's productions of /ihi/ syllables frequently indicated a complete cessation of air flow during /h/ production. This abnormal glottal adductory posture also disturbed normal reinitiation of voicing associated with the terminal /i/ segment which perceptually was judged as a discontinuity between the /h/ and terminal /i/ segment.

The data discussed in this section clearly indicate that deaf speakers mismanage laryngeal functioning during speech. In some cases, the nature of this mismanagement appears to be related to abnormal mechanical adjustments of the larynx which adversely affect the speaker's ability to produce linguistically important parameters, like intonation, stress, and voicing contrasts. Some recent findings by Reilly (1979) are germane to this point. Reilly found that some deaf individuals use durational contrasts to differentiate between stressed and unstressed syllables, primary and weak stress, and prepausal and nonprepausal syllables. As Harris and McGarr (1980) suggest, the use of durational contrasts to signal changes in stress reflect a knowledge of the rules underlying this suprasegmental parameter. The deaf person's inability to control certain respiratory and phonatory processes, however, precludes the normal changes in frequency and intensity associated with varying stress patterns. These findings underscore the need for continued research regarding laryngeal control and adjustment problems of the deaf.

ARTICULATORY ASPECTS

No discussion regarding the speech of the deaf would be complete without treating oral articulatory aspects. Oral articulatory (dis)abilities of the deaf are well documented, and the research findings are remarkably consistent with respect to identifying typical segmental error patterns (cf. Hudgins and Numbers, 1942, Smith, 1972, and Levitt et al. 1980). These error patterns will not be discussed here. Rather, our discussion will center around some recent research studies designed to investigate selected physiological underpinnings of the deaf's misarticulations. We will argue, in concert with Harris and McGarr (1980), that the misarticulations exhibited by deaf speakers reflect a breakdown

in normal interarticulator timing patterns rather than simply inappropriate articulator placements. This is not a new notion. Hudgins and Numbers (1942), in fact, made a similar suggestion almost 40 years ago, which was reaffirmed by Calvert (1961) 20 years ago. Owing probably to the lack of appropriate instrumentation and firm theoretical hypotheses regarding normal articulatory behavior, however, little attention has been paid to articulation dynamics of deaf speakers.

Recent research regarding articulation problems of the deaf clearly reflects (1) the assumption that the appropriate realization of intended speech sounds is the result of complex changes in vocal tract configurations as a function of time, and (2) the importance of appropriate temporal patterns to speech intelligibility (Metz, Samar, et al., 1980). Space does not permit a detailed discussion of normal articulatory dynamics. The reader is encouraged to see such excellent discussions of normal articulatory dynamics as Daniloff et al. (1980) and Kent (1976). Suffice it to say that the temporal patterns realized in normal speech give rise to a highly encoded signal with redundant information about the segments being produced (coarticulatory effects). When this normal temporal pattern is disturbed, speech intelligibility is greatly reduced.

McGarr and Harris (in press) have recently shown that a breakdown in interarticulator timing relationships is, at least, one manifestation of disturbed temporal patterning in the speech of the deaf. These researchers studied orbicularis oris (the sphincter muscle responsible for closing and puckering the lips) and genioglossus (the extrinsic tongue muscle responsible for gross tongue positioning) muscle activity of one normal-hearing and one deaf speaker, using electromyographic (EMG) and acoustical procedures. Each subject produced multiple repetitions of nonsense words that were specifically formulated to provide observations of the relative onsets and offsets of the lip and tongue muscles. The generalized form of these nonsense words was /VCVCVC/, where the consonant was always /p/ and the vowels were either /ə/, /i/ or /a/. Thus, the relative timing relationships between lip and tongue gestures could be determined by observing the action potentials of the two muscles with respect to the acoustic representation of the nonsense word.

In general, McGarr and Harris found that the EMG patterns associated with lip activity of the deaf speaker closely approximated the EMG patterns of the normally hearing speaker. This finding is consistent with previous research (Huntington et al., 1968). Activity of the deaf speaker's genioglossus muscle, however, differed considerably from the normal-hearing speaker. Consider, for example, the onset of genioglossus activity associated with the /pi/ cluster in the nonsense word /əpapip/. The normal-hearing speaker consistently exhibited peak genioglossus acitivity associated with tongue positioning for the /i/ segment coincident with the acoustic /p/ burst release, and the relationship between lip and tongue muscle activity onsets reflected a tight "temporal coupling." In contrast, peak genioglossus activity associated with the deaf speaker's tongue positioning for the /i/ segment frequently followed the acoustic /p/ burst release. Moreover, the time of onset of genioglossus activity was highly variable with respect to orbicularis oris activity. This observed breakdown in interarticulator timing relationships suggest that this deaf speaker has adopted a phoneme-by-phoneme production strategy (McGarr and Harris, in press) that is potentially void of normal coarticulatory patterns. Similar breakdowns in speech timing relationships have been reported by Rothman (1977).

Another procedure that has great potential for studying articulatory dynamics of deaf persons is cinefluorography. Cinefluorographic procedures have provided much important information regarding normal and abnormal articulation processes, and these procedures have recently been applied to the speech of the deaf. Briefly, cinefluorographic procedures involve taking relatively high-speed (60–150 frames/sec) lateral x-ray films of the articulators during specified speech acts. Small radiopaque markers are attached to selected articulators and other landmarks within the oral cavity to provide consistent reference and measurement points. Analysis procedures usually involve computer-assisted frame-by-frame tracking of the radiopaque marker trajectories, which yields a wide va-

riety of spatial and temporal information about the articulators in question (Zimmermann (1980) or Zimmermann and Rettaliata (1981)) for a more specific account of these procedures).

In a recent investigation, Stein (1980) employed cinefluorographic and acoustic procedures to study selected speech gestures of two normally hearing and five deaf speakers. Stein's findings indicate that many of the articulatory movement patterns of the deaf speakers were similar to those of normally hearing speakers. However, between group differences were observed relative to certain parameters associated with consonant production. In particular, the deaf speakers' articulatory movements for consonants were of greater duration and magnitude (vertical displacements) than those of the normally hearing speakers, and the deaf speakers exhibited faster articulatory speeds with respect to lip, tongue tip, and jaw movement. Stein (1980) further observed that voice onset times frequently occurred early relative to initial consonants and that voice offsets occurred late relative to production of voiceless terminal consonants. The deaf speakers also exhibited delayed movement onsets toward the second consonant relative to the steady state portion of the vowel. With respect to vowel production, Stein (1980) noted that the deaf speakers tended to use jaw movement rather than tongue movement to differentiate vowel height. Aberrations of tongue dorsum movement patterns were also observed during certain vowel productions, but these aberrant movements did not seem to be related to general speech intelligibility.

Despite Stein's very detailed analysis of articulatory kinematics, no one articulatory parameter, or group of parameters, could be isolated as a major contributor to the poor speech intelligibility of the deaf speakers. Moreover it is worth noting that Zimmermann and Rettaliata (1981) have reported very similar articulatory kinematic findings during an analysis of a postlingually deafened speaker. In comparison to a normal-hearing control, this postlingually deafened speaker exhibited faster articulatory speeds for the lip, tongue tip, and jaw, delayed tongue dorsum movements relative to jaw and tongue tip movements, longer transition times during

VC gestures, abnormally long vowel durations, vowel height differentiation resulting primarily from jaw displacements and several other gesture-specific differences. Interestingly, Zimmerman and Rettaliata report that all the deaf subjects' test utterances were judged to be phonemically accurate.

In addition to providing some rather intriguing data regarding the role of audition in speech monitoring (Zimmermann and Rettaliata, 1981), the above cinefluorographic findings strongly suggest that the mismanagement of certain articulatory parameters do not completely account for the reduced speech intelligibility of the deaf. Indeed, it appears that certain deviations from normal articulatory dynamics have little impact on speech intelligibility. This may be related to the fact that certain articulatory parameters are highly modulatable (Zimmermann and Rettaliata, 1981) and/or to the perceptual tolerances of listeners experienced with deaf speech (Metz, Schiavetti, and Sitler, 1980). It is equally likely that the speech errors of the deaf are the result of *interactions* among abnormal respiratory, laryngeal, and articulatory processes, and although it may be parsimonious to relate the speech errors of the deaf to the abnormal processes of a single peripheral system, such an approach is probably erroneous. Efforts should be taken to identify these potential interactions in relation to selected speech errors of the deaf.

SUMMARY

At the outset of this chapter we suggested that some speech errors of the deaf may be related to abnormal neuromuscular, biomechanical, and aerodynamic events. The data presented in this chapter seem to support this premise. It is important to realize, however, that much of the research discussed in this chapter focused on only one physiological system. Such research is important. But, research regarding the interactions among the physiological systems supporting speech is clearly needed. This point is underscored by the cineradiographic findings previously discussed. These findings indicate that many of the deaf's articulatory variations during speech do not correlate well with reduced speech intelligibility. The impact of articula-

tory variations on speech intelligibility may only be fully realized when respiratory and laryngeal events are accounted for. It may be that interactions among abnormal respiratory, laryngeal, and articulatory events produce what has come to be termed deaf speech.

In summary, the data discussed in this chapter suggest two major problems regarding the deaf's control of speech production. One problem is abnormal physical posturing of the systems supporting speech. Examples of abnormal physical posturing include initiating speech at very low lung volumes and abnormal abduction of the vocal folds during voiceless consonant productions. Problems of this nature can adversely affect speech intelligiblity. The more serious speech control problem, however, appears to be the deaf's inability to temporally coordinate respiratory and laryngeal activity with articulatory events. Intelligible speech is impossible without these coordinations. Future research will hopefully facilitate our understanding of both postural and coordination problems exhibited by deaf speakers. A better understanding of these problems should lead to the development of more effective remedial regimes and early intervention strategies.

References

Abbs, J.H., and Watkin, K.L. Instrumentation for the study of speech physiology. In N.J. Lass (ed.), *Contemporary Issues in Experimental Phonetics.* New York: Academic Press, 1976.

Benguerel, A.P., Hirose, H., Sawashima, M., and Ushijima, T. Laryngeal control in French stop production: A fiberoptic, acoustical and EMG study. *Folia Phoniatr. (Basel)*, 1978, *30*, 175–198.

Calvert, D.R. Some acoustic characteristics of the speech of deaf children. Doctoral dissertation, Stanford University, 1961.

Catford, J. *Fundamental Problems in Phonetics.* Bloomington, Indiana: Indiana University Press, 1977.

Daniloff, R., Shuckers, G., and Feth, L. *The Physiology of Speech and Hearing: An Introduction.* Englewood Cliffs, New Jersey: Prentice-Hall, 1980.

Fink, B. R. *The Human Larynx: A Functional Study.* New York: Raven Press, 1975.

Forner, L.L., and Hixon, T.J. Respiratory kinematics in profoundly hearing-impaired speakers. *J. Speech Hear. Res.*, 1977, *20*, 373–408.

Gilbert, H.R. Simultaneous oral and nasal airflow during stop consonant production by hearing impaired speakers. *Folia Phoniat.*, 1974, *27*, 423–437.

Harris, K.S., and McGarr, N.S. Relationships between speech perception and speech production in normal hearing and hearing impaired subjects. In J.D. Subtelny (ed.), *Speech Assessment and Speech Improvment for the Hearing Impaired*. Washington, D.C.: A.G. Bell Association for the Deaf, 1980.

Hirose, H., Lisker, L., and Abramson, A. Physiological aspects of certain laryngeal features in stop production. In *Haskins Laboratories Status Report on Speech Research*. New Haven, Connecticut: Haskins Laboratory, 1972, SR-31/32, 183–191.

Hixon, T. Respiratory functioning in speech. In F. Minifie, T. Hixon and F. Williams (eds.), *Normal Aspects of Speech, Hearing, and Language*. Englewood Cliffs, New Jersey: Prentice-Hall, 1973.

Hixon, T., Goldman, M., and Mead, J. Kinematics of the chest wall during speech production: Volume displacement of the rib cage, abdomen, and lung. *J. Speech Hear. Res.*, 1973, *16*, 78–115.

Hixon, T., Mead, J., and Goldman, M. Dynamics of the chest wall during speech production: Function of the thorax, rib cage, diaphragm, and abdomen. *J. Speech Hear. Res.*, 1976, *19*, 297–356.

Hudgins, C.V., and Numbers, F.C. An investigation of the intelligibility of the speech of the deaf. *Genet. Psychol. Monogr.*, 1942, *25*, 289–392.

Huntington, D.A., Harris, K.S., and Sholes, G. An electromyographic study of consonant articulation in hearing impaired and normal speech. *J. Speech Hear. Res.*, 1968, *11*, 147–158.

Hutchinson, J., and Smith, L. Aerodynamic functioning in consonant production by hearing-impaired adults. *Audiol. Hear. Educ.*, 1976, *2*, 16–25.

Kent, R. Models of speech production. In N.J. Lass (ed.), *Contemporary Issues in Experimental Phonetics*. New York: Academic Press, 1976.

Kim, C. A theory of aspiration. *Phonetica*, 1970, *21*, 107–116.

Levitt, H., Stromberg, H., Smith, C., and Gold, T. The structure of segmental errors in the speech of deaf children. *J. Commun. Disord.*, 1980, *13*, 419–442.

Lindquist, J. Laryngeal articulation studied on Swedish subjects. In *Quarterly Progress and Status Report 2-3*. Stockholm: Speech Transmission Laboratory, 1972, 10–27.

Lisker, L. In qualified defense of VOT. *Lang. Speech*, 1978, *21*, 375–383.

Mahshie, J.J. Laryngeal behavior of hearing impaired speakers. Doctoral dissertation, Syracuse University, 1980.

McGarr, N.S., and Harris, K.S. Articulatory control in a deaf speaker. In I. Hochberg, H. Levitt, and M.J. Osberger (eds.), *Speech of the Hearing Impaired: Research, Training, and Personnel Preparation*. Baltimore: University Park Press (submitted, 1981).

Metz, D.E., Samar, V., Parasnis, I., Whitehead R., and Sims, D. Current research on relationships between selected higher order processes and the communication skills and problems of deaf persons. *Am. Ann. Deaf.*, 1980, *125*, 360–365.

Metz, D.E., Schiavetti, N., and Sitler, R.W. Toward an objective description of the dependent and independent variables associated with intelligibility assessments of hearing impaired adults. In J.D. Subtelny (ed.), *Speech Assessment and Speech Improvement for the Hearing Impaired*. Washington, D.C.: A.G. Bell Association for the Deaf, 1980.

Metz, D.E., and Whitehead, R.L. Aberrant laryngeal devoicing gestures produced by deaf speakers: Evidence from high speed laryngeal films. Paper presented to the Acoustical Society of America, Los Angeles, 1980.

Millin, J.P. Therapy for the reduction of continuous phonation in the hard of hearing population. *J. Speech Hear. Disord.*, 1971, *36*, 496–498.

Moll, K., Zimmerman, G.N., and Smith, A. The study of speech production as a human neuromotor system. In M. Sawashima and F. Cooper (eds.), *Dynamic Aspects of Speech Production*. Tokyo: University of Tokyo Press, 1977.

Monsen, R. The production of English stop consonants in the speech of deaf children. *J. Phonetics*, 1976, *4*, 29–42.

Monsen, R., Engebretson, M., and Vemula, R. Indirect assessment of the contribution of subglottal oil pressure and vocal fold tension to changes in fundamental frequency in English. *J. Acoust. Soc. Am.*, 1978, *64*, 65–80.

Monsen, r., Engebretson, M., and Vemula, R. Some effects of deafness on the generation of voice. *J. Acoust. Soc. Am.*, 1979, *66*, 1680–1690.

Reilly, A.P. Syllable nucleus duration in the speech of hearing and deaf children. Doctoral dissertation, City University of New York, 1979.

Rothenberg, M. *The Breath Stream Dynamics of Simple-Released-Plosive Production, Bibliotheca Phonetica VI*. Basel: Karger, 1968.

Rothman, H. An electromyographic investigation of articulation and phonation patterns in the speech of deaf adults. *J. Phonetics*, 1977, *5*, 369–376.

Sawashima, M., Abramson, A., Cooper, F., and Lisker L. Observing laryngeal adjustments during running speech by use of a fiberoptic system. *Phonetica*, 1970, *22*, 193–201.

Shipp, T., and McGlone, R. Laryngeal dynamics associated with voice frequency change. *J. Speech Hear. Res.*, 1971, *14*, 761–768.

Smith, C.B. Residual hearing and speech production in deaf children. In *Communication Science Laboratory Report 4*. New York: City University of New York, 1973.

Sondhi, M.M. Measurement of the glottal waveform. *J. Acoust. Soc. Am.*, 1975, *57*, 228–232.

Stein, D.M. A study of articulatory characteristics of deaf talkers. Doctoral dissertation, University of Iowa, 1980.

Titze, I.R. Comments on the myoelastic-aerodynamic theory of phonation. *J. Speech Hear. Res.*, 1980, *23*, 495–510.

Titze, I.R., and Talkin, D. A theoretical study of the effects of the various laryngeal configurations on the acoustics of phonation. *J. Acoust. Soc. Am.*, 1979, *66*, 60–74.

van den Berg, J.H. Myoelastic-aerodynamic theory of voice production. *J. Speech Hear. Res.*, 1958, *1*, 227–243.

Warren, D.W. Aerodynamics of speech production. In N.J. Lass (ed.), *Contemporary Issues in Experimental Phonetics*. New York: Academic Press, 1976.

Whitehead, R.L. Some respiratory and aerodynamic patterns in the speech of the hearing impaired. In I.

Hochberg, H. Levitt, and M.J. Osberger (eds.), *Speech of the Hearing Impaired: Research, Training, and Personnel Preparation*. Baltimore: University Park Press (submitted, 1981).

Whitehead, R.L., and Barefoot, S. Some aerodynamic characteristics of plosive consonants produced by hearing-impaired speakers. *Am. Ann. Deaf.* 1980, *125*, 366–373.

Whitehead, R.L., and Barefoot, S. Air flow characteristics of fricative consonants produced by normally hearing and hearing-impaired speakers. *J. Speech Hear. Res.* (in review)

Whitehead, R.L., and Metz, D.E. Aberrant laryngeal devoicing gestures produced by deaf speakers: Evidence from acoustic, aerodynamic and glottographic data. Paper presented to the Acoustical Society of America, Los Angeles, 1980.

Zimmermann, G. Articulatory behaviors associated with stuttering: A cinefluorographic analysis. *J. Speech Hear. Res.*, 1980, *23*, 95–107.

Zimmerman, G., and Rettaliata, P. Articulatory patterns of an adventitiously deaf speaker: Implications for the role of auditory information in speech production. *J. Speech Hear. Res.*, 1981, *24*, 169–178.

Chapter 6

Sign Language and Manual Communication

SUSAN D. FISCHER, PH.D.

In this chapter, we shall consider signing as a distinct channel of communication. We shall consider signing in American Sign Language, and how the structure of that language compares with languages such as English. After a brief discussion of the social context of sign language use, we shall turn to the concept of "signing in English," and the relationship between signing in English and the educational process.

EFFECTS OF CHANNEL ON LANGUAGE

If we compare the expression of ideas in a manual/visual channel with their expression in a vocal/auditory channel, it is obvious that there will be advantages and drawbacks to each channel, which can influence the efficiency of different means of expressing the same concept. Both the productive and recep-

tive aspects of the channel must be considered.

In production we have only to compare the speech articulators (larynx, tongue, palate, teeth, and lips) with the sign articulators (arms, hands, face, and torso) to see that for the most part the main sign articulators are orders of magnitude larger and slower moving than the main speech articulators. This is an obvious advantage of speech over signing; however, signing has advantages as well, which natural sign languages, such as American Sign Language (ASL), are known to exploit.

In an early study, Bellugi and Fischer (1972) found that it takes about twice as long to produce a sign as it does to say an English word. These results have been largely confirmed by the more recent work of Grosjean (1979). However, Bellugi and Fischer also found, paradoxically, that the rate of information transmission was the same for spoken

90

English and ASL. How is this possible? If the same information is being transmitted in half the number of units, each unit of ASL obviously contains much more information. The ability to pack more information into a single unit of ASL depends crucially on the advantages of the manual/visual channel. It is possible to produce and perceive many parts of a message simultaneously in signing in a way that is not possible in speech. For example, in ASL, one manual sign (the equivalent of a word) could contain up to five morphemes (units of meaning) occurring simultaneously. Also simultaneously, the facial expression could be showing negation and/or interrogation, while the direction of eye gaze could be expressing a pronoun. For example, if we wanted to say "may I ask you a question?" in ASL, the information that requires six words in English requires only one sign in ASL—but that sign is highly complex, and the sign utterance even more so. There is a specific sign which means "to ask a question." Further, that sign inflects for person and number of both subject and object. At the same time, raised eyebrows show the fact that the signer is asking a question of the viewer, and a slight head nodding softens the question to a request for permission. No information is gained or lost in this case, nor is any time lost. The visual system is equipped to handle complex simultaneously occurring patterns in a fundamentally different way from the auditory system.

Thus, it is possible for the hands, face, and body to produce a complex pattern of visual signals that constitute an efficiently communicable message, while the visual system is able to process that message equally efficiently. This is not to say that speech is strictly sequential or that signing is strictly simultaneous. We know that an individual speech sound has several simultaneous aspects (e.g., place of articulation, manner of articulation, voicing, and tone) and that it is virtually impossible acoustically (and auditorily) to tear two speech sounds apart. Conversely, in a sign utterance, it is clear that signs do follow each other in some order, and even within a sign there is some sense of linearity. It is possible to say, however, that signing (at least naturally occurring signing) has relatively more simultaneity, while speech has relatively more linearity, and that these phenomena are related respectively to the functioning of the visual and auditory systems, as well as to the functioning of the hands and body versus the vocal apparatus.

The structure of a language is shaped by the way it is produced and perceived. This is so much the case for spoken language that we are often blinded to the possibilities for linguistic expression outside of speech. We may be tempted to discount by definition any language that is not produced vocally. However, if a language fits all the other criteria discussed in Chapter 1 and is perfectly adequate to the needs of the community that uses it, we need to permit our definition to include such a language as a language. American Sign Language is one such language—it is the preferred means of communication of a large number of deaf people in the United States and Canada.

HISTORICAL PERSPECTIVE: ASL AND SIGN LANGUAGES

Many people unfamiliar with sign language jump to some unwarranted conclusions about it. Consider, for example, this quotation, from an earlier edition of a reputable text on deafness (Silverman and Lane, 1970, p. 390, in H. Davis and S.R. Silverman's *Hearing and Deafness*):

"It is generally agreed that sign language is bound to the concrete and is rather limited with respect to abstraction, humor, and subtleties such as figures of speech which enrich expression."

This myth, and it is indeed only a myth, is intimately related to another myth, that sign language is iconic, i.e., that there is a direct, nonarbitrary relationship between *all* signs and their referents. It is undeniable that the meanings of *some* ASL signs are more transparent than those of most English words. However, this is not true of all signs; indeed, as Mayberry (1978, p. 404) has pointed out in her chapter in a later edition of the same book quoted above (H. Davis and S.R. Silverman's *Hearing and Deafness*),

"Many signs bear some visual resemblance to what they symbolize, such as the signs *house, book,* and *tree.* From this it follows that if a language can symbolize only what can be drawn in the air, then its ability to symbolize what cannot be seen is severely restricted. Actually, ASL's vocabulary includes numerous abstract concepts, which can be discussed as easily in ASL as in English. Perhaps the characteristics of the manual and visual modalities make the transparency of sign language more striking than the onomatopoeia of oral languages."

It is also probable that sign languages may have started out with rather iconic signs but that through usage by intelligent human beings with physical limitations and a range of ideas, these signs have become more arbitrary over time (Frishberg, 1975). A very brief history may help to clarify things.

Almost anywhere there are even one or two deaf people, some signing system will develop (though we may not want to call it a language at the beginning). Some current examples can be found in Kuschel (1974), Feldman et al. (1978), and in the personal experience of many hearing families with deaf children. In order for a sign *language* to develop, a sort of "critical mass" of deaf people with the opportunity to pass their signing down to future generations appears to be necessary. The first time that we know of where this took place was in the late eighteenth-century in France. L'Abbé de L'Épée founded a school where signing was used. What he did was to take the signs that already existed among the deaf people he had met (*signes naturelles*) and add to them signs which he invented in order to teach French, Latin, and Greek grammar (*signes méthodiques*). He then based the teaching of speech on the knowledge of French that his students had gained through signing, reading, and writing. L'Épée's successor, L'Abbé Sicard, continued this tradition and was ready to pass it on elsewhere. French Sign Language spread to many countries in Europe and, in the early 1800's, to the United States. American Sign Language in the United States, through such institutions as the American School and later Gallaudet College, has had a continuous tradition of more than a hundred years, though ASL is still quite young as languages go. Even in 100 years, however, a language can change quite a bit; so, although one can see similarities between present-day American and French sign languages, the two are not immediately mutually intelligible.[1]

ASL STRUCTURE

Let us focus now on the structure of American Sign Language. We shall talk about phonology (sublexical structure), word meaning, morphology, and syntax. When we discuss signing in English in a later section, most of what we say here about phonology and some of what we say about word meaning will apply.

Phonology

ASL combines signs (which constitute the equivalent of words), fingerspelling (letter by letter spelling of English words "in the air"), and facial and body postures to produce sentences and discourses. If we look at an individual sign, we find that it is analyzable into three or four phonological components which occur simultaneously: a moving handshape (or possibly two), a location (which can be a nonmoving hand as well as part of the face or body), the movement, and the relationship among the hands and the location. The first person to analyze the sublexical structure of ASL was Stokoe (1960). Based on his analysis, he and two colleagues developed a dictionary of ASL signs (Stokoe et al., 1965).[2] Stokoe found groupings of handshapes, locations, and movements that count as the same in ASL. He called these groupings *cheremes* (from the Greek root meaning "handy") instead of phonemes, but the principle is the same as for spoken language phonology. For example, in ASL, except for fingerspelling, which constitutes a special subsystem of ASL, the handshapes for "A" and "S," as well as "T," all count as the same, and just as we found for aspirated and unaspirated consonants in English, there are predictable environments in ASL where "A" and

---

[1] Ironically, use of French Sign Language was discontinued in French schools around 1870—the reduction of French Sign Language to an underground language seems to have hastened linguistic change in sign language in France.

[2] Although Stokoe et al. (1965) contains about 3000 entries, the size of the vocabulary of ASL is actually much larger, due both to omissions and to the noninclusion of a great deal of productive word formation processes.

Figure 6.1.   Handshapes which count as the same in Hong Kong Sign Language.

"S" will occur. For example, a sign made with the fist-shaped hand touching either another hand or a part of the body on the side nearest the palm or first knuckle cannot be an "S" shape; on the other hand, a sign which requires the thumb side of the hand to touch may not be an "A" shape. We can thus say that "A" and "S" are members of the same phoneme class in ASL.[3]

What counts as the same or what counts as different can vary from sign language to sign language, just as it varies from spoken language to spoken language. For example, Figure 6.1 shows two handshapes that count as the same for Hong Kong Sign Language but which count as different in American Sign Language. Figure 6.2, conversely, shows two handshapes that count as the same in American Sign Language but which count as different for Japanese Sign Language finger-spelling.

Analogous to spoken languages, signed languages also have their own particular inventories of elements, in addition to classes of segments that count as the same. For example, just as there are no clicks in English, ASL does not have any signs made in the armpit (one sign meaning "deodorant" may be a counterexample to this claim, but most of the time it will be made *next* to the armpit rather than *in* it.) However, in Hong Kong Sign Language, the armpit is an acceptable location; the Hong Kong sign for "Wednesday" is given in Figure 6.3.

Another example of an element that might occur in another sign language but does not occur in ASL is the shape in Figure 6.4. This shape occurs in Japanese Sign Language, but not in ASL.

Combinations of handshapes, movements, and locations can be *physically* or *linguistically* constrained. A linguistically constrained combination might be found in another sign language, but a physically constrained one is much less likely to be found in another sign language. Much as it is impossible in a spoken language to produce an ingressive fully voiced vowel (i.e., to phonate while inhaling),

---

[3] One reason why "S" and "A" wouldn't be distinctive in ASL is that in *signing* it's hard to see the difference anyway, if the viewer is focusing on the face (Siple, 1978). In fingerspelling, by contrast, the signer focuses the viewer's attention on the hands, thus putting fingerspelling in the area of maximum visual acuity.

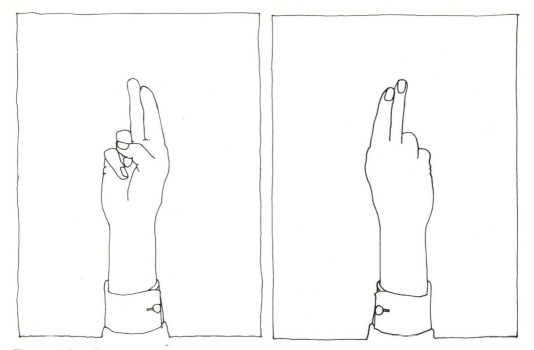

Figure 6.2. Two Japanese Sign Language handshapes which count as the same for ASL.

Figure 6.3. Hong Kong sign for "Wednesday."

Figure 6.4. Japanese Sign Language handshape that does not occur in ASL.

it is physically impossible for a sign to require touching the elbow to the ear. However, it is *linguistically* prohibited in ASL for a "Y" hand to touch the palm of another hand with the extended pinky. This is, however, perfectly acceptable as the sign for "stand" in Hong Kong Sign Language. See Figure 6.5. The sign would be just as unacceptable for ASL as "pferd" is for English.

Another aspect of sublexical structure in which linguists are interested is how one sublexical element influences another in the environment. For example, the English word "input" is almost never pronounced as [input]; rather, the presence of [p] influences the pronunciation of the nasal /n/, and the end result is [imput]. This is a process called *assimilation*, which is common to all languages, including sign languages. An example from fingerspelling is the realization of "E" depending on the environment; if the previous or following letter uses only two fingers (e.g., "V," "N," "H," "R," or "U"), "E" will also be made with two fingers instead of four. We also find a great deal of assimilation in lexical compounds in ASL. (Compounding is a highly productive way of coining new signs in ASL). Figures 6.6 and 6.7 show the indi-

Figure 6.6.   ASL sign for "two weeks."

Figure 6.5.   Hong Kong sign for "stand."

Figure 6.7.   ASL sign for "past."

Figure 6.8.   ASL sign for "two weeks ago."

vidual signs for "two weeks" and "past." Figure 6.8 shows the compound sign meaning "two weeks ago." A complex assimilation process is occurring here; the handshape of the first sign continues over the second; the hand orientation of the second sign is anticipated in the first. The result is a phonological fusion of two signs into one.

In summary, ASL signs have a sublexical structure analogous to the sublexical structure in spoken language. One big difference is that this structure is exhibited simultaneously rather than linearly; however, this is simply a consequence of the modality, as we saw in the first section of this chapter.

Word Meaning in ASL

There will always be problems of translation between any two languages. A naive monolingual speaker of English who is learning French or Spanish may want to know *the* word for "know" or "think" or, in Spanish, "be", when in those languages there is not one word that corresponds in meaning to the English. For "know," there are two—one roughly meaning knowledge of a subject and the other meaning acquaintance, usually with

a person. In the case of "think," there is one word for having an opinion, and another for the process of thinking. In Spanish, there is one word for the equative "be" and another for the "be" of location. Thus the semantic scope of one word in one language may be different from that of another word in another language, as we discussed in Chapter 1. The problem of translation becomes even more complicated when we look at words with multiple meanings. Consider the word "run" in English; if we were translating the following sentences into another language, chances are we would have to use a different word for each of the uses of "run."

(1) Your nose is running.
(2) The motor is running.
(3) You have a run in your stocking.
(4) There's been a run on baby spoons lately.
(5) She will run in a marathon tomorrow.
(6) He runs a private school.
(7) I've got to run now.
(8) The president will not run for reelection.
(9) Even a used car can run $\begin{Bmatrix} \text{into} \\ \text{you} \end{Bmatrix}$ a lot of money these days.
(10) We have some errands to run this afternoon.
(11) "Bye Bye Love" keeps running through my head.
(12) The dyes in natural fabrics have a tendency to run.
(13) Red hair runs in his family.

The list could go on. Like any other language different from English, ASL also has different signs (words) for each of the uses of "run" in (1)–(13). To use one when another is meant may give an ASL user a very different impression from the one intended!

Even if there is a one-to-one correspondence between a word in English and a sign in ASL, the scope of the sign may be different; as in French, ASL has two signs for "think"— one for having an opinion, and the other for the process of reflection. The translation of an English word into sign may have a broader or narrower scope than the English word. For example, the English word "hurt" can be translated into ASL fairly accurately with a sign; however, that sign is limited to physical hurt. To talk about hurt feelings, a signer either uses a different sign entirely or fingerspells H-U-R-T in such a way that it becomes a sign (this process has been extensively researched by Battison (1978)). One example in which the sign has a broader scope than the English word is in the sign that is glossed as "thirsty." This sign does, indeed, refer to a need for liquids; however, it has been metaphorically extended to include the meaning of "having a yen or a longing for." Thus it is perfectly grammatical in ASL to say that you are thirsty for a hamburger; the meaning will be roughly that you haven't had a hamburger for a long time and you sure would like one right now.

Word Formation in ASL

In Chapter 1, we talked a little about two kinds of word formation processes in general: *inflectional*, by which words are changed to fit into sentences, and *derivational*, by which new words are formed out of old ones. In both cases, several morphemes are combined into one word. If we focus on inflectional morphology in ASL, we find that ASL inflects for somewhat different things than does English. For example, English has markers for tense; ASL, by contrast, marks *time* with adverbs, usually at the beginning of a discourse, but not with an inflection on the verb to show grammatical tense. By the same token, English inflects its verbs for singular and plural in the present tense, while ASL inflects verbs for three kinds of plural, as well as for subject and object, for which English must use separate words.

Many of the kinds of grammatical inflections we find in ASL are also to be found in other languages, even if not found in English. For example, in Table 1.2 in Chapter 1, we had examples of *reduplication* to form the plural in Pangasinan. ASL has a totally analogous process for plural information—the only difference is that for ASL the second "syllable" is repeated instead of the first. Thus, the compound sign for "expect," which, broken down into its component parts, means "think + wait", is pluralized ("expect many things") by signing THINK once, and then by repeating the sign WAIT while moving the hands in a horizontal arc (Fischer, 1973; Fischer and Gough, 1978).

What else does ASL inflect for? One thing that may be familiar to people who know something about sign language is what has been called directional verbs. These are verbs

that can inflect for case in much the same way we saw for Swahili in Chapter 1. A representative example is given in Figures 6.9 and 6.10. Figure 6.9 shows someone signing YOU-GIVE-ME, while Figure 6.10 shows the same person signing I-GIVE-YOU. Many ASL verbs can inflect for third person cases similarly by referring to the location of the appropriate referents. These locations may be actual or established by linguistic convention, so that it is possible to inflect verbs for absent referents.

In addition to the plural we have already discussed, ASL also has a very rich system of inflecting for *aspect*. Aspect is a way of marking a verb, distinct from tense, to show focus on certain parts of the action or state. If we define tense as the grammatical marking of time, we find that ASL does not have any tense—it has separate words for marking time, but no grammatical markers. (English has a grammatical marker for present and past, but not for future, for which it uses a separate word, *will*, or the less formal *gonna*). Aspect, by contrast, is concerned with how the action or state is viewed; it is also a grammatical marker, but it can interact with time words or markers. For example, various

Figure 6.9.   ASL sign for "you give me."

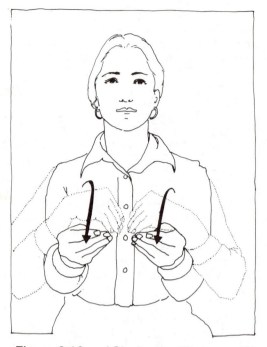

Figure 6.10.   ASL sign for "I give you."

aspectual markers in many languages can focus on the beginning of an action, the "on-goingness" of the action, the end of the action, the speed with which the action is viewed, or the regular repetition of that action. Examples of aspect markers in English are the *be* + *ing* construction, which marks ongoing action, and *have* + *past participle*, which marks the completion of that action, as distinct from the past tense, which marks the time at which the action takes place. A sentence like *I have finished my homework* is in the *present* tense (the past tense would be *I HAD finished my homework*), but it is focusing on the completion of the action, hence our feeling that it is describing something that necessarily must have taken place in the past in order to be over with. In the case of a *have* construction, we are not focusing on the time but on the completive aspect. ASL can mark for many different aspects (more grammatical markings for different aspects than English), such as habitual, continuative, completive, and several others. There are discussions of these in Fischer, 1973, and Klima et al., 1979.

An example of different aspect in ASL can be seen if we focus on the verb READ. The sign for the verb READ is shown in Figure

6.11 and normally is made with two short repetitions of the movement. If that movement is made once with a sweeping motion, the meaning shifts to "read through," a form of the completive aspect. If it is repeated quickly more than three times, it carries the progressive aspect, "reading." If it is repeated slowly with emphasis, it carries the meaning of continuative aspect "keep on reading," and if the sign is made with minimal but intense movement, the meaning changes to "read intensively and incessantly." With the exception of "read" versus "reading," English has no *grammatical* way to express these different aspects; it must resort to periphrastic constructions.

Let us turn our attention now to derivational morphology. This is currently one of the areas in research on ASL that has been receiving the most attention. One of the first explicit discussions of derivational morphology in ASL is Supalla and Newport (1978); they talk about the derivation of nouns from verbs in ASL, in which they found a systematic relationship between pairs of signs like FLY-AIRPLANE versus AIRPLANE, and SIT versus CHAIR.

Figure 6.11.   ASL sign for "read."

In addition to deriving nouns from verbs, there are other often highly complex ways of forming multimorphemic signs. One is compounding, as we mentioned above, by which two signs are juxtaposed and a phonological reduction, such as assimilation, or some loss of movement fuses them into one unit. For example, the sign for "sister" is a phonologically fused compound of GIRL and ALIKE; the sign for "breakfast" is a compound of EAT and MORNING. This is still a productive process; the sign for "inflation" is MONEY + BUILD-UP-FAST, and a compound sign recently came into existence for "gridlock."

In addition to the use of compounds, there is another very common way to form complex words in ASL, namely, the use of *classifiers*. In many languages of the world, when one is handling or counting, it is necessary for the grammar of the language to specify what class of things one is counting or handling. In English, this is all lexical and fairly idiosyncratic; it is rather weird to say (14), unless one is being sarcastic:

(14) I think I'll lug this feather to the other side of the room.

In ASL, as in other languages, such as Navajo, the grammar requires the use of a classifier for such categories as small things, light things, round things, stick-like things (including people), and, in some cases, abstract things. We saw examples of numerical classifiers in Japanese in sentences (20)–(22) in Chapter 1. ASL shows the size, shape, or general dimensionality of objects in many verbs of handling. The handshape classifiers that are incorporated into verbs in ASL function as simultaneous pronouns, abstracting such features as thin and flat from the nouns they refer to, much as an English pronoun such as *she* abstracts the features of animate, female, and subject from the noun it refers back to.

In ASL, although there may be a general all-purpose sign for "open" (just as in Japanese there is a general all-purpose word for "two"), most of the time it is necessary to specify what kind of thing is being opened, and/or with what. Thus, the signs for opening a newspaper, a can, a package, a jar, or a window are all different. There may even be many signs for opening a window, depending on how that window is in fact opened; a sliding window or a jalousie will be opened differently from a double-hung window. A sign like OPEN-REGULAR-WINDOW is in fact made up of two or three sign morphemes: thin-flat-thing, starting in relation to another thin-flat-thing, and then the final act of opening in a particular way. The classifiers here are a recurrent, limited set functioning as pronouns, and they do not in fact necessarily reflect the exact size and shape of their referent any more than *she* reflects the size and shape of *its* referent.

Some signs are even more complicated. The sign TWO-WEEKS-AGO, which we discussed earlier, incorporates the numerical classifier for WEEK, along with the numeral TWO, combined with the sign for PAST. Another example with three meaning elements would be the sign RIDE-IN-VEHICLE (Fig. 6.12). Here we have the base hand, a "C" shape which signifies container, plus a "legs" hand which signifies human being, their relation to each other, then the motion of going—at least a four-morpheme sign. It would be ungrammatical to use the "con-

Figure 6.12.   ASL sign for "ride in a vehicle."

tainer" classifier for talking about riding *on* a vehicle like a bicycle; another classifier would have to be used.

Combining classifiers with motion verbs is a very productive way to coin new signs. Figure 6.13 shows to combination of the classifier signifying thin flat rectangular shape, the "legs" classifier we use for human being, and the orientation of the hands plus a movement, which together mean "skateboard," a relatively recent phenomenon. More discussion can be found in Supalla (1980), Kegl and Wilbur (1976), and McDonald (1981).

We know that different languages are *required* or *permitted* to express some concepts gramatically (i.e., systematically), while other concepts may be expressed less systematically. If we compare ASL to English, we find that certain elements of size and shape must be expressed in ASL but are not required to be expressed in English, and if they are expressed in English, it is not gramatically, but lexically. We shall see in the next section that while ASL expresses the same kind of syntactic complexity as English, it does so in radically different ways.

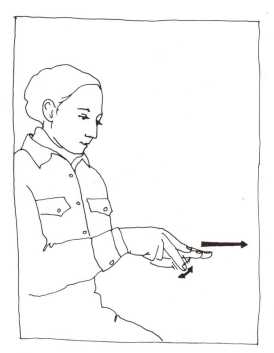

Figure 6.13. ASL sign for "skateboard."

ASL Syntax

Just as languages vary in what must be expressed and what can be expressed grammatically, they also differ in how a particular point will be expressed. One thing that all languages express is basic grammatical relations; these include such notions as subject and object, as well as various kinds of subordination and coordination. There is often a trade-off between complexity in one part of the grammar and simplicity in another. Further, one language may use the morphology to express an idea, while another language uses the syntax or even the phonology. We can see this contrast by comparing English with ASL and some other languages.

How does English express who does what to whom (grammatical relations)? Virtually all distinctions among different parts of the sentence in English are at the level of syntax. Sentences (15) and (16) mean very different things, as do (17) and (18).

(15) Franklin never liked Harry.
(16) Harry never liked Franklin.
(17) He can't tie a knot.
(18) He can't knot a tie.

English, in contrast to ASL and Latin, has no means of marking subject or object except with order; changing the order changes the grammatical relations. English also does not have formal means of marking parts of speech; both *knot* and *tie* can be either nouns or verbs, again in contrast with ASL or Latin. English *inflectional* morphology is almost nonexistent; the syntax thereby must take up the slack, so English has quite rigid word order, a complex lexicon, and a complex interaction among various kinds of word choices. Inflecting languages like ASL and Latin have relatively free word order but a very complex morphological system. (For discussions of word order in ASL, see Fischer, 1974 and 1975 and Liddell, 1981).

We saw in Chapter 1 (see, for example, sentences (17)–(19) in Chapter 1) that what is expressed with an inflection in one language could be expressed with a separate word in another. This is also true in ASL vis-à-vis other languages, and in fact requires us to stretch our linguistic horizons a bit in order to see the parallels between the expression of various syntactic functions in all languages, including ASL.

We saw in Chapter 1 that English expresses the idea of a conditional by means of a subordinator *if*; Japanese expresses it with an inflection on the verb, as can German. ASL expresses conditionals by a combination of shifts in facial expression, body tension, and eyeblinks (Baker and Padden 1978, Coulter, 1979)! English expresses questions with a syntactic rule (subject-auxiliary inversion), separate lexical markers (such as *who* and *what*), and intonation. Japanese keeps the same order for questions and declarative sentences but adds a question marker *ka* at the end of a sentence to make it a question. ASL has some *wh* words but also uses the visual equivalent of rising intonation (rising eyebrows and other concomitant behaviors) to signify questions as well.

Consider the expression of relative clauses, which are sentences functioning as modifiers or specifiers on nouns. English expresses relative clauses by the use of particular relative pronouns, the deletion of the shared noun phrase within the clause, and the placement of the clause after the noun it modifies. Japanese (see sentence (18) in Chapter 1) has no relative pronoun, also deletes the shared noun phrase in the relative clause, and places the relative clause *before* the noun it modifies. In ASL, some relative clauses come before the noun, and some after (the distinction seems to be whether the relative clause contains old information or new information, where the old information type of clause precedes the noun and the new information clause follows it). ASL has the equivalent of relative pronouns, but sometimes the shared noun is deleted in the *matrix* (main) sentence rather than in the relative clause (Liddell, 1978).

In summary, there are equivalent ways of expressing grammatical function in any language. Some languages will have more or less systematic ways of expressing a particular function, and they won't always do it in the same place in the grammar. ASL is no exception to this rule; it has its own means of expressing relations among elements of the sentence, and they are radically different from those in English, though not necessarily different in kind from what one finds in other languages of the world, spoken or signed.

THE SOCIOLINGUISTIC CONTEXT OF SIGN LANGUAGE

Some basic facts about how sign language is learned and used in the United States, and indeed in many countries, reveal a number of singularities, which in turn can affect both the grammar, ultimately, of ASL and the people who use sign language.

Unlike most (though not all—see Fischer, 1978, for discussion) spoken languages, ASL is not strictly native to the majority of people for whom it is a primary means of communication. Only about 7–9% of deaf children have even one deaf parent, and only about one in 10 children born to prevocationally deaf parents is born hearing-impaired (Rainer et al., 1969; , Schein and Delk, 1974; Ries, 1973). Although deafness can be diagnosed very early nowadays, and although many hearing parents are starting to learn to sign as soon as their child's deafness is diagnosed, the vast majority of deaf children are still not exposed to any signing at all until they enter school at age 3 or 5 or even later.

In some ways, the language development (and here we include both sign language and English) of deaf children is somewhat analogous to that of immigrant children who learn a new language "in the streets." Deaf children who attend residential schools are socialized into a language community outside of the classroom which values ASL skill, just as young immigrant children are socialized into the host language more outside of the classroom than in it. Another similarity would appear to be that the older the child is when exposed to a new language, after a point, the harder it will be for that child, or most children, to master the new system completely.

The big difference between immigrant children and deaf children is that immigrant children have a language to start with, and many deaf children do not. Deaf children may have some internal symbolic system, and they may have "home signs" or a fragmentary knowledge of English, but many do not begin learning *any* language until they are older. Immigrant children start learning *some* language at birth.

ASL, then, is a language with few truly "native" users, though there is a much higher proportion of "near-native" users, including hearing children of deaf parents and children who start learning ASL very early, e.g., at residential schools. Age of acquisition and knowledge of ASL or ability to process it efficiently have been found to correlate by Woodward (1973), Newport and Supalla, (1980), and Mayberry et al. (in press).

Attempts to learn ASL are also made by hearing adults, with greater or lesser success. Even with a language base to work from, adults find it harder to learn a new language than children. Speculation as to why can be found in various versions of the critical age hypothesis (Lenneberg, 1967; Krashen, 1975), which argues that not everybody can learn a first or second language after a certain age (scholars disagree what that age is, some argue that the age is 5, others that it is puberty). Now, when we say that not everybody can learn a second language with 100% mastery, that is not to say that nobody can. Some people are extraordinarily good language learners—others are not; and this knack for learning languages does not seem to be related to intelligence. It is probably safe to say, however, that the vast majority of hearing people who try to learn ASL as adults will tend to sign with a "hearing accent," using whatever sign language they have mastered but filling it in with a lot of English.

Until very recently, ASL has been looked down upon as less than a legitimate language. At the same time, ASL is one of the defining features of the deaf subculture, and it is sometimes in the interests of that subculture to keep the language obscure to outsiders. These two factors combine so that when an ASL user is signing to a hearing English user, they will tend to sign as closely to English as they are able, using ASL signs in a roughly English word order, with greater-than-ordinary use of fingerspelling. This makes it difficult for the hearing person to learn ASL (if they are never exposed to it), but at the same time it can help to serve as a bridge. The varieties of signing that serve as an interface between the deaf culture and language and the hearing culture and language are called PSE (Pidgin Sign English). Like any pidgin language, PSE is nobody's first language, and it will be used differently, depending on the first language of the user; i.e., the PSE of the hearing person will differ significantly from the PSE of the

deaf person (Woodward and Markowicz, 1975). Because of time constraints, PSE is what is used most often by interpreters, even those who are trying to use ASL. We shall return to this point a bit later.

SIGN LANGUAGE AND THE EDUCATIONAL PROCESS

In every other major industrialized country in the world, there is a sign language which is significantly different from the spoken language. In some of these countries, especially those which have incorporated the sign modality into the educational system, there is a signed version of the spoken language coexisting with the sign language. In those countries where signing has been forbidden in the classroom as a matter of national policy, there appears to be more variation than one would find in ASL. See, for example, Deuchar (in press). The suppression of sign language in the educational system may also accelerate the changes that naturally occur in the language.

Within the educational setting, there seem to have been three roles for sign language historically. One has been to forbid signing in the classroom, a second has been to base the teaching of the spoken and written language on the student's knowledge of the sign language, and the third is to use the sign channel to introduce the majority language to the community. Each of these approaches has its fervent adherents; however, the somewhat-differing goals and the self-selection involved in parents' selecting the approach for their children make it difficult to determine if one method is to be preferred to any other. Each approach succeeds for some purposes for some students. We will discuss some of the advantages and disadvantages of each approach.

Exclusively Oral Methods

The goal of oral education is to enable the hearing-impaired person to become fully integrated into hearing society. The oral method relies heavily on developing good skills in articulation, speechreading, and use of residual hearing. The advantages of this method are that when it works, the hearing-impaired person can indeed become fully integrated into hearing society. The disadvantage is that not everyone is able to learn a first language from the often-impoverished cues available. Oral methods tend to work best when there is some residual hearing, and when there is an already existing language base, either because the child is postlingually deaf or because the child has deaf parents and learned sign language at home (Mindel and Vernon, 1971). Oral methods also succeed with some profoundly congenitally deaf children. The unanswerable (on all sides) question is how well the successful oral learner would have done in other content areas as well as in articulation, had s/he been permitted the use of sign language in conjunction with oral training.

Bilingual Approach

One promising approach to the use of sign language in the classroom has been to use ASL as a vehicle for teaching English. This has been highly successful at the postsecondary level (Forman and Holcomb, in press) and has been advocated for earlier levels as well. The advantages of this approach are that it takes into account the student's already-existing linguistic knowledge; explanations of important points can be made in the child's native language, so that content learning proceeds apace. The disadvantages are that not all children entering school know ASL; in fact most do not, so there is no native language to build on. The second disadvantage is that it requires that the teacher be fluent in ASL, which most teachers of the deaf are not (Woodward, 1980).

Bimodal Approach

The most commonly used approach to utilizing sign language in the classroom is what is generally called "total communication." Total communication (TC) is a philosophy which advocates gearing the language input to the student and the situation and not necessarily requiring simultaneous input to the child all the time. While this philosophy theoretically admits the utility of using ASL for some children, in practice the TC practitioners tend to employ some version of signed English. They feel that if children see English represented consistently on the hands, as well as on the lips and on the printed page, that

the constant exposure will hasten their acquisition of English in all modalities (Gustason et al., 1972). Signing "in English" (a phrase whose meaning we shall discuss below in some detail) facilitates simultaneous communication (sign and speech) by permitting sign and speech to co-occur; it is impossible to sign ASL while speaking English, as the syntaxes of the two languages are so different. The advantages of total communication are that first, it provides input in as many different modalities as the child can receive. Second, it can serve to reinforce English instruction to have English presented on the hands. Third, it permits flexibility of approach to the learning of different skills. The disadvantages of TC really lie in the way the term itself can be, and has been, misused. If a previously orally oriented school "goes total" without adequate preparation in teacher training or materials and drastically lowers emphasis on other than sign language skills, the linguistic input the children receive will be highly inconsistent. If parents are not involved in learning sign language, the usefulness of signing in the classroom is diminished.

In the last 15 years, more and more schools have introduced some form of signing into the classroom, as part of a TC philosophy. Most of these involve "signing in English," as we mentioned above. Recall that signing is a modality and that it is possible, at least theroretically, to sign English as well as to sign ASL or any other language. There are, however, a number of different approaches to "signing in English," and these may have educational and social consequences.

We discussed Pidgin Sign English (PSE) above as the linguistic interface between deaf hearing people. One way to sign English is to use a modified version of PSE. PSE occurs naturally as a part of the process of communication, but it lacks certain redundancies of both ASL and English; however, it is possible to augment it in a systematic way to produce more strict signed English. This involves using the semantically appropriate ASL signs for the concepts involved and either finger spelling or adding supplementary signs for the functors of English for which there is no direct ASL equivalent. Thus, for example, the sentences in (1)–(13) would be signed in English word order with English endings added to them, but 13 distinct signs for "run" would be used for the 13 different meanings of the word in English. This is essentially the approach advocated by Bornstein (1978).

At the other extreme from a PSE type of approach is the so-called Rochester method, which involves fingerspelling, letter by letter, though quite rapidly, the written representation of spoken English. This is generally viewed as a supplement to an oral approach.

Another very commonly used way of signing English is the invented systems that have developed as part of the advent of TC. The most commonly used version is SEE II (Gustason et al., 1972), and there is an excellent discussion of their use in Wilbur (1978). These systems utilize certain aspects of ASL signs but tie them much closer to English than the PSE type of approach, in the following ways:

1. An attempt is made to have one sign for each English morpheme. Fingerspelling is avoided.
2. These systems follow the "two out of three" criterion: One sign will be used as long as the two English words under consideration share two out of three of spelling, pronunciation, and meaning.

Thus, the 13 sentences in (1)–(13) will use the same sign for "run," as contrasted to the PSE approach which would use 13 different signs.

3. Possible sign vocabulary is enriched by extensive use of *initialization*, whereby a family of signs is created from one by changing the signing handshape to the first letter of the intended English word. This process exists marginally in ASL, though as we have seen, there are other ways to coin new words in ASL as well.

At this point in history, it is difficult to determine any absolute advantages or disadvantages for each of these three possibilities; however, one can make some observations.

How one determines success or failure of any of these systems is largely dependent on how one defines success or failure. In part, this in turn depends on the goals one has for introducing the signing system in the first place. Numerous questions come to mind which may help to clarify some of the issues involved. First, is the goal of the signing

system to be a *model* of English from which the child can internalize the language, a *communication tool* for acquiring knowledge of, among other things, English, or as a way of expressing English once that language has been acquired, perhaps through other means? Second, how important is it that the deaf person be able to participate in both the hearing and deaf cultures? Someone who learns one of the stricter artificial signing systems will have to unlearn a great deal in order to learn ASL, while someone who has learned a more PSE type of system, while having to learn new grammatical markers for ASL, will not have to unlearn some of the principles of the artificial system in order to understand and be understood by most deaf adults. On the other hand (so to speak), *if* it turns out to be the case that the stricter artificial systems facilitate the learning of written or spoken English, then there may be justification for advocating those systems. As of this writing, there are a number of studies (Crandall, 1973; Raffin et al., 1978; Bornstein and Saulnier, 1981) that show fairly conclusively that exposure to signed English morphemes increases the probability of the child's acquiring those morphemes in their signing. However, the missing logical link so far is how that sign acquisition carries over to the child's internalized system of English. It is interesting that even these results hold, given the often inconsistent exposure to those signed morphemes that children often receive (Marmor and Petitto, 1979).

Some form of signing is probably here to stay in most school systems. There is no hard evidence that it adversely affects the acquisition of English or even of speech and lip-reading, and there is some evidence that knowledge of signing facilitates acquisition of reading and writing of English as well as speech and speechreading (Mindel and Vernon, 1971; Moores, 1978; Brasel and Quigley, 1977). However, the introduction of signing into the schools cannot be viewed as an easy substitute for good instruction in all aspects of language use in deaf children. It is just as hard to sign well as it is to speak well, and materials and good teaching are, if anything, more important when one is working across modalities.

SUMMARY

Unlike many of the other language modalities discussed in this book, signing—at least ASL—can be acquired normally and without delay by a child exposed to it early enough; there is no sensory barrier in the way. ASL is a language distinct from English, neither "better" nor worse, neither simpler nor more complex, but different. It is one of the markers of the deaf subculture. ASL is a language; signing is a modality. Thus, it is possible to sign "in English," often as a bridge between the hearing and deaf worlds. In this regard, it is interesting to note that sign language (though probably not ASL, but some form of PSE) is the most popularly taught adult education course throughout the country (*Newsweek*, 1980). The learning of sign language by hearing people in the community serves to reinforce that bridge. Signing is definitely not a panacea for the experiential deficits suffered by people who cannot hear; however, there is evidence that it can facilitate the acquisition of the standard language of the community in many modalities.

References

Baker, C., and Padden, C. Focusing on the non-manual components of American Sign Language. In P. Siple (ed.), *Understanding Language through Sign Language Research*. New York: Academic Press, 1978, 27–57.

Battison, R. *Phonological Borrowing in American Sign Language*. Silver Spring, Maryland: Linstok Press, 1978.

Bellugi, U., and Fischer, S. A comparison of sign language and spoken language. *Cognition*, 1972, *1*, 173–200.

Bornstein, H. Sign language in the education of the deaf. In I.M. Schlesinger and L. Namir (eds.), *Sign Language of the Deaf*. New York: Academic Press, 1978, 333–361.

Bornstein, H. and Saulnier, K. Signed English: A brief follow-up to the first evaluation. *Am Ann. Deaf*, 1981, *126*, 64–72.

Brasel, K., and Quigley, S. Influence of certain language and communication environments in early childhood on the development of language in deaf individuals. *J. Speech Hear. Res.*, 1977, *20*, 95–107.

Coulter, G.R. American sign language topology. Doctoral dissertation, University of California, San Diego, 1979.

Crandall, K. Inflectional morphemes in the manual English of young hearing-impaired children and their mothers. *J. Speech Hear. Res.*, 1973, *21*, 372–286.

Deuchar, M. Variation in British sign language. In J. G. Kyle and B. Woll (eds.), *Proceedings of the Second International Symposium on Sign Language Research*. London: Croom Helm (in press).

Feldman, H., Goldin-Meadow, S., and Gleitman, L. Beyond Herodotus: The creation of language by linguistically deprived deaf children. In A. Locke, (ed.), *Action, Symbol, and Gesture: The Emergence of Language*. New York: Academic Press, 1978.

Fischer, S. Two processes of reduplication in the American sign language. *Found. Lang.*, 1973, *9*, 469–480.

Fischer, S. Sign language and linguistic universals. In C. Rohrer and N. Ruwet (eds.), *Actes du colloque Franco-Allemand de Grammaire Transformationelle*, band II. Tübingen: Max Niemeyer Verlag, 1974, 187–204.

Fischer S. Influences on word order change in American sign language. In C. Li (ed.), *Word Order and Word Order Change*. Austin: University of Texas Press, 1975, 1–25.

Fischer, S. Sign language and creoles. In P. Siple (ed.), *Understanding Language through Sign Language Research*. New York: Academic Press, 1978, 309–331.

Fischer, S., and Gough, B. Verbs in American Sign Language. *Sign Lang. Stud.*, 1978, *18*, 17–48.

Forman, J., and Holcomb, S. Using American sign language. In Sr. F. Solano (ed.), *Proceedings of the Convention of American Instructors of the Deaf*. Silver Spring, Maryland (in press).

Frishberg, N. Arbitrariness and iconicity in ASL. *Language*, 1975, *51*, 696–719.

Grosjean, F. The study of timing in a manual and a spoken language: American sign language and English. *J. Psycholinguist. Res.*, 1979, *8*, 379–405.

Gustason, G., Pfetzing, D., and Zawolkow, E. *Signing Exact English*. Rossmar, California: Modern Signs Press, 1972.

Kegl, J., and Wilbur, R. Where does structure stop and style begin. Syntax, morphology, and phonology vs. stylistic variation in ASL. In S. Mufwene, C. Walker, and S. Steevers (eds.), *Papers from the Twelfth Regional Meeting, Chicago Linguistic Society*. Chicago: University of Chicago Press, 1976.

Klima, E., Bellugi, U., Fischer, S., Pedersen, C., and Newkirk, D. The structured use of space and movement. In E. Klima and U. Bellugi (eds.), *The Signs of Language*. Cambridge, Massachusetts: Harvard University Press, 1979, 272–315.

Krashen, S. The critical period for language acquisition and its possible bases. In D. Aaronson and R. Rieber (eds.), *Developmental Psycholinguistics and Communication Disorders*. New York: New York Academy of Science, 1975.

Kuschel, R. *A Lexicon of Signs from a Polynesian Outliner Island*, Psykologisk Skriftserie, #8. Copenhagen: Psykologisk Laboratorium, Københavns Universitet, 1974.

Lenneberg, E. *Biological Foundations of Language*. New York: John Wiley & Sons, 1967.

Liddell, S. *American Sign Language Syntax*. The Hague: Mouton, 1981.

Liddell, S. Nonmanual signals and relative clauses in American sign language. In P. Siple (ed.), *Understanding Language through Sign Language Research*. New York: Academic Press, 1978, 59–90.

Marmor, G. and Petitto, L. Simultaneous communication in the classroom: How well is English grammar represented? *Sign Lang. Stud.*, 1979, *136*, 99–136.

Mayberry, R. Manual communication. In H. Davis and S.R. Silverman (eds.), *Hearing and Deafness*, ed. 4. New York: Holt, Rinehart & Winston, 1978.

Mayberry, R., Fischer, S., and Hatfield, N. Sentence repetition in American Sign Language. In J.G. Kyle and B. Woll (eds.), *Proceedings of the Second International Symposium on Sign Language Research.* London: Croom Helm (in press).

McDonald, B. Aspects of the ASL verbal system. Doctoral dissertation, SUNY Buffalo, 1981.

Mindel, E., and Vernon, M. *They Grow in Silence: The Deaf Child and His Family.* Silver Spring, Maryland: National Association for the Deaf, 1971.

Moores, D. *Educating the Deaf: Psychology, Principles, and Practices.* Boston: Houghton Mifflin, 1978.

Newport, E.L. Constraints on structure: Evidence from American sign language and language learning. In W.A. Collins (ed.), *Minnesota Symposium on Child Psychology*, vol. 14. Hillsdale, New Jersey: Lawrence Erlbaum Associates, 1981.

Newport, E.L., and Supalla, T. The structuring of language by developmental processes: Clues from the acquisition of signed and spoken language. In U. Bellugi and M. Studdert-Kennedy (eds.), *Signed and Spoken Language: Biological Constraints on Linguistic Form.* New York: Verlag Chemie, 1980.

Raffin, M., Davis, J., and Gilman, L. Comprehension of inflectional morphemes by deaf children exposed to a visual English sign system *J. Speech Hear. Res.*, 1978, *21*, 387–400.

Rainer, J., Altshuler, K., and Kallman, F. (eds.) *Family and Mental Health Problems in a Deaf Population*, Springfield, Illinois: Charles C Thomas, Publisher, 1969.

Ries, P. Association between achievement test performance and selected characteristics of hearing impaired students in special education programs. In *Further Studies in Achievement Tests, Hearing Impaired Students, United States: Spring, 1971.* Washington, D.C.: Office of Demographic Studies, Gallaudet College, Series D, #13, 1973.

Schein, J., and Delk, M. *The Deaf Population of the United States.* Silver Spring, Maryland: National Association of the Deaf, 1974.

Signing up for sign language. *Newsweek*, 1980, *95*, 47.

Silverman, S.R., and Lane, H. Deaf children. In H. Davis and S.R. Silverman, *Hearing and Deafness*, ed. 3. New York: Holt, Rinehart & Winston, 1970, 384–425.

Siple, P. Visual constraints for sign language communication. *Sign Lang. Stud.*, 1978, *19*, 95–110.

Stokoe, W. *Sign Language Structure* Studies in Linguistics Occasional Papers, 8. Buffalo: University of Buffalo Press, 1960.

Stokoe, W., Casterline, D. and Croneberg, C. *A Dictionary of American Sign Language.* Washington, D.C.: Gallaudet College Press, 1965.

Supalla, T. Derivational morphology in ASL. In F. Caccamise and D. Hicks (eds.), *ASL in a Bilingual, Bicultural Context: Proceedings of the Second National Symposium on Sign Language Research and Teaching.* Silver Spring, Maryland: National Association for the Deaf, 1980, 27–45.

Supalla, T., and Newport, E. How many seats in a chair? The derivations of nouns and verbs in ASL. In P. Siple (ed.), *Understanding Language through Sign Language Research.* New York: Academic Press, 1978, 91–132.

Woodward, J., and Markowicz, H. Pidgin sign languages. Paper presented at the Conference on Pidgins and Creoles, Honolulu, 1975.

Woodward, J.C. Implicational lects on the deaf diglossic continuum. Doctoral dissertation, Georgetown University, 1973.

Woodward, J. Some sociolinguistic problems in the implementation of bilingual education for deaf students. In F. Caccamise, and D. Hicks (eds.), *ASL in a Bilingual, Bicultural Context: Proceedings of the Second National Symposium on Sign Language Research and Training.* Silver Spring, Maryland: National Association of the Deaf, 1980, 183–210.

Recommended Reading

Baker, C., and Cokely, D. *American Sign Language: A Teacher's Resource Text on Grammar and Culture.* Silver Spring, Maryland: TJ Publishers, 1980.

Klima, E., and Bellugi, U. *The Signs of Language.* Cambridge, Massachusetts: Harvard University Press, 1979.

Siple, P. (ed.) *Understanding Language through Sign Language Research.* New York: Academic Press, 1978.

Stokoe, W. (ed.) *Sign Language Studies* (a quarterly scholarly journal devoted to research on sign language). Silver Spring, Maryland: Linstok Press.

Wilbur, R.B. *American Sign Language and Sign Language Systems.* Baltimore: University Park Press, 1978.

Chapter 7

English in the Deaf Population

JOSEPH H. BOCHNER, M.A.[1]

The loss of hearing sensitivity in young children alters the character of their linguistic intake, which in turn interacts with their development and maturation and affects the acquisition of language (and speech) to the degree that many deaf children enter adolescence and adulthood without the ability to communicate effectively in English. However, not all hearing impairments have equally devastating effects on language development. Given a child with impaired hearing, the integrity of his linguistic intake, which is associated with the integrity of his sensory capabilities (e.g., the severity and configuration of his hearing loss) and physical properties of the intake itself, interacts with the progression of his cognitive development and neurological maturation (e.g., the child's age at onset of the hearing loss) to determine, in large part, the course and extent of his linguistic growth. Therefore, some hearing impairments have little or no discernible effect on language acquisition (e.g., hearing losses occurring in the latter stages of childhood), while others almost always have a profound and lasting impact (e.g., severe congenital hearing losses). Due to the enormous range of this variation, the hearing-impaired population consists of a widely diverse and extremely heterogeneous mixture of people whose linguistic skills range from the primitive to the highly refined.

This chapter describes the major characteristics of language use, structure, and acquisition in the deaf population by reviewing and evaluating pertinent literature in the area of language and deafness. It is not intended as an exhaustive review of the literature; rather, it is designed to touch upon major works in the field, providing critical analysis of research that has been conducted and, more importantly, providing observational and descriptive data bearing on the problem

---

[1] Currently doctoral candidate at the University of Wisconsin-Madison.

of language and deafness (for other reviews see Swisher, 1976, Norlin and Van Tasell, 1980, Cooper and Rosenstein, 1966, and Kretschmer and Kretschmer, 1978).

In order to discuss language and deafness, however, an explicit definition of terms is necessary. Language, in this chapter, refers to English, while deafness denotes individuals with severe to profound bilateral (peripheral) hearing losses occurring before about two years of age (cf. Lenneberg, 1967). The definition of deafness extends beyond a simple audiometric classification to include chronological age, since it is the interaction of hearing loss, or more properly linguistic intake, with development and maturation that affects the use, structure, and acquisition of English. Although this definition of deafness circumscribes a subset of the hearing-impaired population (i.e., individuals with severe to profound "prelingual" hearing losses), the language characteristics of these individuals are not uniform and invariant. In other words, significant differences among the individuals who comprise the group do exist, and it is important to recognize this fact. Unless otherwise indicated, statements made in this chapter are intended as generalizations which apply to prelingually deaf individuals as a group, and such generalizations are valid descriptions of group characteristics only.

The scope of this chapter encompasses the use, structure, and acquisition of English, and the chapter is organized around these themes. An implicit distinction between linguistic ability and various domains of linguistic performance has been incorporated into the chapter for the purpose of organizing and presenting information. Linguistic ability herein refers to functional knowledge of English (i.e., observations and descriptions of language structure and linguistic competence), while performance domains denote data derived from nonlinguistic procedures (e.g., standardized tests, word counts, error taxonomies, and word associations). Although many important characteristics of the linguistic ability of the deaf are embodied in their spoken and written language performance, most research in these areas has employed procedures unable to observe or describe linguistic competence. Therefore, in order to distinguish true linguistic ability from quasi-linguistic components of performance, separate sections have been devoted to each topic in this chapter.

In the field of linguistics, descriptions of language structure and linguistic competence are normally based on spoken rather than written discourse, since speech is the primary embodiment of natural language. However, given the function of writing in the deaf population, a function which in many ways is analogous to the role of speech in the hearing world, it appears reasonable to consider writing a primary manifestation of language in deaf individuals. In fact, data indicate that various characteristics of the spoken and written language of the deaf are correlated (Goda, 1959). These considerations eliminate the need for strictly distinguishing between spoken and written language in a general discussion of this sort, most importantly in a general discussion of linguistic ability. Moreover, certain characteristics of writing performance (e.g., simple observations of language structure) complement descriptions of linguistic ability and cannot be excluded from them.

Performance characteristics are reviewed first in this chapter, and linguistic ability is covered next, followed by a general discussion of language acquisition in deaf individuals. Finally, the chapter closes with a brief summary and concluding remarks.

PERFORMANCE CHARACTERISTICS

Reading

The reading comprehension skills of deaf children and young adults frequently have been compared to those of individuals with normal hearing, reading comprehension constituting "probably the single most critical area of school achievement for any group of children" (Trybus and Karchmer, 1977, p. 64). Comparative studies of reading performance, which may be traced back to the early part of this century (e.g., Pintner and Patterson, 1917), have typically relied on scores from standardized tests and have consistently resulted in large differences between the performance of deaf subjects and normal-hearing controls matched for age. The distressingly poor performance of deaf students on tests of reading achievement indicates that they are at a considerable educational disadvantage, which stems primarily from linguistic deficiencies rather than from pervasive cognitive or intellectual deficits (Conrad, 1979; Furth, 1971; Moores, 1970a; Pintner and Patterson, 1916).

Test data indicate that the reading achievement of approximately half of the deaf high-school population is below that of an average 9½-year-old hearing child, in other words below a fourth-grade level (Furth, 1966; Cooper and Rosenstein, 1966; DiFrancesca, 1972; Trybus and Karchmer, 1977; Conrad, 1977). This finding has been interpreted as evidence that about half of the young deaf adult population may be considered "functionally illiterate" (Furth, 1966; Conrad, 1977). Consistent with the findings of previous research, the results of a recent comprehensive study reveal that less than 10% of the hearing-impaired 18 year olds in the United States can read at or above an eighth-grade level (Trybus and Karchmer, 1977). As a group, deaf students' average growth in reading achievement has been estimated at less than 0.3 grade equivalents/year (Trybus and Karchmer, 1977; DiFrancesca, 1972), and this growth probably subsides at the time they complete school (Hammermeister, 1971). Thus, many deaf individuals without the benefit of formal post-secondary education enter adulthood reading at or below a fourth-grade level and remain at this plateau throughout their adult lives.

The vocabulary achievement of deaf students, like their performance in the related area of reading, differs markedly from that of hearing norms, with most deaf students 18 years old and younger scoring at or below a fourth-grade level (DiFrancesca, 1972; Cooper and Rosenstein, 1966). In general, the vocabulary performance of deaf people tends to be poorer than their reading achievement, indicating that weaknesses in the area of vocabulary probably contribute to poor reading comprehension (DiFrancesca, 1972; Walter, 1978).

Although decades of research have consistently shown that the reading and vocabulary performance of deaf students is exceedingly low in comparison to that of hearing norms, the English language proficiency of these individuals is substantially lower than that of hearing children achieving similar grade equivalent scores on standardized reading and vocabulary tests (Moores, 1970a; Walter, 1978). For example, an 18-year-old deaf student scoring at the fourth-grade level on a standardized reading or vocabulary test would tend to be less proficient in his use of English than a typical fourth grader with normal hearing. The discrepancy between the linguistic ability of deaf students and that of normal-hearing students performing at comparable grade levels stems from the fact that standardized reading and vocabulary tests measure educational achievement rather than linguistic ability per se and, in so doing, presuppose a level of linguistic proficiency which most deaf children do not possess (Moores, 1970b). The distinction between educational achievement and linguistic ability illustrates the fact that normally hearing children, unlike their deaf counterparts, develop a great deal of linguistic knowledge before reaching school age, without the benefit of formal education (Dale, 1976; Kretschmer and Kretschmer, 1978); whereas academic achievement is highly correlated with formal schooling and, in most cases, is just beginning to develop as a child enters school. Therefore, grade equivalent reading and vocabulary scores may only be considered rough, indirect estimates of the relative linguistic ability of deaf students, with this use and interpretation of achievement test scores being justified by the fact that linguistic ability is a necessary prerequisite for reading and vocabulary achievement and by the fact that reference to hearing norms is explicitly avoided by considering grade equivalent scores "relative values that show relationships between sub-groups of the (deaf) population" (DiFrancesca, 1972, p. 7).

Verbal Associations and Spelling

Word association tests and semantic differential scales, measures derived from behaviorist approaches to the psychology of language, have been administered to deaf children and young adults in attempts to provide insight into their learning of vocabulary and the organization of their lexicons (e.g., Blanton, 1968). Reminiscent of reading and vocabulary achievement data, the basic finding of these studies is that the verbal associations of hearing-impaired subjects differ from those of individuals with normal hearing, with the word associations of deaf subjects often resembling those of younger, hearing children (Blanton, 1968; Koplin et al., 1967; Swisher, 1976). In other words, the results of verbal association studies imply that deaf and normal-hearing individuals differ with respect to the organization and acquisition of lexical information. Both sensory and learning factors (e.g., the role of audition in experiencing the universe and acquiring knowledge, and the role of formal vocabulary teaching as opposed to naturalistic verbal learning) have been mentioned as possible causes of this difference (Blanton, 1968; Nunnally and Blanton, 1966). However, word-sorting data indicate that the difference between the semantic organization of deaf and hearing adolescents is not generalized across the entire lexicon; rather, this difference appears to be limited in large part to semantic domains for which the deaf have little experience, such as words associated with auditory imagery (Tweney et al., 1975).

Unlike deaf individuals' academic achievement in the areas of reading and vocabulary, which has been shown to be severely retarded in comparison to hearing norms, their spelling achievement is relatively advanced. Data have consistently shown that within the limits of their vocabularies, the spelling performance of hearing-impaired students is superior to that of normally hearing children matched for age or reading achievement (Hoemann et al., 1976; Templin, 1948; Gates and Chase, 1926) and is also superior to their own reading achievement (DiFrancesca, 1972). This superiority has generally been attributed to the fact that hearing loss renders children less inclined to commit auditory confusion errors on spelling tasks, auditory confusions constituting the basis of most spelling errors in children with normal hearing (e.g., Read, 1975; cf. Gibson et al., 1970). Rather than using auditory (speech) coding as their primary means of representing written information in short-term memory, many deaf individuals tend to employ visual (orthographic) encoding schemes as well as coding based on the manual alphabet (Conrad, 1973; 1979; Locke and Locke, 1971). In summary, differences exist between the performance of deaf and normal-hearing individuals on verbal association and spelling tasks, and these differences have been atttributed to the effects of hearing loss on learning and information processing.

Writing

As in other performance domains, analysis of the writing of the deaf has frequently been accomplished by comparing the performance of deaf subjects and normally hearing controls along one or more dimensions. Various indices have been devised to assess both quantitative and qualitative aspects of writing performance, with most measures employing enumerative procedures, such as word counts or counts of error and sentence types. The assumptions underlying this research are that the writing performance of deaf and normal-hearing children are directly comparable and that enumerative procedures can provide insight into the use and development of written language in the deaf. Since writing may be considered a primary manifestation of linguistic competence in the deaf but may only be considered a subsidiary linguistic skill in the hearing population, and since enumerative procedures are not sensitive to linguistic ability, the validity of these assumptions is dubious; consequently, the results of this research should be interpreted cautiously. For example, although the performance of deaf teenagers resembles that of younger children with normal hearing on many numerical indices of writing performance (e.g., word counts and counts of sentence types), as has been demonstrated in comparative studies (e.g., Myklebust, 1964; Heider and Heider, 1940), the linguistic abilities of deaf teenagers are not on a par with those of normal-hearing elementary school children (Moores, 1970a). Equating the writing performance of deaf adolescents to that of normally hearing elementary school children is, therefore, a practice which should be avoided, unless clear distinctions are drawn between linguistic competence and writing performance in these two populations (see "Appendix A" to this chapter for an example of a typical composition written by a deaf adolescent).

The results of word count studies indicate that deaf children and adolescents write shorter sentences (i.e., fewer words per sentence) than hearing controls at comparable ages (Heider and Heider, 1940; Myklebust, 1964), using a larger proportion of simple, one-clause sentences and a smaller proportion of multiple-clause constructions than their hearing counterparts (Heider and Heider, 1940). Clear differences between deaf and hearing children have also been observed with regard to patterns of word and phrase usage, with the deaf often repeating the same words and phrases over and over within a discourse (Heider and Heider, 1940; Simmons, 1962; Myklebust, 1964). However, on computations of the total number of words and sentences per composition, differences between deaf and hearing subjects are less definitive due to methodological differences between studies (Swisher, 1976) and to interactions between the hearing status and age of subjects (Myklebust, 1964). Furthermore, the criteria for defining and classifying sentences in writing performance have been arbitrary (e.g., Heider and Heider, 1940) and in some instances subjective and inexplicit (e.g., Myklebust, 1964). Thus, sentence counts, as well as counts of the number of words per sentence, are not as objective, reliable, and valid as they might appear to be.

Quantitative analyses of word classes in written language performance reveal that deaf individuals sometimes use more articles and nouns and fewer adverbs and conjunctions than normally hearing children matched for age, while comparative data on their use of other word classes (e.g., verbs, adjectives, and prepositions) are more problematical, since conflicting results have been reported by different researchers (compare Simmons, 1962, and Myklebust, 1964). Even these findings are mitigated by a number of considerations. Aside from methodological differences between studies (Cooper and Rosenstein, 1966), the results are tempered by interactions between the hearing status and age of subjects, which have been reported for the use of articles and prepositions (Myklebust, 1964), and, more importantly, by the fact that this research has been biased toward classifying words according to the linguistic categories of standard English, rather than nonstandard categories which might have been intended by the deaf (Cooper and Rosenstein, 1966; cf. West and Weber, 1974).

Aside from numerical data collected in comparative studies, the results of other word count research reveal that the sentence and composition length of deaf adolescents and young adults tend to increase with age, and numerical indices pertaining to the diversity of word usage also tend to increase as a function of age (Stuckless and Marks, 1966). However, grammatical errors remain numerous in the writing of deaf 18 year olds, although their number has been shown to have decreased slightly with age (Stuckless and Marks, 1966).

Perhaps the most striking characteristic of the written language of deaf individuals is the proliferation of errors or deviations from the norms of standard English grammar and usage. These errors, or "deafisms" as they are sometimes called, have been classified in terms of nonlinguistic categories of addition, substitution, omission, and order of words (Myklebust, 1964). However, the definitions of these categories have been neither precise nor objective (Cooper and Rosenstein, 1966), nor are the categories mutually exclusive, which is to say that a given error may be classified in more than one way (e.g., the error in the sentence "The dog chased the car and had a flat tire" may be classified either as an omission, omitting the subject of "had," or as a substitution, substituting "and" for a relative pronoun). Such classification schemes, which presuppose that language is simply a linear array of words, are biased toward the norms of standard English, and consequently are not able to provide insight into the phrase and clause structure intended by deaf individuals (Bochner, 1978). Therefore, nonlinguistic error taxonomies reveal more about the subjective impressions which normally hearing adult readers have of written language than they do about the performance of deaf writers.

The results of nonlinguistic error analyses provide little information about writing performance and linguistic behavior, simply indicating that the category of omission is the most frequent type of error committed by deaf children and adolescents, followed in order of decreasing frequency by the categories of substitution, addition, and word order (Myklebust, 1964). In contrast, observational data have consistently revealed pervasive patterns of errors in inflectional morphology (e.g., verb tense and agreement), function words (e.g., articles and prepositions), and other linguistic categories (e.g., phrase and clause structure) in the writing of the deaf (Greenberg and Withers, 1965). Such observations provide direct insight into both writing performance and linguistic ability and therefore are a potentially valuable source of information for students, teachers, and researchers.

Writing skills in deaf children also have been studied to determine the order in which sentence structures and word classes develop in written language (Walter, 1959). Consistent with the results of other research in the area of writing (Myklebust, 1964), data indicate that naming behavior (i.e., the simple juxtaposition of nouns and noun phrases) represents a primitive stage of written language development and that conjunctions and prepositions appear relatively late and are a source of great difficulty (Walter, 1955). Thus, the development of sentence structures and word classes in the written language of deaf children seems to reflect the general characteristics of their writing performance embodied in counts of words, word classes, and sentence types, and as in the area of reading comprehension, much of this development appears to reach a plateau during adolescence or shortly thereafter (Myklebust, 1964).

Spoken Language

Aside from the obvious fact that speech intelligibility is an independent (and perhaps confounding) variable which must be considered when selecting subjects, the basic procedures used in most studies of spoken language performance correspond to those employed in research on writing, and the shortcomings of these studies are identical to those of their counterparts in written language. Moreover, the results of spoken language research parallel those in the area of writing, with word and error count data indicating that deaf children, adolescents, and young adults produce fewer words (both types and tokens) overall, fewer words (types and possibly tokens) within most word classes, shorter sentences, and more errors than normally hearing controls of the same age or

younger (Brannon, 1966 and 1968; Brannon and Murray, 1966; Elliott et al., 1967; Simmons, 1962). In a related finding, hard-of-hearing children and adolescents also have been found to produce much shorter sentences than normally hearing controls (Bamford and Mentz, 1979).

The spoken language of deaf individuals seems to consist primarily of nouns and verbs, indicating a dearth of function words (Goda, 1964; Elliott et al., 1967; Brannon, 1966 and 1968). On the other hand, in what may be a contradictory finding, the use of words and word classes in spoken language seems to be more diverse than their use in writing (Simmons, 1962). Despite these seemingly disparate findings, written productions appear to be longer (i.e., having more total words and words per sentence) than their spoken counterparts (Goda, 1959). When compared to younger children with normal hearing, the overall performance of deaf children on oral language comprehension and production tasks tends to improve relatively slowly as a function of age, with verb forms constituting a major source of difficulty in spontaneous oral production (Pressnell, 1973). In conclusion, data from numerous studies indicate that the expressive language performance of deaf children, like their performance in receptive domains, differs from that of normally hearing children at the same age or younger.

LINGUISTIC ABILITY

Lexical and Morphological Knowledge

Knowledge of words and word classes in deaf children, adolescents, and young adults has been studied experimentally with sentence completion procedures. These indicate that within the limits of their vocabularies, the deaf know a good deal about the gross distributional properties of English lexical items (Odom et al., 1967; MacGinitie, 1964). However, their functional knowledge of semantic information and of finer syntactic properties of lexical items is severely limited (Walter, 1978; Odom et al., 1967). That is, deaf individuals frequently select words from appropiate syntactic categories (i.e., nouns, verbs, articles, prepositions, etc.) to complete sentences, but often choose inappropriate words from within these categories. Therefore, they seem to exhibit a fairly well developed knowledge of category membership, but lack comparable competence with semantic information and with finer syntactic properties of words. Consistent with observations of their written and spoken language performance, these findings demonstrate that function words are a source of great difficulty for the deaf (Odom et al., 1967). In addition, their vocabularies usually are comprised of very few lexical items, being limited to a fraction of the content words acquired by normally hearing children (Walter, 1978; cf. Odom et al., 1967). Furthermore, their knowledge of even the most common content words is seriously deficient (Walter, 1978; cf. Templin, 1966), which is consistent with verbal association and reading and vocabulary achievement data.

Knowledge of various aspects of English morphology (i.e., inflectional endings on nouns and verbs and derivational suffixes) has been studied with sentence completion and comprehension techniques in research indicating that many deaf individuals have not acquired functional (productive) control of various morphological rules, especially derivational rules (Cooper, 1967). Similar procedures have been employed to assess lexical and morphological knowledge in research demonstrating that deaf children and adolescents know relatively more about content words than they do about function words and morphology (Hart and Rosenstein, 1964). Likewise, knowledge of lexical features associated with various types of pronouns (e.g., case, gender, and number features associated with personal, possessive, reflexive, and relative pronouns) has been assessed in a series of multiple-choice, sentence completion tests administered to deaf children, adolescents, and young adults, the results of which indicate that their knowledge of the English pronoun system is incomplete and that knowledge of lexical features is not additive (Wilbur et al., 1976).

Patterns of lexical and morphological errors commonly occur in the writing of deaf individuals (Greenberg and Withers, 1965), and in further research their status has been assessed and compared to knowledge of standard English sentence patterns by eliciting grammaticality judgments from deaf subjects (Quigley et al., 1976c). Consistent with observations of their writing performance, grammaticality judgment data indicate that deaf children, adolescents, and young adults have considerable difficulty with inflectional endings on verbs, as well as with auxiliary forms and the main verbs "have" and "be" (Quigley et al., 1976a). These data also reveal that their judgments are extremely unreliable (cf. Gleitman and Gleitman, 1979). Therefore, their knowledge of lexical (auxiliary forms and the main verbs "have" and "be") and morphological (inflectional) aspects of English verb forms, while tending to increase as a function of chronological age, appears incomplete and unstable, even in young adult members of the population (Quigley et al., 1976a).

Based on observations of written utterances produced by children (Ivimey and Lachterman, 1980; Ivimey, 1976) and the results of a sentence repetition experiment conducted on adolescents (Charrow, 1974), the lexical and morphological abilities of deaf individuals have been described in studies which further document the difficulty they have with function words (especially auxiliary forms, articles, and prepositions) and inflectional morphology (especially verb endings). Since verb forms are not consistently associated with time reference in the language of many deaf children, they may not be analyzable into separate stem and tense morphemes (Ivimey and Lachterman, 1980). Moreover, data on the production of negative and interrogative sentences indicate that auxiliary forms may not comprise a functionally distinct grammatical category (i.e., a separate category of auxiliary forms may not be specifiable in grammatical rules) for many deaf children (Ivimey and Lachterman, 1980). Since these descriptions have been based on observations of utterances produced by elementary school children, they are probably indicative of a relatively early stage of language development, and hence are not likely to be completely generalizable to the population of young deaf adults. Nevertheless, to the extent they are valid descriptions of the linguistic systems of deaf children, they probably can provide insight into the language of deaf adults, especially with respect to patterns of variation between and within individuals. In addition to these descriptions, the distribution (misuse) of articles (Charrow, 1974) and prepositions (Ivimey and Lachterman, 1980) has been found to be highly variable and not readily subject to formal analysis. Furthermore, it appears that some combinations of lexical items function as unanalyzed (or incompletely analyzed) units for many children, e.g., certain verb + preposition collocations (Ivimey and Lachterman, 1980; cf. West and Weber, 1974).

In general, deaf individuals have considerable difficulty with function words and inflectional (and derivational) morphology. Similar findings also have been reported for hard-of-hearing children in an oral recall-repetition experiment (Wilcox and Tobin, 1974) and for a young hard-of-hearing child in a description of her spontaneous oral productions (West and Weber, 1974). While many studies have located specific problem areas in standard English grammar, few have sought to describe the rules (especially nonstandard rules and grammatical categorizations) and patterns of variation which characterize the attempts of hearing-impaired individuals to process and produce English. Descriptive studies of this sort can provide valuable insight into the linguistic ability of deaf people and lead to the development of improved pedagogical methods and materials.

Interrogative and Passive Constructions

The difficulties deaf children, adolescents, and young adults experience with interrogative sentences have been investigated with a grammaticality judgment procedure in research designed to assess knowledge of rules involved in the derivation of questions (Quigley et al., 1974a). This research demonstrates that their conscious knowledge of such rules as subject-auxiliary inversion, "do" support, and WH movement improves with chronological age, yet remains incomplete and somewhat unstable even in young adults. Additionally, this research demonstrates that deaf individuals of all ages exhibit a strong tendency to accept ungrammatical strings introduced by WH question words as gramatically correct interrogatives (e.g., "Who did the dog bite the girl?"), a tendency which probably occurs because such strings contain a contiguous subject-verb-object sequence.

The extent to which these findings are supported by observations of naturalistic utterances is unclear at best, which weakens generalizations pertaining to functional linguistic skills and language structure (Gleitman and Gleitman, 1979; Read, 1978). Another factor tempering such generalizations is the finding that many deaf individuals often seem to comprehend questions, as evidenced by their ability to select appropriate responses on a multiple-choice question-answering task (Quigley et al., 1974a). More importantly, this research presupposes the existence of a separate grammatical category consisting of auxiliary forms. However, such a category may not exist in the language of deaf children (Ivimey and Lachterman, 1980), as noted previously. Therefore, descriptive data pertaining to the status of auxiliary forms (Ivimey and Lachterman, 1980) indicate that the structure of interrogative constructions in the language of many deaf individuals (especially children) may differ greatly from the structure of interrogatives in standard English grammar, which implies the existence of significant inter- and intra-individual variation. Although the status of auxiliary forms cannot be ascertained directly from grammaticality judgment and comprehension data for interrogative sentences, such data are completely consistent with the hypothesis that a separate and distinct category of auxiliary forms does not exist in the English of many deaf children and that such a category may only begin to emerge in a highly unstable form in older children and remain unstable in many adult members of the population.

The difficulty deaf children, adolescents, and young adults encounter with auxiliary forms also is evident in the comprehension and production of passive sentences. The results of comprehension experiments conducted in the United States (Power and Quigley, 1973) and the Netherlands (Tervoort, 1970) indicate a strong tendency to interpret passive sentences as if they were active, a tendency which diminishes as a function of chronological age, yet is not overcome even in young adults. Production data gathered in a multiple-choice, sentence completion task are consistent with this finding, indicating that deaf individuals have considerable difficulty with the lexical and morphological markers which characterize the passive construction (Power and Quigley, 1973). Furthermore, in recalling active and passive sentences, deaf adolescents and young adults commit many errors, especially with function words and morphological endings (Sarachan-Deily and Love, 1974). Taken together, these data clearly demonstrate that many deaf people have a severely limited knowledge of the passive construction. Since the passive construction is associated with a set of lexical (function words, i.e., "be" and "by") and morphological (e.g., "-en") markers and since such forms in general constitute a major source of difficulty for the deaf, it is reasonable to conclude that many of their problems with passive sentences are related to a pervasive difficulty with function words and morphology, especially within the system of verb and auxiliary forms (cf. Quigley et al., 1976a).

In summary, deaf people experience considerable difficulty with interrogative and passive constructions, and this difficulty may arise in large measure because a separate grammatical category consisting of auxiliaries has not been firmly and completely established in their linguistic repertoire.

Multiple-Clause (Multiple-Verb) Sentences

The difficulty deaf children, adolescents, and young adults experience with conjoined clauses has been studied with grammaticality judgment and sentence-combining techniques (Wilbur et al., 1975), while judgmental and comprehension protocols have been employed to investigate their problems with relative clauses (Quigley et al., 1974b; cf. Davis and Blasdell, 1975), and their knowledge of complement constructions has been examined by eliciting grammaticality judgments (Quigley et al., 1976b). Consistent with observations of their naturalistic utterances (e.g., Greenberg and Withers, 1965; Heider and Heider, 1940), the results of these investigations indicate that conjunction poses the least problem for the deaf, that relativization is much more troublesome than conjunction, and that complementation presents the greatest obstacle (Quigley et al., 1976b and 1976c). Much of the difficulty deaf individuals experience with multiple-clause (multiple-verb) constructions manifests itself as a problem in correctly associating verbs with appropriate subject noun phrases in discontinuous arrangements of constituents (i.e., when verbs and subject noun phrases are interrupted by intervening material, such as in center-embedded relative clauses, reduced conjoined clauses, and certain infinitive constructions). This problem is related to a general tendency to impose grammatical closure on any potential subject-verb-object series (i.e., on any contiguous noun-verb-noun sequence), and thereby obliterate distinctions between coordinate and subordinate clauses and active and passive sentences. In general, the difficulty deaf people experience with multiple-clause (multiple-verb) constructions appears to be a manifestation of a pervasive structural anomaly in their language, an anomaly which has been characterized as a tendency to "perceive, produce, and learn syntactic structures by arranging lexical items in a linear-sequential fashion without regard to hierarchical order and without specifying relations of subordination and superordination" (Bochner, 1978, p. 174). This anomaly is reflected in the spontaneous utterances of many deaf individuals (in an utterance such as "The man stepped on the balloon and broke" (for other examples see "Appendix B" to this chapter, Greenberg and Withers, 1965, and Heider and Heider, 1940)) and has been described in research employing judgmental procedures (Bochner, 1978). Furthermore, the description of this anomaly is supported by the results of a phrase recall experiment (Odom and Blanton, 1967), the results of experiments designed to assess the use of language describing temporal order among events (Jarvella and Lubinsky, 1975), and the results of various other studies (Quigley and King, 1980).

Although spread throughout the population, the tendency toward juxtaposing phrases and clauses in linear series is not always consistently manifested between or even within individuals. In other words, the tendency is viewed best as a means of characterizing inter- and intra-individual variation, and in this regard it is possible that under certain circumstances even words may be arranged in linear series without being grouped into constituent units or chunks (e.g., in the early stages of language acquisition, some deaf children exhibit primitive naming behaviors in which nouns are simply listed or juxtaposed in serial order). Unlike the simple juxtaposition of phrases and clauses, a tendency to arrange words in serial order has yet to receive sufficient empirical support to be accepted as a general principle. However, the existence of such a tendency is supported tentatively by the general difficulty the deaf experience with function words and by data indicating that phrase structure does not facilitate word recall in many deaf individuals (Odom and Blanton, 1967). Again, should a tendency to arrange words in serial order exist, it would do so only under certain restricted circumstances, and hence could be considered only as a possible means of describing linguistic variation in the deaf population.

As might be expected, the problems deaf individuals encounter with multiple-clause constructions are related to the pervasive difficulty they experience with function words, such as relative pronouns, conjunctions, and complementizers. For example, certain subordinate clause markers (e.g., "that" and "because") may tend to function as coordinating conjunctions in the language of many deaf people, which is consistent with the notion that phrases and clauses are often arranged in linear (serial) order (Bochner, 1978). In a related area, specifying the reference of nouns and noun phrases appearing in a discourse is a serious problem for many deaf individuals, a problem which typically manifests itself as a chronic misuse of articles but also may involve the misuse of pronouns and the apparent omission of coreferential nouns and noun phrases (Wilbur, 1977; e.g., Greenberg and Withers, 1965). Therefore, in addition to posing a problem for the arrangement of phrases and clauses, the misuse of function words poses a problem for indicating the reference of nouns and noun phrases in discourse as well.

In summary, deaf individuals experience considerable difficulty with multiple-clause (multiple-verb) constructions, exhibiting a general tendency to impose grammatical closure on any contiguous noun-verb-noun sequence. This tendency is related to a grammatical anomaly characterized by the linear (serial) arrangement of phrases and clauses and the misuse of function words.

LANGUAGE ACQUISITION

As noted in the introductory portion of this chapter, primary language development is influenced greatly by the interaction between sensory capabilities and maturation of the central nervous system (cf. Lenneberg, 1967). Sensory mechanisms transmit linguistic information to the brain, information which stimulates and serves as a model for language development. In general, the linguistic information reaching the brain, linguistic intake, is limited by sensory capabilities (channel capacities and physical characteristics of linguistic signals), while the plasticity of the central nervous system is limited by maturation (chronological age), and these limiting factors interact to determine the fundamental course and extent of language acquisition in deaf individuals. Implicit in this scheme is the notion that upon reaching the brain, linguistic intake is processed by an intact central mechanism, a mechanism which presumably is unaffected by peripheral hearing loss.

Despite the use of amplification and exposure to visual representations of linguistic information (e.g., articulatory gestures, print, and manual codes), the linguistic intake of the deaf child generally remains impoverished, deformed, and incomplete (cf. Grewel, 1963, and Liberman, 1974). Hearing aids cannot compensate completely for hearing losses, since they only are able to make selected portions of the speech spectrum audible in a given ear (Niemoeller, 1978). Even with the benefits of amplification, the signal reaching the brain is imperfect in one way or another. Likewise, visual representations of linguistic information differ in many important respects from natural auditory representations. For example, many articulatory movements are not visible, and hence cannot be perceived in speechreading (Perry and Silverman, 1978). Furthermore, conventional orthography differs from speech in that much of the nonsegmental information represented in the speech signal (e.g., intonation, rhythm, duration) is not preserved in orthography (Fries, 1963), and such information may be extremely important for the perceptual segmentation (chunking) of the signal into constituent units during language acquisition (Crystal, 1973; cf. Lashley, 1951, Lenneberg, 1967, Lieberman, 1967, Martin, 1972, Svensson, 1974, and Nooteboom et al., 1978). In addition, many important features of spoken language often are not represented clearly and consistently in the performance of manually coded English; e.g., inflectional endings and function words often are omitted in the production of signs and fingerspelling, whether by accident or by design, and prosodic aspects of speech, such as rhythm, rate, pause, and intonation, are not always preserved in manual signals. Therefore, due to limitations inherent in the sensory mechanisms themselves and in the information they process, the quality and quantity of the linguistic intake of most deaf children are sorely deficient, which probably causes their linguistic percepts to be vastly different from those of normal-hearing children.

A child's knowledge and experience of the environment depend crucially on the integrity of his sensory mechanisms, since these mechanisms serve as channels for the transmission of environmental information to the brain. When conceived in this fashion, hearing loss represents a deficiency in the intake of environmental information (especially linguistic information), and the interaction between sensory capabilities and maturation of the central nervous system may be construed as a classical interaction between environmental and biological variables. The effects of this interaction are illustrated graphically in laboratory experiments in which certain species of birds (e.g., male white-crowned sparrows) are surgically deafened early in life, before their characteristic song patterns have been acquired. Deprived of an external model on which to base their vocalizations and also of auditory feedback of their own voices (i.e., deprived of environmental stimulation and feedback), these birds acquire highly abnormal song patterns in which all species-specific characteristics are lost (Marler, 1975; Nootebohm, 1975). Such experiments illustrate that the intake of environmental information consists of both external models and feedback from one's own productions. Linguistic feedback is therefore considered an important aspect of the language intake of the deaf (cf. Myklebust, 1964), which implies that the learner's productions play an important role in language development (Chapman and Miller, 1975; Clark, 1978). In summary, laboratory experiments conducted on birds clearly have shown that the devastating effects of deafness on normal development are a product of the interaction between biological (age) and environmental (intake) vari-

ables, an interaction in which selected intake activates innate mechanisms at appropriate maturational stages and guides the development of species-specific behaviors and abilities.

A child's age at onset of deafness is the critical biological variable affecting language development, while the quality and quantity of linguistic intake, as well as the reception of linguistic feedback, are the crucial environmental variables. In addition to these primary variables, there are a number of secondary factors which collectively seem to affect language development in very modest ways. These secondary factors are mostly sociolinguistic and affective in nature, although some are related to aspects of cognition and/or correlated with the integrity of linguistic intake. The effects of one such secondary variable, the hearing status of the deaf child's parents, has been examined in studies which indicate that deaf offspring of deaf parents perform slighty better on reading comprehension tests and other indices of performance than deaf offspring of normally hearing parents (Corson, 1973; cf. Quigley, 1979, Brasel and Quigley, 1977, Vernon and Koh, 1970, and Stuckless and Birch, 1966). Other secondary variables include the nature of the deaf child's sociolinguistic contact with the hearing world (cf. Quigley, 1979), his cognitive/learning style (Parasnis and Long, 1979), and the methods, materials, and extent of his communication instruction (Kretschmer and Kretschmer, 1978; Moores, 1978).

The fact that language development in the deaf population is influenced primarily by an interaction (i.e., the interaction between biological and environmental factors) allows for the possibility of enormous individual variation in linguistic ability, variation which presumably correlates most with changes in the primary variables and least with changes in secondary variables. The range of linguistic diversity found in the deaf population probably exceeds that found in any subgroup of the normally hearing population, with individual differences in the use, structure, and acquisition of English presumably stemming from differences in one or both of the primary variables. Clearly, the biological variable, age at onset of deafness, plays a major role; moreover, it can be defined easily and objectively, and its effects are directly observable. Unfortunately, the environmental variable, the quality and quantity of linguistic intake and the reception of feedback, is not as readily definable or measurable, making its effects difficult to isolate and observe. However, certain intake factors (e.g., certain nonsegmental aspects of the speech signal) may be physically altered in order to serve as independent variables in perception/comprehension experiments conducted on normally hearing children, thereby permitting these factors to be isolated and defined, and their effects observed, at least indirectly, with respect to normal language acquisition. Given the nature of the interaction between the primary variables, the deaf child's chances for becoming a competent user of the English language in adulthood depend critically on the integrity of linguistic intake occurring in the preschool years (i.e., before approximately five years of age). In other words, the probability for normal or nearly normal language acquisition appears to increase in proportion to the integrity of early (preschool) linguistic intake, which implies that the most crucial period for primary language acquisition occurs from birth through about five years of age.

The process of language acquisition in the deaf population has been compared both to normal first-language acquisition in hearing children (Myklebust, 1964; Quigley et al., 1976c; Kretschmer and Kretschmer, 1978) and to second-language learning in children and adults (Pintner and Patterson, 1916; Cicourel and Boese, 1972; Charrow and Fletcher, 1973; Goldberg and Boardman, 1974). The latter comparisons generally have presupposed that first- and second-language acquisition are vastly different processes. However, these processes are remarkably similar in a number of important respects, most of which are related to the appearance of learner errors, such as overgeneralizations (Dulay and Burt, 1974 and 1976). Therefore, it is not surprising to discover that language development in the deaf shares many similarities with that occurring in other populations, most notably in first- and second-language learners (Quigley and King, 1980).

Perhaps the major difference between successful first- and second-language acquisition pertains to the lability of learner error patterns, and hence to the plasticity of the learner's linguistic competence. Although errors (e.g., overgeneralizations) occur naturally in both first- and second-language acquisition (Dulay and Burt, 1974 and 1976; Dale, 1976), certain of these commonly persist and become entrenched ("fossilized") in second-language learning (Selinker, 1972; Selinker et al., 1975), while this is not the case for normally hearing children acquiring their primary language(s), in which case all error patterns are extremely plastic (Dale, 1976). In second-language learning, it has been hypothesized that errors which can seriously inhibit comprehension (i.e., "global" mistakes) are more labile and amenable to correction than those which do not (i.e., "local" mistakes) (Burt and Kilparsky, 1975). However, both types of errors (i.e., global and local mistakes) persist in the English of many deaf individuals and resist correction by conventional pedagogical techniques used in deaf education (Greenberg and Withers, 1965; Quigley and King, 1980). For example, errors affecting the ordering of constituents, such as those involved in processing and producing passive sentences (Power and Quigley, 1973; Greenberg and Withers, 1965), and errors in clause structure, such as those pertaining to the distinction between coordinate and subordinate constructions (Bochner, 1978; Greenberg and Withers, 1965 (see "Appendix B" to this chapter for examples of such errors)), can seriously impede comprehension (i.e., they are global mistakes), yet they persist in many deaf learners despite years of instruction. In second-language learners, such errors are not thought to be nearly as persistent and resistant to correction (Burt and Kilparsky, 1975). However, this hypothesis is somewhat tenuous, since it has yet to receive sufficient empirical support to be accepted as a general principle. Language acquisition in a large segment of the deaf population, then, appears to differ from that occurring in *both* successful first- *and* second-language learners in at least one very important respect, the persistence of major structural and processing anomalies (i.e., global mistakes) and their resistance to correction by conventional means.

Despite indications that the linguistic competence of many deaf individuals may become suppressed or plateau at levels well below those attained by successful first- and second-language learners (Myklebust, 1964; cf. Bamford and Mentz, 1979), it has been maintained that the only significant characteristic separating language development in the deaf from that occurring in other populations (especially in normally hearing children) is that their rate of acquisition is much slower (Quigley and King, 1980; Quigley et al., 1976c). These two viewpoints, which may be termed the suppression and rate hypotheses, are not compatible. The suppression hypothesis proposes that the primary interaction between biological (age) and environmental (intake) variables can suppress *both* the rate *and* extent of acquisition, and hence can limit the level of linguistic competence attainable by deaf individuals in adulthood. The rate hypothesis, on the other hand, proposes that the extent of linguistic growth is not limited in any way and therefore predicts that deaf adults eventually will develop mature competence if they are given enough time to compensate for their slow rate of acquisition. The pervasive nature of the errors occurring in the English of the deaf, as well as general characteristics of their linguistic ability and performance outlined earlier in this chapter, indicate that the level of linguistic competence in many deaf individuals is suppressed to the point where progress toward the attainment of mature competence is not simply slow but is limited in an absolute sense to levels well below those attainable by normal first- and second-language learners. Thus, the suppression hypothesis appears preferable to its alternative.

The slow rate and eventual suppression of language development in deaf individuals are thought to stem from the fact that the potential for primary language acquisition diminishes quite dramatically as a function of chronological age (Lenneberg, 1967), which implies that intake (environmental) deficits in early life cannot be completely compensated for in adulthood. Therefore, as stated earlier, the integrity of linguistic intake in the preschool years appears to be the primary factor responsible for suppressing language development in the deaf population.

In summary, the persistence of major structural and processing anomalies and their resistance to correction by conventional methods indicate that language development in many deaf individuals probably is not equivalent to that occurring in either successful first- or second-language learners, this lack of equivalence being associated with the notion that error patterns and linguistic competence are less labile (less plastic) in the deaf than they are in other language-learning populations. Moreover, the pervasive nature of error patterns in general indicates that the rate and extent of language acquisition in many deaf individuals are radically depressed, owing primarily to an interaction between biological (age) and environmental (intake) variables. In short, the effects of deafness on language development cannot be construed simply as a retardation in the rate of acquisition but may be conceived in terms of a generalized suppression of language acquisition and linguistic competence.

SUMMARY

The foregoing discussion has characterized the devastating effects of deafness on the use, structure, and acquisition of English, evaluated research in the area of language and deafness, and defined variables thought to affect language development in hearing-impaired individuals. A conclusion to be drawn from this discussion is that deafness usually imposes severe communicative and educational handicaps on children, handicaps which rarely are overcome completely. Unfortunately, the prospects for eradicating these disabilities are not particularly good (cf. Moores, 1970b). However, the prospects for lessening the communicative and educational deficits of ever greater numbers of deaf children are much better. In other words, a realistic appraisal of the enormous magnitude of the problem of language and deafness in all of its manifestations leads to the inevitable conclusion that communicative and educational barriers cannot be removed completely from the paths of all deaf children in the foreseeable future. However, the prospects for lowering these barriers are steadily improving, and it is reasonable to expect ever-increasing numbers of deaf individuals to enter or move closer to the mainstream of society as our knowledge of the problem of language and deafness advances and as our commitment to the education of deaf children and young adults increases.

Research in the area of language and deafness can contribute much to our knowledge of the role played by environmental (linguistic intake and feedback) factors in language acquisition and also can contribute significantly to the education of the deaf. Three lines of research appear most promising. In one, explicit unbiased descriptions of the language structure (linguistic ability) of deaf individuals at various stages of development (i.e., children, adolescents, and adults) need to be formulated, and any unique aspects of their grammars characterized. Such descriptions should, in principle, attempt to characterize linguistic variation between and within individuals and/or subgroups of the population. In another avenue of research, specific environmental factors (i.e., factors which characterize the quality and quantity of linguistic intake and feedback) need to be precisely defined and their effects estimated. In the third area, the potential for developing new pedagogical techniques and technologies which would compensate for intake deficits and/or facilitate language acquisition needs to be explored. The pursuit of such research promises to enhance our knowledge and thereby contribute to lessening communicative and educational handicaps in larger numbers of deaf children and young adults.

APPENDIX A

Composition of a Deaf 14 Year Old Judged "Average" for That Age by Teacher Judgment[2]

They packed for going to the pinic outside. The little boy wanting to bring our dog. But her mother said to him, "Yes, you can bring our dog in pinic. Then they went with the dog. The dog bark about 3 or 4 time. he excited to go with us. They went out the car. They play baseball. Then they are ready to eat their pinic. They ate sandwishes. They drink their tea or peinch. Her Mother were cooked their hammers with the breads. They have fun to ate their food. They enjoy to have

---

[2] Reproduced with permission from E.R. Stuckless and C.H. Marks, *Assessment of the Written Language of Deaf Students*, 1966.

fun to ate their pinic. They like to have a wonderful pinic. Their dog were excited to have fun to play baseball. The dog try to catch softball. The little girl named is Nancy. The little boy name is Jerry. His Father name is Dale Her Mother name is Freda.

APPENDIX B

Composition of a Young Deaf Adult Exhibiting Confusion between Dependent and Independent Clauses

There was a man named Mr. Koumal which he tried to kill himself. Whenever he thought of some ways to kill himself but he failed. First of all he was drinking that made him to do something foolishy. He tried to shoot but no bullet came out. Then he thought of another way. Later he put a nail in the wall which it was for hanging. But everything he did was wrong. Another idea came up, so then he jumped out of the bridge but a boat moved along that saved his life. He was so desperate that another man robbed him. Somehow after the rob man left which he didn't kill Mr. Kouman. Somehow and somewhat that made him to changed his mind not to commit suicide. He wanted to live and he loved his life and the nature.

References

Bamford, J., and Mentz, L. The spoken language of hearing-impaired children: Grammar. In J. Bench and J. Bamford (eds.), *Speech-Hearing Tests and the Spoken Language of Hearing-Impaired Children*. London: Academic Press, 1979.

Blanton, R.L. Language learning and performance in the deaf. In S. Rosenberg and J.H. Koplin (eds.), *Developments in Applied Psycholinguistics Research*. New York: Macmillan, 1968.

Bochner, J.H. Error, anomaly, and variation in the English of deaf individuals. *Lang. Speech*, 1978, *21*, 174–189.

Brannon, J.B. The speech production and spoken language of the deaf. *Lang. Speech*, 1966, *9*, 127–136.

Brannon, J.B. Linguistic word classes in the spoken language of normal, hard-of-hearing, and deaf children. *J. Speech Hear. Res.*, 1968, *11*, 279–287.

Brannon, J.B., and Murray, T.T. The spoken syntax of normal, hard-of-hearing, and deaf children. *J. Speech Hear. Res.*, 1966, *9*, 604–610.

Brasel, K.E., and Quigley, S.P. The influence of early language and communicative environments on the development of language in deaf children. *J. Speech Hear. Res.*, 1977, *20*, 95–107.

Burt, M.K., and Kilparsky, C. Global and local mistakes.

In J.H. Schumann and N. Stenson (eds.), *New Frontiers in Second Language Learning*. Rowley, Massachusetts: Newbury House, 1975.

Chapman, R.S., and Miller, J.F. Word order in early two and three word utterances: Dose production precede comprehension? *J. Speech Hear. Res.*, 1975, *18*, 355–371.

Charrow, V.R. *Deaf English: An Investigation of the Written English Competence of Deaf Adolescents*, Technical Report No. 236. Stanford, California: Institute for Mathematical Studies in the Social Sciences, Stanford University, 1974.

Charrow, V.R., and Fletcher, J.D. *English as the Second Language of Deaf Students*, Technical Report No. 208. Stanford, California: Institute for Mathematical Studies in the Social Sciences, Stanford University, 1973 (also in *Devel. Psychol.*, 1974, *10*, 463–470).

Cicourel, A.V., and Boese, R.J. Sign language acquisition and the teaching of deaf children. In C.B. Cazden, V.P. John, and D. Hymes (eds.), *Functions of Language in the Classroom*. New York: Teachers College Press, 1972.

Clark, R. Some even simpler ways to learn to talk. In N. Waterson and C. Snow (eds.), *The Development of Communication*. Chichester, England: John Wiley & Sons, 1978.

Conrad, R. Some correlates of speech coding in the short-term memory of the deaf. *J. Speech Hear. Res.*, 1973, *16*, 375–384.

Conrad, R. The reading ability of deaf school-leavers. *Br. J. Educ. Psychol.*, 1977, *47*, 138–148.

Conrad, R. *The Deaf School Child*. London: Harper & Row, 1979.

Cooper, R.L. The ability of deaf and hearing children to apply morphological rules. *J. Speech Hear. Res.*, 1967, *10*, 77–86.

Cooper, R.L., and Rosenstein, J. Language acquisition of deaf children. *Volta Rev.*, 1966, *68*, 58–67.

Corson, H. Comparing deaf children of oral deaf parents and deaf parents using manual communication with deaf children of hearing parents on academic, social, and communicative functioning. Unpublished doctoral dissertation, University of Cincinnati, 1973 (cited in Quigley, 1979 and Kretschmer and Kretschmer, 1978).

Crystal, D. Non-segmental phonology in language acquisition: A review of the issues. *Lingua*, 1973, *32*, 1–45.

Dale, P.S. *Language Development*. New York: Holt, Rinehart & Winston, 1976.

Davis, J., and Blasdell, R. Perceptual strategies employed by normal-hearing and hearing-impaired children in the comprehension of sentences containing relative clauses. *J. Speech Hear. Res.*, 1975, *18*, 281–295.

DiFrancesca, S. *Academic Achievement Test Results of a National Testing Program for Hearing-Impaired Students: United States, Spring 1971*. Washington, D.C.: Gallaudet College, Office of Demographic Studies, 1972.

Dulay, H.C., and Burt, M.K. You can't learn without goofing. In J.C. Richards, (ed.), *Error Analysis*. London: Longman, 1974.

Dulay, H.C., and Burt, M.K. Creative construction in second language learning and teaching. In H.D. Brown (ed.), *Papers in Second Language Acquisition. Lang. Learn.*, 1976, Special Issue No. 4.

Elliott, L.L., Hirsch, I.J., and Simmons, A.A. Language of young hearing-impaired children. *Lang. Speech*, 1967, *10*, 141–158.

Fries, C.C. *Linguistics and Reading*. New York: Holt, Rinehart & Winston, 1963.

Furth, H.D. A comparison of reading test norms of deaf and hearing children. *Am. Ann. Deaf*, 1966, *111*, 461–462.

Furth, H.D. Linguistic deficiency and thinking: Research with deaf subjects 1964–1969. *Psychol. Bull.*, 1971, *76*, 58–72.

Gates, A.I., and Chase, E. H. Methods and theories of learning to spell tested by studies of deaf children. *J. Educ. Psychol.*, 1926, *17*, 289–301.

Gibson, E.J., Surcliff, A., and Yonas, A. Utilization of spelling patterns by deaf and hearing subjects. In H. Levin and J.P. Williams (eds.), *Basic Studies on Reading*. New York: Basic Books, 1970.

Gleitman, H., and Gleitman, L. Language use and language judgment. In C.J. Fillmore, D. Kempler, and W. Wang (eds.), *Individual Differences in Language Ability and Language Behavior*. New York: Academic Press, 1979.

Goda, S. Language skills of profoundly deaf adolescent children. *J. Speech Hear. Res.*, 1959, *2*, 369–376.

Goda, S. Spoken syntax of normal, deaf, and retarded adolescents. *J. Verb. Learn. Verb. Behav.*, 1964, *3*, 401–405.

Goldberg, J.P., and Boardman, M.B. English language instruction for the hearing-impaired: An adaptation of ESL methodology. *TESOL Q.*, 1974, *8*, 263–270.

Greenberg, B.L., and Withers, S. *Better English Usage: A Guide for the Deaf*. Indianapolis: Bobbs-Merrill, 1965.

Grewel, F. Remarks on the acquisition of language in deaf children. *Lang. Speech*, 1963, *6*, 37–45.

Hart, B.O., and Rosenstein, J. Examining the language behavior of deaf children. *Volta Rev.*, 1964, *66*, 679–682.

Hammermeister, F.K. Reading achievement in deaf adults. *Am. Ann. Deaf*, 1971, *116*, 25–28.

Heider, F., and Heider, G. A comparison of sentence structure of deaf and hearing children. *Psychol. Monogr.*, 1940, *52*, 42–103.

Hoemann, H.W., Andrews, C.E., Florian, V.G., Hoeman, S.A., and Jensema, C.J. The Spelling Proficiency of Deaf Children. *Am. Ann. Deaf*, 1976, *121*, 489–493.

Ivimey, G.P. The written syntax of an English deaf child: An exploration in method. *Br. J. Disord. Commun.*, 1976, *11*, 103–120.

Ivimey, G.P., and Lachterman, D.H. The written language of young English deaf children. *Lang. Speech*, 1980, *23*, 351–377.

Jarvella, R.J., and Lubinsky, J. Deaf and hearing children's use of language describing temporal order among events. *J. Speech Hear. Res.*, 1975, *18*, 58–73.

Koplin, J.H., Odom, P.B., Blanton, R.L., and Nunnally, J.C. Word association test performance of deaf students. *J. Speech Hear. Res.*, 1967, *10*, 126–132.

Kretschmer, R.R., and Kretschmer, L.W. *Language Development and Intervention with the Hearing Impaired*. Baltimore: University Park Press, 1978.

Lashley, K.S. The problem of serial order in behavior. In L.A. Jeffress (ed.), *Cerebral Mechanisms in Behavior*. New York: John Wiley & Sons, 1951.

Lenneberg, E.H. *Biological Foundations of Language*. New York: John Wiley & Sons, 1967.

Liberman, A.M. Language processing: State-of-the-art report. In R.E. Stark (ed.), *Sensory Capabilities of Hearing Impaired Children*. Baltimore: University Park Press, 1974.

Lieberman, P. *Intonation, Perception, and Language*. Cambridge: MIT Press, 1967.

Locke, J., and Locke, V. Deaf children's phonetic, visual and dactylic coding in a grapheme recall task. *J. Exp. Psychol.*, 1971, *89*, 142–146.

MacGinitie, W.H. Ability of deaf children to use different word classes. *J. Speech Hear. Res.*, 1964, *7*, 141–150.

Marler, P. On the origin of speech from animal sounds. In J.F. Kavanagh and J.E. Cutting (eds.), *The Role of Speech in Language*. Cambridge: MIT Press, 1975.

Martin, J.G. Rhythmic (hierarchical) versus serial structure in speech and other behavior. *Psychol. Rev.*, 1972, *79*, 487–509.

Moores, D.F. An investigation of the psycholinguistic functioning of deaf adolescents. *Except. Child.*, 1970a, *36*, 645–652.

Moores, D.F. Psycholinguistics and deafness. *Am. Ann. Deaf*, 1970b, *115*, 37–48.

Moores, D.F. *Educating the Deaf: Psychology, Principles, and Practices*. Boston: Houghton Mifflin, 1978.

Myklebust, H.R. *The Psychology of Deafness*. New York: Grune & Stratton, 1964.

Niemoeller, A.F. Hearing aids. In H. Davis and S.R. Silverman (eds.), *Hearing and Deafness*. New York: Holt, Rinehart & Winston, 1978.

Nootebohm, F. A zoologist's view of some language phenomena with particular emphasis on vocal learning. In E.H. Lenneberg and E. Lenneberg (eds.), *Foundations of Language Development, vol. 1*. New York: Academic Press, 1975.

Nooteboom, S.G., Brokx, J., and de Rooij, J. Contributions of prosody to speech perception. In W.J.M. Levelt and G.B. Flores D'Arcais (eds.), *Studies in the Perception of Language*. New York: John Wiley & Sons, 1978.

Norlin, P.F., and Van Tassell, D.J. *Linguistic Skills of Hearing-Impaired Children*, Monographs in Contemporary Audiology, vol. 1, no. 4. Minneapolis, Minnesota: Maico Hearing Instruments, 1980.

Nunnally, J.C., and Blanton, R.L. Patterns of word association in the deaf. *Psychol. Rep.*, 1966, *18*, 87–92.

Odom, P.B., and Blanton, R.L. Phrase-learning in deaf and hearing subjects. *J. Speech Hear. Res.*, 1967, *10*, 600–605.

Odom, P.B., Blanton, R.L., and Nunnally, J.C. Some "cloze" technique studies of language capability in the deaf. *J. Speech Hear. Res.*, 1967, *10*, 816–827.

Parasnis, I., and Long, G.L. Relationships among spatial skills, communication skills, and field dependence in deaf students. *Directions*, 1979, *1*, 26–37.

Perry, A.L., and Silverman, S.R. Speechreading. In H. Davis and S.R. Silverman (eds.), *Hearing and Deafness*. New York: Holt, Rinehart & Winston, 1978.

Pintner, R., and Patterson, D. A measurement of the language ability of deaf children. *Psychol. Rev.*, 1916, *23*, 413–436.

Pintner, R., and Patterson, D. The ability of deaf and hearing children to follow printed directions. *Am. Ann. Deaf*, 1917, *62*, 448–472.

Power, D.J., and Quigley, S.P. Deaf children's acquisition of the passive voice. *J. Speech Hear. Res.*, 1973, *16*, 5–11.

Pressnell, L.M. Hearing-impaired children's comprehension and production of syntax in oral language. *J. Speech Hear. Res.*, 1973, *16*, 12–21.

Quigley, S.P. Environment and communication in the language development of deaf children. In L.J. Bradford and W.G. Hardy (eds.), *Hearing and Hearing Impairment*. New York: Grune & Stratton, 1979.

Quigley, S.P., and King, C.M. Syntactic performance of hearing impaired and normal hearing individuals. *Appl. Psycholinguist.*, 1980, *1*, 329–356.

Quigley, S.P., Montanelli, D.S., and Wilbur, R.B. Some aspects of the verb system in the language of deaf students. *J. Speech Hear. Res.*, 1976a, *19*, 536–550.

Quigley, S.P., Wilbur, R.B., and Montanelli, D.S. Question formation in the language of deaf students. *J. Speech Hear. Res.*, 1974a, *17*, 699–713.

Quigley, S.P., Wilbur, R.B., and Montanelli, D.S. Complement structures in the language of deaf students. *J. Speech Hear. Res.*, 1976b, *19*, 448–457.

Quigley, S.P., Wilbur, R.B., Power, D.J., Montanelli, D.S., and Steinkamp, M.W. *Syntactic Structures in the Language of Deaf Children*. Urbana, Illinois: Institute for Child Behavior and Development, University of Illinois, 1976c.

Quigley, S.R., Smith, N.L., and Wilbur, R.B. Comprehension of relativized sentences by deaf students. *J. Speech Hear. Res.*, 1974b, *17*, 325–341.

Read, C. Lessons to be learned from the preschool orthographer. In Lenneberg, E.H. and Lenneberg, E. (eds.), *Foundations of Language Development*, vol. 2. New York: Academic Press, 1975.

Read, C. Children's awareness of language, with emphasis on sound systems. In A. Sinclair, R.J. Jarvella, and W.J.M. Levelt (eds.), *The Child's Conception of Language*. Berlin: Springer Verlag, 1978.

Sarachan-Deily, A.B., and Love, R.J. Underlying grammatical rule structure in the deaf. *J. Speech Hear. Res.*, 1974, *17*, 689–698.

Selinker, L. Interlanguage. *Int. Rev. Applied Linguistics*, 1972, *10*, 209–231.

Selinker, L., Swain, M., and Dumas, D. The interlanguage hypothesis extended to children. *Lang. Learn.*, 1975, *25*, 139–152.

Simmons, A.A. A comparison of the type-token ratio of spoken and written language of deaf children. *Volta Rev.*, 1962, *64*, 417–421.

Stuckless, E.R., and Birch, J.W. The influence of early manual communication on the linguistic development of deaf children. *Am. Ann. Deaf*, 1966, *111*, 452–460, 499–504.

Stuckless, E.R., and Marks, C.H. *Assessment of the Written Language of Deaf Students*. Pittsburgh: University of Pittsburgh School of Education, 1966.

Svensson, S. *Prosody and Grammar in Speech Perception*.

Stockholm: Monographs from the Institute of Linguistics, University of Stockholm, 1974.

Swisher, L. The language performance of the oral deaf. In H. Whitaker and H.A. Whitaker (eds.), *Studies in Neurolinguistics,* vol. 2. New York: Academic Press, 1976.

Templin, M.C. A comparison of the spelling achievement of normal and defective hearing subjects. *J. Educ. Psychol.,* 1948, *39,* 337–346.

Templin, M.C. Vocabulary problems of the deaf child. *Int. Audiol.,* 1966, *5,* 349–354.

Tervoort, B. The understanding of passive sentences by deaf children. In G.B. Flores D'Arcais and W.J.M. Levelt (eds.), *Advances in Psycholinguistics.* New York: American Elsevier, 1970.

Trybus, R., and Karchmer, M. School achievement scores of hearing-impaired children: National data on achievement status and growth patterns. *Am. Ann. Deaf,* 1977, *122,* 62–69.

Tweney, R.D., Hoemann, H.W., and Andrews, C.E. Semantic organization in deaf and hearing subjects. *J. Psycholinguist. Res.,* 1975, *4,* 61–73.

Vernon, M., and Koh, S.D. Early manual communication and deaf children's achievement. *Am. Ann. Deaf,* 1970, *115,* 527–536.

Walter, G.G. Lexical abilities of hearing and hearing-impaired children. *Am. Ann. Deaf,* 1978, *123,* 976–982.

Walter, J. A study of the written sentence construction of a group of profoundly deaf children. *Am. Ann. Deaf,* 1955, *100,* 235–252.

Walter, J. Some further observations on the written sentence construction of profoundly deaf children. *Am. Ann. Deaf,* 1959, *104,* 282–285.

West, J.J., and Weber, J.L. A linguistic analysis of the morphemic and syntactic structures of a hard-of-hearing child. *Lang. Speech,* 1974, *17,* 68–79.

Wilbur, R.B. An explanation of deaf children's difficulty with certain syntactic structures of English. *Volta Rev.,* 1977, *79,* 85–92.

Wilbur, R.B., Montanelli, D.S., and Quigley, S.P. Pronominalization in the language of deaf students. *J. Speech Hear. Res., 1976, 19,* 120–140.

Wilbur, R.B., Quigley, S.P., and Montanelli, D.S. Conjoined structures in the language of deaf students. *J. Speech Hear. Res.,* 1975, *18,* 319–335.

Wilcox, J., and Tobin, H. Linguistic performance of hard-of-hearing and normal-hearing children. *J. Speech Hear. Res.,* 1974, *17,* 286–293.

Part IV

Assessment of Communication Skills

Chapter 8

Hearing and Speechreading Assessment with the Severely Hearing-Impaired Child

MARY PAT MOELLER, M.S.

Essential to individualized educational planning for hearing-impaired children is a comprehensive, objective evaluation from which strengths and weaknesses in auditory and visual communication can be delineated. Audiologists are more frequently being called upon to serve as members of child-study teams and to contribute to individual habili-

tative planning. In order for the audiologist to contribute in a meaningful way to the child's aural habilitation program, modification of the traditional pediatric service delivery model is needed. The conceived role of the audiologist must be expanded to include an emphasis not only on determining the extent of residual hearing but also on investigating how the child processes connected language through the auditory and visual channels. Since many complex factors influence the child's language learning the audiological evaluation should be viewed as one facet of, and intricately related to, a multidisciplinary effort (Matkin et al., 1979; Matkin, 1980; Moeller and Eccarius, 1980; Johnson et al., 1980).

This chapter explores some practical considerations in meeting the expanding demands of pediatric audiological care. Primarily, the chapter addresses current practices and needs in the assessment of auditory and visual communication skills of young hearing-impaired children with severe and profound losses. The audiologist's role in the habilitative process is viewed within a multidisciplinary model. Methods of modifying traditional procedures, to better assess sensory function, are described.

REVIEW OF PROCEDURES

Numerous recent technological and procedural advances have allowed for the earlier identification of hearing loss and more specific diagnosis of degree and nature of hearing impairment in children. Such advances as the "crib-o-gram" (Simmons, 1977), auditory brainstem response (ABR), and the use of improved systems of follow-up with high-risk screening have contributed to earlier identification and initiation of management with hearing-impaired infants (Mencher et al., 1981; Bentzen and Jensen, 1981). Advances in the use of impedance audiometry (Northern, 1981), ABR (Galambos, 1978; Jacobson et al., 1981) and visual reinforcement audiometry (VRA) (Moore and Wilson, 1978) with infants have led to better specification of degree of residual hearing and differential diagnosis of auditory problems. Progress in diagnosis of hearing loss has also been related to conceptualization of evaluation as an ongoing process and to the increasing availability of a battery of electrophysiological and behavioral audiological tests (Hodgson, 1978). Extended-output audiometers allow for more definitive measurement of residual hearing in severely and profoundly hearing-impaired children (Erber and Alencewicz, 1976; Boothroyd, 1980). Although such procedural advances have contributed to improved pediatric care, many problems still exist in accurately identifying hearing-impaired infants and in providing services to their families. Sweetow and Barrager's (1980) survey of parents of hearing-impaired children revealed continuing concerns for late identification, misleading information conveyed to parents by professionals, counseling deficiencies, and delays in hearing-aid fitting. Continued advances in clinical management of the hearing-impaired child are needed.

Of particular concern is the need for procedures to better evaluate the functional auditory skills of this population. At present, few appropriate tests are available to assess the residual auditory function in hearing-impaired children with limited language (Cramer and Erber, 1974).

Speech Audiometry Measures

Commonly, audiologists have been able to complete only cursory speech audiometric measures with young hearing-impaired children, largely due to this lack of standardized materials and procedures. The audiologist may obtain a speech detection threshold (SDT) easily from the child, since the child need only detect rather than recognize the speech signal. Yet, the potential for underestimating the speech reception abilities of the child (particularly if the audiometric configuration is irregular) contraindicates reliance on the SDT as the sole speech measure. Likewise, pure tone thresholds are poor predictors of word recognition skills, especially for children with pure tone averages ranging from 85 to 100 dB (Erber, 1974c), and must be complemented by additional speech audiometric studies. Boothroyd (1970) reported obtaining SDTs by using discrete phonemic units, grossly representing the spectral range of 500–4 kHz (/u/, /a/, /i/, /ʃ/, /s/). A similar test has been described by Ling (1976). This test can be useful with young children because only a detection task is involved, yet valuable information is obtained because the sounds span a wide frequency region.

Audiologists routinely attempt to measure a speech reception threshold (SRT), and picture identification tasks (Lloyd et al., 1967; Griffing et al., 1967) or object/toy selection tasks (Northern and Downs, 1974, p. 151) are useful with some children as young as three years of age. Spondees may not be recognized, however, by more severely and profoundly hearing-impaired youngsters, since some of these children have such limited functional hearing that they respond to auditory stimuli on a tactual basis. Cramer and Erber (1974) advocated the use of a spondee recognition test to separate those children who respond tactually on the basis of limited low-frequency information from those who are able to hear spectral information. Erber (1977a) has further developed a picture identification task called the Children's Auditory Test (CAT), which contrasts spondees with monosyllables and trochees. This test was also designed for differentiating children who primarily "feel" stimuli from those who "hear" sufficient information to recognize words. Children receiving only tactual information may be able to make stress pattern categorization of the stimuli but will obtain low word recognition scores with the same stimuli.

Other speech measures suggested for use with hearing-impaired children include measures of speech discomfort (UCL) and preferred listening levels (MCL) (Erber and Alencewicz, 1976). Routinely, such data as MCL and UCL are obtained with adults, yet there is a need for standardizing the measurement procedures with children.

DISCRIMINATION MEASURES: PHONEMIC CONTRASTS

Commonly used speech discrimination materials developed for children, such as the Word Intelligibility by Picture Identification (WIPI) (Ross and Lerman, 1970), the N-U Chips (Katz and Elliott, 1978), the Discrimination by Identification of Pictures (DIP) (Siegenthaler and Haspiel, 1966) and the Manchester Picture Vocabulary Test (Watson, 1967) have the advantages both of a clearly defined response mode (picture pointing), which facilitates scoring and interpretation, and of a controlled receptive vocabulary pool. Such tests can be quite useful in the audiologist's battery, yet the vocabulary prohibits use with many children who have limited language skills. For example, Olsen and Matkin (1980) suggested on the basis of

data obtained on normal-hearing preschoolers (Sanderson-Leepa and Rintelmann, 1976) that utilization of the WIPI materials is most appropriate for those youngsters with receptive vocabulary ages measuring at four years and above. The DIP has additional limitations in that it presents only 2 pictures/page and therefore has a high probability for correct chance responses. A closed-set response format has also been found to yield scores higher than those obtained from measures like PBK-50s (phonetically balanced kindergarten word lists) which are open-set. Thus, Olsen and Matkin (1980) suggested that the audiologist interpret speech discrimination test results relative to the particular materials used.

The above tests may also be too difficult for a child with limited hearing, who may perform only at chance level. With another child, who has sufficient residual hearing and vocabularly skills, the use of isolated words only may not reveal sufficient information about his auditory perception of connected speech. It is important for speech perception tasks to be within the confines of the child's attention span, response repertoire, short-term memory, and receptive language level (Keaster, 1971; Olsen and Matkin, 1980); otherwise, scores will reflect not only auditory skills but also other developmental constraints related to the hearing loss. However, tests must also be sufficiently taxing to identify areas of difficulty.

Although most phonemic discrimination measures developed for use with children involve discrimination of minimally paired pictured words, a few other formats have been used clinically. The PBK-50s were developed by Haskins (1949) to meet the need for discrimination word lists controlled to kindergarten-level vocabulary. Like phonetically balanced lists used with adults, this test requires that the child repeat the stimulus word spoken by the examiner, and no familiarization cues are available (open set). This procedure has minimal utility with severely hearing-impaired children, due to their articulatory deficits, limits of their word identification abilities, and receptive vocabulary level. Olsen and Matkin (1980) cautioned that this measure should be used only when the child's receptive vocabulary age is at least comparable to a normal-hearing kindergartener. Boothroyd (1970), however, suggested the use of open-set word repetition tests with children having sufficiently well-developed residual hearing. Rather than scoring the word repeated as correct or incorrect, he utilized a phoneme score, which credits the child for recognizing certain speech sounds, although he may have been unable to recognize the entire word. Boothroyd felt that this method of scoring would be less influenced by the child's language problems, yet the child's articulatory ability used as the response mode may affect analysis.

Tests requiring only discrimination judgments have been useful clinically with children who fail to demonstrate speech sound recognition. Such tests as the Wepman Auditory Discrimination Test (Wepman, 1973), however, require the young child to make a conceptually difficult same/different judgment. In addition, the phonemic contrasts presented are difficult, making this test of limited utility for children with significant hearing loss.

Other paradigms deserve further investigation. The Washington Speech Sound Discrimination Test (Prather et al., 1971) requires that the child make a simple comparison of a model with the stimulus word. For example, the child is shown a picture of "cup" and is asked to determine on successive trials if the examiner says "cup" /kʌp/ (whereupon the child places a chip in the box housing the picture of "cup") or some other stimulus (i.e., Θʌp, whereupon the chip is placed in "other" box). This technique requires few training trials with children as young as three years of age, and controls language level maximally. This paradigm seems quite adaptable to exploring phonemic confusions of the hearing-impaired and perhaps to assessing auditory, visual, and combined processing of small information units. Tests are also needed which will document a child's ability to self-monitor his speech production, particularly in the primary years.

Boothroyd (1970) has further advocated the use of binary choice discrimination tasks for children who fail to demonstrate speech sound recognition. Stimuli are chosen to reflect syllabic pattern, duration, voicing, and first-formant and second-formant frequency discriminations selectively (i.e., ball versus baby, /u/versus/ ʃ /, etc.).

ENVIRONMENTAL SOUND DISCRIMINATION TASKS

Audiologists have traditionally relied on observations of a child's responses to environmental stimuli, gross noisemakers, and filtered environmental sounds to gain further information about functional auditory skills. These procedures have been largely nonstandardized, however, and noisemakers, in particular, are difficult to calibrate with precision. Olsen and Matkin (1980) have found the administration of a test requiring recognition of familiar environmental sounds useful with children who have severely limited language and speech recognition skills. They suggested that the Sound Effects Recognition Test (SERT) be added to the routine auditory perception battery for young hearing-impaired children. The SERT (Finitzo-Hieber et al., 1980) presents three equated subtests of 10 controlled environmental sounds/test through a speech audiometer via tape recording. The child identifies the picture of the stimulus perceived from a closed set of six. For example, the child hears a piano being played, and chooses the picture of *piano* rather than *firetruck* or *doorbell*. Matkin has found this test useful in differentiating functional auditory skills even among nonverbal children (Olsen and Matkin, 1980).

Modifications: Continuing Needs

There are a number of obvious problems with the traditional test battery utilized to assess functional auditory skills in hearing-impaired children. The audiological contribution to aural habilitation of hearing-impaired youngsters would certainly be enhanced by the availability of a developmentally ordered battery of tests of auditory and visual communication, specifically designed for children with limited hearing and language abilities. A number of practical considerations should be addressed in test development selection and use. First, if it is accepted that auditory speech perception evolves from initial reliance on context, situation, and suprasegmentals with gradual attention to phonemic contrasts (Boothroyd, 1980), a comprehensive battery should reflect such levels of auditory development. This may require use of varied tasks and stimuli of varied linguistic complexity (Erber, 1979). Addressing only phonemic discrimination or recognition of single words restricts what can be learned about the child's ability to derive meaning from connected discourse (an essential skill in language learning). At present, few developmentally appropriate measures are available for use with toddlers and preschoolers. Feasible means of exploring auditory skills within the language-learning context are needed.

Tests should also be designed to study the relationships between speech perception and speech production in the hearing-impaired, as well as the effects of speech production training on the child's perceptual skills. In addition, test design should be consistent with current psycholinguistic findings. Task demands should be arranged to reflect the increasing expectation for integration and abstraction, commensurate with cognitive and language maturation of the child. Audiological data should be viewed with respect to the child's overall communicative competency.

EVALUATING THE WHOLE CHILD THROUGH TEAM MANAGEMENT

With young children the need for a team management approach and ongoing assessment is critical. Audiological results cannot be viewed in isolation but must be viewed in light of the child's other developmental behaviors. Several pragmatic approaches have been used clinically to meet the needs of this pediatric population.

Aull-Moeller et al. (1980) and Moeller and Eccarius (1980) describe a multidisciplinary approach by which audiological results are interpreted in conjunction with language and learning measures, and children are managed jointly by a team consisting of an audiologist and an aural rehabilitation specialist. Audiological evaluations and communication assessments are performed. Collective results are plotted on a profile, and the child's relative strengths and weaknesses are determined. Recommendations evolve from joint assessment and input from the child's educators and parents.

Through a multidisciplinary effort, procedures may be developed which more directly assess auditory-linguistic functioning. For example, Aull-Moeller and Garstecki (1977) found that a group of severely hearing-impaired children trained orally were able to improve comprehension of morphological markers by attending selectively to redundant features (e.g., the word "some" was perceptually more salient than the noun plus the marker "s" as a cue for plurality). Several of the children failed to recognize the semantically redundant cues and profitted from "strategy" training. Issues of auditory-linguistic learning such as these need further exploration.

Matkin (1980) has suggested a number of practical approaches which address the "total child" issue. These include behavioral observation, vocabulary screening, and comparative testing.

BEHAVIORAL OBSERVATION

Matkin advised the careful documentation of the following behaviors: (1) the number of trials required to establish a conditioning bond (for visual reinforcement audiometry or play-conditioning procedures), (2) the child's ability to maintain the bond and transfer it across stimuli and activities, (3) the rate of habituation and adaptation to stimuli, (4) the age appropriateness of the response style, and (5) the physiological state of the child.

The issue of careful documentation of response style is germane to all aspects of communication evaluation. Task analysis and careful observation of behavioral responses may reveal strengths and weaknesses in the child's learning style, which may influence processing of information and may be amenable to change. Often, this information is as meaningful as the test scores themselves.

VOCABULARY SCREENING

Matkin further suggested that audiologists screen the receptive vocabulary level of the child, using formal measures (such as the Peabody Picture Vocabulary Test, Dunn, 1959) or informal measures, such as checking the child's auditory-visual recognition of the intended test materials. Such measures assist in determining the most appropriate materials for speech perception testing.

COMPARATIVE TESTING

Matkin (1980) recommended the routine comparison of hearing-aided audiograms with unaided (sound field warble tone) audiograms. He also suggested routine evaluation of the child's auditory-visual perception of the speech materials in addition to auditory-only testing.

Current Procedures

A few procedures have recently been developed to address some of the needs described earlier. The authors' recommendations reflect sensitivity to auditory training procedures and the close interplay of assessment and habilitation.

Trammell et al. (1980) developed the Test of Auditory Comprehension (TAC) to investigate processing of speech at a linguistic rather than a phonemic level. The TAC was designed for, and normed specifically on, hearing-impaired youngsters ranging in age from 4 years to 12 years, 11 months, divided into groups on the basis of pure tone average consisting of (1) moderate losses (41–55 dB), (2) moderately severe losses (56–70 dB), (3) severe losses (71–90 dB), and (4) profound losses (91 dB+). The authors stated that the test was designed to provide a more comprehensive evaluation of auditory function than was previously available, an indication of the child's ability to use audition as an avenue for learning, a predictive measure, and a progress measure (Trammel et al., 1980). The TAC is accompanied by the Auditory Skills Instructional Planning System (Hoverston, 1980), a comprehensive auditory-linguistic training program. A child's performance on the TAC can be used to assist in placing him at the appropriate skill level in the curriculum and to aid in monitoring auditory skill growth.

The TAC includes a screening task and 10 independent subtests, presented in a closed-set, 2–5 alternative forced-choice format. The screening task quickly samples abilities ranging from gross discrimination to recall of complex messages and guides the examiner in the appropriate selection of subtests to be administered or in determination of which subtest to start with. TAC subtests are presented in hierarchical order and measure a variety of skills. These include discrimination of linguistic versus environmental stimuli, gross pattern recognition of familiar speech versus human nonspeech (crying) and environmental sounds, recognition of stereotypic messages, recognition of core noun vocabulary, comprehension of 2- and 4-critical-element messages, sequencing of events, and comprehension of questions following storytelling. Storytelling subtests are presented in both quiet and noise.

Standardization data indicate that children with moderate losses passed on the average, 7.9 subtests; those with moderately severe losses, 6.4 subtests; those with severe losses, 4.6 subtests; and those with profound losses, 2.1 subtests.

The results are visualized in profile form and may be compared to the normative population, relative to specific age and degree of hearing loss. In view of the prescriptive information obtained, it certainly should be considered as a standard procedure in the audiological assessment of hearing-impaired children. Further, comparison of the auditory profile with an auditory/visual profile can be beneficial with the TAC materials.

The TAC meets a number of assessment needs for the older preschool and primary age child. Matkin's experience with this measure reveals that children younger than five have difficulty with the last three subtests, perhaps due to their language limitations (Matkin, 1981). The TAC is the first standardized test to use units larger than words. However, information regarding fine phonemic discrimination (which is not explored in detail on the TAC) and additional measures of the child's ability to assimilate and sequence auditory information may be needed to supplement the TAC results. The speaking rate of the talker on critical elements subtests is prohibitive on the tape for some students, and diagnostic teaching with controlled rate and structuring may be useful. In addition, testing at varied sensation levels may be of interest.

Another recent adaptation of traditional procedures was suggested by Weber and Riddell (1976). These authors adapted the original WIPI (which tests auditory recognition of single words) test items to include a sentence version. They found a number of children who were able to significantly improve a midrange WIPI performance (56–72%) when given the sentence version. For these children, the improved performance more closely resembled teacher judgments of their auditory abilities and seemed to the authors to be a result of the children's ability to perceive conceptual language units easier than isolated elements. Blair (1976) also developed a sentence test to investigate recognition of familiar monosyllables in context. Olsen and Matkin (1980) suggested that although sentence materials may have limitations in the clinical setting, the demands of such tasks may more closely resemble the typical listening demands that the child encounters.

In a three-year study, Bench and Bamford (1979) have developed a series of sentence tests for deaf children by first sampling the spontaneous spoken (picture-elicited) expression of 263 hearing-impaired children, age 8–15. These sentences were used to construct 21 lists of test sentences which, by inference, contain only those words and grammatical structures spoken by the students. Fifty key words related to the gist of the sentence meaning are scored correct if the root of the key word is understood by the tester, i.e., inflections are not required for correctness. Data regarding this test's validity and reliability are very encouraging.

Erber has recently suggested a number of appropriate approaches to more closely ally audiological results with educational needs. One is a diagnostic teaching approach by which the child's ability to detect, discriminate, identify, and comprehend materials of varied complexity and length is assessed. Results are plotted on a matrix to provide the teacher with prescriptive guidance. There is a need for standardized materials consistent with Erber's matrix model. Erber (1980) also recently developed the Auditory Numbers Test (ANT), which was designed as another means of differentiating children who receive tactual information only, from children who receive auditory information. The test requires only that the child identify counted sequences and individual numbers 1–5. Erber reports successful use of this test with children as young as three. Results of this test assist the clinician in determining realistic goals for auditory training. Children who merely feel

sound may require training in stress pattern categorization but may not be expected to make phonemic judgments, for example. Performance on this test may suggest an entry point as well as prognostic information for auditory training.

Informal Adaptations for Very Young Children

Traditional speech discrimination tests are rarely appropriate for use with the very young child. In such cases, audiologists often obtain little or no information about the child's ability to process complex sound stimuli and are restricted to measuring thresholds for tonal stimuli and speech. The information in Table 8.1 and the descriptions below suggest a variety of informal procedures which should be considered as a way of obtaining more meaningful information about the speech perception potential of the young hearing-impaired child. These informal measures are presented in a hierarchy from what is believed to be from the least complex to the most complex stimuli and task demands. The hierarchy is also meant to roughly approximate developmental auditory training stages.

GROSS MEANINGFUL ENVIRONMENTAL SOUNDS

One of the simplest levels of auditory stimuli to use with young children is filtered environmental sound. Tapes of basic environmental sounds are available from Developmental Learning Materials and Northwestern University Audiology Clinic. The child may be taught to associate the sound heard with a realistic toy (rather than a picture, which may be too abstract). For example, the child could answer a toy telephone when he hears the ringing sound, select the stuffed dog when barking is heard, etc.

A number of considerations should be mentioned in reference to the use of any object set task with young children. The objects should be highly realistic, because a young child may not be developmentally ready for recognition of small-scale representational toys, which requires internal representation of the object at a symbolic level (Sheridan, 1964). The set size should also be controlled, since the child's perceptual span is reduced at two to three years of age. The child's teacher or parent may be able to provide useful guidance to the audiologist regarding which particular stimuli elicit responses from the child (certain sounds or words). In the early stages of habilitation, the child's performance is often task-specific, and input from the teacher is quite valuable.

USE OF ONOMATOPOEIA SOUNDS

Onomatopoeic sound stimuli are frequently used in auditory training programs (Pollack, 1970; Clark and Watkins, 1978). These sounds are vocally produced representations of object sounds (i.e., a dog says "woof-woof"; a car makes a motor sound). Again, by use of familiar object sets, gross auditory discrimination skills (e.g., select dog when woof-woof is heard but not when another sound is heard) or auditory identification skills (choose appropriate toy when name sound is heard) can be assessed. Such materials lend themselves to manipulation of prosodic and temporal contrasts, using gross or fine differences in the presentations (i.e., choppy versus continuous stimuli, rising versus falling inflection, etc.). Caution must again be exercised with respect to age and conceptual demands of such tasks. Clark and Watkins (1978) "estimate" that vocal discrimination on the basis of prosodic features emerges in children with severe hearing losses following six months of training but requires considerably more time with profoundly impaired children.

FAMILIAR PROSODIC SIGNALS

It may be of interest to determine if the child recognizes familiar prosodic patterns as signals of events or actions. Game sequences that the mother typically uses with the baby may be structured so that the child's anticipatory responses reveal recognition. For example, as the mother begins the familiar "pat-a-cake" sequence verbally, the child may attempt to clap his hands; prosodic patterns associated with an angry sounding voice may result in inhibiting the child's activity, etc. Again, the child's parent or teacher may be able to advise the audiologist about routines which elicit anticipatory responses. However, at times, it may be difficult to differentiate whether the response was prompted by auditory or situational cue or by the child's recognition of linguistic cues.

PHONEMIC REPRODUCTION

Once a sample of the child's phonemic repertoire has been observed, the audiologist may attempt to involve the child in vocal exchanges. For example, the audiologist may repeat CV syllables to the child /mamama/ and attempt to elicit an imitation of the pattern from the child. Some young children will readily imitate pitch contours, changes in temporal patterns, or gross variations in intensity. Others may accurately imitate the spectral properties of the model. This procedure has limitations, the most obvious of which are the child's production constraints and ability or motivation to imitate. With maturation, however, phonemic/prosodic imitations may be useful. Some examples of possible sequences may be found in the Phonetic Level Speech Evaluation by Ling (1976).

NOUN RECOGNITION WITH OBJECTS AND TOYS

Small sets of objects or toys are used in many clinics (Northern and Downs, 1974) to obtain preliminary measures of vowel and consonant discrimination within the confines of the child's receptive vocabulary. A variety of objects might be made available to evaluate (1) simple spondee recognition, (2) monosyllabic versus polysyllabic stimuli to obtain a gross estimate of pattern perception, and (3) fine consonant discrimination with low-level vocabulary (e.g., "Objects That Rhyme," available from Ideal Company).

SIMPLE COMMANDS AND DIRECTIONS

A standard set of simple directions (accompanied by language development norms) should be available clinically. The examiner selects highly redundant commands within the child's receptive language and expects a motoric or gestural response (i.e., "Wave bye-bye", "Where's your nose?"; "Show me your shoes"). The task demands may be simplified by presenting a "closed-set" or limited number of choices (i.e., instruct the child that "eye, nose, mouth, arm, or tummy" will be said). The type of directions and the number followed should be systematically recorded. Messages like these are included in the Test of Auditory Comprehension (TAC) on the "Stereotyped Messages" subtest. The authors of the TAC feel that such messages are easier for hearing-impaired children to perceive than core noun vocabulary. Yet clinical experience suggests that such may not be the case for profoundly hearing-impaired children. For the very young child, it is difficult to predict whether recognition of words or stereotypic messges will be easier, and perhaps both tasks should be tried.

The selection of which of these informal adaptations should be used is dependent on the child's age, extent of training with hearing aids, and language level. An attempt should be made to define the most difficult level for the child by surveying two or three of these tasks. Diagnostic teaching with materials such as those described above should quickly reveal if the child is able to respond.

Visual and Combined Auditory-Visual Processing

Several of the concepts discussed above also apply to the evaluation of functional visual skills in young hearing-impaired children. Many audiologists have realized the benefits of assessing a child's information reception not only through audition but also through the visual and auditory-visual channels. It should be kept in mind, however, that many of the factors believed to affect lipreading performance have been determined with normal adult subjects (Jeffers and Barley, 1971) or with hearing-impaired adults.

Table 8.1
Informal Adaptations for Assessing Auditory Skills of Very Young Children

Task	Approximate Age[1]	Response	Indicated
Gross environmental sounds	2 years +, with training	Select realistic toy in response to associated sound	For children with limited language comprehension
Onomatopoeia vocal sounds	2 years +, with training	Select toy in response to vocally produced stimuli	Young children requiring maximal auditory contrasts, such as gross temporal or durational contrasts
Familiar prosodic signals	18 months to 2 years +, depending on prior training	Anticipatory reaction to familiar cues	Children who have begun to attach meaning to familiar verbal stimuli
Phonemic reproduction	2 years +, depending on training	Engages in reciprocal vocal imitation	Children able to imitate freely with sufficiently differentiated phoneme repertoire
Noun recognition	2 years +, with training	Selects appropriate toy	Children who have established at least a small core receptive vocabulary and meaningful auditory association
Simple commands and directions	2 years +, with training	Follows through with response specified by command	Children who have established a core receptive vocabulary and sufficient prosodic and key word auditory comprehension

[1] Age ranges stated are based on subjective clinical observation and are highly dependent on age of identification and extent of training. Wide individual differences may be expected, yet in most cases, cognitive, linguistic, and attention prerequisites will need to be well-established for these tasks to meet with success. They will also be highly influenced by extent of residual hearing.

The speechreading performance of children reflects the level of linguistic development much more so than with adults. Thus, both research findings and test results must be considered relative to the language-learning process.

Tests of Speechreading for Use with Children

Table 8.2 summarizes the characteristics of currently used speechreading tests which were designed for evaluating children (after Jeffers and Barley, 1971, pp. 343–378).

A review of the tests reveals that the various tests have met certain needs, yet much further development is required to consider several factors important to language learning and pragmatic communication. Aspects of standardization of the available tests are of particular concern. Measures need to be "updated" in light of current psycholinguistic information in order to tap skills more closely related to emerging discourse abilities.

Some available tests designed for children have strengths in the inclusion of relational directions, comprehension of questions, and variations in set size, all of which place increasing processing demands on the young child. However, many of the included items are those formally "taught" in preschools for hearing-impaired children (i.e., color, number concepts, etc.), and although these skills

Table 8.2
Summary of Speechreading Tests for Children

Test	Standardization Population	Stimuli	Age Factors
Butt and Chreist Speechreading Test[1]	130 hearing-impaired subjects—age range, 2–9 years *Concern:* Standard deviations are wide, obscuring age differences	Informal checklist Object manipulation, words in phrases, question and direction comprehension	Under age 3 Items range in difficulty from 2- to 60-month developmental language level
Craig Lipreading Inventory[2]	243 hearing-impaired students *Concern:* Normative data: divided into categories of preschool versus non-preschool	Word recognition Sentence recognition Multiple-choice, picture identification task	Designed for hearing-impaired children from end of first grade through tenth grade
Cavendar Test of Lipreading Ability[3]	141 normally hearing students, 11–18 years *Concern:* Standardization data on hearing-impaired students not reported	Sentences—response indicated by underlining one word which occurred in the sentence from a closed set of five words	Designed for use with hard-of-hearing school-age children Vocabulary appropriate for grades 1–3
Costello Test of Speechreading[4]	70 hard-of-hearing and deaf students, 9–14 years Significant difference found between deaf and hard-of-hearing groups *Concern:* Relatively small standardization sample	Word and sentence recognition of materials with low and high visibility Word test: Child repeats word spoken Sentence test: Child manipulates dollhouse toys in response to statement	Kindergarten-level vocabulary Normed age 9–12

[1] Butt and Chreist, 1968.
[2] Craig, 1964
[3] Cavender, 1949.
[4] Costello, 1957

are important to measure, they may not reflect the broader range of semantic notions which develop in early language stages. For example, the child's ability to speechread a variety of relational concepts in a phrase (spatial concepts, object functions) may provide insight into his acquisition of two-word combinations in production. A more comprehensive survey of semantic meanings (i.e., recurrence, negation, possession, etc.) would be an important addition to the present focus on labels and attributes. One approach used representational toy manipulation and appears to have merit, as it may allow for investigation of the child's ability to follow connected discourse. Set size, however, must be controlled.

Numerous primary issues remain to be addressed in assessment of speechreading with young children. Suggestions for consideration follow:

1. More systematic study of influence of visual memory constraints on developmental aspects of speechreading acquisition (De Filippo, 1980). Such materials as the Assessment of Children's Language Comprehension (ACLC) (Foster, 1973) have been adapted clinically to study visual and combined reception while controlling stimulus length. The ACLC uses a set of 50 familiar words, which are then used as critical elements in gradually increasing units (2, 3, and 4 critical element length) and paired minimally with distractors.

2. Systematic measurement of length of attention, visual acuity factors (Pollard and Neumaier, 1974) and distractibility. Several studies have isolated additional factors which should be considered in evaluating and planning remediation strategies in the area of speechreading. The reader is referred to these sources for further information:Primary factors which appear to influence language learning through the visual modality and are in need of further study include the acoustic and visual conditions of the environment (Erber, 1971, 1974a), linguistic demands of the materials and differential effects on performance (Erber and McMahan, 1976; Erber, 1977b), issues of relative visibility of phonemes or phoneme units (De Filippo, 1980; Green et al., 1980; Erber, 1974b), degree of hearing loss (Jeffers and Barley, 1971; Erber, 1971), and visual-perceptual skills, such as speed of perception and focus (Jeffers and Barley, 1971).

3. Investigation of speechreading performance in relation to general language abilities and extent of training (Hutton, 1960; Jeffers and Barley, 1971).

4. Diagnostic teaching to examine effects of controlling certain variables (i.e., sentence length, redundancy, visually distinct elements) upon performance.

5. Use of a variety of stimulus materials and attempts to study modality strengths and weaknesses (auditory versus visual versus combined processing). Particular attention should be paid to the contribution of audition to speechreading performance across varied stimuli and response modes (Caccamise et al., 1980). Erber (1977b) suggests studying auditory-visual reception under conditions of varied length, internal redundancy, and syntactic complexity with separate derived scores. (The reader should refer to Erber (1977b) for a comprehensive discussion of adaptive communication strategies.)

GENERAL FACTORS RELATED TO ASSESSMENT OF DEAF CHILDREN

A number of behavioral variables may affect a child's performance on audiological tests. Comprehensive evaluation should include observation of the child's learning strategies, attending skills, etc. Problems in these areas may interfere with auditory and language development, and the audiologist may need to refer the child to other professionals, such as a developmental psychologist, for more comprehensive evaluation. Several of these behavioral characteristics are observed frequently clinically and should be screened for by the audiologist.

Memory Variables

The influence of memory variables has been mentioned above. Careful analysis of auditory and visual short-term and long-term memory is essential in communication evaluation. Types of test materials utilized may influence results, and care in test selection must be exercised. For example, Wilson et al. (1975), in reviewing neuropsychological studies of hearing-impaired children, found that hearing-impaired children performed poorer than normals on visual memory tasks, using verbal material, which might be facilitated by labeling or previous experience. In the absence of norms for the hearing-impaired, such tests must be interpreted cautiously.

Impulsive Response Style

One aspect of impulse control according to Harris (1978) is the ability to plan ahead in a careful and organized fashion. Harris (1978) has found impulsivity to be a common problem in young deaf children. This finding is in need of replication, but the issue should be considered relative to possible effects on a child's test performance. The audiologist should note how well the child scans the available responses and plans or checks his responses. Providing structure (insisting that he look at each item, repeating, etc.) to the child may improve his test performance.

Attention to Relevant Stimuli

Some hearing-impaired children present subtle attention problems which make it difficult for them to discover what is the most relevant stimulus dimension in a task. For example, the child may be easily distracted by other interesting dimensions and fail to realize that all the varied shapes presented are the same color. The child's selective "focus" may not be in line with the examiner's. Ability to focus selectively on what is important is essential to auditory training, as well. One three-year-old severely hearing-impaired youngster was able to achieve 100% recognition of a large set of familiar objects under conditions of strict structuring and ideal acoustic treatment. Her carryover to the classroom (with a controlled S/N ratio) of a similar task was quite deficient, since she had difficulty sorting out the relevant auditory dimension in the context of increased visual distraction. She also attended to prosodic or phonetic features indiscriminately. Other children who appear to have difficulty sequencing auditory information have been found later to be unaware that sequence was a dimension to be attended to and subsequently responded well to "strategy" training. A child who has difficulty "focusing" should be referred for diagnostic teaching.

Other Aspects of Attention

A child's ability to deal with increased visual or auditory distraction (figure-ground) should be monitored. Control of classroom environment or materials may be necessary. Children with specific visual scanning deficits may have difficulty not only with speechreading but also with making important, subtle discriminations, such as an addition from a subtraction sign in math. School-age children who appear to be having particular problems in attending to find visual differences should be referred for visual and learning evaluations.

SUMMARY

The need for an expanded role of the audiologist in rehabilitative care of hearing-impaired children has been emphasized in this chapter. Such a role involves the audiologist in evaluation of the hearing-impaired child's *functional* auditory and speechreading skills. Problems with traditional approaches to evaluation have been described, and recent developments and continuing needs have been considered. Recognition of the limitations of current approaches and involvement of audiologists in the design of educationally relevant materials for ongoing evaluation of the child are critical needs.

The audiological contribution to the child's habilitation program may be maximized by involving audiologists more routinely and directly in a multidisciplinary effort. The audiological data should be shared and viewed in relation to the child's broader communication competencies and needs.

Recent improvements in test design have reflected the close interplay of assessment and habilitation. The audiologist should continually be attuned to determining the child's progress over time, using tools which will reflect developmental processes. Informal behavioral observation of learning strategies, attention skills and other variables should be considered in analyzing results. The audiologist must also remain sensitive to the child's overall developmental needs.

References

Aull-Moeller, M.P., and Garstecki, D.G. Comprehension of plural morphemes by hearing impaired children. Paper presented at the Annual Convention of the Americal Speech and Hearing Association, Chicago, November 1977.

Aull-Moeller, M.P., Matkin, N.D., Kroese, J., and Hook, P.E. Individualized teacher in-service: A multi-disciplinary model. *Volta Rev.*, 1980, *82*, 430–439.

Bench, J., and Bamford, J. (eds.) *Speech-Hearing Tests and the Spoken Language of Hearing-Impaired Children.* London: Academic Press, 1979.

Bentzen, O., and Jensen, J.H. Early detection and treatment of deaf children: A european concept. In G. Mencher and S. Gerber (eds.), *Early Management of Hearing Loss*. New York: Grune & Stratton, 1981.

Blair, J.C. The contributing influences of amplification, speechreading and classroom environments on the ability of hearing impaired children to discriminate sentences. Doctoral dissertation, Northwestern University, 1976.

Boothroyd, A. Audiological evaluation of severely and profoundly deaf children. In G. Fant (ed.), *International Symposium on Speech Communication Ability and Profound Deafness*. Washington, D.C.: A. G. Bell Association for the Deaf, 1970.

Boothroyd, A. as quoted in G. Hoverston (coordinator), *Auditory Skills Curriculum*. Los Angeles: Foreworks, 1980.

Butt, D.S., and Chreist, F.M. A speechreading test for young children. *Volta Rev.*, 1968, *70*, 225–244.

Caccamise, F., Johnson, D.D., Hamilton, L.F., Rothblum, A.M., and Howard, M. Visual assessment and the rehabilitation of hearing-impaired children and adults. *J. Acad. Rehabil. Audiol.*, 1980, *13*, 78–101.

Cavender, B.J. The construction and investigation of a test of lipreading ability and a study of factors assumed to affect the results. Unpublished master's thesis, Indiana University, 1949.

Clark, T., and Watkins, I. *The Ski-Hi Model*, produced by Project Ski-Hi for U.S. Office of Education, P.L. 91-230, Title IV, Part C. Logan, Utah: Project Ski-Hi, 1978.

Costello, M.R. A study of speechreading as a developing language process in deaf and in heard of hearing children. Unpublished doctoral dissertation, Northwestern University, 1957.

Craig, W.N. Effects of preschool training on the development of reading and lipreading skills of deaf children. *Am. Ann. Deaf*, 1964, *109*, 280–296.

Cramer, K.D., and Erber, N.P. A spondee recognition test for young children. *J. Speech Hear. Disord.*, 1974, *39*, 304–311.

De Filippo, C.L. Memory for articulated sequences and lipreading performance of deaf observers. Unpublished doctoral dissertation, Washington University, 1980.

Dunn, L. *Peabody Picture Vocabulary Test*. Circle Pines, Minnesota: American Guidance Services, 1959.

Erber, N.P. Auditory and audiovisual reception of words in low-frequency noise by children with normal hearing and by children with impaired hearing. *J. Speech Hear. Res.*, 1971, *14*, 372–381.

Erber, N.P. Effects of angle, distance and illumination on visual reception of speech by profoundly deaf children. *J. Speech Hear. Res.*, 1974a, *17*, 99–112.

Erber, N.P. Visual perception of speech by deaf children: Recent developments and continuing needs. *J. Speech Hear. Disord.*, 1974b, *39*(2), 178–185.

Erber, N.P. Pure-tone thresholds and word-recognition abilities of hearing impaired children. *J. Speech Hear. Res.*, 1974c, *17*, 194–202.

Erber, N.P. Evaluating speech reception ability in hearing impaired children. In F. Bess (ed.), *Childhood Deafness: Causation, Assessment and Management*. New York: Grune & Stratton, 1977a.

Erber, N.P. Developing materials for lipreading evaluation and instruction. *Volta Rev.*, 1977b, *79*, 35–42.

Erber, N.P. An approach to evaluation auditory speech perception ability. *Volta Rev.*, 1979, *81*, 16–24.

Erber, N.P. Use of the auditory numbers test to evaluate the speech perception abilities of hearing-impaired children. *J. Speech Hear. Disord.*, 1980, *45*, 527–532.

Erber, N.P., and Alencewicz, C. M. Audiological evaluation of deaf children. *J. Speech Hear. Disord.*, 1976, *41*, 257–267.

Erber, N.P., and McMahan, D.A. The effects of sentence context on recognition of words through lipreading by deaf children. *J. Speech Hear. Res.*, 1976, *19*, 112–119.

Finitzo-Hieber, T., Gerling, I.J., Matkin, N.D., and Skalka, E. A sound effects recognition test for the pediatric audiological evaluation. *Ear Hear.*, 1980, *1*, 271–276.

Foster, R., Giddau, J., and Stark, J. *Assessment of Children's Language Comprehension*. Palo Alto, California: Consulting Psychologists Press, 1973.

Galambos, P. Use of the auditory brainstem response (ABR) in infant testing. In S. Gerber and G. Mencher (eds.), *Early Diagnosis of Hearing Loss*. New York: Grune & Stratton, 1978.

Green, K.W., Green, W.B., and Holmes, D.W. Speechreading abilities of young deaf children. *Am. Ann. Deaf*, 1980, *125*, 906–908.

Griffing, T., Simonton, K., and Hedgecock, L. Verbal auditory screening for preschool children. *Trans. Am. Acad. Ophthalmol. Otolaryngol.*, 1967, *71*, 105–110.

Harris, R.I. Impulse control in deaf children: Research and clinical issues. In L.S. Liben (ed.), *Deaf Children: Developmental Perspectives*. New York: Academic Press, 1978.

Haskins, H. A phonetically balanced test of speech discrimination for children. Unpublished master's thesis, Northwestern University, 1949.

Hodgson, W.R. Tests of hearing-birth through one year. In F.N. Martin (ed.), *Pediatric Audiology*. Englewood Cliffs, New Jersey: Prentice-Hall, 1978.

Hoverston, G. (Coordinator) *Auditory Skills Curriculum*. Los Angeles: Foreworks, 1980.

Hutton, C. A diagnostic approach to combined techniques in aural rehabilitation. *J. Speech Hear. Disord.*, 1960, *25*, 267–272.

Jacobsen, J.T., Seitz, M.R., Mencher, G., and Parrot, V. Auditory brainstem response: A contribution to infant assessment and management. In G. Mencher and S. Gerber (eds.), *Early Management of Hearing Loss*. New York: Grune & Stratton, 1981.

Jeffers, J., and Barley, M. *Speechreading*. Springfield, Illinois: Charles C Thomas, Publisher, 1971.

Johnson, D., Caccamise, F., and Kadunc, N.J. Development of communication individualized educational programs (CIEP) for deaf secondary-level students. *J. Acad. Rehabil. Audiol.*, 1980, *13*, 32–50.

Katz, D.R., and Elliott, L.L. Development of a new children's speech discrimination test. Paper presented at the American Speech and Hearing Association Convention, San Francisco, 1978.

Keaster, J. as quoted in J. Jeffers and M. Barley, *Speechreading*. Springfield, Illinois: Charles C Thomas, Publisher, 1971, p. 333.

Ling D. *Speech for the Hearing Impaired Child: Theory and Practice*. Washington, D.C.: A.G. Bell Association for the Deaf, 1976.

Lloyd, L.L., Reid, M.J., and McManis, D.L. The effects of response mode on the SRTs obtained from retarded children. *J. Aud. Res.*, 1967, *7,* 219–222.

Matkin, N.D. Personal communication, 1981.

Matkin, N.D. A critical assessment of current practices in the audiologic management of preschool children. In J. Subtelny (ed.), *Speech Assessment and Speech Improvement for the Hearing Impaired.* Washington, D.C.: A.G. Bell Association for the Deaf, 1980.

Matkin, N., Hook, P., and Hixson, P. A multidisciplinary approach to the evaluation of the hearing impaired. *Audiology*, 1979, *4,* No. 7.

Mencher, G., Baldursson, G., and Mencher L. Prologue: The way we were. In G. Mencher and S. Gerber (eds.), *Early Management of Hearing Loss.* New York: Grune & Stratton, 1981.

Moeller, M.P., and Eccarius, M. Evaluation and intervention with hearing-impaired children: A multi-disciplinary approach. *J. Acad. Rehabil. Audiol.*, 1980, *13,* 13–31.

Moore, J.M., and Wilson, W. Visual reinforcement audiometry (VRA) with infants. In S. Gerber and G. Mencher (eds.), *Early Diagnosis of Hearing Loss.* New York: Grune & Stratton, 1978.

Northern, J.L. Impedance measurements in infants. In G. Mencher and S. Gerber (eds.), *Early Management of Hearing Loss.* New York: Grune & Stratton, 1981.

Northern, J.L., and Downs, M.P. *Hearing in Children.* Baltimore: Williams & Wilkins, 1974.

Olsen, W., and Matkin, N.D. Speech audiometry. In W.F. Rintelmann (ed.), *Hearing Assessment.* Baltimore: University Park Press, 1980.

Pollack, D. *Educational Audiology for the Limited Hearing Infant.* Springfield, Illinois: Charles C Thomas, Publisher, 1970.

Pollard, G., and Neumaier, R. Vision characteristics of deaf students. *Am. Ann. Deaf*, 1974, *119,* 740–746.

Prather, E., Miner, A., Addicott, M., and Sunderland, L. *Washington Speech and Discrimination Test.* Danville, Illinois: Interstate Printers, 1971.

Ross, M., and Lerman, J. A picture identification test for hearing-impaired children. *J. Speech Hear. Res.*, 1970, *13,* 44–53.

Sanderson-Leepa, M., and Rintlemann, W.F. Articulation function and test re-test performance of normal-learning children on three speech discrimination tests: WIPI, PBK 50, and NU Auditory Test No. 6. *J. Speech Hear. Disord.*, 1976, *41,* 503–519.

Sheridan, M.D. Development of auditory attention and language symbols in young children. In C. Renfrew and K. Murphy (eds.), *The Child Who Does Not Talk.* London: Clinics in Developmental Medicine, 1964.

Siegenthaler, B., and Haspiel, G. *Development of Two Standardized Measures of Hearing for Speech by Children*, Cooperative Research Program, Project #2372. Washington, D.C.: U.S. Office of Education, 1966.

Simmons, F.B. Automated screening test for newborns: The crib-o-gram. In B.G. Jaffe (ed.), *Hearing Loss in Children.* Baltimore: University Park Press, 1977.

Sweetow, R.W., and Barrager, D. Quality of comprehensive care: A survey of parents of hearing impaired children. *A.S.H.A.*, 1980, *22,* 841–847.

Trammell, J.L., Farrar, C., Francis, J., Owens, S.L., Schepard, D.E., Thies, T.L., Wilten, R.P., and Faist, L.H. *Test of Auditory Comprehension.* Los Angeles: Foreworks, 1980.

Watson, T.J. *The Education of Hearing-Handicapped Children.* Springfield, Illinois: Charles C Thomas, Publisher, 1967.

Weber, S., and Riddell, R.C. A sentence test for measuring speech discrimination ability in children. *Audiol. Hear. Educ.*, 1976, *2,* 25, 27, and 30.

Wepman, J.M. *Auditory Discrimination Test.* Cambridge, Massachusetts: Language Research Associates, 1973.

Wilson, J., Rapin, I., Wilson, B., and Van Denburg, F. Neuropsychologic function of children with severe hearing impairment. *J. Speech Hear. Res.*, 1975, *18,* 634–652.

Chapter 9

Hearing and Speechreading Evaluation for the Deaf Adult

DONALD G. SIMS, PH.D.

In general, because of their clients' limited residual hearing, audiologists dealing with deaf people will find that the focus of evaluation will be on the degree of communication handicap and the benefit derived from amplification rather than on the establishment of the probable site of auditory lesion. Au-diologists focus on (re)habilitative assessment and training, describing the deaf person's ability to communicate via oral/aural means to teachers, parents, administrators, vocational rehabilitation counselors, other professionals, and potential employers. Also, they soon realize that the real-life communicative significance of a 40% auditory speech sound discrimination score and a 90-dB average hearing loss is not well understood.

This chapter discusses current auditory and speechreading evaluation practices for the adult deaf person. A profile system which attempts to functionally catagorize student communication performance is described. Finally, since there is a need to develop new tests for the deaf client, basic test validation procedures are reviewed.

PURE TONE TESTING

Pure tone testing with the deaf adult is accomplished with standard audiometric techniques (Green, 1978) with two exceptions. First, standard audiometers frequently do not provide sufficient intensity for the tonal stimuli to reach the threshold of profoundly deaf persons. Erber (1976) suggests the use of an auxiliary amplifier to extend the range of hearing level to 125 dB. Boothroyd and Cawkwell (1970), however, caution that thresholds measured at these high levels may actually be tactile rather than auditory, particularly at frequencies below 2000 Hz.

Second, pure tone bone conduction thresholds are usually not obtainable, again due to audiometer and tactile response limits. Rossi and Sims (1977) have reported the utility of using tympanometry with deaf persons in order to determine the presence of middle ear pathology which would be otherwise undetectable by normal audiometric testing methods. The use of the acoustic reflex to clarify the interpretation of positive tympanometry results can be limited by the severity of the hearing loss because the absence of the acoustic reflex may be due to (1) inaudibility of the stimulus, (2) congenital absence of the normal reflex arc mechanism, or (3) the presence of a conductive hearing loss. Rossi and Sims (1977) and Djupesland (1976) have discussed some strategies to overcome these reflex testing problems through the use of accessory amplifiers and examination of cutaneous reflexes. The reader is also referred to McCandless (1979) for a description of how the acoustic reflex may be used as a substitute for the speech loudness discomfort level measurement in the hearing-aid evaluation for

setting saturation sound pressure levels of the hearing aid.

SPEECH AUDIOMETRY

For speech audiometry, some modifications of standard clinical practices are required. First, the deaf client should not be required to respond orally, since the examiner may misunderstand his/her speech articulation. Usually, the responses should be written or signed to the examiner. Johnson and Yust (1976) have described a speech audiometry response system used at the National Technical Institute for the Deaf, which consists of a 12-alternative push-button panel for students to indicate their response choice. That choice is registered in the examiner's room on a similar box via 1 of 12 labeled lights. The system works with a cassette tape player of the type which can be synchronized to a slide projector. The cue tones on the control track of the cassette tape player which are normally used for changing a slide projector are used in this device to trigger a "listen now" cue light. This replaces the use of a carrier phrase in normal speech audiometry which deaf persons may confuse with the stimulus item. The response system can be used for any multiple-choice task by simply changing the front panel overlay on the client's response box to indicate the test choices.

Speech Reception Threshold (SRT)

The purpose of the SRT with the adult deaf population in most cases is not to confirm pure tone threshold average results. The primary purpose of the SRT with the deaf is to establish the gain in speech reception provided in the aided versus unaided conditions. It may also be used in the hearing-aid evaluation to select an aid or aid setting which maximizes the SRT. Finally, on a functional communication basis, Ventry et al. (1971, p. 207) have reported that the speech threshold, measured with spondaic words, roughly corresponds to the minimum stimulus intensity at which conversation will be understood. If the deaf person wearing an aid is able to give an SRT at intensity levels less than the average intensity level for speech (approximately 60-dB HL), prognosis for significant oral/

aural communication achievement is considerably brightened.

In order to achieve a valid response, a selected set of spondaic words will be used. This can be accomplished by familiarizing the client with the selected list of words at a most comfortable listening level (MCL). Words that are not understood by the client, even after review, should be eliminated from the test list. The operating principle should be to use as many words from the standard W-1 test lists as possible in order to maintain test validity as an estimate of conversational speech threshold. Certainly, when less than 10 spondaic words can be reliably repeated at MCL, attempting an SRT will result in lowered validity but may still be useful for within student comparisons for amplification.

Because the spondee words have a steep performance-intensity function (Hirsh et al., 1952), variability around threshold is maximized, and subsequently (if all spondee items are of near-equal difficulty), threshold is almost an all-or-none type of response. For the severely or profoundly hearing-impaired, however, this steep performance-intensity function may not be found due to speech discrimination limitations. Consequently, a psychophysical procedure for threshold estimation is needed which can efficiently home in on the more variable threshold encountered in this population. The Levitt and Rabiner (1967) adaptive procedures have been working well at NTID and have been recommended for speech audiometry by Bode (1975 and 1978), and Steele et al. (1978).

Since this may be unfamiliar, the following detail is given. The threshold determination procedure is similiar to bracketing and begins at MCL for speech or plus 15 dB re the speech detection threshold (SDT). One spondaic word is given per step of attenuation. The attenuator is always moved in 5-dB steps except on the first series of steps downward (getting softer) from the MCL toward threshold. This run downward is made in 10-dB steps to save time. The strategy of manipulating attenuation then remains the same throughout the test. When a correct response is obtained, the hearing-loss dial is decreased (softer), and for an incorrect response the dial is increased (louder). The tester simply records the decibel values on the hearing-loss dial when a reversal of attenuation direction is called for. In this manner, i.e., ascending and descending in hearing level by 5-dB steps, 6 points of reversal of attenuation are obtained. If the reversal points do not appear to be consistent, more reversal points may be obtained. Only the last 4 reversal points are used, and they are averaged to obtain the SRT. In practice, this threshold determination method is quick to administer (one to two minutes) and highly reliable (Plomp, 1979).

Speech Detection Threshold (SDT)

Frequently when the clinician fails to obtain the SRT, a speech detection threshold (SDT) or speech awareness threshold is substituted as a measure of speech sound sensitivity and gain for amplification. The SDT, however, may be subject to quite divergent results, depending on any number of factors. Hirsh (1952) and Hirsch and Chaiklin (1959) state that the SDT is 10 dB lower in intensity than the SRT. Beattie et al. (1975) found that when "ba ba" was the stimulus, "SRT could be estimated by adding 8 dB to the SDT." They caution, however, that these findings are taken from normal-hearing subjects and that this relationship might very well be different for the hearing-impaired. Frisina (1962) found that among Gallaudet College students, the SDT correlated most closely with the 500-Hz pure tone air conduction threshold. I have found that the SDT with running speech as the stimulus correlated best with the 250-Hz threshold (r, .81; N = 632) among the NTID student population. The difference between the SDT and the 250-Hz thresholds was only 3 dB, with the standard deviation of the difference at 10 dB.

Boothroyd (1972) and Ling and Ling (1978) suggest that selected phonemes can be used in an SDT task to estimate residual hearing from 250 to 4000 Hz (see Chapter 8 of this text, concerning the 5-Sound Test).

In general, the SDT is highly related to audiometric configuration and the speech stimulus used for the test. Thus the SDT is not a direct substitute for the SRT, since results depend on the test conditions.

In order to improve test-retest consistency, it is recommended that recorded running speech be used as the stimulus for the SDT.

Thresholds should be obtained by following the standard bracketing technique for pure tone thresholds. Most importantly, the clinician should be careful not to interpret the results for rehabilitative purposes in the same manner as for the SRT.

Loudness Discomfort Level (LDL)

It is common to find a range between the SDT and loudness discomfort of 10 dB with the deaf listener. Measurement of loudness discomfort levels (LDLs) for speech is often used to specify hearing-aid saturation sound pressure level (SSPL 90). The SSPL 90 should be set not so high as to cause discomfort or hearing discrimination rollover (Jerger and Hayes, 1977), yet it should be set sufficiently high for speech to be heard at a sensation level providing optimal speech intelligibility. Beattie et al. (1980) and Beattie and Sheffler (1981) review the influence of (1) instructions to the listener, (2) hearing sensitivity, (3) listener experience, and (4) psychophysical technique as important influences on the LDL measurement. However, little work has been done with the severe or profoundly hearing-impaired.

Beattie and Sheffler (1981) have summarized a series of LDL experiments and have recommended procedures for measurement as follows: Connected discourse from a male speaker is initially presented at MCL. Loudness is then varied in 6–10-dB increments every 7 seconds until discomfort is signaled or the audiometer limit is reached. The intensity is decreased 10 dB, and an ascending presentation mode is instituted in which the speech is raised 2 dB for every 7-second listening interval. This latter procedure is repeated three times in succession, and the LDL is taken at the median intensity of the three trials. Instructions to the client should include the notions that (1) it is important to understand the talker, (2) the judgment should be made on the basis that the listener would be listening for at least 15 minutes, (3) it is important to listen to speech intensities that are definitely too loud as well as too soft, (4) the comfort and success of the hearing-aid fitting depend on the listener's careful judgment, and (5) the loudness will be controlled during the test by the listener pointing upward for louder, downward for softer, and horizontal for no change in level.

Most Comfortable Listening Level (MCL)

The measurement of the MCL is important, first, for setting the gain of a hearing aid so conversational speech levels can be heard comfortably and, second, to determine the hearing level at which to present speech discrimination tests. The convention of presentation at 30–40-dB Sensation Level is usually not possible due to the limited dynamic range of the deaf client. Using MCL in this manner is reasonable in view of recent research reporting that maximization of speech discrimination scores may occur at or near the MCL (Budacki and Hipskind, 1979; Erber and Witt, 1977). Finally, the MCL in combination with the LDL measure can be used to establish the presence of loudness tolerance problems. The literature agrees that measurement of these responses is prone to bias due to the starting level of the stimulus and test instructions. Dirks and Kamm (1976) and Ventry and Johnson (1978) report that differences as great as 20 dB may be obtained between ascending and descending MCLs. Ventry and Johnson recommend a descending procedure as more reliable and more closely related to the maximum speech discrimination score with their hearing-impaired listeners. They suggest using spondee words presented initially at the listener's LDL minus 5 dB and decreased in 5-dB steps until the listener signals that the MCL has been reached. Following the listener's first report, the intensity is increased by 10 dB and then decreased in 5-dB steps until MCL is again reported. This procedure continues until the lowest intensity level at which three MCL judgments, not necessarily consecutive, are obtained. Instructions to the listener are essentially to raise the finger when "the words become soft enough to be most comfortable. . . . The words will get louder or softer again. Each time the words are comfortable to listen to raise your finger. Choose the level by pretending that you are listening to the radio and the words are comfortable."

Cox (1980) and Hawkins (1980) suggest that for hearing-aid fitting purposes, frequency-specific stimuli are necessary because "the SSPL of a hearing aid varies as a function of frequency and because LDL's for hearing-impaired persons may also change across frequency. If speech is used, the client may be responding to a selected frequency region where the intensity of the speech is greater and/or in a region where the LDL is at a lesser intensity." They suggest the use of filtered ⅓-octave bands of continuous speech or narrow-band noise as stimuli. They also make specific suggestions as to how to equate the real ear versus 2-cc hearing-aid coupler differences, so that the clinician can examine the standard hearing-aid response curves from the 2-cc coupler and know how that translates to average eardrum sound pressure (see Chapter 20 for a detailed discussion).

Auditory Speech Reception/ Discrimination

Revoile and Pickett (Chapter 2) underscore the notion that speech discrimination testing which stops at obtaining a simple number of words correct is not sufficient to plan (re)habilitation of the deaf client. Listeners with the same score have very different perceptual capacities for perceiving phonemic distinctive features. These differences are related not only to the amount of hearing loss and audiometric configuration (Jones and Studebaker, 1974; Erber, 1976) but also to the frequency and temporal resolving power of the impaired ear (Risberg, 1976). Further, knowledge of the language must also be taken into account when the hearing-impaired listener has to fill in missing words to understand the message. Here is where word or sentence reception scores help to determine the functional communication status of the individual. It is essential to assess speech reception skill on a distinctive feature basis AND on a functional word, phrase, and/or sentence basis. These types of results lead to potential answers to questions regarding the handicap of deafness for communication.

Table 9.1 presents a set of word reception tests which have proven useful over a broad range of severely and profoundly hearing-impaired persons. These tests are arranged roughly in order of difficulty. Only recently published citations are given.

WORD PATTERN RECOGNITION

In general, digit and spondee discrimination tests serve to differentiate whether the deaf listener can utilize gross time and intensity cues (which are probably tactually perceived (Erber, 1978 and 1980a) or whether the listener can use acoustic/spectral information. For example, the stimulus "42" may be identified among the foils of "5, 2, 3, and 1" on the basis of tactually perceived duration of the target, but if the stimulus were "2" and the foils were the same, identification could involve vowel perception abilities (Webster and O'Shea, 1980; Erber, 1978). Cramer and Erber (1974) have also devised a list of spondaic words with equal time envelopes for the two syllables which cannot be distinguished tactually but could be easily discriminated by acoustic/spectral information. Erber (1980b) also suggests methods for detailed evaluation of whether intensity/time patterns in syllables and sentences can be used by deaf listeners. He also indicated (1976) that once the hearing loss exceeds 95 dB, word recognition abilities are much less likely. If tactile/intensity cues are the limit of the auditory perception ability, training is indicated for the refinement of these skills for suprasegmental detection as an aid in speechreading.

SYLLABLE AND WORD DISCRIMINATION

Syllable discrimination and distinctive feature discrimination are reviewed in Chapter 2. Word identification skills are often possible with deaf listeners if small-enough answer sets are used. With the deaf adult, these tests are used mainly for determining the phonemic distinctive features the listener is able to use. Jones and Studebaker (1974), Risberg (1976), Sims (1975), and Webster and O'Shea (1980) have used rhyme test formats in this regard. Risberg's test items were designed to assess (1) one- versus two-syllable discrimination (possible with hearing losses up to 100 dB), (2) the ability to use formant frequency information below 1500 Hz (possible with average hearing losses of up to 90 dB), (3) the ability to use high-frequency, formant-2 vowel information (possible with hearing loss of up to 80 dB at 2000 Hz), and (4) the ability

TABLE 9.1
Assessing Auditory Reception of Severely Hearing-Impaired Adults

Test/Stimulus	Response Mode	Additional Information	(Re)habilitative Consequences
Digits (Erber, 1980b; Webster and O'Shea, 1980)	Small set for multiple choice	Gross intensity, temporal patterns	Tactile training assessment
Spondees, trochees (Cramer and Erber, 1974; Johnson, 1976)	Small set for multiple choice	Stress pattern perception or word identification	Can distinguish whether to pursue prosidic feature discrimination (tactile) or acoustic speech discrimination
Syllable/word (Webster and O'Shea, 1980)	4–6 Alternative Multiple choice	Initial/final consonant perception	Phoneme drill planning and assessment
Sentences (Spin Test) (Kalikow, Stevens, and Elliot, 1977)	Closed set	Interaction with language competence	Functional description of communication handicap with high face-validity
Sentences (CID Everyday Sentences) (Sims, 1975)	Open set	Interaction with language competence	Functional description of communication handicap with high face-validity
Word tests (PB-50, W-22)	Open set	Comparison with main body of research and clinic practice	?
All of the above in background noise			Improves relationship to real world listening conditions

to use timing of noise energy, as in discrimination among [s, st, and t] (possible for hearing losses averaging 90 dB or less), and (5) the ability to distinguish [n] from [l] and between voiced versus voiceless plosives, e.g., [p and b] (possible with an average hearing loss of <70 dB). The rhyme test format allows many deaf listeners to score meaningfully in contrast to PB open-set tests in which approximately 70% of NTID students have scored 0% correct.

SENTENCE RECEPTION TESTS

Sentence length tests have great appeal because of the high face-validity with regard to assessment of functional speech reception skill. The CID Everyday Sentences Test (Davis and Silverman, 1970) has been extensively used at NTID as part of the communication profile system (Johnson, 1976). The CID sentences are scored by the percentage of 50 key words correctly written down. These key words are embedded in a test form consisting of 10 sentences. Ten forms of the test are available. The disadvantage of this type of test is that English competence may help or hinder the score (Bamford, 1979). And, no phonetic analysis of the responses is possible

due to the influence of the other words in the sentence upon the probability of a correct response for a given word. However, the test is somewhat "easier" than the PB word tests, in that NTID students score an average of 30% better on the sentence test (Sims, 1975).

SPEECHREADING ASSESSMENT

As in the case of hearing, speechreading can be evaluated on four levels: (1) vowel and consonant perception, (2) word perception, (3) sentence reception, and (4) continuous speech comprehension. Results are used to plan therapy in each of these areas as elements of a typical speechreading lesson. Berger (1972) and Jeffers and Barley (1971) present comprehensive reviews of most tests.

Testing Factors

RECORDED VERSUS LIVE VOICE TESTS

Sims and Jacobs (1976) found that a live presentation of test materials in the sentence format resulted in an average 14% improvement over the results of a video-taped version of the same test with the same speaker. Berger

(1972) suggests that these differences may be due to the two-dimensional versus three-dimensional viewing conditions for the filmed versus live presentation. Another possible factor in the live testing situation is that the tester waits for eye contact from the speechreader, and thus the speechreader has the advantage of an anticipatory set.

FAMILIARITY

Live testing may include the factor of familiarity with the tester. A teacher may want to test in this manner in order to describe clinically how the student might perform in a face-to-face situation after familiarization with the speaker and the situation. Lloyd and Price (1971) have also found that scores for deaf students improved as a function of familiarity with the test sentences.

VISION

Hardick et al. (1970) determined that visual acuity poorer than 20/40 significantly reduced speechreading scores. Since there is an increased incidence of visual problems among the deaf, it is thus important to rule out visual problems before testing and training begin (see Johnson et al., 1981, for a comprehensive review of the incidence of visual problems and assessment procedures).

Consonant and Vowel Tests

Consonant viseme (Fisher, 1968) reception with the severely hearing-impaired is similar to that of normally hearing viewers. However, profoundly deaf individuals vary widely in performance (Erber, 1972; Sims and Montgomery, 1977). Clinically useful paradigms for assessment and the planning of therapy have been described by Binnie et al. (1976). Basically, they involve determining whether the client discriminates place of articulation. Walden et al. (1977) have shown that a few hours of drill can improve visual reception to a point where the person is making confusions only within viseme categories. Visual vowel and diphthong discrimination has been studied recently by Wozniak and Jackson (1979), who showed that diphthongs are easier than vowels to identify. They suggest beginning analytic vowel discrimination training with diphthongs.

Word Tests

Most testing has used PB words; scores typically are about 30% correct with wide individual variation (Binnie, 1976). The Craig (1964) and Mykelbust-Neyhus (1971) tests of lipreading have subtests for word identification with the deaf population. Jacobs uses a word level test to determine a speechreader's skill in discriminating among homophonous words (Sims and Jacobs, 1976). Typically, word tests are used as the format for determining vowel and/or consonant discrimination abilities, as in administering a version of a rhyme test with visual-only clues.

Sentence Tests

Sentence tests have the highest face-validity with regard to assessing the functional ability to communicate. The tests frequently used are the Utley (1946), the John Tracy (Taaffe, 1957), the Craig Lipreading Inventory (1964), and the Diagnostic Test of Speechreading (Myklebust and Neyhus, 1971). At NTID we have used the CID Everyday Sentences Test (Jeffers and Barley, 1971; Johnson, 1976). It appears to distribute students normally about a mean score of 50% correct and therefore is useful for initial placement of students in speechreading classes. For assessment of the results of training, the Jacobs Test (Sims and Jacobs, 1976) has been useful because it is somewhat less difficult than the CID Everyday Sentences Test and appears to be more sensitive to gains made as a result of training.

Although one may assume a minimum fourth- to sixth-grade achievement level in English reading and writing skills, with the NTID adult population, it is important to take care that the content of sentence tests do not contain constructions which exceed the syntactic competence of the deaf person; as failure to speechread these items may be confounded with failure to understand them in any modality (see Chapter 7 by Bochner). (To my knowledge, none of these tests have been analyzed for syntactic complexity).

Connected Speech

De Filippo and Scott (1978) have described a new approach to speechreading assessment, using the technique of shadowing the talker. That is, the parameter being measured is how fast the listener can repeat back exactly what the talker said, verbatim. This technique was used by them to evaluate the efficacy of an electrotactile speechreading aid (see Chapter 3). Perhaps for deaf clients with good speech intelligibility and English, this test would appear to have better face-validity than does a written response typically used in conventional testing. I have found it useful for teaching future teachers of the deaf how to improve their visual intelligibility in the classroom by assigning pairs of teachers to speechread each other using an article from a magazine. Such strategies as spelling, repeating, slowing articulation, and slight exaggeration of articulatory movements are used to obtain the verbatim shadow response.

AUDIOVISUAL SPEECH RECEPTION

In everyday communication, audition and vision are usually available. Thus, this condition should not be overlooked as it often is in routine audiometric evaluations. Whereas the mildly to severely hearing-impaired person generally improves speechreading reception with auditory cues, the profoundly hearing-impaired listener appears to benefit much less from the auditory portion of a combined auditory and visual test stimulus (Sims and Montgomery, 1977; Erber, 1979). Erber (1972) found that severely hearing-impaired individuals could distinguish voiceless from voiced stops and nasal consonants from oral listening alone but that profoundly deaf people could not. While the normal-hearing and severely hearing-impaired groups achieved nearly perfect consonant recognition through combined auditory-visual reception (AV), the profoundly deaf group's AV performance was similar to visual-only scores. Walden et al. (1975) found that adding sound to speechreading tests improved the perception of duration, place of articulation, frication, and nasality features for moderately hearing-impaired listeners. Word recognition usually improves 19–28% for the severely deaf and 1–15% for the profoundly deaf according to Erber (1975). Sentence reception also improves with sound (Craig, 1964). Data from Johnson (1976) at NTID has shown a 23%

increase in the proportion of students scoring better than 54% on the CID Everyday Sentences Test (Fig. 9.1) when sound is combined with visual cues. We have also observed approximately 9% of an entering class of NTID students (N = 291) whose reception of the CID Everyday Sentences was poorer when viewing them in the AV mode than in the visual mode. This could result from several factors: (1) error in test-retest measurement, (2) error in test results caused by a less than optimal amplification fitting, (3) "masking" from defective and possibly contradictory residual hearing cues, (4) students' unfamiliarity with amplified sound due to infrequent or no use of amplification, and (5) attentional strategies employed by the listeners to ignore auditory information.

Depending upon the needs of the individual, the same word, sentence, or phoneme level tests given for speechreading evaluation are usually administered with sound for AV testing. As in any auditory or speechreading test, the results are dependent on the speaker, the stimulus, and the response task (Binnie et al., 1976). Therefore, video-taped tests are recommended for precise and reliable documentation of the results of training. The tester needs only to turn the picture and/or sound on to change conditions of testing from auditory, to visual, to auditory-visual testing.

PROFILE ASSESSMENT

Assessment of communication with deaf adults requires analysis of test results across multiple modalities of expression and reception of language. Any given professional dealing with a deaf client may not have a complete understanding of how to interpret all of the raw scores in a discipline that is unfamiliar. One way to bring all of this testing into a coherent picture is to utilize a profile schema in which raw scores are summarized on some kind of a common scale. NTID began use of a profile system in 1972 for the following purposes: (1) to have the means for rapid identification of each student's communication performance strengths and weaknesses in order to plan a tentative program of therapy (Johnson and Caccamise, 1981), (2) to be able to more easily counsel students and consult with instructors regarding the test

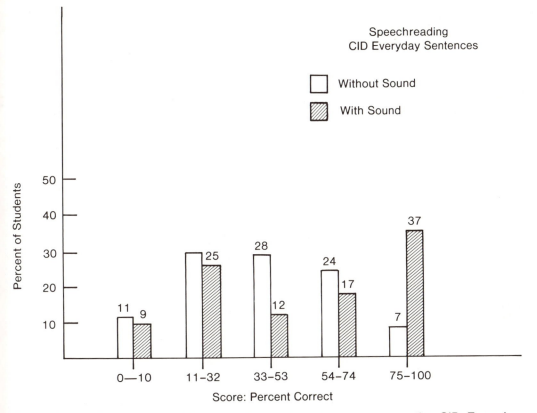

Figure 9.1. Visual and auditory-visual speechreading scores on the CID Everyday Sentences Test (N = 243 entering NTID students, 1975 (after Sims and Jacobs, 1976)).

results and subsequent rationale for communication training, (3) to be able to summarize population histories and trends for descriptive study of factors contributing to student communication skills (Conklin et al., 1980; Sims et al., 1980), and (4) to provide information for program development and management on the basis of student needs for instruction and other clinical services. Note that the above uses of the profile system do not include either detailed diagnostic assessment, or pre-post training assessment. A second diagnostic battery of tests must be utilized in addition to the performance profile system (Johnson and Crandall, in press). For example, Binnie (1976) suggests a diagnostic profile for speechreading, and Subtelny (Chapter 10 of this text) outlines the many diagnostic determinations necessary for complete specification of a deaf person's speech disorders.

The NTID profile test battery includes instruments for assessing hearing (speech) discrimination, speech reading with and without sound, manual reception (signed English without voice or lip movement), simultaneous (signed English and speech) reception, English reading comprehension, English writing intelligibility, and speech intelligibility (Johnson, 1976). The tests are constructed where possible from the CID Everyday Sentences in order to maximize face-validity with regard to functional communication. Raw scores for each instrument are converted into five profile ranks. Each rank is accompanied by a descriptor of functional communication performance as follows: Profile 5—the complete content of the message is received or expressed; Profile 4—most of the content of the message is received or expressed with some difficulty; Profile 3—about half of the message is received or expressed appropriately, with great difficulty; Profile 2—only an occasional word or phrase is received or expressed; and Profile 1—none of the message is received or expressed. All testing is completed under optimum communication conditions with regard to background noise, lighting, and talker clarity. Interpretation of the above descriptors should be made with these conditions in mind. The conversion of raw scores for speech reading with and without sound, manual reception, and simultaneous reception are all based on the number of key words correctly identified on the CID Everyday Sentences as follows: Profile 5, 75–100% correct; Profile 4, 54–74% correct; Profile 3, 33–53% correct; Profile 2, 11–32% correct; and Profile 1, 0–10% correct. The hearing (speech) discrimination profile and receptive/expressive English language profiles involve multiple tests and are described by Johnson (1976). Much more work needs to be completed to verify the functional communicative validity between the descriptors of functional communication and the raw score ranges of the profile instruments. Results of field tests in two secondary schools for the deaf have indicated its utility with students down to age 14 (Johnson and Kadunc, 1980).

Communication Individualized Educational Plans

The profile system has proven useful for setting up a sequence of communication training (Johnson, 1981) at NTID. With the profile system, one may, for example, scan the rankings of an individual student and quickly determine the strengths and weakness across the major communication modalities, which would not be predicted on the basis of an audiogram, scholastic achievement tests, and IQ measures typically available in school files. Also, subgroups of students with similar communication characteristics may be used as a means to set up reasonable educational objectives for a student with similar entering communication skills (Johnson and Kadunc, 1980).

INSTRUCTIONAL ASSESSMENT

In working with deaf people in the area of communication training, one frequently finds that conventional, off-the-shelf tests are not appropriate because of limited residual hearing or English factors. Also, because of these limited skills or abilities, it becomes important to have a very close correspondence between what is practiced in therapy and what is eventually tested to determine if any gains have been made. For example, if the teacher has drilled on auditory discrimination of the voicing and nasality distinctive features, one may not necessarily expect large gains in other distinctive feature catagories. Thus it is often necessary to construct tests to match the curriculum. The danger with this approach is that one may design a test with such close correspondence to the curriculum that there is no assurance that auditory discrimination skill has improved over and above what the student has memorized. Snell and Mapes (1980) have described a pre-post auditory training assessment scheme that appears to work well under these limitations (see Chapter 19 of this text by Durity).

Also, in spite of the best efforts in test development and validation, one should be aware that performance on a one-shot test of 25–50 items may not demonstrate the results of limited training. In these cases it may be much more informative to utilize single subject, or time-series designs (Kratochwill, 1978; Ventry and Schiavetti, 1980) which show increments in skill over time devoted to drill. For example, response latency for a discrimination drill on perception of nasality can be measured fairly simply. If the latency of response goes down, one can infer that increment in skill is taking place. Once the latency plateaus, one may infer that maximal skill has been achieved and training can move on to another area. It should be emphasized that reaching the plateau may take a few minutes or several hours of concentrated practice which may represent only 20 or 2000+ trials. Peterson (1980), for example, found that one severely hearing-impaired subject was still improving in distinctive feature reception after 2000 trials, using an amplitude compression hearing aid. This process is greatly facilitated with programmed self-instruction and automation, so that several hundred trials may be easily accomplished in one sitting.

TEST DEVELOPMENT

Following is a summary of some of the general steps used in test development. Procedures such as these should be completed on the new tests that the clinician develops in order to insure that valid and reliable measurement of therapeutic effects can be made. There are two key requirements for test instrumentation in speech and hearing: first, the test should be precise enough to reliably detect individual differences (Thorndike and Hagen, 1969); and second, validation procedures should be completed on the same population that will be measured following therapy as the variability associated with repeated measurements may be quite different among various hearing-loss groups.

Figure 9.2 presents a flow chart of some of the steps in test validation. The first stage in this procedure is to establish content validity (see Cronbach, 1970, for a detailed discussion). As discussed above, content validity has to do with being certain that one is testing the desired skill and that the response mode of the test corresponds closely with the training task. Since pretest and posttest gains are to be measured, two forms of the test will be needed. In order to achieve maximum efficiency and reliability, and minimize test-retest error, a pool of test items forming a prototype test are pared down by item analysis to two forms which contain items of equal difficulty. The two forms should correlate highly and have no significant mean score differences.

If the tester desires to relate the test results to the larger domain of speech reception, a concurrent validity measure should be administered to the target population at the same time as the prototype test is administered in its pilot form. Typically, to satisfy this validity consideration, one would give another speech discrimination test, such as the PB words or CID Everyday Sentences Test. However, established measures of speech discrimination, when used with deaf persons, usually results in a majority of scores at the 0% correct level; thus one may not assume that statistics for normal distributions will be applicable for validation purposes.

Though not often done because of methodological difficulties, the establishment, of criterion validity (Magnusson, 1966, p. 153) is highly desirable. This procedure allows one to classify persons into categories of observable changes in communication behavior as a result of treatment. Thus the real world

value or practical significance can be established. Typically, an outside criterion judgment is made by "experts." For example, the tester could ask classroom teachers to rate their students' skills on a 5-point, poor-to-excellent scale of auditory speech reception skill. These ratings would then be correlated to the prototype test to establish criterion validity. If the teacher rankings are reliable, the correlations are significant, and if there are enough persons in each rank category, the prototype test results can be used to describe observable differences in communication function. Then, when a student's posttest scores improve beyond the standard error of the test AND into a range of scores associated with an observable change, one may be in a good position to declare the training to be effective.

There is one further step, however, which must be accomplished. Thornton and Raffin, (1978) suggest that the error of measurement for each subgroup of the hearing-impaired population may vary substantially and should be accounted for. This can be assessed by examination of the distribution of the test scores on the two final forms of the test. The standard error of measurement should be calculated for each subgroup. From that a confidence interval can be established for test results which are beyond the error of measurement and thus statistically significant (Cronbach, 1970, p. 151).

In summary, hearing and speechreading evaluation with deaf adults is not evaluation of a single population with similar characteristics. In spite of limited residual hearing, the variability of communication function among deaf individuals is wide. That is why adequate assessment practices and procedures are so necessary in order to plan and measure the effectiveness of communication training. The professional dealing with a deaf client must also be cognizant of evaluation procedures across the disciplines of audiology, speech pathology, linguistics, and education in general. Though profile systems have some problems, they are a great help in the assessment and planning of communication training because one may broaden his or her perspective on the needs of the deaf person without undue study of the details of test interpretation in an unfamiliar discipline.

It is my hope that this chapter raises the

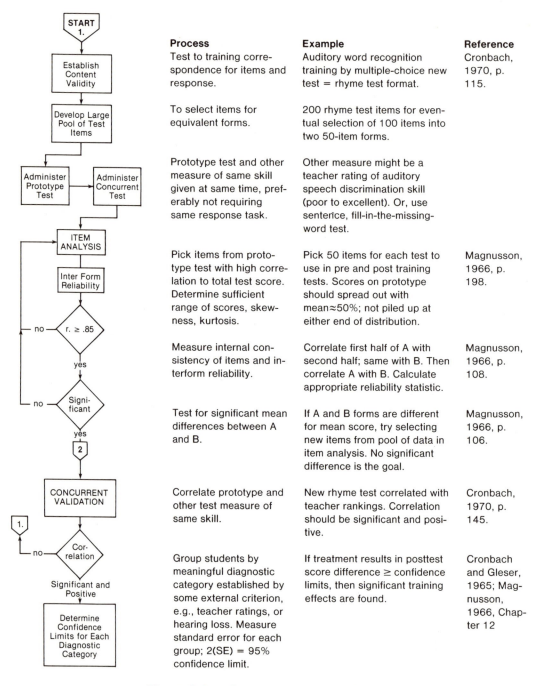

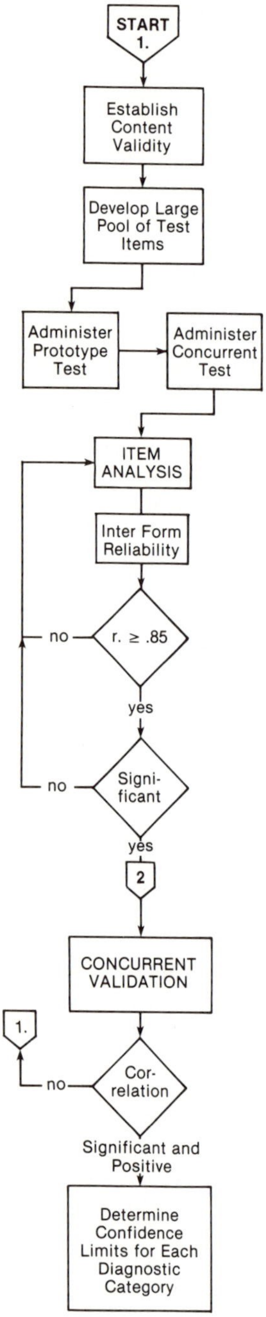
START 1.
Establish Content Validity
Develop Large Pool of Test Items
Administer Prototype Test
Administer Concurrent Test
ITEM ANALYSIS
Inter Form Reliability
r. ≥ .85
no
yes
Signi-ficant
no
yes
2
CONCURRENT VALIDATION
1.
no
Cor-relation
Significant and Positive
Determine Confidence Limits for Each Diagnostic Category

Process	Example	Reference
Test to training correspondence for items and response.	Auditory word recognition training by multiple-choice new test = rhyme test format.	Cronbach, 1970, p. 115.
To select items for equivalent forms.	200 rhyme test items for eventual selection of 100 items into two 50-item forms.	
Prototype test and other measure of same skill given at same time, preferably not requiring same response task.	Other measure might be a teacher rating of auditory speech discrimination skill (poor to excellent). Or, use sentence, fill-in-the-missing-word test.	
Pick items from prototype test with high correlation to total test score. Determine sufficient range of scores, skewness, kurtosis.	Pick 50 items for each test to use in pre and post training tests. Scores on prototype should spread out with mean≈50%; not piled up at either end of distribution.	Magnusson, 1966, p. 198.
Measure internal consistency of items and interform reliability.	Correlate first half of A with second half; same with B. Then correlate A with B. Calculate appropriate reliability statistic.	Magnusson, 1966, p. 108.
Test for significant mean differences between A and B.	If A and B forms are different for mean score, try selecting new items from pool of data in item analysis. No significant difference is the goal.	Magnusson, 1966, p. 106.
Correlate prototype and other test measure of same skill.	New rhyme test correlated with teacher rankings. Correlation should be significant and positive.	Cronbach, 1970, p. 145.
Group students by meaningful diagnostic category established by some external criterion, e.g., teacher ratings, or hearing loss. Measure standard error for each group; 2(SE) = 95% confidence limit.	If treatment results in posttest score difference ≥ confidence limits, then significant training effects are found.	Cronbach and Gleser, 1965; Magnusson, 1966, Chapter 12

Figure 9.2. Concepts in test development.

consciousness of professionals dealing with the communication problems of the deaf so that they will no longer routinely accept audiometric reports for deaf people which have pure tone results and nothing else, under the guise that no further communication assessment was possible due to the extent of the hearing loss.

References

Bamford, J. Methodological considerations and practical aspects of the BKB sentence lists. In J. Bench and J. Bamford (eds.), *Speech-Hearing Tests and the Spoken Language of Hearing-Impaired Children*. London: Academic Press, 1979.

Beattie, R., and Sheffler, M. Test-retest stability and effects of psychophysical methods on the speech loudness discomfort level. *Audiology*, 1981, *20*, 143.

Beattie, R., Svihovec, D., Carmen, R., and Kunkel, H. Loudness discomfort level for speech: Comparison of two instructional sets for saturation sound pressure level selection. *Audiology*, 1980, *1*, 197.

Beattie, R., Svihovec, D., and Edgerton, B. Relative intelligibility of the CID spondees as presented monitored live voice. *J. Speech Hear. Disord.*, 1975, *40*, 84.

Berger, K. *Speechreading: Principles and Methods*. Baltimore: National Educational Press, 1972.

Binnie, C. Relevant aural rehabilitation. In J. Northern (ed.), *Hearing Disorders*. Boston: Little, Brown, 1976.

Binnie, C. Jackson, P., and Montgomery, A. Visual intelligibility of consonants. A lipreading screening test with implications for aural rehabilitation. *J. Speech Hear. Disord.*, 1976, *41*, 530–539.

Bode, D. Adaptive speech testing applied to hearing impaired listeners. Paper presented at the Convention of the American Speech and Hearing Association, San Francisco, 1978.

Bode, D., and Carhart, R. Estimating CNC discrimination with spondee words. *J. Accoust. Soc. Am.*, 1975, *57*, 1216–1218.

Boothroyd, A. Audiological evaluation of severely and profoundly deaf children. In G. Fant (ed.), *International Symposium on Speech Communication Ability and Profound Deafness*. Washington, D.C.: A.G. Bell Association for the Deaf, 1972.

Boothroyd, A. Speech perception and sensorineural hearing loss. In M. Ross, and T. Giolas (eds.), *Auditory Management of Hearing Impaired Children*. Baltimore: University Park Press, 1978.

Boothroyd, A., and Cawkwell, S. Vibrotactile thresholds in pure tone audiometry. *Acta Otolaryngol. (Stockh.)*, 1970, *69*, 381–387.

Budacki, R., and Hipskind, N. The relationship between MCL and speech discrimination. Paper presented at the American Speech, Language and Hearing Association Convention, Atlanta, 1979.

Chaiklin, J. The relation among three selected auditory speech thresholds. *J. Speech Hear. Res.*, 1959, *2*, 237–243.

Conklin, J., Subtelny, J., and Walter, G. Analysis of the communication skills of young deaf adults over a two year interval of technical training. *Am. Ann. Deaf*, 1980, *125*, 388–393.

Cox, R. Procedure for establishing limiting levels in hearing aid fitting. Paper presented at the American Speech, Language and Hearing Association Convention, Detroit, 1980.

Craig, W. Effects of preschool training on the development of reading and lipreading skills of deaf children. *Am. Ann. Deaf*, 1964, *109*, 280–296.

Cramer, K., and Erber, N. A spondee recognition test for young hearing impaired children. *J. Speech Hear. Disord.*, 1974, *39*, 178–185.

Cronbach, L. *Essentials of Psychological Testing*, ed. 3. New York: Harper & Row, 1970.

Cronbach, L., and Gleser, G. *Psychological Tests and Personnel Decisions*. Chicago: University of Illinois Press, 1965.

Davis, H., and Silverman, R. Central Institute for the Deaf Everyday Sentences. In *Hearing and Deafness*, ed. 3 Appendix. New York: Holt, Rinehart & Winston, 1970.

De Filippo, C., and Scott, B. A method for training and evaluating the reception of ongoing speech. *J. Acoust. Soc. Am.*, 1978, *63*, 1186–1192.

Dejupesland, G. Nonacoustic reflex measurement-procedures, interpretations and variables. In A. Feldman, and L. Wilber (eds.), *Acoustic Impedance and Admittance*. Baltimore: Williams & Wilkins, 1976.

Dirks, D., and Kamm, C. Psychometric functions for loudness discomfort and most comfortable loudness levels. *J. Speech Hear. Res.*, 1976, *19*, 613–628.

Erber, N. Auditory, visual, and auditory-visual recognition of consonants by children with normal and impaired hearing. *J. Speech Hear. Res.*, 1972, *15*, 413–422.

Erber, N. Auditory-visual perception of speech. *J. Speech Hear. Disord.*, 1975, *40*, 481–492.

Erber, N. Audiologic evaluation of deaf children. *J. Speech Hear. Disord.*, 1976, *41*, 257–267.

Erber, N. Vibratory perception by deaf children. *Int. J. Rehabil. Res.*, 1978, *1*, 27–37.

Erber, N. Auditory-visual perception of speech with reduced optical clarity. *J. Speech Hear. Disord.*, 1979, *22*, 212–223.

Erber, N. Auditory evaluation and training of hearing impaired children. *J. Natl. Student Speech, Lang. Hear. Assn.*, 1980a, *1*, 6–20.

Erber, N. Use of the auditory numbers test to evaluate speech perception abilities of hearing impaired children. *J. Speech Hear. Res.*, 1980b, *45*, 527–532.

Erber, N., and Witt, L. Effects of stimulus intensity on speech perception by deaf children. *J. Speech Hear. Disord.*, 1977, *42*, 271.

Fisher, C. Confusions among visually perceived consonants. *J. Speech Hear. Res.*, 1968, *11*, 796–800.

Frisina, R. Audiometric evaluation and its relation to habituation and rehabilitation of the deaf. *Am. Ann. Deaf*, 1962, *107*, 478.

Green, D. Pure tone air-conduction testing. In J. Katz (ed.), *Handbook of Clinical Audiology*, ed. 2. Baltimore: Williams & Wilkins, 1978.

Hardick, E., Oyer, H., and Irion, P. Lipreading performance is related to measurements of vision. *J. Speech Hear. Res.*, 1970, *13*, 92–100.

Hawkins, D. The effect of signal type on the loudness discomfort level. *Ear Hear.*, 1980, *1*, 38–41.

Hirsh, I. *The Measurement of Hearing*. New York: McGraw-Hill, 1952.

Hirsh, I., Davis, H., Silverman, R., Reynolds, E., Eldert, E., and Benson, R. Development of materials for speech audiometry. *J. Speech Hear. Disord.*, 1952, *17*, 321–337.

Jeffers, J., and Barley, M. *Speechreading*. Springfield, Illinois: Charles C Thomas, Publisher, 1971.

Jerger, J., and Hayes, D. Diagnostic speech audiometry. *Arch. Otolaryngol*, 1977, *103*, 216–222.

Jerger, J., and Northern, J. (eds.) *Clinical Impedance*

Audiometry, ed. 2. American Electromedics Corp., 1980.

Johnson, D. Communication characteristics of a young deaf adult population: Techniques for evaluating their communication skills. *Am. Ann. Deaf*, 1976, *121*, 409–424.

Johnson, D., and Caccamise, F. Rationale and strategies for planning communication individualized educational programs (CIEP) for deaf students. *Am. Ann. Deaf*, 1981, *126*, 370–381.

Johnson, D., Caccamise, F., Rothblum, A., Hamilton, L., and Howard, M. Identification and follow-up of visual impairments in hearing-impaired populations. *Am. Ann. Deaf*, 1981, *126*, 321–360.

Johnson, D., and Crandall, K. The adult deaf client and rehabilitation. In J. Alpiner, (ed.), *Handbook of Adult Rehabilitative Audiology*, ed. 2. Baltimore: Williams & Wilkins (in press).

Johnson, D., and Kadunc, N. Usefulness of the NTID communication profile for evaluating deaf secondary level students. *Am. Ann. Deaf*, 1980, *125*, 337–349.

Johnson, D., and Yust, V. Rationale and design for a student response system. In D. Johnson and W. Castle (eds.), *Info Series II*. Rochester, New York: National Technical Institute for the Deaf, 1976.

Jones, K., and Studebaker, G. Performance of severely hearing impaired children on a closed response, auditory speech discrimination test. *J. Speech Hear. Res.*, 1974, *17*, 531–540.

Kalikow, D., Stevens, K., and Elliot, L. Development of a test of speech intelligibility in noise using sentence materials with controlled word predictability. *J. Acoust. Soc. Am.*, 1977, *61*, 1337–1351.

Kratochwill, T. *Single Subject Research*. New York: Academic Press, 1978.

Levitt, H., and Rabiner, L. Use of a sequential strategy in intelligibility testing. *J. Acoust. Soc. Am.*, 1967, *42*, 602–612.

Ling, D., and Ling, A. *Aural Habilitation*. Washington, D. C.: A.G. Bell Association for the Deaf, 1978.

Lloyd, L., and Price, J. Sentence familiarity as a factor in visual speech reception (lipreading) of deaf college students. *J. Speech Hear. Res.*, 1971, *14*, 291–294.

Magnusson, D. *Test Theory*. Reading, Massachusetts: Addison-Wesley, 1966.

McCandless, G. Real-ear measures of hearing aid performance. In P. Yanik (ed.), *Rehabilitation Strategies for Sensorineural Hearing Loss*. New York: Grune & Stratton, 1979.

Myklebust, H., and Neyhus, A. *Diagnostic Test of Speechreading*. New York: Grune and Stratton, 1971.

Peterson, P. Further studies of perception of amplitude-compressed speech by impaired listeners. Master's thesis, M.I.T., 1980.

Plomp, R., and Mimpen, A. Improving the reliability of testing the speech reception threshold for sentences. *Audiology*, 1979, *18*, 42–52.

Risberg, A. Diagnostic rhyme test for speech audiometry with severely hard of hearing and profoundly deaf children. In *Quarterly Progress and Status Report 2-3*. Stockholm: Speech Transmission Laboratory, 1976, 40–58.

Risberg, A., and Agelfors, E. Information extraction and information processing in speech-reading. In *Quarterly Progress and Status Report 2-3*. Stockholm: Speech Transmission Laboratory, 1978, 62–82.

Risberg, A., Agelfors, E., and Boberg, G. Measurements of frequency-discrimination ability of severely and profoundly hearing-impaired children. In *Quarterly Progress and Status Report 2-3*. Stockholm: Speech Transmission Laboratory, 1975, 40–48.

Rossi, D., and Sims, D. Acoustic reflex measurement in the severely and profoundly deaf. *Audiol. Hear. Educ.*, 1977, *3*, 6–8.

Sims, D. The validation of the CID Everyday Sentence Test for use with the severely hearing impaired. *J. Acad. Rehabil. Audiol.*, 1975, *8*, 70–79.

Sims, D., Gottermeier, L., and Walter, G. Factors contributing to the development of intelligible speech among prelingually deaf persons. *Am. Ann. Deaf*, 1980, *125*, 374–381.

Sims, D., and Jacobs, M. Speechreading evaluation and the National Technical Institute for the Deaf. Paper presented at the Convention of the A.G. Bell Association for the Deaf, Boston, 1976.

Sims, D., and Montgomery, A. Multidimensional analysis of auditory and visual perception among the profoundly hearing impaired. Paper presented to the 94th Meeting of the Acoustical Society of America, Miami, 1977.

Steele, J., Binnie, C., and Cooper, W. Combining auditory and visual stimuli in the adaptive testing of speech discrimination. *J. Speech Hear. Disord.*, 1978, *43*, 115–122.

Stephens, S., Blegvad, B., and Krogh, H. The value of some suprathreshold auditory measures. *Scand. Audiol.*, 1977, *6*, 213–221. (Also published in *Am. Ann. Deaf*, 1980, *125*, 374–381.)

Taaffe, G. A film test of lipreading. *John Tracy Clinic Res. Papers*, November 1957, ii.

Thorndike, R., and Hagen, E. *Measurement and Evaluation in Psychology and Education*. New York: John Wiley & Sons, 1969.

Thornton, A., and Raffin, M. Speech discrimination scores modeled as a binomial variable. *J. Speech Hear. Res.*, 1978, *21*, 507–518.

Utley, J. A. test of lipreading ability. *J. Speech Hear. Discord.*, 1946, *11*, 109–116.

Ventry, I., Chaiklin, J., and Dixon, R. *Hearing Measurement*. New York: Appleton-Century-Crofts, 1971.

Ventry, I., and Johnson, J. Evaluation of a clinical method for measuring comfortable loudness for speech. *J. Speech Hear. Disord.*, 1978, *43*, 149–159.

Walden, B., Prosek, R., Montgomery, A., Scherr, C., and Jones, C. Effects of training on the visual recognition of consonants. *J. Speech Hear. Res.*, 1977, *20*, 130–145.

Walden, B., Prosek, R., and Worthington, D. Auditory and audiovisual feature transmission in hearing-impaired adults. *J. Speech Hear. Res.*, 1975, *18*, 272–280.

Webster, J., and O'Shea, N. Current developments in auditory speech discrimination tests for the profoundly hearing impaired at NTID. *Am. Ann. Deaf*, 1980, *125*, 350–359.

Wozniak, V., and Jackson, P. Visual vowel and diphthong perception from two horizontal viewing angles. *J. Speech Hear. Res.*, 1979, *22*, 354–365.

Chapter 10

Speech Assessment of the Adolescent with Impaired Hearing

JOANNE D. SUBTELNY, PH.D.

THEORY AND PRINCIPLES OF ASSESSMENT

DIAGNOSTIC SYSTEM

SPEECH INTELLIGIBILITY
    PROCEDURE FOR SECURING SAMPLES
    ANALYSIS PROCEDURE
    ORAL READING

EVALUATION OF SUPRASEGMENTAL FEATURES
    PROSODY
    VOCAL PITCH
    QUALITY

ASSESSMENT OF SEGMENTAL FEATURES

INTERRELATIONSHIPS BETWEEN PERCEPTION AND PRODUCTION

This chapter is directed to speech/language pathologists working with hearing-impaired adolescents in the mainstreamed secondary environments of the United States. The primary objective in this writing is to supply practical information which will assist in assessing some of the rather unique combinations of communication problems encountered. As theoretically acknowledged in rehabilitation literature (Davis, 1977), the magnitude and complexity of the individual's communication problems necessitates an integrated team approach for optimal efficiency in evaluation and training. Unfortunately, the recommended blend of professional expertise is not always available. As a consequence, the speech/language pathologist needs considerable insight and skill in gaining answers to many pertinent questions, such as:

1. Does the speaker know and use the English linguistic system?

2. How much speech can the adolescent comprehend by audition, by vision, and by combined use of audition and vision?
3. Is amplification adequate?
4. Which basic processes of speech production are impaired and to what degree?
5. Which phonological features can be produced consistently, inconsistently, or not at all?
6. What is the relationship between the adolescent's speech perception and speech production?

Although the questions posed relative to language and speech reception are addressed extensively in other chapters, some discussion of linguistic and auditory assessment is included here. Such discussion is required to interpret speech observations and integrate training in speech reception, language, and speech production.

In writing from the clinical viewpoint, the author has drawn from personal experience, borrowed heavily from research in areas of deafness, and applied information from related areas to the specific problem of the hearing-impaired adolescent. The content is organized to discuss theory and principles of assessment, the diagnostic system, speech intelligibility, evaluation of suprasegmental and segmental features of speech, and the interrelationships between perception and production in hearing-impaired adolescents.

THEORY AND PRINCIPLES OF ASSESSMENT

The faulty speech of the hearing-impaired adolescent within the mainstreamed setting is considered to result primarily from imperfect auditory perception and from instruction which has failed to optimally utilize residual hearing, vision, and other sensory cues (tactile-kinesthetic) to supplement impaired audition in the process of learning language. This conclusion is based upon a simple communication model specifying that speech is the outward manifestation of inner language. The learning of language requires acoustic impulses faithfully transmitted to the central nervous system where they can be processed, interpreted, and stored as linguistic units within the central nervous system. Speech production requires that neuromuscular impulses are sequentially released to the speech mechanism, thereby affecting muscular movements which result in sounds generated with spectral and temporal features approximating those stored in auditory memory (Borden and Harris, 1980, p. 137).

This accounting of speech perception and production mediated by the central "black box" or cognitive organizer, which represents the core or integrator in language learning (Hollis et al., 1976), emphasizes the intimate relationship between perception and production as it relates to language learning and speech acquisition. The model also serves to establish a broad reference considered essential to satisfactory diagnosis of speech in the adolescent with impaired hearing. This applies simply because spoken language, a rule governed communication system, is learned primarily through hearing speech. Speech is considered a conversion of language into sound. The communicative adequacy of speech is therefore a direct expression of the speakers' "knowledge of meanings (semantics) formalized into structure (syntax, morphemes, phonemes) that is finally encoded into the sounds of speech" (Borden and Harris, 1980, p. 8).

In early developmental stages of speech acquisition, auditory perception precedes production. In later stages, auditory feedback continues to facilitate learning, but tactile-kinesthetic-proprioceptive feedback begins to play a more dominant role in the habituations and generalization of motor responses (Johnson, 1980, p. 38).

Speech learning is best conceived as progressing in syllable or "clusters of sounds" units rather than by phonemes. A great deal of practice is required to habituate the neuromuscular responses so that simpler speech tasks may be integrated into more complex patterns and eventually internalized to achieve a level termed automaticity by Ling (1976). Streng et al., (1978, pp. 40–41) similarly emphasize that speech learning for the hearing-impaired child implies conscious practice of hierarchical order of simple speech tasks before a child "can get it all together." The child "learns to speak by speaking, not by swimming or signing or watching the teacher talk.... Well established motor speech skill must be developed in order to speak automatically."

Practice of articulatory sequences has formed the basis for most procedures in traditional speech correction for many years. Deviant articulation has been corrected by these systematic procedures requiring the speaker to produce a sound under different stimulus conditions and with progressive increases in complexity (Elbert et al., 1967; Garrett, 1973; McReynolds and Bennett, 1972; Pollack and Rees, 1972; Ruder and Bunce, 1981). The success attained in well-designed programs for correction of articulation defects has led McLean to conclude that in articulation, "clusters of phones (sounds) are integrated at motor levels below the cognitive level.... The overall history of success in symptomatologic therapy, and the significantly good results attained in all programmed therapy systems attacking the phoneme in coarticulation contexts, clearly seem to indicate that phones and phoneme boundaries are 'learned by doing'. . . . In the case of phonology, the motor production itself contributes heavily to the full learning of the rules of the system [McLean, 1976, pp. 358–359]."

Success in speech development utilizing a highly systematic approach at the surface structure level has also been reported with deaf children (Ling, 1976; Novelli-Olmstead, 1979) and with young adults with impaired hearing (Lieberth and Subtelny, 1978; Subtelny et al., 1980a). Although the learning of other aspects of language (semantic, syntactic, and morphological) is generally not approached through practice drills, various studies indicate that the learning of phonology of a second language (Chastain and Woerdehoff, 1968; Chastain, 1970 and 1972; Neufeld, 1980) or the correction of phonology in normally hearing and hearing-impaired speakers can and is facilitated by structured practice drill at the surface structure level. Compositely, these reports suggest that the speech errors of many hearing-impaired adolescents in the mainstream may not be language (phonemic) deficiencies but rather motoric (phonetic) deficiencies or combined phonemic and phonetic deficiencies.

This suggestion is supported by consistent research evidence showing that the speech of the deaf is more intelligible during sentence rather than single isolated word production (Brannon, 1964; Hudgins, 1949; Subtelny, 1977; Thomas, 1963). For hearing speakers with articulation defects the opposite situation is observed—speech is perceptually more deviant during continuous speech production (Faircloth and Faircloth, 1970). This observation is explained by the increased difficulty in producing sounds within a dynamic context which more clearly reveals aberrations in coarticulatory activity.

In most deaf speakers, coarticulation is grossly deviant, yet intelligibility is somehow better in sentence context than in single word utterances. This may be interpreted as some evidence that the linguistic (phonemic) base may be frail, but it is supportive of an even weaker phonetic underpinning—a premise which seems consistent with data showing significant negative correlations between

phonetic error and intelligibility in hearing-impaired speakers (Brannon, 1966; Markides, 1970; Monsen, 1978; Smith, 1975; Subtelny, 1977).

Two common characteristics in the speech of the hearing-impaired further the suggestion of a primary phonetic basis for the speech disorder. These characteristics are:

1. The tremendous distortions in the temporal features of speech described as vowel prolongations (Hudgins and Numbers, 1942; John and Howarth, 1965); extended durations of articulatory contacts (Angelocci, 1962; Li, 1980); abnormal pause (Nickerson, 1975; Osberger, 1978); slow articulatory movements (Calvert, 1962; Monsen, 1978); and excessively slow rates of syllable articulation (Forner and Hixon, 1977; Stevens et al., 1978); and

2. A high incidence of articulatory errors reported as omissions (occurring at word, phrase, and sentence endings and as elements within consonant blends) and distortions, resulting from faulty tongue placement and aerodynamic control (Geffner and Freeman, 1980; Hudgins and Numbers, 1942; Markides, 1970; Nober, 1967; Smith, 1975).

In the typical error pattern of the hearing-impaired child, omissions and distortions predominate and tend to be consistent. In this regard, the pattern fits the description of a "phonetically based disorder" (Johnson, 1980, p. 122). In adolescents, however, consistent substitution errors generally are proportionately lower in incidence. When these errors occur, they most frequently involve voicing errors, glottal stops, and/or neutralization of vowels. This latter error is described as a postural fault (Stevens et al., 1978), which has been confirmed by spectrographic studies of vowels indicating reduction in tongue movement during speech as shown in Figure 10.1.

Radiographic study of deaf speakers (Li, 1980) has provided visual information which substantiates the physiological descriptions and the acoustical specifications of defects (Fig. 10.2). There also is limited electromyographic data indicating that a primary factor contributing to the unintelligibility of deaf speech is a failure to control interarticulatory programming (Harris and McGarr, 1980).

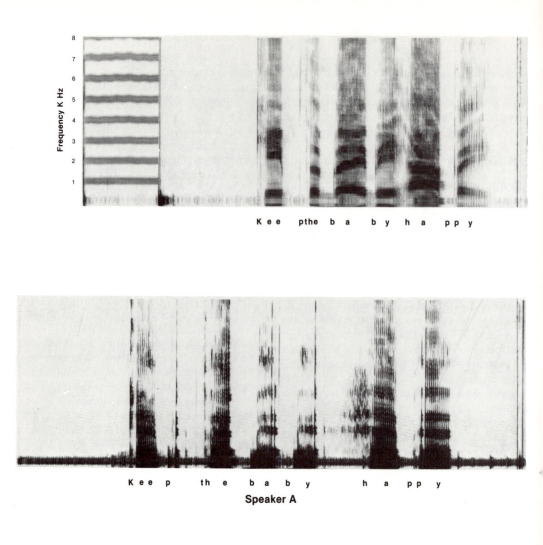

Keepthe ba by ha ppy

Keep the ba by ha ppy

Speaker A

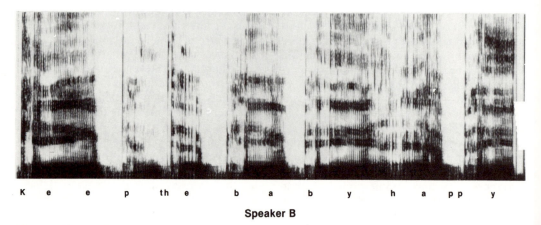

K e e p th e b a b y h a pp y

Speaker B

Figure 10.1. Spectrograms of sentences produced by a normal-hearing man (*top*) and by two different deaf men. The spectrogram of the sentence produced by Speaker A displays glottal stops at syllable boundaries and as substitutions for bilabial stops. The rather flat or nonvarying pattern of formant relationships during utterances of Speakers

158

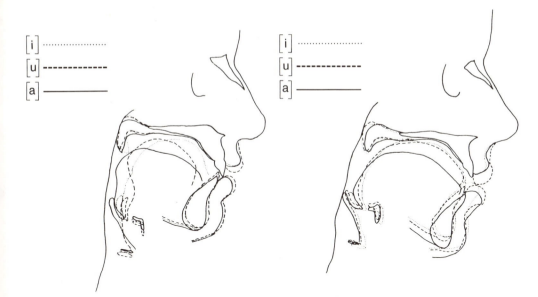

Figure 10.2.   Superimposed tracings of cephalometric films secured while a normal-hearing (*left*) and a deaf adult female (*right*) sustained phonations of vowels [i], [u], and [ɑ]. Respective vowel phonations of the deaf speaker are physiologically differentiated from the normal-hearing speaker by a neutralized or centralized position of the tongue within the oral cavity, marked retraction of the epiglottis toward the posterior pharyngeal wall, elevation of the hyoid bone, and by a greater-than-normal vertical dimension between the hyoid bone and laryngeal sinus which is anatomically delineated superiorly by the false (ventricular) folds and inferiorly by the vocal folds (Courtesy of Dr. Walter Li).

Further support for this premise is found in Monsen's (1978) spectrographic measures of voice onset times in deaf talkers which indicate faulty programming of laryngeal and articulatory activity. This latter fault frequently is manifested in the deaf speaker's inability to physiologically differentiate voiced-voiceless cognates and by the tendency to intrude the schwa after release of a voiced stop in final position.

Compositely, there are many factors suggesting a general phonetic disability in the hearing-impaired adolescent which may be attacked at the surface structure level to develop tactile-kinesthetic feedback associated with the appropriate articulomotor responses. Training strategies focused at the surface

structure level to correct phonetic errors differ from strategies employed to correct phonemic (language) errors at the cognitive level. For this reason, assessment procedures must be broad enough to differentiate phonetic and phonemic errors. The procedure to define the phonetic level of competence must also be comprehensive enough to specify feature as well as phoneme production and perception.

Since the fundamental purpose of the speech assessment is to serve as the basis for instruction, the assessment should objectively identify areas of weakness which independently or interdependently reduce the communicative competence and confidence of the hearing-impaired adolescent. A satisfactory assessment requires an evaluation of how well

---

A and B indicates a restricted range of tongue movements. Approximately equal durations of stressed and unstressed syllables in the word "baby" are also displayed in both deaf speakers. Note the abnormal vowel prolongations and undifferentiated voicing and temporal features for [p] and [b] displayed in the spectrogram of Speaker B.

a person can hear and understand speech, as well as an evaluation of how well a person can produce speech. In the broadest reference, these evaluations would involve auditory comprehension of speech in the presence of environmental noise and the intelligiblity of spoken discourse within a conversational setting. Such evaluations are perhaps the most practical indices of an adolescent's competence in aural/oral communication. As such, they are subjective but provide considerable information pertaining to the individual's ability to hear, cognitively organize, and linguistically translate acoustic signals into appropriately sequenced neuromuscular impulses required to produce spoken English with appropriate semantic, syntactic, and grammatical features.

It is assumed that the speech/language pathologist working within a mainstreamed, secondary environment or within a specialized educational setting will have access to student information. Physiological and psychological evaluations as well as educational histories offer pertinent information to assist in speech assessment. From the educational history many significant facts related to speech skill can be determined. Age of diagnosis, use of amplification, parental involvement, socioeconomic level, and quality and quantity of educational intervention are all factors which will influence the communicative status, the attitudes, and the motivation of hearing-impaired adolescents to learn or improve speech.

From the psychological viewpoint, Coleman (1960) has stressed three factors as key determinants of effective learning. These are the characteristics of the student, the nature of the task to be learned, and the procedures used to facilitate and evaluate learning. In considering the characteristics of the hearing-impaired adolescent, psychologists have emphasized that motivation, personality traits, and background level of existing skills are powerful factors which influence what a student is willing to learn, what he can learn, and how efficiently he will learn it. If speech/language pathologists within a mainstreamed environment accept the essential validity of this concept, getting to know the adolescent as a person becomes a very high priority. Assessments of personality traits, interests,

and personal attitudes toward hearing and speech problems may be just as important as assessments of speech, auditory, and linguistic skills.

Although Moores (1978) and Cohen (1978) have addressed the psychosocial complexities encountered by the hearing-impaired adolescent, there appears a dearth of literature dealing with the adolescent's attitudes toward personal problems in communication. Pronovost (1978) stresses the extreme importance of understanding the adolescent's attitudes toward communication and refers to an inventory to assess attitudes toward communication (Libbey, 1978). In self-assessment of speech intelligibility, Libbey found that 20% of the adolescents reported that people "understand all of my speech"; 39% reported that people "understand most of my speech." Compositely, these figures indicate that almost 60% of the adolescents studied in mainstreamed environments had self-perceptions of speech skill considerably better than intelligibility levels as judged by teachers of the hearing-impaired (Jensema et al., 1978). The indicated differences in the speech intelligibility status of adolescents may be partially explained by differences in the populations studied and by inherent differences between self and teacher perceptions of skill.

In order to pursue differences between self and teacher perceptions of communicative skill, a questionnaire in multiple-choice format (Table 10.1) was administered to a representative group of 57 late adolescents entering NTID. Assuming that level of competence may exert some influence upon attitude and motivation to learn speech, questions were posed to determine student estimates of their own competence in speech and speech reading, and their attitudes toward the importance of speech and the value of individualized speech training. Questionnaire responses were then correlated with professional ratings of speech intelligibility and measures of speechreading with sound. Self-ratings and professional ratings of speech intelligibility were significantly rated (r, .68). Self-ratings of speechreading skill and percentage scores for key word recognition in speechreading were also significantly related (r, .60). Although both correlations are positive, it cannot be assumed that all students

Table 10.1

Examples of Multiple-Choice Questions to Sample Student Attitudes toward Competence in Communication, Value of Individualized Speech Training, and the Importance of Speech

A. People understand:
   1. Nothing I say
   2. A few words
   3. About half of my words
   4. Almost everything I say
   5. Everything I say

B. I think my speech is:
   1. Never good enough
   2. Usually not good enough
   3. Sometimes O.K.; sometimes not O.K.
   4. Usually good enough
   5. Always good enough

C. When I read lips and listen, I understand:
   1. Nothing
   2. Very little—only a few words
   3. About half of what is said, but I get the general idea
   4. Most of what is said
   5. Almost everything

D. Individual speech training is:
   1. Never helpful—just a waste of time
   2. Usually not helpful
   3. Probably helpful when I have time to practice
   4. Usually helpful
   5. Always very helpful

E. My future job will require:
   1. No talking
   2. Very little talking
   3. An average amount of talking
   4. A lot of talking
   5. Talking most of the time

have realistic attitudes about their own expressive and receptive competence. Some students underestimate, others overestimate their skill. Since attitudes influence motivation to learn speech, it is important to recognize and deal with discrepancies between what students can do in speech and what they think they can do. A paper and pencil questionnaire is not the best method to assess attitudes, but such instruments can be used formally or informally within an interview or conversational setting to yield the desired information.

In the NTID study (Subtelny, 1976), positive attitudes toward speech therapy, the importance of speech, and use of speech were all significantly related to speech intelligibility ratings, i.e., positive attitudes toward speech were associated with good speech. At this juncture, one cannot determine whether positive attitudes were responsible for the development of good speech or whether good speech was instrumental in the development of positive attitudes. Ideally, functional speech is its own reward, fostering increased motivation for further refinement of skill.

When responses to the questionnaire were studied relative to other skills, it became clear that motivation (as indicated by responses) and the degree of improvement achieved in therapy are influenced by the adolescent's present level of competence in speech, which in turn is partially influenced by the associated degree of auditory handicap. In general, late adolescents with meager skills in speech, auditory discrimination, and speech reading are not motivated to take advantage of opportunities for instruction unless counseling, instruction, and the environment are conducive to improving attitudes as well as skill levels.

By adolescence, self-conceptions of hearing and speaking competence have been formulated, albeit these may or may not be valid. In assessment, the examiner should determine how the adolescent personally perceives his/her communicative competence. After evaluation, the assessment information should be interpreted in a constructive, objective way to help the adolescent understand realistically current levels of performance and what can be achieved with continued training and diligence.

In accordance with Coleman's philosophy and current principles of assessment, a primary objective is to determine the adolescent's present level of existing skill in communication. This pertains simply because motivation to learn and the character and scope of training provided are greatly influenced by present levels of communicative competence and by the potential to achieve competence.

Determination of competence at the teenage stage of development is facilitated by higher levels of cognitive and linguistic development which improve the validity and reliability of audiological, speechreading, and speech evaluations and which also provide varied channels for use in multisensory training. To illustrate: The literate adolescent probably has learned some orthographic system other than English to indicate sound-symbol relationships. Since an orthographic system is of great value in training audition, speechreading, and speech, the adolescent's ability to use the diacritical marking system recommended in the mainstreamed environment should be evaluated. This can be done simply by asking the student to write a series of words as they sound (rat, rate, write, wrote, right, etc.) or to produce a string of words written with diacritical markings.

Although speech and hearing specialists have expertise in working with the International Phonetic Alphabet, its use with hearing-impaired adolescents should be avoided. The phonetic alphabet will not reinforce the system advocated by teachers of English, hence it may confuse rather than help students.

With an adolescent, errors in production may be corrected by writing in diacritical symbols and by explaining in physiological terms. The adolescent also can develop a functional knowledge of audition and phonological rules to assist in training. In summary, adolescents are capable of understanding their communication problems as well as the "why" and "how" of assessment and remedial procedures.

The evaluations of attitudes, orthographic skill, speech, language, and speech perception must be interpreted and integrated to develope remedial plans and to forecast potential for improvement. This requires considerable insight and experience. It is not implied that all the requisite information can or should be accumulated and analyzed in one or several sessions. Speech evaluation should be an ongoing process which permits the examiner to assess progress, modify priorities, and alter teaching strategies when indicated. Without objective measures and careful analysis of data, evaluations and reevaluations cannot offer the direction needed, nor can the teacher assess personal competence as the facilitator of learning.

DIAGNOSTIC SYSTEM

At its most fundamental level, an auditory-vocal communication channel consists of perception, linguistic translation (central integration), and production. A sensory input (stimulus) progresses through a cognitive/association (integrating) process in the brain to mediate a response output. Current thinking regarding hierarchical levels of integrative processing provides a good reference from which to structure diagnostic procedures for hearing-impaired adolescents. These young people frequently have compounded difficulties in speech perception, linguistic processing, and speech production. Hollis et al. (1976) have described the hierarchical levels of linguistic processing relative to an auditory-speech (input-output) communication channel as follows:

1. At the imitative level, the stimulus input (audiovisual model of a word spoken by the teacher) is the same as the response output (spoken word of the listener).
2. At the nonimitative level, the response to the stimulus is symbolic. For example, the stimulus input (printed word) is a different sensory model than the response output (word spoken by the learner).
3. At the constructive or generative level of cognitive/association function, the stimulus input (picture) may sample the learner's ability to arrange and produce words in appropriate sequence for the response output (verbal description). To do this, the learner must have memory for the vocabulary (semantic items) needed; knowledge of structural linguistic rules (syntax, morpheme, and phonemes); and satisfactory neuromuscular programming to produce an intelligible utterance appropriate to the visual stimulus input.
4. The transformative level is the highest level of cognitive/association. At this level, the stimulus input (picture or story) may sample the speaker's ability to produce words properly sequenced as in a conventional constructive or generative respsonse, as well as the ability to make additions or transformations resulting in a creative or original verbal response.

Since these levels deal with both auditory-visual and visual-motor channels of communication, they are used to conceptualize the assessment procedure for hearing-impaired adolescents. Optimal communication training for many adolescents with severe hearing loss requires individualized analysis of capabilities of varied levels of performance within both auditory-vocal and visual-motor channels of communication. This point becomes very apparent when a primary educational goal is to develop an alternate sensory input mode because audition cannot be efficiently utilized in language and/or speech learning.

The speech component in the assessment system is outlined by listing the parameter evaluated and the associated stimulus employed to elicit response (Table 10.2). For each parameter, progression in difficulty is incorporated. For example, intelligibility at the basic level calls for repetition, an imitative response to an audiovisual stimulus. At the oral reading level, a nonimitative response is elicited from a visual stimulus of print. For spontaneous speech and conversation responses, the generative and transformational levels, less structured stimuli in pictorial or verbal form are used to elicit speech requiring progressively greater skill in formulation.

Because speech performance is known to be influenced by the nature of the task imposed by the stimulus, assessment procedures should sample intelligibility at the varied levels indicated. For example, speech may be very intelligible when an auditory and visual model is used as stimulus. Although this response may indicate good auditory-visual memory for sound sequences, efficient speech reception via combined audition and speech reading, and acceptable motoric skill in production, the response does not indicate that speech will be equally intelligible during oral reading. When the audiovisual model is replaced by the visual stimulus, speech may retain intelligibility because the speaker has good articulation facilitated by the cues provided in print. However, this again does not indicate that intelligibility would be comparably good when speech is formulated spontaneously without access to print.

The same principle in hierarchy of skill requirement is projected for the assessment of suprasegmental and segmental features. To illustrate: The suprasegmental features of prosody, pitch, intensity, and voice quality

Table 10.2

Stimuli to Evaluate Varied Parameters and Varied Levels of Speech Performance in Hearing-Impaired Adolescents

Parameter	Stimulus
Intelligibility	
Conversation	Interpersonal communication
Spontaneous speech	Pictures or film strip
Oral reading	Story, paragraph or sentences
Repetition	Sentences of varying length and complexity
Suprasegmental features	
Prosody	Spontaneous speech; oral reading, word/syllable repetition
Intonation	Statements and questions
Stress	Words and syllables
Pitch (register and control), intensity, rate, control of air expenditure, voice quality (breathy, tense, nasal, pharyngeal)	Spontaneous speech, oral reading, word/syllable repetition
Segmental features	
	Spontaneous speech; articulation words and sentences; word/syllable repetition
Vowels	Contrasts for diphthongs and vowels; long vowels and short vowels in words and CVC syllables
Consonants Manner	Contrasts for glides, nasals, stops, fricatives, and affricates in words and VCV syllables
Voicing	Contrasts for stops, fricatives, and affricates in words and VCV syllables
Place	Contrasts progression from front to back in words and VCV syllables

are assessed at repetition, oral reading, and spontaneous levels *before* evaluating the segmental features of vowels and consonants categorized by manner, voicing, and place. This ordering to evaluate production of segmental features is recommended because it follows the order of progressive difficulty in the auditory discrimination of features as defined by Boothroyd (1976 and 1978), Erber (1974), Pickett et al. (1972), and Risberg (1976). For each segmental feature, levels of difficulty in performance are similarly structured to progress from production of words and syllables in repetition (imitative level) to oral reading of articulation test words and sentences (nonimitative level) to spontaneous speech (generative level).

The word and syllable repetition tasks are designed also to assess contrasts in production and perception within each feature at progressive levels of difficulty. For example, minimal contrasts in VCV paradigms, such as [aba] − [aza] may be used as a same-difference auditory task and as an imitative production task to evaluate manner differentiation. Similarly, [apa] − [aba] and [apa] − [ata] may be used respectively to assess perception and production of voicing and place features. All repetition tasks first require an auditory and visual model with directions to "watch and listen carefully." The task may then be varied to the "listen only" condition. Considerable information pertaining to auditory and visual reception of suprasegmental and segmental aspects based on distinctive features may be accumulated in this way. The purpose of evaluating both perception and production at this very basic level is to facilitate a clinical comparison between the two skills which will assist in determining whether speech performance is commensurate with auditory perception of speech and in determining focal areas for remedial effort.

Perceptual ratings with descriptors ranging on a scale from 1 (very poor) to 5 (normal) are recommended to assess intelligibility and suprasegmental aspects of speech. The reliability and validity of such rating to evaluate the speech of hearing-impaired adolescents have been found to be satisfactory (Subtelny et al., 1980b). Training in the rating procedure, which involves practice in listening and

rating, is needed because several deviant features often coexist and interrelate within the speech pattern. Experience is required to analyze and then synthesize perceptual features so that the examiner can determine which basic processes (respiratory, phonatory, articulatory) are deviant. This determination is needed to establish priorities in training.

SPEECH INTELLIGIBILITY

Although various procedures have been described to analyze language samples (Lee, 1974; Lee and Canter, 1971; Myklebust 1964; O'Donnell et al., 1967; Streng et al., 1978), authorities seem to agree that further work is needed to standardize procedures in obtaining samples (Wilson, 1969) and to develop better analysis techniques (Byrne, 1978). Considering these facts, only general guidelines are suggested to assess the spoken language of the adolescent with severe hearing impairment.

The spoken language sample is mandatory and serves several purposes. First and commonly, the oral language sample is secured to describe the language used by the student in order to plan a program of remediation for both language and speech and to serve as a basis to evaluate progress in remediation. Second, within the hearing-impaired population, the sample is used as the most practical referent for intelligibility ratings and/or measurements. Third, the samples provide a context from which other parameters of speech may be evaluated at a generative or transformational level of performance. The "other parameters" should include phonology (segmental features) in spontaneous context and suprasegmental features.

The phonological analysis of the spontaneous speech samples may be compared with the results of articulation testing to identify phonemes which are correctly produced within structured situations but are not correctly produced in spontaneous speech. The knowledge that a feature or group of phonemes has not carried over into conversational use provides clear clinical direction.

Much of the information derived from analysis of spontaneous speech, particularly as it relates to the inflection or marking of nouns and verbs, helps to differentiate problems in speech from problems in language. The sounds (bound morphemes) used to indicate plural and possession for nouns /s, z, es, ez/ and to indicate verb tense /ed, t, ing/ are not only difficult to hear but also difficult to see. Since hearing-impaired speakers commonly err by dropping sounds at word, phrase, and sentence endings (Hudgins and Numbers, 1942; Levitt et al., 1976; Smith, 1975), the question becomes why. The errors may be partially attributed to faults in audition (perception), to faults in learning some of the morphological features of English (linguistic processing), and/or to faults in respiratory and articulatory control (production). If word endings are not accurately perceived, hearing-impaired adolescents frequently have great difficulty in learning and using grammatical rules for construction regardless of their skill in production.

By comparing speech during spontaneous production and during oral reading, it is possible to gain some impression of the basis for common errors. When oral reading is much more intelligible than spontaneous speech, the speaker probably has not internalized grammatical and syntactical rules adequately for communicative purposes, even though articulation may be adequate. To illustrate: An adolescent may produce /s/ and /z/ adequately on articulation test items but fail to produce these phonemes for pluralization or possession of nouns in conversational discourse. In this case, language rather than speech instruction is indicated, which should assist in the carryover of articulatory skill into conversational speech.

Procedure for Securing Samples

Before recording speech, some general observations about the quantity and quality of responses should be made. During conversations, is repetition requested frequently? Does comprehension require writing? Are most verbal responses single words, short phrases, or sentences? Are phrases grammatically correct? Is the student comfortable in conversation? If good rapport has not been established, it is far better to defer the recording until a later date. The speaker's attitude and feelings can have a marked effect upon the quantity and quality of the recording.

Pictures, a sequence of pictures, or short film strips appropriate to the age and interest of the student may be used to stimulate speech production which is supposed to sample common usage. In selecting an appropriate stimulus for a specific student, the needs of the speaker may well be considered within the reference expressed by Miller and Yoder (1972). The speaker needs (1) something to say, (2) a way to say it, and (3) a reason for saying it. Adolescents generally speak more freely about their own activities at home with family and at school with friends. The simple direction, "Tell me what you did today," is sometimes sufficient. On the other hand, at the communicative level of function, no stimulus will elicit speech from an adolescent who is resistant and has no desire to communicate orally. Whichever stimulus is selected, the directions should be presented clearly, repeated, and reinforced in writing as indicated.

In order to assure that the oral language sample can be analyzed to fulfill all purposes, recordings should be made with good equipment maintaining a constant mouth-to-microphone distance in a quiet environment. If the speaker does not use a drop in intonation to mark sentence endings, it will be difficult to determine where one sentence ends and the next begins. When this problem is anticipated, the speaker should be directed to pause briefly between sentences. From the recordings, scripts should be obtained and checked against the tape as often as is necessary to assure accuracy of transcription and to rate the suprasegmental aspects of the utterance.

Both directions and the procedures for obtaining and analyzing samples should be standardized (Darley, 1978) so that changes in performance over time can be attributed to the speaker rather than to the examiner. Since portions of the recording may be unintelligible, the examiner should note the stimulus used and any additions to the primary stimulus, if such were needed to achieve the minimum of 50 utterances recommended for analysis (Byrne, 1978; Lee and Canter, 1971; Lee, 1974).

Analysis Procedure

Fundamentally, the examiner needs to determine what aspects of the linguistic system are deficient and to define the general length, complexity, and intelligibility of utterances. At the adolescent stage of development within a mainstreamed setting, this need may be adequately met by a rather simple, straightforward analysis which lends the clinical direction sought. In the first step, the words produced are listed, categorized, and counted relative to grammatical component, as described by Byrne (1978). Nouns, pronouns, verbs, adjectives, and adverbs (contentives) are listed and counted separately. All other words, articles, prepositions, and conjunctions (the functors) are also categorized and counted. A percentage of use for each grammatical component is then established and compared with normative data (Berry, 1969; Lee, 1974) to identify disproportionate or deficient grammatical usage.

When errors occur, the words listed in grammatical categories should be phonetically transcribed to provide the examiner with a list of words currently used but incorrectly produced. This information, gleaned from the current speaking vocabulary, identifies early targets for correction from the phonological aspect. By focusing phoneme correction on words and phrases already within the speaker's repertoire, carryover of skill into conversational use may be greatly facilitated.

Further analysis of sentence structure yields additional insight as to which syntactic and grammatical features should be addressed in therapy. For example, after categorizing noun and verb phrases, the examiner can determine the following: Are the phrases in correct order? Are they complete? Are functors omitted? Are nouns and verbs in agreement? Are nouns inflected properly to indicate possession and number? Is tense correctly marked in regular and irregular verb forms? Are contractions used? Are reversals used appropriately in question forms? What percentage of the utterances are complete sentences? What level of intelligibility is achieved during spontaneous speech generation?

Definitive responses to these questions will assist in (1) combining targets for language and speech correction; (2) formulating descriptions of competence in speech to communicate with "significant others" in the stu-

dent's environment, thereby facilitating reinforcement of speech/language instruction; and (3) comparing levels of intelligibility during spontaneous speech with other measures, as previously described.

Oral Reading

To determine speech intelligibility during oral reading, the adolescent should be familiarized with material which is commensurate with reading competency. Preferably, one of the passages specifically designed for the purpose of speech evaluation should be used.[1] After orienting the student relative to purpose, procedure, and material, recordings are made and played back to one or several listeners who judge or rate how much of the message can be understood. A scale with descriptors is generally used to facilitate numerical ratings which may be averaged for several judges to determine a single index of intelligibility.[2]

An alternative procedure of the rating system, commonly used to assess a great variety of speech and voice disorders, involves recording of words produced in isolation or within sentence contexts. In this instance, the listeners write the words or sentences as understood, so that a percentage score of word intelligibility can be determined.

Many factors are known to affect the intelligibility of speech produced by hearing-impaired speakers. Some of these factors are attributed to characteristics of the listener, to the nature of the stimulus, and to the presentation of the stimulus. For example, the intelligibility of speech produced by the deaf is higher when the listener is experienced in listening to deaf speech (Asp, 1975; Hudgins

---

[1] The following passages for oral reading were prepared to measure speaking rate and to provide a quick survey of a speaker's ability to produce all of the sounds in speech: *Arthur, the Young Rat* (Williams et al., 1978, p. 276); *My Grandfather* (Van Riper, 1963, p. 484); and *The Rainbow Passage* (Fairbanks, 1960, p. 127).

[2] Descriptors for the Speech Intelligibility Rating Scale used at NTID are as follows: 5, speech is completely intelligible; 4, speech is intelligible with the exception of a few words or phrases; 3, with difficulty, the listener can understand about half the content of the message (intelligibility may improve after a listening period); 2, speech is very difficult to understand—only isolated words or phrases are intelligible; 1, speech is completely unintelligible.

and Numbers, 1942; McGarr, 1978). Intelligibility is also higher when the speaker reads aloud rather than speaks spontaneously (Calvert and Silverman, 1975) and when the speaker uses words within short phrases or sentence context rather than words in isolation (Miller et al., 1951; O'Neill, 1957 and 1975).

Intelligibility or comprehension is also influenced by visual cues of the speaker. Erber (1972), Ling (1978), and Johnson (1976) have stressed the fact that comprehension is improved for the hearing-impaired when speechreading and audition are combined. Speech intelligibility is also related to the speaker's degree of hearing loss (Boothroyd, 1970; Markides, 1970; Smith, 1975), configuration of loss (Ling and Ling, 1978; Risberg and Martony, 1972), hearing-aid use (Walter and Sims, 1978), and articulatory proficiency, as mentioned previously. These observations suggest a clustering of interrelated skills in speech, hearing, and speechreading as has been described for hearing-impaired students aged 10–14 years (Levitt et al., 1976). Study of these same skills in late adolescent students attending NTID (Subtelny and Walter, 1975) supports a similar observation of clustering (Fig. 10.3).

In Figure 10.3, means for measures of hearing discrimination, articulation, and speechreading with sound are graphed for 274 NTID students grouped on the basis of speech intelligibility ratings. The *dashed* and *dotted lines*, graphing corresponding means for articulation and speechreading, show a strong relationship (r, .69) between the two measures. Both measures (articulation and speechreading) are also highly correlated with intelligibility ratings (r, .80 and .81, respectively). The remarkable difference is that the means for articulation tend to be slightly higher than the corresponding means for speechreading for each speech grouping. Means for both articulation and speechreading are considerably higher than means for speech discrimination, but both are significantly related (r, .46 and .53) to measures of discrimination (*solid bold line*). Measures of speech discrimination and ratings of speech intelligibility were also significantly related (r, .58).

Despite limitations and difficulties, intelligibility ratings and measures are justified to provide a practical overall index of speech proficiency and a rather crude reliability and validity check on related communication measures. Since interrelationships between parameters have been established, measures in hearing, articulation, intelligibility, and speechreading may be used to predict associated skill or potential to develop skill in a related area (Johnson and Caccamise, 1981).

EVALUATION OF SUPRASEGMENTAL FEATURES

Prosody

Prosody, sometimes referred to as suprasegmental features, is defined as the intonation and stress patterns in speech which are superimposed upon the smaller speech sound segments combined in words, phrases, and sentences. Both intonation and stress contribute to the intelligibility of contextual speech. Intonation (variations in vocal pitch) is used to mark the ending of a phrase, to differentiate a question and statement, to show feeling, and sometimes to change in meaning. Stress, created by subtle changes in pitch, duration, and intensity of a syllable or word, similarly shows feeling and can change the meaning of a word (con′duct, ′con duct) or of a sentence (*I* will go, I *will* go).

The early developmental mastery of suprasegmental features (Berry, 1969; Menyuk, 1972) should not obscure the remarkable precision required to modify respiration, phonation, and articulation appropriately for normal prosodic features. The complex preplanning needed when sentences are linguistically formulated and produced provide a rational basis for the severe problems that many deaf speakers have in blending sounds, syllables, words, and phrases together within normal time constraints.

Since standardized clinical tests to evaluate prosody are not currently available, prosody is generally assessed by judgmental ratings. Such judgments can be secured from spontaneous speech, from oral reading, and from words in the short sentence contexts formulated to contrast questions and statements and to vary word and syllable stress. Short sentences, as described by Sussman and Hernandez (1979), are recommended to assess

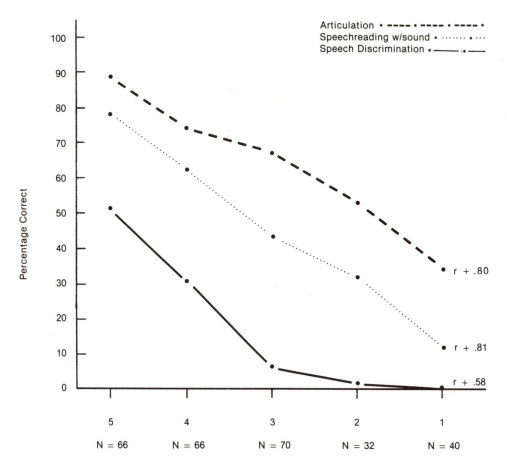

Figure 10.3. Means for measures of articulation, speechreading with sound, and speech discrimination, with students grouped on the basis of speech intelligibility ratings. Test material included the CID Everyday Sentences Test to determine percentage scores for key word recognition in speechreading and speech discrimination. The Arizona Articulation Proficiency Scale was used to determine percentage measures for sounds correctly produced (N = 274 students entering the National Technical Institute for the Deaf, 1972–73).

both auditory perception and production of prosodic features.

Vocal Pitch

Pitch, intensity, and voice qualities of tenseness and breathiness are all related to laryngeal function. For this basic reason, a quality deviation such as breathiness, attributed to faulty approximation of folds during tone generation, is commonly associated with reduced intensity, whereas excessive vocal tension generally is associated with an elevated pitch.

Because of the complex interrelationships existing between varied perceptual features identified with voice production, discrete perceptual ratings are needed to quantitatively and qualitatively assess the varied features to provide some priorities and direction for instruction. To illustrate: Consider aberration in pitch register and pitch control, which are common in deaf speakers (Angelocci et al.,

1964; Boone, 1966; Martony, 1968; McGarr and Osberger, 1978; and Zaliouk, 1960). The fundamental frequency of vocal fold vibration is determined by the tension and elasticity of the folds and by subglottal air pressure which is the power supply setting the folds in vibration. Stretching or increasing tension on the folds is effected by the cricothyroid muscles and by longitudinal tension indirectly applied to the folds via the suprahyoid muscles, which elevate the folds from above, or the infrahyoid muscles, which depress the folds from below. Since an abnormally high pitch register is identified with an aberrantly high vertical position of the larynx (Shipp, 1975) effected by muscle groups located above rather than below the larynx, assessment of pitch register should specify degree and direction of deviation from an optimal level in order to indicate a proper remedial procedure.

As stated, vocal pitch is controlled during phonation by vocal fold tension and by *subglottal air pressure*. When marked fluctuations in pitch occur during speech, the problem does not necessarily reflect an abnormally high laryngeal position but rather an inability to coordinate respiratory and phonatory muscles. Simply because remedial strategies (to relax vocal tension or to gain control of respiration) differ dependent upon causative factors, separate ratings of pitch register and control are recommended.

Quality

In conventional voice examinations, quality is identified and then quantitatively assessed both during continuous speech and during sustained vowel phonations, with variation in quality noted as pitch and intensity are progressively raised or lowered in singing or counting (Fairbanks, 1960; Morris and Spriestersbach, 1978). Although hearing-impaired adolescents generally are not requested to sing, observations of quality during continuous speech and sustained vowel phonation are required. This is particularly important because studies of voice disorders have shown that the quality defects, said to be perceptually and acoustically based in vowels, may be more apparent during continuous speech than during sustained vowel production (Boone, 1971; Carney and Sherman,

1971; Sherman and Linke, 1952). Calvert (1962), whose study of deaf voice quality was no exception in this regard, attributed his findings to the very slow articulatory movements observed in deaf speakers and to the influence of the phonetic environment (coarticulation) upon vowel production and perception.

The interactive effects of articulation, phonation, and respiration may be illustrated by a consideration of one common fault in deaf speakers—the overaspiration of stop and fricative consonants in initial positions (Hudgins, 1946; Hutchinson and Smith, 1976; Whitehead and Barefoot, 1980). This fault has been attributed to inept teaching and to the habitual use of excessively high intraoral pressure for constrictive consonant production said to increase tactile feedback for the deaf speaker. The overaspiration in articulation distorts the temporal features and lends a breathy quality to the speech pattern, which may not be related to laryngeal malfunction or faulty approximation of the folds.

In order to differentiate deviant articulatory and phonatory function, judgments of quality during sustained phonation of vowels [i] [u] [ɑ] requiring extremes in tongue position should be compared with judgments of the same vowels combined in VCV syllables with the intervocalic consonants varied progressively to sample respective features of manner and voicing. In these imitative tasks, the conditions under which the quality varies can be determined.

In order to confirm an impression that breathiness is related to articulation rather than phonation, words from the Iowa Pressure Test (Morris et al., 1961) may be read or repeated by the speaker. Since words on this test were specifically selected because of high intraoral pressure requirements, breathiness should become increasingly apparent if the disturbance is articulatory in nature.

In order to confirm an impression that breathiness is laryngeal in origin, the maximum duration in sustaining a vowel may be timed. According to Fox (1978), if normal coordination of respiration and phonation exists, a speaker should be able to sustain a vowel with relative constant pitch and intensity for 6–10 seconds without strain. When phonation cannot be sustained for 6 seconds, the examiner attempts to identify one of the following conditions:

1. The folds are not approximating, or they are late in approximating after considerable glottal flow has occurred;
2. The folds are excessively tense and overadducting to restrict glottal flow;
3. Inhalation is too shallow to sustain phonation; or
4. Air is simultaneously expired through both oral and nasal tracts.

Any one or a combination of these conditions will adversely affect quality and prosody by altering respiration during speech, which is frequently deviant in hearing-impaired speakers (Forner and Hixon, 1977; Whitehead, in press). Remediation of the problem will logically depend upon which condition is causative. For this reason, timing phonation, determining the rate of syllable and word production, and observing respiration during continuous speech production should be included in assessment procedures when voice quality and prosody are deviant.

The general procedures described to assess breathiness may be applied to evaluate other voice qualities, i.e., vocal tension, nasal resonance, and pharyngeal resonance, as described by Boone (1966).

ASSESSMENT OF SEGMENTAL FEATURES

Articulation testing is the conventional method of evaluating segmental features as an aid to planning speech therapy. Fundamentally, the examiner strives to determine the speaker's ability to produce a wide range of speech sounds in varied positions and contexts. There are acknowledged difficulties and limitations in making such determinations and in interpreting the information to plan speech instruction for hearing-impaired adolescents.

One limitation in articulation testing relates to the basic difference in performance for production of a sound in single words as opposed to production of the sound in contextual speech. Another limitation is the small size of the phonetic sampling generally obtained. Still another limitation, especially as it would apply to hearing-impaired speakers, is the stimulus to production. As elaborated

elsewhere, producing a single word in response to print or picture stimulus requires lesser cognitive and linguistic skill than producing the word spontaneously in conversation. Despite limitations, testing of articulation in word and sentence contexts is highly recommended when supplemented with other observations of speech skill within conversational contexts and also within VCV and CVC syllables when further information is needed.

Articulation tests provide an organized system to assess all phonemes produced in desired contexts so that patterns of error can be defined. Since type of error, consistency, and error position within words all appear to exert variable effects upon intelligibility, the pattern of error determined by standardized procedures should be undertaken. In these procedures, stimulus presentations may be varied to elicit both spontaneous and imitative responses in word and/or sentence contexts.

Standardized assessments of stimulability (Turton, 1976) may also be made to assist in target selections. Other factors influencing target selection include phoneme perception, visibility, motoric complexity in production, and frequency of occurrence in conversational English. With hearing-impaired adolescents, target selection is facilitated by administering a test, such as the Fisher-Logemann Test of Articulation Competence (Fisher and Logemann, 1971), which provides an analysis of production by distinctive features, i.e. manner, voicing, and place. The results can then be directly related to a feature analysis of auditory perception.

Distinctive features defined by Singh (1976) as "the physical (articulatory or acoustic) and psychological (perceptual) realities of the phoneme" are described as underlying phoneme recognition and production. Sounds are said to be perceived as bundles of features and produced by combining requisite features. For this reason, analysis of auditory perception and production on a simplified (phonetic) feature basis is clinically recommended for an adolescent speaker with auditory impairment. A comparison of feature perception and production serves well to focus remediation on auditory and/or speech training to correct a feature violation, which may be common to several phonemes in auditory perception and in production, or exclusively noted in perception or production.

This recommendation is supported by a basic relationship which exists between auditory perception and speech production in speakers with normal hearing (Winitz, 1969, 1975, and 1980) and impaired hearing (Boothroyd, 1976; Markides, 1970); by an expanding body of research relating perception of features to pure tone response in normal and hearing-impaired subjects (Bilger and Wang, 1976; Caccamise, 1973; Pickett, 1979; Walden and Montgomery, 1975); and by research showing that speech remediation is most efficient if training is focused upon features rather than phonemes (McLean, 1976; McReynolds and Bennett, 1972).

INTERRELATIONSHIPS BETWEEN PERCEPTION AND PRODUCTION

In discussing articulatory disorders in hearing populations, most authorities (McDonald, 1980; Turton, 1976; Van Riper, 1963) recommend that auditory discrimination be included with the testing of articulation and stimulability. When speakers are known to have impaired audition, the relative importance of testing speech reception from sentence to phoneme levels becomes even more important. Recognizing that phonemes and features are in some respects rather well differentiated acoustically and physiologically, it is hypothesized (1) that some features will be perceived with a higher degree of accuracy than others, (2) that features perceived with greater accuracy will be produced more intelligibly, and (3) that performance in both perception and production will be related to the extent of hearing loss.

Based on these projections, phoneme perception and production in CV contexts were comparatively studied in a group of 160 young adults attending NTID (Subtelny, in press). Students were categorized by degree of hearing loss to study relationships between perception and production before and after combined speech and auditory training. The results of testing phoneme identification (Jones et al., 1976) and production showed that scores for both perception and production became progressively lower as the degree of hearing loss increased. Scores for percep-

tion were consistently lower than the corresponding scores for production in all groups of subjects. Pattern of performance in perception and production were also revealed when consonants were grouped by manner features.

Since some manner features are perceived and produced with greater accuracy than others and since the relationship between perception and production varies with degree of loss, it is strongly recommended that diagnosis involve separate analyses of consonant perception and production so that these relationships can be studied within the reference of subject's degree of hearing loss. Through this type of analysis, the clinician can determine whether training should focus on perception, production, or involve training in both perception and production. The recommended analysis also helps identify target features for improvement and provides base line data permitting the teacher and student to determine changes in performance incident to training.

An example may clarify these diagnostic implications. Speaker D in Figure 10.4 had a discrimination score for words in sentence context of 28% and a pure tone average of 88 dB, with cutoff at 8 kHz. As shown in Figure 10.4, this speaker had comparatively poor perception of plosives, fricatives, and sibilants and had below-average (for adolescent speakers with comparable degrees of loss) production skill for these three groups of consonants. Compositely, these observations suggested that therapy should combine auditory and production training focused on plosive-fricative differentiations.

Measures of perception and production after this speaker received 28 hours of individualized training revealed significant improvement for both plosives and fricatives. Perception and production of glides also improved significantly, although this manner group was not targeted in training.

The overall results of this study indicate that relatively large gains in consonant production can be achieved as a result of training. Smaller but significant gains in consonant perception were associated with improvements in production, but vowel perception and production improved minimally. When the sample was subdivided on the basis of auditory discrimination, greater gains for

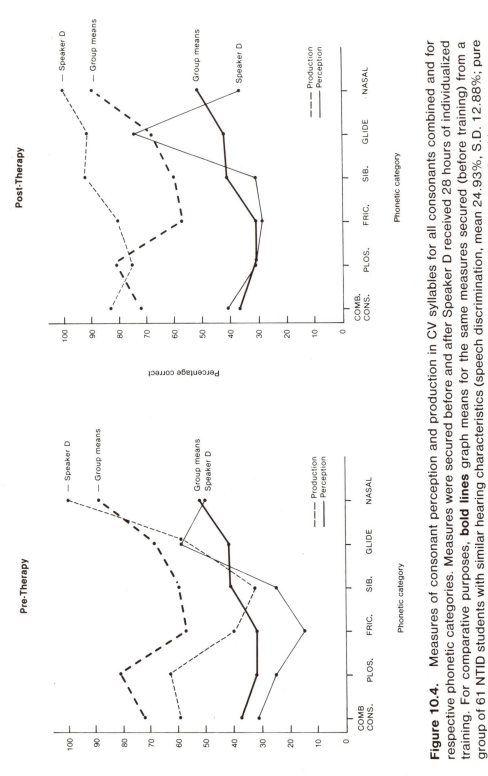

Figure 10.4. Measures of consonant perception and production in CV syllables for all consonants combined and for respective phonetic categories. Measures were secured before and after Speaker D received 28 hours of individualized training. For comparative purposes, **bold lines** graph means for the same measures secured (before training) from a group of 61 NTID students with similar hearing characteristics (speech discrimination, mean 24.93%, S.D. 12.88%; pure tone average, mean 85.03 dB, S.D. 13.46 dB). By comparing the measurements for Speaker D with group means, remarkable improvements in perception and production are evident after training.

most speech measures and for auditory discrimination were identified with students who had some discrimination for speech.

In overview, these findings offer support for Ling's clinical statement that training in production will improve perception (Ling, 1976). The results also agree with data reported by Ling and Maretic (1971) and by Novelli-Olmstead (1979). Consistent gains in production and perception can be achieved if audiological information is used prescriptively to improve phoneme perception and if target selection and training strategies are based upon prescriptive information provided by assessing both perception and production.

In summary, successful planning of communication training for the hearing-impaired adolescent requires appropriate procedures to assess the individual as a person, his/her functional use of language, and his/her characteristics of hearing and speech. Some guidelines for assessment have been suggested for varied parameters and for varying levels of performance. It is projected that broader gains in communication can be achieved by integrating speech, language, speechreading, and auditory training with relative emphasis determined by respective assessments.

References

Angelocci, A.A. Some observations on the speech of the deaf. *Volta Rev.*, 1962, 9, 403–405.

Angelocci, A.A., Kopp, G.A., and Holbrook, A. The vowel formants of deaf and normal hearing eleven to fourteen-year old boys. *J. Speech Hear. Disord.*, 1964, 29, 156–170.

Asp, C.W. Measurement of aural speech perception and oral speech production of the hearing-impaired. In S. Singh (ed.), *Measurement Procedures in Speech, Hearing, and Language*. Baltimore: University Park Press, 1975.

Berry, M.F. *Language Disorders of Childen: The Bases and Diagnosis*. New York: Appleton-Century-Crofts, 1969.

Bilger, R.C., and Wang, M.D. Consonant confusions in patients with sensorineural hearing loss. *J. Speech Hear. Res.*, 1976, 19, 718–748.

Boone, D.R. Modification of the voices of deaf children. *Volta Rev.*, 1966, 11, 686–692.

Boone, D.R. *The Voice and Voice Therapy*. Englewood Cliffs, New Jersey: Prentice-Hall, 1971.

Boothroyd, A. *A Distribution of Hearing Levels in the Student Population of the Clarke School for the Deaf*, SARP Report #3. Northampton, Massachusetts: Clarke School for the Deaf, 1970.

Boothroyd, A. *Influence of Residual Hearing on Speech Perception and Speech Production by Hearing-Impaired Children*, SARP Report #26. Northampton, Massachusetts: Clarke School for the Deaf, 1976.

Boothroyd, A. Speech perception and sensorineural hearing loss. In M. Ross and T. Giolas (eds.), *Auditory Management of Hearing-Impaired Children*. Baltimore: University Park Press, 1978.

Borden, G.J., and Harris, K.S. *Speech Science Primer: Physiology, Acoustics, and Perception of Soeech*. Baltimore: Williams & Wilkins, 1980.

Brannon, J.B. Visual feedback of glossal motions and its influence on the speech of deaf children. Doctoral dissertation, Northwestern University, 1964.

Brannon, J.B. The speech production and spoken language of the deaf. *Lang. Speech*, 1966, 9, 127–136.

Byrne, M.C. Appraisal of child language acquisition. In F. Darley and D. Spriestersbach (eds.), *Diagnostic Methods in Speech Pathology*. New York: Harper & Row, 1978.

Caccamise, F.C. An analysis of hearing-impaired persons' responses to C/i syllables under three test modes. Doctoral dissertation, University of Washington, Seattle, 1973.

Calvert, D.R. Deaf voice quality: A preliminary investigation. *Volta Rev.*, 1962, 9, 402–403.

Calvert, D.R., and Silverman, S.R. *Speech and Deafness*. Washington, D.C.: A.G. Bell Association for the Deaf, 1975.

Carney, P.J., and Sherman, D. Severity of nasality in three selected speech tests. *J. Speech Hear. Res.*, 1971, 14, 396–407.

Chastain, K.D. A methodological study comparing the audio-lingual habit theory and the cognitive code-learning theory: Continued. *Mod. Lang. J.*, 1970, 54, 257–266.

Chastain, K.D. Behavioristic and cognitive approaches in programmed instruction. In H.B. Allen and R.N. Campbell (eds.), *Teaching English as a Second Language: A Book of Readings*. New York: McGraw-Hill, 1972.

Chastain, K.D., and Woerdehoff, F.J. A methodological study comparing the audiolingual habit theory and the cognitive code-learning theory. *Mod. Lang. J.*, 1968, 52, 268–279.

Cohen, O.P. The deaf adolescent: Who am I? *Volta Rev.*, 1978, 80, 265–274.

Coleman, J.C. *Personality Dynamics and Effective Behavior*. Chicago: Scott, Foresman, 1960.

Darley, F.L. Appraisal of acquired language disorders. In F.L. Darley and D.C. Spriestersbach (eds.), *Diagnostic Methods in Speech Pathology*. New York: Harper & Row, 1978.

Davis, J. *Our Forgotten Children: Hard-of-Hearing Pupils in the Schools*. Minneapolis: Bureau of Education for the Handicapped, Department of Health, Education, and Welfare, 1977.

Elbert, M., Shelton, R.L., and Arndt, W.B. A task for evaluation of articulation change: 1. Development of methodology. *J. Speech Hear. Res.*, 1967, 10, 281–288.

Erber, N.P. Auditory, visual and auditory-visual recognition of consonants by children with normal and impaired hearing. *J. Speech Hear. Res.*, 1972, 15, 423–438.

Erber, N.P. Pure-tone thresholds and word-recognition abilities of hearing-impaired children. *J. Speech Hear.*

Res., 1974, *17*, 194–202.

Fairbanks, G. *Voice and Articulation Drillbook*, ed. 2. New York: Harper & Row, 1960.

Faircloth, M.A., and Faircloth, S.R. An analysis of the articulatory behavior of a speech defective child in connected speech and in isolated-word responses. *J. Speech Hear. Disord.*, 1970, *33*, 51–61.

Fisher, H.B., and Logemann, J.A. *The Fisher-Logemann Test of Articulation Competence.* Boston: Houghton Mifflin, 1971.

Forner, L.L., and Hixon, T.J. Respiratory kinematics in profoundly hearing-impaired speakers. *J. Speech Hear. Res.*, 1977, *20*, 373–408.

Fox, D.R. Evaluation of voice disorders. In S. Singh and J. Lynch (eds.), *Diagnostic Procedures in Hearing, Language, and Speech.* Baltimore: University Park Press, 1978.

Garrett, E.R. Programmed articulation therapy. In W.D. Wolfe and D.J. Goulding (eds.), *Articulation and Learning.* Springfield, Illinois: Charles C Thomas, Publisher, 1973.

Geffner, D.S., and Freeman, L.R. Speech assessment at the primary level: Interpretation relative to speech training. In J. Subtelny (ed.), *Speech Assessment and Speech Improvement for the Hearing Impaired.* Washington, D.C.: A.G. Bell Association for the Deaf, 1980.

Harris, K.S., and McGarr, N.S. Relationships between speech perception and speech production in normal-hearing and hearing-impaired subjects. In J. Subtelny (ed.), *Speech Assessment and Speech Improvement for the Hearing-Impaired.* Washington, D.C.: A.G. Bell Association for the Deaf, 1980.

Hollis, J.H., Carrier, J.K., and Spradlin, J.E. An approach to remediation of communication and learning deficiencies. In L. Lloyd (ed.), *Communication Assessment and Intervention Strategies.* Baltimore: University Park Press, 1976.

Hudgins, C.V. Speech breathing and speech intelligibility. *Volta Rev. 1946, 48,* 642–644.

Hudgins, C.V., and Numbers, F.C. An investigation of the intelligibility of the speech of the deaf. *Genet. Psychol. Monogr.*, 1942, *25*, 289–392.

Hudgins, C.V. A method of appraising the speech of the deaf. *Volta Rev.*, 1949, *51*, 597–638.

Hutchinson, J.M., and Smith, L.L. Aerodynamic functioning in consonant production by hearing-impaired adults. *Audiol. Hear. Educ.*, 1976, 16–25.

Jensema, C.J., Karchmer, M.A., and Trybus, R.J. *The Rated Speech Intelligibility of Hearing Impaired Children: Basic Relationships and Detailed Analysis*, Series R, Number 6. Washington, D.C.: Gallaudet College, Office of Demographic Studies, 1978.

John, J.E., and Howarth, J.N. The effect of time distortions on the intelligibility of deaf children's speech. *Lang. Speech*, 1965, *8*, 127–134.

Johnson, D.D. Communication characteristics of a young deaf adult population: Techniques for evaluating their communication skills. *Am. Ann. Deaf*, 1976, *121*, 409–424.

Johnson, D.D., and Caccamise, F.C. Rationale and strategies for planning communication individualized education programs (CIEP) for deaf students. *Am. Ann. Deaf*, 1981, *126*, 370–381.

Johnson, J.P. *Nature and Treatment of Articulation Disorders.* Springfield, Illinois: Charles C Thomas, Publisher, 1980.

Jones, K., Whitehead, R., Bancroft, J., and Sims, D. The performance of students at the National Technical Institute for the Deaf on an auditory speech perception test. Paper presented at the American Speech and Hearing Association Convention, Houston, 1976.

Lee, L.L. *Developmental Sentence Analysis.* Evanston, Illinois: Northwestern University Press, 1974.

Lee, L.L., and Canter, S.M. Developmental sentence scoring: A clinical procedure for estimating syntactic development in children's spontaneous speech. *J. Speech Hear. Disord.*, 1971, *36*, 315–340.

Levitt, H., Stark, R., McGarr, N.S., Carp, J., Stromberg, H., Gaffney, R.S., Barry, C., Velez, A., Osberger, M.J., Leiter, E., and Freeman, L. Language communication skills of deaf children, 1973–76. In *Proceedings of Language Assessments for the Hearing Impaired: A Work Study Institute.* Rome, New York: New York State Education Department, New York School for the Deaf, 1976.

Li, W. A comparative cephalometric and cineradiographic study of speech produced by hearing and deaf women. Master's thesis, Eastman Dental Center and the University of Rochester, 1980.

Libbey, S. Attitudes toward communication of "mainstreamed" hearing-impaired adolescents. Master's thesis, Boston University, Department of Special Education, 1978.

Lieberth, A., and Subtelny, J. The effect of speech training on auditory phoneme identification. *Volta Rev.*, 1978, *80*, 410–417.

Ling, D. *Speech and the Hearing-Impaired Child: Theory and Practice.* Washington, D.C.: A.G. Bell Association for the Deaf, 1976.

Ling, D. Auditory coding and recoding: An analysis of auditory training procedures for hearing-impaired children. In M. Ross and T. Giolas (eds.), *Auditory Management of Hearing-Impaired Children.* Baltimore: University Park Press, 1978.

Ling, D., and Ling, A. *Aural Habilitation: The Foundations of Verbal Learning in Hearing-Impaired Children.* Washington, D.C. A.G. Bell Association for the Deaf, 1978.

Ling, D., and Maretic, H. Frequency transposition in the teaching of speech to deaf children. *J. Speech Hear. Res.*, 1971, *14*, 37–46.

Markides, A. The speech of deaf and partially-hearing children with special reference to factors affecting intelligibility. *Br. J. Disord. Commun.*, 1970, *5*, 126–140.

Martony, J. On the correction of the voice pitch level for severely hard of hearing subjects. *Am. Ann. Deaf*, 1968, *113*, 195–202.

McDonald, E.T. Disorders of articulation. In R.J. Van Hattum (ed.), *Communication Disorders: An Introduction.* New York: MacMillan, 1980.

McGarr, N.A. The difference between experienced and inexperienced listeners in understanding the speech of the deaf. Doctoral dissertation, City University of New York, 1978.

McGarr, N., and Osberger, M. Pitch deviancy in intelligibility of deaf speech. *J. Commun. Disord.*, 1978, *11*, 237–247.

McLean, J.E. Articulation. In L.L. Lloyd (ed.), *Communication Assessment and Intervention Strategies*. Baltimore: University Park Press, 1976.

McReynolds, L., and Bennett, S. Distinctive feature generalization in articulation training. *J. Speech Hear. Disord.*, 1972, *37*, 462–470.

Menyuk, P. *The Development of Speech*. New York: Bobbs-Merrill, 1972.

Miller, G.A., Heise, G.A., and Lichten, W. The intelligibility of speech as a function of the context of test material. *J. Exp. Psychol.*, 1951, *41*, 329–335.

Miller, J., and Yoder, D. A syntax teaching program. In J. McLean, D. Yoder, and R. Schiefelbush (eds.), *Language Intervention with the Retarded: Developing Strategies*. Baltimore: University Park Press, 1972.

Monsen, R.B. Toward measuring how well deaf children speak. *J. Speech Hearing Res.*, 1978, *21*, 197–219.

Moores, D.F. *Educating the Deaf—Psychology, Principles, and Practices*. Boston: Houghton Mifflin, 1978.

Morris, H.L., and Spriestersbach, D.C. Appraisal of resonance. In F.L. Darley and D.C. Spriestersbach (eds.), *Diagnostic Methods in Speech Pathology*, ed. 2. New York: Harper & Row, 1978.

Morris, H.L., Spriestersbach, D.C., and Darley, F.L. An articulation test for assessing competency of velo-pharyngeal closure. *J. Speech Hear. Res.*, 1961, *4*, 48–55.

Myklebust, H. *The Psychology of Deafness*. New York: Grune & Stratton, 1964.

Neufeld, G.G. On the adult's ability to acquire phonology. *TESOL Q.*, 1980, *14*, 285–298.

Nickerson, R.S. Characteristics of the speech of deaf persons. *Volta Rev.*, 1975, *77*, 342–362.

Nober, E.H. Articulation of the deaf. *Except. Child.*, 1967, *33*, 611–621.

Novelli-Olmstead, T. Production and reception of speech by hearing-impaired children. Master's thesis, McGill University, Montreal, 1979.

O'Donnell, R.D., Griffin, W.J., and Norris, R.C. *Syntax of Kindergarten and Elementary School Children: A Transformational Analysis*, Research Report #8. Champaign, Illinois: NCTE Committee on Research, 1967.

O'Neill, J.J. Recognition of intelligibility test materials. *J. Speech Hear. Disord.*, 1957, *22*, 87–90.

O'Neill, J.J. Measurement of hearing by tests of speech and language. In S. Singh (ed.), *Measurement Procedures in Speech, Hearing and Language*. Baltimore: University Park Press, 1975.

Osberger, M.J. The effect of timing errors on the intelligibility of deaf children's speech. Doctoral dissertation, City University of New York, 1978.

Pickett, J.M. Perception of speech features by persons with hearing impairment. *Curr. Issues Linguist. Theory*, 1979, *9*, 721–736.

Pickett, J.M., Martin, E., Johnson, D., Smith, S., Daniel, Z., Willis, D., and Otis, W. On patterns of speech feature reception by deaf listeners. In G. Fant (ed.), *International Symposium on Speech Communication Ability and Profound Deafness*. Washington, D.C.: A.G. Bell Association for the Deaf, 1972.

Pollack, E., and Rees, N. Disorders of articulation: Some clinical applications of distinctive feature theory. *J. Speech Hear. Disord.*, 1972, *37*, 451–461.

Pronovost, W.L. Communicating with the world-at-large. *Volta Rev.*, 1978, *80*, 301–318.

Risberg, A. Diagnostic rhyme test for speech audiometry with severely hard of hearing and profoundly deaf children. In *Quarterly Progress and Status Report*. Stockholm: Speech Transmission Laboratory, 1976, *3*, 40–58.

Risberg, A., and Martony, J. A method for classification of audiograms. In G. Fant (ed.), *Speech Communication Ability and Profound Deafness*. Washington, D.C.: A.G. Bell Association for the Deaf, 1972.

Ruder, K.R., and Bunce, B.H. Articulation therapy using distinctive feature analysis to structure the training program: Two case studies. *J. Speech Hear. Disord.*, 1981, *46*, 59–65.

Sherman, D., and Linke E. The influence of certain vowel types on degree of harsh voice quality. *J. Speech Hear. Disord.*, 1952, *17*, 401–408.

Shipp, T. Vertical laryngeal positions during continuous and discrete vocal frequency change. *J. Speech Hear. Res.*, 1975, *18*, 707–718.

Singh, S. *Distinctive Features: Theory and Validation*. Baltimore: University Park Press, 1976.

Smith, C. Residual hearing and speech production in deaf children. *J. Speech Hear. Res.*, 1975, *18*, 795–811.

Stevens, K.N., Nickerson, R.S., and Rollins, A.M. On describing the suprasegmental properties of the speech of deaf children. In D.L. McPherson and M.S. Davis (eds.), *Advances in Prosthetic Devices for the Deaf: A Technical Workshop*. Rochester, New York: National Technical Institute for the Deaf/Rochester Institute of Technology, 1978.

Streng, A.H., Kretschmer, R.R., and Kretschmer, L.W. *Language, Learning and Deafness*. New York: Grune & Stratton, 1978.

Subtelny, J.D. Is it ever too late for deaf adults to improve their speech? Paper presented at the A.G. Bell Association for the Deaf Convention, Boston, Massachusetts, 1976.

Subtelny, J.D. Assessment of speech with implications for training. In F.H. Bess (ed.), *Childhood Deafness: Causation, Assessment and Management*. New York: Grune & Stratton, 1977.

Subtelny, J.D. Patterns of performance in speech perception and production. In I. Hochberg, H. Levitt, and M.J. Osberger (eds.), *Speech of the Hearing Impaired: Research, Training and Personnel Preparation*. Baltimore: University Park Press (in press).

Subtelny, J.D., Orlando, N.A., and Webster, P.E. Evaluation of speech training at the postsecondary level. In J. Subtelny (ed.), *Speech Assessment and Speech Improvement for the Hearing Impaired*. Washington, D.C.: A.G. Bell Association for the Deaf, 1980a.

Subtelny, J.D., and Walter, G.G. An overview of communication skills of NTID students with implications for planning rehabilitation. *J. Acad. Rehabil. Audiol.*, 1975, *8*, 33–50.

Subtelny, J.D., Whitehead, R.L., and Orlando, N.A. Description and evaluation of an instructional program to improve speech and voice diagnosis of the hearing impaired. *Volta Rev.*, 1980b, *82*, 85–95.

Sussman, H., and Hernandez, M. A spectrographic analysis of the suprasegmental aspects of the speech of hearing-impaired adolescents. *Audiol. Hear. Educ.*, 1979, *5*, 12–16.

Thomas, W. Intelligibility of the speech of deaf children. In *Proceedings of the International Congress on the Education of the Deaf*, Document No. 106, 1963.

Turton, L.M. Diagnostic implications of articulation testing. In D. Wolfe and D. Goulding (eds.), *Articulation and Learning*, Springfield, Illinois: Charles C Thomas, Publisher, 1976.

Van Riper, C. *Speech Correction: Principles and Methods*, ed. 4. Englewood Cliffs, New Jersey: Prentice-Hall, 1963.

Walden, B.E., and Montgomery, A.A. Dimensions of consonant perception in normal and hearing-impaired listeners. *J. Speech Hear. Res.*, 1975, *18*, 444–455.

Walter, G., and Sims, D. The effect of prolonged hearing aid use on the communicative skills of young deaf adults. *Am. Ann. Deaf*, 1978, *123*, 548–554.

Whitehead, R. Some respiratory and aerodynamic patterns in the hearing impaired. In I. Hochberg, H. Levitt, and M.J. Osberger (eds.), *Speech of the Hearing Impaired: Research, Training and Personnel Preparation*. Baltimore: University Park Press (in press).

Whitehead, R., and Barefoot, S. Some aerodynamic characteristics of plosive consonants produced by hearing-impaired speakers. *Am. Ann. Deaf*, 1980, *125*, 366–373.

Williams, D.E., Darley, F.L., and Spriestersbach, D.C. Appraisal of rate and fluency. In F.L. Darley and D.C. Spriestersbach (eds.), *Diagnostic Methods in Speech Pathology*, ed. 2. New York: Harper & Row, 1978.

Wilson, M.E. A standardized method for obtaining a spoken language sample. *J. Speech Hear. Res.*, 1969, *12*, 95–102.

Winitz, H. *Articulatory Acquisition and Behavior*. New York: Appleton-Century-Crofts, 1969.

Winitz, H. *From Syllable to Conversation*. Baltimore: University Park Press, 1975.

Winitz, H. Auditory knowledge and articulation disorders of the hearing impaired. In J. Subtelny (ed.), *Speech Assessment and Speech Improvement for the Hearing Impaired*. Washington, D.C.: A.G. Bell Association for the Deaf, 1980.

Zaliouk, A. Falsetto voice in deaf children. *Curr. Prob. Phoniatr. Logopedics*, 1960, *1*, 217–226.

Chapter 11

English Skill Assessment with the Severely Hearing-Impaired

GERARD G. WALTER, ED.D.

EXPERIENCE

VOCABULARY
    SIZE OF LEXICON
    KNOWLEDGE OF MORPHEMES
    INFLECTED WORDS
    WORD FLEXIBILITY

SYNTAX
    STRUCTURAL CATEGORIES
    WITHIN CATEGORY ASSESSMENT

RECEPTIVE AND EXPRESSIVE SKILLS
    RECEPTIVE SKILLS
    EXPRESSIVE SKILLS
        STIMULUS MATERIALS
        GRAMMATICAL CORRECTNESS
        VOCABULARY USE
        ORDER OF IDEAS

A severe to profound impairment in the auditory mechanism makes the learning of English (or any other auditorily based language) a monumental task for the afflicted individual. A majority of hearing-impaired people do not achieve levels in reading and writing comparable to their hearing peers. Swisher (1976), Moores (1970), Cooper and Rosenstein (1966), and Trybus and Karchmer (1977) have all reviewed the literature on English skills of deaf children and come to the same conclusion: In reading, writing, and speaking, the deaf child lags several years behind the hearing child. Furthermore, given the late age at which many linguistic structures still are not mastered by hearing-impaired children, it is likely that these children are experiencing more than simple retardation in development. In fact, some studies comparing the psycholinguistic abilities of deaf and hearing children have concluded that deaf persons may be using rules to process English that are different from the rules used by their hearing peers (Tweney and Hoemann, 1973; Sarachan-Deily and Love, 1974; Bochner, 1978). Moores (1971) has stated, " . . . it is evident that the language ability of deaf students differs from that of hearing both quantitatively and qualitatively [p. 21]."

These results suggest that it might be unreasonable to assume that a deaf student, scoring at an eighth grade level on a standardized reading test, would behave linguistically like a 13-year-old hearing student reading at grade level. It follows that a simple grade equivalency score on a reading test would provide little information concerning how a particular deaf student approaches a reading task. Furthermore, it has been suggested that standardized reading tests yield spuriously high scores for deaf students (Moores, 1971). It seems, then, that what is necessary is a more diagnostic approach to evaluating deaf individuals' English performance beyond mere comprehension and grammatical scores on standardized tests. What is needed is a multifaceted assessment approach to evaluating the English skills of individual hearing-impaired persons. The importance of a multivariate approach to assessing competency in English has been noted on many authors. Chall (1958) specifically states that

"of the diverse stylistic elements that have been reliably measured and found significantly related to difficulty, only four types can be distinguished: vocabulary, sentence structure, idea density, and human interest [p. 157]."

Following the lead of Chall, and others, this paper will attempt to outline a series of variables that must be attended to when choosing or developing test instruments to use with hearing-impaired individuals. As such, the chapter will discuss three broad areas: vocabulary, syntax, and experiential-level. Beyond these three areas, the chapter will move to discuss the applications of each of these in a receptive English task (reading) and in an expressive English task (writing). In this way, it is expected that the reader will be able to achieve a sensitivity to those variables that must be appreciated when evaluating English skills of severe and profoundly hearing-impaired individuals.

EXPERIENCE

In teaching English, instructors have traditionally emphasized vocabulary building and syntactical understanding as the most important components of the curriculum. However, language is also dependent, to some degree, on the social context and the experience an individual brings to the language learning situation (Ervin-Tripp, 1968). The role of experience is usually assumed, and its contribution to being a competent user of English is seldom systematically considered.

For most hearing students who already know, implicitly, the rules of the language and have a relatively large vocabulary, the nature of the content used in English instruction is probably relatively minor. Such may not be true for the severely to profoundly hearing-impaired person. Before discussing evaluating vocabulary and syntactic skills, let's more clearly define what is meant by this concept of experience.

Experience is best defined as that body of information a student brings with him/her to the learning activity. It is all the stored information about the content used in the exercise, and would incorporate such things as space-time relationships, reality versus fantasy, significance, interrelationships, etc. In a sense, it is the way the student orders his world and the relationships among persons, places, and events.

Consider for a moment an exercise in which students are asked to write about a drawing of the Statue of Liberty. As a teacher, you have received the following two paragraphs for two separate students.

(1) This picture is a statue of a king holding a club. It must be big, because he goes into the sky. There is an airplane and clouds in the picture.
(2) This is a picture of the Statue of Liberty. It is in New York City, and it is very tall. It was given to the U.S. by France as a sign of friendship. It is a great symbol for the U.S.

In the two paragraphs above, there certainly are no problems with English, but the knowledge the student was able to bring to bear on producing the first paragraph greatly limited what could be said, the vocabulary choice, and perhaps even the syntactic constructions available for use. The same functions are operating when we read. In the production and comprehension we must bring to bear not only our linguistic competence but also all our experiential knowledge. While I like to think of myself as a competent user of English, I have great difficulty understanding the writings of the Existentialists.

If we have made the point of what we mean by experience, then how do we go about measuring it in hearing-impaired individuals? Unfortunately, there are no tests which can be used. As an instructor, you should always be asking yourself, "Will the materials I am using to evaluate English skills inhibit the English productivity of the students?" Are you expecting them to read and write about materials for which they have no adequate basis of knowledge?

It must be remembered that much of the information that hearing learners take in comes through audition and reading. We depend heavily on these modes, and it is just these avenues of communication with which the hearing-impaired person has difficulty. As teachers, we must always question whether it is English we are measuring or the student's world knowledge. Try putting yourself in the position of the severely to profoundly hearing-impaired individual writing about the Statue of Liberty (or any other unknown concept) when the individual has never seen the Statue of Liberty or had anyone explain to him its significance. It would be very difficult to explain what the picture represents. It is my opinion that English production is impaired when such unfamiliar stimuli are used in English testing.

We must also be aware of such things in all tasks given to a severely to profoundly hearing-impaired person. We are so often concerned about syntactic and vocabulary levels that we seldom stop to consider whether the information presented is within the student's level of comprehension. This question is fundamental to all areas of assessment and must be given attention any time we set out to evaluate skill levels in English.

VOCABULARY

The importance of vocabulary knowledge for the development of English competency has been distinctly described by J.B. Carroll (1971):

"Much of the failure of individuals to understand speech or writing beyond the elementary level is due to deficiency in vocabulary knowledge. It is not merely the knowledge of single words and their meanings that is important, but also the knowledge of the multiple meanings of words and their grammatical functions [p. 175]."

Klare (1963) has stated, "Vocabulary is rather generally agreed upon as the important factor in reading difficulty."

Assessment of vocabulary skills has always been linked to English skill, especially reading comprehension and general IQ development. Consider the including of separate vocabulary tests in batteries, such as the California Achievement Tests (Tiegs and Clark, 1963), the Gates-McGinitie Tests (Gates and McGinitie, 1965), and the Stanford Achievement Tests (Kelly et al., 1964), not to mention their inclusion in individual intelligence tests, such as the Wechsler and the Stanford-Binet. Use of such standardized measures with hearing-impaired readers has continually demonstrated that the average hearing-impaired school leaver scores at levels similar to that of a hearing fourth grader (Cooper and Rosenstein, 1966; DiFrancesca, 1972; Trybus and Karchmer, 1977).

In a more recent study, Walter (1978) used a criterion reference technique for evaluating vocabulary knowledge based on frequency of occurrence of a word in printed English. In comparing hearing and deaf children (ages 10–14), the levels achieved by the oldest hearing-impaired group (14 years) were far below the levels achieved by the youngest hearing group (10 years).

While there is much data to support the handicapping effects severe to profound hearing impairment has on vocabulary development, there exists little research that attempts to detail exactly the nature of the vocabulary difficulty for hearing-impaired students. Attempts to define exactly the nature or extent of the vocabulary deficiency is not a simple task. The following discussion is intended to provide the reader with a set of guidelines to consider when designing a test to measure vocabulary skills or when choosing a test currently available on the market.

Size of Lexicon

As described above, much of the past research has depended upon norm reference tests to determine the amount of deficit resulting from hearing impairment. The difficulty with such testing is that very little information about what words a student really knows and does not know is impossible to acquire. What is needed is a way of determining exactly what words in the English lexicon a student knows. Estimates of the frequency of use of words in English have been made by Thorndike and Lorge (1944), Kucera and Francis (1967), and Carroll et al. (1971). These frequency estimates provide a basis for determining which words in English are used most often, thus those which should be most important to know.

If one examines the word lists defined above, it immediately becomes evident that they contain a great deal of redundancy by using derivatives, inflections, compounds, etc. Add to this the presence of function words, such as "the" (the most frequently occurring word in English), "a," "but," "will," "is," etc., and the size of the lexicon expands beyond just root words. While knowledge of the words falling into these classes are important for achieving competence in English, their meanings are difficult to assess. As a starting point, what is needed is a way of defining, for measurement purposes, the content words that are important to know in English.

Durphy (1974) has provided a definition of a basic root word which excludes proper nouns, derivatives, inflections, compounds, archaic words, foreign words, and technical terms. As a result, he has demonstrated that there must be about 12,300 basic words in English. He has extended his work to show that the average high school senior knows about 7,000 of these words, and the average student at the end of the third grade knows about 2,000 of these basic words. By using various stratefied sampling techniques (such as that described by Walter, 1976), an approach could be developed to evaluate the number of words a student knows from a predefined list without testing knowledge of all words in the list. It would seem logical, especially for hearing-impaired students, that development of a vocabulary is related to the amount of visual exposure (through print and fingerspelling) they have had with the English lexicon. We might expect that they would have a better chance of knowing the words they encounter most often. A first step in evaluating vocabulary must be to determine which words a student knows. However, complete evaluation of vocabulary skill does not end here.

Knowledge of Morphemes

The ability of an individual to apply morphemic rules greatly expands the size of a working vocabulary. When one starts with the basic words in a person's vocabulary and adds the dimensions of morphological knowledge, vocabulary abilities are greatly improved. For this reason a complete assessment of vocabulary skill must entail an evaluation of a student's ability to apply morphological rules to his working basic vocabulary. Consider the words in Table 11.1.

From an assessment point of view, it probably is not necessary to evaluate each of the nine words in Table 11.1 in order to determine a person's vocabulary knowledge. Two things would, however, be necessary: first, assessment of which of the basic root words is understood, and second, assessment of knowledge of the morphological rules that can be applied to these words. With such information in mind about a student, the teacher can make some judgments as to the abilities a student has in using various basic words in the English lexicon.

In this area, Dixon (1976) has developed a program for teaching morphological spelling. Just as in teaching spelling, individual assessment of morphological ability can contribute to the knowledge of a student's vocabulary abilities.

Inflected Words

Related to the concept of knowledge of morphemic expansion of words is the knowledge a student has of a change in meaning as a result of inflection. Does the student know the difference in meaning between work and worked, box and boxes, or blue, bluer, and bluest? Again, as with morphemic analysis, information about a student's ability to inflect words can provide some basic information about working vocabulary size. It would seem

Table 11.1
Examples of Changed Meaning by Using Morphological Rules

Basic	Related	Related
to employ	employee	employable
to fix	fixer	fixable
to assist	assistant	assistance

that such information could be evaluated independently and assembled to extend knowledge about vocabulary abilities of a given individual.

Word Flexibility

The area of word flexibility entails evaluating how a student can use a word in multiple meaning environments. Given the same graphical form, "run," as used in Chapter 6, can a student understand the meaning of "run" when printed in each of the following sentences?

You have a *run* in your stocking.
There's been a *run* on baby spoons lately.
She will *run* in a marathon tomorrow.
I've got to *run* now.
The president will not *run* for reelection.
Even a used car can *run* you a lot of money.
We have some errands to *run* this afternoon.
The dyes in natural fabrics have a tendency to *run*.

Such flexibility in vocabulary usage is the key to being able to comprehend printed messages. Again, by using a basic word list such as defined above (Durphy, 1974), it would be an important part of any vocabulary assessment procedure to know how a student can use a given graphical form in a variety of contexts.

In summarizing, keep in mind we do not advocate use of norm reference tests to evaluate vocabulary skills. Such tests give little information about what a student knows and where he is having difficulty with the English lexicon. We suggest a three-dimensional approach to vocabulary assessment. The first accounts for basic or root word knowledge, the second the morphological and inflection abilities of the student, and the third, the ability to use words in a flexible manner in different parts of speech and with a variety of meanings. By gaining such assessment knowledge, the instructor or diagnostician can determine what instruction must be provided and how long the road to remediation will be.

SYNTAX

The third area which must be assessed in order to gain information about English competence is the knowledge a person has about the syntax of the English language. Given the general lack of achievement in English by deaf students, it is not surprising to discover they do not exhibit competence in the English syntactic system. Yet, to develop a test to evaluate each of the structures would result in an instrument that could not be realistically administered to a subject within the constraints of time or space. The only realistic approach is to sample a set of English syntactic structures and develop a technique to evaluate the sampled structures.

Structural Categories

A series of studies by Quigley et al. (1976) has culminated in the development of the *Test of Syntactic Abilities* (1978). The test, in its final form, evaluates eight structures and was normed on a national sample of deaf students ranging in age from 10 to 18 years. Table 11.2 presents a list of structures evaluated by the test of syntactic abilities.

Using the above categories, Quigley et al. (1976) have demonstrated that for all structures, the youngest hearing group (10 year olds) outperformed the oldest deaf group (18 year olds). However, more important than demonstrating an overall deficit in comprehension of syntactic structures is that the test battery provides information about specific structures. For example, even on tests of question formation on which hearing 10-year-old students scored 100%, 18-year-old deaf students scored only 78%.

A first step in attempting to measure syntactic abilities is to choose those syntactic categories which are appropriate to the task at hand. It must be stressed that to measure all categories is probably counterproductive

Table 11.2

Structure Evaluated by the *Test of Syntactic Abilities* (1978)

Complementation
Conjunction
Disjunction
Negation
Pronominalization
Question formation
Relativization
Verb systems

and unnecessary. The diagnostician must be judicious in making a choice.

Within Category Assessment

The English language is not as simply organized as the categories defined above might imply. Within each of the categories, there are levels of measurement which can take place. For the purpose of this paper, let us consider just one category: relativization. The structure of relativization can differ depending on its position in the sentence, the nature of the relative pronoun used, and the characteristics of the sentence of which it is a part.

When choosing or writing a test, the teacher must be aware of exactly what is being measured. If you are writing questions about relativization, you must be aware of the different forms that relativization can take. To evaluate only one or two forms might result in overgeneralization about the student's abilities, thus missing input in some needed area of instruction. For example, hearing-impaired students generally perform much better with relativization of "who" forms than with "that" forms.

It is impossible, within the limits of this paper, to define completely a total structure of syntax for the English language. It might even be questionable whether such a description has yet been completely documented. There are, however, some excellent works that provide such information. For further reading in this area, the interested individual is referred to Akmajian and Heny (1975), Bresnan (1978), and Stockwell et al. (1973). By reference to these sources the reader should be able to determine structures that will point the direction along which assessment in the syntactic area can proceed. To attempt measurement of syntax without clear-cut directions should not be attempted.

After selection of the appropriate structures and the various aspects of that structure, the diagnostician can move to develop and/or select an appropriate instrument to accomplish individual assessments.

RECEPTIVE AND EXPRESSIVE SKILLS

A great symbol of freedom stands in New York Harbor. It was a gift from France, and was completed in 1886. The Statue of Liberty was sculpted by Frederic A. Bartholdi and took twelve years to complete. It represents freedom and has been a beacon of hope for millions of people coming to the United States during the age of immigration from 1850–1920. It is a major symbol of freedom of life, liberty and the pursuit of happiness in the United States.

In the previous parts of this paper we have discussed three important areas to which an individual must attend when writing or choosing tests of English. We have not discussed whether the tests are of a reading or writing nature. Evaluation of English skills must proceed to look at both the receptive ability of the individual, primarily through reading,[1] and the expressive skills, primarily through writing.[2] The final parts of this chapter will discuss evaluating of English skills in both the receptive and expressive modes.

Receptive Skills

Reading is a major source of input used for learning in our society. Persons with low-level reading skills have difficulty in reading printed directions, newspapers, and magazines, not to mention the wide variety of texts used in schools. Severe to profound deafness results often in the affected individual having difficulty learning to read. The Office of Demographic Studies (Trybus and Karchmer, 1977) report that the average reading and grade level for hearing-impaired high-school seniors is at about the fourth grade; certainly this is not at the desirable twelfth-grade level. In order to analyze reading abilities for hearing-impaired students, a teacher must be cognizant of the interaction of factors effecting comprehension. Goodman (1970) refers to reading as a psycholinguistic guessing game, an interaction between thought and language. He views the reader as bringing not only language skills to their reading tasks, but also cognitive skills and experience.

Frank Smith (1973) points out that the best decoders are not necessarily the best comprehenders. Reading is more than a simple perceptual task—word identification is not read-

---

[1] It is recognized that hearing, speechreading, and signing in English are also ways the hearing-impaired individual receives information.

[2] It is recognized here that speaking and signing in English also are part of expression in English.

ing. Once words are identified, the reader must be able to apply both lexical and syntactical knowledge in order to extract meaning. Even when meanings have been assigned to individual words, the meaning of the entire passage is not necessarily clear. A reader must also have knowledge about how particular words function syntactically and how they relate semantically to the entire context.

To illustrate this point, let us take the passage at the beginning of this section. From an experiential point of view, some assumptions are made: these include information about New York harbor, France as a country, the United States as a country, age of immigration, etc. There are vocabulary demands throughout, such as beacon, symbol, sculptured, etc. Some of the syntax rules contained in this passage, which must be known and understood, are aspects of pronominalization, conjunction, and verb tense agreement. In order to comprehend meaning from such a passage, all the elements defined earlier in this chapter must be brought together.

In assessing receptive skills in English, we seldom look at the specific linguistic skills. Rather, we are concerned with the various levels of comprehension, specifically with the ability of a student to do some or all of the following: remembering details, sequencing events, determining the main idea, making inferences, and evaluating critically.

While the ability to perform at each of these levels may or may not be related to the linguistic competence of the individual, it is important for the diagnostician to determine the language components in such behaviors. Only by knowing the linguistic capabilities of the subject, and the characteristics of the stimulus materials, can the tester make some inference about the behavior of reading comprehension. Pearson (1974–75) has pointed out that sentence length (a poor measure of syntactic complexity) and word frequency (a measure of word difficulty) are the factors most commonly assumed to contribute to reading difficulty, but that no single study has "employed a design that permits one to measure the effects of either factor as well as the unique effects due to their interaction [p. 161]."

What is left is for the evaluator to remain aware of the fact that evaluating comprehension skills must be done by taking into account all of the aspects of assessment that the previous parts of this paper have discussed. To lose sight of the integration of these aspects in the comprehension process is to bias judgments about the behavior of the individual during the reading task. While it may not be possible to evaluate all aspects at one time, a diagnostician must be aware of the fact that these elements interact with each other and play their own idiosyncratic roles in the reading behavior of an individual. Only through observation that keeps in mind all of these can the teacher or diagnostician hope to be helpful in remediating the comprehension problems of a student. The next part of this paper will discuss a similarly difficult task, that of evaluating English in the expressive mode.

Expressive Skills

In a sense, expressive proficiency in English is easier to evaluate than are comprehension aspects. In expression—written, spoken, or signed (provided the channel is intelligible)—we see the results of the competence level of the producer. Such is not the case with comprehension aspects of language. Since writing is the easiest channel to address in a chapter such as this, we will limit our remarks to that single modality, although what is said should be equally applicable to speaking and signing in English.

STIMULUS MATERIALS

Crucial to acquiring any sample of a person's productive English is a thorough understanding of the nature of the stimulus which is used to acquire such a sample of behavior. The diagnostician must be careful to choose a stimulus which is within the realm of experience of the individual, so that the individual may properly bring together the elements of vocabulary and syntax in producing the written composition. Experience has shown that it is often better to provide an individual with a stimulus rather than to allow the person to produce one. Often, attempts by an individual to choose a topic do not allow for enough limitation or enough specificity about what to write. In addition, it has been our experience that providing a picture, picture series, or short film and asking the hearing-impaired student to produce a story or write a composition about what has been observed is very effective. This approach allows the individual to pick an aspect of the stimulus without having to struggle with choosing a topic. Also, such an approach eliminates the possibility that reading difficulty will inhibit a person from understanding the stimulus and the details of the directions for writing. Again, the evaluator is cautioned in the choice of a stimulus. In referring to the compositions at the beginning of this section, it's clear that the second composition demonstrates an understanding of the meaning of the stimulus material, but the first composition demonstrates very little understanding of the meaning of the picture and is merely placing words on a paper in an attempt to cope with what has been observed. For this reason, it is important that an appropriate stimulus be well thought out before any attempt is made at acquiring a sample of students' writing.

GRAMMATICAL CORRECTNESS

Certainly, the most often evaluated portion of a hearing-impaired individual's written composition is that of grammatical correctness. It is beyond the scope of this paper to determine approaches to assessing grammatical correctness in written compositions. The readings suggested earlier can provide some guidance for the diagnostician in evaluating grammatical correctness in written compositions. The problem in providing such assessments is not so much to identify where a mistake in grammatical correctness has occurred (this is usually readily apparent to the competent user of English) but to determine exactly what the intent of the producer was when the grammatical error was made and, finally, weigh the effect of a grammatical error on the overall intelligibility of the composition. Table 11.3 presents an abbreviated version of such an ordering of error types, based on the work of Crandall (1980).

From Table 11.3 it can be seen that the errors of punctuation and spelling probably do not affect the intelligibility of the written material as greatly as do those of deleting content elements or of producing words with no apparent syntax. While this is a simplification in terms of the English grammatical system, it does illustrate what must be done in order to categorize errors in production of the English language.

Table 11.3

A Sample Ordering of Grammatical Errors (Crandall, 1980)

Acceptable English
Mechanical errors
Inflectional morpheme errors
Derivational morpheme errors
Free function errors
Sematic contention stem error
Structural errors
Multiple structure errors
Unconventional English
Unrecognizable English

VOCABULARY USE

Also, when a student produces written materials, it is important that the evaluator attend to the level of vocabulary used by the student in his written expression. It seems, for compositions produced by hearing-impaired persons, that we pay strict attention to the grammatical errors of their writing but seldom pay direct attention to the choice of words made by the students. Much is to be learned about the ability and flexibility a student demonstrates in use of the linguistic system by attending to the appropriate choice of words. Techniques such as type token ratio and average frequency distribution of words used have been attempts to assess the productive vocabulary of students. Again, an instructor needs to attend to the type of error a student is making in vocabulary. Is it the wrong word that is used, the wrong inflection of a word, or an inappropriate meaning form of the word? Add to this the difficulties associated with using a word that may be just slightly inappropriate for the specific context, and the teacher can gain a great deal of evaluative information concerning word use by the students in written English.

ORDER OF IDEAS

As is indicated in the beginning of this paper, the role of the experiential level of the subject cannot be underestimated. Similarly, the ideas that a student uses in a composition are important. Ordering of these ideas can be considered within the total composition, within a paragraph, or within a sentence. Too often, we become so involved with trying to evaluate the grammatical and vocabulary difficulties of students' productions that we seldom evaluate whether or not the ideas a student is expressing are appropriate and in appropriate logical order. It is important, despite the difficulties in syntax and vocabulary, that students learn to order their ideas within a composition. This is an aspect to be evaluated with hearing-impaired students. It is often said, even in instructing hearing students, that much of the difficulty they experience in producing written English is related to the ability to properly put their ideas down in a good order. It is important that this area of assessment be incorporated into any evaluation of student-produced English materials.

SUMMARY

This chapter has attempted to specify techniques a teacher or diagnostician can use to evaluate the English skills of severely to profoundly hearing-impaired individuals. It must be stressed that techniques seldom exist that can evaluate all the areas discussed. It is recommended that the diagnostician select those which are most applicable to the particular student in the particular area under consideration, and then search out existing instrumentation or develop their own instrumentation for use in the situation.

Development of good and adequate testing instruments is a long and arduous task. This does not, however, invalidate the use of individually developed and prepared tests. This is especially appropriate if the diagnostician is thoroughly familiar with the goals of the assessment and the needs for remedial work to further remediate the specific problem.

References

Akmajian, A., and Heny, F. *An Introduction to the Principles of Transformational Syntax.* Cambridge, Massachusetts: MIT Press, 1975.

Bochner, J. Error, anomaly, and variation in the English of deaf individuals. *Lang. Speech,* 1978, *21,* 174–189.

Bresnan, J. A realistic transformational grammar. In M. Halle, J. Bresnan, and G.A. Miller (eds.), *Linguistic Theory and Psychological Reality.* Cambridge, Massachusetts: MIT Press, 1978.

Carroll, J.B. *Learning from Verbal Discourse in Educational Media: A Review of the Literature,* ETS RM 71-61. Princeton, New Jersey: Educational Testing Service, 1971.

Carroll, J.B., Davies, P., and Richman, B. *Word Frequency Book.* New York: Houghton Mifflin, 1971.

Chall, J.S. Readability: An appraisal of research and application. In *Bureau of Educational Research Monographs.* Columbus, Ohio: Ohio State University, 1958.

Cooper, R.L., and Rosenstein, J. Language acquisition of deaf children. *Volta Rev.,* 1966, 45–46.

Crandall, K.E. *Written Language Scoring Procedures.* Rochester, New York: National Technical Institute for the Deaf, 1980.

DiFrancesca, S. *Academic Achievement Test Results of a National Testing Program for Hearing Impaired Students: United States, Spring, 1971.* Washington, D.C.: Gallaudet College, Office of Demographic Studies, 1972.

Dixon, R. *Morphographic Spelling Program.* Eugene, Oregon: E-B Press, 1976.

Durphy, H.F. *The Rationale, Development, and Standardization of a Basic Word Vocabulary Test,* DHEW Publication No. HRA 74-1334. Washington, D.C.: Government Printing Office, 1974.

Ervin-Tripp, S. An analysis of the interaction of language, topic and listener. In J.A. Fishman (ed.), *Reading in the Sociology of Language.* The Hague: Mouton, 1968.

Gates, H.I., and McGinitie, W.H. *Gates McGinitie Reading Tests.* New York: Teachers College Press, 1965.

Goodman, K.S. Reading: A psycholinguistic guessing game. In H. Singer and R.B. Ruddell (eds.), *Theoretical Models and Processes of Reading.* Newark, Delaware: International Reading Association, 1970.

Kelley, T., Madden, R., Gardner, E., and Rudman, H. *Stanford Achievement Tests—Advanced Battery.* New York: Harcourt, Brace & World, 1964.

Klare, G.R. *The Measurement of Readability.* Ames, Iowa: Iowa State University Press, 1963.

Kucera, H., and Francis, W.W. *Computational Analysis of Present-Day American English.* Providence, Rhode Island: Brown University Press, 1967.

Moores, D. Psycholinguistics and Deafness. *Am. Ann. Deaf,* 1970, *115,* 37–48.

Moores, D.F. *An Investigation of the Psycholinguistic Functioning of Deaf Adolescents,* Research Report no. 18. Minneapolis: University of Minnesota, Research and Development Center in Education of Handicapped Children, 1971.

Pearson, P.D. The effects of grammatical complexity on children's comprehending, recall, and conception of certain semantic relations. *Reading Res. Q.,* 1974–75, *10,* 155–192.

Quigley, S.P., Wilbur, R.B., Power, D.J., Montanelli, D.S., and Steinkamp, M.W. *Syntactic Structures in the Language of Deaf Children.* Urbana, Illinois: University of Illinois, Urbana-Champaign, 1976.

Sarachan-Deily, A.B., and Love, R.J. Underlying grammatical rule structure in the deaf. *J. Speech Hear. Res.,* 1974, *17,* 689–698.

Silverman-Dresner, T., and Guilfoyle, G. *Vocabulary Norms for Deaf Children.* Washington, D.C.: A.G. Bell Association for the Deaf, 1972.

Smith, F. *Psycholinguistics and Reading.* New York: Holt Rinehart, and Winston, 1973.

Stockwell, R.P., Schachter, P., and Partee, B.H. *The Major Syntactic Structures of English.* New York: Holt, Rinehart & Winston, 1973.

Swisher, L. The language performance of the oral deaf. In H. Whitaker and H.A. Whitaker (eds.), *Studies in Neurolinguistics,* vol 2. New York: Academic Press, 1976.

Test of Syntactic Abilities. Beaverton, Oregon: Dormac, Inc., 1978.

Thorndike, L.L., and Lorge, I. *The Teachers Word Book of 30,000 Words.* New York: Bureau of Publications, Teachers College, Columbia University, 1944.

Tiegs, E.W., and Clark, W.W. *California Reading Tests.* Monterey, California: California Test Bureau, 1963.

Trybus, R.J., and Karchmer, M.A. School achievement scores of hearing-impaired children: National data on achievement status and growth patterns. *Am. Ann. Deaf,* 1977, *122,* 62–69.

Tweney, R.D., and Hoemann, H.W. The development of semantic associations in profoundly deaf children. *J. Speech Hear. Res.,* 1973, *16,* 309–318.

Walter, G.G. Lexical abilities of hearing and hearing-impaired children. *Am. Ann. Deaf,* 1978, *123,* 976–982.

Sign Language Assessment

NANCY HATFIELD, PH.D.

Over the past fifteen years there has evolved an increased understanding of the positive impact of American Sign Language (ASL) and manual codes for English (MCE) (used along and in conjunction with speech) on the psychosocial, cognitive, language, communication, and general educational development of deaf and hard-of-hearing persons (Caccamise et al., 1978; Holcomb, 1971; Schlesinger and Meadow, 1972; Siple, 1978; Vernon, 1969; Weiss et al., 1975; Wilbur, 1976). This increased understanding has been a major factor in the trend toward the inclusion of sign language as part of a "total" approach to the education of persons with hearing losses (Jordan et al., 1976). This trend, in turn, has lead to an increased need for the assessment of language and communication skills of deaf and hard-of-hearing persons to include sign language (ASL and MCE) and simultaneous communication.

Prior to the last decade the hearing status of a subject's parents was usually a good predictor of sign language proficiency. The majority of deaf children with deaf parents were fluent in American Sign Language

(ASL), the manual-visual language used by the deaf community in the United States, having acquired it as a native language. By contrast, the majority of deaf children of hearing parents had little or no knowledge of sign language in early childhood. Many, however, learned ASL later in life, either upon enrolling in a residential school for the deaf or upon graduating from high school and coming into contact with the deaf community (Meadow, 1975; Woodward, 1973a). As a result, many deaf people with hearing parents also had some ASL skills by adulthood, with degree of proficiency likely related to such variables as age of acquisition, language acquisition environment, and attitudinal factors.

In recent years attempts to improve the English proficiency of the deaf have led to the development of artificial sign language systems that attempt to more closely approximate English. Although all tend to use English word order, these systems vary a great deal. Some represent English words by using English morphology as a basis for combining ASL signs; thus, the word "cowboy," which is represented by one sign in ASL, is signed "cow" + "boy." In addition, invented signs are used in varying degrees to represent English affixes and words for which no formal ASL signs exist. Other systems approximate a natural form of code switching which occurs when deaf ASL users sign to hearing (or deaf) people who "know" sign language but whose dominant or native language is English; this has been called "Pidgin Sign English" (PSE) (Reilly and McIntire, 1980; Woodward, 1973b). Usually, ASL signs are retained and supplemented with fingerspelling and invented signs for English affixes. One way to characterize the relationships among ASL, PSE, and the various forms of artificial sign systems is to represent them on a two-dimensional continuum with ASL at one end and English at the other (see Figure 12.1). Although the lexicons of ASL and these systems often overlap, the syntax and morphology vary greatly. Artificial sign language systems have been taught to parents and teachers in the hope that deaf children will acquire English, represented in signed form, as a native language (Schlesinger and Meadow, 1972; Schlesinger, 1978). An increasing number of programs for deaf children have adopted some type of English sign system, a trend documented by Moores (1978).

Previous assumptions regarding sign language acquisition and proficiency within the deaf population, therefore, appear to be tenable no longer. In the past the sign language skills of deaf adults may have involved primarily ASL as the dominant language with ability to code switch and sign "in English," a secondary skill dependent on a variety of factors, some known and some unknown. At the present time, however, the hearing-impaired population may be developing varying skills in at least two languages, with one language in many modalities: ASL, English in signed form, and English as used by the hearing population (spoken, heard, read, and written). In other words, a good proportion of the hearing-impaired population may be functioning bilingually. There may exist a group of deaf people for whom English in signed form is learned as a first language and ASL as a second language. For other deaf people, ASL may function as the first, or dominant, language with English in signed form a second language. Finally, there may be deaf people equally skilled in ASL and English in signed form as well as deaf people proficient in neither. If Meadow's variable "linguistic mode and ability" is to be adequately treated in research on deafness, it is important to distinguish between skill in ASL and skill in English within the manual mode,

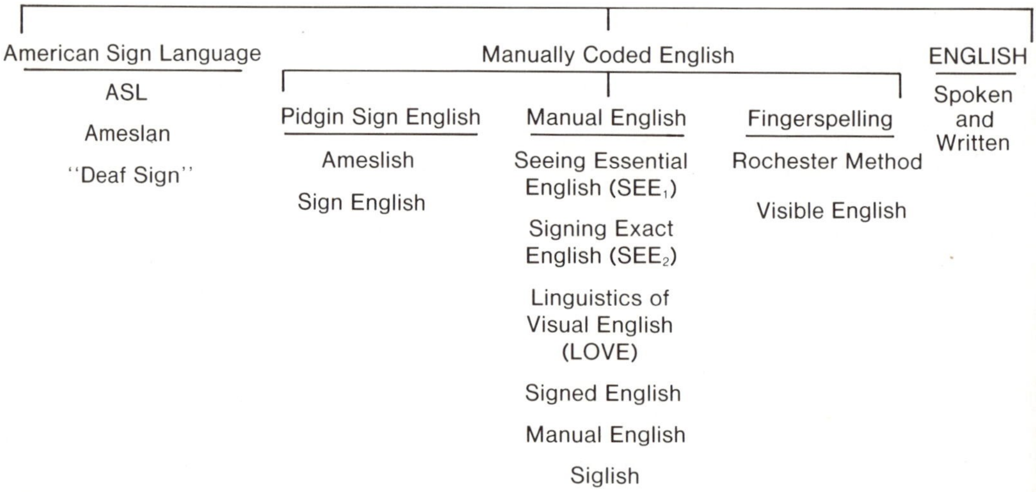

American Sign Language	Manually Coded English			ENGLISH
ASL	Pidgin Sign English	Manual English	Fingerspelling	Spoken and Written
Ameslan	Ameslish	Seeing Essential English (SEE$_1$)	Rochester Method	
"Deaf Sign"	Sign English	Signing Exact English (SEE$_2$)	Visible English	
		Linguistics of Visual English (LOVE)		
		Signed English		
		Manual English		
		Siglish		

Figure 12.1. ASL-English language continuum (based on Stokoe, 1972; Caccamise and Newell, 1978).

and to determine subjects' relative proficiency in the two languages.

EFFECTS OF MANUAL COMMUNICATION ON OTHER SKILLS

Much of the sign language research conducted in the past has investigated the effects of manual communication on the development of other skills: speech and speechreading, written English, academic achievement in general, and personal-social adjustment. Most of these studies compared deaf children of deaf parents (who as a group are exposed to sign language from birth) and deaf children of hearing parents (who as a group are not exposed to sign language from birth). In general, deaf children exposed to manual communication at home and/or in school outperformed children educated by oral-aural methods alone in the skills listed above (Schlesinger and Meadow, 1972; Stuckless and Birch, 1966; Vernon and Koh, 1970). Several different hypotheses have been offered to account for these results: (1) Knowledge of "sign language" provides a linguistic base which facilitates acquisition of English as a second language (Charrow and Fletcher, 1974); (2) In the case of deaf children with deaf parents, greater parental acceptance of deafness results in a less traumatic adjustment to deafness (Corson, 1973; Meadow, 1968a and 1968b); and (3) Richer linguistic, social, and cognitive experiences through use of a shared communication system within family and/or school enhance all aspects of development (Liben, 1978).

Although as a group deaf children exposed to sign language outperform those not exposed to sign language, they still perform at levels far below their hearing peers in English skills (Brooks, 1978; Furth, 1966) and in general academic achievement (Lane, 1976). These facts raise another question: Are the effects of manual communication on other skills different if the proficiency involved is in MCE rather than ASL? The above studies either assumed that deaf children of deaf parents acquired ASL as a native language, or they failed to adequately define "sign language" and to differentiate between fluency in ASL and MCE. It may be that knowledge of MCE more readily transfers to other English skills than knowledge of ASL. A study by Brasel and Quigley (1977) pursued this line of research. They compared the performance of four groups of deaf children on the language subtests of the Stanford Achievement Test and the Test of Syntactic Ability (Quigley and Power, 1971). Two of the groups had deaf parents; one group reportedly used sign language that more closely approximated English grammatical structure (manual English, or ME, group), and one reportedly used ASL (average manual, or AM, group). The other two groups had hearing parents; the children in one group were given intensive oral training (intensive oral, or IO, group), and the others were not (average oral, or AO, group). The comparison of the four different groups yielded results consistent with previous research: The children of deaf parents (ME and AM groups) outperformed children of hearing parents (IO and AO groups). However, the ME group also performed significantly better than the other three groups on almost all measures. The method used to group subjects was questionable; judgments as to group placement were based on the English skills of parents as determined by their written responses to questionnaire items, and on parents' reports of the type of manual communication they used with their children, which could not be verified. In addition, socioeconomic status of the groups varied. Nevertheless, these findings suggest that there may in fact be differential effects of sign language, depending on whether a child is fluent in ASL or MCE, and underscores the need to differentiate between these language skills.

ASSESSMENT OF ASL AND MCE

ASL and MCE as Communication Modes

Another body of sign language research has compared the relative efficiency of various communication modes in transmitting information to deaf people. Most of these studies compared spoken English alone, various forms of MCE (with and without speech), and fingerspelling. The focus here is on those studies which attempted to differentiate between ASL and MCE skill. The three studies that did compare ASL and forms of MCE (Higgins, 1973; Mayberry, 1976; Murphy and Fleischer, 1977) are flawed by one or more of the following: (1) inadequate definition of terms, such as "sign language," so that it is impossible to determine what is being tested; (2) inappropriate elicitation and test development techniques that make it doubtful the languages purportedly being assessed are actually represented in test stimuli; (3) inappropriate test format, e.g., one that requires written response, so that performance in the sign language modes is confounded with performance in written English; and (4) failure to consider the interaction of subjects' varying linguistic skills with the communication modes tested.

The purpose of Higgins' (1973) study was to compare the comprehensibility of factual information presented in three communication methods, all without voice: fingerspelling, American Sign Language (ASL) "in its colloquial form," and "Siglish," a method of signing "much closer to English than colloquial signing" (Higgins, 1973, p. 47). Thirty-seven undergraduate students at Gallaudet College were randomly assigned to a fingerspelling group, a Siglish group, or an ASL group. Each of two factual passages adapted from written materials was recorded without voice on video tape by a hearing signer in the three communication methods identified above. After reading printed instructions, subjects viewed the two video-taped passages presented in one of the three communication methods and then completed 10 printed multiple-choice questions for each passage. The performance of the Siglish group was significantly superior to both of the other groups.

Mayberry (1976) compared the oral, manual, and combined oral-manual language skills of eight first-born normally hearing children, aged 3 to 7 years, of deaf parents who communicated mainly via "manual language" in the home. Manual language was defined as ASL interspersed with fingerspelling of items for which there is no standard sign. "Combined oral-manual language" referred to the simultaneous use of speech and manual communication, so presumably involved a form of MCE. The Utah Test of Language Development (UTLD) (Mecham et al., 1967) was used to test both expressive and receptive oral, ASL, and MCE skills. The

Peabody Picture Vocabulary Test (PPVT) (Dunn, 1965) was used to test receptive oral, ASL, and MCE vocabulary. To assess ASL, the author, a native signer with normal hearing, administered the tests to each child manually without verbalization. The children were required to respond manually. Combined language skills were tested by using a combination of MCE and speech in administering the same two tests. The children were allowed to respond orally, manually, or in any combination of manual and oral language. In summary, the children's oral language performance profiles showed no significant deficits and were not related to parental use of oral or manual language. Manual language performance ranged both above and below expectations. Some vocabulary items were specific to manual or oral language vocabulary inventories. Manual language proficiency appeared to be inversely related to parental use of oral language.

In one of the few studies that recognized subjects' linguistic skills as a variable to consider, Murphy and Fleischer (1977) compared the comprehension of what they termed "Ameslan" and "Siglish" by students with different sign language preferences. The authors defined Ameslan following Fant (1972) as " . . . the sign language used by nearly all (signing) deaf people in the United States. It does not follow the English grammatical scheme and is a wholly different language from English." Siglish was defined as " . . . a sign language that follows the English grammatical system. It is English presented visually on the hands, rather than orally by the voice [Fant, 1972]." Subjects were 29 profoundly deaf students enrolled at California State University at Northridge (CSUN). Each student stated a sign language preference based on his or her preferred reading of signs when communicating with deaf friends in a social setting; 16 preferred Ameslan and 13 preferred Siglish. Two lectures were written and audio-taped by two CSUN professors, who also constructed a 10-item multiple-choice test for the lecture. An interpreter rehearsed each audio tape prior to the experiment to ensure strict adherence to the syntax of each language (Ameslan and Siglish). Each preference group was broken into two subgroups; one received the two treatments in

Ameslan, while the other received the two lectures in Siglish. In each test situation the interpreter interpreted the material live from the audio tape as he would in a normal classroom setting. After each lecture the students completed the written multiple-choice test.

No significant differences were found. Those who preferred Ameslan and received Siglish did as well as those who preferred Ameslan and received Ameslan. The authors concluded that despite stated preferences, these CSUN students performed as a bilingual group with about equal facility in two distinct manual languages, ASL and Siglish. Since these students had to have above average English skills to be admitted to CSUN, this is probably an accurate conclusion.

The studies described above suggest that individuals making comparisons between languages must (1) have sufficient understanding of and respect for those languages, (2) ensure that the target languages are actually obtained in test stimuli through appropriate talent selection and elicitation procedures, (3) avoid bias toward one language in test instructions and procedures, and (4) consider subjects' linguistic skills as a variable affecting their comprehension of those languages.

Effects of Language Background on Reception of ASL and MCE

In a study comparing receptive ASL and MCE skills of deaf college students, Hatfield et al. (1978) attempted to correct for the problems discussed above. In this study, two short stories of approximately equal length were taken from Hoemann (1975). Video tapes were made of each story signed in ASL and MCE. Eleven true-false questions signed in the same language as the preceding story were included on each video tape as a test of comprehension. The person who signed the stories and questions is a hearing daughter of deaf parents skilled in both MCE and ASL. All students entering the National Technical Institute for the Deaf were administered a test of manual reception which requires written translations of 10 MCE sentences (CID Everyday Sentences Test; see Caccamise, 1976). Students who were judged from the results of this test to be skilled receivers of

sign language participated in the study. These students were then presented the two videotaped stories. Each student saw both stories, one in ASL and one in MCE, with the order of presentation of language and story counterbalanced. Students responded to true-false questions by circling the appropriate answer on a printed answer sheet. Prior to presentation of the video tapes, students completed a language background questionnaire. From Woodward's (1973a) work in sociolinguistics and ASL, a six-item questionnaire was developed to gather data on students' language backgrounds (e.g., parental hearing status, age of acquisition).

Based on questionnaire responses, students were divided into three groups, high, medium, and low. Each group differed in language background characteristics. Students in the high group (n = 23) had deaf parents and one or more other deaf family members, learned to sign at age 3 or younger from family, attended a residential school for the deaf for at least part of their schooling, and preferred to use ASL when communicating with friends. A student from the medium group (n = 112) typically had hearing parents, one family member who was deaf, learned to sign from friends between the ages of 5 and 10, attended a residential school for the deaf, and preferred to communicate with friends using ASL and/or simultaneous communication (speech and signs together). A typical student in the low group (n = 84) had hearing parents, no other deaf family members, learned to sign from teachers or friends at age 16 or older, attended public schools or day classes for the deaf, and preferred to use simultaneous communication or speech alone when communicating with friends.

As expected, there were significant differences in performance on the signed stories between groups with differing language backgrounds. The high group made the fewest errors overall, and the low group made the most errors overall ($p \le .001$). There was also a significant language by group interaction ($p \le .01$), with the low group making fewer errors on the MCE than the ASL story and the other two groups performing about equally on both.

In a follow-up study that compared reception of stories presented in two MCE systems, one that incorporated linguistic features of ASL (e.g., use of space, incorporation of manner, pronoun referencing) and one that did not (Hatfield et al., 1980), results described above were replicated. That is, the high group made fewer errors overall than either the medium group or the low group. Subjects performed equally well on the two MCE systems. These findings suggest that in decoding MCE, deaf subjects do rely on features associated with spoken/written English (e.g., word order, affixes, tense markings) and are therefore truly "bilingual" in ASL and MCE. They also provide further support for the notion that deaf people exposed to both ASL and MCE from an early age develop better proficiency in both languages than those who are not as exposed.

Taken together these studies suggest that some deaf students function bilingually and that their language backgrounds have an effect on their sign language skills. However, the relative contributions of the different language background variables to prediction of ASL and MCE skills cannot be determined from the two studies, and many questions remain. For example, are there two or three variables that account for most of the variance in understanding ASL? Which variables are most highly related to fluency in MCE? Furthermore, if deaf students do function bilingually, can methods used traditionally to measure relative skill in two spoken languages be adapted to measure relative skill in two signed languages?

In order to provide information as to which language background variables may be related to ASL and MCE proficiency and how these skills may best be measured, literature on the description and measurement of bilingualism is reviewed below, followed by research on variables associated with bilingual functioning.

DESCRIPTION OF BILINGUALISM

Bilingualism has been described in numerous ways, depending on the discipline involved and the purposes of a particular author. Definitions range from those such as Thiery's (1978) definition of a true bilingual as " ... someone who is taken to be one of themselves by the members of two different linguistic communities, at roughly the same social and cultural level" (p. 146), to those such as Weinreich's (1953) definition of bilingualism as "the practice of alternately using two languages." Albert and Obler (1978) point out that vague definitions of bilingualism leave several issues unresolved; for example, does "use" of a language entail any minimal fluency criterion, and what modalities should be considered in the evaluation of "using languages alternately?" Acknowledging these issues, Macnamara (1967) defines the bilingual as a person who possesses at least one of the language skills (speaking, writing, listening, and reading) to even a minimal degree in the second language. For example, he would consider as bilingual an educated native speaker of English who can also read a little French. This description assumes that bilingualism is a continuum, or series of continua, which varies among individuals along a variety of dimensions. Thus, bilingual proficiency may vary from minimal competency in one of the four language skills to complete mastery of all aspects of more than one language (balanced bilingualism).

The term "balanced bilingualism" refers to native proficiency in both languages (Albert and Obler, 1978) or equal skill in two languages (Macnamara, 1967). This condition is so rare that some writers doubt its existence (Thiery, 1978). Most bilinguals are "nonfluent"; i.e., they possess sufficient skill in the second language for successful basic communication but are perceived by themselves and others as not possessing native-like control of the languages (Segalowitz and Gatbonton, 1977). The language that is more pervasive and pivotal is called the dominant language. Although the dominant language is usually the first language learned, this is not always the case (Lambert, 1978; Stokoe, 1972). For example, a deaf person may be exposed to MCE from age 6 and learn ASL at age 12, yet by adulthood be dominant in ASL.

Another distinction, one originally identified by Weinreich (1953), may be made between compound and coordinate bilingualism. These constructs are generally interpreted as reflecting the degree of semantic overlap between the two language systems within the individual. As Hornby (1977, p. 5) summarizes, coordinate bilinguals " . . . have separate (and different) semantic systems, while compound bilinguals are taken to simply have two distinct modes of expression (the two languages) for a single underlying semantic network." However, Hornby and others assert that this distinction is no longer useful, since it is likely confounded with context for language learning, which in turn is probably confounded with age of acquisition.

For purposes of this paper, bilingualism is defined as even minimal competency, receptive and expressive, in two varieties of sign language used by deaf people in America: American Sign Language (ASL) and manually coded English (MCE). The focus is on assessing the relative ASL and MCE proficiency of deaf people with varying language backgrounds.

Many different approaches have been used to measure degree of bilingual proficiency, or language dominance. Some of these are discussed below, along with considerations for adapting them as measures of bilingual sign language skill.

MEASUREMENT OF BILINGUALISM

Macnamara (1967) discusses two basic approaches to measuring degree of bilingualism: direct testing and indirect testing. Direct measures of bilingual proficiency include tests of reading comprehension, vocabulary, writing, speaking, and listening. The problems associated with directly testing language skills in just one language are numerous and complex, not to mention trying to measure comparable skills in two languages. These problems include deciding which dialects to test and developing valid and reliable tests for a particular population of bilinguals (since, for example, tests of French standardized on a monolingual French population may be invalid for use on a French-English bilingual population). To avoid these difficulties, researchers have devised indirect methods to measure degree of bilingualism. Most of these measures are based on the premise that bilinguals generally perform the same task more efficiently in their dominant language. Four types of indirect measures are classified by Macnamara: rating scales, fluency tests, flexibility tests, and dominance tests. Mea-

sures representative of each type are discussed below.

Rating Scales

Two measures of bilingualism frequently used are language background questionnaires (LBQ) and self-rating scales. Most questionnaires are based on the work of Hoffman (1934) and ask questions about a subject's language usage patterns in the home and community. Hoffman reported significantly high correlations between children's bilingual questionnaire scores and interview ratings as to extent of bilingual background. Arsenian (in Macnamara, 1969) cited validity estimates of $r = .80$ obtained by correlating LBQ ratings and ratings of linguistic proficiency made by interviewers. Many subsequent studies involving indirect measures of bilingualism have based their validity on correlations with LBQ ratings. However, in a study using stepwise multiple regression analysis, Macnamara (1969) found that LBQ ratings were relatively poor predictors of language proficiency measures (e.g., reading comprehension, vocabulary, intonation). He cautioned that social and attitudinal factors may affect responses to questions, thereby attenuating the predictive power of the LBQ. Self-ratings, in which the subject rates his or her speaking, listening, writing, and reading skills in each language, were found to be predictors of Macnamara's criterion measures.

Fishman and Cooper (1969), using bilingual Spanish-English subjects, assessed the relationship among 124 measures of bilingualism (e.g., listening comprehension, word-meaning given a category, LBQ ratings, self-ratings). They found that self-reports on proficiency and usage were the best predictors of their criteria (accentedness, reading, Spanish repertoire range, and English repertoire range). However, the social pressures that distort LBQ ratings may also distort self-ratings, an important consideration in the context of measuring bilingual sign language skills.

Two problems inherent in using rating scales to measure sign language skills are the prejudice and lack of awareness often found within the deaf community regarding the linguistic status of ASL and MCE. A deaf person may label another's use of ASL as "ungrammatical" signing or "bad English," having adopted a bias against ASL commonly found in the deaf education establishment. Likewise, some political factions consider MCE "not a real language," "artificial," and "impossible to use." A deaf person may also be unaware that s/he uses different sign languages in different situations and may even deny knowledge of ASL (Stokoe, 1972). Another indication of this lack of awareness is that there is no uniform terminology among deaf people for referring to the two languages. This does not mean that self-ratings and questionnaires cannot be useful in determining a deaf person's bilingualism. A global self-rating of sign language skill, e.g., "How well do you sign," on a 5-point scale, may correlate highly with other measures of ASL and/or MCE skill.

Language background questionnaires could also provide information helpful in indirectly determining proficiency in ASL and MCE. Indirect questions in conjunction with demographic information (e.g., on parental hearing status), rather than direct questions à la Hoffman (1934) regarding language usage (e.g., "Does your mother sign to you in ASL or MCE?"), may provide the data necessary to determine if a person is more likely to be proficient in MCE, ASL, or both. For example, in the studies discussed earlier (Hatfield et al., 1978 and 1980) language background information was useful in differentiating among students with varying ASL and MCE proficiency. Important questions to ask would concern parental hearing status and use of manual communication, age of sign language acquisition, and residential school attendance.

Fluency Tests

Numerous measures of bilingualism involve "fluency," i.e., speed of responding to verbal stimuli or speed of verbal production in two languages. Rao (1964) and Dornic (1978) designed tests that measured overall time necessary to follow short simple directions. For example, bilingual subjects in Dornic's study were instructed first in one language and then the other to check off a series of test items defined by position, value, shape, or color. Even with the simplest form of the test, speed of responding was a reliable

index of language dominance, as measured by self-ratings and interviewer ratings. In Ervin's (1961) picture-naming task, subjects matched labels with pictures of common objects; times obtained correlated highly with years of experience in the two languages. Determining language dominance by reaction time tests was first described in Lambert (1955). In this study, response latencies were compared for three groups of bilinguals with differing language histories: undergraduate French majors, graduate French majors, and a group of French natives whose second language was English. The three groups differed reliably in speed of response to instructions in each language, as measured by button-pressing latencies.

Lambert et al. (1959) developed a battery of indirect tests which measured (1) the time taken to recognize words in each language, (2) the relative fluency of giving free associations to stimulus words in each language, and (3) the relative speed of reading words and translating words from one language to the other (knowledge of interlanguage equivalence). All but one of these tests (speed of translation) were intercorrelated and could be interpreted as measuring a single factor: language dominance or balance.

Lambert (1978) summarized the results of these two studies as follows: bilinguals who were balanced in speed of pushing buttons on command in two languages were also balanced in fluency of associating, in perceiving words, and in reading in two languages. Attitudinal factors, as well as cultural and personality characteristics, were also found to be related to language dominance. In Macnamara's (1969) study, Lambert's "speed of reading" measure was a powerful predictor of all four language skills criteria. Two of Lambert's other fluency tests, word naming and word completion, were weak predictors of bilingual proficiency. Further support for the validity of reaction time measures of bilingualism is provided by the work of Genesee et al. (1978). French-English bilinguals who were balanced according to self-reports, native-speaker judgments, and speed of encoding in the two languages were also balanced in speed of responding in a language recognition task.

Adapting the reaction time test of Lambert

et al. to a group testing solution, Scherer and Wertheimer (1964) developed an "assimilation of meaning" test to assess " . . . the ease with which more complex meanings could be assimilated in the subjects' two languages" (p. 140). A series of obviously true or false statements (e.g., "Water runs uphill") were played rapidly, first in one language and then in the other. Subjects indicated whether the statement was true or false. Scores based on mean number correct in each language correlated with measures of listening comprehension as well as with a combined index of language proficiency.

Measuring speed of response to verbal stimuli appears to be a reliable and valid method of determining relative language proficiency. Differences in response times were related to language background factors (e.g., years of experience with the second language, usage patterns), certain personality characteristics, self-ratings, and interviewer ratings in the studies discussed above. A major consideration in adapting fluency tests to measure sign language bilingualism is the need to test facility beyond the word level. Because the vocabularies of ASL and MCE are shared to some extent, tests that measure latencies for word recognition, for example, are inappropriate. However, a test like Scherer and Werthheimer's (1964) that uses sentence stimuli might be effectively adapted to measure relative skill in receiving ASL and MCE sentences.

Flexibility Tests

Macnamara's (1967 and 1969) "richness of vocabulary" test, which measures ability to find near-synonymous paraphrasings of a stimulus phrase (e.g., "The reason I did it," "He is drunk"), is based on the notion that bilinguals have more ways of expressing a concept in their strong language than in their weak language. Subjects comprised three distinct groups of Irish-English bilinguals: (1) native Irish speakers who had learned English at school and in the English-speaking environment of Ireland; (2) native English speakers who had their secondary schooling in preparatory colleges in which half the students were native Irish speakers and all college work was conducted in Irish; and (3) native English speakers who had been edu-

cated throughout in English but had learned Irish in school for not less than 12 years. A "richness of vocabulary" score accounted for 80% of the variance in the criterion "degree of bilingualism," as measured by experience in the two languages.

A "word detection" test described in Lambert et al. (1959) may also be classified as a flexibility test. Subjects were required to find as many French and English words as possible embedded in a long nonsense word, e.g., DANSONODEND. Four test stimuli were presented tachistoscopically for one-second intervals. The score assigned each subject was percentage of English words detected minus percentage French words detected. Comparative facility in word detection correlated positively with degree of bilingualism, as determined by a response time measure. In Macnamara's (1969) study, however, word detection contributed significantly to only 4 of the 15 regressions performed: those in which vocabulary scores, spelling scores, speech grammar scores, and writing grammar scores were the criteria.

Obviously, a word detection test would be inappropriate for assessing sign language proficiency. A "richness of vocabulary" test has possibilities, however, since idioms in ASL and MCE may vary greatly. The test could be based on the number of ways that skilled users of ASL and MCE could sign a particular concept in a limited period of time. Again, however, lack of awareness of differences between ASL and MCE, lack of experience in paraphrasing ASL, and attitudinal factors could affect results.

Dominance Tests

In a dominance test the bilingual reads aloud a list of words which occasionally contains a visually ambiguous word, i.e., one which could belong to either of two languages (e.g., "pipe" or "silence" in English and French). In Lambert et al. (1959), subjects dominant in English or French tended to give the ambiguous words an English or French pronunciation, respectively. Balanced bilinguals, who presumably were not set to respond in either language, responded about equally often in French and English. The degree and direction of response set was positively correlated with degree of bilingualism, as measured by the original reaction time test described in Lambert (1955). Again, this type of test would be inappropriate for use with an ASL-MCE bilingual group, due to the shared lexicons of ASL and MCE.

Four types of indirect measures of bilingualism have been reviewed here: rating scales, fluency tests, flexibility tests, and dominance tests. Of these, rating scales and fluency appear to be most readily adaptable to measurement of bilingual sign language skills.

Variables Associated with ASL-MCE Proficiency

A major complication in viewing sign language skills from a bilingual perspective is that many deaf children are not proficient in any language in the preschool years; i.e., a large number of deaf children enter school with essentially no native language. The exceptions are the small number of deaf children with deaf parents who learn ASL as a native language, an unknown number of deaf children with hearing parents who learn MCE within the home from an early age, and the few deaf children who attain early competency in oral-aural English skills. By early adulthood, however, the majority of deaf people have developed some degree of proficiency in ASL and/or MCE (Rainer et al., 1963). The work of Meadow (1972), Woodward (1973a), and others suggests that sign language bilingualism is probably related to age of acquisition, language learning context (e.g., home versus residential schools for the deaf), and social-emotional factors (e.g., attitudes toward ASL and MCE).

Woodward (1973a) showed that linguistic variation in sign language (from a variety closer to ASL to a variety closer to English) correlated with four selected social variables: (1) hearing status (deaf or hearing), (2) parental hearing status (deaf or hearing), (3) age of acquisition of sign language (before or after age 6), and (4) education (college or no college). A person whose signing tended to be more like ASL than MCE was deaf, had deaf parents, learned to sign before age 6, and attended college. The most important social variable for ASL-MCE sign variation seemed to be deafness, followed by parental hearing status, education, and age of sign language

acquisition. Woodward's data involved informant's intuitions regarding the "acceptability" of certain linguistic structures; i.e., it was not the author's intention to determine the relationship of these social variables to subjects' receptive or expressive ASL or MCE skills. A deaf informant could, for example, judge certain sign features "unacceptable" yet be proficient in understanding both ASL and MCE.

The studies of Hatfield et al. (1978a and 1978b) suggest similar grouping of variables related to receptive proficiency in ASL and MCE, although again the relative contributions of each variable cannot be ascertained. Hatfield's language background variables replicated two of Woodward's (parental hearing status and age of acquisition) with the addition of several others: (1) hearing status of other family members, (2) source of sign language input, (3) type of schools attended, and (4) sign language preference. All subjects were deaf and attended college. The first variable was added because in families with hearing parents but with another deaf family member (e.g., a grandparent or sibling), chances seemed better that the deaf child had learned some form of sign language more closely approximating ASL. The second variable was added on the assumption that if hearing teachers were the sign instructors, it was more likely that the child had learned MCE than ASL. "Type of schools attended" was added based on Meadow's (1972) observation that for the majority of deaf children with hearing parents, transmission of deaf culture (including sign language socialization) takes place in residential schools for the deaf. This phenomenon is due to the fact that deaf parents tend to send their deaf children to residential schools, and these children form the linguistic group from whom other children learn ASL. On the other hand, if a deaf child of hearing parents attended day classes in which MCE was used as a communication mode, his or her dominant language is more likely to be MCE than ASL. The final variable, sign language preference, was included as a gross index of a person's attitudes toward ASL and MCE. However, it is likely that the other variables are related to attitudes toward sign language as well. Deaf people with deaf parents, or those with hearing parents who attended residential schools for the deaf, are more likely to have positive attitudes toward sign language than subjects with hearing parents who did not attend residential schools or who attended strict oral programs that prohibited any use of manual communication. The latter may tend to hold more positive attitudes toward MCE than ASL (Padden and Markowicz, 1975).

Much of the previous research involving deaf subjects and sign language (as an independent or dependent variable) has failed to take into account the existence of two different varieties of sign language: one distinct from English (ASL) and the other more closely approximating English (MCE). In the past, only children of deaf parents learned a sign language from infancy; the language learned was usually ASL. Deaf children of hearing parents tended to learn ASL at other points in the life cycle, either upon enrollment in a residential school or following graduation from high school. However, an increasing number of educators and parents are learning and using MCE as a communication mode with deaf children from infancy. As a result, the deaf population in the United States may be functioning bilingually in the signed modality to an increasing extent. If this is the case, researchers must recognize differences between ASL and MCE, as well as subjects' varying skills in these two languages, when investigating the following: signed languages as communication modes, effects of sign language on other skills, and sign language assessment.

It seems appropriate to look to the literature on bilingualism in spoken languages for a theoretical framework from which to view bilingualism in signed languages. This body of literature, coupled with sociolinguistic research on sign language, provides us with some general language background variables that may be related to varying degrees of proficiency in ASL and MCE. It also provides us with methods that may be adapted to measure relative skills in two signed languages.

References

Albert, M.L., and Obler, L.K. *The Bilingual Brain: Neuropsychological and Neurolinguistic Aspects of Bilingualism.* New York: Academic Press, 1978.

Brasel, K., and Quigley, S. Influence of certain language and communication environments in early childhood on the development of language in deaf individuals. *J. Speech Hear. Res.*, 1977, *20*, 95–107.

Brooks, P.H. Some speculations concerning deafness and learning to read. In L. Liben (ed.), *Deaf Children: Development Perspectives.* New York: Academic Press, 1978, 87–101.

Caccamise, F. Manual communication skills assessment and program planning for NTID students. In *Proceedings of the 47th Meeting of the American Instructors of the Deaf*, 1976, 610–615.

Caccamise, F., Hatfield, N., and Brewer, L. Manual and simultaneous communication: Research and implication. *Am. Ann. Deaf*, 1978, *123*, 803–823.

Caccamise, F., and Newell, R. *Terminology and a Brief Description for Sign Language/Manual Communication Systems.* Rochester, New York: Rochester Institute of Technology, NTID, 1978.

Charrow, V., and Fletcher, J. English as the second language of deaf children. *Dev. Psychol.*, 1974, *10*, 463–470.

Corson, H. Comparing deaf children of oral deaf parents and deaf parents using manual communication with deaf children of hearing parents on academic, social, and communicative functioning. Unpublished doctoral dissertation, University of Cincinnati, 1973.

Dornic, S. The bilingual's performance: Language dominance, stress, and individual differences. In D. Gerver and H.W. Sinaiko (eds.), *Language Interpretation and Communication.* New York: Plenum Press (NATO Conference Series II), 1978, 259–271.

Dunn, L. *The Peabody Picture Vocabulary Test.* Circle Pines: American Guidance Service, 1965.

Ervin, S. Learning and recall in bilinguals. *Am. J. Psychol.*, 1961, *74*, 446–451.

Fant, L. *Ameslan: An Introduction to American Sign Language.* Northridge, California: Joyce Motion Picture Co., 1972.

Fishman, J., and Cooper, R. Alternative measures of bilingualism. *J. Verb. Learn. Verb. Behav.*, 1969, *8*, 276–282.

Furth, H. *Thinking without Language.* New York: Free Press, 1966.

Genesee, F., Hamers, J., Lambert, W., Momonen, L., Seitz, M., and Starck, R. Language processing in bilinguals. *Brain Lang.*, 1978, *5*, 1–12.

Hatfield, N., Caccamise, F., Brewer, L., Menkis, P., and Siple, P. Assessment of receptive skills in American Sign Language and manually coded English. In F. Caccamise and D. Hicks (eds.), *American Sign Language in a Bilingual, Bicultural Context.* Silver Spring, Maryland: NAD, 1980.

Hatfield, N., Caccamise, F., and Siple, P. Deaf students' language competencies: A bilingual perspective. *A.A.D.*, 1978, *123*, 847–851.

Higgins, E. An analysis of the comprehensibility of three communication methods used with hearing impaired students. *A.A.D.*, 1973, *118*, 46–49.

Hoemann, H. *The American Sign Language.* Silver Spring, Maryland: NAD, 1975.

Hoffman, M.N. *The Hoffman Bilingual Schedule.* Teachers College Press, 1934.

Holcomb, R. Three years of the Total Approach—1968–1971. *Report of the Proceedings of the Forty-Fifth Meet-*

ing of the Convention of American Instructors of the Deaf. Washington, D.C.: U.S. Government Printing Office, 1971, 522–530.

Hornby, P. Bilingualism: An introduction and overview. In P. Hornby (ed.), *Bilingualism: Psychological, Social, and Educational Implications.* New York: Academic Press, 1977, 1–13.

Jordan, I.K., Gustason, G., and Rosen, R. Current communication trends at programs for the deaf. *Am. Ann. Deaf,* 1976, *121,* 527–532.

Lambert, W.E. Measurement of the linguistic dominance of bilinguals. *J. Abnorm. Soc. Psychol.,* 1955, *50,* 197–200.

Lambert, W.E. Psychological approaches to bilingualism, translation, and interpretation. In D. Gerver and H. Sinaiko (eds.), *Language Interpretation and Communication.* New York: Plenum Press, 1978, 131–143.

Lambert, W.E., Havelka, J., and Crosby, C. The influences of language acquisition contexts on bilingualism. *J. Abnorm. Soc. Psychol.,* 1959, *56,* 239–243.

Lane, H. Academic achievement. In B. Bolton (ed.), *Psychology of Deafness for Rehabilitation Counselors.* Baltimore: University Park Press, 1976.

Liben, L. Developmental perspectives on the experiential deficiencies of deaf children. In L. Liben (ed.), *Deaf Children: Developmental Perspectives.* New York: Academic Press, 1978, 195–215.

Macnamara, J. The bilingual's linguistic performance—A psychological overview. *J. Soc. Issues,* 1967, *23,* 58–77.

Macnamara, J. How can one measure the extent of a person's bilingual proficiency? In L. Kelly (ed.), *Description and Measurement of Bilingualism: An International Seminar, University of Moncton, June 6–14, 1967.* Toronto: University of Toronto Press, 1969, 80–97.

Mayberry, R. An assessment of some oral and manual language skills of hearing children of deaf parents. *A.A.D.,* 1976, *121,* 507–512.

Meadow, K. Early manual communication in relation to the deaf child's intellectual, social, and communicative functioning. *A.A.D.,* 1968a, *113,* 29–41.

Meadow, K. Parental responses to the medical ambiguities of deafness. *J. Health Soc. Behav.,* 1968b, *9,* 299–309.

Meadow, K. Sociolinguistics, sign language, and the deaf subculture. In T.J. O'Rourke (ed.), *Psycholinguistics and Total Communication.* Washington, D.C.: NAD, 1972, 19–33.

Meadow, K.P. The development of deaf children. In E.M. Hetherington (ed.), *Review of Child Development Research,* vol. 5. Chicago: University of Chicago Press, 1975.

Mecham, M., Jex, L., and Jones, J. *The Utah Test of Language Development.* Salt Lake City: Communication Research Associates, 1967.

Moores, D.F. *Educating the Deaf: Psychology, Principles, and Practices.* Boston: Houghton Mifflin, 1978.

Murphy, H., and Fleischer, L. The effects of Ameslan versus Siglish upon test scores. *J. Rehabil. Deaf,* 1977, *11,* 15–18.

Padden, C., and Markowicz, H. *Crossing cultural groupo boundaries into the deaf community.* Paper presented at the Conference on Culture and Communication,

Temple University, Philadelphia, Pennsylvania, 1975.

Quigley, S., and Power, D. *Test of Syntactic Ability, Rationale, Test Logistics, and Instructions.* Urbana, Illinois: Institute for Research on Exceptional Children, 1971.

Rainer, J., Altshuler, K., and Kallman, F. *Family and Mental Health Problems in a Deaf Population.* New York: Columbia University, Department of Medical Genetics, 1963.

Rao, R. Development and use of Directions Test for measuring degree of bilingualism. *J. Psychol. Res.,* 1964, *8,* 114–119.

Reilly, J., and McIntire, M. ASL and PSE: What's the difference? In F. Caccamise and D. Hicks (eds.), *American Sign Language in a Bilingual, Bicultural Context.* Silver Spring, Maryland: NAD, 1980.

Scherer, G., and Wertheimer, M. *A Psycholinguistic Experiment in Foreign Language Teaching.* New York: McGraw-Hill, 1964.

Schlesinger, H. The acquisition of signed and spoken language. In L. Liben (ed.), *Deaf Children: Developmental Perspectives.* New York: Academic Press, 1978, 69–85.

Schlesinger, H., and Meadow, K. *Sound and Sign: Childhood Deafness and Mental Health.* Berkeley, California: University of California Press, 1972.

Segalowitz, N., and Gatbonton, E. Studies of the nonfluent bilingual. In P. Hornby (ed.), *Bilingualism: Psychological, Social, and Educational Implications.* New York: Academic Press, 1977, 77–89.

Siple, P. (ed.). *Understanding Language through Sign Language Research.* New York: Academic Press, 1978.

Stokoe, W.C., Jr. Sign language and bilingualism. In W. Stokoe (ed.), *Semiotics and Human Sign Languages.* The Hague: Mouton, 1972, 154–174.

Stuckless, E.R., and Birch, J. The influence of the early manual communication on the linguistic development of deaf children. *Am. Ann. Deaf,* 1966, *111,* 452–462.

Thiery, C. True bilingualism and second language learning. In D. Gerver and H. Sinaiko (eds.), *Language Interpretation and Communication.* New York: Plenum Press, 1978, 145–153.

Vernon, M. Sociological and psychological factors associated with profound hearing loss. *J. Speech Hear. Res.,* 1969, *12,* 541–563.

Vernon, M., and Koh, S. Effects of early manual communication on achievement in deaf children. *A.A.D.,* 1970, *115,* 527–536.

Weinreich, U. *Language in Contact.* New York: Publications of Linguistic Circle, 1953.

Weiss, K., McIntyre, C., Goodwin, M., and Moores, D. *Characteristics of young deaf children and intervention programs,* Research Report #91. Minneapolis: Research Development, and Demonstration Center in Education of Handicapped Children, University of Minnesota, 1975.

Wilbur, R. The linguistics of manual languages and manual systems. In L. Lloyd (ed.), *Communication Assessment and Intervention Strategies.* Baltimore: University Park Press, 1976.

Woodward, J. Some observations on sociolinguistic variation and ASL. *Kansas J. Sociol.,* 1973a, *9,* 191–200.

Woodward, J. Some characteristics of pidgin sign English. *Sign Lang. Stud.,* 1973b, *3,* 39–46.

Chapter 13

Individual Educational Planning and Public Law 94-142

RICHARD L. BALDWIN, ED.D.
MARY E. CAMPBELL, PH.D.

MULTIDISCIPLINARY EVALUATION

INDIVIDUALIZED EDUCATIONAL PROGRAMS

PROGRAMMATIC OPTIONS

REASSESSMENT AND PLANNING

THREE-YEAR COMPREHENSIVE EVALUATION

Since the beginning of time man has passed on his culture, has taught youth the mores of society, and has organized persons so that a delineation of responsibility is interspersed within the population. So it is with education. People have accepted their responsibility to educate the youth of society, to pass along the culture, and to prepare children for the adult role. They have agreed to provide funds so that schools can be built, teachers hired, and curricula developed. They have passed state and federal laws and regulations which provide a structure to deliver education. They have also established a means of preparing professionals to take on the responsibility of educating youth.

When our forefathers wrote the constitution, they gave the responsibility of education to the states. Each state accepted this responsibility and today in communities all across the United States can be found agencies providing education for youth. In addition to the public sector, private educational programs have been developed. Many of these are backed by religious groups, and several operate schools for the handicapped.

Providing an education for all has been an evolutionary phenomenon. Education for the wealthy, males, and the nonhandicapped preceded the involvement of the social issues which gave rights to women, minority students, and the handicapped. People in the United States experienced a social revolution in the 1960's and 1970's. Many factors converged at this time and resulted in legislation which has affected services to the handicapped. Cruickshank (1975) has stated that the historical development of services to the handicapped has been related to social change, including changing attitudes toward handicapped persons. Thomas Jordan (1962) has observed "that the best index of maturity in society is the attention it pays to its handicapped, its poor, its abandoned." As a nation we are indeed beginning to reach such a mature state.

With the passage of the Education of All Handicapped Children Act (Public Law 94-142) in 1975 and the Rehabilitation Act of 1973 (Section 504), the rights of every handicapped individual has come much closer to being honored.

"It is the purpose of this act to assure that all handicapped children have available to them . . . a free appropriate public education which emphasizes special education and related services designed to meet their unique needs, to assure that the rights of handicapped children and their parents or guardians are protected, to assist states and localities to provide for the education of all handicapped children, and to assess and assure the effectiveness of efforts to educate handicapped children."

United States Congress
Education of All Handicapped Children
Act of 1975
Public Law 94-142

"No otherwise qualified individual in the United States . . . shall, solely by reason of his handicap, be excluded from participation in, be denied the benefit of, or be subject to discrimination under program of activity receiving federal financial assistance."

United States Congress
Section 504 of the Rehabilitation Act of 1973
Public Law 93-112

Rules and regulations have been promulgated by the Bureau of Education for the Handicapped, United States Office of Education, and states. Therefore, local and intermediate school districts are required to conform to these rules if they wish to receive federal funds. The states may have additional laws, rules, and special guidelines which may be even more rigorous than those in the federal law. At the very least, the federal law provides a structure for planning and implementing programs and services for handicapped individuals from 3 to 21 years of age. It also provides the right to due process and other protection under the law. DuBow (1977) has summarized the provisions which are included in the requirement that an individualized educational program (IEP) be developed for each child on an annual basis. The law requires that an IEP be reviewed on an annual basis (1) with both teacher and parent involvement in the process, (2) the establishment of procedures to assure that the evaluation and testing of students are nondiscriminatory, (3) the right of due process on the part of parents, including meaningful involvement in decisions affecting their child, and (4) the removal of various kinds of barriers which threaten to limit educational opportunities.

The remainder of this paper will consider each of these areas in detail. For more discussion on the application of the law and its implication for hearing-impaired students, the reader is referred to an article by Stuckless and Castle (1979).

Since each student is an individual, the specific evaluation and planning must be tailored to each child's specific needs. Therefore, it must be emphasized that there is no typical hearing-impaired child. Positions taken in this chapter are suggestive in nature and to be molded or modified to address the unique needs of each child or situation. There is no one way to evaluate or teach all children. No two IEP meetings will be alike, no two teachers will impart knowledge or skills in the same manner. The children educators refer to as being hearing-impaired are children first and hearing-impaired second. They do not always present themselves free from additional handicaps, and they emit behaviors unique to their personalities. Therefore, take caution to apply the concepts and ideas presented in this chapter to the child where applicable and not to every child as if a child must fit a specific mold.

A first step in planning for a student identified as being handicapped is that of assessing the student's present level of functioning. Planning a program and teaching the student most effectively is contingent upon the quality of the information used to best assess the student's skills, specific needs, and the order and method in which these needs may be developed most effectively. Although there are other areas which must be considered in planning, this chapter will concentrate on the IEP as it relates to communication training.

MULTIDISCIPLINARY EVALUATION

In order to effect a change in communication behavior, the teacher must first understand the current behavior. Without a knowledge of the present, one can hardly progress to an improved state in the future.

Federal regulations mandate that prior to the determination of eligibility, suspected handicapped persons be evaluated by a multidisciplinary evaluation team or group of persons, including at least one teacher or other specialist with knowledge in the area of suspected disability. Section 300.532 of the regulations for Public Law 94-142 requires:

"State and local educational agencies shall ensure, at a minimum, that (a) tests and other evaluation materials: (1) are provided and administered in the child's native language or other mode of communication, unless it is clearly not feasible to do so; (2) have been validated for the specific purpose for which they are used, and (3) are administered by trained personnel in conformance with the instructions provided by their producer; (b) tests and other evaluation materials include those tailored to assess specific areas of educational need and not merely those which are designed to provide a single general intelligence quotient; (c) tests are selected and administered so as best to ensure that, when a test is administered to a child with impaired sensory, manual, or speaking skills, the test results accurately reflect the child's aptitude or achievement level or whatever other factors that test purports to measure, rather than reflecting the child's impaired sensory, manual, or speaking skills (except where those skills are the factors which the test purports to measure); (d) no single procedure is used as the sole criterion for determining an appropriate educational program for a child; (e) the evaluation is made by a multidisciplinary team, a group of persons including at least one teacher or other specialist with knowledge in the area of suspected disability; (f) the child is assessed in all areas related to the suspected disability, including, where appropriate, health, vision, hearing, social and emotional status, general intelligence, academic performance, communication status, and other abilities."

State regulations may dictate who shall serve on the multidisciplinary evaluation team for children suspected of being hearing-impaired. For example, minimal composition of this team in Michigan is an audiologist and otolaryngologist. Other qualified professionals who can provide diagnostic information include the teacher of the deaf, the regular classroom teacher, speech and language specialists, the psychologist, social worker, and others.

After the multidisciplinary team has been determined, it is important for this team to assure that the suspected hearing-impaired person is assessed in all areas related to the suspected disability, including, where appropriate, health, vision, hearing, social or emotional status, general intelligence, academic performance, communication status, and motor disabilities. This handbook and this chapter specifically deal with communication training, so this will receive detailed attention; however, the team should assess all appropriate areas. Communication is a two-way experience requiring both the expression and reception of information. Other chapters in this book detail assessment in each of these areas.

On the expressive side, the assessment of a hearing-impaired child's communication status may, where appropriate, include ability to write in English, the ability to use sign language, and the ability to speak. Each of these things must be attended to when considering the ability of the student to express himself. It is important to evaluate the child in the mode of communication normally used by the child. To evaluate a child's use of sign language when this is a foreign language to him/her is not appropriate. Likewise, preprimary children would not be candidates for evaluation in written language. To limit evaluation of expression to only speech, written English or sign language would be to provide an incomplete picture of a student's expressive communication skills if the student has some competency in all of the aforementioned modes.

On the receptive side we must go beyond hearing assessment typically furnished for the hearing-impaired child by the audiologist, which includes pure tone thresholds, speech discrimination scores, and tympanography. We may, if appropriate, also consider a student's ability to receive information through spoken language or sign language, perhaps the ability to use an oral or a sign language interpreter, the ability to read printed materials in English, the ability to speechread, and the ability to hear and speechread in combination. These areas should be reviewed when evaluating the student's receptive capabilities. For detailed analyses on these areas, the reader is referred to other chapters in this book.

The purpose of such an evaluation is to determine the strengths and weaknesses of the suspected handicapped person. A knowledge base is prerequisite to planning a program of remediation, therapy, or instruction. Results of the multidisciplinary evaluation offer a base line for reevaluating the effects which will indicate if the person has progressed, regressed, or remained stable in their communicative behavior. Information from this initial evaluation and its reevaluation then serves as a starting point for future direction in modification of the individualized instructional program.

Often overlooked is the fact that the parent can play an important role in the evaluation process. The parent and siblings are both participants and observers of a student's communication outside of school experience. Interviews with these family members can help to determine the means used to communicate with the child in the home, in and out of the home, and in school settings. Not only how language is conveyed but also what is conveyed is equally important. Attitudes toward communication and feelings about its importance are critical to a total understanding of the child's communicative behavior.

The federal regulations require that state and local educational agencies ensure that the evaluation procedures provide for tests and materials that are administered in the child's native language, have been validated for the specific purpose for which they are used, and are administered by trained personnel. Also, the regulations require that the tests and other evaluation materials have validity which is adequate for the particular disability being evaluated. Validity is often difficult to assess for sensory-deprived students. As a result, the input from the parents and other family members can serve to qualify further the results of the formalized testing.

So far we have considered the evaluation process as the base line of receptive and expressive communication behavior. We have determined that assessment is a team effort and that evaluation materials used by the team must adhere to state and federal regulations. We also emphasized the importance of involving the parent in the evaluation process, and we listed some assessment areas which must be considered. The next step in the process is to incorporate this information into a vehicle that will lead to strategies aimed at modifying communication behavior. This vehicle is the individualized education program or IEP.

INDIVIDUALIZED EDUCATIONAL PROGRAMS

The IEP is developed at a meeting which is convened by the public agency responsible for providing special education programs and services to handicapped persons. Participants at this meeting include a representative of the public agency and the child's teacher. The parent must be invited, and a member of the multidisciplinary evaluation team must be a participant, or at minimum, someone who can discuss and explain the evaluation procedures and results. In Michigan, for example, this meeting is called an individualized educational planning and placement committee or IEPC. This committee determines if the child is eligible for special education programs and services and, if eligible, what program and services are necessary to provide a child with a free and appropriate public education.

When the participants convene to write an IEP, the first item to be addressed is a statement of the child's present levels of educational performance. Obviously, any evaluation which is as thorough as the ones suggested in this book would be quite lengthy. What must be written, however, is some specific findings from the multidisciplinary evaluation team that suggests future development in terms of the individual's communication status.

The second component of the IEP is a statement of annual goals, including short-term instructional objectives. This is where planning comes to the fore. Given the status of the child's communication behavior, the goals and objectives for improving communication skill must be stated. It is at this point that the directions for change are defined.

It should be noted that methods, techniques, and materials are not required components of the IEP. These variables are the prerogative of the school district and the teacher assigned to work with the child. Public agencies can identify these specifics in an IEP if they wish, but if they do, they bind themselves to the provision of service. If methods and materials are stated and then not used, the parent has the resource of requesting a hearing or perhaps filing a complaint. Philosophies, methods, techniques, and materials are administrative decisions and should not be addressed in the IEP.

Another component of the IEP is the specific identification of the special education programs and services to be provided to the child. Each state submits to the Office of Special Education (OSE) a federal annual program plan (FAPP) which specifies the special education programs and services provided in each state which are available to eligible handicapped students. Finally, the IEP is to contain a statement reflecting the extent to which the student will be able to participate in regular educational programs.

One of the most important acts by the public agency is the notification of parents of the course of action proposed by the public agency relative to the handicapped or suspected handicapped student. This notice must contain the following:

"(1) A full explanation of the procedural safeguards available to the parent;
 (2) A description of the action proposed or refused by the agency, an explanation of why the agency proposes or refuses to take the action, and a description of any options the agency considered and the reasons why those options were rejected;
 (3) A description of each evaluation procedure, test, record or report the agency uses as a basis for their proposal or refusal; and
 (4) A description of any other factors which are relevant to the agencies proposal or refusal."

This notice must be written in language understandable to the general public and must be

"(B) Provided in the native language of the parent or either mode of communication used by the parent, unless it is clearly not feasible to do.
 (C) If the native language or other mode of communication of the parent is not a written language the state or local educational agency shall take steps to ensure:
  (1) That the notice is translated orally or by other means to the parent in his or her native language or other mode of communication;
  (2) That the parent understands the content of the notice, and
  (3) That there is written evidence that the requirements in paragraph (C) (1) and (2) of this section have been met."

   Section 300.505 of the regulations for Public Law 94-142.

For the hearing-impaired, it may be necessary to provide an oral or a manual interpreter at IEP meetings or to visit the home to translate these rights and notices to parents and/or the handicapped person.

There is one right of the parent that deserves particular mention in this treatise on the federal mandate and communication assessment and training. This is the right to an independent educational evaluation at public expense if the parent disagrees with the public agency's evaluation and if the public agency does not wish to convene a hearing to show that its evaluation is appropriate.

Once the parent has been notified of the public agency's intent to provide specific special education programs and services and the IEP is complete with current status and direction in the form of goals and objectives, either the parent or the public agency can approve of this plan, or either party can request a hearing. If a hearing is not requested, the child is assigned to special education and related services so that the teaching process may begin or continue.

PROGRAMMATIC OPTIONS

After consideration of the child's eligibility for special education, and a review of the multidisciplinary evaluation team report, a decision of appropriate special education programs and services must be made. There are a variety of educational settings for hearing-impaired children. The traditional residential school for the deaf remains a part of the educational continuum; however, its role is being altered by the increased establishment of programs in the public schools. More and more public schools are establishing programs in the local districts. This growth is in response to the sociological, psychological, and legal impact of educating and/or placing handicapped persons in the least restrictive environment. The "state school for the deaf" has a role in the continuum, but the traditional role will probably be altered in the years ahead.

Public school programs have been in existence for years in both urban and rural areas. There is a decided advantage in developing "center" programs so that there can be a grouping of children large enough to adequately provide curricular experiences for them.

In areas where there is a smaller concentration of hearing-impaired students, classrooms tend to have less homogeneous groupings. Therefore, continual evaluation of each student's needs and creative ways to provide instruction are necessary. Often such programs are located in regular school settings. The expertise of regular classroom teachers and support personnel may be utilized, but they cannot be expected to do an adequate job without orientation and training, guidance, and support. This assistance for gaining the understanding and skills necessary falls on the teacher of the hearing-impaired and on the administrator. The danger of utilizing regular school personnel, even where appropriate, is that they may not have been assisted in preparing for the pupils or, even more unfair, that the students cannot function successfully in that particular situation. Placement of students in an environment in which they can achieve success is critical.

For hearing-impaired students, placements often emphasize the use of models of communication. Being familiar with the particular methods and philosophies used by the various programs is useful in planning. Viewing the student's needs and the amount of direct support necessary to develop each individual's communication skills is essential. To put a student into a self-contained classroom may be appropriate for one student who needs a great deal of direct teaching, but it may not be appropriate for another. Placements such as classrooms within a regular school or in the regular classroom itself offers advantages but, no doubt, will not offer as much direct support from a teacher of the hearing-impaired. Knowing one factor, such as the child's hearing loss, should not alone determine placement. It has been our experience that some profoundly hearing-impaired students function very successfully with minimum support in a regular school setting. On the other hand, some students with only moderate hearing impairments have great difficulty in even self-contained situations.

Preschool children are often seen within the home setting. Teachers of the hearing-impaired may work with the child and his/her parents to meet the beginning educational needs in other than a school environment. One advantage to the home program model is the close and frequent contact the teacher

has with the parents. An opportunity for parent involvement and for assisting the parent in expanding the child's learning experiences provides a real plus to the home model of delivery. Parents have a much more dominant role in the develoment of objectives to be written in the IEP.

Another placement option for the public school and/or the parents is the private sector. There are a number of private residential and day programs for deaf children available in this country. Some states allow districts to contract with these schools as a means of fulfilling their responsibility to provide each handicapped child with a free and appropriate education. Other states may not use the public tax dollar to support private education.

The continuum of educational programs and services may include such environments as resource rooms, transitional classrooms, or teacher consultant services. Some schools may employ oral or sign language interpreters to provide the deaf child with a means of receiving and transmitting language in the educational setting.

Each student is to be viewed as a unique individual, and a setting appropriate for his/her learning style should be available whether the appropriate site is a residental, day, special class, regular class, or whether the student needs to receive the services of a teacher, consultant, audiologist, or a speech pathologist. Irregardless of the educational setting or the personnel providing the instruction or service selected for the student, strategies need to be developed to accomplish the goals and objectives identified in the IEP.

The objectives and strategies which have been identified do not require a particular methodology or curriculum but rely on the teacher to utilize his/her knowledge and skill in instructing the student. The creativity of the teacher, the knowledge of a process needed, and the utilization of resources coupled with teaching skills are extremely critical if the most is to be made of each student's potential.

REASSESSMENT AND PLANNING

In keeping with federal mandates of Public Law 94-142, each handicapped student's progress is to be reviewed at least annually. The review not only provides the opportunity to update student progress records and other observations and achievement data but also provides the opportunity to plan for future needs. Minimally, the child's teacher and someone who represents the public agency must be in attendance. The parent or the student, if he is 18 or older, must be invited, and every effort should be made to include them in the meeting. Others who have useful information may also be invited. The value of this periodic review is in the opportunity it provides for evaluating the previous plan and making necessary adjustments for future programming.

THREE-YEAR COMPREHENSIVE EVALUATION

A federal regulation in the *Federal Register* of August 23, 1977, indicates that an evaluation of the student is to be conducted every three years, or more frequently if requested or if conditions warrant it. This regulation is especially helpful for maintaining current otological and audiological evaluations as well as for determining the quality and appropriateness of the child's personal hearing aid. This information is critical and should be obtained at least every year, if possible.

SUMMARY

This chapter has identified the pressures of a society which responds to the moral obligations to include the education of the handicapped individuals under the protective laws of the land. The requirements and implications of sections of Public Law 94-142 have been described in some detail. There is no doubt that the persons who designed the law have the welfare of the handicapped persons at heart. It is up to those who have direct responsibility for students to make the laws work to their advantage. Hopefully, by following some of the processes described in this chapter and in other chapters of this book, better services in terms of communication skill development for hearing-impaired individuals can be met.

References

Cruickshank, W.M. The development of education for exceptional children. In W.M. Cruickshank and G.O. Johnson (eds.), *Education of Exceptional Children and Youth*, ed. 3. Englewood Cliffs, New Jersey: Prentice-Hall, 1975.

DuBow, S. Public Law 94-142. *Am. Ann. Deaf*, 1977, *122*, 468–469.

Jordan, T.E. *The Exceptional Child.* Columbus, Ohio: Charles E. Merrill Books, 1962.

Stuckless, E.R., and Castle, W.E. The law and its implications for mainstreaming. In M.E. Bishop (ed.), *Mainstreaming: Practical Ideas for Educating Hearing-Impaired Students.* Washington, D.C.: A.G. Bell Association for the Deaf, 1979.

Part V

Speech Training

Chapter 14

Speech Improvement by the Deaf Adult: Meeting Communicative Needs

SIDNEY M. BAREFOOT, M.S.

DETERMINING SPEECH NEEDS

ESTABLISHING PRIORITIES AND PROGNOSIS

SELECTING FORMAT: INDIVIDUAL, GROUP, OR SELF-INSTRUCTION?
    INDIVIDUAL SPEECH THERAPY
    GROUP SPEECH INSTRUCTION
    SELF-INSTRUCTION AND/OR SELF-PRACTICE

PROVIDING INSTRUCTION FOR DIFFERENT NEEDS

EVALUATING SPEECH IMPROVEMENTS

As a group, deaf adults experience numerous and varied difficulties with their speech. This is indicated, in part, by data regarding speech intelligibility. Although definitions of intelligibility vary among studies, it can be generalized that currently, most deaf children reach adulthood with speech that cannot be completely understood by a normally hearing listener (Jensema et al., 1978; Libbey and Pronovost, 1980; Walter, 1980).

Typically, speech intelligibility ratings are valuable but do not portray a complete picture of a deaf person's spoken communication competence. Even those deaf speakers whose words can be correctly understood may not be using those words to communicate effectively. Difficulties with oral syntax, discourse organization, interpersonal dynamics, social appropriateness, and other parameters of spoken communication may compound the overall nature of "intelligibility."

In essence, the speech communication difficulties experienced by deaf adults are complex, and in many cases, their speech patterns are well habituated. Whatever the reasons for this persistent picture of speech difficulties (and a myriad of explanations have been proposed), it is not to be assumed that deaf adults are content with their level of speech skills. It is also not to be assumed that deaf adults cannot improve their speech.

The problem posed for speech/language pathologists (to be called "therapists" in this chapter), other professionals, and the deaf adults themselves is how to achieve meaningful improvements in speech. To accomplish this, there is a need for professionals and deaf persons who seek their services to view the speech improvement process with careful regard for two critical factors: (1) personal and social maturity levels of the adult learner, and (2) limited instructional time available.

Consideration for these factors can influence the focus of assessment and the course of instruction. A sense of urgency may lead to new efficiences of effort with constant attention to real, well-prioritized communication needs. The challenge is to discern what aspects of speech development are most needed and what improvements are possible for each individual.

DETERMINING SPEECH NEEDS

Van Riper (1966), in relating his successes and failures in speech therapy, recounted, "Over and over again I have failed because I have not asked two crucial questions: 'What is it that this person needs?' and 'What is it that he needs from me?' [p. 277]." Such questions apply well to situations in which a deaf adult requests assistance from a speech therapist.

"Speech needs" should not be confused with other terms used by speech pathologists, such as "disorder," "abnormality," or "problem." Such terms are usually externally imposed on the deaf person, vary in objectivity, and may not relate to the person's reasons for requesting assistance. The term "speech need" is used in this chapter to mean any aspect of speaking that is important for an individual deaf person to acquire and use in his or her own communication situations. Speech needs may be related to word or sentence intelligibility, discourse organization, situational pragmatics, or other parameters of spoken communication. Such speech needs are practical needs selected from the communication circumstances of each deaf person. Although they are not necessarily equivalent to speech "abnormalities" detected by trained listeners, they may be related. In contrast, however, some speech "errors" may present no functional communication problems, and some undeveloped skills may be judged by the deaf person to be "nice but not needed." To apply Van Riper's questions, the speech therapist may ask, "What new functional speech skills, if any, are important for this deaf individual to acquire?" and "What is my helping role?"

In determining speech needs, the interplaying roles of the deaf adult and the speech therapist emerge. Seldom are clients initially able to describe the exact nature and extent of their speech difficulty. Equally seldom do professionals initially understand the personal communication circumstances of an individual client. For communicative speech needs to be accurately determined, considerable information must be shared between these parties. This process may be facilitated for deaf adults if the professional has a thorough understanding of speech as a sensori-motor, linguistic, and interpersonal communication process. Equally important, the therapist needs a good understanding of both deafness and stages of adult development. Failure to understand either factor may result in a learning process poorly suited to the deaf and/or to adults.

Even young children may offer some indication of their general communication needs. Their adult family and professionals who bear the responsibility for directing communication growth can benefit from insightful use of such information. As the child matures, the value of these expressions of self-analysis does not diminish, but their nature changes, reflecting psychological maturation. This maturation is noteworthy in any speech assessment process, since with normal adolescence and adulthood comes a developing role as self-evaluator and decision-maker, a role that may change throughout adulthood. Knox (1977) in describing normal adult development, indicated that many psychological factors proceed through lifelong evolution, including ego, self-concept, and personality with associated decision-making, goal-setting, level of autonomy, and roles in interpersonal relationships.

Chickering (1972) in describing the development of the young adult, stressed the role of emotional independence, claiming, "The road to emotional independence begins with disengagement from the parents, proceeds through reliance on peers, and ends with personal autonomy [p. 59]." Such adult autonomy, Chickering indicated, does not require complete independence but rather the "recognition and acceptance of interdependencies [p. 77]."

The development of these psychological factors by deaf adolescents or adults has limited documentation. Cohen (1978) reported that deaf adolescents have a special identity struggle as they interact with family, peers, and both the deaf and hearing community. There are also indications that deaf adolescents may enter adulthood with major gaps in their knowledge of personal and social information (Emerton et al., 1979), but additional research is needed in this area.

Speech therapists who recognize the importance of understanding the psychological development of their adult deaf clients, nevertheless, do not have a comprehensive information base from which to operate. They must learn much about deaf adulthood from the deaf themselves, recognizing individual characteristics and generalizing when possible. Certainly, as deaf adults seek assistance with their speech, they bring with them their own degree and type of independence. Speech therapists can benefit from recognizing, using, and promoting the growth of that independence. Out of such may come self-driven speech learning, self-motivated speech practice, and self-applied skills in communication situations. Failure to capitalize on the potential for independence, particularly with young adults, may result in their passive acceptance of externally imposed "speech exercises" with little carryover of skills into meaningful situations.

As Chickering (1972) indicated, there is also a need for the development of adult interdependencies. This applies directly to communication improvement, since communication is both a tool and a product of interdependency. As these relationships evolve in a deaf adult's life, it may require greater interdependence with hearing people. Higgins (1980), in describing the "deaf community," noted the variability among deaf adults in their active participation in a deaf community and in their feelings as "outsiders" to hearing people. The position of deaf adults relative to these two "communities" may well influence their interest in developing interdependencies. In speech instruction, considerable interdependence should develop between the deaf client and the normally hearing speech therapist. Optimal speech learning requires a blending of the therapist's knowledge and professional skill and the client's knowledge of self. Communication of this knowledge, by whatever means and modalities, becomes the foundation of their interdependence.

An example of interdependence is the ongoing diagnostic process which allows for descriptions of speech and judgments of communication effectiveness. The therapist may report precise information to the deaf adult and, in effect, tell what is acoustically lacking or what is physiologically needed to improve. However, deaf persons are the ultimate prac-

tical determiner of their personal needs for speech. They relate the professional information to their personal needs and then make decisions, ranging from acceptance of their current speech level to a strong desire to develop new skills. Deaf adults' descriptions of their speech needs are also ongoing and may change as professionals, peers, family, or circumstances are persuasive. Ideally, speech instruction is flexible, so that the recognized communication need always remains the basis of learning.

ESTABLISHING PRIORITIES AND PROGNOSES

As speech needs are determined by deaf adults, they are generally determined to be multiple. There may be a need to improve articulation, voice, pronunciation, organization of spoken ideas, vocabulary, grammatical structures, sensitivity to different interpersonal situations, and self-confidence in speaking situations. While it is true that these factors are all intricately interwoven and must be seen as a whole, it is not always possible to give equal attention to all parameters simultaneously. The improvement process often requires sufficient prioritization of needs to allow for focused attention.

When prioritizing speech needs with deaf adults, it is important to recognize that functionality can be important from the onset of instruction. Such functionality is the communicative use of any speech parameter in situations important to the speaker. Long-term investments in less functional "subskills" of speech, such as phoneme articulation drills at the syllable level, may not have sufficient benefit to warrant extended learning time. This appears to contradict good models of speech production for deaf children. For example, Ling (1976) stressed that speech production skills should be developed by deaf children in their natural order (as developed in normal children), beginning with respiratory/phonatory control followed by normal sequences of phonetic and phonological development. To some extent, this process can and sometimes must also be followed by deaf adults learning speech. Physiologically, certain subskills, such as breath support, phonation control, and articulation, must be adequate before intelligible sentence production is possible. However, one must be careful about overusing the ideal child development or "prerequisites" model when working with deaf adults. This is related to the second major problem discussed earlier, limited instructional time. Currently, the typical opportunity for focused speech instruction for deaf adults may not exceed 2 hours/week or, if extended, 100 hours/year. Often, instruction times have irregularities throughout the year and do not progress for more than a few years at maximum. This reality, although harsh, should result in a learning plan for adults that prioritizes maximum functional speech gain, even at the cost of some subskill precision. Many deaf adults who improve their speech errors prefer to "move on" to learn new skills rather than correct all aspects of the original task. This can be a valid preference if it allows for the building of functional successes. In an extreme contrast, therapists who automatically respond to an articulation test and begin working with adults in intensive articulation drill one phoneme at a time, hoping to "build toward conversation later" may find phonetic success with only a few phonemes in a year, with little phonological-level success and no improvement in spontaneous speech intelligibility. Such priorities can result in wasted efforts if they do not meet a functional speech need. Thus, speech therapists working with deaf adults are placed in a position of idealist and pragmatist, bridging their knowledge of physiological necessities with their awareness of time limitations and learner characteristics.

Considering the importance of communicative speech success to many deaf adults, the prioritizing of speech needs can be related to prognoses for improvement. Some prognostic clues may be revealed in these adults' personal description of their speech need. For example, an adult with poor speech intelligibility may indicate high motivation to develop only a limited set of intelligible phrases and also express motivation to develop the requisite articulation skills. For this learner, the strength of the motivation may result in an intense effort to succeed in difficult tasks. While the /ch/ sound can be difficult for deaf adults to learn, the /ch/ may be especially important to a speaker named Charles. With this focused desire, the /ch/ or an intelligible

approximation may be quickly developed with enough accuracy to achieve success in a business introduction. In contrast, phonemes normally easy to develop might never be produced by this person who did not consider them part of a personal speech need. For more intelligible deaf speakers, their perceived speech needs may exclude articulation altogether, as they might prefer to develop their organization skills or oral language.

It can be seen that there is strong and constant value in knowing the broader speech needs of each adult learner. Without some use of this information, technically trained professionals and their clients may embark on an instructional process that disappoints all participants.

For the assessor to understand the perspective, attitudes, desires, and intentions of the learner, exploratory interviewing may be necessary. This allows the client to organize and verbalize thoughts about these personal factors, perhaps for the first time. Successful introspection may be a key contributor to self-selection of speech goals, self-motivated speech learning, and/or self-acceptance.

Clinical research is needed to develop interviewing techniques that succeed with deaf adults. While questionnaires have their role, written questions may only test the deaf person's reading abilities and not ellicit meaningful answers. Live interviews in the adult's preferred communication mode are a good, if time-expensive, option.

It is important that the interviewing process support the therapist's goal of fostering the client's thoughtful self-exploration. Questioning and probing are more likely to succeed in a conversational context rather than in a cross-examination format. By using a number of questions at an appropriate language level, it may be helpful to probe for the following information:

1. What is the personal history of deafness (type, severity, onset/cause)?
2. What mode(s) of communication has been previously used in
   A. the home?
   B. schooling?
   C. social/business interaction with the deaf?
   D. social/business interaction with hearing people?
3. Are hearing aids used? Why or why not? If

used, how frequently? Are they functioning properly?

4. How much speech instruction has been received previously?
5. How much speech is used now? Where? With whom?
6. Why is speech instruction wanted?
7. Are there additional reasons for seeking instruction (i.e., college credit, financial support, etc.)?
8. Are the speech needs immediate or investments in the future?
9. What does the family (parents, spouse, etc.) think about speech instruction now?
10. If speech instruction were begun, with whom would speech be practiced?
11. Is a particular instructional format (group, individual, self-instructional) desired? Why?
12. If only one new speech skill could be developed, what particular skill would be chosen? Why?

These questions can bring factors to light which will influence judgments of prognosis for speech improvement and help prioritize instructional goals. A review of each of these questions may illustrate their potential value.

Personal history questions may reveal that the client's hearing loss is rapidly progressive. This may indicate to the therapist that auditory-based speech instruction and practice, while ideal for many deaf adults, should receive low priority for this person and that top priority should instead be given to a confidence-building speech maintenance program. If additional physical disabilities or other complicating factors are revealed, priorities can be further influenced.

Information about previously used modes of communication can be very revealing. Mode flexibility, social patterns, and type or extent of speech needs may be suggested. However, such information requires careful interpretation. For example, if speech is used in the home and with hearing people while all other communication is through signing and fingerspelling, this may indicate a well-applied communication flexibility if there is some proficiency with each mode. However, the same response may also indicate that speech is nearly unintelligible, voluntary contact with hearing people is rare, and the only secure affiliation is with nonspeaking deaf friends. These two contrasting possibilities can greatly influence prognoses and instruc-

tional priorities. In the first case, conversational speech skill expansion may be appropriate, whereas in the second case, a basic orientation to speaking with hearing people may be necessary, including an exploration of feelings and attitudes about speech and speakers.

Questions about hearing aids are important in prioritizing instruction which uses residual hearing. Aid repairs, replacements, or first-time purchases may become preinstructional priorities. In cases of less-than-sufficient aid use, priority may be given to opportunities for experimentation with different aids and decision-making about future aid use.

Descriptions of past speech instruction may also influence priorities. The orally trained adult who has had 18 years of speech therapy may need some of the same skills as adults with little previous training. However, differences in their attitude and approach to more instruction may require different instructional strategies. Past instruction may have varied influences on future learning. In some cases, experienced learners have plateaued in skill and/or "had enough speech classes." In other cases, their experience and continued interest makes the learning process rapid and efficient.

The nature and extent of current speech use can suggest a prognosis for speech learning, carryover, and communicative practice. In cases in which speech is used only with speech therapists (a real possibility), speech instruction may be advised against, or instructional goals may be focused on expansion of the communicative environment. Adults with a number of well-defined uses for speech may present a better prognostic picture.

Reasons for wanting speech instruction vary widely and may influence the prioritizing process. Ideally, deaf adults will want to learn as much speech as possible to communicate effectively in many situations. However, more restricted desires may also be positive ("I have a hearing girl friend"). Less positively, indications of external pressures (parental and others) or whimsical gambling may also be revealed.

Additional reasons sometimes prompt deaf adults to seek speech instruction. College credits, financial support, and parental approval may have more appeal than speech improvement itself. While this suggests a poor prognosis, priorities may be arranged to motivate the client to develop speech for its personal communicative value.

The immediacy of speech use is worth examining when prioritizing needs. Vaguely expressed needs for "speaking better in the future" may be clues to unrealistic expectations and limited vitality for intense, immediate learning. In contrast, learners who currently feel communicative needs for speech and intend to practice each new skill can be provided excellent learning opportunities.

Family opinion is important to many deaf adults, even those with well-established independence and identity. Family attitudes toward speech learning may be positive, negative, or neutral. In cases of strong family support for motivated learners, instructional opportunities may be broad. However, when there is a strong disagreement with family about the merit of speech instruction, priority may be given to orientation or "experimental" instruction to let the adult test the learning process.

Questions about potential speech practice opportunities can isolate the "classroom speaker" from the gregarious person who will initiate and expand speaking experiences throughout instruction. In some cases, deaf or hard-of-hearing friends may be the only people available for practice. Implications of this limitation may warrant some preinstructional discussions to assess prognosis.

When attitudes about instructional format are explored, adults may have slight preferences or none at all. However, others may express strong convictions for or against a particular format. Reasons may be objective or biased, but their discussion may greatly assist in prioritizing instruction.

Questions which solicit the client's top priority for speech can reveal as much information about the learner as about the needs. Self-analysis skills, logic, clarity of thought, motivation, and other factors influencing learning may be indirectly assessed as the client answers the question. Inabilities to even understand the question ("What is a speech skill?") may indicate a severe lack of understanding of speech. Inabilities to answer the question may suggest a poor knowledge of

self. Clear, concise, and realistic answers can catapult the teacher and learner into exciting action.

While this type of questioning may be used to establish original priorities, it may also be used throughout instruction to detect shifts in attitude or needs which may necessitate changes in instructional priorities. Generally, this prioritizing process is intended to help select goals for a deaf client. However, in cases in which the demand for speech services exceeds the professional's case load, prioritizing may be needed to select among clients, providing service to those who need it and want it most and who stand the best chance of progressing.

SELECTING FORMAT: INDIVIDUAL, GROUP, OR SELF-INSTRUCTION?

When attempting to develop new speech skills, deaf adults may prefer different learning formats. Each format has its merits but only if well matched with student interests and capabilities.

Individual Speech Therapy

Individual speech therapy may be strongly preferred over group formats by some learners. In part, this may be due to the individualistic nature of the problem, or it may be more related to attitude. Particularly for deaf adults who do not see themselves as "speaking" deaf persons, privacy and individual professional attention may be preferred to exposure to peers in group instruction. For adults with relatively poor speech intelligibility and a strong sence of belonging in a deaf community, there may be a need to provide individualized time to experiment with speech and determine how speaking affects personal feelings. Individual speech therapy can also be a favorite format of therapists who find that on a one-to-one basis, they can deeply explore the individual nature of the speech need and provide tailor-made assistance and personal support to the learner.

Group Speech Instruction

Group speech instruction may be the result of both idealistic and pragmatic influences. Practically, it allows a limited number of professionals to serve a larger number of clients. Recognizing the program constraints that many speech therapists face, group learning can be the only viable alternative. However, it is also not without its superior assets, if properly designed and offered to deaf adults.

In groups, there can be increased opportunities for analysis and application of communication. For students with a relatively well established oral language base and adequate speech reception skills, a group format may promote interstudent practice in speechreading, listening, speaking, discourse organization, interpersonal dynamics, and other complementary skills. Peer observations can assist learners in assessing their needs, selecting learning goals, and evaluating improvements. However, the strength of group instruction is not to be assumed in all group situations. If improperly organized, groups may confuse or frustrate participants. There is a danger of unskilled speakers, with limited speech discrimination abilities, providing errant performance feedback to other students. In public-speaking instruction, for example, students may be encouraged to present speeches to the deaf class in an oral mode. While this may be an attempt to practice for a future hearing audience, it can be unproductive for a class "audience" which cannot adequately receive the oral messages of their peers.

Self-Instruction and/or Self-Practice

Self-instruction and/or self-practice has also been provided in speech instruction for deaf adults. At the National Technical Institute for the Deaf (NTID), learning and practice modules have been used in a specially designed self-instruction lab (McQuay and Cascarelli, 1980) to complement communication courses. Speech materials are used to support instruction in pronunciation, telephone use, conversational speech, speech therapy, vocabulary-oriented speech courses, and others. Independent speech instruction may be amenable to video tape or computer-assisted instruction. Independent practice opportunities are particularly well suited to learners having sufficient hearing discrimination to monitor their own speech. However, learners with less hearing may also record their speech which can be judged later by the therapist or naive listeners. Visual feedback by using such instruments as the Speech Spectrographic Display (Stewart et al., 1976) has been applied to speech learning by deaf adults (Maki, 1980) and may be amenable to independent practice situations.

While practice labs suit the needs for simulated communication experience, other instructional formats may provide more direct communication practice. Such "live" opportunities may be in varied settings, structured or unstructured, supervised or independent, and formally or informally evaluated. McMahon (1980a) developed a speech communication logging system in which deaf adults were free to choose their speech experiences but then systematically self-reported the communicative results. When functional speech goals are given high priority, this type of communication practice is eminently logical. It carries the advantages of self-initiative and quantifiable accountability, both of which are important factors for long-term speech improvement.

PROVIDING INSTRUCTION FOR DIFFERENT NEEDS

In answering Van Riper's question about the client, "What is it that he needs from me?," professional assistance in clarifying speech needs may be enough. In some cases, professional input may indicate that speech instruction is not needed, due to high skill levels, extremely poor prognosis, or other restrictive factors. Such clarifications may be a valuable service to deaf adults. However, instruction may instead be clearly recommended, with speech needs described and prioritized, yet the client's question remains, "How can you help me?" The answer may be completely dependent on the characteristics of each learner and their unique speech need.

The deaf adult with *unintelligible speech* is, of course, the special teaching challenge. It would be easy to "write-off" such adults as poor candidates for speech instruction, regardless of their motivation levels. However, if deaf adults have a need to communicate with hearing people, this broad need at least has room for intelligible speech in special situations. For this level of speech learners, the speech learning process should dovetail into the larger communication process, perhaps by combining instruction in expressive writing, nonverbal communication, speech, and oral language with instruction in receptive reading, nonverbal communication, speechreading, and listening.

In addition, basic strategies for clarifying information and coping with communication breakdowns with normally hearing people may be needed. Kelly and Subtelny (1980) developed an instructional process to improve such interpersonal communication (IPC) skills of deaf adults, including practice with social introductions, information clarifying, identification of emotions, problem-solving, and adapting to different types of interaction. Fortunately, some IPC skills acquired by the adult for use with hearing people may also improve their skills with other deaf people.

Deaf persons with the most limited speech may also have limited knowledge of the social and linguistic customs of normally hearing people. They may need to learn that these hearing people place high value on brief spoken greetings ("How ya doing?") or rhetorical responses ("Fine"). They may need to distinguish the situational contexts that make some expressions socially inappropriate. A basic awareness of idioms and slang (Smith and Subtelny, 1976) could be helpful. Attention to linguistic flexibility may be needed to prevent exaggerated or unnecessary "written English" forms ("I am fine" versus "Fine").

Deaf adults in this group are likely to be seriously in need of basic improvements in respiration, phonation, and articulation. Unfortunately, due to limitations in time and/or learner potential, compromises may be necessary in subskill accuracy if the goal is to make limited utterances communicative. In this delicate trade-off, the therapist gives every speech skill its maximum chance for growth, but the accountability rests in communicative progress, not in subskill development.

For the unintelligible adult speaker, speech reception abilities are not likely to be strong. However, these limited skills should be maximally used and developed for functional speech support, including audition, speechreading, and reception of nonverbal communication. In some cases, note-writing and speaking combinations may be developed. It is also possible that spoken names and social or emergency phrases and expressions to complement common business communication may be used without writing.

In general, the seemingly "unintelligible" speaker need not consider speech as useless. Careful, well-prioritized instruction may develop important new skills. Positive communication experiences may prove the usefulness of these skills to the learner. If new speech use, however limited, is found by the deaf adult to make a communicative difference, speech intelligibility will have taken a sizable leap forward.

At a higher speech level is the deaf adult with *several intelligible phrases, even overall semi-intelligibility.* As a communicator with hearing people, this adult is somewhat different from the previous, lower group. Speech is more likely to be used (although that cannot be assumed, as negative experience may have resulted in a nonuse of speech regardless of available skill). Speechreading and/or listening skills may be higher, possibly good enough to assist in self-monitoring speech and understanding others. As with all deaf speakers, reading and writing abilities may range from low to superior levels. However, oral language skills are difficult to judge for this group, considering their poor word intelligibility.

A recent effort has been made to rate the "message intelligibility" of deaf adults in their spontaneous speech (Card et al., 1980). Audio recordings of NTID students telling a story based on a series of pictures were rated by speech pathologists on a one-to-five scale with half-point intervals, the same scale as used at NTID for rating word intelligibility (Subtelny, 1977). These ratings were intended to reflect the number of ideas or concepts understood by the listener. Data are currently being collected to further investigate this instrument. It may be particularly interesting and important also to explore the "live" message effectiveness of this low-level speaker. Hearing "listeners" in live situations often supplement their hearing with some level of speechreading and observation of nonverbal communication, thereby understanding more of the deaf speaker's message. To capitalize on this in instruction, therapists may investigate the potential for improving the message intelligibility of these deaf speakers through complementary attention to speech intelligibility, nonverbal communication, syntax, vocabulary, and IPC skills.

Certainly, instruction for this group may include all of the skills needed by the lowest level of speakers. However, in many cases, their speech repertoire is more extensive, intelligibility is possible in longer utterances, and interaction with hearing people is less dependent upon writing; thus, instructional opportunities may be broader. In some cases, intelligibility or social effectiveness may be increased with the reduction of a major obstacle, such as pitch problems or vocal tension. Spector et al. (1979) described an effective training program to reduce vocal tension in adult deaf speakers.

Communication instruction may be interdisciplinary, as has been reported by Whitehead and Burke (1981). They report significant gains in speech intelligibility when group instruction was provided to deaf adults having some speech but overall poor speech intelligibility and whose speech reception abilities were also low. This 10-week course combined an audiologist and speech pathologist as a team providing basic strategies for functional communication with hearing people. Classroom activities and field trips successfully supported training in functional speech intelligibility and speechreading as well as developing particular language expectations in special situations.

It can be seen that there are multiple possibilities for speech improvements by this level of speaker. They are deserving of considerable instructional attention and creative new approaches.

The next higher group consists of adults with *speech that is semi-intelligible or may include only a few unintelligible words or phrases.* Speakers in this category may have a range of speech skills, including various competencies with voice and articulation, although a strong respiratory/phonatory/articulatory base is usually established. Speech instruction may, nevertheless, still be needed due to remaining articulation errors, breathiness, vocal tension, pitch problems, or errors in prosody and other suprasegmental features.

This type of speaker still has not reached a comfortable level wherein their speech is consistently understood. Overall communication effectiveness may be poorer than is suggested by word intelligibility ratings or articulation scores. This may be due to a history of "speech training" with little experience in communicating with hearing people. Inappropriate or underdeveloped oral language patterns may reduce message intelligibility, including syntax, vocabulary, and organization of ideas. Fortunately, many deaf adults are ready to attack these skills, particularly when motivated by the taste of communication successes never before achieved.

Direct attention to the pragmatics of speech is important for all levels of speaker, but certainly for deaf adults whose word intelligibility is high enough to allow for many conversations with hearing people. Ling (1980) stated, "Pragmatic analysis is concerned with the specification and classification of the purposes or functions language can be made to serve [p. 256]." Kretschmer and Kretschmer (1980) described the development of pragmatics in hearing-impaired children. Among the functions addressed were conversational presuppositions of speaker and listener, conversational devices, and conversational strategies. Prutting (1979), in describing normal and disordered communication development, provided a stage process model for the development of pragmatics skills. In reviewing research related to communication competence in adults, Prutting noted that several definitions of competence have been proposed, describing rules which speakers and listeners observe in their conversations. In theory, such principles may depend on the partners, settings, or conversational purposes. However, as Prutting observed, there is a lack of base line data regarding specific behaviors which contribute to adults' communication competence. Certainly, this is true for deaf adults as well. Speech therapists must therefore explore the communication experiences of their deaf clients to determine if communication difficulties are restricted to phonological, syntactic, or semantic needs, or if they are also (or instead) related to breakdowns in conversational dynamics.

Some effort has been made to assess deaf

adult's knowledge of interaction principles. Kelly (1975), in describing an IPC course offered to NTID students, indicated that its development was guided by assessment information obtained from NTID students, using a questionnaire. Kelly sampled student knowledge of such factors as social introductions, conversations, discussions, problem situations, and job interviews. McMahon (1980b), in developing instruction for conversational speech, employed a behavioral checklist for use by teachers and other professionals working with students to determine possible student needs. This screening device included several functional speech skills and interaction behaviors. McMahon also informally assessed students' abilities in discourse organization, particularly the sequencing of sentences occurring in spoken dialogue. More investigation is needed in this area, both to define components of pragmatics needed by deaf adults and to attempt their improvement. Such rigor is particularly needed for deaf adults who have already developed a strong speech base, including several aspects of oral language, yet still lack an overall communication effectiveness in conversations with hearing people.

Some of this group of "almost and sometimes intelligible" speakers seems particularly vulnerable to a performance lag that belies their true capabilities. Such a gap may also exist at other levels of speech ability, but for this higher group, there is opportunity to make significant communication gains by applying many of their existing skills while developing new ones. These learners are poorly served by professionals who accept weak performance. An environment is needed that demands full use of speaking potential, particularly in educational settings in which other modes are easier. McMahon, in developing conversational speech instruction, focused his interest on deaf adults whose speech intelligibility ratings when speaking spontaneously were poorer than when reading orally. The objectives were to enhance functional conversational effectiveness by developing abilities in speaking clearly, using correct English, organizing ideas, and speaking with confidence. This type of instruction may be needed by many deaf adults who

possess skills but who fail to apply them adequately when they are most needed.

There are several other areas in which this type of speaker can build on an already-strong speech base. One such area is pronunciation. It is often difficult for deaf adults to independently learn the pronunciation of new vocabulary. Spelling is often misleading or otherwise unhelpful, as in "debt," "ocean," and "antique." Nutter (1975) reported instruction at NTID in the use of pronunciation symbols used in Merriam-Webster dictionaries. Pschirrer (1980a), in refining this instruction, reported that deaf adults were able to learn these sound-symbol relationships and apply them to unfamiliar vocabulary. While an adequate speech base is needed (semi-intelligibility or better), Pschirrer found that auditory discrimination was not required to learn and use these symbols. In part, their learning can be supported by the use of visual memory devices (Pschirrer, 1980b).

Students with better than semi-intelligible speech who have some hearing discrimination for speech are in a particularly advantageous position for developing spoken communication competence. Castle (1980) developed an NTID course in telephone training, wherein students are taught several functional telephone communication strategies in addition to basic telephone information. Gustafson (1980b) developed a speech course to support this telephone course, reporting significant improvements in speech intelligibility during phone use. This type of instruction can be highly motivating for adults as they experience a broadening communication effectiveness when making business or personal telephone calls. Other speech-related instruction reported for this type of deaf speaker includes communication through songs and poems (Schmalz et al., 1980), spoken general vocabulary (Humphrey et al., 1979), and spoken technical vocabulary (Miller, 1975). The use of hearing is particularly valuable in these programs, as they can be supported by self-practice using audio tape materials.

For deaf adults who possess sufficient skill in speech and speech reception, it is possible to use those strengths to build other communication areas while simultaneously improving speech. For example, Kelly and Whitehead (1981) reported experimental English instruction with deaf adults having relatively good speech intelligibility and speech reception but low levels of reading and writing. Receiving instruction in an oral and written mode, these adults significantly improved their written English while also improving oral grammar and word intelligibility in spontaneous speech.

In general, it can be seen that for this group of speakers, specific speech skills may vary widely in spite of similarities in intelligibility. Although learning opportunities, such as singing and telephone use, may be most suited to speakers at the upper end of the intelligibility range, this entire group of deaf adults is in a position to develop several new skills and apply existing skills in new communication situations.

At the *highest level of intelligibility*, the deaf adult is usually able to interact successfully with hearing people in a variety of situations. However, such success is often not as frequent or as universal as many deaf speakers would prefer. This may be due to lingering word intelligibility problems or sensitivity to hearing people's reactions to their intelligible but unusual manner of speaking. Instruction may address these needs, including articulation, pitch, and rate. In cases in which speech is resistant to change, instruction may focus on self-acceptance and improved interpersonal relations with hearing people. Even at this high level, flexible switching of modes and strategies may be necessary to accommodate communication breakdowns. It is particularly embarrassing for these speakers to get stuck on an unintelligible word and not know how to resolve the problem.

Intelligible hearing-impaired adults may also benefit from instruction and experience in group leadership (Kelly and Subtelny, 1978), public speaking (Gustafson, 1980a), job interviewing, and other activities which require organization of ideas, clarity of message, versatility in speech reception, and broad sensitivity to nonverbal aspects of communication. Instruction suited to less-intelligible speakers may also be appropriate for this high group, such as singing, poetry reading, spoken vocabulary development, pronunciation, and telephone training.

As the entire spectrum of deaf adults is reviewed for speech improvement potential, it can be seen that although communicative opportunities may be better for the more-intelligible speakers, spoken communication improvement is possible at all levels. There can be tremendous satisfaction for the client and therapist when such progress is realized. This places special importance on the process of evaluation, as it is the key to satisfying "believability."

EVALUATING SPEECH IMPROVEMENTS

Success is that ultimate goal of learners and teachers. For deaf adults, judgments of success need not be restricted to any speech parameter, particularly to a single measure of overall intelligibility. For many adults, improvement that fills one critical communicative need is true success. Ideally, the evaluation of both speech needs and speech improvements is an ongoing process throughout instruction. Like the preinstructional assessment, it includes professionals and nonprofessionals, informal and formal measures. When speech is evaluated for improvement, the findings can have tremendous impact at any learning stage. Success may build new successes. The detection of growth serves not only to reward past efforts but also to motivate for future attempts.

The McMahon (1980a) speech logging system described earlier serves as an assessment tool for improvement as the deaf adult reports individual speech experiences and rates listener understanding of that speech. Importantly, it is a type of systematic introspection that can be used throughout life. It can be complemented by professional input, but it is not professional-dependent.

Silverman (1977) decribed a systematic procedure for assessing speech therapy outcome that includes several practical criteria. The procedure requires that the speech therapist examine the therapy method used and respond to several evaluation questions. These questions presented by Silverman attempt to evaluate the effects of therapy on the client's communicative and noncommunicative behaviors, as well as the attitudes of the client, clinician, family, and others toward therapy and its effects. The investment of the client and clinician are also evaluated, as well as the probability of relapse following the termination of therapy. Although Silverman applied this approach to stuttering therapy, it has potential applications to deaf adults who have attempted speech improvement.

It is important that if successful speech improvement is claimed, its definition should be made clear. Success may occur in different areas, including word intelligibility, message intelligibility, and interpersonal effectiveness. There is also situation-specific success. Speakers who fail in noisy restaurants may succeed in a quiet bank. Success should also be rated for consistency. A one-time use of a pluralization rule with /z/ may not be regarded as success if five following attempts were not correct. There is also generalized success. For example, the letters "ph" may be described in the classroom as the /f/ phoneme but may be practiced only in the word "phone." Later, spontaneous use of /f/ in "graph" may indicate successful generalization.

In any assessment of speech, if the therapist offers input, accuracy and honesty are critical. Unwarranted praise and overstated success can be as harmful as undetected progress. For many deaf adults, speech improvement may seem impossible. As they try to learn, they will want to know if their judgments of improvement are accurate. The therapist's objectivity, honesty, and candor is being tested. As interdependent adults, the learner and therapist may influence their mutual success by the way they mutually assess their work.

SUMMARY

There are several indications that deaf adults can make speech improvements which may enhance their adult lives and which can be accomplished within limited instruction time and/or initiated for long-term independent development.

Attention as been focused on two important factors that influence speech instruction for adults: constant attention to communicative speech experiences and constant awareness of time limitations. The focus on com-municative speech is certainly not restricted to adults but may well be encouraged for deaf children as well. The time factor, fortunately, is potentially more generous for children then for adults, although in all cases, efficiency is critical.

Any overview of the current speech status of deaf adults must reveal their serious, wide-ranging needs for better speech skills. Hopefully, improved speech learning by deaf children will steadily reduce the communication needs they take into adulthood.

References

Card, S.C., Spector, P.B., and Walter, G.G. A comparison of three measures of speech intelligibility of the hearing-impaired. Paper presented at the New York State Speech and Hearing Association Convention, Monticello, New York, 1980.

Castle, D.L. *Telephone Training for the Deaf* (course materials). Rochester, New York: National Institute for the Deaf, Rochester Institute of Technology, 1980.

Chickering, A.W. *Education and Identity*. San Francisco: Jossey-Bass Publishers, 1972.

Cohen, O.P. The deaf adolescent: Who am I? *Volta Rev.*, 1978, *80*, 265–274.

Emerton, R.G., Hurwitz, T.A., and Bishop, M.E. Development of social maturity in deaf adolescents and adults. In L. Bradford and W. Hardy (eds.), *Hearing and Hearing Impairment*. New York: Grune & Stratton, 1979.

Gustafson, M.S. Advanced communication for group presentation: Learning and speaking about hearing impairment. *Am. Ann. Deaf*, 1980a, *125*, 413–416.

Gustafson, M.S. *Speech for Telephone Communication* (internal report). Rochester, New York: National Technical Institute for the Deaf, Rochester Institute of Technology, 1980b.

Higgins, P.C. *Outsiders in a Hearing World: A Sociology of Deafness*. Beverly Hills, California: Sage Publications, 1980.

Humphrey, B.A., Subtelny, J.D., and Whitehead, R.L. Description and evaluation of structured speaking and listening activities for hearing-impaired adults. *J. Commun. Disord.*, 1979, *12*, 253–263.

Jensema, C., Karchmer, M., and Trybus, R. *The Rated Speech Intelligibility of Hearing-Impaired Children: Basic Relationships and a Detailed Analysis*, Series R, Number 6. Washington, D.C.: Gallaudet College Office of Demographic Studies, 1978.

Kelly, J.F. NTID training program in interpersonal communication. *J. Acad. Rehabil. Audiol.*, 1975, *8*, 131–133.

Kelly, J., and Keatch, S. *Effects of Concurrent and Complimentary Training in Spoken and Written Language* (internal report). Rochester, New York: National Technical Institute for the Deaf, Rochester Institute of Technology, 1981.

Kelly, J., and Subtelny, J.D. *Interpersonal Communication II: Group Discussion* (course materials). Rochester,

New York: National Technical Institute for the Deaf, Rochester Institute of Technology, 1978.

Kelly, J., and Subtelny, J.D. *Interpersonal Communication* (course materials). Rochester, New York: National Technical Institute for the Deaf, Rochester Institute of Technology, 1980.

Kelly, J.F., and Whitehead, R.L. Integrated spoken and written English instruction for the hearing-impaired. Poster session at the Convention of American Speech, Language, and Hearing Association, Los Agneles, California, 1981.

Knox, A.B. *Adult Development and Learning.* San Francisco: Jossey-Bass Publishers, 1977.

Kretschmer, R.R., and Kretschmer, L.W. Pragmatics: Development in normal-hearing and hearing-impaired children. In J.D. Subtelny (ed.), *Speech Assessment and Speech Improvement for the Hearing-Impaired.* Washington, D.C.: A.G. Bell Association for the Deaf, 1980.

Libbey, S.S., and Pronovost, W. Communication practices of mainstreamed hearing-impaired adolescents. *Volta Rev.,* 1980, *82,* 197–220.

Ling, D. *Speech and the Hearing-Impaired Child: Theory and Practice.* Washington, D.C.: A.G. Bell Association for the Deaf, 1976.

Ling, D. Integration of diagnostic information: Implications for speech training in school-aged children. In J.D. Subtelny (ed.), *Speech Assessment and Speech Improvement for the Hearing-Impaired.* Washington, D.C.: A.G. Bell Association for the Deaf, 1980.

Maki, J.E. Visual feedback as an aid to speech therapy. In J.D. Subtelny (ed.), *Speech Assessment and Speech Improvement for the Hearing-Impaired.* Washington, D.C.: A.G. Bell Association for the Deaf, 1980.

McMahon, M.A. Logging spoken English experiences: A strategy for carryover. Paper presented at the Teachers of English to Speakers of Other Languages Convention, San Francisco, 1980a.

McMahon, M.A. *Refinement of Conversational Speech* (course materials). Rochester, New York: National Technical Institute for the Deaf, Rochester Institute of Technology, 1980b.

McQuay, K.C., and Cascarelli, L.S. A self-instruction lab for developing communication skills of deaf postsecondary students at NTID. *Am. Ann. Deaf,* 1980, *125,* 406–412.

Miller, T.D. Job related speech and language training. *J. Acad. Rehabil. Audiol.,* 1975, *8,* 126–130.

Nutter, M.M. Development of pronunciation skills. *J. Acad. Rehabil. Audiol.,* 1975, *8,* 122–125.

Prutting, C. Process /ˈprä│, ses/n: The action of moving forward progressively from one point to another on the way to completion. *J. Speech Hear. Disord.,* 1979, *44,* 3–30.

Pschirrer, L. *Pronunciation Training for Students with Poor Hearing Discrimination* (internal report). Rochester, New York: National Technical Institute for the Deaf, Rochester, Institute of Technology, 1980a.

Pschirrer, L. Using imagery to teach independent pronunciation skills to deaf college students. *Am. Ann. Deaf,* 1980b, *125,* 855–860.

Schmalz, K., Card, S., and Subtelny, J.D. *Communicating through Songs and Poems* (course materials). Rochester, New York: National Technical Institute for the Deaf, Rochester Institute of Technology, 1980.

Silverman, F.H. Criteria for assessing therapy outcome in speech pathology and audiology. *J. Speech Hear. Res.,* 1977, *20,* 5–20.

Smith, J.M., and Subtelny, J.D. *Idioms and Slang* (course materials). Rochester, New York: National Technical Institute for the Deaf, Rochester Institute of Technology, 1976.

Spector, P.B., Subtelny, J.D., Whitehead, R.L., and Wirz, S.L. Description and evaluation of a training program to reduce vocal tension in adult deaf speakers. *Volta Rev.,* 1979, *81,* 81–90.

Stewart, L., Larkin, W., and Houde, R. A real-time sound spectrograph with implications for speech training for the deaf. Paper presented to the IEEE International Conference on Acoustical Speech and Signal Processing, Philadelphia, 1976.

Subtelny, J.D.: Assessment of speech with implications for training. In F.H. Bess (ed.), *Childhood Deafness: Causation, Assessment and Management.* New York: Grune & Stratton, 1977.

Van Riper, C.V. Success and failure in speech therapy. *J. Speech Hear. Disord.,* 1966, *31,* 276–279.

Walter, G.G. *Profile History for Speech Intelligibility* (internal report). Rochester, New York: National Technical Institute for the Deaf, Rochester Institute of Technology, 1980.

Whitehead, B.K., and Burke, M.E. *Strategies to Aid Functional Communication of Hearing-Impaired Young Adults* (internal report). Rochester, New York: National Technical Institute for the Deaf, Rochester Institute of Technology, 1981.

Chapter 15

Use of Speech Training Aids

JUDITH L. BRAEGES, M.S.
ROBERT A. HOUDE, PH.D.

Intelligible speech is based on the speaker's ability to produce the phonetic distinctions required by the speech code. A person's auditory monitoring of these phonetic distinctions in his own speech and in the speech of others, plays a primary role in normal speech development. Lacking sufficient self-monitoring capabilities, the hearing-impaired individual learning the speech code must depend on *external* monitoring for indication that his production attempts are correct or in error.

The primary function of a speech display in speech training with the hearing-impaired is to provide the required external monitoring by exhibiting phonetic distinctions which would otherwise be perceived ambiguously or not be perceived at all by the deaf person. A device which could clearly and consistently display a large number of the phonetic distinctions of speech should have a role in speech training for the hearing impaired. Such a device may provide assistance to the teacher's phonetic analysis and instructions

to the student or may be used directly by the hearing-impaired person to substitute for inadequate phonetic discrimination skills.

A speech display which would be useful in teaching speech to the hearing-impaired has been the goal of applied speech science for the past five decades, and the number and variety of aids that have resulted from these efforts are overwhelming. Since the beginning of the modern electronic era (1920), there have been more than 100 different speech training aids developed. Almost all of these have been considered, by their developers, to be significant contributions in the area of speech training. However, few of them have been formally evaluated. Very few have had a significant impact on teaching speech to the deaf, and none have come into widespread use. The reasons for this failure are varied. One problem is the erroneously high expectations of both teachers and engineers for immediate dramatic improvements through the use of an aid. There is no basis for expecting aids to do more than assist the teacher. The assistance role of speech aids may, however, allow for more efficient and effective use of the teacher's time. An additional problem is the absence of clinically developed and tested procedures for using speech aids. The objective descriptions of the capabilities of training aids, which are provided by speech scientists and engineers and are phrased in the esoteric terms of electronic signal processing, are difficult to relate to clinical applications. Thus, the teacher is confronted with the problem of evaluating the assets and liabilities of specific aids and then relating this information to the requirements of the teaching task. Little if any guidance is available for making a rationale choice among the various aids.

EVALUATION OF SENSORY AIDS

Before attempting to provide information which may be useful to the clinician in assessing the assets and liabilities of sensory aids, it is important to categorize the properties of aids. A convenient categorization results from the questions: (1) How is information displayed by the sensory aid? and (2) what information is displayed?

Table 15.1 presents some contemporary sensory aids categorized on the basis of these two factors. The horizontal axis presents information relative to "how the information is displayed" and includes visual, tactile, and auditory parameters. The relative effectiveness of visual, tactile, and/or auditory displays is not completely understood, although various researchers advocate one sense modality over another (Liberman et al., 1968; Ling, 1976; Ling and Ling, 1978). Sensory aids which display an interval of speech are believed to be more effective for correcting speech than are aids which display only an instant of speech, because with the latter it is impossible to demonstrate how speech characteristics change over time. The speech information which is displayed may be stored for detailed study, as is common with visual displays, or it may be transient, as is usual for tactile and auditory displays. The availability of storage is beneficial, when an aid is to be used for analysis and teaching, because it allows the information to be measured, studied, and discussed. Aids which do not provide storage of the speech information

may be beneficial as speech reception aids. The use of such speech reception aids, which may be considered to be auditory substitution devices wearable in natural communication environments, will not be discussed here. Only information relative to sensory aids used in structured speech training situations will be considered.

Data regarding the type of information displayed is presented on the vertical axis of Table 15.1 and is divided into acoustic and articulatory speech displays. The speech characteristics which are presented on these acoustic or articulatory displays are ranked from the complete representation of speech (such as complete spectrum or vocal tract configurations) to the single parameter characteristics (such as wave form or voicing). The specific aids listed in Table 15.1 include only those which are believed to be currently in use. The numbers which follow each aid refer to a table of information in Appendix 1. For information on the large number of aids which are no longer in use, the reader is referred to a thorough compilation presented in Levitt et al. (1980).

Clinical Properties

Although Table 15.1 presents a convenient organization of the various features of speech training aids, it does not provide information relative to the clinical applicability of the devices. When identifying the usefulness of speech aids, it is necessary to consider: (1) the ease of use of the aid, and (2) the correct/error distinctions which can be reliably made on the speech aid.

EASE OF USE

This characteristic relates to the difficulty and/or ease of operating the device. Questions which must be addressed are: Is the speech training aid comfortable to use, or is it irritating and a source of distraction to the student and the teacher? Are the number of controls and the difficulty of their adjustment so great that the user is discouraged from working with it? The concern about hardware usability, which relates to the complexity of the operating controls, is essentially a subjective judgment which changes significantly as the user acquires more experience with the instrument.

Table 15.1
Speech Training Aids*

What Information Is Displayed?	How Is Information Displayed?				
	Stored Interval		Single Instant or Average		
	Visual	Tactual	Visual	Tactual	Auditory
Acoustic Displays					
Multichannel spectrum information	BTL-VST-I, 1 BLT-VST-II, 2 SSD, 3	Spens, 4, 7	Lucia, 5, 19 BBN Display System (M), 6 SonA-Match, 45	ORI Tactile Vocoder, 8, 9 Teletactor, 7, 9, 10 Mesa, 7, 11 Optacon Spectrum Display, 12	
Formant frequency		Kirman, 13	Pickett, 14		Reeder, 15
Spectrum centroid				Sentiphone, 7, 16	
Fricative spectrum centroid	VSTA (M), 17		Boothroyd S Ind., 18 S.I. Am. S Ind., 5, 19		Guttman, 44
Pitch	IPPI, 22 VSTA (M), 17 Visi-Pitch (M), 7, 45 PM-100 Intonation Trainer (M), 20 Vocal II (M), 21 BBN Display System (M) 6		S.I. Am. Pitch Ind., 5, 19 Florida, 23 Light-A-Pitch, 45 Boothroyd Pitch Ind., 18	Stratton, 24	Vilchur, 25
Nasality	VSTA (M), 17 BBN Display System (M), 6 Boothroyd Nasal/Oral Comparator, 18		Tonar, 26 S.I. Am. Nasal Ind., 5, 19 Boothroyd Nasal Ind., 18		
Intensity (speech envelope)	VSTA (M), 17 BBN Display System (M), 6 Visi-Pitch (M), 7, 45 Vocal II (M), 21 PM-100 Intonation Trainer (M), 20		Voice-Lite, 27 VLI, 28 Boothroyd Int. Ind., 18	Fonator, 7, 33 NTID Tactile Aid, 34 Goldstein, 35	
Selected speech features	Boothroyd Voicing Ind., 18		Upton, 29 Cornett, 30	Miller, 36 SRA-10, 7, 37	
Acoustic waveform displays			Pronovost, 31 Video-Articulator, 32		

Table 15.1 (*continued*)

What Information Is Displayed?	How Is Information Displayed?				
	Stored Interval		Single Instant or Average		
	Visual	Tactual	Visual	Tactual	Auditory
Articulatory Displays Vocal tract con-figuration			Crighton, 40 Wakita, 41		
Tongue position			Fletcher, 42		
Lingua-palatal contact	Electro-Palato-graph, 38 Fletcher, 39				
Laryngeal function			Fourcin, 43		

* (M) indicates device appears as multiple entries; numbers refer to information entries in Appendix 1.

Another factor which relates to the usability of a speech training device is the availability of clinically designed procedures for using the specific instrument. Availability of such procedures may be considered a principal factor which determines whether a device will be used or not. Effective drill and practice procedures for use with speech training aids must be given careful consideration when evaluating the usefulness of an aid. The software should be examined as critically as the hardware.

CORRECT/ERROR DISTINCTIONS THAT AN AID CAN MAKE

This characteristic determines the extent of an aid's applicability to speech training. By considering the set of all target/error pairs which commonly occur in speech training with the hearing-impaired, it is possible to determine systematically an aid's ability to display each pair clearly and consistently. Thus, it is possible to compare and rate the potential use of different aids.

The common target/error problems in speech training for the hearing-impaired are presented in Table 15.2. These data were compiled from a study of the speech production characteristics of students in a residential school for the deaf (Houde, 1980b). The studies of deaf articulation by Levitt (in press), Smith (1975), Angelocci et al. (1964), and Hudgins and Numbers (1942) were also considered in compiling these data. The errors listed are limited to those which are persistently produced by students when attempting the target phoneme. A variety of additional speech errors occur in the speech of the hearing-impaired, but they are usually modified with simple correction procedures. These errors have not been included in Table 15.2. Consonant errors are categorized according to a set of articulatory error characteristics suggested by Levitt (in press). Vowel and suprasegmental errors are grouped in conventional categories.

The range of speech training problems for which a speech display is relevant is directly related to the completeness of the speech information the aid displays. A device which displays only intensity (speech envelope) information is unable to provide phonetic analysis and feedback for sounds which are distinguished by spectral differences. Further, it is not possible for a time-averaged spectrum without storage to differentiate sounds on the basis of voice onset time.

In determining the utility of a speech training aid, it is important to calculate the number and the relative effect of the speech problems which the aid is capable of serving. This concept is of extreme importance when determining the value or usefulness of a speech training aid.

Table 15.2
Common Errors

Consonants

Target	Voiced/Voiceless State	Voiced/Voiceless Timing	Velar State	Velar Timing	Major Misarticulation	Overreconstricted
ba		p, bᵖ	m	mb		
da		t, dᵗ	n	nd	g, click	
ga		k, gᵏ	ŋ	ŋg	d	
pa		b, pᵇ	m			
ta		d, tᵈ	n		k, ṭ	
ka		g, kᵍ	ŋ		t, ṭ	
ma			b	mb		
na			d	nd	ŋ	
va	f	vf, fv, fvf	ƞ		v△, vv△, v△v
ða	θ	ðθ, θð, θðθ				d, ð̠d, d̠ð
za	s	zs, sz, szs				d, zd, dz, z△
ʒa	ʃ	ʒʃ, ʃʒ, ʃʒʃ				dʒ, ʒdʒ, ʒd, z, d
fa	v	fv, vf, fvf	ƞ			f△, ff△, f△f
θa	ð	θð, ðθ, ðθð				t, θt, tθ
sa	z	sz, zs, szs				t, s△, st, ts
ʃa	ʒ	ʃʒ, ʒʃ, ʒʃ				
ha					χ, hə, ə̥	
dʒa	tʃ					d
tʃa	dʒ					t
ab	p	b⁻p	m	b⁻m, mb		
ad	t	d⁻t	n	d⁻n, nd	g, click	
ag	k	g⁻k	ŋ	g⁻ŋ, ŋg	d, h	
ap	b	b⁻p	m	mp		
at	d	d⁻t	n	nt	k, ṭ	
ak	g	g⁻k	ŋ	ŋk	t, ṭ	
am			b	mb, b⁻m		
an			d	nd, d⁻n	ŋ	
aŋ			g	ŋg, g⁻ŋ	ng	
av	f	vf, fv, fvf	ƞ		v△, vv△, v△v
að	θ	ðθ, θð, θðθ				d, ð̠d, d̠ð
az	s	zs, sz, szs				d, zd, dz, z△
aʒ	ʃ	ʒʃ, ʃʒ, ʃʒ				dʒ, ʒdʒ, ʒd, z, d
af	v	fv, vf, fvf	ƞ		f△, ff△, f△f
aθ	ð	θð, ðθ, ðθð				t, tθ, θt
as	z	sz, zs, szs				ts, st, t, s△
aʃ	ʒ	ʃʒ, ʒʃ, ʒʃ				ʃ△, ʃt, ʃ△ʃ, s
adʒ	tʃ					d
atʃ	dʒ					t

△, plosive release; ‗, dental; ', palatalized; ', simultaneous glottal stop; ᵥ, voiced; ˇ, sloppy; ˜, nasal; |, pause; ⁻, unreleased stop; ƞ, voiced nasal fricative; ?, glottal stop; ə, schwa; ₒ, voiceless.

226

Underconstriction	Substitution or Addition of Glottal Stop	Addition of Pause, Vowel, or Glide	Omission	Target
ð, l, s, st, ŏd, dð, dz, zd	?, b?, b'	bwa, bja, əb	—	ba
χ̠, χ, χg, χ̠g, gχ̠	?, d?, d'	əd	—	da
	?, g?, g'	əg	—	ga
θ, s, st, θt, tθ, t⁻s	?, p?, p'	p|, əp, pwa, pja	—	pa
χ̠, χk, kχ̠	?, t?, t'	t|, ət	—	ta
	?, k?, k'	k|, ək	—	ka
ɱ		m|, əm	—	ma
l, ĩ, ŏ̠		n|, ən	—	na
v̌		v|, əv	—	va
ð̌		ð|, əð	—	ða
ž̧ʒ		z|, əz	—	za
ǯ		ʒ|, əʒ	—	ʒa
f̌		f|, əf, fwa, fja₋	—	fa
θ̌		θ|, əθ	—	θa
š, ʃ		s|, əs	—	sa
ʃ		ʃ|, əʃ	—	ʃa
		h|, əh	—	ha
ʒ	?, dʒ?, d'ʒ	dʒ|, ədʒ	—	dʒa
ʃ	?, tʃ?, t'ʃ	tʃ|, ətʃ	—	tʃa
θ, l, ð̌, s, zd, dð, dz, ŏd	?, b'	|b, bə, uwb, ijb	—	ab
χ̠, χ, gˣ, ˣg	?, d'	|d, də	—	ad
	?, g'	|g, gə	—	ag
θ, s, st, t⁻s, θt, tθ	?, p'	|p, pə, uwp, ijp	—	ap
χ̠, χk, k⁻χ	?, t'	|t, tə, uwt	—	at
	?, k'	|k, kə, uwk	—	ak
l, ĩ, ŏ̠		|m, mə, uwm, ijm	—	am
		|n, nə, uwn, ijn	—	an
	?	|ŋ, ŋə	—	aŋ
v̌		|v, və, uwv, ijv	—	av
ð̌		|ð, ðə, uwð, ijð	—	að
ž̧, ʒ		|z, zə, uwz	—	az
ǯ		|ʒ, ʒə, uwʒ	—	aʒ
f̌		|f, fə, uwf, ijf	—	af
θ̌		|θ, θə, uwθ, ijθ	—	aθ
š, ʃ		|s, sə, uws	—	as
ʃ		|ʃ, ʃə, uwʃ	—	aʃ
ʒ	?, d'ʒ	|dʒ, dzə	—	adʒ
ʃ	?, t'ʃ	|tʃ, tʃə	—	atʃ

Table 15.2 *(continued)*
Common Errors

Semivowels and Glides

Target	Overconstriction	Misarticulation		Addition or Substitution of		Excessive Nasality	Omission
		Major	Minor	Schwa	Glottal Stop		
la	d, ld, dl n, nl, ln			∂l	?, ?l	ĩ	—
al	d, ld, dl n, nl, ln			l∂	?	ĩ	—
ra			w	∂, ∂r	?, ?r		—
ar			ɚ	r∂, ∂	?		—
wa		bw, pw	r	∂w	?, ?w		—
ja		g, ŋ	i	∂, ∂j	?, ?j		—

Vowels and Diphthongs

Target	Substitution of Near or Far Neighbor or Central Vowel	Substitution of Diphthong	Inappropriate Pitch Rise	Excessive Nasality
Vowels	Yes	Yes	On high vowels	Yes
Diphthongs	Yes	Glide too long	On high vowels	Yes

Suprasegmental Phonemic Elements

Elements	Errors
Syllable pitch	Pitch too low on stressed syllable Pitch too high on unstressed syllable Pitch too low on stressed syllable in emphasized word
Pitch contour	Inappropriate falling, rising, sustained or stressed syllable contour at terminal juncture
Relative intensity/duration contour	Stressed syllable too quiet or too short Unstressed syllable too loud or too long

Speech Quality Factors

Factors	Errors
Pitch average	Too high/Too low
Intensity average	Too loud/Too quiet
Syllable rate (duration) average	Too slow (Too long)
Laryngeal quality	Breathy/Tense
Average nasality	Hypernasal

Rating Specific Aids

There are approximately 600 individual target/error pairs listed in Table 15.2. Thus, testing how accurately an aid displays each of these pairs is an obvious impracticality. It is possible, however, to predict how effectively an aid may differentiate all the target/error pairs by using a smaller set of elementary distinctions. This smaller set consists of (1) *speech envelope differences*, (2) *differences in voicing and voicelessness*, (3) *nasality differences*, (4) *differences in spectral features*, (5) *differences in pitch and intensity*, and (6) *differences in speech quality*. These six elementary capabilities of a speech training aid can be determined by the Short Test of Elementary Error Discrimination (STEED).

Short Test of Elementary Error Discrimination (STEED)

Speech Envelope Tests (Intensity)

I_1	boo/boot (released)	Detects the release of a complete articulatory closure (e.g., differentiates one from more than one syllable released by stops)
I_2	allay/away	Detects the release of a partial articulatory closure, and the change in envelope level due to a change in voicing
I_3	two/do	Distinguishes an initial voiceless plosive from a voiced plosive
I_4	poppa/pop (released)	Distinguishes sounds which differ in duration and in average intensity
I_5	ban/ran	Distinguishes sounds whose speech envelopes differ in initial or final rate of change

Voice/Voiceless Tests

V_1	I/shy	Distinguishes sustained voiceless sounds from voiced sounds
V_2	oh/toe	Detects the occurrence of very short duration voiceless sounds
V_3	Ann/van	Distinguishes sustained voice fricative sounds from voiced sounds
V_4	Sue/zoo	Distinguishes sustained voice fricative sounds from fricative sounds

Nasality Tests

N_1	me/bee	Distinguishes errors in velar state (open versus fully closed)
N_2	me/mbee	Detects errors in the timing of the velar closure or release in nasal sounds

Spectrum Tests

S_1	see/she	Distinguishes s/ʃ substitutions
S_2	be/ba	Distinguishes far-neighbor front vowel substitution
S_3	do/da	Distinguishes far-neighbor back vowel substitution
S_4	Ed/add	Distinguishes near-neighbor front vowel substitution
S_5	fought/foot	Distinguishes near-neighbor back vowel substitution
S_6	down/Don	Distinguishes substitution of diphthongs
S_7	use (verb)/ooze	Distinguishes addition of glides
S_8	way/ray	Distinguishes errors differentiated by very small spectral change

Suprasegmental Tests (Pitch and Intensity)

P_1	spot[1]/spot[2] (1 and 2 differ in pitch by only one note on the musical scale, such as do/re, re/mi, . . .)	Distinguishes the difference in syllable pitch corresponding to a difference in stress
P_2	now?/*now* (emphasized)	Distinguishes differences in terminal pitch contour
L_1	contract (noun)/contract (verb) (pitch monotone)	Distinguishes syllables on the basis of syllable loudness and syllable duration

Speech Quality Tests
(Use any short phrase; vary the trials by test measure only)

Q_1	Normal pitch range/Half an octave higher	Distinguishes error in average pitch
Q_2	Normal loudness/Too loud	Distinguishes error of excessive loudness
Q_3	Normal loudness/Too quiet	Distinguishes error of insufficient loudness
Q_4	Normal rate/Too slow	Distinguishes error of a too slow speaking rate
Q_5	Normal nasality/Hypernasality	Distinguishes hypernasality errors
Q_6	Normal voice/Breathy voice	Distinguishes error due to a breathy voice
Q_7	Normal voice/Tense voice	Distinguishes error due to a tense voice

TEST PROCEDURE

(1) Adjust the sensory aid so that it is clear and comfortable, as suggested in the user's manual. With some aids, specific conditions, such as microphone placement, may be crucial to the display of selected speech distinctions. It is important that the manufacturer's recommendations be followed.

(2) When evaluating speech aids which do not have storage, particularly tactile aids, the tester's hearing should be masked, and a second person should utter the word pairs. Because the displayed signal occurs simultaneously with the spoken signal and is not stored for analysis, if the tester hears the speech, it is difficult to separate the information received through the aid from that received auditorially. The tester's judgment of the distinction between test elements must be based only on the information from the aid.

(3) Say the first pair of test elements, "boo/boot", with a clear pause between. Care must be taken to control the nontest parameters (e.g., intensity, duration, pitch) so that each pair differs only by the single parameter being tested.

(4) Decide if the display of "boo" and "boot" are clearly different. Descriptions of the distinguishing features of correct and error productions may be supplied with the aid. If not, the tester must say the contrastive pair a number of times, and attempt to identify if and how the phonetic difference between the two elements is displayed. On certain aids it will not be possible to distinguish between the elements of all 30 test items. Marginal or slight differences which may be perceivable are usually not effective when teaching students. The displayed differences must be clear and consistent to be usable. The tester should continue with each item until the distinction, or lack of distinction, has been verified.

(5) Repeat this same procedure for each of the 30 test items of the STEED.

Rating of Three Representative Aids

The STEED procedure was used to rate three common types of sensory aids: (1) a single channel vibrotactile aid, (2) a pitch and intensity visual display, with storage, and (3) a visual spectrum display, with storage. The results are presented in Table 15.3.

TEST INTERPRETATION

Each test item clearly and consistently distinguished in the STEED indicates a group of correct/error pairs which may be discriminated when using the specific sensory aid. The sets of errors represented by each test item are presented in Table 15.4.

USE OF SENSORY AIDS WHEN TEACHING SPEECH

The previous section provided a procedure for rating and comparing sensory aids for training speech with the hearing-impaired. By using the tests, a teacher can decide how suitable a particular aid might be for the specific needs of the hearing-impaired students s/he is working with.

The primary asset of a sensory aid is that it displays phonetic distinctions. The teacher should use this information to analyze students' attempts at speech and to teach speech production. The hearing-impaired person can use the information to assist in the perception of phonetic distinctions which are usually missed or ambiguous. Further, such a feedback tool could be used by the hearing-impaired person to evaluate and practice speech production independently.

We have developed materials and procedures for using a speech display to assist these three speech training activities, i.e., error analysis, production teaching, and production drill. The role played by the aid in these activities is illustrated in the following hypo-

Table 15.3
STEED Ratings for Three Representative Aids

Test Item		Single-Channel Vibrotactile Display	Pitch and Intensity Visual Display with Storage	Visual Spectrographic Display with Storage
Intensity				
boo/boot	I_1	x	x	x
allay/away	I_2			x
do/to	I_3		x	x
poppa/pop	I_4			x
ban/ran	I_5			x
Voiced/Voiceless				
I/shy	V_1		x	x
toe/oh	V_2		x	x
Ann/van	V_3		x	x
Sue/zoo	V_4			x
Nasality				
me/be	N_1	x	x	x
mbe/me	N_2		x	x
Spectrum				
see/she	S_1			x
be/ba	S_2			x
do/da	S_3			x
Ed/add	S_4			
foot/fought	S_5			
Don/down	S_6			x
use (v.)/ooze	S_7			x
way/ray	S_8			x
Suprasegmental				
do/re	P_1		x	
now?/*now*	P_2	x	x	x
'contract/con'tract	L_1	x	x	x
Speech Quality				
Pitch range	Q_1	x	x	x
Loud	Q_2		x	x
Quiet	Q_3		x	x
Slow	Q_4	x	x	x
Hypernasal	Q_5			
Breathy	Q_6	x		x
Tense	Q_7			x
Summary **Number of Errors Discriminated**				
Consonants		147/500 (29%)	257/500 (51%)	500/500 (100%)
Vowels and Diphthongs		2/70 (3%)	17/70 (24%)	47/70 (67%)
Suprasegmentals and Quality		19/26 (73%)	23/26 (88%)	22/26 (85%)
Totals		168/596 (28%)	297/596 (50%)	569/596 (95%)

thetical case, which is a composite of many actual teaching experiences.

Ron is 10 years old and profoundly deaf. He routinely wears binaural amplification and communicates by a combination of semi-intelligible speech and rudimentary sign language.

A screening articulation test revealed that he produces voiceless fricatives for both voiced and voiceless fricative targets. With an in-depth evaluation of his /f/ and /v/ productions, it is found that occasionally his /v/ attempts sound somewhat better though not actually correct. It is difficult to decide just what he is doing during

Table 15.4
Errors Tested by Each Test Item

Test Items	Voice/Voiceless Errors	Velar Errors	Errors of Overconstriction	Errors of Underconstriction
I$_1$		f. stops f. nasals	i. stops f. fricatives /l/, v. fricatives	stops f. affricates
I$_2$		i. stops f. nasals	i. fricatives i. v. fricatives i. affricates /l/	stops
I$_3$	i. stops	i. nasals		
I$_4$		f. v. stops	f. affricates	f. stops
I$_5$	f. stops	f. stops	i. fricatives i. v. fricatives /l/	i. nasals i. affricates
V$_1$			fricatives v̄. affricates	stops
V$_2$	i. stops	i. v̄. stops f. stops	f. fricatives	i. /d/
V$_3$		v. fricatives /v/	v. fricatives v. affricates	v. fricatives v. stops
V$_4$	fricatives affricates		f. v. fricatives	
N$_1$	nasality errors in all nasals, stops, v. fricatives, vowels, diphthongs, /l/			
N$_2$	errors in timing of velar closure or release in nasals			
S$_1$	overconstriction of ʃ, underconstriction of s			
S$_2$	substitution of far neighbor vowels for front vowels			
S$_3$	substitution of far neighbor vowels for back vowels			
S$_4$	substitution of near neighbor vowels for front vowels			
S$_5$	substitution of near neighbor vowels for back vowels			
S$_6$	substitution of diphthongs			
S$_7$	substitution or addition of glides in stops, fricatives			
S$_8$	all errors differentiated by very small spectral changes			

Test Items	Major Articulation or Configuration Errors	Addition or Substitution of Glottal Stop	Addition of Pause, Vowel or Glide	Omission
I₁	ng/ŋ ah/ag	i. stops i. affricates /ŋ/, f. /l/ f. /r/	i. stops affricates nasals fricatives	f. stops f. affricates
I₂			fricatives nasals /l/	fricatives v. fricatives i. affricates i. nasals i. /l/
I₃		i. v̄. stops		i. v̄. stops
I₄		f. stops	f. stops f. affricates	
I₅	bwa/wa pwa/wa ga/ja	/l/, /r/ /j/, /w/	v. fricatives f. /tʃ/	f. nasals
V₁				fricatives f. /dʒ/
V₂	pwa/wa	i. v̄. stops		i. v̄. stops f. stops
V₃				v. fricatives v. affricates
V₄				
P₁	syllable pitch errors			
P₂	pitch contour errors, inappropriate pitch rise in vowels			
L₁	syllable loudness errors			
Q₁	average pitch errors			
Q₂	voice too loud			
Q₃	voice too quiet			
Q₄	syllable rate too slow			
Q₅	hypernasality			
Q₆	breathy voice			
Q₇	tense voice			

these marginally correct trials. Ron is given a list of simple words beginning with /v/ to record on the Speech Spectrographic Display (SSD). This is a visual display which instantaneously records and stores a spectrogram of the student's speech (see Fig. 15.1). His dominant error, /f/, is easily identified and analyzed (no voicing during the frication). The marginal productions are also clearly seen on the visual display as attempts which start as /f/ but have a brief period of voicing during the frication, just before the vowel begins. This is seen as a voicing bar below the irregular vertical lines of frication (Fig. 15.2). A count is taken of the /f/ and /fv/ errors as a base line measure.

As production teaching begins, auditory, visual, and tactile cues as well as verbal descriptions are used, but Ron is still not able to produce a correct /v/. The SSD is used and through various demonstrations he is taught that the dark bar at the bottom of his recorded spectrograms shows that he has used his voice and that the irregular vertical lines show that he is releasing the air of the fricative. He is told, "You must make both the air and the voice at the same time." He experiments, trying to coordinate these two aspects of the production. The teacher explains each production, relating what he hears and feels to what he sees on the display. He quickly learns to associate the feeling and sound of his correct production with the correct visual representation. Figure 15.3 shows a typical attempt during production learning.

Once Ron is able to spontaneously produce the /v/ in simple consonant-vowel contexts at approximately a 30% correct rate, frequent production explanations from the teacher are no longer needed. The task has become one of drilling the production. He begins to work with the SSD independently. Using worksheets listing simple word assignments, he sits at the SSD, recording each attempt. He looks for the presence of the voicing bar in his /v/ attempt to verify its correctness. This simple criteria—presence versus absence of the unbroken dark bar—is used by this student as he practices the target production repeatedly. The teacher regularly tests his production skill, and his performance on these tests determines his passing on to words offering more difficult phonetic contents. The extensive number of trials with feedback required to stabilize Ron's target production is delivered with the SSD rather than by the teacher, whose time is thus free to teach other skills. As Ron works independently with the SSD, the teacher monitors and guides his work and encourages carryover of the /v/ production to his spontaneous language use.

Figure 15.1. Speech Spectrographic Display (courtesy of Spectraphonics, Inc.).

The methods and procedures for using the SSD which were illustrated in the above example were developed by analyzing the requirements of the various activities of structured speech training and relating them to the characteristics of this specific training aid. The analysis suggested possible applications which have been developed through experimental work with hearing-impaired students ranging from 6 to 20 years of age (Houde and Braeges, in press; Braeges, 1980).

The analysis of the components of structured speech training could be used as a basis for developing procedures for the use of other speech training aids. The questions which must be answered are: (1) What are the major components of structured speech teaching? (2) What characteristics of aids are of particular benefit to each activity? (3) How may an aid be used at each step?

Framework for Developing Sensory Aid Procedures

Although there are a number of different approaches to structured speech training with the hearing-impaired (Haycock, 1933; Ewing and Ewing, 1964; Ling, 1976), nearly all methods have three main activities in common: (1) error analysis, (2) production teaching, and (3) production drill.

ERROR ANALYSIS

In most structured speech training programs, once the target skill to be developed has been selected, the student's error production is analyzed to determine the way it differs

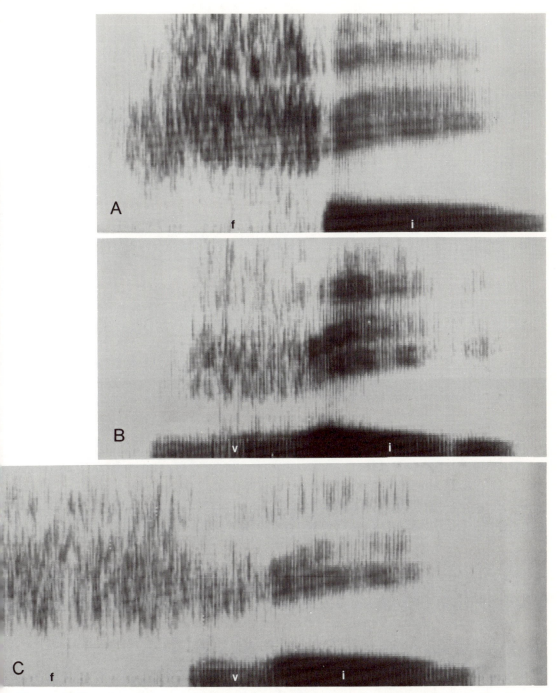

Figure 15.2. *A* and *B*, spectrograms of correct [f] and [v], respectively. *C*, production of error [fv].

Figure 15.3. Typical student spectrogram during development of [v] phoneme.

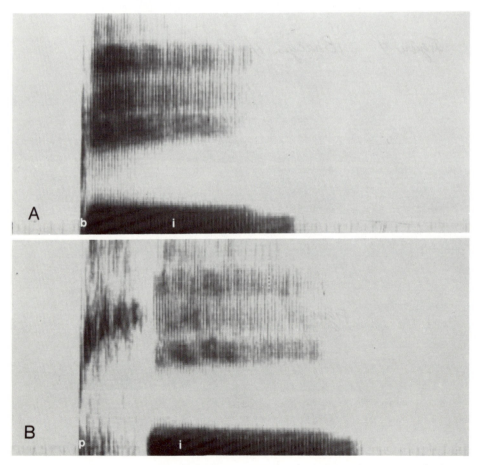

Figure 15.4. *A* and *B*, spectrograms of correct [b] and [p], respectively.

from the correct production. This analysis is the basis for the corrective directions that are given to the student. Traditionally, this analysis is performed by the ear of the teacher and is usually sufficient for many errors. The error may be described by relating it to a reference set of other phonetic productions, i.e., in terms of substitution, omission, or distortion. The teacher does not need assistance from an outside monitor, such as a speech display, to describe these "simple" errors.

Many productions in the speech of the deaf, however, are not easily perceived by ear alone. Deaf speakers often produce distinctions based on parameters which differ from the standard phoneme feature distinctions of English. Because we tend to perceive categorically (Lisker and Abramson, 1967), production errors which do not result in a change of one whole phoneme are often difficult to analyze. Such marginal productions are common in the speech of the deaf. An example of this error is /p^b/ for /p/. The error production is not clearly /b/ or /p/ and is usually caused by the deaf speaker producing a voice onset time (VOT) which is too long for a clear /b/ but too short to be an unambiguous /p/. Such a production may be identified by the teacher as something between /b/ and /p/, but the accurate analysis of such extraphonemic errors in articulatory terms is very difficult.

A speech training aid which displays the continuous range of phonetic parameters (e.g., range of VOT error productions, as shown on an SSD) rather than categorical representations (e.g., voiced versus unvoiced judgment as shown on a VSTA (Stewart et al., 1973) could assist in the identification and analysis of ambiguous VOT productions. The phonetic distinction /p/ versus /p^b/ is clearly displayed by a sound spectrograph. Figure 15.4 presents spectrograms of correct productions of /p/ and /b/. Figure 15.5 presents a /p^b/ production by a hearing-impaired speaker. The length of the VOT of the correct and error productions can be measured over a number of trials to identify an objective measurement of the VOT necessary for an unambiguous /p/ production.

Similarly, an aid which displays pitch vary-

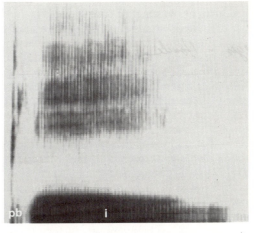

Figure 15.5. Spectrogram of typical [p^b] error.

ing in time can assist in the analysis of pitch contour productions, which are often difficult to evaluate perceptually beyond the simple correct/error judgment. A device which provides storage permits objective measurements and analysis of the nature of the errors. Figure 15.6 presents a Visi-Pitch tracing of a terminal contour.

As tools to aid in the analysis of error

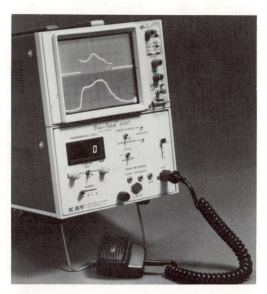

Figure 15.6. Visi-Pitch display of terminal contour (courtesy of Kay Elemetrics Corp.).

productions, parametric speech displays must be used with some caution. A parametric display presents isolated features, or parameters, of the speech signal. Such an aid identifies a specific feature of the signal, "decides" how to describe that feature, and displays the result of the decision. For example, a pitch frequency display "decides" what the frequency of the speech signal is and then displays it. A nonparametric instrument presents the speech signal as is, and the interpretive decisions must be made by the user.

Parametric displays may, at times, present inappropriate information. For example, what is perceived as an acceptable pitch may be displayed as being unsatisfactory. (This can occur when there is a sudden intensity drop in the student's voice.) The parametric display exhibits a decision but does not indicate the validity of that decision.

Speech displays can be of considerable assistance in the analysis of errors if they freeze the display (storage) for objective analysis and measurement. In addition, the amount of signal analysis incorporated within the aid

determines its relative contribution to the analysis task. In general, the less processed the signal, that is, the more complete the representation of the speech production, the greater the amount of information provided for analysis.

PRODUCTION TEACHING

In this step of structured speech training the teacher must communicate to the students how to use their articulators to correctly produce the target. Traditional methods include auditory modeling, diagrams, and verbal descriptions. Because of the abstract and dynamic nature of the desired productions, it is often difficult to communicate the necessary information to the hearing-impaired student by using traditional methods. A speech display may be used as an additional communication tool if it directly displays articulatory activity or can be clearly related to it.

A speech aid which displays information in articulatory terms is the Electro-Palatograph (Fig. 15.7). A thin artificial palate imbedded with electrodes is placed in the

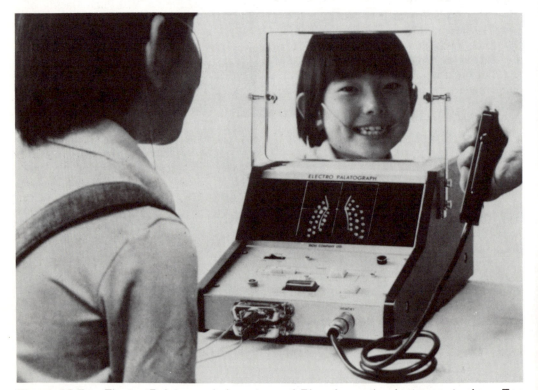

Figure 15.7. Electro-Palatograph (courtesy of Rion Acoustics Instruments, Inc., Torrance, California).

student's mouth. Lights on a display board show the points of tongue/palate contact. The desired points and duration of contact can thus be shown directly to the student. Although the accuracy of this display is lessened because saliva can trigger the electrodes in the absence of tongue contact, this direct articulatory representation of speech production is potentially very useful.

Although not a direct articulatory display, the SSD representation of the speech signal can be related to the student's articulation and therefore used to develop production skills. For example, correction of the substitution of /d/ for /t/ can be facilitated by first having the student record /t/ in isolation. The teacher explains that the vertical lines show aspiration, and the light space at the bottom shows there was no voicing. Next, the student is told to record "/t/–pause–/i/". The importance of the light space (no voicing) after the /t/ release and before the vowel is stressed. The student is helped, through repeated trials, to retain the brief absence of voicing after release while decreasing the length of his pause before the vowel (Fig. 15.8). The instantaneous visual representation of the exaggerated production enables the student to direct his attention to the precise sound and feeling of the important parameter, the delayed onset of voicing. This instantaneous feedback may assist the student in making the association between the production motor activity and its tactile-proprioceptive and auditory sensations. The instantaneity of a speech display may be a critical factor in developing the student's internal self-monitoring ability.

In order to be a useful teaching tool, a sensory aid must be accurate. It must display phonetic distinctions with a high level of clarity and consistency because its function at this step of speech training is the development of the student's understanding of the task. Uncertainty introduced by an unclear or inconsistent display is frustrating to both the student and the teacher.

PRODUCTION DRILL

Once the student understands how to produce the target correctly, he must practice it to develop his skill to an automatic level. Feedback relative to his attempts serves to reinforce the correct productions and thus increase the frequency of their occurrence. The amount and degree of feedback changes through the course of the student's progress. Early in therapy, the error rate is high, and right/wrong feedback may not be explicitly given after each attempt. This would be too punishing to the student. Correct productions are clearly noted and reinforced, but many errors are only implicitly identified, in part by the more complex, directive feedback they prompt from the teacher. As the student's skill improves, the percentage of simple feedback increases, and the more complex analytic feedback decreases. At some point the simple feedback alone is sufficient. This point of development is the drill phase. A speech display which provides clear, consistent simple feedback in an easy-to-use way can provide a means of independent work to the student. A system in which the SSD is used to deliver large amounts of independent drill in phonetic production is a regular part of the speech program at the Rochester School for the Deaf (Houde, 1980a; Altman et al., 1981). It has been found that student learning rates are approximately equal whether the drill has been delivered by a teacher or by the SSD. Because students can work relatively independently with a speech display, one teacher can monitor three or four students at one time, thus significantly multiplying the amount of drill available to each student.

As the student's production skill improves, the problem of weaning him from the external feedback must be addressed. The student's independent evaluation of his speech is necessary for the spontaneous use of the learned skills. The question of the development of self-monitoring skills in conjunction with the use of an external feedback device has been noted by Maki (1980). In this study, students at the National Technical Institute for the Deaf received feedback from an instantaneous spectrographic display (SSD) during alternate blocks of drill. They were required to judge their own productions without external feedback during the non-SSD blocks. Speech production and judgment skills improved during both the SSD and non-SSD blocks. These data suggested that the use of learned skills did not require the presence of the visual feedback. The development of self-monitoring skills, and their

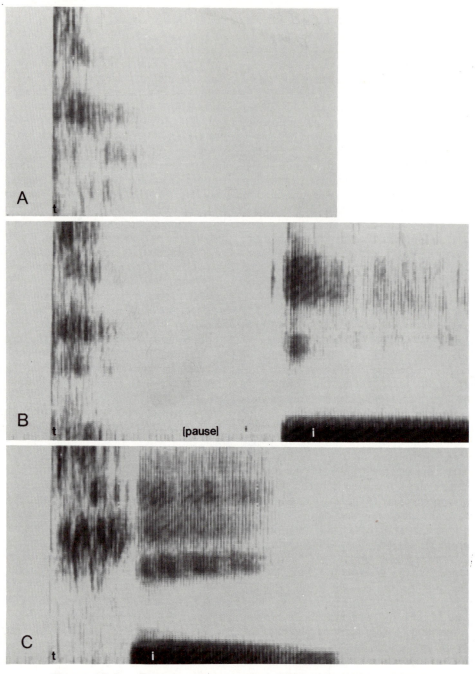

Figure 15.8. Sample spectrograms of [t] production teaching.

relationship to the use of sensory feedback aids, require further study.

Regardless of the particular activity in which a speech training aid is used, concern is often raised about a student's ability and willingness to work with such instruments.

We have found that initially an aid's novelty in the speech training situation motivates the student. As this novelty wanes, the assignments can be varied, and the materials made more interesting (Altman et al., 1981). The Computer Based Speech Training Aid (Nick-

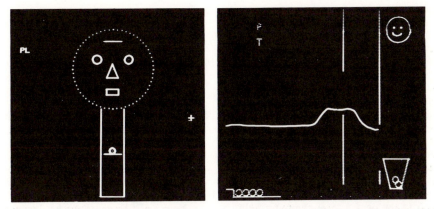

Figure 15.9. Motivating displays used by Computer Based Speech Training Aid (courtesy of A.G. Bell Association for the Deaf).

erson and Stevens, 1973; Boothroyd et al., 1975) used smiley faces and visual games to motivate the student (Figure 15.9). In addition, the objective feedback supplied by a device may be accepted by the student with a greater level of confidence than the teacher's feedback (Maki, 1980). Frequently, the student's improving skill is obvious to him. This increased confidence and skill result in sustained interest and motivation to improve.

SUMMARY

Sensory aids can be useful in teaching speech skills to hearing-impaired students. The ability of speech displays to exhibit phonetic distinctions and thus assist in differentiating between correct and incorrect productions may be adapted to the three major activities of speech training: error analysis, production teaching, and production drill. All aids, however, do not serve these purposes equally well. The various characteristics of the different speech aids make them particularly useful in one or another of these teaching activities.

This chapter has provided a framework for organizing the great array of sensory aids which exist. A procedure has been suggested to compare and rate different aids in their ability to exhibit the phonetic distinctions important in speech training. This information may be used as a basis for selecting aids for teaching. Examples are provided of the actual use of sensory aids in each of the three main activities of speech training, and particular characteristics of aids which are of interest to each activity are identified. This material may serve as a basis for developing methods and procedures for the use of sensory aids in the task of teaching speech to the hearing-impaired.

APPENDIX 1

Speech Training Aids

1. Bell Telephone Laboratories, Visible Speech Translator-I.
   Potter, R.K. Visible patterns of sound. *Science*, 1945, *102*, 463–470.
   Potter, R.K., Kopp, G.A., and Green, H.C. *Visible Speech*. New York: VanNostrand, 1947. Reprinted as Potter, R.K., Kopp, G.A., and Kopp, H.G. *Visible Speech*, New York: Dover Publications, 1966.
2. Bell Telephone Laboratories, Visible Speech Translator-II.
   Stark, R.E., Cullen, J.K., and Chase, R.A. Preliminary work with the new Bell Telephone Visible Speech Translator. *Am. Ann. Deaf*, 1968, *113*, 205–214.
   Stark, R.E. Teaching /ba/ and /pa/ to deaf children using a real-time spectral display. *Lang. Speech*, 1972, *15*, 14–29.
3. Speech Spectrographic Display. Available from Spectraphonics, Inc., 1531 St. Paul Street, Rochester, New York, 14621.
   Stewart, L.C., Larkin, W.D., and Houde, R.A. A real time sound spectrograph with implications for speech training for the deaf. In *Proceedings of the 1976 IEEE International Conference on Acoustics, Speech, and Signal Processing.* New York: IEEE Press, 1976, 590–593.
   Houde, R.A., and Braeges, J.L. A role for

sensory aids in formal speech training for the deaf. In *Proceedings of the Conference on the Speech of the Hearing-Impaired*, City University of New York, November 1979. Washington, D.C.: A.G. Bell Association for the Deaf (in press).

4. Spens, K.E. Preliminary results from experiments on recognition of spectral patterns on a vibrator matrix with different time windows. In *Quarterly Progress and Status Report 2–3*. Stockholm: Speech Transmission Laboratory, 1976.

5. Risberg, A. Visual aids for speech correction. *Am. Ann. Deaf*, 1968, *113*, 178–194.

6. Nickerson, R.S., and Stevens, K.N. Teaching speech to the deaf: Can a computer help? *IEEE Trans. Audio Electroacoust.*, 1973, 445–455.
    Boothroyd, A., Archambault, P., Adams, R.E., and Storm, R.D. Use of a computer-based system of speech training aids for deaf persons. *Volta Rev.*, 1975, *77*, 178–193.

7. Spens, K.E. Tactile speech communication aids for the deaf: A comparison. In *Quarterly Progress and Status Report 4*, Stockholm: Speech Transmission Laboratory, 1980.

8. Engelmann, S., and Rosov, R. Tactual hearing experiment with deaf and hearing subjects. Except. Child., 1975, *41*, 243–253.

9. Oller, D., Payne, S.L., and Gavin, W.J. Tactual speech perception by minimally trained deaf subjects. *J. Speech Hear. Res.*, 1980, *23*, 769–778.

10. Saunders, F.A., Hill, W.A., and Simpson, C.A. Speech perception via the tactile model: Progress report. In *Proceedings of the 1976 IEEE International Conference on Acoustics, Speech, and Signal Processing*. New York: IEEE Press, 1976, 594–597.

11. Sparks, D., Kuhl, P., Edmonds, A., and Gray, G. Investigating the MESA (Multipoint Electrotactile Speech Aid): The transmission of segmental features of speech. *J. Acoust. Soc. Am.*, 1978, *63*, 246–257.

12. Goldstein, M.H., and Stark, R. Modifications of vocalizations of preschool deaf children by vibrotactile and visual displays. *J. Acoust. Soc. Am.*, 1976, *59*, 1477–1481.

13. Kirman, J.H. Tactile perception of computer-derived formant patterns from voiced speech. *J. Acoust. Soc. Am.*, 1974, *55*, 163–169.

14. Pickett, J.M., and Constam, A. A visual speech trainer with simplified indication of vowel spectrum. *Am. Ann. Deaf*, 1968, *113*, 253–258.

15. Reeder, K. A low-frequency formant speech code for the hearing impaired. Unpublished doctoral dissertation, Brighman Young University, 1975.

16. Traunmuller, H. The Sentiphone. In *Proceedings of the Conference on Speech Processing Aids for the Deaf*, Gallaudet College, 1977 (in press).

17. Stewart, L.C., Houde, R.A., and Larkin, W.D. The VSTA: An approach to the speech training instrumentation problem. Paper presented at the Proceedings of the Cranahan Conference on Electronic Prosthetics, Lexington, Kentucky, 1973.

18. Boothroyd, A., and Damashek, M. *Development of Small Speech Training Aids*, S.A.R.P. #23. Northhampton, Massachusetts: Clarke School for the Deaf, 1976.

19. Available from S.I. America, 255 South 17th Street, Philadelphia, Pennsylvania 19103.

20. Available from Voice Identification, Inc., P.O. Box 714, Somerville, New Jersey 08876.

21. Available from Madsen Electronics, 1807 Elmwood Ave., Buffalo, New York 14207.

22. Dolansky, L., Phillips, N.D., and Bass, A.D. An intonation display system for the deaf. In G. Fant (ed.), *International Symposium on Speech Communication Ability and Profound Deafness*. Washington, D.C.: A.G. Bell Association for the Deaf, 1972, 283–293.

23. Available from Saber Inc., Suite 216-N, 2020 North Atlantic Avenue, Cocoa Beach, Florida 32931.

24. Stratton, W.D. Intonation feedback for the deaf through a tactile display. *Volta Rev.*, 1974, *76*, 26–35.

25. Vilchur, E., and Killian, M.C. Auditory aid to deaf speakers in monitoring fundamental voice frequencies. *J. Acoust. Soc. Am.*, 1976, *59* (Suppl. #1): 569 (abstract).

26. Fletcher, S.G., and Bishop, M.E. Measurement of nasality with Tonar. *Cleft Palate J.* 1970, *7*, 610–621.

27. Available from Behavioral Controls, Inc., P.O. Box 480, Milwaukee, Wisconsin 53201.

28. Available from Linguisystems, Inc., Suite 806, 1630 Fifth Avenue, Moline, Illinois 61265.

29. Pickett, J.M., Gengel, R.W., Quinn, R., and Upton, H.W. Research with the Upton Eyeglass Speechreader. In G. Fant (ed.), *Proceedings of the 1974 Stockholm Speech Communications Seminar*. New York: John Wiley & Sons, 1974.

30. Cornett, R.O., Beadles, R., and Wilson, B. Automatic cued speech. In *Proceedings of the Conference on Speech Processing Aids*

for the Deaf, Gallaudet College, 1977 (in press).

31. Pronovost, W., Yenkin, L., Anderson, D.C., and Lerner, R. The Voice Visualizer. *Am. Ann. Deaf*, 1968, *113*, 230–238.

32. Available from Amera, Inc., 2515 North 1600 East Street, Logan, Utah 84321.

33. Available from Siemens Hearing Instruments, Inc., 685 Liberty Avenue, Union, New Jersey 07083.
    Schulte, K. The use of supplementary speech information in verbal communication. *Volta Rev.*, 1978, *80*, 12–20.

34. Connors, S., and McPherson, D.L. A vibrotactile training program for the deaf using a single vibrator. In D. McPherson (ed.), *Advances in Prosthetic Devices for the Deaf*. Rochester, New York: National Techical Institute for the Deaf, 1978, 208–217.

35. Goldstein, M.H. Tactual stimulation in speech reception: Experience with a non-auditory child. In *Proceedings of the Conference on the Speech of the Hearing Impaired*, City University of New York, November 1979 (in press).

36. Miller, J.D., Engebretson, A.M., and DeFilippo, C.L. Preliminary research with a three channel vibrotactile speech reception aid for the deaf. In G. Fant (ed.), *Proceedings of the 1974 Stockholm Speech Communications Seminar*. New York: John Wiley & Sons, 1974.

37. Available from Scott Instruments, 815 N. Elm Street, Denton, Texas 76201.
    Scott, B.L. Development of a tactile aid for the profoundly hearing impaired. In M. Henoch (ed.), *Aural Rehabilitation for the Elderly*. New York: Grune & Stratton, 1979.

38. Available from Rion Acoustic Instruments, Inc., 912 West 223 St., Torrance, California 90502.
    Kiritani, S., Kakita, K., and Shibata, S. Dynamic palatography. In M. Sawashima, and F.S. Cooper (eds.), *Dynamic Aspects of Speech Production*. Tokyo: University of Tokyo Press, 1977.

39. Fletcher, S.G., Hasegawa, A., McCutcheon, M.J., and Gilliom, J.D. Use of lingua-palatal contact patterns to modify articulation in a deaf adult speaker. In D. McPherson (ed.), *Advances in Prosthetic Devices for the Deaf*. Rochester, New York: National Technical Institute for the Deaf, 1978.

40. Crichton, R.G., and Fallside, F. Linear prediction model of speech production with applications to deaf speech training. *Proc. Inst. Elect. Eng. Contr. Sci.*, 1974, *121*, 865–873.

41. Wakita, H. Direct estimation of the vocal tract shape by inverse filtering of acoustic speech wave forms. *IEEE Trans. Audio Electroacoust.*, 1973, AU-21, 417–427.

42. Fletcher, S. Orometric measurements and modifications of deaf speech. *IEEE Spectrum*, 1981, *5*, to appear.

43. Fourcin, A.J., and Abberton, E. First applications of a new laryngograph. *Med. Biol. Illus.*, 1975, *21*, #3.

44. Guttman, N., Levitt, H., and Bellefleur, P.A. Articulatory training of the deaf using low frequency surrogate fricatives. *J. Speech Hear. Res.*, 1970, *13*, 19–29.

45. Available from Kay Elemetrics Corp., 12 Maple Ave., Pinebrook, New Jersey 07058.

References

Altman, E., Antimore, D., DeBold, J., Heaney, N., Koch, J., and Skrobach, I. Independent visual feedback drill integrated with speech training for the deaf. Paper presented at the Convention of American Educators of the Deaf, Rochester, New York, 1981.

Angelocci, A., Kopp, G., and Holbrook, A. The vowel formants of deaf and normal hearing eleven- to fourteen-year-old boys. *J. Speech Hear. Disord.*, 1964, *29*, 156–170.

Boothroyd, A., et al. Use of a computer-based system of speech training aids for deaf persons. *Volta Rev.*, 1975, *77*, 178–193.

Braeges, J. Spectrographic analysis for the diagnosis of the articulation errors of deaf children. Paper presented at the New York State Speech and Hearing Association Convention, April 1980.

Ewing, A., and Ewing, E. *Teaching Deaf Children to Talk*. Manchester: Manchester University, Press, 1964.

Haycock, G.S. *The Teaching of Speech*. Washington, D.C.: Volta Bureau, 1933.

Houde, R.A. Evaluation of independent drill with visual aids for speech training. In J.D. Subtelny (ed.), *Speech Assessment and Speech Improvement for the Hearing Impaired*. Washington, D.C.: A.G. Bell Association for the Deaf, 1980a.

Houde, R. An analysis of the articulation skills of deaf children. Paper presented at New York Speech and Hearing Association Convention, 1980b.

Houde, R., and Braeges, J. Independent drill: A role for speech training aids in the speech development of the deaf. In *Proceedings of the Conference on the Speech of the Hearing Impaired*, City University of New York, November, 1979 (in press).

Hudgins, C., and Numbers, F. An investigation of the intelligibility of the speech of the deaf. *Genet. Psychol. Mono.*, 1942, *25*, 289–392.

Levitt, H. Acoustic characteristics of the speech of deaf children: Factors affecting intelligibility. In *Proceedings of the Conference on the Speech of the Hearing Impaired*, City University of New York, November 1979 (in press).

Levitt, H., Pickett, J., and Houde, R. (eds.) *Sensory Aids for the Hearing Impaired.* New York: IEEE Press, 1980.

Liberman, A., Cooper, F., Shankweiler, O., and Studdert-Kennedy, M. Why are speech spectrograms hard to read? *Am. Ann. Deaf,* 1968, *113,* 127–133.

Ling, D. Speech and the Hearing Impaired Child: Theory and Practice. Washington, D.C.: A.G. Bell Association for the Deaf, 1976.

Ling, D., and Ling, A. *Aural Habilitation: The Foundations of Verbal Learning in Hearing Impaired Children.* Washington, D.C.: A.G. Bell Association for the Deaf, 1978.

Lisker, L., and Abramson, A. Some effects of context on voice onset time in English stops. *Lang. Speech,* 1967, *10,* 1–28, 1967.

Maki, J. Visual feedback as an aid to speech therapy. In J. Subtelny (ed.), *Speech Assessment and Improvement for the Hearing Impaired.* Washington, D.C.: A.G. Bell Association for the Deaf, 1980.

Nickerson, R., and Stevens, K. Teaching speech to the deaf: Can a computer help? *IEEE Trans. Audio Electroacoust.,* 1973.

Smith, C. Residual hearing and speech production in deaf children. *J. Speech Hear. Res.,* 1975, *18,* 795–811.

Stewart, L.C., Houde, R.A., and Larkin, W.D. The VSTA: A approach to the speech training instrumentation problem. Proceedings of the Cranahan Conference on Electronic Prosthetics, Lexington, Kentucky, 1973.

Chapter 16

Functional Speech Therapy for the Deaf Child

ANN K. LIEBERTH, M.A.

The ability to articulate sounds in itself is a biomechanical marvel. Coordination of respiration, phonation, and articulation in the act of speaking involves muscles, nerve fiber firings, and split-millisecond timing between events. Phonemes must be combined rapidly to produce intelligible utterances. The cycle is completed, when the syntax and semantics are processed, by using a common phonological and semantic rule system. This enables the listener to extract meaning and produce a response. The fact that most of us develop the skill of articulation with few problems and no direct, formal teaching adds to the amazement of it all.

The complex nature of the act of speech

production makes teaching this skill to others who have not developed it or who are producing phonemes in error difficult. The problems of developing speech in a prelingually deaf child are particularly baffling to the speech pathologist. The task becomes monumental when influenced by an inadequate or nonfunctional auditory feedback system.

BACKGROUND INFORMATION

"Throughout the recorded history of education of the deaf, the desirability of equipping the deaf person with spoken language has seldom if ever been questioned [Calvert and Silverman, 1975, p. 1]." As one surveys the literature, no matter what the philosophy of communication, the value of teaching speech to the deaf is seldom ignored, nor are discussions of the teaching of that skill eliminated. "To reduce or abandon our best efforts in teaching speech to deaf persons is to deny them the opportunity for an achievement unique to man—the development of an acoustic code that enables a human being to communicate with his fellow human being in a distinctive way that is not possible through any other mode of communication [Calvert and Silverman, 1975, p. 2]."

Many methods have been developed to teach deaf children to speak. As can be seen in Table 16.1, which summarizes methods of teaching speech to the deaf, trends appear and disappear. The methods may be classified into (1) multisensory, (2) unisensory, (3) methods using technical devices to transform speech into a more visible form, (4) methods using written, signed, or fingerspelled symbols to represent speech, and (5) approaches using a combination of any or all of the above. Within each classification, we can identify analytic (sound-by-sound) approaches as well as synthetic (whole-word) approaches. An understanding of the variety and development of methods of teaching speech to the deaf is important if one is to create a theoretical framework for effective intervention strategies.

Multisensory Methods

"Speech is a visuo-motor-kinetic activity. Perception and production of speech require the use of all modalities, each developed to the maximum level [French, 1971, p. 212]." This is the underlying theme of the methods of teaching speech classified as multisensory. Touch, speechreading, audition, and representations of speech are used in various combinations to develop receptive and expressive oral language. Speech production is dependent on, and shaped by, speech perception. The perception of speech is seen as the utilization and integration of the total sensory features of the sound (Calvert and Silverman, 1975, p. 159).

Visible speech, Zaliouk's method (1954), the Association Phoneme method, and Rau's method (1960) use written, printed, fingerspelled, or other symbol systems to represent what is happening during the act of speech. Ling (1976, p. 4) envisions the development of speech primarily as auditory-based, but stresses the importance of the role of multiple sensory modalities in developing and maintaining speech skills.

Researchers hypothesized that a "system overload" may result from the use of multisensory methods in teaching speech to the deaf. Two reasons were offered for this hypothesis: (1) a child cannot attend to multiple stimuli presented quickly, remember them, and integrate the different stimuli into a percept (meaning is attached to stimuli); and (2) stimuli arising from the various concurrent signals (auditory, visual, tactile, motokinesthetic) are different. Certain aspects of each sensory input are more crucial than others in forming a percept. These crucial elements are not similar across sensory modalities (Ling, 1976).

Unisensory Methods

In the unisensory methods, audition is the primary channel used in speech training. These methods (labeled aural methods, unisensory methods, auditory methods, and acoupedics) gained recognition in the 1960's (Calvert and Silverman, 1975, pp. 148–166). Advocates of these approaches believe that use of lipreading, taction, or motokinesthesis in speech training creates a dependence on these senses and serves as a detriment to the development of listening skills. Audition, on the other hand, is best suited for the devel-

Table 16.1
Methods of Speech Training

Methods	Characteristics
Multisensory	
Babbling method (Avondino, 1919)	Syllable drill as vehicle for development of speech
Visible speech (Bell, 1932)	Symbol system
TVA (tactile-visual-auditory) (French, 1971)	All sensory inputs used to maximum
Zaliouk (1954)	Visual-tactile system; represents movements of articulation
Rau (1960)	Fingerspelling integrated with phoneme teaching
Association Phoneme (McGinnis, 1963)	Written, printed, or pictures used to teach speech—analytic
Ling (1976)	Multisensory, sequenced, systematic; phonological and phonetic level development
Unisensory	
Pure oralism/auditory stimulation	Analytic; speechreading and home training also emphasized
Acoustic (Goldstein, 1939)	Emphasis on audition
Krug (Moores, 1978)	Written and spoken labeling of objects in child's environment; motokinesthetic
Language association—element of natural language	Speech learned through activity
Acoupedic (Pollack, 1964)	Audition facilitates speech development
Auditory global (Goldstein, 1939)	Synthetic; connected speech is always used as stimulus

opment of speech skills, the primary characteristics of which are acoustic (Ling, 1976, p. 22; Berg, 1976, p. 138; Siebert, 1980, p. 104). The basic tenets of these methods are (1) that all deaf persons have some amount of residual hearing and (2) that the speech of the deaf person who has been trained with audition as the primary input is superior in intelligibility than that of the deaf person trained through any other channel (Moores, 1978, p. 230). The child is trained to use audition alone in perceiving the speech patterns he is asked to produce.

Orthographic Systems

The methods mentioned previously concentrate on the development of production skills utilizing speech reception (either a symbol or visual, auditory, or tactile input) as the primary avenue of instruction. Thus, early in the history of teaching speech to the deaf, the correlation between speech reception and speech production was recognized. Yet, intelligible speech was not achieved by the majority of deaf children. This inspired the continual search for other methods of teaching speech to deaf children.

From Alexander M. Bell's (1914) attempts at making speech more visible came the development of other symbol systems to represent speech sounds. Among these are the Fitzgerald Key, Northampton Charts, International Phonetic Alphabet, International Teaching Alphabet, and the use of diacritical markings. Magner (1971, p. 251) believed that the choice of one of the symbol systems is not nearly as important as continued use of one system. Often the therapist who works with the child a limited number of hours is the only person that uses the orthographic system with the child. Thus, the child has only limited practice in the use.

Ling (1976, pp. 56–60) believes that the use of an orthographic symbol system in teaching speech to the deaf can impede rather than enhance progress. Ling's arguments are summarized in the following:

1) Use of any system of writing is developmentally inappropriate in teaching speech to deaf children. Children are not ready motorically and neurologically for reading and writing until age 4 or 5. 2) The written forms used to represent speech are clumsy and bizarre. The systems chosen represent the "sound" of language but do not represent in all cases the traditional use of the symbols in reading. Hence, the children had to learn that there were two orthographic symbol systems—one to apply in reading, and one to use in speaking or learning speech. 3) Some proponents of the use of a symbol system in teaching speech advocate teaching reading and writing before introducing speech production. This may waste valuable time during the critical period for language and speech learning. 4) If speech, reading, and writing are taught at the same time, the development of three different skills is required of the child. 5) The use of the written form overburdens the child's memory system. 6) The written form, as used by most therapists, ignores the suprasegmentals.

Pike (1945) has attempted to solve this latter concern, developing a separate marking system to indicate prosodic features. Ling (1976, p. 56) and Ling and Ling (1978, p. 143), however, have identified analytic features of an orthographic symbol system as a primary culprit in causing many of the speech characteristics of the deaf which have been noted by Hudgins and Numbers (1942) and Nickerson (1975). The child becomes dependent on a symbol system rather than on automatic production of meaningful speech.

He learns to produce the phonemes represented by the symbols on command, but functional use in everyday communication is limited (Vorce, 1971, p. 226; Ling, 1976, p. 56).

The appearance of cued speech (Cornett, 1967) was applauded as a nonwritten symbol system for representing the speech sounds of English in developing receptive and expressive skills in the deaf child. The system, comprised of hand positions and configurations, was designed to aid speechreading. Again, this system had some merits in improving speech reception which, in turn, would hopefully improve speech production. The primary criticism of this method is that attention to the visual signal detracted from or confused the auditory signal reception (Ling and Clarke, 1975). Cued speech is attractive in that it is learned easily by the child, the teacher, the therapist, and the parent. The problem comes in the applicability of the system in everyday communication.

Technical Devices

The shortcomings of using a written or cued form in teaching speech, as well as technological advances, encouraged the development of a better means of representing the speech signal in a visible or tactile form. This area offered hope to those interested in developing intelligible speech in the deaf. The rationale used in development of speech training aids are that (1) a pattern or model can be presented to or compared by the student for production and (2) the teacher can intervene and pinpoint the student's errors (Pickett, 1971). See Chapters 3 and 15 for detailed discussion of tactile and visual aids.

SPEECH TRAINING FOR THE DEAF CHILD

The problem in speech training for the hearing-impaired child lies in the fact that those responsible for that training want to use *the* method of *their* choice for the child. The expectation is that if a method has worked for one child, it will work for all deaf children. If failure occurs, however, it is generally not believed to be the result of the training method. The choice of training approach should be based on (1) appropriateness for the child, (2) provision of maximum opportunity for the child to develop auditory skills, (3) provision for assessment of other disabilities which may impede progress in speech development, (4) provision for ongoing assessment of the child's progress, and (5) provision for alternative techniques if necessary (Calvert and Silverman, 1975, pp. 166–167). The choice of method, therefore, should be based on what the child brings to the intervention process, not what we instill upon him.

The following description is not of a method of speech training. It has not been subjected to experimental design or research because of the flexibility and variability of its application. Rather, it is a definition and description of possible approaches to the development of some essentials of speech production. As stated previously in this text, the method of speech training should vary with the child's needs, environment, abilities and disabilities.

Speech production includes respiration, phonation, resonation, articulation, and the addition of the suprasegmental features of pitch, rate, rhythm, and loudness. Ling (1976, p. 3) groups these parameters into phonetic level skills and phonological level skills. Phonetic level skills include the ability to (1) control intensity, duration, and voice frequency during vocalization, and (2) produce, repeat, and alternate segmental patterns within syllables. These skills are necessary, although not exclusive, prerequisites for the development of spoken language. Phonological skills include the ability to use the segmental and suprasegmental features of speech in meaningful contexts (Ling, 1980). An effective program of speech training should include training on both the phonetic and phonological levels.

The objectives of speech training with the child, the description of which will follow, include the following: (1) to develop the ability to vocalize and use voice meaningfully; (2) to develop a controlled, pleasant, and relaxed voice quality; (3) to develop vocalization with proper pitch, intensity, and duration; (4) to develop imitative ability in respect to speech production; (5) to develop control of and appropriate physiological coordination between articulation, respiration, phonation, and resonation in the production of speech; (6) to develop maximal use of

residual hearing in receptive and expressive communication; (7) to develop a multisensory cue system to aid reception and production of speech; (8) to develop articulation of phonemes in contexts that are meaningful to the child; (9) to develop use of the skills mastered at the phonetic level in spontaneous speech; and (10) to develop the recognition that speech is an effective means of controlling one's environment to satisfy personal needs (Siebert, 1980, pp. 106–107). With the objectives in mind, intervention strategies will be suggested for the deaf child.

The steps in training should be geared to the child's abilities and needs in achieving the objectives listed above. They include (1) establishment of vocalization, (2) control of suprasegmentals (breath control and support, duration, increasing complexity of vocal duration, intensity, pitch, and rhythm), and (3) phoneme training (imitative level, syllable level, word level, and sentence level). In all steps in the program, perception training precedes production training.

Establishing Vocalization

In this stage of increasing and modeling vocalization, we must not ignore the significance of the relationship between perception and production. Every opportunity should be exploited to integrate auditory and vocal development. It is not enough to "talk, talk, talk" at this stage. The child's auditory skills require more than stimulation if they are to develop and be used to their maximum potential in communication. The child's responses to voice can be developed through stimulus-response reinforcement techniques. When the child responds to voice with a look or a glance, that behavior should be rewarded until it can be elicited consistently. We are assuming, of course, that the child is aided or has sufficient residual hearing to make this response. When the basic response to voice is established, the child should be taught to differentiate voices (Daddy's versus Mommy's). Responses to durational aspects of vocalization may be developed through many creative techniques. The materials and activities used must be (1) attractive but not distracting to the child, (2) developmentally appropriate, (3) integrated with response shaping in production training, (4) realistic, and (5) use speech or human vocalization as the stimuli. The child's efforts—both successful and unsuccessful—should be confirmed, modeled, and reinforced through visual, auditory, and tactile input. The child's responses will be guided, elicited formally, and finally spontaneous.

"Before any formal speech work is begun, it is imperative that some vocalization be present [Siebert, 1980, p. 107]." Hearing-impaired babies are capable of vocalizations, as demonstrated through the acts of coughing, laughing, crying, sneezing, and cooing. These are natural and involuntary vocalizations involving simple muscle coordinations. Without the reinforcement of hearing his own voice and the voice patterns of others, a deaf child's vocal play decreases or ceases. The therapist must reestablish the child's voluntary use of vocalization. Techniques include social reinforcement of the child's use of vocalization, and the provision of voice patterns for the child to imitate. Involuntary vocalizations provide a starting point during which reinforcement of the use of voice may occur. Tactile or visual devices, such as a vibrator or a sound-sensitive light, provide further information to the child in reference to what response is desired. The child is tickled, thus stimulating him to laugh. The use of voice during laughter is rewarded. Activities should quickly move to those which stimulate the use of voice—play activities, "need" activities (the child has to use voice to obtain something). The visual or tactile aid that was used during involuntary vocalization may be used to provide a consistency in the response-reinforcement paradigm.

The parents' response to normal vocalizations of the child provide positive reinforcement and serve to increase the quantity, quality, and length of his vocalizations. For example, the child comes to the father with a toy that is broken or a box that will not open. If the child uses vocalization during his "request" for help, a smile, pat, or simple acknowledgment of the child can serve as a reinforcer. If the child is capable of voluntary use of voice, withholding the item requested, ignoring the child, or requesting or reminding him to use his voice before the request is filled can be effective in training meaningful use of voice. The parents should be instructed in techniques for increasing vocalization, enhancing variety (pitch and duration) in vocalized patterns, and increasing meaningful use of vocalization.

Ling (1976) sets the following criteria for this phase:

"1) spontaneous production of at least 12 voluntary vocalizations in the course of a three minute observation period when the child is stimulated through active play, 2) the consistent use of voice to attract attention, and 3) vocalization in response to a question or when asked to imitate [p. 196]."

Control of Suprasegmentals

The next step in the intervention process should be voluntary control of the suprasegmental features of voice: duration, intensity, and pitch. These parameters were discussed earlier but only as they occurred involuntarily. As the child becomes more social, the use of suprasegmentals in everyday conversation should be developed for the purpose of self-expression. Auditory, tactile, and visual feedback aids can be incorporated in developing control of the suprasegmental features of voice. The therapist should determine which of the input modes or all she will use in this aspect of training.

BREATH CONTROL AND SUPPORT

Speech pathologists have recognized the correlation between unintelligible speech and poor breath control and support. Thus blowing and deep-breathing exercises are used to foster better control of air expenditure during speech. Bell (1914) and Ptacek and Sander (1963) found no relation between blowing and phonation skills in normally hearing subjects. Thus, the use of blowing exercises as a therapeutic technique in teaching breath control and support to deaf infants is questionable.

Hudgins (1937) has an excellent list of suggestions for the development of breath control and support. The parents may teach the child to imitate the concept of continuous voicing of the vowels with constant pitch and intensity by using a "whisper lite" or sound-sensitive light. Other tactile devices, such as a bone oscillator through which speech is delivered to the child's hand, can also be employed to introduce the target behavior to the child. The target becomes not only meaningful use of voice and voice patterns but also identification, understanding, and auditory association of voice and voice patterns used in everyday conversation.

DURATION

In the initial phase of training in this area, the child acts merely as a receiver who is guided to some action based on what the therapist does with her voice. This affords a perfect opportunity for the integration of auditory training in durational aspects of vocalization. After receptive skills in identification of vocal duration have reached the therapist's criterion level, the child is asked to produce a variety of duration patterns in his use of voice, first on the imitative level, then elicited, and finally in spontaneous utterances used in play or everyday communications.

Various activities may be used to aid in the development of this skill. A toy car can be moved along a "highway"; string can be removed from an empty oatmeal box as long as vocalization occurs; airplanes can be moved along a cardboard "sky"; lines can be traced on paper, connecting items (such as a dog with a dog house) emphasizing one continuous movement per continuous vocalization. Variations in duration may be taught through activities or games, such as musical chairs (this involves audition as well); "Mother May I"—where the child moves as long as the therapist is vocalizing; moving cars along a "highway", moving boats in a "river," etc. Emphasis should be placed on continuous movement with continuous vocalization.

Ling (1976) sets the following criteria for the skill of vocal duration:

"1) sustain a vocalization for at least three seconds; 2) imitate separate vocalizations differing in duration, each on one breath; and 3) imitate up to four separate vocalizations differing in duration all in one breath [p. 201]."

INCREASING COMPLEXITY OF VOCAL DURATION

From this base, the child should be led to the production of alternating durational patterns on one breath. Again, auditory training should be integrated with production training. Tracing a path in a sand box, tracing the child's finger on a strip of sandpaper, and moving a train along different lengths of track are examples of some activities that can be used to teach the child this skill both receptively and expressively. Training should be expanded to reach the criterion performance of the production of four separate syllables of four different durations on one breath. The use of different transportation items, a "running" relay race are examples of activities that can be used to achieve mastery of this stage of development.

INTENSITY

Intensity is another suprasegmental feature of voice that should be included in speech training of the deaf infant. The objective is the conscious control and appropriate use of intensity patterns in spontaneous utterances. In order to achieve this objective, activities and targets should be sequenced, so that mastery of use of one skill leads to facilitation of production as well as perception of another, until the objective has been achieved. Various targets, such as the ability to whisper, the ability to alternate loud and soft voices, the ability to use prolonged soft and loud vowels, and the ability to alternate intensity patterns within one breath grouping, are suggested by Ling (1976, pp. 204–206) as subskills to be developed in the mastery of control of intensity. Unconscious control of each subskill should be attained before the target behavior is changed.

Auditory training should be integrated in each level of development. The child should be able to identify and discriminate loud and soft voice usage. The child can be introduced to the concept by discrimination training with loud and soft sounds. He listens to a drum; if it sounds loud, he can pick up an index card with a large drum drawn on it. If the drum is hit softly, he can choose an index card with a small drum drawn on it. Similarly, if the child hears the therapist saying "hello" in a loud voice, the child chooses an index card, picturing a person with a large mouth. If the child hears the therapist saying "hello" in a soft voice, he can choose an index card with a picture of someone with a small mouth. Use of loud voice should not be construed to mean use of tense, a forced phonation either on the part of the therapist or on the part of the child.

Therapists often use music as one of the stimuli in teaching perception and production of intensity. It should be remembered that we are teaching control and appropriate use of vocal intensity; therefore, the use of music has little or no significance to production training. Various techniques can be used to teach the production of vocal intensity. Activities include having the children call to Mom, Dad, siblings, or peers; "calling" a toy dog; using pictures of children talking loud and whispering for the child to imitate; and "duck, duck, goose" (whispering the word duck and using a loud voice on the word goose).

PITCH

When a deaf infant first begins to use voice (previously identified as reflexive or involuntary voicing as used in crying, laughing, or vocal play), the pitch used is within normal range. Only when the infant is deprived of audition—both auditory feedback and auditory input—does the use of pitch deteriorate and the range narrow to produce the "typical" monotone, flat quality of deaf voices. The most important feature in therapeutic intervention in this area is consistent use of appropriate amplification at the earliest possible age. The major problem in intervention becomes the close relationship between changes in intensity and changes in pitch. The therapist must guard against production of the two parameters simultaneously when presenting a model for the child to imitate.

Auditory identification of pitch change as produced by the therapist or parent is a necessary prerequisite for development of production skills. At first the two different pitches produced by the therapist should be at least an half octave apart. The child is asked to identify if the sound heard is high or low. The stimuli used should be voiced and not a sound produced by a musical instrument, since the objective is to develop control and use of pitch variety in spontaneous utterances.

The next step is actual imitated production by the child of pitch changes. The child imitates the therapist's production of a high-pitched and low-pitched voice. Emphasis

should be placed on tension-free production of the desired pitch at a constant intensity level. The child is then taught to produce a number of pitch changes within his pitch range on one breath. Training in audition should be interspersed with production training at all levels, thus modeling the response for the child into an auditory feedback cue system. As perception skills are sharpened, improvement in production and control of pitch through self-monitoring will follow.

RHYTHM

As an important contributor to intelligibility, rhythm or the timing of phonemic combinations and breath groupings should now be developed as a part of suprasegmental feature and phonological training. Rhythm is affected by the rate of syllable utterance and requires proper grouping, accent, and phrasing of syllables. Speech rhythm is not like musical rhythm; therefore, the value of training using musical rhythm exercises in developing rhythm in speech is questionable.

As with all other stages, training in perception precedes training in production. The child should be presented with a variety of vocalized rhythm patterns using vowels or syllables. He is to identify the rhythm pattern using audition only. Stimuli such as big circles for "stressed" vowels and little circles for "unstressed" vowels drawn on an index card from which the child can choose the pattern heard can be used effectively. The child can reproduce a rhythm pattern presented by the therapist on a drum or with rhythm sticks.

Nursery rhymes are excellent in receptive training. What infant does not like listening to the rhythm and repetitions in nursery rhymes?

Syllable practice involving various rhythm, accent, and phrasing patterns should be introduced. Emphasis in production should be on rhythmic, tension-free production of alternating CV combinations with control and appropriate application of intensity, accent, and breath groupings on the imitated, elicited, and spontaneous levels.

Phonemic Training

Training in the suprasegmentals should not be put aside as the therapist begins formal training in production of consonant-vowel alternations. They remain to be trained in word, phrase, sentence, and conversational contexts for it is in these contexts the suprasegmentals are used in spontaneously generated utterances by the child. The initial control of these features has been taught and now the features should be applied appropriately in phonological contexts.

The stimuli for training suprasegmental parameters of voice have been vowels and, sometimes, consonant-vowel combinations. The focus was *not* on correct articulation of the phonemes but on production of the suprasegmental feature. Delay of phonemic training until these features are present at the unconscious level in the child's phonetic repertoire is not only necessary but also developmentally appropriate. A child engages in vocal play long before he begins to babble or combine closed and open vocalizations.

IMITATIVE LEVEL: CONSONANT/ VOWEL PRODUCTION

Imitations of vowels produced by the therapist must be present before consonant-vowel combinations are introduced. The child should demonstrate a physical as well as a social readiness for this training. Imitated productions should vary in duration, pitch, and intensity. Meaningful vowel productions—"uh, oh," "ah," "oo," "ow"—should be incorporated as part of this perception and production training.

Alternation of consonant-vowel combinations should be the next target behavior for its developmental significance and direct relationship to the types of respiratory and phonatory controls needed in speech production. The first target should be a single consonant-vowel utterance. An effective technique for the above process is the use of the utterance "boo." What parent has not played this with their child? It is not surprising that this game is taught to the infant on imitated, elicited, and spontaneous levels.

Controlled consonant-vowel repetitions should then be introduced. The target behavior becomes rhythmic, connected alternations of one CV combination. Ling (1976) sets the criterion at 3 syllable repetitions/sec. He cites the need for research into whether this diadokokinetic rate is adequate for CV combinations (Ling, 1980, p. 247). The target behavior is the *smooth*, relaxed, controlled alternation of consonants and vowels with no pauses between each repetition. This parallels the babbling stage of speech development in which motoric patterns of utterances are practiced and matched by the infant with what he hears. The complexity of the target behavior increases as the child is asked to produce different CV combinations, with the vowel constant, alternately at a rate of 3 syllables/sec (batada) on one breath and with constant pitch and intensity.

SYLLABLE TRAINING

When the child can produce the vowels and diphthongs with appropriate control and imitation of suprasegmental features, syllable training can commence. "While repetition of meaningless syllables (drills) will not produce speech, it is possible that when the motor system has not been 'programmed' to perform some of the necessary activities for the production of speech, special practice may be needed [Vorce, 1971, p. 236]." The emphasis in these syllable drills is on automaticity, rhythm, and breath control. Consonant-vowel combinations are repeated until fluency is an integral part of the utterance. Ling (1976) states that "speech patterns should be rehearsed until it takes conscious attention to produce them inaccurately [p. 89]." This rehearsal develops orosensory motor patterns and auditory patterns which are necessary prerequisites in the development of lasting speech skills. Practice of all combinations of consonants and vowels is necessary, due to allophonic variations existing as phonemes are combined. Releasing (CV) and arresting (VC) combinations should be taught. The importance of including syllable drill is only overshadowed by the movement from syllable drill to correct production in functional words as quickly as possible. This can be done by developing understanding and use of CV and VC words, such as up, boo, bye, hi, me, off, no, shoe, etc., in meaningful contexts.

At the word, phrase, and sentence levels, speech and auditory training can be integrated with language training. Items introduced as language development activities can be "loaded" with the phoneme being developed. The items can be trained auditorially as well as expressively. The training session becomes integrated with all activities serving to meet the varied goals of the session. It has been the author's experience that carryover is much greater because the child's speech, language, and listening skills are all being monitored and reinforced during the training session. The child becomes more aware of monitoring his own speech and language as they are continually being used during the session. The parents become more skilled at encouraging carryover in the home because they have observed speech, language, and auditory training being integrated in each of the activities of the session.

ORDER OF TRAINING

Determiners for order of consonant development include the following:

"1) relative ease with which the consonant may be assimilated into well-established, breath-grouped voice and vowel patterns; 2) relative salience of the sensory cues by means of which the consonants may be differentiated; 3) the extent to which they share features in common; 4) their relative organic differences; and 5) their developmental order [Ling, 1976, p. 120]."

Training should proceed from CVC words to bisyllabic words, to two word utterances, and into connected language. The key to training in these later stages is constant attention to the child's needs as they occur in his spontaneous utterances. This requires constant evaluation of the child's utterances by parent and therapist. Automaticity of production at lower levels is the key to the stability of the child's productions at the higher levels. As the child's vocabulary grows and his expressive language competence increases, the intervention needs in the area of speech production change. For example, as the child learns the past tense or pluralization rules, speech training (as well as auditory training) may be necessary in teaching the morphological endings that must be present in the utterance to carry the semantic information.

In summary, "to be optimally effective, speech training has to begin early, be undertaken frequently and consistently, and be systematically carried out so that it rapidly enables the child to use speech as an effective means of communication [Ling, 1976, p. 149]."

PARENTAL INVOLVEMENT

One of the most important factors relative to speech training for the deaf infant is the parent. Mary New, developer of the Lexington School program, believes that both counseling and home training are necessary requirements of any speech training program through which the *maximum potential* of the child may be realized (French, 1971, p. 207). Speech pathologists should not envision themselves as the only deliverers of speech training. Some speech pathologists feel uncomfortable with teaching speech to the deaf and believe that bringing a parent into the training program would create confusion, frustration, and a lack of appropriate intervention. Thus, parents often remain as uninformed observers. The role of the speech pathologist is to assist the parent in gaining information and confidence. Magner (1971, p. 248) believes that one function of speech pathologists is to lead parents to discover appropriate training techniques and to evaluate the use of these techniques. Ling and Ling (1978, p. 9) state that the "parents can do more than the professional to help the child develop verbal skills in early infancy."

The importance of parent training should be recognized by the professional who is responsible for training the deaf infant. Many programs, however, do not provide for parent involvement. This is often due to a lack of knowledge about the composition of such programs and/or a lack of sufficient funds.

A Parent Program

From the time the child is identified as hearing-impaired, the parents should be involved in the decision-making process as well as with other parents of hearing-impaired infants. At the time of initial diagnosis, the parents should be given a little "technical" information and a list of names on a "parent hot line." This "hot line" consists of parents with hearing-impaired children, who live in the same geographical area. The "new parents" should be scheduled for a second meeting with a speech pathologist and audiologist one week after the initial diagnosis has occurred. At the second meeting, the child must be reevaluated, and the diagnosis and test procedures explained. Through such a procedure, parents should be better able to assimilate the basic information about their child and the program because of reduced emotional stress. At the second meeting, the parents should be the facilitators of the discussion. It must be an unhurried opportunity for the parents to become acquainted with the problem of deafness, the professional, the clinic, and their own role in the intervention process.

GROUP MEETINGS

Once a month, a group meeting of parents should be held with the speech pathologist/audiologist serving as an advisor. The parents are to be responsible for planning the agenda of each meeting, which may be either social or informational. Also, during school vacations, siblings may meet as a group for social and informational purposes. The parents of each child should be seen individually by the speech pathologist once a month, usually at their home. At that time, progress reports should be delivered by both the parents and the therapist, mutual goals and objectives for intervention plans for the next month set, and questions and individual problems addressed. Parents should also be observed interacting with their child in a daily living activities in which auditory, speech, and language development principles are demonstrated.

Some possible programs which a parent group may want to arrange include a panel of deaf adults to discuss their experience; an otolaryngologist to discuss anatomy and physiology of the ear; a psychologist to discuss discipline techniques; a pediatrician and a dentist to discuss preparing children for medical and dental treatment; a psychologist to discuss parental attitudes and feelings about handicapped children; etc.

OTHER ACTIVITIES

It is helpful if the parents become involved in educating the public with regard to deafness. This may be accomplished by preparing and distributing a list of behavioral signs that may indicate a hearing loss and by organizing a parent "hot line", referred to earlier in this paper. The parents may participate in newspaper interviews and radio and TV spots for hearing and speech month and various fund-raising campaigns. Further, they may work on legislation for the handicapped and raise money for equipment for the clinic.

STAFF REQUIREMENTS

The program suggested above may be staffed by one audiologist, one speech pathologist, and a dedicated group of parents of hearing-impaired children in a community speech and hearing clinic. The attendance and membership in such a group may fluctuate as the hearing-impaired children move to other programs. The parents of children who have "graduated" to other programs may wish to maintain their membership in the infant program to offer and receive support from others.

RESEARCH NEEDS

As one surveys the literature regarding teaching speech to the deaf, one is struck with amazement at the paucity of research-based studies in this area. The status of our knowledge, skills, and techniques have literally remained at a standstill for the past 50 years.

Moores (1978) summarizes the present status of speech training for the hearing-impaired as follows:

"1) knowledge about the processes by which deaf children acquire speech is virtually non-existent;

2) information on the use of speech by deaf individuals in natural situations is almost completely anecdotal;

3) educators of the deaf, as a group, make no distinction between speech development and speech remediation;

4) no valid, reliable diagnostic speech tests have been developed for the deaf. Those commonly used have been designed for hearing individuals;

5) there is inadequate understanding, in qualitative and quantitative terms, of the speech of deaf children; the classic study of speech intelligibility (Hudgins and Numbers) was reported in 1942, and results are based on the reading of ten simple sentences.

6) to the best of the author's knowledge, no study has ever been conducted comparing the effects of different techniques or methods of teaching speech to the deaf;

7) as a general rule, methods of teaching speech to the deaf in the United States have neither a theoretical [n]or pragmatic base [pp. 224–225]."

Several problems alluded to by Moores (1978) stand out as deserving immediate attention. Carefully controlled data-based studies of methodologies in teaching speech to deaf infants and preschoolers are paramount if speech pathologists are to be successful in their efforts. The relationship between the developing phonological system and the syntactic and semantic aspects of language must be studied. The results gleaned from such an investigation would provide information on the development of the phonemic system and assessment of prosodic and assimilative features of speech (Vorce, 1971, p. 226). Ongoing assessment techniques should be developed so that speech behaviors can be sequenced to meet the objectives. Assessment tools and techniques must be developed and documented to provide in-depth, reliable, and valid measures of the hearing-impaired child's strengths and weaknesses in the area of speech. Data-based studies on the use of instrumentation in teaching speech to the deaf preschooler appear necessary before further technological developments and refinements may be made, so that visual information on the nature of speech production could be useful to the infant. Another important area of research relates to methods of individualizing instruction within structured programs of speech training. It is generally agreed that there is no one method of speech training that is suitable for each hearing-impaired child. The question must be answered relative to how we can plan for and use appropriate intervention strategies based on the needs of each child. Longitudinal studies of hearing-impaired children receiving structured speech training programs would provide guidelines for future intervention and information relative to the development of speech skills by deaf children. The causal factors involved in deafness and their relation to prognosis in terms of the hearing-impaired child's ability to understand and use spoken language is an area that may hold information for the speech pathologist, audiologist, and parents involved in long-range planning. Other areas open to research include behavior characteristics of children and their relation to speech training methods; parent and teacher involvement in successful speech training with the deaf child; and conditions other than hearing impairment that impede success in speech.

SUMMARY

Speech training for the hearing-impaired child is indeed a complex task. At the very heart of this training is the child and the child's parents. It is the child and all that constitutes his environment that will serve as the "soil" in which the "seeds" of speech skills will develop. Ignorance of the child and his environment is one of the greatest injustices to the child and one of the greatest hindrances to the development of durable and usable speech skills. Some of the other factors that have been cited as contributing to the attainment of intelligible speech are

1. a *positive* attitude toward the value of oral communication;
2. effective and skillful teachers;
3. a systematic speech program;
4. appropriate amplification and maximal development of residual hearing;
5. adequate experience using speech;
6. development of an effective auditory-kinesthetic feedback system;
7. transfer of automatic phonetic skills to the phonological level;
8. supportive, informed, and cooperative parents (Golf, 1980, p. 146).

We must focus our efforts in all these areas but not fool ourselves into believing success is assured if all the above factors are achieved. "Degree of hearing impairment, intelligence, parental concern and ability and additional handicaps as assessed on initial diagnosis cannot reliably indicate whether a child will be able to communicate verbally [Ling and Ling, 1978, p. 7]." We are unable to totally rule out other factors which we have blindly ignored as we totally commit our efforts to following "the method." "No approach should ever be so rigid as to preclude spontaneous development, to limit the child's opportunity to communicate by speech or to detract from his urge to do so [Ling, 1976, p. 119]."

With these thoughts in mind, consider Alexander Graham Bell's statement, "One of the greatest achievements in the world is that of a child born deaf who learns to talk [in *Statements on Deafness*, 1979]."

References

Avondino, J. The babbling method. *Volta Rev.*, 1919, *21*, 273–282.

Bell, A. *English Visible Speech in 12 Lessons*, ed. 6. Washington, D.C.: Volta Bureau, 1932.

Bell, A.M. Vocal physiology, the principles of speech and dictionary of sounds. *Volta Rev.*, 1914, *16*, 65–78.

Berg, F. *Educational Audiology: Hearing and Speech Management.* New York: Grune and Stratton, 1976.

Calvert, D., and Silverman, S.R. *Speech and Deafness.* Washington, D.C.: A.G. Bell Association for the Deaf, 1975.

Cornett, O. Cued speech. *Am. Ann. Deaf*, 1967, *112*, 3–13.

French, S. The acquisition of speech. In L. Connor (ed.), *Speech for the Deaf Child: Its Knowledge and Use.* Washington, D.C.: A.G. Bell Association for the Deaf, 1971.

Goldstein, M. *The Acoustic Method for the Training of the Deaf and Hard-of-Hearing.* St. Louis: Laryngoscope Press, 1939.

Golf, H. Summary comment: Principles, objectives, and strategies for speech training. In J.D. Subtelny (ed.), *Speech Assessment and Speech Improvement for the Hearing Impaired.* Washington, D.C.: A.G. Bell Association for the Deaf, 1980.

Hudgins, C.V. Voice production and breath control in the speech of the deaf. *Am. Ann. Deaf*, 1937, *82*, 338–363.

Hudgins, C., and Numbers, F. An investigation of the intelligibility of the speech of the deaf. *Genet. Psychol. Monogr.*, 1942, *25*, 389.

Hutchinson, J., and Smith, L. Language and speech of the hearing impaired. In R. Schow and M. Nerbonne (eds.), *Introduction to Aural Rehabilitation.* Baltimore: University Park Press, 1980.

Ling, D. *Speech and the Hearing Impaired Child: Theory and Practice.* Washington, D.C.: A.G. Bell Association for the Deaf, 1976.

Ling, D. Integration of diagnostic information: Implications for speech training in school-aged children. In J.D. Subtelny (ed.), *Speech Assessment and Speech Improvement for the Hearing Impaired.* Washington, D.C.: A.G. Bell Association for the Deaf, 1980.

Ling D., and Clarke, B. Cued speech: An evaluation study. *Am. Ann. Deaf*, 1975, *120*, 480–488.

Ling, D., and Ling, A. *Aural Habilitation: The Foundations of Verbal Learning in Hearing Impaired Children.* Washington, D.C.: A.G. Bell Association for the Deaf, 1978.

Magner, M. Techniques of teaching. In L. Connor (ed.), *Speech for the Deaf Child: Its Knowledge and Use.* Washington, D.C.: A.G. Bell Association for the Deaf, 1971.

McGinnis, M. *Aphasic Children: Identification and Education by the Association Method.* Washington, D.C.: A.G. Bell Association for the Deaf, 1963.

Moores, D. *Educating the Deaf: Psychology, Principles, and Practices.* Boston: Houghton Mifflin, 1978.

Nickerson, R. Characteristics of the speech of deaf persons. *Volta Rev.*, 1975, *77*, 342–362.

Pike, K. *The Intonation of American English.* Ann Arbor, Michigan: University of Michigan Press, 1945.

Pickett, J. Speech science research and speech communication for the deaf. In L. Connor (ed.), *Speech for the Deaf Child: Its Knowledge and Use.* Washington, D.C.: A.G. Bell Association for the Deaf, 1971.

Pollack, D. Acoupedics: A unisensory approach to auditory training. *Volta Rev.*, 1964, *66*, 400–409.

Ptacek, P., and Sander, E. Maximum duration of phonation. *J. Speech and Hear. Disord.*, 1963, *28*, 171–182.

Rau, F. *Teaching Pronunciation to the Deaf.* Moscow: Institute of Defectology, 1960.

Siebert, R. Speech training for the hearing impaired: Principles, objectives, and strategies for preschool and elementary levels. In J.D. Subtelny (ed.), *Speech Assessment and Speech Improvement for the Hearing Impaired.* Washington, D.C.: A.G. Bell Association for the Deaf, 1980.

Statements on Deafness. Washington, D.C.: A.G. Bell Association for the Deaf, 1979.

Vorce, E. Speech curriculum. In L. Connor (ed.), *Speech for the Deaf Child: Its Knowledge and Use.* Washington, D.C.: A.G. Bell Association for the Deaf, 1971.

Zaliouk, A. A visual tactile system of phonetical symbolization. *J. Speech Hear. Disord.*, 1954, *19*, 190–207.

Part VI

Receptive Training

Integration of Auditory Training with Speech and Language for Severely Hearing-Impaired Children

MARIETTA M. PATERSON, M.SC.

HISTORICAL OVERVIEW OF AUDITORY TRAINING
ELECTRONIC HEARING AIDS

A MODEL FOR AURAL (RE)HABILITATION
STIMULI IN CONTEXT

TEACHING THROUGH EVALUATION AND INDIVIDUALIZED INSTRUCTION
FIVE-SOUND TEST

STRATEGIES AND TECHNIQUES FOR AURAL REHABILITATION
ORGANIZING AURAL REHABILITATION
LANGUAGE-RELATED TRAINING
UTILIZING SEMANTIC/SYNTACTIC INFORMATION
SUPRASEGMENTAL PATTERNS
FOLLOWING DIRECTIONS
AUDITORY COMPREHENSION
AUDITORY SEQUENTIAL MEMORY
PRESENTATION OF MATERIALS
ROLE REVERSAL

DIAGNOSTIC TEACHING BY USE OF ACOUSTIC AND ARTICULATORY DATA
SYLLABLE AND WORD DISCRIMINATION AND IDENTIFICATION
SYLLABLE DISCRIMINATION
STRESS PATTERNS
VOICE DISCRIMINATION
WORD-LEVEL DISCRIMINATION, IDENTIFICATION, AND COMPREHENSION

The use of audition is the fastest, easiest, and most direct means of acquiring spoken language. It is auditory input in the presence of communicative experience which plays the primary role in the speech and language development of hearing children. Although researchers are not agreed as to precisely how a hearing infant becomes a talking, communicative being by age 4, there does seem to be consensus that the human brain is especially attuned to process spoken language (Fry, 1975, p. 140; Lenneberg and Lenneberg,

1975, p. 18). Spoken language is normally received at the brain via the auditory channel. The brain is able, stage by stage, to develop awareness of the acoustic cues underlying linguistic distinctions and thus to separate the patterns which make up language. Similarly, it is through audition that the child experiments with and monitors motor speech production as development proceeds from babble to conversation. In order to recognize (perceive) and produce (use expressively) speech patterns, the child must have adequate if not consistent exposure to oral language in a context which is meaningful to him. By age 4 the hearing child has integrated auditory experience with speech and spoken language sufficiently to have learned most of the auditory discriminations and many of the rules implicit in language and is able to communicate effectively orally.

Most hearing-impaired children have intact central nervous systems, and therefore the brain capacity for processing spoken language following normal developmental steps is assumed (Lenneberg and Lenneberg, 1975, p. 148; Ling and Ling, 1978, p. 2). We know also that the majority of hearing-impaired children *do* have sufficient residual audition to benefit from wearing hearing aids (Boothroyd, 1976, p. 26; Ling, 1976, p. 86; Ross and Giolas, 1978, pp. 10, 137 and 182). Given this, the critical factor in the acquisition of oral language for the hearing-impaired must be the amount and quality of auditory experience available, just as it is for the hearing child. Speech sounds must be heard loudly enough and often enough in real-life situations, so that the brain can associate sounds with meaning.

Many severely to profoundly hearing-impaired children do learn to communicate through spoken language in spite of their defective hearing (Ling, 1978, p. 113; Whetnall and Fry, 1971, p. 204). Early auditory-oral experience in a good parent-infant habilitative program encourages the development of speech and spoken language in a normal fashion in an environment where auditory experience is integrated with speech production skills and spoken language. The key to successful learning is often more related to the quality and quantity of the intervention than to the amount of hearing loss.

Aural (re)habilitation is the means by which hearing-impaired children are enabled to maximize the use of their residual audition. Aural habilitation entails work with young children learning speech and spoken language for the first time (approximately 0–5 years). Aural rehabilitation assists the older child (approximately 6 years and up) to maximize the use of residual audition even when the optimum developmental learning time may have passed. Efficient use of therapeutic time prohibits the retracing of all developmental stages for the older child. However, the older child has the advantages of greater maturity and attentiveness, wider interests and knowledge of the world, and more developed cognitive and academic abilities with which teaching can be integrated—all of which promote more streamlined teaching and progress. Structured lessons for the older child (6 years and up) can include auditory-oral language experience activities and specific auditory discrimination training through speech production practice to let the child become consciously aware of distinctions he did not previously recognize or produce. The greatest problem in later education lies in the remedial or corrective nature of the teaching, which often involves replacing habitual and inadequate patterns with new behaviors.

This chapter will explore some of the parameters involved in auditory-oral learning for the older, mainstreamed severely to profoundly hearing-impaired child. The objective is to support the contention that auditory training is inexorably linked with motor speech skill and spoken language in the (re)habilitation of the hearing-impaired child regardless of age. Practical suggestions for an integrated aural rehabilitation program will be offered, drawn from clinical experience with severely to profoundly hearing-impaired mainstreamed children.

HISTORICAL OVERVIEW OF AUDITORY TRAINING

The concept of training the listening ability of a hearing-impaired person has existed for over 200 years. In the eighteenth century, otologists and educators working in Europe were developing the notion that a hearing-impaired person must learn how to hear.

Ernaud, in Paris in 1761, believed "that total deafness did not exist and that auditory perception would increase with listening practice", and a Portuguese, Jacobo Pereira, used speaking tubes and ear trumpets for auditory training of speech/sound discrimination. The use of these primitive amplifiers continued into the next two centuries. Urbantschisch, in Germany in the nineteenth century, used residual audition to train the auditory discrimination of words and sentences. In nineteenth-century England, Wilde and Toynbee did similar work. They believed that "constant ear practice would be expected to yield improvement." By the early twentieth century, training the listening of hearing-impaired children through the use of speaking tubes had become common in many schools. The literature on this early work is reviewed in detail in Wedenberg (1951) and DiCarlo (1964). The emergence of modern auditory training begins with the electronic hearing aid.

Electronic Hearing Aids

The appearance of electronic hearing aids in the 1930's began to have a dramatic effect on the lives of many hearing-impaired children. Many who benefited from amplication had thresholds of hearing that could not be reached before. The early group hearing aids were very heavy, cumbersome, and nonportable. Typically, these instruments were housed in a special room which became the "auditory training room," (Ewing, 1967, p. 16). Thus, listening practice was kept separate from the daily routine and life experience of the students. Isolation of auditory training through necessity in the early days of amplification fostered the notion that listening can be divorced from experience and taught as a separate skill. Modern hearing aids make this notion obsolete.

The advent of the miniaturization of hearing aids about 30 years ago has made it possible for many hearing-impaired children to learn spoken language from simple exposure to the sound patterns of spoken language all day, every day. Other children, because of greater hearing loss or too late a start, need additional specific auditory training as well as amplified auditory experience in order to make meaningful use of residual audition

(Ling, 1978, p. 130; Ross and Giolas, 1978, p. 182).

A MODEL FOR AURAL (RE)HABILITATION

Advanced hearing-aid technology has forged ahead of the ability of most programs to exploit these advances in the effective use of residual audition. Generally, there is poor auditory management and uncertainty about what exactly to do for "auditory training" which has resulted in low standards being set for the children's aural rehabilitation (Boothroyd, 1976, p. 26; Ross and Giolas, 1978, pp. 10, 209, and 296). Contributing to this dilemma is the fact that there has not yet been a comprehensive model to follow for the delineation of the stages of auditory skill acquisition and the integration of these skills with speech and spoken language acquisition (Ross and Giolas, 1978, p. 182). As intimated above, there is a need to distinguish between auditory experience on the one hand and auditory training on the other. The former implies development of speech perception skills in meaningful situations, and the latter implies specific discriminations to be taught and then generalized.

The literature on speech reception and the use of the auditory channel in acquiring spoken language by hearing-impaired children is increasing continually (Fry, 1975; Lenneberg and Lenneberg, 1975; Ross and Giolas, 1978, p. 11; Borden and Harris, 1980, p. 161). The model of speech reception learning/training suggested by Hirsh (1970) and detailed by Ling (1978, p. 183) and Ling and Ling (1978, pp. 157–159) is proposed in this chapter. In brief, this model suggests the following:

1. Auditory speech reception requires the processing of sequential yet overlapping stages of detection, discrimination, identification, and comprehension of meaningful verbal stimuli.
2. The development of these auditory skills is maximixed when combined with motor speech production by the child.
3. Normal stages of oral language acquisition should be followed in the programming of the meaningful training stimuli.

Our experiences with this model have resulted in some changes in the traditional approaches to auditory training. Many auditory training curricula or guidelines include the discrimination of environmental or nonverbal sounds. It is implied that greater skill at discriminating a bell from a whistle will somehow assist in the perception and discrimination of speech sounds (Lovell and Stoner, 1960; Office of the Los Angeles County Superintendent of Schools, 1976; Northcott, 1977; Pollack, 1971). This idea cannot be supported. The brain does have hemispheric specialization for the reception of speech and nonspeech sounds (Liberman et al., 1967), and thus, it is likely that it uses different strategies to process each type of acoustic information. Further, speech and environmental sounds have vastly different temporal characteristics. Certainly, learning to discriminate environmental sounds may have some importance in itself, but there is no evidence that it will promote improvement in speech discrimination.

Stimuli in Context

The need to teach children to use their hearing in meaningful situations and in conjunction with speech and language skills is relatively new. For example, Kelly's (1953) text of materials is comprised of lists of words and alphabet letters which are to be drilled. However, some evidence suggests that little transfer into everyday life will occur through drilled practice of lists of words (Doehring and Ling, 1971). Kelly's approach is similar to the traditional and largely abandoned method of expecting students to learn a foreign language by memorizing long lists of vocabulary. Practice in listening, imitating, identifyng, and comprehending spoken language in context is what helps one to acquire fluency in any tongue. Among the most comprehensive auditory training programs currently available is that published by the Los Angeles County school system (*Auditory Skills Curriculum*, 1976). It includes various types of listening skills arranged in sequential order of difficulty. However, this material, in spite of its noteworthy organization, fails to integrate auditory skills with systematic evaluation and teaching of speech, incorporation of verbal responses in auditory activities, and fostering of the use of audition throughout the day.

Some researchers have suggested that speech production helps perception of spoken language (Lieberth and Subtelny, 1978; Novelli-Olmstead, 1979). Yet many past studies have not required a verbal response in the training tasks. Berg's (1978) program of auditory training emphasizes the reciprocity between listening training and speech production (and visual training when necessary). But he does not describe procedures for integrating auditory training with speech production and language knowledge. In fact, no one has studied these procedures in an empirical manner. Hence the current approach to auditory training remains inadequate, since it does not promote development of dynamic, continuous speech reception and production as found in normal conversation.

TEACHING THROUGH EVALUATION AND INDIVIDUALIZED INSTRUCTION

Through evaluation of each student's speech, spoken language, and auditory capacity, short-term and long-term teaching goals can be established, and individual needs can be incorporated into the planning of rehabilitation. Systematic diagnostic teaching will permit the teacher to monitor the effectiveness of the program and to modify teaching techniques or strategies to accommodate students' individual differences. Detailed assessment of speech, language, and hearing are covered elsewhere in this book (Part IV). However, the author would like to detail the use of Ling's Five-Sound Test as an essential day-to-day assessment tool.

Five-Sound Test

The five sounds [u, a, i, ʃ, s] are those used in the Five-Sound Test created by Ling (1978, p. 98). These were chosen to represent the entire range of speech sounds from the lowest to the highest frequency.

Use of this test is an indispensable tool for the teacher/clinician to utilize (1) to verify the functioning of a hearing aid (an essential step in an auditory-oral lesson) and (2) to establish effective listening distance or earshot.

Administration of the test is easy and requires no special materials with children age 6 or older. One simply instructs the child to listen and clap his hands when he hears a sound. The test can be used for detection (child only claps) and discrimination (child responds verbally). The sounds should be presented both close to the child and from increasing distances. Some children will be able to hear all or some of these sounds from a distance of 10 feet, while for others these sounds may only be audible at 6 inches. This is the very information the teacher needs to know in order to do auditory work within an effective listening distance. Further details on the test are provided by Ling and Ling (1978, p. 98) and in a video tape produced by Ling (1981).

STRATEGIES AND TECHNIQUES FOR AURAL REHABILITATION

It is beyond the scope of this chapter to detail an entire program of auditory-oral learning. However, a sample of suggested strategies and techniques used successfully in work with mainstreamed severely to profoundly hearing-impaired children will be briefly presented.

Organizing Aural Rehabilitation

Structured intervention provides an opportunity to program for the individual's needs. A typical lesson might include (1) a hearing-aid check, (2) the Five-Sound Test, (3) phonetic level speech practice, (4) auditory discrimination of syllables related to the speech practice, (5) specific phonological teaching of speech sounds, (6) auditory exercise involving the phonological stimuli, (7) language experience activities incorporating specific semantic/syntactic or pragmatic goals, and (8) setting of targets for home practice.

Although target areas can be subdivided mentally by the teacher to facilitate planning, the implication is that the entire session be conducted in a normal conversational manner (auditorily) as much as possible, with the provision of visual (lipreading) and tactile cues as necessary to supplement audition.

Language-Related Training

The following are specific examples of strategies which integrate auditory training with spoken language development.

UTILIZING SEMANTIC/SYNTACTIC INFORMATION

In English, new information is found at the end of the sentence (Clark and Clark, 1977, p. 360). This is also usually the word most easily retained by many hearing-impaired children who have poor auditory memory. Many severely-to-profoundly hearing-impaired students need a slightly longer time to process speech, especially when they have not been exploiting their residual audition to the utmost, so that the last word or piece of information is often the part retained. Thus, building auditory skills should progress through basic sentence patterns which draw the student's attention to target items. (Even when the child is learning to auditorily discriminate *dog* from *boy*, it is best done in a natural phrase rather than in isolation; therefore, "Where is the dog?" or "Give me the dog" is preferable to saying the word "dog"). For example, ask the child to discriminate auditorily between the following pairs of sentences:

Find the *dog*. versus Find the *boy*.
Find the *dog eating*. versus Find the *dog jumping*.
The boy who is eating is *tall*. versus The boy who is eating *plays hockey well*.

SUPRASEGMENTAL PATTERNS

This training activity improves the ability to determine whether an utterance is a question, statement, or command by listening for suprasegmental information—intonation pattern, stress, duration, and intensity cues. Few children have difficulty with this skill which provides essential contextual information.

FOLLOWING DIRECTIONS

Training the ability to comprehend an auditorily presented command improves auditory sequencing and memory span. Sentence patterns found in commands are relatively simple and consistent in their word-ordering and intonation patterns. They offer a meaningful and useful framework for listening comprehension practice while quickly engaging the student in an increasingly more complex and abstract task as new pieces of information are added. The following are examples of a suggested hierarchy:

(A) Give me the _____ . Give me the
_____ and the _____ .
Give me both the _____ and the
_____ but not the _____ .

Groups B and C can be started after only a little practice with the first two parts of (A).

(B) Put the _____ in (on, under, behind)
the _____ . Put the _____
in the _____ and the _____
in the _____ .

(C) Circle (underline, put a cross on) the
_____ .
Circle the first one and underline the second.

AUDITORY COMPREHENSION (CONCRETE TO ABSTRACT)

This training improves the ability to identify something, someone, some place, or some action when given concrete, descriptive, and abstract clues. The following suggested strategies should be used concurrently with other aspects of aural rehabilitation as soon as the student begins to have some language which he can identify and comprehend auditorily. In order to complete these structured language experiences, the student's associative vocabulary will be tapped and increased. Through auditory selection and auditory description and identification, the student's auditory comprehension can be improved.

Auditory Selection

For this activity, items (pictures, materials, objects) are selected from a group of known items by using progressively more abstract clues. For example:

Where's the banana? (banana versus ball, cup, dog)
Show me something long and yellow (banana versus car, pencil, book)
Find the thing that you can eat (banana versus car, pencil, book)
I want something that is a fruit (banana versus car, tiger, house)
This object grows in hot, tropical countries. Monkeys love to eat them.
You can peel this, but you won't cry!
Part of this thing is very slippery!

Auditory Description/Identification

A game can be played in which each player takes turns guessing a hidden object or picture. At the easiest level a predetermined sequence of auditorily presented clues is given to help the child organize his thinking. As the student gains confidence and experience in asking questions to determine information, the "crutch" of using a predetermined sequence can be removed. The language can be adapted to the level appropriate for each child. The following is an example of categories to be worked through.

Aim: To identify a particular unknown animal.
Category
or group: Is this a/an _____? (vehicle, sport, profession, place, animal, etc.)
Size: Is this animal _____? (large, small, bigger than, smaller than)
Color: Is this animal _____? (yellow, brown, white)
Specific
characteristics: How many _____ does it have? (legs, feet)
Does it have a _____? (tail, horn, tusk, bill, wings)
Does this animal have _____? (fur, hide, scales, feathers)
Food: Does this animal live _____? (in the jungle, on the farm, in the forest, in the North, in the desert)

AUDITORY SEQUENTIAL MEMORY

Finally, training is presented to improve the ability to comprehend, sequence, and retell a story which has been presented auditorily. Storytelling activities involve creative thinking and the ability to utilize many abstract levels of language, i.e., description, temporal adjustment, making inferences, making deductions, and drawing conclusions. Several different hierarchical stages of storytelling can be described which integrate auditory and spoken language skills progressing from the concrete to the abstract level.

Stage 1. Improve the ability to listen to and repeat a story composed of three to four pictures. With the picture hidden, the teacher recounts the action in one or several simple sentences. The student listens and repeats what he has heard, so that both he and the teacher can verify his auditory comprehension. Then, with the student looking at the picture and lipreading (if necessary), the teacher can repeat the dialogue. The teacher can determine if the pictorial context completes the auditory message by asking the student again for a verbal imitation of the stimulus. All the pictures are presented in this way until the story is complete. Spontaneous and natural verbal exchange should be encouraged during the structured practice to allow for linguistic expansion. As a last step, the student can then resequence the jumbled up pictures and try to retell the story simply.

Stage 2. Improve the ability to listen to and repeat in one's own words a story presented one picture at a time.

Stage 3. Improve the ability to listen to and retell in one's own words a story which the student has heard, without interruption.

Stage 4. Student and teacher can create stories containing rich, expressive dialogue and use of abstract thought and language.

Presentation of Materials

Activities in individual teaching are basically three-phased. At this practical "how to" level, one must control the time frame of the activity, its content, and the verbal interactions one wishes to promote. The suggested three phases are (1) presentation of materials, (2) exploitation of materials, and (3) removal of materials. Presentation involves getting the toys, pictures, and materials on to the table in an interesting fashion which implicates the student immediately and allows verbal interaction to occur. Mode of presentation and particular objectives can vary as much as the teacher's creativity. A young child could, for example, be asked to feel an object in a bag and guess what it is by listening to auditory clues; or the stimulus could be pictures with each person present having two which they would, in turn, describe to their neighbor. Another strategy, the teacher could hide the object completely and give clues, asking the student to repeat what he heard. Asking the student to give a verbal response should be a technique employed in all parts of the session to encourage verbal interchange, to verify auditory receptive difficulty, and to allow incidental speech correction. Once on the table, the materials can be used again in many ways to consolidate targets, perhaps just matching of like objects of opposite concepts, building a puzzle together, playing con-

centration or "go fish," or playing at shopping, cooking, building. A specific syntactic structure could be taught. For example, toy cars, trucks, and little people could be manipulated, and appropriate language models used, to teach the passive construction, i.e., "The car was hit by the truck" versus. "The truck hit the car." In this instance, as in many language experience situations, more natural dialogue can develop by actually making pretend accidents occur, so that the child is encouraged in spontaneous expression as well as in comprehension and imitation of the specific syntactic/semantic structures being taught.

One should not simply remove objects or materials from the table to go to the next activity. Whenever possible use this time to verify your teaching, e.g., by asking the student to pick up the appropriate picture or objects after auditory identification. Also, auditory memory can be quickly assessed for the known items used, by asking the child to select and sequence them up to 5 in a row. Let the student practice placing objects left to right in reading sequence and give him a chance after a single presentation to select those he is sure of and, on a second presentation, to go back and fill in the missing items. The students develop confidence and start making more and more educated guesses as their auditory skills grow.

Role Reversal

It is unnecessary for the teacher/clinician to always be the dominant person. Role reversal allows the student to take a turn playing teacher. This is both enjoyable and an opportunity to show how well they can do. Use of this technique at the syllable discrimination level allows the teacher and student to work on listening and speech production in the context of the same activity. For example, the teacher gives the auditory stimulus for two rows of blocks representing [da] and [ma], and the student indicates by selection which syllable he heard. After satisfactorily completing that once or twice, the teacher can ask the student to say the syllables while the teacher listens. This throws the responsibility of making a really good attempt to say those syllables on the child and to do the best he can at that moment.

Similarly in language work, flow of conversation is more natural if the student is not always answering questions but is also actively participating in asking questions and commenting on occurrences.

DIAGNOSTIC TEACHING BY USE OF ACOUSTIC AND ARTICULATORY DATA

The structure of a set, or grouping of specific speech sounds, as outlined below, neatly organizes both acoustic-phonetic (which can indicate how well or how poorly sounds or parts of sounds are heard) and articulatory-phonetic (which relates to how and where sounds are made) information for evaluating and teaching purposes. The teacher/clinician can determine the child's capacity to discriminate, can pinpoint areas of uncertainty and weakness in his listening, can relate the results of any particular auditory training task to the information of the Five-Sound Test, and can also analyze why the student's production of one of the phonemes is poor and thus better devise strategies for correction. It is the combining of articulatory with acoustic data which is important for auditory discrimination. Just as the syllable is the most appropriate unit for motor speech practice, so can syllable practice be valuable in consolidating this knowledge and bringing the child's attention to salient features he may never have been aware of.

The following is an abbreviated summary of acoustic data relevant to the sample set:

Manner: Acoustic cues for manner contrasts are audible and discriminable for students with residual audition which extends up to 1000 Hz.

Place: Some acoustic cues for place distinctions are audible and discriminable for students with residual audition which extends up to 2000 Hz. All place distinctions would be rendered audible with audition up to 4000 Hz.

Voicing: Acoustic cues for voicing are audible and discriminable for students with residual audition up to 1000 Hz.

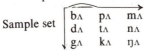

Sample set

bʌ	pʌ	mʌ
dʌ	tʌ	nʌ
gʌ	kʌ	ŋʌ

Vertically, each group forms a class of phonemes which have two distinctions in common (manner and presence or lack of voicing) and one distinction which differentiates them (place). Within class, auditory discrimination based on place difference will be difficult for students with very limited hearing (see above). However, students can learn to understand why certain sounds are easily confused when practice with this set is undertaken.

Horizontally, or across class, each group in the set is differentiated by manner and /or voicing. Thus, while they have place in common, they are more discriminable than the vertical sets.

An example of the use of set is with the very common substitution error of [ba] for [ma] and/or the use of these two sounds when only one was intended (mba for either ma or ba). Faulty discrimination and production can be due to one or more of the following errors in auditory discrimination and poor motor speech control:

1. The student is not auditorily aware of the nasal/non nasal contrast and therefore does not monitor it in speech production.
2. The [b] intrusion occurs because the stop/continuant distinction has not been established at the articulatory or motor speech level.
3. The child is unaware that less tension is required for the production of [m] than for [b].

Correction of this confusion must begin with auditory detection and discrimination. The Five-Sound Test can be used to verify if the child is able to detect both [m] and [b]. Adequate amplification at 200–500 Hz would allow perception of both sounds (Ling, 1976; Pickett, 1980). If the child is able to detect the two sounds, one can then proceed to the discrimination task. Once discrimination ability is established, successive motor speech practice will be more meaningful with the child monitoring his production through his hearing.

Distinctions related to suprasegmentals can be taught through other sets involving intensity, duration, and voice frequency difference. Vowels can be arranged in sets differing in place of production and their acoustic parameters. Other consonant sets can be formulated by using contrasts within and between manner, place, and voicing features. Sets of consonant blends can be arranged according to a variety of criteria, including whether they are initial, final, or medial and the blending process involved.

Higher levels of auditory reception cannot be achieved simply by syllable practice. Thus, as soon as the discrimination of particular syllables has been achieved, the child should be expected to discriminate, identify, and comprehend verbal material which includes what he has already learned. Such work leads naturally to the development of auditory sequential processing without which the child cannot interpret the spoken message.

Syllable and Word Discrimination and Identification

SYLLABLE DISCRIMINATION

Improve the ability to discriminate (by use of acoustic cues for manner, place, and voicing) small differences between sounds presented in single and multiple syllables, i.e., manner—da versus na; place—di versus gi; voicing—dada*di* versus dada*ti*.

STRESS PATTERNS

Improve the ability to auditorily identify stress patterns of English. These patterns are auditorily identifiable because they contain much low-frequency acoustic information, such as duration, heavier intensity, and some pitch change on the stressed syllable. Syllable practice can readily be transferred into words and sentences, e.g.:

Ba ba	Í know	péncil, Míchael, Shé is
ba Ba	I knów	a dóg, abóut
BA BA	nó! nó!	ráincoát, íce créam
BA baba	Í don't know	mótor boat,óvercoat
ba ba Ba	I don't knów	Put it thére! Turn it óff!
ba Ba ba	I dón't know	banána, tomáto

VOICE DISCRIMINATION

Improve the ability to auditorily distinguish between nasal and oral voice quality. Encourage the student to listen to and judge his own voice quality. This is not as difficult as it may sound, as older students are able to discriminate a nasal, fuzzy voice from a clear, oral, forward-sounding voice. This is critical for clearing up nasality in speech production. If one is sure that a student can tell when he is speaking too nasally, one can expect better self-monitoring.

WORD-LEVEL DISCRIMINATION, IDENTIFICATION, AND COMPREHENSION

The following is a suggested hierarchy of word discrimination tasks which involve the technique of selection from a known group:

1. Improve the ability to select one known item from a group of known items all varying in acoustic properties and syllable length, i.e., a boat, an airplane, a sheep, a banana, a classroom.
2. Improve the ability to discriminate between pairs of words which rhyme or which are acoustically similar, i.e., boat versus goat; father versus brother; evergreen versus overshoe (analysis of the latter pair shows that because of the similarity of syllable number, stress, and acoustic properties of various syllables, they would be a minimal pair for children addressed in this chapter).
3. Improve the ability to select one known item from a group of known items with initial consonants similar but with different vowels and final consonants. The words can now be more similar in syllable length, e.g., "down, dough, dime, dart, dancer, demon."
4. Improve the ability to select one known item from a group of known items with the initial consonant varying in manner with the remainder of the word rhyming or acoustically very similar, i.e., bean, mean, scene, dream, team or hitting, sitting, knitting.
5. Improve the ability to select one known item from a group of single syllable known items with varying manner and place contrasts in final position, e.g., "kick, kill, kit, king, kid, kiss."

These activities are similar to those typically classified under auditory training. They are intended to be transferred into a meaningful, communicative context for further reinforcement.

SUMMARY

In summary, this chapter has presented a brief overview of some of the major factors involved in the development of audition, speech, language, and later academic skills for severely to profoundly hearing-impaired children. The need to integrate this knowledge has been stressed. At the same time, however, it should be recognized that there is insufficient data in print today to structure a syllabus which would be applicable for auditory work with children of different age groups and abilities. More comprehensive models of auditory training and experience remain to be developed. Such models are essential if future hearing-impaired children are to reap optimal benefit from the technological advances made in the past few decades.

References

Berg, F.S. *Listening Handbook*. New York: Grune and Stratton, 1978.

Boothroyd, A. The role of hearing in education of the deaf. Northampton, Massachusetts: Clarke School for the Deaf, 1976.

Borden, G., and Harris, K. Speech perception. In *Speech Science Primer*, chap. 5. Baltimore: Williams & Wilkins, 1980.

Clark, H., and Clark, E. *Psychology and Language*. New York: Harcourt Brace Jovanovich, 1977.

DiCarlo, L.M. *The Deaf*. Englewood Cliffs, New Jersey: Prentice-Hall, 1964.

Doehring, D.G., and Ling, D. Programmed instruction of hearing-impaired children in the auditory discrimination of vowels. *J. Speech Hear. Res.*, *14*, 1971, 746–754.

Ewing, I.R. *Lipreading and Hearing Aids*. Manchester: Manchester University Press, 1944.

Fry, D.B. Phonological aspects of language acquisition in the hearing and the deaf. In E.H. Lenneberg and E. Lenneberg (eds.), *Foundations of Language Development*, vol. 2. New York: Academic Press, 1975.

Hirsh, I.J. Auditory training. In H. Davis and S. Silverman, (eds.), *Hearing and Deafness*. New York: Holt, Rinehart & Winston, 1970, pp. 346–359.

Kelly, J.C. *A Clinician's Handbook for Auditory Training*. Washington, D.C.: A.G. Bell Association for the Deaf, 1973.

Lenneberg, E.H., and Lenneberg, E. (eds.) *Foundations of Language Development*, vol. 2. New York: Academic Press, 1975.

Liberman, A.M., Cooper, F.S., Shankweiler, D.P., and Studdert-Kennedy, M. Perception of the speech code. *Psychol. Rev.*, *74*, 1967, 431–461.

Lieberth, A., and Subtelny, J.D. The effect of speech training on auditory phoneme identification. *Volta Rev.*, *80*, 1978, 410–417.

Ling, D. *Speech and the Hearing-Impaired Child: Theory and Practice*. Washington, D.C.: A.G. Bell Association for the Deaf, 1976.

Ling. D. Auditory coding and recoding. In M. Ross and T. Giolas (eds.), *Auditory Management of Hearing-Impaired Children*. Baltimore: University Park Press, 1978.

Ling, D. *The 5-Sound Test*, video tape produced at McGill University, 1981. (Available on request from John Roston, Instructional Communication Centre, McGill University, Montreal, Canada).

Ling, D., and Ling, A.H. *Aural Habilitation: The Foundations of Verbal Learning in Hearing-Impaired Children*. Washington, D.C.: A.G. Bell Association for the Deaf, 1978.

Lovell, E.L., and Stoner, M. *Play it by Ear*. Los Angeles: John Tracy Clinic, 1963.

Northcott, W.H. *The Hearing Impaired Child in the Regular Classroom*. Washington, D.C.: A.G. Bell Association for the Deaf, 1973.

Novelli-Olmstead, T. Production and reception of speech by hearing-impaired children. Unpublished master of science thesis, McGill University, 1979.

Office of the Los Angeles County Superintendent of Schools. *Auditory Skills Curriculum*. Los Angeles: Foreworks, 1976.

Pickett, J.M. *The Sounds of Speech Communication*. Baltimore: University Park Press, 1980.

Ross, M., and Giolas, T.G. (eds.) *Auditory Management of Hearing-Impaired Children*. Baltimore: University Park Press, 1978.

Wedenberg, E. Auditory training of deaf and hard of hearing children. *Acta Otolaryngol.[Suppl. 94] (Stockh.)* 1951, 7–82.

Whetnall, E., and Fry, D.B. *The Deaf Child*. London: Whitefriars Press, 1971.

Chapter 18

Visual Communication (Speech-reading) for the Severely and Profoundly Hearing-Impaired Young Adult

MARJORIE ADAMSON JACOBS

Teaching speechreading to severely and profoundly hearing-impaired young adults who wish to improve or strengthen speechreading and aural-oral communication skills is both challenging and rewarding. Instructors will find that the severely or profoundly hearing-impaired adult's primary mode of communication, sensory capabilities, linguistic and communicative competencies, life experiences, education, family, socioeconomic and cultural background, aptitudes, and abilities are extremely diversified. A review of the literature reveals that research has been focused on several areas related to evaluations, the sender (speaker), the receiver (speechreader), the message (code), and the environment. However, an in-depth review of the literature is not within the scope of this chapter and the reader is referred to the bibliography for further study. Discussion will be limited to an overview of visual communication, factors that contribute to speechreading proficiency and effective aural-oral communication, with implications for instruction. Suggestions will be made for developing instructional methods and materials for live and self-instruction. Discussion will also focus upon the valuable contribution of contextual, associational nonverbal and verbal language cues to speechreading profi-

ciency and the development of communication strategies. Desirable teacher characteristics and the use of video tapes for speechreading instruction will be described. For the purpose of brevity, "young severely and profoundly hearing-impaired adults" will also be referred to as "young adults" or "students."

VISUAL COMMUNICATION: AN OVERVIEW

Visual communication is a broad term which encompasses a myriad of sensory stimuli that may impact upon the mind of a hearing or hearing-impaired person to create impressions, feelings, ideas, and meaning. One tends to think of visual communication for the severely or profoundly hearing-impaired person either in terms of speechreading (lipreading) or manual language. However, visual communication can also include nonverbal language cues which may be associated with the environment in which the communication act takes place, the participants, time, and the social distance between the participants. Space cues may not conform to the social distances described by Hall (1963, 1969) because of the hearing-impaired adult's need to get closer to the speaker for optimal viewing and listening conditions. Visual communication may also incorporate graphics, telecommunication devices, electronic handwriters, "real-time" graphic displays, computers, television, video tapes, and movies (Pickett, 1981; Castle, 1981; Stuckless, 1981). Forms of visual communication that are cues to aid speechreading are Upton's Eyeglasses (Upton, 1968) and the hand-to-mouth systems reported by Cornett (1967, 1970, 1972), Schulte (1972), Børrild (1972), Fant (1972), and Jenson (1971). The motor-kinesthetic cue system described by Jenson (1971) is used by many teachers to aid speech production and cues phonemes by place and manner of articulation. Fingerspelled letters made close to the lips may also be used to quickly aid identification of phonemes, homophenes, orthographic pronunciation symbols, or key words. While these various aids and techniques can aid reception of speech by the severely or profoundly hearing-impaired person, the emphasis in this chapter will be upon some of the factors which are related to proficiency in speechreading and educational procedures for improving speechreading skill.

SPEECHREADING: A DEFINITION

Speechreading is a visual, oral-language communication skill that enables a person to obtain linguistic information by watching the sequential, articulatory movements of a speaker's lips, jaws, adjacent facial musculature, and facial expressions. Speechreading is highly dependent upon the sensory capabilities of the speechreader and his/her information-processing abilities related to perception, memory, and thinking. Speechreading as a communication skill is also dependent upon the speechreader's ability to utilize non-verbal and verbal associational cues. These cues may be related to the speaker, the message, and the environment (Jacobs et al., 1982). Speechreading, like listening, is not a passive process. It requires the active participation of the speechreader through mental and physical alertness and an *"attentional set"* for *speech communication*.

Contribution of Sensory Information to Speechreading

Speechreading for the majority of severely and profoundly hearing-impaired young

adults is dependent upon sensory information received from auditory, tactile, and kinesthetic senses. Thus, the continuous use of sensory aids, such as appropriately fitted and working hearing aids, vibrotactile units, transposer aids, and induction loop and radio transmission systems provides most, but not all, hearing-impaired young adults with cues that supplement or complement the visual reception of speech (Boothroyd, 1977; Connors and McPherson, 1978; Walter and Sims, 1978). While studies have indicated that the degree of hearing loss is an important factor in speechreading proficiency (Erber, 1972a; Donnolly, 1969; Johnson, 1978, p. 198), one continues to see profoundly hearing-impaired young adults utilizing speechreading with sound cues that enable them to receive all or most of everyday spoken messages. The number of incoming NTID students who are unable to utilize sound cues effectively for improved speechreading with sound ability has for several years remained at approximately 10%. An informal study investigated the effects of speechreading training upon this group. The results suggest that with continuous use of appropriately fitted and working hearing aids, approximately half of the students improve their speechreading with sound ability while the remaining half are unable to do so or do not wish to use hearing aids for physiological or psychological reasons (Jacobs and Johnson, 1976; Jacobs, 1977). These findings have implications for training and indicate the need for investigation into the student's reasons for lack of hearing aid use, appropriateness of fitting, best ear fitting, condition of hearing aid and hearing aid reevaluation if student desires it, *before* instruction begins.

Listening Behavior and Speechreading Skill

The ability to maintain sustained auditory and visual attention is an important factor related to speechreading lengthy, connected discourse using speechreading with sound cues. Mira (1970) investigated the application of the conjugate reinforcement method as a direct measurement of the listening behavior of hearing-impaired children. The investigator found that hearing-impaired children vary in their listening behavior, and listening patterns could not be predicted from pure tone losses or training differences. This method of measuring listening ability has implications for speechreading with sound training.

PRIMARY FACTORS IMPORTANT TO SPEECHREADING PROCESS AND PROFICIENCY

Jeffers and Barley (1971, p. 20) consider three primary factors to be highly important to the speechreading process and to speechreading proficiency. These are related to the speechreader and are (1) visual-perceptual proficiency, (2) the ability to synthesize information necessary to make perceptual and conceptual closure, and (3) thought flexibility to revise tentative decisions regarding the content of the message.

VISUAL PERCEPTUAL PROFICIENCY

Visual Acuity

Visual acuity must be within normal limits or corrected to within normal limits to enable the speechreader to see the fine, sequential, articulatory movements of speech. Students with visual problems may need preferential seating to enable them to see the speaker's face. The student should be the best judge of the viewing situation. However, some students may need encouragement to take the initiative and obtain favorable seating.

Visual acuity may be affected by distance, angle, illumination, and fatigue, and these factors may be expected to affect speechreading ability. The reader is referred to Caccamise et al. (1981) for recommendations related to optimising the use of vision for communication and learning.

Distance and Viewing Angle

Speechreading proficiency may be affected by distance and angle between the speechreader and speaker (Erber, 1972b; Watson 1974). Distances may vary between speechreader and speaker, but generally up to 10 feet is considered to be a good distance, with 5–8 feet being a "conversational" distance appropriate for instructional purposes. The speechreader is the best judge of preferred distance in class or individualized therapy. For most speechreaders, watching the

speaker at horizontal viewing angles of 0–45° is preferred. If a circular table is used for instruction, the instructor may wish to change the seating to give students practice from different angles, for example, profile viewing.

Factors such as distance, angle, illumination, and fatigue may be expected to affect speechreading ability. The reader is referred to Caccamise, Meath-Lang and Johnson, 1981, for recommendations related to optimising the use of vision for communication and learning.

Illumination

Erber (1974, 1979a) recommends that the amount of light on the teacher's mouth should be similar to the amount of light on the face for optimizing speechreading. Light sources behind the speaker, such as a brightly lit window, cause the speaker's face to be in a shadow (Jacobs, 1974; Jacobs et al., 1978). The phenomenon of light and dark adaptation may have to be considered if the teacher is using slides, movies, or video tapes. Time must be allowed for the student's eyes to adapt to the change in lighting. Dark adaptation refers to the time of the increase in sensitivity of the eyes when lighting is terminated (for example, walking into a darkened movie theater). Light adaptation refers to the change in luminence when going from dark to light (Sanders, 1971, p. 115). The course of dark adaptation is longer than that of light adaptation.

Visual Problems

The incidence of visual defects among the severely and profoundly hearing-impaired population has been well documented (Lawson and Myklebust, 1970). Among hearing-impaired college students, studies show an estimated incidence of 31% for visual pathologies and 58% for acuity, color and binocular problems (Johnson et al., 1981). Frey and Krause (1971) found the incidence of deficiency in color-discrimination among the deaf to be twice that of the general population. Even though there is a high incidence of color deficiency among the severely and profoundly hearing-impaired population, a study on color-form discrimination indicates that most deaf subjects prefer color (Suchman, 1966).

Experience has shown that the majority of

young hearing-impaired adults who use video tapes for self-instruction prefer color to black and white television (Jacobs, 1975). However, some students prefer black and white. In view of the incidence of color deficiency among severely and profoundly hearing-impaired young adults, instructors should investigate student's preference and be alert to the possibility of color deficiency and visual problems.

Visual Memory

Visual memory plays an important role in the speechreading process and is considered by Jeffers and Barley (1971, p. 159) to relate to the ability to revise and formulate decisions for perceptual closures. The speechreader must *perceive* the articulatory patterns from the speaker's mouth and jaw movements, *retain* the patterns sequentially in short-term memory, *code* into linguistic units by using inner language coding systems, *synthesize* the information with associated sensory and related contextual cues, *match* with information in permanent memory, for final message identification. This is a somewhat-simplistic description of a complex subject which has been discussed in detail in Chapter 4. For further clarification, the reader is referred to the information-processing model of audio-visual speech perception described by Risberg and Agelfors (1978), and Sanders (1971, pp. 13–27; 1976, pp. 1–32)

De Filippo (1980) suggests visual sequence memory training with articulatory shapes to strengthen and develop the visual and viseme coding systems of the dominant sense of profoundly hearing-impaired children. *Segments* of instruction related to visual memory training are desirable to *increase* the *sensory information* available to the speechreader in speech perception.

Visual Perception of Consonants and Vowels

The visual perception of place of articulation of consonants, vowels and diphthongs is very important to speechreading. The more phonemes the severely or profoundly hearing-impaired adult can recognize, the less he/she has to fill in by guessing, using linguistic information or other associational cues. The reader is referred to a recent study by Walden et al. (1981) on the effects of training on speech recognition by hearing-impaired adults with high frequency hearing losses. A significant increase was found in auditory-visual sentence recognition after auditory or visual consonant training. This is an area worthy of investigation among the severely and profoundly hearing-impaired population. Visual perception of consonants has been studied by Woodward (1957) and Woodward and Barber (1960). Four sets of visually contrastive consonants were found. The studies of Binnie et al. (1976), Erber (1972a) and Walden et al. (1974) indicate that under normal conditions, subjects with normal hearing and also those with hearing impairments are able to correctly recognize place of articulation in consonant-vowel syllables. Binnie et al. (1976) identified nine categories of recognition and suggested training be given only if subjects fail to meet criterion level performance.

Franks and Kimble (1972) in a study of visual perception of 32 consonant clusters in nonsense syllables found that they were incorrectly perceived 89% of the time. The consonant clusters were seen most frequently as single consonants. Franks found five contrastive groups. Sounds in the final position were identified with greater accuracy. They were speechread correctly 45% of the time, compared to 29% (initial) and 15% (medial) in the triple clusters. Franks suggested that, for training purposes, the teacher should select consonant clusters easily identified and contrast them with less discriminable clusters within contrastive groups. A suggestion for training consonant cluster identification for English language reinforcement is to utilize final consonant blend patterns as morphological markers for plurals and verb tenses. For example, "s" added in lau*ghs*, li*fts*, shi*fts* (see Fries, 1978, p. 17, for lists).

Jackson et al. (1976) studied the visual perceptual features underlying vowels, using subjects with normal hearing, and identified five perceptual patterns of vowel lipreading. The categories agree with those of Jeffers and Barley (1971, pp. 62–78). These are: (1) lip extension versus rounding; (2) vertical lip separation; (3) general size of opening; (4) vertical movement from the first to the second nucleus of diphthongs; and (5) size of opening of the second diphthong nucleus. Categories (1) and (3) have meaning for diphthong movements. Visual vowel recognition was found to correlate highly with speechreading skill. Wozniak and Jackson (1979) found diphthong stimuli easier to identify than vowel stimuli at two angles of observation (0° and 90°). Confusion tended to shift towards the stressed vowel element of the diphthong. The majority of the severely and profoundly hearing-impaired population have residual hearing that should enable them to discriminate most of the vowels.

The stressed vowel, which is the core of the syllable, contributes to the transmission of *rhythm*, *stress*, and *meaning* in connected discourse. When the speaking rate is increased, the stressed vowels are usually preserved, while the unstressed vowels may be "glossed" over and replaced by the schwa [ə]. This is often evident when presenting a specific word in isolation and using it in connected speech.

For these reasons, vowel and diphthong discrimination practice is extremely important for the severely and profoundly hearing-impaired population.

THE SPEAKER

"The speaker ... he is a thing to be seen, a being of action to be noted and read through the eye"—Charles Henry Woolburt (1927, p. 8).

Speaker characteristics that facilitate speechreading are mobile lips (Stone, 1957), appropriate gestures and facial expressions (Arthur, 1962; Berger et al., 1970, while inappropriate gestures appear to lower speechreading proficiency (Popelka and Berger, 1971). O'Neill (1951) found that the speaker who conveyed the most information by speechreading was also the most intelligible under auditory conditions. Good articulation tends to slow down vowel duration and aids auditory-visual speech perception. It is suggested that the speaker talk naturally at a normal speaking rate during instruction and for all oral communication (Tucker, 1979; Rosenstein, 1972), giving appropriate intonation and stress to facilitate comprehension of the message. Poor speechreaders may need a slower rate, shorter sentences, and simple syntactical structures. Good speechreaders may need a slower rate when speechreading long connected speech or technical language. As skill improves with practice, a normal speaking rate should be used. Speechreading and oral communication are facilitated when the speaker and speechreader become familiar with each others speech patterns and mannerisms.

ADDITIONAL FACTORS THAT CONTRIBUTE TO EFFECTIVE ORAL COMMUNICATION

Effective oral communication is not only dependent upon the speechreader's ability to receive and process linguistic and nonverbal information, but upon factors associated with the speaker and speechreader in their changing roles of sender-receiver during communication. These factors are related to: (1) understanding the topic and expectations of *spoken* language, which may be based upon linguistic skills, knowledge, and life experiences in similar situations, (2) understanding the purpose of the communication encounter, (3) understanding the participant's roles and point of view; (4) positive self-concept, (5) warmth and empathy between participants, (6) the ability to send clear feedback cues (verbal and nonverbal), (7) sensitivity to communication difficulties and prompt utilization of strategies to ensure communication does not break down, and (8) the ability to take a chance and *guess* to make sense out of a conversation when parts are missing. Blesser's (1974) description of a "synthetic generalist" is a perfect description of attributes observed in a proficient speechreader. These factors have implications for classroom instruction related to the development of communication strategies. The reader is referred to the texts of Hughey and Johnson (1975) and Brooks (1971) for further study on the dynamics of speech communication.

A common factor observed in good speechreaders and effective communicators is a sense of humor, a wonderful asset which not only puts the participants at ease, but enables a severely and profoundly hearing-impaired adult to cope with frustrations when they do occur.

THE ENVIRONMENT

Sizing Up the Situation

Situational cues can provide nonverbal information to facilitate anticipation and expectations of spoken language. The speechreader's ability to *visually scan* and size up the situation and understand the speaker's role will provide an *"attentional set"* for social or formal communication. Different kinds of environments may need special strategies to ensure optimal viewing and listening conditions for oral communication. For example, strategies used in a quiet office will be different from the kinds of strategies used in a large hall or theater.

Auditory Distractions

Auditory distractions may affect speechreading ability (Leonard, 1962). The speechreader's ability to use his/her hearing aid may also be affected resulting in greater reliance on speechreading. Achieving the maximum speechreading proficiency possible for young adults who use hearing aids, and will be working in a noisy environment, is an important consideration for planning remediation. The effect of noise on speech perception by the hearing and hearing-impaired participants, and the hearing-impaired young adult's ability to monitor his/her vocal loudness in noise are also factors to be considered. The hearing participant in the communication event may also be relying on speechreading. These factors have implications for remediation and communication strategies instruction. It can be anticipated that speechreading will be enhanced if the environment is not too aurally distracting.

Visual Distractions

Visual distractions may also affect speechreading by drawing the speechreader's attention away from the face, especially if the distraction is more interesting than the speaker. In some situations, and for training purposes, setting up distractions (visual or auditory) may cause the speechreader to focus his/her concentration more closely on the speaker during speech communication.

MOTIVATION

Worthington (1956, cited in Berger, 1972, p. 113) investigated the relationship between the lipreading ability of congenitally deaf high-school students and certain personality factors. The study showed a strong relationship between lipreading and level of aspiration on a motor task performance but not with degree of adjustment measured on a personality inventory. Costello (1964) studied individual differences in speechreading among deaf children (11–15 years of age) and suggested that attitude toward communication is of considerable importance in speechreading skill development among deaf children. Better speechreading skill was found among children who reported a positive attitude toward speech and speechreading by their parents and deaf peers. A positive attitude toward aural-oral communication by parents (and professionals) may be expected to facilitate aural-oral communication. The use of speech and speechreading for community and on-the-job communication may help to alleviate any feelings of isolation experienced by the hearing-impaired adult (Jacobs, 1975).

A positive attitude toward improving oral communication has been found among NTID students who show a significant gain after instruction, and among proficient speechreaders (see Table 18.1). Negative attitudes may also change after a young adult has had work experiences (Taylor, 1980).

Thus, interest and motivation should strengthen speechreading and overall aural-oral communication skills among severely and profoundly hearing-impaired young adults. However, as any experienced and observant teacher knows, what a person may say about his/her motivation may not necessarily be a positive indicator of motivation. Miles (1960) found that individuals who expressed the most eagerness to learn, learned the least. Motivation that is intense may be accompanied by a distracting emotional state which can interfere with a person's ability to learn, especially difficult tasks of discrimination (Hilgard, 1956, pp. 486–487; Hilgard and Blower, 1975, pp. 608–609). If young adults are to acquire good speechreading skills, they must be motivated to do so in a reinforcing environment (Calvert and Silverman, 1975). This means that individual instruction must be planned, the young adult should be fully aware of objectives, take an active part in learning and goal setting, and experience success and failure. Hilgard and Blower (1975) indicate in their discussion of the principles of stimulus-response theory that conflicts and frustrations arise in the process of learning difficult discriminations and in social situations. These frustrations have to be recognized and resolved by student and instructor. It is through failure in a nonthreatening classroom environment that young adults learn to use individual coping strategies, develop the confidence necessary to overcome communication barriers, and avoid communication breakdowns. These are essential factors for carryover outside the classroom situation.

CONTRIBUTION OF NONVERBAL LANGUAGE CUES TO SPEECHREADING PROFICIENCY

One might anticipate that it would not be necessary to give instruction to develop sensitivity and awareness of nonverbal language cues in young, severely and profoundly hearing-impaired adults. However, people vary a great deal in their ability to receive, interpret, and send nonverbal language cues (Coleman, 1949; Tagiuri et al., 1953). Levine (1976) has pointed out a common misconception, that understanding of nonverbal language comes naturally to a growing child. Meanings attached to nonverbal language, like verbal language, have to be learned (Wood, 1976). Kretschmer (1981, p. 196) also referred to the importance of nonverbal framing in normal language development and the implications for a unisensory versus a multisensory approach to language acquisition. The reader is referred to Mays and LaFrance (1978) for a review of the literature on the acquisition of nonverbal language and the distinction between personal expression and shared interactional codes. Research among diverse groups suggests that sensitivity to nonverbal stimuli may be expected to increase with age, training and practice (Rosenthal et al., 1979, pp. 338–341). Nonverbal communication and its role in human communication should be utilized to its fullest in visual communication training from childhood through adulthood.

Johnson (1975, 1978, p. 200) has shown that there is considerable variation among the severely and profoundly hearing-impaired young adult population in ability to receive, express, and interpret nonverbal language. Inability to express and receive nonverbal language may be expected to seriously limit the speechreader's ability to communicate effectively in social situations and with fellow workers. It is desirable to incorporate into speechreading instruction, teaching methods directed toward developing students' sensitivity to nonverbal language cues (Jacobs et al., 1982). This may be accomplished through discussion, observation, interpretation, and expression.

According to Birdwhistell (1970, p. 7), membership in a social or cultural group is highly dependent upon an individual's mastery of a nonverbal language communication system as well as the verbal system. He also estimates that less than 35% of social meaning is transmitted through words, 65% coming from nonverbal language (1970, p. 2). Mehrabian (1971, p. 43) places even less emphasis on verbal language, estimating that 7% of meaning comes from words, 55% from facial expressions, and 38% from vocal cues. Body cues other than facial expressions were not included in this study. The importance of developing a heightened sensitivity and awareness of nonverbal language cues to speechreading proficiency among the severely and profoundly hearing-impaired population (and instructors) cannot be overemphasized.

Nonverbal language cues available to the speechreader are many and varied (Jacobs et al., 1982; Sanders, 1971, pp. 115–128). These may be associated with the participants in the communication act in their changing roles of speechreader-listener and speaker, as well as with the environment in which communication is taking place. Nonverbal language cues are most effective in communicating feelings, attitudes and relationships (Watzlawick et al., 1967). Nonverbal communication also contributes to real impressions of people; for example, meeting strangers (Barker, 1942). Sometimes the nonverbal message contradicts the message, and under these circumstances people tend to believe the nonverbal message (Mehrabian, 1967, p. 331). Bugental et al. (1970) studied the perception of contradictory meanings conveyed by verbal and nonverbal channels and found that children do not learn to interpret conflicting messages until they are well into their teens. This would seem to be an area of research worthy of investigation in the severely and profoundly hearing-impaired young adult population (see Rosenthal et al., 1979).

Contextual Cues and Speechreading Proficiency

Arthur (1962) used filmed test materials to investigate the value of nonverbal contextual cues (gestures, facial expressions, and objects) to speechreading skill among adult subjects with hearing impairments or normal hearing. Speechreading skills were found to be significantly higher with contextual cues than without such cues. Berger et al. (1970) and Popelka and Berger (1971) also reported that gestures made a significant contribution to speechreading skill. Popelka and Berger (1971) found that adding inappropriate gestures to the lip movements resulted in decreased understanding when compared to lip movements alone. Popelka and Berger (1971) also studied the effects of extrafacial gestures, using a face mask so that only the lips were visible. It was shown that extrafacial gestures positively influenced proficiency in speechreading.

Use of Nonverbal Language Cues during Instruction

During speechreading instruction, appropriate nonverbal language cues can greatly facilitate speechreading. However, for some students, hand movements and gestures may need to be limited during speechreading practice to facilitate *close visual attention* to the face. Hand gestures should be minimized for poor speechreaders receiving basic instruction, and gradually introduced as students' skill and confidence in speechreading ability improve.

Experience has also shown that adults who have sustained a severe or profound hearing loss of recent origin are easily distracted by hand gestures during speechreading practice. An "eye sweep" from the face to the hand is frequently observed. This is understandable. The adult who is in the process of learning to shift from the auditory to the visual modality is on the horns of a dilemma. He/she does not know if the instructor is about to sign, fingerspell, gesture, or if the movement is a mannerism. Thus, it is important to discuss the *mode* of communication to be used during segments of instruction, especially for adults receiving basic speechreading instruction.

Experience has also shown that adults who have recently sustained a severe or profound

hearing impairment vary a great deal in their ability to acquire functional speechreading skills. For some adults it may take years to acquire the ability to focus visual attention on the speaker's face, view the speaker within the context of the communication situation, selectively filter out irrelevant visual stimuli, attend to relevant cues and shift from one communication mode to another to obtain the most information.

Nonverbal language cues are particularly important for the speechreader-listener as they relate to the semantic and pragmatic aspects of conversation. Nonverbal language cues may also be an indication of the suprasegmental features of spoken language that convey meaning, such as intonation, stress and juncture. Nonverbal language cues may also be cues to punctuation—for example, a question mark, exclamation point, or period. An investigation by Greene (1963) into the ability of unskilled lipreaders to lipread the accented syllables of polysyllabic nonsense words found that accent and placement could be identified through lipreading. Aspects of the pragmatics of language such as turn taking, opening and closing a conversation, how a person intends his/her message to be understood by the speechreader-listener (such as a question, request, promise, command, statement) can be inferred from facial expressions, gestures, touch, body movements, eye contact, withdrawal of eye contact, as well as the prosodic features in the verbal message. The reader is referred to the literature for an in-depth discussion of the pragmatics of language (Clark and Clark, 1977, pp. 25–40; and to the text of Searle, 1969).

It is hoped that these aspects of nonverbal communication will direct the reader's attention to their significance for instruction and to the speechreader's comprehension of the intended meaning of the speaker in conversation.

APPROACHES TO INSTRUCTION

English Competency and Speechreading

The English language competency of the speechreader is one of the numerous variables associated with the speechreading process (Berger, 1972, p. 200; Jeffers and Barley, 1971, pp. 33–34). Fehr and Trotter (1975) used various syntactical structures for evaluating speechreading. Subjects were college students with normal hearing. The authors concluded that speechreading is enhanced if there is control of syntactical structures when communicating with hearing-impaired individuals, either in an educational setting or by television. Hull (1976) suggests a linguistic approach to teaching speechreading. Subtelny and Walter (1975) found that low profiles in language and speech intelligibility predict poor speechreading ability. It can be anticipated that possession of a functional linguistic system will provide the speechreader with additional information to aid in message identification, facilitate anticipation, and help to fill in missing parts of speech. Good English skills are the foundation for learning aural-oral communication skills.

Speechreading has been used as an avenue for developing linguistic skills for centuries. Dodd's study (1976) on the phonological systems of severely and profoundly deaf children found evidence to suggest that lipreading was a major input to the deaf child's phonological system. Speechreading for the deaf child also has been described as a developing language process (Costello, 1957; Frisina, 1954). Speechreading proficiency can therefore be expected to improve with language comprehension (Lowell, 1960; Kretschmer, 1976).

Jeffers and Barley (1971, p. 7–8) describe the teaching of English language skills concurrently with speechreading instruction as "language-speechreading" or "concurrent instruction." English language-speechreading instruction is therefore directed toward improving or strengthening spoken, read, and written English according to individual needs.

The principle of teaching English language skills concurrently with speechreading, in a systematic manner, according to student's specific English language needs has been incorporated into a pilot speechreading "complement" course to formal English instruction concurrently being taught at NTID (Forman et al., 1980). Instruction utilizes the aural-oral skills of the student for learning specific English syntax and morphology in live instruction, and 1 hour a week of additional practice with a video-taped speechreading exercise. English instruction is provided by an English instructor and speechreading by an audiolo-

gist. Speechreading instruction in a speechreading "complement" course may *tend* to be more analytical than a traditional speechreading course because *specific grammatical structures* are emphasized in receptive and expressive language. Care must be taken that *spoken language* does not become *stilted*; instruction too analytical, and thus interfere with speechreading proficiency (Jeffers and Barley, 1971, p. 28; Berliner, 1980). Grammatical concepts currently being acquired should relate to everyday or career-related language.

Reinforcing English Language Concepts in Speechreading Instruction

Speechreading instruction should closely follow English grammatical concepts being learned by the young adult. This allows the teacher to focus on *familiar* linguistic structures and incorporate them into instructional materials. Conversational techniques may be used by teachers in a speechreading "complement course" to foster learning and usage of specific grammatical structures. These techniques are similar to the "linguistic conversations," described by Van Uden (1981, pp. 210–249). According to Van Uden (p. 210), "linguistic conversation" refers to conversation in which the main topic is the semantic and grammatical structure of language, the primary focus being the discovery of the structure of language. Conversations between instructor and student may also be incorporated into traditional speechreading courses to reinforce English grammatical structures according to student's needs. Conversations related to building empathy and rapport through discussion of attitudes and feelings are referred (with great sensitivity) as "heart-to-heart" conversations by Van Uden (1981, p. 210). These conversations are very much a part of teacher-student interaction and are excellent for speechreading practice.

The importance of speechreading instructors possessing a good knowledge of linguistics and psycholinguistics becomes evident (Crandall, 1978). Of considerable importance is a clear understanding of the complex interaction of phonology and syntax with the pragmatic, semantic and intellectual activities of the receiver (speechreader-listener) and the sender (speaker) during speech communication. The interaction of these four dimensions of spoken language leads to the identification and comprehension of the speaker's intended meaning and is essential for effective communication (Clark and Clark, 1977, pp. 25–40).

The similarities between the speechreading process and reading comprehension strategies have long been known (Jeffers and Barley, 1971, pp. 4–8). Recently, Williams (1978) studied the relationship between reading and speechreading, using high-school subjects with normal hearing. *Word-by-word* reading was found to be a significant characteristic of *poor readers* and *poor* speechreaders. Speechreading training might therefore include the use of remedial-reading instructional strategies. This is an area worthy of further study for the adult speechreader.

In traditional speechreading instruction, *segments* of analytical teaching at the syllable or word-for-word recognition level are *stages* in skill development. The primary objective is to improve the young adult's speechreading skill and speed of recognition for the goal of *effective oral communication*. Instruction focuses upon quick comprehension of *spoken language*, looking for the main idea and the "gist" rather than word-for-word recognition, anticipating the speaker's meaning from available contextual, nonverbal, and verbal language cues and utilizing communication strategies. English language skills may be reinforced through writing and reading, using written worksheets, overhead transparencies, or the blackboard, by teacher "feedback," and eliciting correct English grammatical structures in conversation.

Some students enrolled in English language-speechreading "complement" courses may need further instruction in traditional speechreading courses. Many young adults may need other communication skills instruction, such as speech therapy, technical communication, interpersonal communication, conversational skills refinement, or public speaking. Such instruction is necessary to enable students to develop confidence and to practice their speechreading, listening, speaking skills, and communication strategies in conversational contexts both inside and outside the classroom.

Participation in theater courses, dramatic productions, and musical activities can also contribute to the student's awareness of nonverbal language cues and sense of rhythm. These activities are highly recommended. They also help to build the student's self-confidence and self-esteem. Both qualities are necessary for effective communication.

Methods and Materials for Instruction

For all levels of speechreading competency, instructional materials and methods may relate to three primary factors associated with the speechreading process. These areas are (1) visual perception (attention, memory, speed and closure), (2) synthetic ability, and (3) thought flexibility. The following discussion presents methods and suggestions for stressing each of these areas.

Visual perception exercises may include digits, words, and phrases. For the advanced speechreader, connected speech may be used for visual memory training. Exercises to facilitate the speechreader's ability to synthesize fragmented speech patterns into "wholes" utilize sentences, paragraph exercises, stories, and conversation. Connected speech exercises may be in a monologue or dialogue form.

Thought flexibility training utilizes homophenous word exercises. These exercises encourage students to think of alternate responses if a message does not make sense within the context of a particular topic or situation (Jeffers and Barley, 1971, pp. 22 and 201). It is recognized that some drill and practice is necessary for certain materials. It has been found that by giving *short drill exercises* and using a *variety* of materials, boredom and fatigue are alleviated. The teacher must be flexible to use whatever instructional methods are necessary to improve or strengthen skills.

Space limitations prevent a detailed discussion, but it must be stressed that *context* is vitally important for presenting all sentence materials. Each practice sentence must have a contextual cue. Cues may be an illustration of a situation, discussion of the roles of the participants, the setting or the topic. Key words may be presented for ideas. Key words may appear in the sentence or be related to the sentence (like crossword puzzle cues). An imaginative instructor can turn a list of seemingly unrelated sentences into a dramatic oral interpretative reading. Unrelated sentences are good practice materials for training flexibility and mental alertness to sudden changes of topic that occur in conversational speech. Good phrasing and rhythm must always be maintained. When necessary and appropriate, attention should also be directed to the speechreader's use of appropriate rhythm and stress. This can also be achieved by the instructor "feeding back" the correct intonation, supplemented by the use of symbols written on the blackboard or hand signals to indicate stress and intonation contours. Oral interpretative readings may be utilized by teacher and student to develop prosodic awareness.

It is important that the student's *natural expression* is encouraged during speechreading instruction. Constant interruption for correction may result in a negative effect on student's spontaneous expression if used too frequently. This means that the speaker (instructor), must use a repertoire of strategies to aid reception without stopping expression. For example: "I didn't understand the last word. Please repeat it for me" or, "Did you say . . . , or . . . ?" "Shaping" spontaneous utterances using strategies, and conversational techniques which focus upon the appropriateness of the response, will not disrupt communicative interaction between participants.

All practice materials should be reviewed for unfamiliar vocabulary, idiomatic expressions (two-word verbs), and, whenever necessary, definitions with examples should be given. A pretest should be given to evaluate the young adult's understanding of the definitions of technical vocabulary to be used in career-related practice materials.

Suggestions for Instructional Materials

Instruction may be taken from the following areas, in stepwise fashion, according to the speechreading skill of the young adult.

1. Orientation response to speech through nonverbal and verbal language. This can be achieved by saying the student's name and using eye contact.
2. Encourage and develop "attentional" set for the reception of speech (speechreading-listening readiness).
3. Phoneme identification training to bring skill level to at least within homophenous categories.

Suggested order is from visible to less visible from the following groups. The symbols for the vowels are Webster's Pronunciation Symbols. The reader is referred to Franks and Kimble (1972) for consonant cluster categories.

VOWELS
Very Easy to Speechread:
/ü/boot, /ō/ boat, /ər/ bird, /aů/ now, yü / menu, /ů(ə)r/ sure, /ô(ə)r/ door
Easy to Speechread:
/ô/ law, ôi (boy), ē (bee), ī(fly), ā (mail), ä (hot)
Difficult to Speechread:
/e(ə)r/ (air), /i(ə)r/ (fear), /i(ə)r/ fire
Very Difficult to Speechread:
/a/ (bat), /ə/ (but), /e/ (bet), /i/ (bit), /ů/ (book)

CONSONANTS
Very Easy to Speechread:
/m p b -mp -mb/, f v -gh ph-/, /th/
Easy to Speechread:
/w wh/, /sh zh (measure) ch j/, /qu-/
Difficult to Speechread:
/l n t d -nt -nd/, /y/, /s/, /r/
Very Difficult to Speechread:
/h/, /g k -ng/, /x/

Training may relate to the following areas:

(1) Memory for articulated, sequential speech movements using visually contrastive digits, letters, days of the week, months, dates, rhyming words (feel-wheel-meal), add-an-item-or-phrase sentences, and connected speech (see Smith, 1974, and Light, 1978, for suggestions).

(2) Quick word or phrase recognition exercises. Materials consist of visible-to-less visible contrastive consonants, diphthongs, vowels, and consonant clusters in various positions, using words of one syllable length or longer. Function words frequently occur in the English language and these can be utilized in prepositional phrases for quick recognition of word patterns. For example; *in* the desk. . . . *by* the desk.

(3) Quick identification of practiced words in sentences.
Example: Put the (weeds, seeds, *beads*, deeds) in the box. Technical vocabulary related to the student's career may also be utilized for quick word recognition exercises. Morphological structures related to English language instruction may also be used.
Example:—less and —ful adjectives such as careless—careful.
—contrastive two-word verbs such as look up—look over.
—present and past verb tenses such as fight—fought.

It may be necessary to direct the speechreader's

attention *briefly* to visual cues of mouth patterns *prior to* segments of vowel and consonant discrimination practice. For example, muscle movements at the mouth corners, and the direction of the lower lip and jaw. Visual aids, such as a drawing of a face or a video tape of a speaker, viewed closeup, full-face, or profile view may be utilized. For example, comparing the vowels *ee - aw* (*feel - fall*).

A technique to make word recognition exercises more interesting and thought-provoking is to have the student identify the stimulus word, and give back association words, synonyns, antonyms or use of the practice word in a sentence. This technique provides further insight into the speechreader's understanding and usage of language. The reader is referred to Clark (1970, pp. 271–286) for further study related to word associations and linguistic theory.

Homophene Identification Exercises

Homophene identification exercises may be utilized for many objectives. For example, to direct the student's close visual attention to the lips and face, to show voice-voiceless contrasts, to improve visual memory of spoken word patterns, to reinforce spelling patterns, to develop thought flexibility, and to demonstrate the importance of context to differentiate meaning. While homophenes may look similar on the lips they are not produced exactly the same on the lips (Roback, 1961), and they are not alike in meaning. Experience has shown that homophenes may be differentiated on the basis of linguistic and situational cues. The reader is referred to a study by Albright and Hipskind (1971), cited by Berger (1972, p. 101), related to visibility and the contribution of linguistic cues to speechreading performance. Experience has shown that it is best to use a closed-set response for poor speechreaders when presenting homophene identification exercises utilizing variations in vowel spelling patterns.

Example: Teacher says: pail. Student watches closely and chooses the words that look like the stimulus word: (a) fail, (b) *sale*, (c) *mail*, (d) *tale*, (e) *bail*

The reader is referred to Jeffers and Barley (1971, p. 201) for additional methods and materials for instruction. Modifications may have to be made according to the student's speechreading skill.

Sentence Recognition Exercises

These exercises relate to training in building expectations of spoken language through association of ideas, using contextual cues. Sentence recognition exercises incorporate language associated with familiar everyday life situations, introductions, student's interests, on-the-job social conversation, job interview questions, committee procedures and terminology, technical language appropriate to the student's career or used in cooperative job experiences while the student is in academia. Sentences should vary in length and syntactical complexity according to the English competencies of the speechreader (Clouser, 1976; Schwartz and Black, 1967). Different forms of sentences may be used, such as declarative, imperative, and interrogative. Various question forms should be practiced. Idioms, slang, and multiple meaning words may also be utilized. Specific English grammatical structures may be incorporated into everyday or technical language sentences.

Connected Discourse Exercises

This may include a sequence of related short sentences for basic speechreaders, or short paragraphs for intermediate speechreaders. Stories, dialogues, excerpts from plays or movies may be utilized for advanced speechreaders. Discussions of local, national, and international news, topics of interest, life skills, hobbies, a synopsis of a movie or play currently being shown, book reviews, the lyrics of popular songs and poetry are appropriate for connected discourse speechreading exercises.

Comprehension testing using a question and answer format should follow the presentation of connected discourse material. Questions may be designed to elicit answers which reinforce grammatical structures concurrently being learned in English instruction. Questions may be formulated to encourage the speechreader to draw inferences and make predictions as in the language-experience approach to teaching reading (Stauffer, 1980, pp. 188–198; Maxwell, 1974). Questions may be used to explore and stimulate the student's thinking skills at three levels: the concrete (literal) level, the abstract (critical) level, and the personal opinion (interpretative) level. Examples of questions are: (a) at the literal level: How many ... ; How much ... ; When ... ; Where ... ; What ... ; Who ... ; or instructions such as: Name ... ; List ... ; (b) at the critical thinking level: Why ... ; How ... ; and (c) at the opinion level: What would you ... ; How would you ... ; Why do you think ... ; What problems do you think ... ? Students should also be encouraged to ask questions at these levels.

Connected discourse may also include on-the-job situations related to technical or general areas. For example, a staff meeting to discuss vacation policy or an interview for a job. Video-taped exercises are an excellent medium for presenting longer materials, such as stories. A live question and answer period follows the self-instruction practice. The development of balloon-captioning (Murray, 1979) has proved to be a useful method for stimulating kinesthetic and rhythmic awareness which are important for speechreading. Popular songs can be captioned and lip synchronized with the music (with permission).

From this discussion it can be seen that a speechreading instructor may utilize different methods and materials related to the primary factors that contribute to speechreading proficiency, according to student's abilities and needs. Speechreading materials may also relate to other courses being taken by the young adult, or general interests. The writer went through one quarter utilizing segments of speechreading instruction which related to parables from the Bible. Students were taking a course on religion and expressed interest in discussing various parables.

Instruction Related to Associational Cues and Communication Strategies

Speechreading instruction may also include discussions about speechreading, factors that may affect speechreading ability, strategies to overcome communication difficulties, and the contribution of associational verbal or nonverbal cues to speechreading proficiency.

Instructors should use their ingenuity to generate stimulating conversations, explore attitudes, or discuss difficult speechreading situations encountered by students and the kinds of strategies used. Role-playing activities with dramatization of situations that might be encountered in daily life or on the job will facilitate and enliven instruction in the areas of strategy skill development and nonverbal language reception and expression.

Awareness of associational nonverbal and verbal language cues and their relationship to communication strategies should be reinforced throughout instruction. The teacher may have to purposefully contrive situations, limit his/her own strategies and place the speechreader in the position of having to take the initiative.

Individual strategies will vary according to the young adult's aural-oral communication abilities, his/her confidence to take the initiative to use strategies, and understanding the roles and relationships of the participants in a particular communication situation. Some students may need to discuss ways to tactfully make suggestions for optimal viewing and listening conditions, especially in situations related to future employment. The most important strategy will be the young adult's ability, at the onset of communication, to tell the hearing person about his/her hearing loss, use of a hearing aid (or nonuse), and suggest the best ways to communicate with each other. Most frequently used strategies may include: (1) choosing preferential seating; (2) finding a quiet place; (3) suggesting a change of posture or the situation to obtain better lighting; (4) requesting verification of the topic or information, through repetition, questions, or confirmation; (5) requesting that the speaker spell a misunderstood word or name; (6) writing letters or numbers in-the-air; (7) writing; (8) requesting a slower speaking rate; (9) asking the speaker to talk louder; (10) asking a hearing friend or fellow worker to take notes at a meeting; (11) requesting that the group leader at a meeting provide an outline of topics before the meeting; (12) requesting that the group leader repeat questions or comments which may be spoken out of the speech reader's visual or auditory range; (13) using manual language for quick associational cues between participants who understand this communication mode; and (14) using predetermined (unobtrusive) hand (or facial) signals to indicate appropriate or inappropriate vocal loudness for the acoustic environment. Many of these strategies may also be used by the hearing person. The reader is referred to Schwartzberg (1975), Jacobs et al. (1978), Berger (1972, p. 199), and Ballantyne (1981) for suggestions.

Methods of Response

Methods of response may be in written, oral-imitation, or oral comprehension modes (with or without written or spoken cues). Thus, for the young adult, perception of stimulus materials may be at the level of detection/orientation, discrimination, identification, and comprehension (see Erber, 1977 and 1979b).

At the imitation-oral stage, the poorer speechreader is encouraged to say familiar practice items *simultaneously or as closely as possible* with the instructor. This technique facilitates visual sequencing through close attention to spoken word patterns. It also utilizes the visual, auditory, tactile, and kinesthetic senses (see Bunger, 1932, p. 45). Some students at this stage may first need a slower rate and repetitions. Others may need to read the practice items first, for familiarization with materials. The important oral-imitation stage has implications for training. The responses of the young adult can give insight into visual sequencing abilities. In the *delayed* imitation-oral stage, the student repeats the practice item *after* the instructor stops speaking. These techniques, used in reverse, may also be used to improve the speechreading skills of oral interpreters when voicing for deaf persons.

The technique of shadowing connected speech, that is, repeating word-for-word what the speaker says, has been reported by Cherry (1953) and Moray (1969, p. 49) in studies of selective listening. A similar tracking procedure, potentially useful for speechreading training, has been reported by De Filippo and Scott (1978). This procedure was used to train and evaluate the reception of ongoing speech with vibrotactile and electrotactile aids to lipreading. The two subjects used in the study (the authors) had normal hearing (see Chapter 9). This technique may also be useful for oral interpreter training.

Thus, a speechreading lesson may include several of the various instructional methods discussed in this section (Fig. 18.1). It is also apparent that evaluations should incorporate identification and/or comprehension of items related to the phonemic, word, sentence, and connected speech levels for appropriate instructional planning of methods and materials. Evaluations of speechreading may also include assessment of speechreading ability with contextual cues, and sentences varying in linguistic complexity.

Fatigue

Instructors should be on the alert for signs of fatigue and allow students to relax for a few moments when necessary. This is very important for students who may be using video tapes for self-instruction.

CLASSROOM COMMUNICATION

An oral environment is important for improving and strengthening aural-oral communication skills. Students must have the opportunity for continuous practice in reception and expression of spoken language if they are to improve their skill (Berger (1972, p. 200); Calvert and Silverman (1975, pp. 50–55)). This means that the instructor must provide language-generating experiences with the roles of speaker (sender) and speechreader (receiver) *changing* during interpersonal communication. An oral environment is conducive to the development and practice of communication strategies. Strategies must not only be teacher-initiated, but student initiated. It is in the "sheltered" classroom environment, through successful experiences, that students build confidence in their ability to use aural-oral communication, and learn to use strategies for effective communication outside the classroom.

Poor Speechreaders Receiving Basic Instruction

Modifications have to be made in teaching strategies for the poor speechreader who may be receiving basic instruction. The poor speechreader (not including adults with hearing impairment of recent origin), is primarily manual in his/her preferred mode of communication and has poor speech intelligibility. The important factor to be considered is that the student is receiving instruction because of a *personal need* and *motivation* to communicate orally through speechreading,

MATERIALS AND METHODS OF RESPONSE

TASK / STIMULUS / RESPONSE with or without cues	VISUAL PERCEPTION — Visual scanning, attention, memory, speed of perception, perceptual closure			CONCEPTUAL CLOSURE — Association training, predictions, synthesis of associational cues, communication strategies		
	Syllables Digits Letters Rhyming words Sentences: · add a phrase · add an item Connected speech:	Consonants Consonant Clusters Diphthongs Vowels Words Word Pairs/Groups Phrases Technical Vocabulary	Homophenes: Words Sentences	Sentences: Everyday Language Idioms, Slang Specific English Syn. & morph. structures	Sentences: Technical — Job-Related	Connected Speech: Paragraphs Stories Conversations Technical Specific English Syn. & morph. structures
Written: Multiple choice, Complete the sentence, Key words, Situational cues, Questions						
Oral: Imitation · Simultaneous · Delayed						
Oral: Comprehension Questions: Literal meaning concrete level, Critical meaning abstract level, Opinions, Interpretation, Dialogue						

Discussion: Associational verbal and nonverbal cues · Associational Cues Booklet (Jacobs et al 1981, in publication). Role-playing activities. Mime. Excerpts from movies.
Speechreading Strategies: Speechreading Strategies Booklet (Jacobs et al. 1978). Role-playing activities (pairs, group).

Figure 18.1. Speechreading instruction: Materials and methods of response. *Syn.*, syntactical; *morph.*, morphological.

listening, and speech. Establishing good rapport between teacher and student is essential. For this reason, it is suggested that poor speechreaders should continue with the same instructor until skill improves to a "gist" level (33–53% on the CID Everyday Sentences Test), or "plateaus" in his/her ability. From the "gist" level, instruction may be offered with different teachers for speaker variety.

The instructor's task is to make the student feel comfortable, to give the practice necessary to improve speechreading ability for target "survival" language skills, encourage communication strategies and reinforce English syntactical and morphological structures according to need.

There will be times (especially in the early stages of instruction or if frustration is observed), when the instructor will use manual language to aid discussions which may be related to instruction, speechreading, associational cues, strategies, or to give a contextual cue to facilitate quick association of ideas.

Fingerspelled letters, formed close to the lips, may be used as a quick visual aid to differentiate phonemes, homophenes, or misunderstood words.

If the student is to improve speechreading and oral communication skills, speech must be encouraged. Experience has shown that the use of speech increases as the student's skill improves and success is experienced. Speechreading and speech are closely related and the student must have the opportunity to practice speech. Therefore, it is suggested that all segments of practice materials be given without signs or fingerspelling but with the supportive help of contextual cues—spoken and written.

Students should understand that instruction may begin with written responses, but after familiarization with materials and skill improves, an oral response will be expected. Familiarization with materials to be practiced is essential. Live instruction requiring a written or an oral response must always follow self-instruction exercises. The oral response may be "same or different," an exact repetition of the stimulus sentence, an appropriate answer to a question, a follow-up related sentence, or dialogue. As familiarity with materials and instructor's speech patterns increases, written worksheets decrease. However, practice items continue to be reinforced through writing and reading, using an overhead projector with transparencies, or a blackboard.

The *power of the written word* as a visual aid to speechreading and English reinforcement cannot be overemphasized. Speechreading, listening, speaking, writing, and reading are communication modes which will be most used in future employment and should therefore be emphasized throughout instruction. However, during instruction, students may be observed reinforcing learning and retention of practice items, using manual language, speech (vocalizing or subvocalizing) or simultaneously using speech and manual language. The reader is referred to Conrad (1979, pp. 131–139) for further study related to the inner language coding systems used in the memorization of linguistic materials.

USE OF VIDEO-TAPED EXERCISES

Experience has shown that group instruction needs to be supplemented with individualized self-instruction and practice for many students (Jacobs, 1975). Poor speechreaders enrolled in basic courses may experience anxiety and frustration when placed in a communication situation in which they have never experienced success. Video-taped exercises for self-instruction, given prior to live instruction, can help to alleviate feelings of pressure between student and speaker. Practice with a video-taped exercise familiarizes the student with materials to be practiced live. Video tapes allow the student to practice at his/her own pace. In a group situation, poorer speechreaders tend to slow down the amount of material that can be practiced. Better speechreaders become bored waiting for the repetitions.

When poor speechreaders received self-instruction practice supplemented by individual or group instruction they improved their postcourse gains by an average of 28%, com-

pared to 15% in a group situation without self-instruction (Stuckless, 1980). Utilizing video-taped exercises of technical language, it is possible for a group of six students to practice speechreading in different areas of interest. Video-taped exercises are also a means of providing practice with a variety of speakers and different viewing angles; for example, full face versus profile.

A classroom that is set up with six booths for self-instruction and a circular table for group or individual work is ideal (Johnson, 1976) (Fig. 18.2). Thus, six students using self-instruction materials from different academic areas can work in the same classroom. This arrangement allows instructors the flexibility to utilize instructional materials for individual needs, and to give group or individual practice (Figs. 18.3 and 18.4).

Another benefit from using self-instruction as an adjunct to live, individual or group instruction is that students develop independent study habits in learning situations designed to give immediate reinforcement and successful experiences.

The availability of video-taped exercises also means that students can make up missed classes or receive additional practice for homework assignments. A typical video-taped exercise might consist of a speaker saying a series of 10–25 sentences one at a time. Poor speechreaders need shorter segments. The speechreader's task is to identify each sentence, using a written response. The student corrects his/her response by watching a caption of the sentence after the answer attempt. Students are encouraged to circle errors and write the correct words above an incorrect response.

The response task can be as simple as a multiple-choice task, as difficult as a completely open-set response, or a comprehension task, such as answering a question related to the stimulus sentence. An English assignment can follow the speechreading task, such as making pronoun substitutions or using pronouns to separate a separable two-word verb. Intermediate difficulty items can be set up with a key word or situational cue written on the response worksheet to facilitate association of ideas, anticipation and sentence identification. Students are encouraged to think of the speaker as a "talking

Figure 18.2. Speechreading classroom.

Figure 18.3. Miss Sara Bishop (student) using self-instruction materials in accounting course.

Figure 18.4. Mrs. Marjorie Jacobs and Miss Sara Bishop during live practice.

teacher" and repeat stimulus items either *with* or *after* the speaker, *after* writing, or when *correcting* from the caption. Poor speechreaders may need to master receptive skills first before expression is expected.

An important consideration when developing video-taped materials is that language is constantly changing (Michaels and Ricks, 1980). Therefore, video-taped materials need to be reviewed periodically and brought up to date. This is especially important for technical language.

Video-taped exercises can provide practice for hearing-impaired adults in nursing homes and hospitals. For hearing-impaired children, the addition of situational cues (cartoons, real life, or captioned) may be utilized to enhance speechreading skill, use of nonverbal or verbal cues, and strategies. Balloon captioning (Murray, 1979) offers promise as a visual aid for developing awareness of the suprasegmental features of speech among hearing-impaired children who can read. Among the hearing population, personal experience has shown that video tapes can be a source of practice for nurses who have to communicate with patients who are unable to write or use voice. Video tapes may also be used for profoundly hearing-impaired adults who have undergone cochlear implant surgery.

Computer-Assisted Instruction

In 1973, the writer collaborated on a project to evaluate computer-assisted instruction for speechreading (Houde et al., 1974). The positive results on this preliminary investigation indicated that this form of technology can be successfully utilized for speechreading instruction. Sims et al. (1979) have developed a computer-assisted, interactive version of this type of video tape, using speechreading exercises developed by the writer which purport to improve student motivation and tailor the amount of practice to the difficulty level. Implementation of this system is now under way, using an inexpensive microcomputer. The reader is referred to Von Feldt (1978) and Richardson (1981) for further review of the literature.

RESULTS OF TRAINING

Speechreading has been described as a successive discrimination task (Brehman, 1965). Practice effects can be seen as a result of training for students who are motivated to improve and maintain their skill. The author tabulated the results of 18 hours of instruction for 152 students (Table 18.1). These students received instruction from different instructors in basic, intermediate, or advanced courses (Jacobs, 1976 and 1977) from different instructors. Students were administered the

CID Everyday Sentences Tests (Johnson, 1976) before and after instruction. Though no experimental controls were applied to the collection of these data and caution is advised in interpretation, one may see trends toward useful gains for most students in communication function as measured by the CID Everyday Sentence Test administered in a combined auditory and visual mode.

However, Stuckless (1980), in a review of research at NTID, reported on a study by Conklin et al. (1976) related to the influence of manual communication learned by students after they entered NTID on their existing speech and lipreading skills. Data were collected on 78 randomly selected entering students over a period of two to three years. Thirty-three students had received one or more quarters of speechreading training. No significant changes were found in speechreading performance. Stuckless suggests that attention be directed to the possibility that gains in proficiency in speechreading may disappear in time unless regularly reinforced.

These suggestions were confirmed in an informal study of students who showed a 15% or better gain after training (n = 75). The results for speechreading without sound (6½ months to 2½ years after training) indicated that, overall, 45% of the students had dropped to precourse level, with the greatest drop among the better speechreaders (54–75% precourse score on the CID Everyday Sentences Test). In this group, 78% were at precourse level, compared with approximately 30% of the students in the 11–53% range of precourse performance. Thus, it is important to provide an aural-oral communication environment and/or training support so that the severely and profoundly hearing-impaired person has the opportunity to continuously practice speechreading, listening and speaking skills; not only for everyday language, but also for the technical language of his/her career choice. A logging system designed as a tool to facilitate self-assessment of speech to aid carryover of communication skills in everyday situations has been described and utilized successfully by McMahon (1980). A similar system to document oral communication experiences and strategies may also be utilized for speechreading instruction.

It is suggested that evaluation of speechreading, hearing, vision, and speech skills

Table 18.1
Results of Training after 16 Hours of Instruction (CID Everyday Sentence Test)[a]

Pretest Score	n	Number with 15% or Better Gain Without Sound	Number with 15% or Better Gain With Sound
0–10	13	6 (46%)	8 (62%)
11–32	36	14 (39%)	24 (67%)
33–53	68	48 (71%)	58 (85%)
54–74	36	14 (39%)	36 (100%)
75–100	—	—	—
	153	82 (54%)	126 (82%)

[a] Score = percentage of key words correctly identified.

should be carried out periodically throughout life. A "refresher" course of instruction may be offered to the adult who wishes to maintain or strengthen aural-oral communication skills.

CHARACTERISTICS OF SPEECHREADING TEACHERS

Specific academic and professional credentials are not the only qualifications necessary to teach speechreading to severely and profoundly hearing-impaired young adults. Speechreading does not simply involve someone standing in front of a class "mouthing" words and sentences like a parrot. Speechreading is a complex visual receptive skill that must be considered within the context of the dynamics of speech communication. Desirable characteristics and guidelines for teachers have been described by Jeffers and Barley (1971, pp. 39 and 237), O'Neill and Oyer (1961, pp. 7–8), and Berger (1972, pp. 197–199). This discussion will focus upon the personal characteristics and emotive ability found to be desirable for teaching this highly important oral communication skill to severely and profoundly hearing-impaired adults.

Speechreading instructors, ideally, should possess the personal characteristics of an oral interpreter (Northcott, 1977 and 1979; Jacobs, 1978) and the emotive ability of an actor or actress (without overacting). These characteristics are especially important for teaching poor speechreaders who need optimum viewing conditions. Desirable personal characteristics include mobile lips (especially a well-defined upper lip), clear enunciation without overexaggeration of lips and tongue, an expressive face, natural gestures and bodily postures appropriate to the content of the message. Instead of overexaggerating the mouth and tongue movements, it is preferable to talk naturally (Tucker, 1979). However, exaggeration (without distortion), may be necessary in some circumstances. Franks (1979) investigated the influence of exaggerated mouth movements on speechreading and found they enhanced speechreading in people with normal hearing and also in hearing-impaired subjects. Excessive dropping of the mandible to show articulatory movements did not enhance speechreading.

It is desirable that the teacher be skillful in using appropriate pauses, emphasis, phrasing, and intonation. Experience producing hundreds of speechreading video tapes has shown that considerable coaching has to be given to some speakers to elicit good phrasing and intonation when using longer sentences and connected speech materials. Meaningful pauses at the end of a phrase enable the speechreader to see visual cues to punctuation, such as lips in a resting position, and to be aware aurally of silences associated with pauses. These factors are especially important if the speechreader misses a word or phrase. A pause also creates anticipation and allows the speechreader to focus on the next phrase (or sentence) to pick up the threads of the conversation.

It has been suggested that immediate reproductive memory is limited in terms of "chunks" rather than single elements (Miller, 1956). Phrasing, which the writer considers to be a form of chunking, may be expected to facilitate information processing. Using phrasing appropriate to the content, and a slower rate when requested, may give the severely and profoundly hearing-impaired person additional "thinking" time to process and carry out the semantic procedures necessary to arrive at the speaker's meaning. Allowance for "thinking time" is an important consideration when a teacher may be teaching new unfamiliar vocabulary or using complex technical language (Nichols and Stevens, 1957). Various linguistic structures may also take longer to process. The reader is referred to the text of Clark and Clark (1977, pp. 133–173, 449–483) for further reading.

Use of Makeup

When necessary, the subtle use of makeup to emphasize the speaker's lips is suggested, especially if the upper lip is thin and rigid. "Matte" colors appear to be more visible and less affected by different kinds of lighting than pale frosted hues.

Makeup for male or female speakers should be considered if communication occurs within a public setting, such as a hall or theater. Important factors that can affect visibility are lighting and distance. White lighting may cause the face to look washed out. The reader is referred to Corson (1975, p.

243) for more information and an excellent in-depth discussion of this frequently over-looked subject.

Makeup for Television

Special studio makeup is desirable for talent on speechreading video tapes, especially for blondes with light skin tones. Facial contours and hair tend to blend and there is no focal point for viewing. The best lipstick color for female speakers for television are the subtle shades of bronze, cinnamon, coffee and amber recommended by Corson (1975, p. 243). Blue and orange hues, dark reds, and lip gloss should be avoided (Faucher, 1980). Experience has shown the light application of a "coffee"-colored lipstick for male speakers with moustaches or beards helps to emphasize the lips, especially the upper lip, and looks fairly natural. Moustaches and beards should "frame" but not cover the lips. Male instructors with mobile lips and deep voices are ideal for teaching speechreading to the severely and profoundly hearing-impaired young adult.

Faucher (1980) recommends the use of eye makeup to enhance the eyes of female subjects, suggesting brown or gray eyeshadow rather than light blue or green. Enhancing the speaker's eyes is desirable. Eye expressions convey important nonverbal language cues to the speechreader. The important consideration is that the application of makeup should be underplayed, retaining the natural appearance of the subject (Shepard, 1981).

Clothing for Television

For upper torso viewing it is recommended that the speaker's clothing be plain and not patterned. Patterns create difficulty for the speechreader in reading the captions if the stimulus sentence is captioned while the speaker is on the screen. Plain colors, such as brown, dark green, dark orange, black, navy blue, or burgundy, are suggested. If video tapes are to be used for basic speechreaders, the speaker should not wear bright distracting jewelry and hair should be kept off the face in the lower jaw region. These recommendations are based upon experience and the suggestions of Talley (1981), producer-director of numerous speechreading productions.

SUMMARY

Visual communication (speechreading) for the severely and profoundly hearing-impaired young adult is directed toward the primary objective of improving or strengthening oral communication. For some adults the objectives may be to achieve "gist" levels for speechreading target "survival" language, to increase awareness of the contribution of associational cues and to use communication strategies. For others, the objectives may be to improve speechreading ability for longer-length connected speech or technical communication. Speechreading instruction may also be utilized for teaching and reinforcing the adults' understanding of the pragmatic aspects of conversation and the usage of English syntax and morphology.

Speechreading has been shown to be a multifaceted and complex subject, to be viewed for instructional purposes within the parameters of interpersonal speech communication. To improve the severely or profoundly hearing-impaired young adult's aural-oral communication skills (speechreading, listening, and speaking) requires an instructor who is conscious of all the elements discussed in this chapter. It also requires an instructor who is sensitive to the needs of the young adult and has the flexibility to try different teaching methods. Above all, to show real improvement requires a *motivated* young adult with a *positive attitude* toward oral communication, as well as a certain art on the part of the teacher.

It is hoped that the material in this chapter will inspire teachers to develop challenging, interesting and innovative speechreading lessons which relate not only to the student's specific needs, abilities, special interests, linguistic skills, life skills, and future career, but to the cultural, political, and social aspects of the world.

References

Albright, P., and Hipskind, N.M. A comparison of visibility and speechreading performance between matched English sentence and Slurvian utterances. Paper presented at the American Speech and Hearing Association convention, 1971. Cited in K.W. Berger, *Speechreading: Principles and Methods.* Baltimore: National Educational Press, 1972, 101.

Arthur, R.H. The effect of contextual and noncontextual motion pictures on the speechreading proficiency of comparable adult males, Ph.D. dissertation, University of Florida, 1962.

Ballantyne, D.L. The Young Deaf Professional at Work: The Start of the Career. Paper presented at the National Technical Institute for the Deaf. Rochester Institute of Technology, Rochester, N.Y., March 25, 1981.

Barker, R. The social interrelations of strangers and acquaintances. *Sociometry*, 1942, *5*, 169–179.

Berger, K.W. *Speechreading: Principles and Methods*. Baltimore: National Educational Press, 1972.

Berger, K.W., Martin, J., and Sakoff, R. The effect of visual distractions on speechreading performance. *Teacher Deaf*, 1970, *68*, 384–387.

Berliner, K.I. Individual differences in speechreading ability: Cognitive variables. Ph.D. dissertation, Claremont Graduate School, 1980. In *Dissertation Abstracts*, 1980, *09-B*, 4528.

Binnie, C.A., Jackson, A.P., and Montgomery, A. Visual intelligibility of consonants. A lipreading screening test with implications for aural rehabilitation. *J. Speech Hear. Disord.*, 1976, *41*, 530–539.

Birdwhistell, R. *Kinesics and Context Essays in Body Motion Communication*. Philadelphia: University of Pennsylvania Press, 1970.

Blesser, B. Discussion: perceptual and conceptual strategies. In R.E. Stark (ed.), *Sensory Capabilities of Hearing-Impaired Children*. Baltimore: University Park Press, 1974, 118–119.

Boothroyd, A. Sensory aids. In J. Burton (ed.), *Hearing Loss in Children*, chap. 49. Baltimore: University Park Press, 1977, 699–714.

Børrild, K. Cued speech and the mouth hand system. A contribution to the discussion. In G. Fant (ed.), *International Symposium on Speech Communication Ability and Profound Deafness*. Washington, D.C.: Alexander Graham Bell Association for the Deaf, 1972, 231–240.

Brehman, A.E. Programmed discrimination training for lipreaders. In *Symposium on Research and Utilization of Educational Media for Teaching the Hearing Impaired*. Washington, D.C.: Department of Health Education and Welfare, 1965.

Brooks, W.D. *Speech Communication*. New York: William C. Brown, 1971.

Bugental, D., Kaswan, J.W., and Love, L.R. Perception of contradictory meanings conveyed by verbal and nonverbal channels. *J. Pers. Soc. Psychol.*, 1970, *16*, 647–655.

Bunger, A.M. *Speechreading—Jena Method*. Danville, Illinois: Interstate Press, 1932, 43.

Caccamise, F., Meath-Lang, B., and Johnson, D.D. Assessment and use of vision: critical needs of hearing-impaired students. *Am. Ann. Deaf*, 1981, *126* (No. 3), 361.

Calvert, D.R., and Silverman, S.R. *Speech and Deafness*. Washington, D.C.: Alexander Graham Bell Association for the Deaf, 1975, 50–55.

Castle, D.L. Telecommunication and the hearing impaired. *Volta Rev.*, 1981, *83* (No. 5, September), 275–284.

Cherry, E.C. Some experiments upon the recognition of speech with one and with two ears. *J. Acoust. Soc. Am.*, 1953, *25*, 975–979.

Clark, H.H. Word associations and linguistic theory. In J. Lyons (ed.), *New Horizons in Linguistics*. Baltimore: Penguin Books, 1970, 269–278.

Clark, H.H., and Clark, E.V. *Psychology and Language: An Introduction to Psycholinguistics*. New York: Harcourt-Brace-Jovanovich, 1977, 25–40, 133–173, 449–483.

Clouser, R.A. The effect of vowel-consonant ratio and sentence length on lipreading ability. *Am. Ann. Deaf*, 1976, *121*, 513–518.

Coleman, J.C. Facial expression of emotion. *Psychol. Monogr.*, 1949, *63*, 1–36.

Conklin, J., Subtelny J., and Walter G. Speech, lipreading, and manual communication during residency at NTID. Paper presented at NTID Mini-Convention, February 1976.

Connors, S., and McPherson, D. A vibrotactile program for the deaf. Paper presented at Poster Session, ASHA Convention, San Francisco, 1978.

Conrad, R. Chap. 5: Deafness and memory span, pp. 115–139, and chap. 7: Lipreading, pp. 176–203, In *The Deaf School Child: Language and Cognitive Functions*. New York: Harper & Row, 1979.

Cornett, R.O. Cued speech. *Am. Ann. Deaf*, 1967, *112*, 3–13.

Cornett, R.O. Effects of cued speech upon speechreading. In G. Fant (ed.), *International Symposium on Speech Communication Ability and Profound Deafness*. Washington, D.C.: Alexander Graham Bell Association for the Deaf, 1970, 222–230.

Cornett, R.O. Cued speech parent training and follow-up program. *Contract #OEC-8009 137-4348-(019) and (615)*. Washington, D.C.: Office of Education, 1972.

Corson, R. Make up for other media. In *Stage Makeup*, Chap. 21, Ed. 5. New York: Appleton-Century-Crofts, 1975, 241–248.

Costello, M.R. Individual differences in speechreading. In *Report of the Proceedings of the International Congress on Education of the Deaf and the 41st Meeting of the Convention of American Instructors of the Deaf*. Washington, D.C.: U.S. Government Printing Office, 1964, 317–321.

Crandall, K.E. Reading and writing skills and the deaf adolescent. *Volta Rev.*, *1978*, *5*, 319–332.

De Filippo, C. Memory for articulated sequences and lipreading performance of deaf observers. Ph.D. dissertation, Washington University, 1980.

De Filippo, C.L., and Scott, B.L. A method for training speech reception. *J. Acoust. Soc. Am.*, 1978, *63* (No. 4, April).

Dodd, B. The phonological systems of deaf children. *J. Speech Hear. Disord.*, 1976, *41*, 185–198.

Donnolly, K. An investigation into the determinants of lipreading of deaf adults. *Int. Audiol.*, 1969, pp. 501–508.

Erber, N.P. Auditory and visual and auditory-visual recognition of consonants by children with normal and impaired hearing. *J. Speech Hear. Res.*, 1972a, *15*, 413–422.

Erber, N.P. Effects of distance on visual reception of speech. *J. Speech Hear. Res.*, 1972b, *15*, 848–857.

Erber, N.P. Effects of angle, distance and illumination on visual reception of speech by profoundly deaf children. *J. Speech Hear. Res.*, 1974, *17*, 99–112.

Erber, N.P. Developing materials for lipreading evaluation and instruction. *Volta Rev.*, 1977, *79*, 35–42.

Erber, N.P. Illumination factors in the design of classrooms for deaf children. *Volta Rev.*, 1979a, *81*, 226–235.

Erber, N.P. An approach to evaluating auditory speech perception ability. *Volta Rev.*, 1979b, *81*, 16–24.

Fant, G. "Q" Codes. In G. Fant (ed.), *International Symposium on Speech Communication Ability and Profound Deafness.* Washington, D.C.: Alexander Graham Bell Association for the Deaf, 1972, 261–268.

Faucher, C. How to do straight TV make-up—a primer. *Educational and Industrial Television*, May 1980, 36–40.

Fehr, J., and Trotter, W. Visual perception by speechreaders of selected syntactic structures. *J. Percept. Mot. Skills*, 1975, *41*, 31–34.

Forman, J., Durity, R., Jacobs, M. Interdepartmental paper National Technical Institute for the Deaf, Rochester Institute of Technology, Rochester, N.Y., 1980.

Franks, J.R. The influence of exaggereted mouth movements on lipreading. *Audiol. Hear. Educ.*, 1979, Dec./Jan., 12–16.

Franks, J.R., and Kimble, J. The confusion of English consonant clusters in lipreading. *J. Speech Hear. Res.*, 1972, *15* (No. 3).

Frey, R.M., and Krause, I.B. The incidence of color blindness among deaf children. *Except. Child.*, 1971, *5*, 393–394.

Fries, C.C. *Teaching and Learning English as a Foreign Language.* Ann Arbor, University of Michigan Press, 1978, p. 17.

Frisina, D.R. Speechreading. In *A Report on the Proceedings of the International Congress on Education of the Deaf and the 41st Meeting of the Convention of American Instructors for the Deaf*, Washington, D.C.: U.S. Government Printing Office, 1954, 191–207.

Greene, J.D. An investigation of the ability of unskilled lipreaders to determine the accented syllable of polysyllabic words. Unpublished master's thesis, Michigan State University. Cited by O'Neill, J.J., and Oyer, H.J.: Aural rehabilitation. In J. Jerger (ed.), *Modern Developments in Audiology*, Ed. 2, Chap. 7. New York: Academic Press, 1973, 227.

Hall, E.T. A system of notation of proxemic behaviors. *Am. Anthropol.*, 65, 1963, 1003–1026.

Hall, E.T. *The Hidden Dimension*. New York: Doubleday, 1969, 10–15.

Hughey, J.D., and Johnson, A.W. *Speech Communication Foundation and Challenges*. New York: Mcmillan, 1975.

Hilgard, E.R., and Blower, J. *Theories of Learning*. Englewood Cliffs, N.J.: Prentice Hall, 1975, 608–609.

Hilgard, E.R. *Theories of Learning*. New York: Appleton-Century-Crofts, 1956, 486–487.

Houde, R., Computer-Assisted Instruction for Speechreading: A Pilot Project. Interdepartmental Communication to D.D. Johnson, Communication Division Project NTID, Rochester Institute of Technology, Rochester, N.Y., 1974.

Hull, R. A linguistic approach to the teaching of speechreading: theoretical and practical concepts. *J. Acad. Rehabil. Audiol.*, 1976, 9, 14–19.

Jackson, P.L., Montgomery, A.A., and Binnie, C.A. Perceptual dimensions underlying vowel lipreading performance. *J. Speech Hear. Res.*, 1976, *19*, 796–812.

Jacobs, M. Facilitating Oral Communication in the Classroom. A working paper. Presented at the Mini-Convention, National Technical Institute for the Deaf, Rochester Institute of Technology, Rochester, N.Y., 1974.

Jacobs, M. Programmed self instruction in speechreading. *J. Acad. Rehabil. Audiol.*, 1975, 8 (Nos. 1 and 2, April-October), 1975.

Jacobs, M. The effectiveness of speechreading training at NTID. A working paper presented at the NTID Mini Convention. National Technical Institute for the Deaf, Rochester Institute of Technology, Rochester, N.Y., 1977.

Jacobs, M. Oral Education: A Historical Overview. A working paper. Presented at a workshop for Oral Interpreters, sponsored by the American Association for the Advancement of Science and the Alexander Graham Bell Association for the Deaf. Houston, Tex. Sponsored by Alexander Graham Bell Association, 1978.

Jacobs, M., Clymer, E.W., and Buckley, M. Speechreading Strategies. National Technical Institute for the Deaf, Rochester Institute of Technology. Rochester, N.Y., 1978.

Jacobs, M., Clymer, E.W., Buckley, M., Woolever, D., Young, M., Castle, T., and Yates, W.E. *Associational Cues*. Rochester, New York: National Technical Institute for the Deaf, Rochester Institute of Technology, 1982.

Jacobs, M., and Johnson, D.D. NTID Interdepartmental communication. Rochester Institute of Technology, Rochester, N.Y., 1976.

Jeffers, J., and Barley, M. *Speechreading (Lipreading)*. Springfield, Ill.: Charles C Thomas, 1971.

Jenson, P.M. The relationship of speechreading and speech. In L.E. Connor, (ed.), *Speech for the Deaf Child, Knowledge and Use*. Washington, D.C.: Alexander Graham Bell Association for the Deaf, 1971, 273, 276–278.

Johnson, D.D. The adult deaf client and rehabilitation. In J.G. Alpiner (ed.), *Handbook of Rehabilitative Audiology*, Chap. 8. Baltimore: Williams & Wilkins, 1978, 172–221.

Johnson, D.D. Communication learning centers at NTID. In *Info Series 2: Equipment Designed to Improve the Communication Skills of the Deaf*. Rochester, N.Y.: National Technical Institute for the Deaf, 1976.

Johnson, D.D. Communication characteristics of NTID students. *J. Acad. Rehabil. Audiol.*, 1975, 8, 17–32.

Johnson, D.D. Communication characteristics of a young deaf adult population: Techniques for evaluating their communication skills. *Am. Ann. Deaf.*, 1976, *121*, 409–424.

Johnson, D.D., Caccamise, F., Rothblum, A.M., Hamilton, L.F., and Howard, M. Identification and follow-up of visual impairments in hearing impaired populations. *Am. Ann. Deaf*, 1981, *126*, 321–360.

Kretschmer, R.R. Language acquisition. In R. Frisina (ed.), *A Bicentennial Monograph on Hearing Impairment. Trends in the U.S.A.* Washington, D.C.: Alexander Graham Bell Association for the Deaf, 1976.

Kretschmer, R.R. Reaction to 7 and 8. In A.M. Mulholland (ed.), *Oral Education Today and Tomorrow*. Washington, D.C.: Alexander Graham Bell Association for the Deaf, 1981.

Lawson, L.J., and Myklebust, H. Ophthalmological deficiencies in deaf children. *Except. Child.*, 1970, *37*, 17–20.

Leonard, R. The effects of continuous auditory distractions on lipreading performance, M.A. thesis, Michigan State University, 1962. Cited in: K.W. Berger, *Speechreading: Principles and Methods*. Baltimore: National Education Press, 1972, 105.

Levine, E.S. Psycho-cultural determinants in personality development. *Volta Rev.*, 1976, *78*, 265.

Light, J.B. *The Joy of Listening: An Auditory Training Program*. Washington, D.C.: A.G. Bell Association for the Deaf, 1978.

Lowell, E.L. Research in speechreading: some relationships to language development and implications for the classroom teacher. In *Proceedings of the 39th Meeting of the Convention of American Instructors of the Deaf*. Washington, D.C.: U.S. Government Printing Office, 1960, 68–75.

Mays, C., and LaFrance, M. On the acquisition of nonverbal communication: a review. *Merrill-Palmer Q.*, 1978, *24*(4), 213–228.

Maxwell, M. Teaching reading as a problem-solving activity. *Am. Ann. Deaf.*, 1974, *6*, 721–723.

McMahon, M. Logging spoken English experiences: Strategies for carryover. Paper presented to Teachers of English to Speakers of other Languages Conference, San Francisco, March 1980.

Mehrabian, A. Orientation behaviours and nonverbal attitude communication. *J. Commun.*, 1967, *17*, 331.

Mehrabian, A. *Silent Messages*. Belmont, Calif.: Wadsworth Publishing, 1971.

Michaels, L., and Ricks, C. *The State of the Language*. Berkeley, California: University of California Press, 1981.

Miles, M.B. Human relationships, training processes and outcomes. *J. Counsel. Psychol.*, 1960, *7*, 301–306.

Miller, G.A. The magical number seven plus or minus two: some limits on our capacity for information processing. *Psychol. Rev.*, 1956, *63*, 81–97. Cited in: E.R. Hilgard and G.H. Bower, *Theories of Learning*. Englewood Cliffs, N.J.: Prentice-Hall, 1975, 584–586.

Mira, M. Measurement of the listening of hearing impaired children. *J. Speech Hear. Res.*, *13* (No. 1, March), 1970.

Moray, N. *Attention: Selective Processes in Vision and Hearing*. London: Hutchinson Educational Ltd., 1969, 49.

Murray, R. Reinforcement of speech through the balloon captioning of song lyrics. *Am. Ann. Deaf*, 1979, *124*, 656–662.

Nichols, R.G., and Stevens, L.A. *Are You Listening?* New York: McGraw Hill, 1957, 79–81.

Northcott, W.H. The oral interpreter: a necessary support specialist for the hearing impaired. *Volta Rev.*, 1977, *79*, No. 3.

Northcott, W.H. Guidelines for the preparation of oral interpreters: support specialists for hearing impaired individuals. *Volta Rev.*, 1979, *81*, 135–145.

O'Neill, J.J. Contributions of the visual components of oral symbols to the speech comprehension of listeners with normal hearing. Doctoral dissertation, Ohio State University of Speech, 1951. Cited in: J.J. O'Neill and H.J. Oyer, *Visual Communication for the Hard of Hearing*. Englewood Cliffs, N.J.: Prentice-Hall, 1961, 47.

O'Neill, J.J., and Oyer, H.J. *Visual Communication for the Hard of Hearing*. Englewood Cliffs, N.J.: Prentice-Hall, 1961, 7–8.

Pickett, J.M. Speech technology and communication for the hearing impaired. *Volta Rev.*, *83* (No. 5, September), 1981.

Popelka, G.R., and Berger, K.W. Gestures and speech reception. *Am. Ann. Deaf*, 1971, *116*, 434–436.

Richardson, J.E. Computer assisted instruction for the hearing impaired. *Volta Rev.*, *83* (No. 5, September), 1981.

Risberg, A., and Agelfors, E. Information extraction and information processing in speechreading. In *Quarterly Progress and Status Report 2-3*. Stockholm: Speech Transmission Laboratory, 1978.

Roback, I.M. Homophenous words. M.A. thesis, Michigan State University, 1961. Cited by J.J. O'Neill and H.J. Oyer, In J. Jerger (ed.), *Modern Developments in Audiology*, Ed. 2. New York: Academic Press, 1973, 226.

Rosenstein, J. How shall he be taught? A panel presentation. *Volta Rev.*, *74*, 557–558.

Rosenthal, R., Hall, J.A., DiMatteo, R., Rogers, P.L., and Archer, D. *Sensitivity to Nonverbal Communication. The PONS Test*. Baltimore: The Johns Hopkins University Press, 1979.

Sanders, D.A. *Aural Rehabilitation*. Englewood Cliffs, N.J.: Prentice-Hall, 1971, 115–128.

Sanders, D.A. A model for communication. In L.L. Lloyd (ed.) *Communication Assessment and In Teneation Strategies*, Chap. 7. Baltimore: University Park Press, 1976.

Schulte, K. Phoneme transmitting manual system (PMS). In G. Fant (ed.), *International Symposium on Speech Communication Ability and Profound Deafness*. Washington, D.C.: Alexander Graham Bell Association for the Deaf, 1972, 255–260.

Schwartz, J.R., and Black, J.W. Same effects of sentence structures on speechreading. *Central States Speech J.*, 1967, *18*, 86–90.

Schwartzberg, J. Some thoughts on communication. *Volta Rev.*, *77* (No. 1, January), 1975.

Searle, J.R. *Speech Acts*. New York: Cambridge University Press, 1969.

Shepard, J. A few makeup suggestions: Personal Communication. Producer/Director, Instructional Television Department, NTID, Rochester Institute of Technology, Rochester, N.Y., 1981.

Sims, D., Von Feldt, J., Dowaliby, F., Hutchinson, K., and Myers, T. A pilot experiment in computer assisted speechreading instruction utilizing the Data Analysis Video Interactive Device (DAVID). *Am. Ann. Deaf*, 1979, *124*, 618–624.

Smith, C. *Auditory Memory Exercises and More Auditory Memory Exercises*. Washington, D.C.: Alexander Graham Bell Association for the Deaf, 1974.

Stauffer, R.G. *The Language Experience Approach to Teaching Reading*, Ed. 2. New York: Harper & Row, 1980.

Stone, L. Facial clues of context in lipreading. In E. Lowell (ed.), *John Tracy Clinic Research Papers*, Los Angeles, 1957, 11.

Stuckless, E.R. A review of research at NTID, 1967–1976. National Technical Institute for the Deaf, Rochester Institute of Technology, Rochester, N.Y., 1980.

Stuckless, E.R. Real-time graphic display and language development for the hearing-impaired. *Volta Rev.*, *83* (No. 5, September), 1978.

Subtelny, J., and Walter, G.G. An overview of the communication skills of NTID students with implications for planning rehabilitation. *J. Acad. Aural Rehabil.*, 1975, *8*, 33–50.

Suchman, R.G. Color-form preference, discriminative accuracy and learning of deaf and hearing children. *Child Dev.*, 1960, *37*, 439–451.

Tagiuri, R., Blake, R.R., and Bruner, J.S. Some determinants of the perception of positive and negative feelings in others. *J. Abnorm. Soc. Psychol.*, 1953, *48*, 585–592.

Talley, S. (Personal communication, 1981.) Presently, Engineer, KECH, TV 22, Salem, Oregon; previously Producer-Director, Instructional-Television Department, National Technical Institute for the Deaf, Rochester, N.Y.

Taylor, P.L. Data Processing Job Activities. An Internal Report, National Technical Institute for the Deaf, Rochester Institute of Technology, Rochester, N.Y., 1980.

Tucker, B. Please speak normally! *Volta Rev.*, 1979, *81*, 45–46.

Upton, H.W. Wearable eyeglass speechreading aid. *Am. Ann. Deaf*, 1968, *113*, 222–229.

van Uden, A.M. The conversational method and the control of language. A chapter for the didactics of language for deaf children. In A.M. Mulholland (ed.), *Oral Education Today and Tomorrow*. Washington, D.C.: Alexander Graham Bell Association for the Deaf, 1981.

Von Feldt, J.R. A national survey of the use of computer and assisted instruction in schools for the deaf. Unpublished manuscript, National Technical Institute for the Deaf, Rochester Institute of Technology, Rochester, N.Y., 1978.

Walden, B.E., Prosek, R.A., and Worthington, D. Predicting audio-visual consonant recognition performance of hearing-impaired adults. *J. Speech Hear. Res.*, 1974, *17*, 270–278.

Walden, B.E., Erdman, S.A., Montgomery, A., Schwartz, D.M., and Prosek, R. Some effects of training on speech recognition by hearing-impaired adults. *J. Speech Hear. Res.*, *24* 1981, (No. 2, June), 207–216.

Walter, G.G., and Sims, D.G. The effect of prolonged hearing aid use on the communication skills of young deaf adults. *Am. Ann. Deaf*, 1978, *123*, 548–554.

Watson, J.M. An experimental study to test for optimum facial angle for televised speechreading lessons. M.A. thesis, California State University, Long Beach, 1974.

Watzlawick, P., Beavin, J., and Jackson, D. *Pragmatics of Human Communication*. New York: Norton, 1967.

Williams, A.M. The relationship between two visual communication systems: Reading and lipreading Ph.D. dissertation, Hofstra University, 1979.

Wood, B.S. *Children and Communication*. Englewood Cliffs, N.J.: Prentice-Hall, 1976, 175–206.

Woodward, M.F. Linguistic methodology in lipreading. In E. Lowell (ed.), *John Tracy Clinic Research Papers*, Los Angeles, 1957, No. 4, 1–32.

Woodward, M.F., and Barber, C.G. Phoneme perception in lipreading. *J. Speech Hear. Res.*, 1960, 212–222.

Woolburt, C.H. *The Fundamentals of Speech*, Ed. 3, revised by J.F. Smith. New York: Harper and Brothers, 1927, p. 5.

Worthington, A.M.L. An investigation of the relationship between lipreading ability of congenitally deaf high school students and certain personality factors, M.A. thesis, Ohio State University, 1956. Cited in K.W. Berger, *Speechreading: Principles and Methods*. Baltimore: National Educational Press, 1972, 113.

Wozniak, V.D., and Jackson, P.L. Visual and vowel diphthong perception from two horizontal viewing angles. *J. Speech Hear. Res.*, 22(2), 1979, 354–365.

Auditory Training for Severely Hearing-Impaired Adults

RICHARD P. DURITY, M.A.

The purpose of this chapter is to present some approaches to developing an auditory training program for severely to profoundly hearing-impaired adults. Auditory training is herein defined as an instructional program for hearing-impaired individuals which is designed to maximize the use of residual hearing for the purpose of greater participation in the auditory (communication) environment.

Because this chapter focuses on *auditory* training, it is necessary to limit the discussion to individuals who can process at least some acoustic information auditorily. For those hearing-impaired individuals who respond only vibrotactilely to acoustic stimulation, tactile sensory aids as a supplement to speech-reading and speechreading training are recommended. The reader is referred to De Filippo, Chapter 3, and Erber, 1979, p. 257, for methods of differentiating whether a client is making acoustic or tactile speech sound discriminations, and for training procedures.

Numerous auditory training programs have been developed and reviewed (Nerbonne and Schow, 1980; Berg, 1976). However, many of these programs fail to meet the unique set of factors which the severely to profoundly hearing-impaired adult brings to a training session: (1) the heterogeneity of the population, (2) the relatively short length of time the adult is available for training and, (3) the relevance of the training to the individual's everyday communication needs.

One factor that contributes to the heterogeneity of the severely to profoundly hearing-impaired client is the age of onset of the hearing loss. Onset can range from congenital, prelingual deafness through recently acquired, postlingual deafness. Another variable is the level of speech discrimination ability. For example, there are clients with severe to profound hearing loss who achieve relatively good scores on the W-22, PB word lists and those who cannot identify any words through audition. Another contributing variable is the age at which the individual began using amplification and the consistency with which amplification was used. Finally, the individual's skill is influenced by previous training history. Some have received consistent aural habilitation services throughout their educational history, while many have not had the benefit of consistent training.

The second factor which must be considered is the amount of time available for training. Unlike the young hearing-impaired child, the adult does not have sufficient time or motivation for extensive programming over a number of years. The adult consumer of aural rehabilitation services demands relevance in the training program to everyday communication needs. Paradoxically, the instructor must acknowledge the fact that auditory skill development requires a systematic hierarchial approach with the challenge of making the more basic discrimination drill materials relevant to the everyday communication situation encountered by adults.

One question often asked is why should one attempt auditory training with the adult client who has passed the critical auditory language learning period? The deaf adult may have experienced years of auditory deprivation which may have left the cortical auditory processes nonfunctional (Kyle, 1978). The answer can only be found by examining the results of training on an individual basis. A good prognostic indicator for the success of auditory training is the client's motivation to improve auditory skills. The quality of such a prognosis assumes that the clinician is able to demonstrate to the client that perception of sound contributes to more

successful oral/aural communication. The benefits of one training program for deaf adults have been demonstrated by Snell and Managan (1976), Mapes and Moreau (1978), and Robbins (1980).

What follows will be a discussion of (1) the processes which are considered important in auditory skill development, (2) the sensory modalities to be emphasized in training, and (3) an example of two training programs for the adult client.

COMPONENT PROCESSES IN THE PERCEPTION OF SPEECH

The multidimensional aspects involved in the processing of speech are paramount considerations in the development of a comprehensive auditory training curriculum. It is theorized that speech perception involves both a primary process equivalent to auditory and phonetic feature analysis and a secondary linguistic process based on perceptual expectancies and internal conceptual information (Sanders, 1977; Lehiste, 1972). The primary processing represents a low-level analysis of the sensory input which permits internal representation of the physical acoustic stimulus. The secondary processing represents a high-level analysis which attempts to confirm linguistic and contextual expectancies from the sensory information being extracted. Researchers in visual perception, reading, and problem solving (Parasnis and Samar, Chapter 4; Palmer, 1975; Stevens and Rumelhart, 1975; Eisenstadt and Kareev, 1975) refer to primary processing as "bottom-up" processing and to secondary processing as "top-down" processing.

In speech perception, "bottom-up" processing involves a succession of analyses of sensory information from the cochlea to the cortex. "Top-down" processing involves the way in which linguistic knowledge and contextual constraints affect the interpretation of the available sensory information. "Bottom-up" and "top-down" processing occur simultaneously" and "interact in such a way that information about the results of higher level analyses can be used to resolve uncertainties at the phonological level [Foss and Hakes, 1978, p. 95]." This theory of perception is consistent with the analysis by synthesis model set forth by Halle and Stevens (1962) (Stevens and Halle, 1967) and Miller's (1962) model of speech perception (Norman, 1969 and 1976). Further evidence for the "top-down"/"bottom-up" theory can be found in the neurological structures of the auditory system. Berry's (1969) description of bidirectional bundles of neural fibers indicates that complex analyses take place along the entire auditory pathway and that these analyses are controlled by both high-level and low-level neurological structures. Just as the concept of "bottom-up" and "top-down" processing is essential in speech perception by persons with normal hearing, it should also be addressed in an effective auditory training curriculum for severely to profoundly hearing-impaired individuals.

Given the complexity of the auditory perceptual process, numerous factors contribute to the perception of speech. The following is a description of some of the factors and a discussion of the effects of severe and profound hearing loss on these factors.

Frequency Discrimination

Frequency is one of the parameters of the acoustic signal that plays an important role in the perception of both the segmental (individual speech sounds) and suprasegmental (intonation, rhythm, and stress) features of speech. At the segmental level, many researchers have acknowledged that for normal listeners, individual phoneme identification is dependent on frequency (Delattre et al., 1952; Cooper et al., 1952; Miller and Nicely, 1955; Hirsch, 1967; Liberman et al., 1967; Lindblom and Studdert-Kennedy, 1967; Levitt, 1978). At the suprasegmental level, frequency information is important in signalling the intonational characteristics of a phrase or sentence (Lieberman, 1967; Levitt, 1978; Fry, 1978). As an example, Ross et al. (1973) have shown that frequency information contributes to the recognition of the speaker's emotional intent.

The ability of severely hearing-impaired listeners to detect and then discriminate frequency has been shown to have a significant effect on their ability to understand speech. Ling and Ling (1978) relate the deaf child's ability to detect individual speech sounds to the frequencies the child can hear. DiCarlo

(1962) demonstrated that poor frequency discrimination ability in hearing-impaired subjects resulted in poor speech discrimination for PB words. Risberg and his colleagues confirmed that for severely and profoundly deaf subjects, speech discrimination for spondees deteriorates when frequency discrimination is worse than 7% at 1000 hertz (Risberg et al., 1975 and 1977). For listeners with severe hearing loss, they found large variations in frequency discrimination ability ranging from nearly normal to moderately poor. For listeners with thresholds poorer than 100 dB, frequency discrimination ability was poor, equivalent to that obtained vibrotactually from the hand (Erber, 1980). Risberg and Agelfors (1978) also demonstrated that hearing impairment could have adverse affects on the identification of intonation contours. Researchers have discovered that frequency discrimination is poorer for high frequencies than for low frequencies and is also poorer at greater levels of hearing loss (Zurek and Formby, 1981). Villchur (1977) found that speech intelligibility was "badly impaired" when he simulated the type of frequency discrimination perturbations which are thought to be typical of deaf listeners. In terms of auditory training, the role of frequency discrimination in understanding speech, needs to be considered. Gengel (1973) reports on a limited number of hearing-impaired subjects whose frequency discrimination ability improved following training.

Intensity Discrimination

Another parameter in the acoustic signal which is important for understanding speech is intensity. The relative intensities of individual speech sounds are considered important in phoneme identification (Fletcher, 1953 and 1970; Sanders, 1971 and 1977; Levitt, 1978; Boothroyd, 1978; Fry, 1978). Likewise, the relative intensities of the formants in the acoustic signal have been found to be important cues for identifying individual phonemes (Delattre et al., 1952; Fletcher, 1970). Variations in intensity are important at the suprasegmental level in that they contribute to the identification of the stressed and unstressed words in an utterance (Levitt, 1978 and 1979).

For many severely to profoundly hearing-impaired listeners, the ability to use intensity for speech discrimination may be disturbed. One possible cause of the discrimination difficulty is recruitment. For ears with recruitment, the perception of loudness increases more rapidly with an increase in physical intensity than it does in normal ears. The effect is one of exaggerating the loudness differences within the acoustic signal. In normal listeners, Villchur (1974 and 1977) has simulated profound deafness as well as the loudness relationships perceived by deaf subjects with recruitment. He found that amplified speech was perceived as intermittent and that intelligibility was destroyed. In one article Villchur (1974) included a recording simulating the distorted loudness relationships perceived by deaf listeners. Perturbations of intensity relationships demand serious consideration in terms of the aural rehabilitative needs of severely to profoundly impaired listeners.

Temporal Discrimination

The temporal aspects of the acoustic signal also have perceptual significance for understanding speech. Many features of individual phonemes, especially voicing and frication, are signaled by duration (Denes, 1955; Lisker and Abramson, 1964; Berry, 1969; Fletcher, 1970; Levitt, 1978). Durational aspects of the acoustic signal also cue stressed syllables in utterances as well as mark syntactic units and phrases. The rhythmic patterns of spoken utterances are cued, in part, by durational information (Levitt, 1978; Fry, 1978; Streng et al., 1978; Harris and McGarr, 1980). The ability of listeners to distinguish the order of occurrence of speech sounds (temporal sequencing ability) has also been recognized as significant in speech perception (Hirsch, 1967; Berry, 1969).

Information about the severely hearing-impaired listeners' ability to use durational cues is limited. Erber (1979) suggests that deaf listeners may be using durational information to distinguish vowels. He suggests that at high intensity levels such discrimination ability is available to the deaf individual vibrotactually and may not reflect auditory skill. Therefore, it is difficult to evaluate the severely to profoundly hearing-impaired listener's ability to perceive durational cues. Ling (1974) reported on a study of the temporal sequencing

abilities of hearing-impaired children. For verbal stimuli, the impaired listeners were poorer at distinguishing sequence of occurrence than normal-hearing children.

Frequency, Intensity, and Temporal Integration

Because of the dynamic multidimensional nature of the speech signal, it is artificial to isolate the physical parameters of the signal which are perceptually important. In fact, the perception of speech involves the integration of all of the dimensions of the acoustic signal. As an example of this type of integration at the segmental level, formant transitions or rapid changes in formant frequency have been shown to be important cues for phoneme identification (Liberman, 1957; Harris et al., 1958; Liberman et al., 1967; Lindblom et al., 1967; Strange et al., 1976). This body of research has shown that the extent of change in formant frequency, the rate of change in formant frequency, and the relative intensities of the formants in transition, all contribute to the perceptual process. In summary, formant transitions are perceptual cues which combine frequency, intensity, and durational parameters. The interdependence of acoustic parameters is also evident in the suprasegmental aspects of speech. As an example, the perception of syllabic and word stress is the result of durational, frequency, and intensity variation (Ling and Ling, 1978; Levitt, 1979).

There is evidence that severe to profound hearing loss reduces the ability of hearing-impaired listeners to discriminate formant transitions (Danaher et al., 1973; Danaher and Pickett, 1975). Danaher and her colleagues suggest that this inability may be caused by low-frequency masking resulting from the high-intensity listening levels required by listeners with severe to profound losses. Yet Godfrey and Millay (1978) have found perception of rapid spectral changes is also difficult for some moderately impaired listeners and that this phenomenon is independent of stimulus frequency or stimulus intensity level. The inability of some hearing-impaired listeners to discriminate formant transitions is evidence that the integration of various acoustic parameters for speech perception may be difficult for severely to profoundly impaired listeners. Whether this affects perception of suprasegmental features requires further investigation.

Selective Attention

Auditory selective attention refers to the listener's ability to select a significant auditory stimulus of interest from a background of irrelevant stimuli. One of the results of selective attention is the establishment of a figure/ground relationship with the incoming auditory stimulus (Sanders, 1977). The listener attends to one particular pattern, and other auditory stimuli become background (Norman, 1976).

Difficulties in selective attention demand consideration in auditory training for severely hearing-impaired individuals. In everyday listening situations, the hearing-impaired person is dependent on hearing aids. Yet, as a study by Tillman, Carhart, and Olsen (1970) has shown, hearing aid systems reduce speech intelligibility in noise for both normal and hearing-impaired listeners. This finding alone suggests that selective attention is an important concern for the hearing aid user. An additional finding by Tillman et al. (1970) demonstrated that the masking effects of competing speech on speech intelligibility were greater for sensorineurally impaired listeners than for normals. These researchers found that the hearing-impaired listeners required a plus 18-dB signal-to-noise ratio to achieve a 40% discrimination score, while normal listeners could obtain this score with a minus 12-dB signal-to-noise ratio. Villchur's (1977) work with processed speech supports the findings reported by Tillman et al. (1970). Villchur simulated recruitment and high-frequency hearing loss in normal listeners and determined that speech spectrum noise had a more significant effect on intelligibility than would occur in the nonsimulated condition. Ross and Giolas (1978) provide an excellent summary of the effects of noise on hearing-impaired listeners and also suggest ways that these effects can be reduced.

The effects of noise on attentional demands during auditory processing have been demonstrated in a study by Downs and Crum (1978). They asked normal hearing subjects to perform two different tasks simultaneously: (1) an auditory learning task, and (2) a reaction-time task with a visual stimulus. They found that even though subject performance on the auditory learning task remains constant under increasingly degraded listening conditions, performance on the visual reaction-time task deteriorated as the listening conditions became poorer. These findings suggest that for normals the increased effort required to attend selectively under degraded listening conditions has adverse effects on the performance of other tasks. Given the special vulnerability of the hearing-impaired listener in noise, the demands of selective attention are highly significant.

MODALITIES FOR TRAINING

Audition and Vision

Formal auditory training exercises may properly emphasize a unisensory approach for a substantial amount of the drill activity. This insures that maximum attention is devoted to the auditory stimulus and improves the chances that the auditory system is being trained to its full capability. It is suggested that speechreading be added only if the student is having significant difficulty with the auditory exercises. Adding the visual stimulus reduces the ambiguity of the auditory signal (Erber, 1972; Binne et al., 1974). Once the pattern for recognition has been established in the auditory/visual mode, the student has a better chance of mastering the materials when the auditory mode alone is reintroduced. Also, combined auditory/speechreading exercises contrasted with speechreading alone serve to reinforce the functional importance of good auditory skills when the students recognize that audition can facilitate speechreading.

Sign Language

As with speechreading, signing and fingerspelling should only be used if the student is having significant difficulty with the combined auditory/visual message. Once the student has mastered the material in a combined manual, auditory, and speechreading mode, the manual cues followed by the speechreading cues should be removed to promote full development of auditory skill.

Audition and Speech

Concurrent with the auditory exercises, students are encouraged to practice their speech. Ling and Ling (1978, p. 157) have stated, "The most efficient way to develop speech is through the use of residual hearing. Conversely, one of the most efficient ways to develop auditory discrimination skills is through the teaching of speech." By repeating the stimulus items to themselves following the listening task, students are able to improve their own productions and reinforce the auditory patterns they have just heard. In many cases, students should be capable of speech productions they have not mastered auditorily. Therefore, with listening materials that are especially difficult, students should be encouraged to say the stimulus items before attempting the listening task. Recently, Durity and Evans (1982) integrated formalized speech training with auditory training activities. Students work on speech lessons which parallel the auditory materials, thereby reinforcing auditory skill development. The inclusion of formalized speech training also permits the student to identify the relationship between auditory training and improvement in expressive skills.

PROGRAMMED SELF-INSTRUCTION

Instruction must be individualized to meet the full range of auditory training needs of the severely hearing-impaired adult population. Individualized instruction can be costly if the only way it can be accomplished is by one-on-one instruction. Most aural rehabilitation centers do not have the resources for a significant amount of individual auditory training. The use of modules of programmed self-instruction (PSI) has been found useful in the development of programs of auditory training to meet individual needs. PSI also has some other advantages. For example, it allows pacing of the instructional stimuli such that students can be perceptually "ready" for the next stimulus. This is often not the case in group or individual auditory training. Self-pacing in programmed instruction allows the student to measure progress through the materials on an immediate feedback basis, thus providing a positive motivational influence.

The instructor's involvement is integral to the PSI process. The instructor (1) helps the students select materials according to the students' needs and interests, (2) provides motivational support, and (3) provides assistance to students having difficulty with the materials.

In order to insure the success of a PSI approach to auditory training, appropriate facilities are essential. At the National Technical Institute for the Deaf (NTID) a special classroom, the Auditory Learning Center (ALC), was designed to support the auditory training curriculum. The ALC is designed with sound absorptive materials, including carpeting and an acoustically tiled ceiling. The ALC has nine individual auditory training carrels. The PSI exercises are recorded on audio tape cassettes. The equipment necessary for use of these materials is described in Johnson (1976b), and the design of an individual auditory training carrel is shown in Figures 19.1 and 19.2.

The audio tape cassettes for the PSI exercises are played back on an audio cassette playback unit. This tape cassette unit has a very useful "review" feature which facilitates repetition of practice stimuli. The signal is sent through an amplifier, and the students may choose to listen through headphones or through the induction coil of their own aids. A stimulus number readout unit provides a digital indication of the stimulus item that the students are listening to and allows them to verify their location on the audio cassette.

For supplemental teacher directed exercises, students are encouraged to use the environmental microphone setting on their personal aids. This setup allows the students to practice in a situation which includes the background noise in the ALC. If live presentation in an ideal listening situation is desired, an auxillary microphone can be jacked into the amplifier for one-on-one practice within the auditory training carrel. The auxillary microphone setup also permits the students to practice and monitor their own speech during PSI exercises with the audio tape cassettes. For a more general description of various types of auditory training equipment, see Rubin (1979) and Ling and Ling (1978).

AUDITORY TRAINING METHODS

At NTID, depending on auditory abilities, students may enroll in either the Level I or Level II Auditory Training Program. Class size usually ranges from three to seven stu-

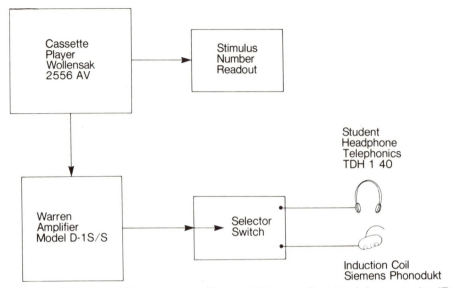

Figure 19.1. Diagram of hardware in the individual auditory training carrels. (Reproduced with permission from D. Johnson, *Info Series 2*, 1976b, p. 66.)

dents and classes meet two hours per week for ten weeks.

In both the Level I and Level II self-instruction programs, students must achieve an 80% correct mastery of the material or repeat the exercise up to three times. If the 80% level of performance is not attained by the third trial, the students work individually with the instructor. Two instructional techniques which facilitate mastery of difficult listening exercises are (1) addition of the speechreading component, and/or (2) requesting that the student practice saying the stimulus items prior to listening. With this assistance, student performance usually improves to the extent that the students can proceed with the next exercise.

Auditory Training Level I

The Level I Program (Snell, Mapes, Hutchinson, et al., 1979) emphasizes the "bottom-up" processes in auditory perception, which were described at the beginning of this chapter. The approach is analytic in nature in that the emphasis is on feature recognition at the phonetic or segmental level rather than at the phonological or suprasegmental level. With the Level I curriculum, the students train on the recognition of consonants or consonantal

distinctive features in monosyllabic words. A second but equally important aspect of the course is training in the use of oral/aural communication strategies. As such, students are encouraged to utilize the skills they are practicing (listening, speechreading, and speech) not only in the classroom but in everyday communication situations.

POPULATION SERVED

The course is recommended for students with the following characteristics: (1) pure tone average (either 2 frequency or 3 frequency) less than 100 dB; (2) hearing discrimination less than 25% on the CID Everyday Sentences (Johnson, 1976a; Davis and Silverman, 1970); (3) NTID Speech Intelligibility Profile Rating (Johnson, 1976a) less than or equal to 3.5 on a scale of 5, where a rating of 5 indicates good speech skills, and a rating of 1 indicates poor skills; and (4) hearing aid use all or most of the time.

Effectively, this means that the Level I Program is designed for students with severe and profound hearing loss who derive some acoustic benefit from amplification and have very poor hearing discrimination, poor speech, and intermediate to poor skills in speechreading. The program has been found

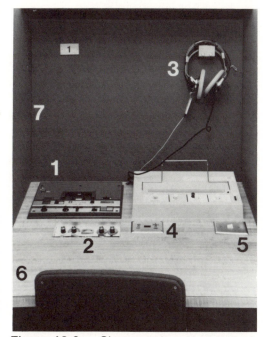

Figure 19.2. Close-up view of an individual auditory training carrel in the Additory Training Center. The carrel includes (*1*) an audio cassette playback unit (Wollensak Model 2556AV), (*2*) an amplifier (Warren Model D-1S/S), (*3*) headphones (Telephonics Model TDH 1 40) and induction coil (Siemens Phonodukt), (*4*) a stimulus number readout unit and two selector switches, (*5*) a master power on-off switch, (*6*) a student work area, and (*7*) special acoustical partitions. (Reproduced with permission from D. Johnson, *Info Series 2*, 1976b, p. 65.)

especially effective with students whose speech evidences greater problems with articulation than with voice, intonation, or pitch.

PRE/POST TESTS

The Level I Placement Test and the Fisher-Logemann Test of Articulation Competence (Fisher and Logemann, 1971) are administered at the beginning and end of the course. Results from these tests are useful in (1) assigning auditory exercises that are appropriate to the students' needs and (2) evaluating pre/post improvement in the students'

auditory and speech skills as a result of training.

The Level I Placement Test is a closed-set auditory identification test. The 60 items are randomly selected from the training materials in the Level I program. The Placement Test yields percent correct scores for each of the auditory distinctive feature categories in voicing, nasality, and sibilancy as well as a total score. The students' task is to listen for a single word and select the correct response from a closed set of four printed alternatives on the response sheet.

The single word subtest of the Fisher-Logemann Test of Articulation Competence assesses the abilities of the students to produce consonants and vowels in a monosyllabic context. The test yields a distinctive feature analysis of the students' articulation errors and allows the instructor to evaluate errors in place of articulation, manner of articulation, and voicing.

Diagnostically, the results of the Placement Test combined with the results of the Fisher-Logemann permit the students and the instructor to determine which distinctive feature categories the students have mastered and those categories which need to be trained. Specific scores on the Fisher-Logemann are seldom used for placement purposes. Rather, the instructor reviews the students' articulation errors to obtain an overall feel for the students' mastery of the features of voicing, nasality, and sibilancy. As an example, student I has the following pretest scores:

Level I Placement Test

Feature Category	% Correct
Voicing	90
Nasality	65
Sibilancy	30

Fisher-Logemann Test of Articulation

Type of Substitution Errors	Number of Errors
Voiced/Voiceless	Minimal
Nasal/Nonnasal	Moderate
Sibilant/Nonsibilant	Significant

Clearly, student I has mastered the voicing feature, both productively and receptively, but has incomplete mastery of the skills needed to detect or produce the nasal/nonnasal contrast and little or no mastery of the sibilant/nonsibilant contrast. Therefore, the instructor might recommend that student I begin training for the feature category in which there is incomplete mastery. Student I would be building from an area of relative strength, and progress to increasingly more difficult areas. Student I would begin with the nasality materials, and progress to the more difficult sibiliancy materials. The instructor might also recommend a second option where student I would begin work in the weakest skill area and later work on areas of less difficulty. This option is based on the philosophy that remediation in the weakest skill areas will have a greater impact on overall hearing discrimination ability. The decision about which option to choose depends on the instructor's philosophical bias, the students' bias about which approach will be most beneficial, and the students' motivation to train on a particular feature category based on their own perceived need.

The Placement Test has also been shown to be useful in evaluating improvements in listening skill as a result of Auditory Training Level I. Durity and Evans (1982) found that for most students, scores on the Placement Test improve, following training. Most students showed the greatest improvement for the feature category areas in which they trained. Those students who did not show improvement on the Placement Test showed improvement in other communication skill areas, including articulation, as measured by the Fisher-Logemann; speechreading, as measured by the Jacobs Everyday Sentences Speechreading Test (Sims and Jacobs, 1976); and overall speech intelligibility, as measured by the Clarke Intelligibility Test (Magner, 1972).

TRAINING MATERIALS

Materials for the Auditory Training Program Level I were developed for use in the following areas: (1) auditory distinctive feature recognition of consonants, (2) visual distinctive feature recognition of consonants, and (3) oral/aural communication strategies.

Auditory Distinctive Feature Recognition of Consonants

The auditory distinctive feature exercises help the students learn to identify consonants according to three contrastive categories: (1) voiced/voiceless, (2) nasal/nonnasal, and (3) sibilant/nonsibilant. For each category a four-stage sequence of auditory exercises has been developed.

Figure 19.3 shows the three feature categories and the four stages within each category and gives an example of the stimulus for each stage within each category.

Stage 1 (shown in Fig. 19.3) is comprised of exercises in which the students listen to two words and determine if the two words are the same or different. In the example, the students see *game* followed by *game/came* on their response sheet. The students know that the first word heard will be *game* and the second word may either be the same (*game*) or different (*came*). In this case the students hear *game/came*, recognize that the two words are different, and circle the correct response *came*.

Stage 2 consists of a short-term retention task which contains exercises that are slightly more difficult. The students hear five words. The first word heard will be the same as one of the next four words. The students' task is to determine which of the subsequent four words is the same as the first word as shown in Figure 19.3. In the example the students see the first word *came* printed on the response sheet followed by the numerals *2, 3, 4, 5*. The students listen to the speaker say five words: *came, name, came, game, lame.* The students recognize that the third word the speaker says is the same as the first word the speaker says (*came*) and circle *3* as the correct response.

Stage 3, the long-term retention task, builds on the skills acquired in both the short-term task and same/different task. The students are required to listen for a target word. The speaker says a list of four words, and the students must identify which one is the target word. In the example in Figure 19.3, the students read the target word *came* on the response sheet. Students listen to the speaker say a list of four words: *name, game, lame, came;* the students then determine that the fourth word, *came,* is the same as the target word, *came,* and circle the correct response, *4.*

Stage 4, the identification task exercises, is the most difficult. The task is a closed-set response task. The students listen for a word

Feature Category	Sequence of Exercises			
	Stage 1 Same/Different Task	Stage 2 Short Term Retention Task	Stage 3 Long Term Retention Task	Stage 4 Identification Task
1. Voicing	Response Sheet: game game came Auditory Stimulus: game came Correct Response: game came game	Response Sheet: came 2 3 4 5 Auditory Stimulus: came name came game lame Correct Response: came 2 3 4 5	Response Sheet: came 1 2 3 4 Auditory Stimulus: name game lame came Correct Response: came 1 2 3 4	Response Sheet: game came lame name Auditory Stimulus: came Correct Response: game came lame name
2. Nasality	Response Sheet: when when wet Auditory Stimulus: when when Correct Response: when when wet	Response Sheet: when 2 3 4 5 Auditory Stimulus: when when wet well wed Correct Response: when 2 3 4 5	Response Sheet: when 1 2 3 4 Auditory Stimulus: when wed well wet Correct Response: when 1 2 3 4	Response Sheet: wet well wed when Auditory Stimulus: when Correct Response: wet well wed when
3. Sibilancy	Response Sheet: pit sit pit Auditory Stimulus: pit sit Correct Response: pit sit pit	Response Sheet: sit 2 3 4 5 Auditory Stimulus: sit knit sit pit kit Correct Response: sit 2 3 4 5	Response Sheet: sit 1 2 3 4 Auditory Stimulus: pit kit sit knit Correct Response: sit 1 2 3 4	Response Sheet: kit knit sit pit Auditory Stimulus: sit Correct Response: kit knit sit pit

Figure 19.3. Auditory Training Level I: Auditory Distinctive Feature Exercises.

and pick the correct response from a list of four possible responses. In Figure 19.3, the students read the set of four possible choices—*game, came, lame, name*—on the response sheet. The speaker says one of the four words, *came*. The students circle the correct response, *came*.

In addition to the voicing category, similar materials are available for each stage in the nasality and sibilancy categories.

Visual Distinctive Feature Recognition of Consonants

The visual feature exercises were designed to meet the needs previously outlined for combined auditory/visual training. These exercises teach students to classify the consonants according to the following visual distinctive feature categories: (1) bilabial, (2) lip protrusion, (3) lingual alveolar and lingual velar, (4) interdental, (5) labiodental.

Students speechread monosyllabic consonant-vowel-consonant (CVC) words in both the with and without sound conditions, and learn to recognize the initial and final consonants according to the five feature categories. The presentation mode may be live with the instructor or on video tape. Either mode allows for group or individual presentation of the materials. The visual exercises may be used concurrently with the auditory feature exercises, or they may be presented prior to introducing the auditory exercises. The visual exercises increase students' motivation for auditory skill development as students realize that audition can reduce the ambiguities inherent in the visual signal.

Oral/Aural Communication Strategies

Concurrent with the visual and auditory exercises, students receive training and practice in using communicative strategies that will facilitate successful communication with hearing people. Students entering the Level I Program with poor expressive and receptive skills, in combination with poor mastery of alternative strategies, experience many unsuccessful attempts at communication. The purpose of this third component of the Level I Program is to help students develop the strategies necessary for successful oral/aural communication. This is achieved through classroom discussion, observation, and real life experiences.

In the classroom, students learn to accept responsibility for the communication situation especially with a hearing person who has limited experience in communicating with the hearing-impaired. Students learn strategies for manipulating the way in which information is given and received. The following is the sequence of strategies which are discussed in the classroom.

The first expressive strategy entails speaking. Students with limited expressive skills are encouraged to use short concise sentences and to speak slowly. Visual cueing, such as natural gestures, facial expressions, body language, and situational cues, should be incorporated. Receptively, students are taught methods for encouraging hearing people to use concise sentences and to speak slowly. Students develop an awareness of how visual cues can facilitate understanding.

If normal speaking, listening, and speechreading attempts are unsuccessful, students learn next to try repeating information, requesting repetition of only the most salient information. If repetition fails, students learn how to rephrase the same message, incorporating appropriate visual cues. Many deaf students are surprised to find that this strategy is successful.

The use of oral and/or visual spelling may be another strategy that is successful if communication is unsuccessful. Spelling difficult or new words aloud or drawing the letters in the air so the hearing person can read them, may facilitate communication. For receiving difficult words, oral and/or visual spelling may be requested.

The final strategy students learn is telegraphic writing. Telegraphic writing is the use of only key words to decrease writing time and increase communicative efficiency. Students practice ways of incorporating speaking with telegraphic writing. Ways to assist the hearing communicator in using appropriate writing strategies for oral/aural communication are also discussed.

Captioned video tapes of successful and unsuccessful communication situations allow students to critically evaluate the use of a variety of communication strategies. From these activities, students learn to identify when and why communication breaks down and how to use appropriate strategies. Students are also encouraged to observe occurrences in their everyday situations to determine if good strategies promote successful communication.

In order to encourage the development and use of oral/aural strategies, students complete at least four individual meetings with hearing people during the course. Formal evaluations of these 15-minute meetings are completed by the students and the hearing person they meet. The effective use of strategies and the students' acceptance of responsibility for the communication situation are evaluated. The following are examples of the types of questions on the evaluation form which provide the instructor with valuable feedback:

1. Did the student repeat or rephrase to further communicate or clarify an idea? _____
   If yes, at whose suggestion?
   a) yours
   b) student's
2. How did the student confirm specific information?
   a) listening and speechreading
   b) requesting repetition
   c) requesting you to slow down
   d) requesting rephrasing
   e) requesting oral or visual spelling
   f) requesting writing
   g) other _____

The first of the meetings is typically with a hearing person who is familiar with the individual. Provided students are successful in using strategies during the first meeting, subsequent meetings are arranged with increasingly less familiar people. In this way, students refine the use of oral/aural strategies. Students receive feedback following each meeting, concurrent with classroom discussions and observations. Recently, Burke and Whitehead (1981) have reported on similar training and its effectiveness.

Auditory Training Level II

The Level II Program (Snell, Mapes, O'Shea, et al., 1979) emphasizes more "top-down" processing than the Level I Program. As such, training focuses on improvement in sentence recognition. Higher levels of auditory perceptual analysis are reinforced, including the use of linguistic and situational contexts. Training materials are related to social topics typical of situations a young adult might encounter. As with Level I, a second aspect of the course helps students improve the use of oral/aural communication strategies.

POPULATION SERVED

The Level II course is recommended for students with the following characteristics: (1) hearing discrimination greater than 25% and less than 70% on the CID Everyday Sentences (Johnson, 1976a; Davis and Silverman, 1970); and (2) hearing aid use all or most of the time. Effectively, this means the Level II Program is designed for students with severe hearing loss who have fair to good hearing discrimination and who consistently depend on audition for communication. The target of this program is the students who need refinement in the use of auditory skills.

PRE/POST TESTS

The Moreau Auditory Test (Robbins, 1980) and the Level II Pre/Post Test (Mapes and Moreau, 1978) have been developed to measure precourse to postcourse gains as a result of Auditory Training Level II.

The Moreau Auditory Test (MAT) is an open-set response task composed of ten novel sentences which students have never heard or practiced. The sentences, however, include key words from the 20-training units in the Level II curriculum. Thus, even though the students do not practice the actual test sentences, they do receive training on many of the component words in different sentential and situational contexts. Following presentation of the stimulus sentences, students transcribe what they have heard. The test is scored according to the number of words correct.

Administered at the beginning and end of the course, the MAT has been shown to be useful in evaluating gains in the auditory recognition of sentences as a result of the Level II course. Robbins (1980) found that students improved an average of 14.6% on the MAT following the ten-week Level II Training Program (see Fig. 19.4). This is contrasted with an average of only 3.6% improvement on the MAT for a control group which did not receive training.

The Level II Pre/Post Test is an open-set response task composed of 90 stimulus sentences. Students receive an individualized form of the test, depending on which six units are selected for the students' training program. Sixty of these sentences (ten sentences from each of six training units) are sentences that the students practice during the training program. The remaining 30 sentences (five sentences from each of six training units) are novel, untrained sentences (probe sentences) which contain key words from the training units and are topically related to their respective units. On the Level II Pre/Post Test, students listen to each sentence and transcribe what they hear. The test is scored according to the number of total sentences correct. The test yields three different scores: (1) percent of total correct, (2) percent of trained sentences correct, and (3) percent of untrained probe sentences correct.

Like the MAT, the Level II Pre/Post Test has been found useful in demonstrating gains in auditory skill as a result of the Level II Program. As shown in Figure 19.4, Mapes and Moreau (1978) reported average gains of 61.9% on trained sentences following the ten-week course, contrasted with a gain of only 6.8% for controls not enrolled in the course. Mapes and Moreau also showed that following training, students showed an average of 33.5% improvement on the probe sentences versus only 8.6% improvement by the control group.

The Level II Pre/Post Test has also been useful in determining how long gains in sentence recognition are retained following training. In a study by Snell and Managan (1976), gains in the recognition of trained sentences were retained for a period of at least ten weeks. Retention was shown to be greatest for students with higher levels of hearing discrimination skill.

The Level II Pre/Post Test may also be useful in assigning units for training. Students

TEST	EXPERIMENTAL SUBJECTS	CONTROL SUBJECTS
Moreau Auditory Test (Robbins, 1980)	15 (N = 17)	4 (N = 5)
Level II Pre/Post Test (Mapes and Moreau, 1978)		
1. Training Sentences	62 (N = 42)	7 (N = 7)
2. Probe Sentences	34 (N = 42)	9 (N = 7)

Figure 19.4.   Level II mean gain scores in percent.

who perform well on the pretest for a particular unit may not need to train on that unit. A more difficult unit for training may be substituted.

TRAINING MATERIALS

The PSI materials for the Auditory Training Level II Program consist of a total of 20 units arranged in two packages.

Package A contains ten units on social topics, such as dorm life, vacationing, and working. Sentences in the units in Package A average four to six words in length. The vocabulary does not exceed a sixth-grade reading level (Dale and O'Rourke, 1976). Units in this package are especially useful for students who have relatively poor hearing discrimination (25–40% on the CID Everyday Sentences) because only short sentences are used.

Package B contains ten units on more sophisticated social and academic subjects. Topics include apartment life, banking, history, and space travel. Package B differs from Package A in that sentence materials in Package B average eight to ten words in length and do not exceed an eighth-grade reading level (Dale and O'Rourke, 1976). The units in Package B are designed for students with relatively good hearing discrimination (50–70% on the CID Everyday Sentences) because the sentences are longer. Units from both packages may be selected for training by students with hearing discrimination between 40% and 50%, and other students who need further practice.

The structure of a unit is shown in Figure 19.5. Students proceed sequentially through each stage of the self-instruction units. Beginning with the Vocabulary Definitions, students study written definitions of selected key words which will appear later in the listening

practice. When students feel familiar with the definitions, the written Vocabulary Test is self-administered. This test is a matching task, and students must achieve a score of 80% correct to pass. Independent work is encouraged on the vocabulary tasks.

Following successful completion of the Vocabulary Test, students proceed with Key Word Practice for the unit. Students can choose from a number of practice options on this listening task, such as either randomly ordered or sequentially presented sentences, with or without the presence of a printed list of key words taken from the practice sentences. When students can recognize the words auditorily, the Key Word Test is self-administered. For this test, the words are presented randomly, without the key word list, and written responses are recorded on an answer sheet. Students score the test and must achieve a score of 80% correct to proceed with the Sentence Practice in Quiet.

For Sentence Practice in Quiet students listen to ten recorded sentences related to the unit topic. The sentences include the ten key words previously practiced. As with Key Word Practice students may choose random order or sequential practice with or without the written list of sentences. When students feel capable of recognizing all ten sentences auditorily, the Sentence Test in Quiet is self-administered.

The Sentence Test in Quiet consists of the ten practice sentences plus five novel, unpracticed probe sentences. The probe sentences are topically related to the unit and contain many of the key words from the unit. Students listen to the randomly ordered sentences and transcribe what they hear on a response sheet. Students score the practice sentences from an answer key and the instructor scores the probe sentences. A score of 80%

**AUDITORY TRAINING LEVEL II
UNIT STRUCTURE**

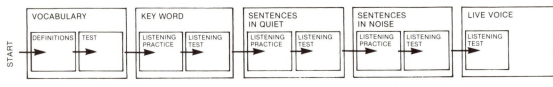

Figure 19.5.

correct on the practiced sentences is required before proceeding to the Sentence Practice in Noise.

The procedure for Sentence Practice in Noise follows exactly the procedure for Sentence Practice in Quiet. The same recorded sentences are presented in the presence of cocktail party noise at an average signal-to-noise ratio of plus 10 dB. Due to the difficulty of this task for many hearing-impaired listeners, it may not be appropriate for students with relatively poor hearing discrimination and may be omitted if students experience excessive frustration. Provided students can successfully complete the practice task, the Sentence Test in Noise is administered.

The instructor may choose to include a Live Voice Test of the practice materials. This provides an indication of whether the training effects are generalized to another speaker.

Students complete six units of the type described in Figure 19.5 during the ten-week course. Units are selected according to the students' interest in the topic, difficulty of material relative to the students' auditory skill, and reading level.

In order to promote the use and development of oral/aural strategies, a series of group discussions may be introduced by the instructor. Subjects for discussion may range from communication problems with hearing people to current events.

The Levels I and II Programs provide a means by which the auditory skills of the severely to profoundly deaf adult may be improved through both analytic/segmental discrimination drill as well as through synthetic, sentence level identification procedures. Aspects of these programs address many of the component processes in speech perception which were discussed earlier in this chapter. It is recognized that these programs only partially fulfill the auditory training needs of deaf adults. Numerous aspects of training remain to be explored. For example, further training in the discrimination of the suprasegmental aspects of the acoustic signal could assist the deaf person in the recognition of syntactic units, increase the redundancy of the message, and thereby improve comprehension (Nerbonne and Schow, 1980, p. 99). Incorporating specific English grammatical structures with auditory drill materials is currently being explored as a method for reinforcing English skill development (Forman and Durity, 1981; Durity et al., 1979).

In the future it is highly recommended that the means for evaluating the results of training be given more attention. First tests must be developed which not only provide a general measure of word recognition ability but are also sensitive to the subcomponents of the particular type of training. There is also a great need to demonstrate that auditory training with the severely to profoundly deaf is significant functionally in everyday communication (see Chapter 9 of this text).

References

Berg, F.S. *Educational Audiology; Hearing and Speech Management.* New York: Grune & Stratton, 1976.

Berry, M.F. *Language Disorders of Children: The Bases and Diagnoses.* New York: Appleton-Century-Crofts, 1969.

Binne, C.A., Montgomery, A.A., and Jackson, P.L. Auditory and visual contributions to the perception of consonants. *J. Speech Hear. Res.,* 1974, *17,* 619–630.

Boothroyd, A. Speech perception and sensorineural hearing loss. In M. Ross and T.G. Giolas (eds.), *Auditory Management of Hearing-Impaired Children: Principles and Prerequisites for Intervention.* Baltimore: University Park Press, 1978.

Burke, M.E., and Whitehead, B.H. Strategies to aid functional communication of hearing impaired young adults. Paper presented to the annual convention of the American Speech-Language-Hearing Association, Los Angeles, 1981.

Cooper, F.S., Delattre, P.C., Liberman, A.M., Borst, J.M., and Gerstman, L.J. Some experiments on the perception of synthetic speech sounds. *J. Acoust. Soc. Am.,* 1952, *24*(6), 597–606.

Dale, E., and O'Rourke, J. *The Living Word Vocabulary.* Elgin, Illinois: Field Enterprises Educational Corporation, 1976.

Danaher, E.M., Osberger, M.J., and Pickett, J.M. Discrimination of formant frequency transitions in synthetic vowels. *J. Speech Hear. Res.,* 1973, *16,* 439–451.

Danaher, E.M., and Pickett, J.M. Some masking effects produced by low frequency vowel formants in persons with sensorineural hearing loss. *J. Speech Hear. Res.,* 1975, *18,* 242–260.

Davis, H., and Silverman, S.R. *Hearing and Deafness,* ed. 3. New York: Holt, Rinehart & Winston, 1970.

Delattre, P., Liberman, A.M., Cooper, F.S., and Gerstman, L.J. An experimental study of the acoustic determinants of vowel color; observations on one and two-formant vowels synthesized from spectrographic patterns. *Word,* 1952, *8*(3), 195–210.

Denes, P. Effect of duration on the perception of voicing. *J. Acoust. Soc. Am.,* 1955, *27*(4), 761–764.

DiCarlo, L.M. Some relationships between frequency discrimination and speech perception performance. *J. Aud. Res.*, 1962, *2*, 37–49.

Downs, D.W., and Crum, M.A. Processing demands during auditory learning under degraded listening conditions. *J. Speech Hear. Res.*, 1978, *21*, 702–714.

Durity, R., and Evans, D. Integration of basic auditory training and speech training (working paper). Rochester, New York: National Technical Institute for the Deaf, 1982.

Durity, R., Forman, J., and Jacobs, M.A. Integration of speechreading and English Level 2 instruction (working paper). Rochester, New York: National Technical Institute for the Deaf, 1979.

Eisenstadt, M., and Kareev, Y. Aspects of human problem solving: The use of internal representations. In D.A. Norman and D.E. Rumelhart (eds.), *Explorations in Cognition*. San Francisco: W.H. Freeman & Co., 1975.

Erber, N. Speech correction through the use of acoustic models. In J.D. Subtelny (ed.), *Speech Assessment and Speech Improvement for the Hearing Impaired*. Washington, D.C.: A. G. Bell Association for the Deaf, 1980.

Erber, N.P. Auditory, visual, and auditory-visual recognition of consonants by children with normal and impaired hearing. *J. Speech Hear. Res.*, 1972, *15*, 413–422.

Erber, N.P. Speech perception by profoundly deaf hearing-impaired children. *J. Speech Hear. Disord.*, 1979, *44*, 255–270.

Fisher, H.B., and Logemann, J.A. *Fisher-Logemann Test of Articulation Competence*. Boston: Houghton Mifflin, 1971.

Fletcher, H. *Speech and Hearing in Communication*. Princeton, New Jersey: D. Van Nostrand, 1953.

Fletcher, S.G. Acoustic phonetics. In F.S. Berg and S.G. Fletcher (eds.), *The Hard of Hearing Child*. New York: Grune & Stratton, 1970.

Forman, J.D., and Durity, R.P. Assessment of grammatical skills for speechreading instruction. *J. Acad. Rehabil. Audiol.*, 1981, *14*, 239–251.

Foss, D.J., and Hakes, D.T. *Psycholinguistics: An Introduction to the Psychology of Language*. Englewood Cliffs, New Jersey: Prentice-Hall, 1978.

Fry, D.B. The role and primacy of the auditory channel in speech and language development. In M. Ross and T.G. Giolas (eds.), *Auditory Management of Hearing-Impaired Children: Principles and Prerequisites for Intervention*. Baltimore: University Park Press, 1978.

Gengel, R.W. Temporal effects in frequency discrimination by hearing-impaired listeners. *J. Acoust. Soc. Am.*, 1973, *54*(1), 11–15.

Godfrey, J.J., and Millay, K. Perception of rapid spectral change in speech by listeners with mild and moderate sensorineural hearing loss. *J. Am. Audiol. Soc.*, 1978, *3*(5), 200–208.

Halle, M., and Stevens, K.N. Speech recognition: A model and a program for research. *I.R.E. Trans. Information Theory*, 1962, *IT-8*, 155–159.

Harris, K.S., Hoffman, H.S., Liberman, A.M., Delattre, P.C., and Cooper, F.S. Effect of third-formant transitions on the perception of the voiced stop consonants. *J. Acoust. Soc. Am.*, 1958, *30*(2), 122–126.

Harris, K.S., and McGarr, N.S. Relationships between speech perception and speech production in normal-hearing and hearing-impaired subjects. In J.D. Subtelny (ed.), *Speech Assessment and Speech Improvement for the hearing Impaired*. Washington, D.C.: A.G. Bell Association for the Deaf, 1980.

Hirsch, I.J. Information processing for speech and language: The significance of serial order of stimuli. In F.L. Darley (ed.), *Brain Mechanisms Underlying Speech and Language*. New York: Grune & Stratton, 1967.

Johnson, D. Communication characteristics of a young deaf adult population: Techniques for evaluating their communication skills. *Am. Ann. Deaf*, 1976a, *121*, 409–424.

Johnson, D. Communication learning centers at NTID. In D. Johnson and W. Castle (eds.), *Info Series 2*. Rochester, New York: National Technical Institute for the Deaf, 1976b.

Kyle, J.G. The study of auditory deprivation from birth. *Br. J. Audiol.*, 1978, *12*, 37–39.

Lehiste, I. The units of speech perception. In J.H. Gilbert (ed.), *Speech and Cortical Functioning*. New York: Academic Press, 1972.

Levitt, H. The acoustics of speech production. In M. Ross and T.G. Giolas (eds.), *Auditory Management of Hearing-Impaired Children: Principles and Prerequisites for Intervention*. Baltimore: University Park Press, 1978.

Levitt, H. Speech acoustics. In L.J. Bradford and W.G. Hardy (eds.), *Hearing and Hearing Impairment*. New York: Grune & Stratton, 1979.

Lieberman, A.M., Some results of research on speech perception. *J. Acoust. Soc. Am.*, 1957, *29*, 117–123.

Liberman, A.M., Cooper, F.S., Shankweiler, D.P., and Studdert-Kennedy, M. Perception of the speech code. *Psychol. Rev.*, 1967, *74*, 431–461.

Lieberman, P. Intonation and the syntactic processing of speech. In W. Wathen-Dunn (ed.), *Models for the Perception of Speech and Visual Form*. Cambridge, Massachusetts: MIT Press, 1967.

Lindblom, B.E.F., and Studdert-Kennedy, M. On the role of formant transitions in vowel recognition. *J. Acoust. Soc. Am.*, 1967, *42*(4), 830–843.

Ling, D. Perception of complex stimuli by children. In R.E. Stark (ed.), *Sensory Capabilities of Hearing-Impaired Children*. Baltimore: University Park Press, 1974.

Ling, D., and Ling, A.H. *Aural Habilitation*. Washington, D.C.: A.G. Bell Association for the Deaf, 1978.

Lisker, L., and Abramson, A.S. A cross-language study of voicing in initial stops: Acoustical measurements. *Word*, 1964, *20*, 384–422.

Magner, M.E. *A Speech Intelligibility Test for Deaf Children*. Northampton, Massachusetts: Clarke School for the Deaf, 1972.

Mapes, F.M., and Moreau, R. The use of decoy sentences to measure auditory training gains. Paper presented to the annual convention of the American Speech and Hearing Association, San Francisco, 1978.

Miller, G.A. Decision units in the perception of speech. *I.R.E. Trans. Information Theory*, 1962, *IT-8*, 81–83.

Miller, G.A., and Nicely, P.E. An analysis of perceptual confusions among some English consonants. *J. Acoust.*

Soc. Am., 1955, *27*(2), 338–352.

Nerbonne, M.A., and Schow, R.L. Auditory stimuli in communication. In R.L. Schow and M.A. Nerbonne (eds.), *Introduction to Aural Rehabilitation*. Baltimore: University Park Press, 1980.

Norman, D.A. *Memory and Attention: An Introduction to Human Information Processing*. New York: John Wiley & Sons, 1969.

Norman, D.A. *Memory and Attention: An Introduction to Human Information Processing*. ed. 2. New York: John Wiley & Sons, 1976.

Palmer, S.E. Visual perception and world knowledge; notes on a model of sensory-cognitive interaction. In D.A. Norman and D.E. Rumelhart (eds), *Explorations in Cognition*. San Francisco: W.H. Freeman & Co., 1975.

Risberg, A., and Agelfors, E. On the identification of intonation contours by hearing impaired listeners. In *Quarterly Progress and Status Report 2-3*. Stockholm: Speech Transmission Laboratory, 1978, 51–61.

Risberg, A., Agelfors, E., and Boberg, G. Measurements of frequency-discrimination ability of severely and profoundly hearing impaired children. In *Quarterly Progress and Status Report 2-3*. Stockholm: Speech Transmission Laboratory, 1975, 40–48.

Risberg, A., Agelfors, E., and Ericson, L. Psychoacoustic tests for the evaluation of speech perception ability. *Scand. Audiol.*, 1977, *Suppl. 8*, 210–215.

Robbins, R.M. The development of a new test to measure precourse to postcourse gains in intermediate auditory training (working paper). Rochester, New York: National Technical Institute for the Deaf, 1980.

Ross, M., Duffy, R.J., Cooker, H.S., and Sargeant, R.L. Contribution of the lower audible frequencies to the recognition of emotions. *Am. Ann. Deaf*, 1973, *118*(1), 37–42.

Ross, M., and Giolas, T.G. Issues and exposition. In M. Ross and T.G. Giolas (eds.), *Auditory Management of Hearing-Impaired Children Principles and Prerequisites for Intervention*. Baltimore: University Park Press, 1978.

Rubin, M. Auditory training systems in perspective. In L.J. Bradford and W.G. Hardy (eds.), *Hearing and Hearing Impairment*. New York: Grune & Stratton, 1979.

Sanders, D.A. *Aural Rehabilitation*. Englewood Cliffs, New Jersey: Prentice-Hall, 1971.

Sanders, D.A. *Auditory Perception of Speech*. Englewood Cliffs, New Jersey: Prentice-Hall, 1977.

Sims, D.G., and Jacobs, M.A. Speechreading evaluation at the National Technical Institute for the Deaf. Paper presented to the convention of the A.G. Bell Association for the Deaf, Boston, 1976.

Snell, K.B., and Managan, F. The effectiveness of auditory training at the National Technical Institute for the Deaf. Paper presented to the annual convention of the American Speech and Hearing Association, Houston, 1976.

Snell, K., Mapes, F., Hutchinson, K., Durity, R., Clymer, W., Young, M., and Lichty, D. *Basic Auditory Training Curriculum*. Rochester, New York: National Technical Institute for the Deaf, 1979.

Snell, K., Mapes, F., O'Shea, N., Moreau, R., Hutchinson, K., Clymer, W., Young, M., and Lichty, D. *Intermediate Auditory Training Curriculum*. Rochester, New York: National Technical Institute for the Deaf, 1979.

Stevens, A.L., and Rumelhart, D.E. Errors in reading: Analysis using an augmented transition network model of grammar. In D.A. Norman and D.E. Rumelhart (eds.), *Explorations in Cognition*. San Francisco: W.H. Freeman & Co., 1975.

Stevens, K.N., and Halle, M. Remarks on analysis by synthesis and distinctive features. In W. Wathen-Dunn (ed.), *Models for the Perception of Speech and Visual Form*. Cambridge, Massachusetts: MIT Press, 1967.

Strange, W., Verbrugge, R.R., Shankweiler, D.P., and Edman, T.R. Consonant environment specifies vowel identity. *J. Acoust. Soc. Am.*, 1976, *60*(1), 213–224.

Streng, A.H., Kretschmer, R.R., and Kretschmer, L.W. *Language Learning and Deafness: Theory, Application, and Classroom Management*. New York: Grune & Stratton, 1978.

Tillman, T.W., Carhart, R., and Olsen, W. Hearing efficiency in a competing speech situation. *J. Speech Hear. Res.*, 1970, *13*, 789–811.

Villchur, E. Simulation of the effect of recruitment on loudness relationships in speech. *J. Acoust. Soc. Am.*, 1974, *56*(5), 1601–1611.

Villchur, E. Electronic models to simulate the effect of sensory distortions on speech perception by the deaf. *J. Acoust. Soc. Am.*, 1977, *55*(5), 665–674.

Zurek, P.M., and Formby, C. Frequency-discrimination ability of hearing impaired listeners. *J. Speech Hear. Res.*, 1981, *46*, 108–112.

Chapter 20

Hearing Aid Evaluation and Orientation for the Severely Hearing-Impaired

ROBERTA MOREAU ROBBINS, M.A.
JACLYN GAUGER, M.A.

Hearing aid evaluation, the process of selecting appropriate amplification for a given individual, has a history like the treatment of the common cold; there are numerous approaches, all with some merit and few that could be called perfect. Most approaches have been based on a primary objective of improving "intelligibility of speech" as was recommended by Davis et al. (1946). Most can also be classified as either comparative or prescriptive in approach. Some professionals have even suggested that dwelling on the hearing aid evaluation itself is not as valuable as listener interaction and counseling.

COMPARATIVE APPROACHES

Perhaps the earliest and most well known comparative approach to hearing aid evaluation is that of Carhart (1946). For each individual, Carhart recommended comparing several aids in terms of (1) effective gain or aided speech reception threshold, (2) tolerance limit, (3) efficiency in noise, and (4) word discrimination using the W-22 word lists. Although, through the years, this approach has received its share of criticism, it continues, with a multitude of variations, to be used in clinical settings throughout the country.

Zerlin (1962) recommended a paired comparison approach to hearing aid evaluation using six hearing aids. Speech in noise was recorded on tape through each aid and was then played back through phones allowing the listener to quickly switch from one aid to another to make his/her comparisons.

Although this approach may have great intuitive appeal, it has one very serious shortcoming. Recording a signal through a hearing aid and playing it back through earphones creates a resonance at about 3000 Hz and has a low frequency filtering effect. The earphone also has a broad resonance between 400 and 1000 Hz (Cox, 1976).

Millin (1975) stressed the importance of allowing the listener to try at least one real commercial hearing aid during the evaluation. He also felt that a training period with each aid was necessary prior to administering speech discrimination tests with the aid. Probably his most important recommendation, however, was to use a constant presentation level of 60 dB SPL (a fairly normal conversational level) for aided speech testing.

Jerger and Hayes (1976) have recommended comparing hearing aid performance across several message-to-competition ratios. Synthetic sentences are presented at 60 dB SPL while a continuous discourse masker is presented at 40, 50, 60, 70, and 80 dB SPL. The listener selects the synthetic sentences from a list of 10. The percent correct at each signal-to-competition ratio is plotted. The resulting plot for each aid is compared. The percent correct at −10 dB message-to-competition ratio has been found to correlate most highly with success with amplification. Interestingly, success with amplification also declined with age and increased with a more sloping hearing loss.

Some attention has also been paid to another unique comparative approach to hearing aid evaluation: the master hearing aid. The use of a master hearing aid has been found to be unsatisfactory by many audiologists because of the often poor correlation between the master hearing aid and its corresponding commercial aid. Levitt and Collins (1980) have recently developed a protocol for the prescriptive fitting of a wearable master hearing aid that would hopefully overcome some of these problems. The approach, still in the research stage, also attempts to merge both the comparative and prescriptive approaches to hearing aid evaluation.

PRESCRIPTIVE APPROACHES

Very early in the history of hearing aid evaluation, comparative approaches were criticized in the Harvard Report (Davis et al., 1946) and the Medical Research Council Report (1947) for being wasteful of time and effort. Both reports recommended a universal hearing aid with a flat to moderate high frequency response for almost all hearing-impaired listeners. Because so many of the subjects in these studies had conductive losses, the results and recommendations are no longer considered relevant to our present population of hearing aid candidates. Again in the 1960's, however, comparative approaches come under attack for being invalid and unreliable (Shore et al., 1960; Resnick and Becker, 1963). With our growing knowledge of hearing loss, prescriptive approaches to hearing aid evaluation began to gain momentum.

Current understanding of desirable gain characteristics of hearing aids began with studies indicating that most listeners select a hearing aid use gain level of approximately one half to two thirds of their hearing loss (McCandless, 1974; Millin, 1965). These findings indicated that it is not desirable to provide gain to restore threshold to 0 dB HL but rather to amplify speech to a comfortable listening level. Most prescriptive approaches to hearing aid evaluation are aimed at meeting this later goal.

Childers et al. (1975) recommended that the frequency shaping in a hearing aid match the individual's equal loudness contour. The obtaining of equal loudness contours, however, can be very time consuming and would require that the hearing aid have a variable slope depending on listening level. This is because for most hearing-impaired listeners as sensation level increases, the equal loudness contours tend to flatten out. Building hearing aids with variable frequency responses dependent on input level is, however, electronically feasible. At this time, the advantages of using this type of circuitry have not been clearly enough demonstrated for its acceptance and use by the hearing aid industry.

Pascoe (1975) has also studied the effects of frequency response on hearing discrimination. Subjects with gradually sloping losses were tested under five conditions: (1) uniform gain as measured in a 2-cc coupler, (2) gain with a 6 dB/octave rise as measured in a 2-cc coupler, (3) uniform functional gain, (4) uniform hearing level, and (5) simulation of a commercial hearing aid. Results clearly showed the uniform hearing level condition to provide the best auditory discrimination. The simulation of a commercial aid produced the poorest hearing discrimination. It should also be noted that this study suggested that the area between 2.5 and 6.3 kHz was especially important for hearing discrimination. Most commercial hearing aids provide gain only to 4 or 5 kHz.

Berger (1976) has developed a "cookbook" approach to prescribing hearing aids involving no comparative testing. Threshold and uncomfortable listening levels are determined at frequencies of 125, 250, 500, 1000, 2000, 3000, and 4000 Hz. A formula then allows for the computation of desirable gain and maximum output at each frequency. If there is a dynamic range of 45 dB or greater at 500 and 1000 Hz, peak-clipping is recommended. If the uncomfortable listening level (UCL) minus operating gain is less than 70 dB, the use of compression is recommended. If there is no measurable hearing at 2000 Hz, no amplification is provided at this frequency and additional gain is recommended at 250 Hz. This last recommendation is very important when considering the severe and profoundly hearing-impaired. Some of the appealing aspects of Berger's approach are that he considers amplifier and earmold characteristics, cosmetic preference, and cost. To find an aid that meets the desired characteristics, however, may not always be an easy task.

Ross (1975) has also developed a prescriptive approach for preverbal children. Both threshold and UCL are measured at octave intervals from 250 to 4000 Hz. If possible, most comfortable listening level (MCL) is also measured. If this is not measured, a halving procedure is used to estimate MCL. These values are converted to SPL and plotted with an assumed 64 dB SPL average speech spectrum. Gain is then computed by subtracting the speech spectrum level at each frequency from the individual's MCL or halved estimate of MCL at each frequency. The maximum power output of the hearing aid is also set not to exceed the measured UCL at any frequency.

It is worth pointing out that in most clinical settings, it is probably some combination of the comparative and prescriptive approaches that is used most often. A compliment to those procedures is listener involvement and counseling.

USER JUDGMENTS AND COUNSELING

Randolph (1976) examined objective performance on word discrimination tests versus subjective accuracy. Using this approach, the listener is asked not only to respond to the word stimulus but also to judge whether or not the response is accurate. This allows for valuable subjective comparisons between hearing aids when objective speech discrimination test results are equivocal among hearing aids.

Resnick and Becker (1963) feel that patient counseling in the area of hearing aid acceptance is crucial. Other researchers have chosen to look via questionnaires at general communicative functioning and how that is affected by the use of amplification. The Hearing Measurement Scale (Noble and Atherly, 1970), Social Hearing Handicap Index (Ewertsen and Birk-Nielsen, 1973), Scale of Self-Assessment of Hearing Handicap (High et al., 1964), Speech Discrimination Assessment Scale (Lamb, 1971), and the Expanded Hearing Loss Scale Questionnaire (Schein et al., 1965) were developed to assess hearing handicaps. Interestingly, many correlate well with pure tone average. Later, the value of such scales for prehearing and posthearing habilitation assessment and in hearing aid evaluations was noted. The Denver Scale of Communicative Function (Alpiner et al., 1975) and the Hearing Performance Inventory (Giolas et al., 1979) were designed specifically with these goals in mind. In fact, the Hearing Performance Inventory has been suggested to be useful in hearing aid evaluation and counseling with the severe and profoundly hearing-impaired (Owens and Fujikawa, 1980).

The simple number of approaches to hearing aid evaluation attests to the state of the art regarding our understanding of hearing aid fitting. It is not unusual for audiologists to complain of the poor electroacoustic quality of hearing aids, but if that is ever to change we, as a profession, must first define precisely what is most desirable in a hearing aid. Ross (1972, p. 653) concluded a discussion of hearing aid evaluation: "Probably the theoretically 'best' aid rarely if ever gets recommended; this result awaits the electroacoustic millenium, but until then the hearing aid evaluation seems to offer the best hope of approaching this goal." At present the hearing aid evaluation does offer the best hope of approaching this goal of the "best" fit, however electroacoustic advancements in hearing aids await our further understanding of the needs of the impaired ear. We seem to know what is "sufficient" but not what is "optimal" for speech sound discrimination and understanding through hearing aids.

HEARING AID EVALUATION WITH SEVERE AND PROFOUNDLY HEARING-IMPAIRED PERSONS

Unfortunately, there are still some professionals who feel that there is no purpose in fitting a hearing aid to the profoundly hearing-impaired individual. This is a saddening injustice when considering that there are those totally deaf (no measurable hearing at any frequency) persons who would undergo cochlear implant surgery to receive extremely minimal auditory cues, while others with measurable hearing are being denied amplification because of professional bias. At the National Technical Institute for the Deaf, interested students who were previously unsuccessful hearing aid users are enrolled in "Orientation to Hearing Aids," a course including both instruction in the care, use, and

maintenance of hearing aids and an ongoing hearing aid evaluation. Many of these students are profoundly hearing-impaired and the majority accept amplification. See "Orientation to Hearing Aids" at the end of this chapter.

DiCarlo (1964), Pollack (1970), Rupp (1971), and Smith (1972) have stressed the need for early and prolonged use of amplification coupled with a good oral/aural environment. Ross (1975, p. 208) states, "For most hearing-impaired children, the early and appropriate selection and use of amplification is the single most important habilitative tool to us."

Sims et al. (1980), in a study of profoundly hearing-impaired (pure tone average = 90 dB HL) college students, found a relationship between the occurrence of functional speech and prolonged hearing aid use coupled with an aural/oral educational environment. Walter and Sims (1978) found that among college age deaf students those who had used hearing aids for 10 or more years had better speech reading with sound and better speech production than did their matched peers who had used hearing aids for less than 10 years. In a study of factors affecting improvements in speech production by deaf college students, it was found that relative use of hearing aids and amount of individualized speech instruction provided were most highly related to improvements in speech production (Conklin et al., 1980).

The rationale for fitting hearing aids to this population is clear. Before discussing an approach to hearing aid evaluation, however, there is a need to review some of the characteristics that make this population unique.

Special Chracteristics of the Severe to Profoundly Hearing-Impaired Individual

Because of the early onset of handicapping sensorineural deafness (Simmons, 1980), most severe and profoundly hearing-impaired persons have below average speech and language skills. The average deaf adult has a fourth-grade reading level (Cooper and Rosenstein, 1966; DiFrancesca, 1972). Vocabulary and understanding of idioms are also below average. Auditory speech recognition is often very poor. For these reasons many traditional speech recognition tests are inappropriate; some because the language is too difficult, others because the discrimination task is too difficult. (See Chapter 9 on assessment of hearing.)

Most severe to profoundly hearing-impaired individuals have recruitment or limited dynamic range. They, therefore, require an aid with both high gain and some form of output limiting whether it be peak clipping or amplitude compression. This requirement for high gain subsequently limits the flexibility in acoustical modifications of earmolds because of feedback problems. Most earmolds for this population must be full-shell type molds with thick walled tubing and no vents. Earmold filters can, however, be used. A small piece of lamb's wool in the hearing aid tone hook has often been helpful in "smoothing out" the 1000-Hz peak found in many hearing aids. This 1-kHz peak is often involved in the reduced dynamic range of hearing-impaired persons. A number of filters are also available commercially. See Killion (1981).

For good or bad, most severe to profoundly hearing-impaired persons encountered in a hearing aid evaluation will have had some experience with hearing aids. In the past, body worn hearing aids were often overfitted, i.e., aids provided up to 140 dB maximum power output, which resulted in aids being uncomfortably loud. This naturally discouraged many hearing aid users. With this kind of past experience, a hearing aid evaluation could be made more difficult. Even for those persons who have been successful hearing aid users, it should not necessarily be assumed that they have a good understanding of hearing aid care and maintenance or that they have consistently worn good working hearing aids. Bess (1977) found that, among hearing aids worn by public school children, 27% of the instruments were faulty, 48% produced excessive total harmonic distortion, and 25–30% did not agree with manufacturer's specifications. Other studies (Coleman, 1972; Gaeth and Lounsbury, 1966; Zink, 1972) have shown that 40–50% of hearing aids worn by children in educational settings performed unsatisfactorily.

Corner audiograms (no measurable hearing beyond 1000–2000 Hz) are also frequently found in this population creating some unique fitting requirements. Berger (1976) has recommended that when no measurable hearing exists at 2000 Hz, no amplification should be provided at this frequency and additional gain should be provided at 250 Hz. Yanick (1979) has also recommended providing no amplification beyond 3000 Hz when there is little or no measurable hearing in this frequency range. In a study (Darbyshire and Reeves, 1969) with children who had a 55-dB loss at 250 Hz and at least a 95-dB loss above 2000 Hz it was found that they performed about the same (55% and 58% respectively on the Manchester Picture Vocabularly Test) with a flat or falling hearing aid frequency response. With a rising frequency response, they performed the poorest (37%).

Ling (1964) has suggested that amplification should be extended down to 70 Hz in low noise situations with children having little hearing above 500 Hz. Later, Lickie and Ling (1968) and Ling (1969) studied the effects of extending low frequency amplification to 80 Hz versus 300 Hz. They found that extending the low frequency amplification improved the perception of certain suprasegmental features such as syllabic structure and stress but not intonation. It also improved the detection of certain voiced phonemes and the identification of vowels within words but not the identification of consonants.

Northern and Downs (1974, p. 232), on the other hand, have cautioned against the use of too great an amount of low frequency amplification. They suggest that low frequency amplification be extended to 100 Hz when there is no residual hearing above 1000 Hz. They also stress that *most* hearing-impaired children need amplification with high frequency emphasis.

Also within this population are those persons whose only responses to sound are vibrotactile. Some of these persons have been assisted in their speech-reading ability by the use of a "vibrotactile hearing aid" (Connors and McPherson, 1980; Decker and Folsom, 1978). Readers may wish to consult other research completed in this area, including Erber (1978), Kricos (1977), Nober (1967), and Pickett (1963).

This population of severe to profoundly hearing-impaired persons is also suspected to have greater masking abnormalities and pitch perception disorders (Villchur, 1978b). Little has been done to date to systematically measure and use this kind of frequency and temporal information in the hearing aid evaluation.

Hearing Aid Evaluation Methods

In this section an approch to hearing aid evaluation with adults and children with some verbal skill will initially be recommended. This will be followed by a recommended procedure to be used with the preverbal child.

With an individual possessing some verbal skill, it is possible to greatly increase the listener's involvement in the evaluation procedure.

Prior to selecting trial hearing aids, it is necessary to determine whether the fitting will be monaural or binaural and what the goal of the hearing aid fitting is. Binaural fittings are recommended whenever possible; however, when the two ears are quite different in threshold loss and discrimination ability, it is not always advisable to fit two aids. Often, for financial reasons, it is necessary to do a monaural fitting. As a rule of thumb, with this population, it is better to fit the better ear when fitting only one ear. Realistic expectations of the hearing aid fitting should then be agreed upon by both the audiologist and the hearing aid user. For many, the hearing aid will improve speech understanding, but for others, speech will never be made functionally intelligible with a hearing aid. Other expectations may include: improved speechreading, a better link with the auditory environment, improved voice control, etc.

Three or four aids should be selected for evaluation. The selection of gain and frequency response specifications of the aid should be based on a goal of making audible, at a comfortable level, as much of the speech spectrum as possible without exceeding the patient's tolerance level at any frequency. Gengel et al. (1971) and Ross (1975) have recommended hearing aid evaluation procedures with children with this same goal in mind. Much of the following is adapted from their procedures.

The calculation of desired gain and frequency response should begin by converting the patient's threshold, most comfortable listening level, and uncomfortable listening level at each frequency to SPL and plotting these values with a plot of the average speech spectrum. See Fletcher (1972) for data on average speech spectrum. At each frequency, the gain needed to bring the speech spectrum to the patient's most comfortable listening level can easily be computed and hearing aid maximum power output can be set just below the patient's tolerance level (Fig. 20.1). Corrections must then be made for differences in real ear versus 2-cc coupler gain. Corrections in Figure 20.1 are adapted from the findings of Killion and Monser (1980). It is likewise crucial to include corrections for earmold variations. Also remember that it is usually undesirable to provide high frequency amplification to persons having little or no high frequency hearing. These persons may desire additional low frequency amplification (Darbyshire and Reeves, 1969; Lickie and Ling, 1968; Ling, 1964, 1969; Berger, 1976; Yanick, 1979).

The evaluation procedure begins by presenting running speech at a constant level of 64 dB SPL while the listener, using a bracketing procedure, adjusts the hearing aid volume to a comfortable level. This is completed by simply asking the listener to adjust the hearing aid volume control back and forth until he feels that the speech is at a comfortable level. All additional testing will be completed with the hearing aid volume at this setting. Testing should include the determination of (1) threshold at each frequency with the use of either warbled tones or narrow bands of noise, (2) a speech reception threshold or a speech awareness threshold if is not possible to obtain a speech reception threshold, (3) uncomfortable listening level for continuous speech, and (4) auditory speech discrimination ability. To expedite this procedure, technology now allows for the determination of aided gain to a fairly accurate degree in only 30 seconds with the use of a miniature microphone that is inserted into the ear canal before the earmold is inserted (Harford, 1980a and 1980b). The microphone measures $4 \times 5 \times 2$ mm and can easily be used in most adult ear canals. Children who have used hearing aids for some time may also have ear canals large enough to accommodate the microphone. Utilizing this mea-

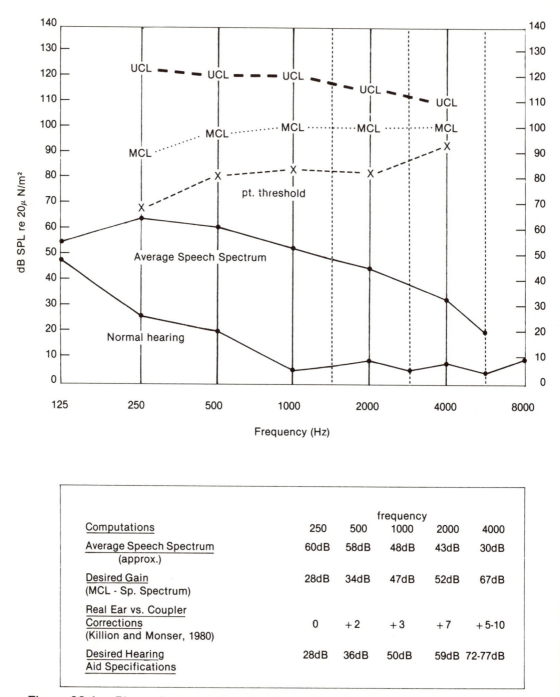

Figure 20.1. Plot and computations for desired hearing aid gain by frequency. MCL, most comfortable listening level; UCL, uncomfortable listening level.

surement technique it is possible to quickly make adjustments in tubing size, tone and maximum power output (MPO) to obtain desired aided gain prior to making any other measurements (i.e., speech reception threshold, uncomfortable listening level, and speech discrimination). The audiologist will look for the aid which (1) makes the greatest portion of the speech spectrum audible, (2) provides the greatest dynamic range, and (3) produces the best speech discrimination. Generally, we would expect the first and last of these to correlate quite highly. The type of speech discrimination test used can vary greatly depending on the listener's age, linguistic ability, and hearing ability. For children, a spondee same/different test, or a spondee discrimination test (Johnson, 1976), numeral tests (Webster and O'Shea, 1980; Erber, 1980), or the Word Intelligibility by Picture Identification (WIPI) Test (Ross and Lerman, 1971) might be used. For older children and adults, a wide variety of discrimination tests might be used. Examiners may also wish to make

use of a speechreading test with sound. The reader is encouraged to review Chapter 9 on assessment of hearing and speechreading.

The listener should then be given the opportunity to try each of the aids in a number of environments, including school, home, and out-of-doors. This will allow him/her an opportunity to evaluate the hearing aid not only on its clarity for speech but also on its telecoil response, cosmetic appeal, and microphone placement. The listener should then record his perceptions of each hearing aid on a form such as that shown in Figure 20.2 The *Orientation to Hearing Aids* package (Gauger, 1978) contains another example of a hearing aid record booklet for the recording of obser-

HEARING AID TRIAL
RESPONSE SHEET

Name: _____ Date: _____
Trial No.: _____ Ear: _____

Hearing Aid Manufacturer _____
Hearing Aid Model _____
Hearing Aid Serial No. _____
Hearing Aid Settings:
          M.P.O. _____
          Tone _____

1. Do you like the hearing aid?   YES   NO   UNSURE
2. Is the hearing aid loud enough?   YES   NO   UNSURE
3. Is the hearing aid too loud?   YES   NO   UNSURE
4. Can you hear your voice?   YES   NO   UNSURE
5. Does your voice sound normal?   YES   NO   UNSURE
6. Does the hearing aid have feedback?   YES   NO   UNSURE
7. Can you hear the TV?   YES   NO   UNSURE
8. Does the hearing aid make speechreading easier?   YES   NO   UNSURE
9. Does the hearing aid feel comfrotable on your ear?   YES   NO   UNSURE
10. Can you hear wind with the aid?   YES   NO   UNSURE
11. Does the wind noise bother you?   YES   NO   UNSURE
12. Does the hearing aid have an echo?   YES   NO   UNSURE
13. Does the aid have a clear sound?   YES   NO   UNSURE
14. Is the earmold comfortable?   YES   NO   UNSURE
15. Are the controls easy to use?   YES   NO   UNSURE
16. How is the "T" response?   GOOD   FAIR POOR
17. How many hours per day did you use the hearing aid?   _____ HOURS
18. How long do the batteries last?   _____ DAYS
19. What volume setting did you use?   1/4   1/3   1/2
                                                               2/3   3/4   Full
20. Is this the best aid you have tried so far?   YES   NO   UNSURE

Comments: _____
_____
_____

Figure 20.2. Sample hearing aid trial response sheet.

vations on each trail aid. See the discussion on "Orientation to Hearing Aids" at the end of this chapter.

Although we feel that listener input and involvement are important parts of the hearing aid evaluation, the reader should be aware of some of the conflicting literature in this area. There is some evidence (Hedgecock, 1949) that listeners perform best with preferred hearing aid characteristics, but more evidence suggests that listeners do not perform well with hearing aid characteristics they choose as comfortable. Watson and Knudsen (1940) found that listeners are likely to prefer characteristics that accentuate the frequencies they hear best without amplification. Darbyshire and Reeves (1969) found that children chose characteristics as comfortable that generally did not produce the best discrimination. Punch and Beck (1980) found that subjects with sloping losses preferred greater extended low frequency emphasis in their aids. Because other studies have suggested that low frequency amplification may cause upward spread of masking, there was some concern that listener quality judgments should not be part of the hearing aid evaluation. It should be remembered, however, that these subject judgments were made in quiet laboratory settings and not after trials with real commercial aids in "real" environments. In a "real" environment, these same subjects may have found they preferred less low frequency emphasis. Thus, it is recommended that the final hearing aid selection be based on both hearing aid test results and patient input.

Some other factors that may play an important role in the final selection of a hearing aid are: FM capabilities, telecoil response, cosmetic factors, microphone placement, and length of warranty.

User instruction on the care, use, and maintenance of the hearing aid(s) should be an ongoing process throughout the evaluation. For further information on user instruction and counseling regarding hearing aids, the reader is referred to "Orientation to Hearing Aids" at the end of this chapter.

With the preverbal child, it is not possible to have the degree of patient input recommended for the older child or adult. The goal of providing gain to make audible the greatest amount of the speech spectrum possible, however, remains. The procedure described above for selecting desirable gain and frequency response characteristics becomes the primary approach to the hearing aid evaluation with this population.

AMPLITUDE COMPRESSION IN HEARING AIDS

Recent research suggests that the use of amplitude compression in hearing aids for the severely hearing-impaired may hold great promise for future hearing aid fittings.

Because of the very limited dynamic range that most severe and profoundly hearing-impaired persons have, the use of some form of amplitude compression in hearing aids has become fairly common. In 1946, Hallowell Davis first suggested that the use of amplitude compression was superior to peak clipping as a means of limiting maximum acoustic output in hearing aids. Amplitude compression eliminates the harmonic distortion inherently produced by peak clipping. In the more than 30 years since that time, a number of approaches to amplitude compression have been investigated.

In present commercial aids, the most common form of compression used is limiter compression. A limiter compressor has a high knee of compression and a high compression ratio. In other words, the compression circuitry is not activated until fairly high levels have been reached, and then the ratio is so high that at this level gain is essentially limited. Therefore, the input-output function of a limiter compressor is very similar to that of a peak clipping device (Fig. 20.3). The compressor, however, has less harmonic distortion.

Much research with compression amplification has focused not on limiter compressors but on compressors active throughout a larger operating range. These compressors are designed to actually compress the speech range into an individual's dynamic range and not simply to limit the maximum acoustic output of the hearing aid.

Caraway and Carhart (1966) studied the effects of linear compression active throughout the entire operating range on intelligibility in normal and moderately hearing-im-

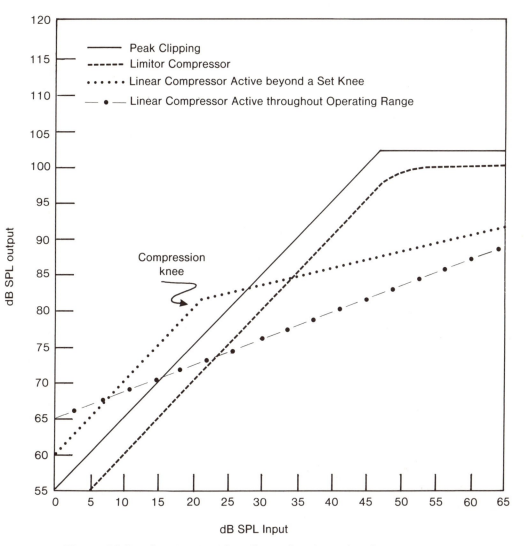

Figure 20.3. Input-output functions of various signal processors.

paired subjects. Their 48 subjects included 12 with normal hearing, 12 with labyrinthine hydrops, 12 with otosclerosis, and 12 with presbycusis. Spondees and Northwestern University Auditory Test No. 4 (NU #4) words were compressed, recorded on tape, and played back to subjects in quiet at sensation levels 0, 8, 16, and 24 dB. Compression ratios included 1:1 (linear amplification, no compression), 2:1 (2-dB increase in input results in 1-dB increase in output), and 3:1. The frequency response of the amplifier was flat with a range from 250 to 5000 Hz. The study yielded the following results: (1) compression did not affect speech reception threshold; (2) there was a small trend for compression to improve discrimination over linear amplification; however, this trend was not statistically significant; and (3) there was no significant difference in discrimination scores between 2:1 and 3:1 compression.

In 1971, a study very similar in design was completed by Burchfield using 36 subjects with unilateral sensorineural hearing losses with either partial or complete recruitment as measured by the alternate bilateral loudness balance (ABLB) test. In this study, 2:1 and 3:1 compression ratios significantly improved discrimination scores over linear or 1:1 amplification. Both the 2:1 and 3:1 compression ratios yielded similar discrimination scores. The discrepancy in test results between these two studies is probably related to the difference in degree of hearing loss and recruitment in the subject populations—those with greater hearing loss receiving greater benefit from compression amplification.

In 1977, Vargo, using a similar research design, studied discrimination in 12 normal and 12 Ménière's disease subjects using compression ratios of 1:1, 2:1, and 5:1. Discrimination was studied in quiet with consonant-nucleus-consonant (CNC) words at 10, 20, and 30-dB sensation levels re: speech reception threshold. His results showed no improvement in discrimination with compression as opposed to linear amplification. Little difference was found between 2:1 and 5:1 compression.

Thomas and Sparks (1971) introduced a new concept to this area of study by combining both output limiting and frequency shaping (high pass filtering) in the same instrument. Although they used peak clipping in their device, they found that filtered/clipped speech resulted in better discrimination scores in hearing-impaired subjects than did unmodified speech.

Much more recently, Young et al. (1980) experimented with whitened (high frequencies and low frequencies equated in intensity) and compressed speech. Normal hearing subjects were tested on discrimination of CNC words with whitened, whitened and 3:1 compressed, and whitened and 10:1 compressed speech. Testing was completed under three signal-to-competition ratios: 0 dB, +8 dB, and +12 dB (speech babble added prior to any processing). Although whitened and compressed speech produced poorer speech identification scores in noise than did unmodified speech, the difference was minimal (greatest difference = 9.6%). Remember also that these subjects had normal hearing and should not have shown benefit from compression. The exciting result of this study was that compression of speech in the presence of noise did not have a serious detrimental effect on intelligibility. Also, extreme compression ratios (10:1) did not interfere with intelligibility.

In a 1973 study, Yanick custom matched compression ratio to the hearing-impaired individual's dynamic range. Resulting compression ratios ranged from 1.6:1 to 3.2:1 for 12 hearing-impaired subjects. When comparing the custom fit compression hearing aid to those subject's personal linear hearing aids, the compression aid resulted in improved speech reception threshold, improved identification on PB-50 words, improved dynamic range, and elevated tolerance thresholds.

In that same year (1973) Villchur completed probably the most comprehensive and extensive study of compression amplification undertaken to that time. Villchur felt that the "ideal amplification could be realized theoretically by dividing the signal into an infinite number of frequency bands and compressing the signal in each band independently. The compression ratio for each band would be adjusted to offset the subject's particular loudness-function derangement at that frequency, and the gain for each band after compression would be adjusted to set the signal slice at its proper level" (p. 1648). In order to approach this on a practical level, he used a two-frequency band compression amplifier with postcompression equalization (frequency shaping). He also set the compression circuitry such that compression was not active throughout the entire operating range but only after input levels reached a level 10 dB above the lowest speech level in each frequency band. By thus raising the level of the compression knee, Villchur was able to eliminate some of the deleterious effects of noise. For each of six hearing-impaired subjects, compression ratio was computed for each frequency band independently, using the following approach:

"The span between the subject's threshold and equal loudness contour was compared at each half-octave to the span between normal threshold and the 74-phon equal-loudness contour.... The average ratio between normal and abnormal spans in each channel determined the compression ratio settings [Villchur, 1973, p. 1651]."

The average computed compression ratios were 2.2:1 for the low frequency band and 3.5:1 for the high frequency band. Subjects were then allowed to adjust the compression ratio to comfortable levels. Average subject adjusted compression ratios were 2.1:1 for the low frequency band and 2.8:1 for the high frequency band. The compressed signal was then equalized such that at each frequency the signal was placed within the individual's dynamic range.

Subjects were tested on CVC syllables that had been recorded in a reverberant environment, in quiet and at +10 dB signal to noise ratio (noise added prior to compression). Presentation levels were at MCL − 10 dB and MCL − 20 dB. Speech identification scores were better in all conditions with processed (compressed and equalized) versus unprocessed (treble boost only) speech.

Yanick (1976a), using a very similar compressor, compared unprocessed speech (bass roll-off only), single band compressed and equalized speech, and double band compressed and equalized speech for their effects on intelligibility in subjects with flat losses and ski-slope losses. In both subject groups, a great improvement in discrimination was found with the two-band compression/equalization. In fact, single band compression/equalization resulted in discrimination scores not very dissimilar to the scores obtained with unprocessed speech. This was found despite the fact that the flat loss group, the compression ratios for the low and high bands were very similar (i.e., 2.4:1 and 2.8:1). This study would suggest that most persons who would benefit from compression would receive greater benefit from two-band compression.

More recently, Yanick (1976b) also found that the additional use of an expansion mode below the compression threshold in the low frequency band will result in even greater improvement in discrimination. Expansion functions essentially opposite to compression, such that a decrease in input will result in a proportionately larger decrease in output. If the expansion mode is activated just below the lowest speech level, the ambient noise should be reduced to a level that is no longer bothersome (Fig. 20.3). The improvement in speech discrimination is believed to be a reflection of the resulting improvement in the signal-to-noise ratio. One major complaint with the use of compression was that the relative level of background noise increased, especially during periods of no speech signal, even though the speech intelligibility was im-

proved. The use of an expansion mode below the compression threshold tends to alleviate this situation and make the use of compression amplification more comfortable.

Byrne and Walker (1979), in a recommended approach to fitting multichannel compression amplification to persons with moderate hearing losses, have also recommended the use of expansion below compression. Unfortunately, at the time of this writing, there are no subject data available from their study.

In general, results of recent research with multichannel compression seem to suggest that this form of amplification may hold great promise for future wearable hearing aids, especially for the severely hearing-impaired. There is still, however, a need to more precisely define the desirable and essential parameters to be incorporated into a wearable hearing aid. Before any additional research in this area is undertaken, those variables that seem to be clearly related to success with compression amplification should be understood.

The time parameters involved in the attack and release from compression seem to be very crucial. Research has suggested that attack times from 1 to 5 msec and release times from 20 to 30 msec are most desirable for use in compression amplification (Carhart and Lynn, 1963; Nabelek and Robinette, 1975; Villchur, 1973; Yanick, 1976a and 1976b).

The speech discrimination test used in research may also play an important role in the success or failure demonstrated with compression. Villchur (1978a and 1979) has suggested that the use of monosyllables in speech discrimination tests used with compression research may show no advantage to compression because they are by nature "precompressed." Monosyllables spoken while monitoring speech on a volume unit (VU) meter will not possess the dynamic range incurred in general conversational speech; therefore, the advantage offered by compression would not be demonstrated.

The subject population used in compression amplification research is also very much related to the outcome. Subjects with only moderate losses and fairly large dynamic ranges may find compressed speech easier to listen to or more confortable but may not demonstrate this advantage on a discrimination test. This is because, even without compression, these subjects may be able to increase the intensity of speech to a level that allows them to hear the weaker phonemes in the language without the stronger phonemes exceeding their tolerance threshold. In reviewing Caraway and Carhart's (1966) study that showed no advantage to compression, we see that the average discrimination score on NU #4 words for the 36 hearing-impaired subjects using linear amplification was 81.7%. The average pure tone average was 47.7 dB. Clearly, many of these subjects did not have a need for compression amplification. These same subjects would also show no advantage to many of today's high gain hearing aids, but that does not mean there is no need for these aids.

Another variable that has not received a great deal of attention in compression research but may be a very crucial one is practice time. For a severely hearing-impaired person who has never heard many of the weaker phonemes in the language, the making audible of these sounds with compression does not guarantee that s/he will be able to apply linguistic value to this new information without some unspecified amount of practice time. Peterson (1980) has stressed the importance of practice time in his study of compression amplification. Early research findings with two-band compression amplification at the National Technical Institute for the Deaf also suggest that, with severe to profoundly hearing-impaired students, practice or training with compressed speech may be essential to the demonstration of advantages to this type of processing.

ORIENTATION TO HEARING AIDS

The Need

The severely to profoundly hearing-impaired young adult population has a poor history of hearing aid use. Many in this population discarded amplification "because the aid broke." As a result, there is a need to inform the young adult deaf population about the workings of personal amplification, its maintenance procedures, and how to troubleshoot minor problems in order for them to become relatively self-sufficient in these areas. All too often, parents, who have always been the target of information giving, maintain this role as their offspring go on to post-secondary schooling or a job. Several authors have supported the need for information to be imparted to the hearing aid user in a logical, organized fashion (Kasten and Warren, 1977; Hodgson, 1978; Kasten 1978). One such program, *Orientation to Hearing Aids (OHA)*, was developed to help meet the need (Clymer et al., 1979).

Target Populations

At the National Technical Institute for the Deaf (NTID) at the Rochester Institute of Technology (RIT), three subsets of the college-age deaf student population have been identified as needing some form of hearing aid orientation: (1) students with limited and/or negative experiences using amplification, (2) students who use amplification all or most of the time, and (3) students who use amplification less than all or most of the time.

The first group, those with limited and/or negative experiences, have, understandably, very little knowledge of the benefits of hearing aids, earmolds, batteries, maintenance procedures, troubleshooting procedures, or guarantees and insurance plans. Approximately 15% of each incoming class of new students ($n = 320$) fits into the category of students who have not used amplification in the previous 3 years and do not currently have a hearing aid. Of those students, approximately 83% are interested in trying amplification again. The remaining 17% are simply not motivated to try hearing aids again, even when it is stressed that they do not have to accept a hearing aid as a result of the process. The OHA curriculum package was initially developed over a period of years to meet the needs of the students who arrived at NTID (mean age of 19.2 years) without amplification, had not used any in the previous 3 years, and were willing to try again (Galloway, 1975; Gauger and McPherson, 1978, Gauger, 1980).

The second group, students who use amplification all of the time (defined as a minimum of 7–8 hours daily), was tested with the pretest materials utilized in the OHA course offered at NTID (to be described in this section). It was found that they knew more about hearing aids than the students in the first group, however few students were able to meet the predetermined criteria for competency (80% correct on a written test). Thirty-four entering students were pretested within their first few weeks on campus. They were given the OHA instructional books to read and study while they were on a quarter "break" and posttested later. The average test scores are reported for the five topics included in the OHA package:

Book	$\bar{X}$ Pretest	$\bar{X}$ Posttest
Hearing Aids and What They Do	37%	65%
Earmolds and Hearing Aid Batteries	42%	66%
Maintenance and Care of Hearing Aids	46%	72%
Troubleshooting Hearing Aid Problems	52%	75%
Consumer Information: Hearing Aids	50%	68%

The average posttest scores show improvement over the average pretest scores, but most students did not reach the 80% level. Six of the 34 students passed all five posttests after reading and studying on their own. This suggests that students who are "successful" hearing aid users lack some basic information and need teacher contact to ensure learning.

The third group, students who have their own hearing aids but use them less than 5 hours per day, will not be discussed in detail here. They do need some type of orientation to hearing aids, but the fitting problem must be solved as well. This is an interesting group because many of them have new hearing aids. It is an area which needs more attention and is currently handled at NTID as a "diagnostic" hearing aid check which could result in the recommendation of a new hearing aid, or a modification of their own instrument whenever possible.

In summary, the primary target population for a full-fledged OHA course at NTID has been those students in the first group, mainly because the second group has been "getting along" (sometimes not too well), and the third group is extremely difficult to motivate (students in this third group have historically dropped the course or simply never showed up for class).

Tasks Involved

In order for any hearing aid user to be as self-sufficient as possible, there are a number of physical tasks which need to be mastered. In this program, these physical tasks are linked with cognitive information which has been broken down into five areas. This listing is called the "Performance Checklist" (Table 20.1).

In the OHA curriculum package, these physical tasks (or psychomotor activities) can

Table 20.1
Orientation to Hearing Aids Performance Checklist

HEARING AIDS AND WHAT THEY DO
1. Insert earmold correctly
2. Attach earmold to hearing aid
3. Insert earmold with hearing aid attached
4. Adjust volume control for most comfortable listening
5. Name outside parts and controls

EARMOLDS AND HEARING AID BATTERIES
1. Wash earmold with appropriate medium
2. Choose correct battery for hearing aid
3. Test battery
4. Insert battery correctly
5. Know how to use recharger (based on interest and need)

MAINTENANCE AND CARE OF HEARING AIDS
1. Turn switch on *Off* when putting aid on and taking it off (or open battery case or turn volume control down)
2. Know when plastic tube should be replaced
3. Clean battery surfaces with eraser

TROUBLESHOOTING HEARING AID PROBLEMS: IDENTIFY
1. Broken hook
2. Dead battery
3. Weak battery
4. Battery in upside down
5. Inappropriate battery size
6. Hole in plastic tube
7. Cracked case
8. Frayed cord (if applicable)
9. Plugged earmold opening

CONSUMER INFORMATION: HEARING AIDS
1. Contact with vocational rehabilitation counselor
2. Fill out guarantee form; know when it ends and what it covers
3. Fill out insurance form; know when it ends and what it covers

be demonstrated as needed by the audiologist. The student is then either formally or informally evaluated to determine whether the performance of the task is at a satisfactory level (i.e., habitual, accurate, internalized, generalized). The student is simultaneously proceeding through a hearing aid evaluation, with the same audiologist, as described elsewhere in this chapter, and reading the series of five instructional books, corresponding to the five areas of psychomotor activities. With few exceptions, students are able to complete this list of activities within a 10-week period, meeting once a week with the audiologist for 50 minutes (separate from the hearing aid evaluation time).

Description of One Orientation Program

The two major aspects of the course are (1) the hearing aid evaluation/loan process and (2) the informational/instructional process. The first aspect is described separately in this chapter; however, there is a great deal of overlap with the informational/instructional process.

There are five information books (Fig. 20.4) which the student reads at a rate of one per week, slower or faster depending on the individual. The titles of the books are:

Hearing Aids and What They Do / 1
Earmolds and Hearing Aid Batteries / 2
Maintenance and Care of Hearing Aids / 3
Troubleshooting Hearing Aid Problems / 4
Consumer Information: Hearing Aids / 5

Additionally, there are three other books: a *Student Manual*, describing course goals, expectations, grading policies, schedules; a *Hearing Aid Record* book, in which the audiologist describes each hearing aid loaned and the student answers 20 questions about experiences borrowing each one; and an *Audiologist Manual*, which is a curriculum guide, including pretest and posttest keys, suggestions for discussions, and background information for teaching the course.

The student is pretested on the course objectives and is then presented with each book and the coinciding psychomotor tasks in the performance checklist. After discussion and/or expansion of the topics and an opportunity

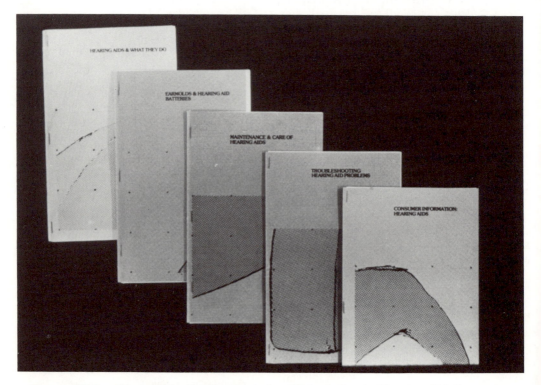

Figure 20.4. Five self-instruction texts for "Orientation to Hearing Aids" course.

for the student to ask questions, the posttest for a given book is administered. A passing score of 80% is required before moving on to the next book. The student may restudy and take the posttest again within a few days.

This process continues until all five instructional books have been completed. At the audiologist's discretion, this course may be taught in a small group (from 2 to 5 students) or individually. The hearing aid evaluation/loan process, naturally, is conducted individually.

As the entire process nears completion, the student makes a decision regarding acceptance of amplification. If, after adequate time and trials with hearing aids, the student decides that s/he would prefer not to begin using amplification, that is accepted by the audiologist. The student enrolls in the course with that understanding, and it is important to abide by it. The option is always there for the student to change his/her mind at a later date.

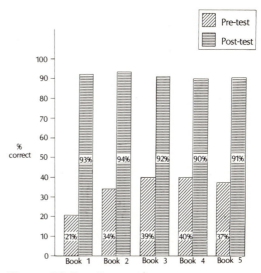

Figure 20.5. Pre- and post-test mastery learning test results (N = 87) of the five "Orientation to Hearing Aids" texts.

Results

The students are pretested and posttested on the course content. The posttests occur at the end of the designated time period for reading and study (usually 1 week) and separately for each of the five books. The results of a group of 87 students (as taught by 8 instructors) are seen in Figure 20.5. The pretest scores are similar with the exception of Book 1: *Hearing Aids and What They Do.* The average posttest scores all exceed the minimum passing criterion of 80%. A small number of students (N = 10) was given a second set of posttests 1 week after the end of the course was finished and again 6 months later. The results indicate that, while the average scores do not remain at the 90–94% levels, they hover around the 80% passing criterion (±5%). The performance checklist items are satisfactorily completed by every student.

Of the students who complete the course, 75% accept either monaural or binaural amplification. The vast majority of the hearing aids recommended are the behind-the-ear style. The most prevalent reasons for nonacceptance of amplification are: audiokinetic nystagmus Tullio phenomenon (Shambaugh, 1967, p. 345) and/or difficulty tolerating sound.

After the course is over and a hearing aid(s) has been recommended, the instructor continues to send the student hourly charts at 5–20-week intervals, depending on the instructor. The hourly chart is used for recording the number of hours per day for a week the aid(s) is worn. The instructor determines the week to be recorded hoping to capture an "average" week. The return rate is not very high, but Figure 20.6 shows the average number of hours per day that students report they are wearing their new hearing aid(s). It is known, however, that some students who initially accepted amplification have stopped using it. Instructors often learn about this by seeing students in other classes, meetings, or informally.

Instructor Reactions

Since the OHA curriculum package was developed in the present format, 18 instructor/audiologists have utilized the materials while teaching the course. A series of interviews was conducted with an initial group of 6 instructors who had not been involved in the development of the package. The interview consisted of 14 questions about the course itself and the materials in the curriculum package, asked of the audiologists by nonaudiologists who were involved in the course development. There were varied re-

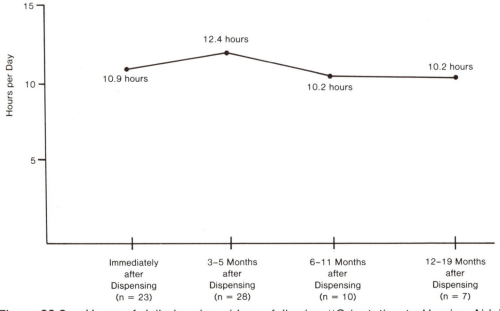

Figure 20.6. Hours of daily hearing aid use following "Orientation to Hearing Aids" course.

actions, based on teaching style and personal preference, but on the whole the audiologists interviewed felt that most of the materials enhanced the teaching/learning process as well as the hearing aid selection and fitting.

Some audiologists prefer to teach the course with a small group of students meeting together for the instructional aspect. Others prefer to have individual meetings. The materials allow for either arrangement. Additional learning aids such as word games and crossword puzzles have been developed by creative audiologists to teach or quiz the vocabulary in each book and reinforce the reading material. Some audiologists add other related material to the course, such as anatomy and physiology of the ear, or causes of hearing loss. Overall, it appears that the student's motivation and the audiologist's attitude toward the course interact to help determine the success of the teaching/learning process.

Recommendations for Developing a Program of Hearing Aid Orientation

After working with a large group of young deaf adults, the first recommendation naturally becomes, "Start early." Even 5-year-olds learn to become aware of their hearing aids, and what happens when a battery dies; or how it feels if the earmold is not inserted properly. The adults around them obviously need some form of orientation as well. Start with easy tasks, but let them become habitual. Parents and teachers are significant influences on young hearing aid users, so gain their attention, respect, and cooperation early.

As both the youngster and the adults in his/her environment master the basic tasks, add more difficult concepts and tasks one or two at a time. Demonstrate how these new tasks are related to those already learned, and why they are necessary. Teach by demonstration and experience. Let the hearing-impaired third-grader "listen" to his/her own hearing aid(s) with a dead battery in it. It is amazing how poignant that experience can be.

References

Alpiner, J., Cheverette, W., Glascoe, G., Metz, M., and Olsen, B. The Denver Scale of Communication Function, 1974. In M. Pollack (ed.), *Amplification for the Hearing Impaired.* New York: Grune & Stratton, 1975.
Berger, K.W. Prescription of hearing aids: a rationale. *J. Am. Audiol. Soc.,* 1976, 2, 3.

Bess, F.H. Condition of hearing aids worn by children in a public school setting. In *The Condition of Hearing Aids Worn by Children in a Public School Program.* HEW Publication No. (OE)77-05002. Washington, D.C.: U.S. Government Printing Office, 1977.

Burchfield, S.B. Perception of amplitude compressed speech by persons exhibiting loudness recruitment. Dissertation 1971, M.S.U., *Dissertation Abstracts International,* 1971, *32,* 1675-B.

Byrne, D., and Walker, G. Proposed method for selecting amplification for a multichannel hearing aid with expansion, compression and limiting facilities, for persons with moderate hearing impairments. Canberra, Australia: Information Report No. 58, National Acoustical Laboratories, Commonwealth Dept. of Health, Australian Government Publishing Service, 1979.

Caraway, B.J., and Carhart, R. Influence of compressor action on speech intelligibility. *J. Acoust. Soc. Am.,* 1966, *41,* 6.

Carhart, R. Tests for selection of hearing aids. *Laryngoscope,* 1946, *56,* 780–794.

Carhart, R., and Lynn, G. Influence of attack and release in compression amplification on understanding of speech in hypocusics. *J. Speech Hear. Disord.,* 1963, *28,* 2.

Childers, R.L., Jansen, J.W., and Sweetman, R.H. The effect of loudness contour spectrum shaping on speech intelligibility. Paper presented at the annual ASHA Convention, Washington, D.C., 1975.

Clymer, W., Gauger, J., and Young, M. Orientation to hearing aids package. *Hear. Aid J.,* 1979, *32,* 5.

Coleman, R.F. Stability of children's hearing aids in an acoustic preschool. Final Report, Project 522466, Grant No. OEG-4-71-0060. Washington, D.C.: U.S. Dept. of H.E.W., 1972.

Conklin, J.M., Subtelny, J.D., and Walter, G.G. Analysis of the communication skills in young deaf adults over a 2-year interval of technical training. *Am. Ann. Deaf,* 1980, *125,* 388–393.

Connors, S., and McPherson, D. A vibrotactile training program for the deaf using a single vibrator. In D. McPherson and M. Davis (eds.), *Advances in Prosthetic Devices for the Deaf: A Technical Workshop for the Deaf* (NTIS No. PB80-131196), 1980.

Cooper, R. L., and Rosenstein, J. Language acquisition of deaf children. *Volta Rev.,* 1966, *68,* 58–67.

Cox, R. Spectral changes produced by earmold-cushion reproduction in hearing aid processing signals. Paper presented at the annual ASHA Convention, Houston, Tex., 1976.

Darbyshire, J., and Reeves, V. The relationship between pure-tone audiograms, frequency response curves, and optimum listening levels—a pilot investigation. *Sound,* 1969, *3,* 37–39.

Davis, H., Hudgins, C.V., Marquis, R. J., et al. The selection of hearing aids. *Laryngoscope,* 1946, *56,* 85–115, 135–163.

Decker, N., and Folsom, R. A tactile method for increasing speechreading abilities: two case studies. *Audiol. Hear. Educ.,* 1978, *4,* 1, 14–18.

DiCarlo, L.M. *The Deaf.* Englewood Cliffs, N.J.: Prentice Hall, 1964.

DiFrancesca, S. Academic achievement test results of a national testing program for hearing-impaired students, United States, Spring, 1971. Washington, D.C.: Gallaudet College, Office of Demographic Studies, 1972.

Erber, N.P. Vibrotactile perception by deaf children. *Int. J. Rehabil. Res.,* 1978, *1,* 27–37.

Erber, N.P. Use of the auditory numbers test to evaluate speech perception abilities of hearing-impaired children. *Speech Hear. Disord.,* 1980, *45,* 527–532.

Ewertsen, H.W., and Birk-Nielsen, H. Social hearing handicap index. *Audiology,* 1973, *12,* 180–187.

Fletcher, H. *Speech and Hearing in Communication.* Huntington, N.Y.: Krieger, 1972.

Gaeth, J.H., and Lounsbury, E. Hearing aids and children in elementary schools. *J. Speech Hear. Disord.,* 1966, *31,* 283–289.

Galloway, A.L. A review of hearing aid fittings on young adults with severe to profound hearing impairment. *J. Acad. Rehabil. Audiol.,* 1975, *8,* 95–100.

Gauger, J. Orientation to hearing aids. Paper presented to the 49th Meeting of the Convention of American Instructors of the Deaf, 1980.

Gauger, J., and McPherson, D. A support system for hearing aid evaluations. *J. Acad. Rehabil. Audiol.,* 1978, *11,* 66–90.

Gauger, J.S. *Orientation to Hearing Aids.* Washington, D.C.: Alexander Graham Bell Association for the Deaf, 1978.

Gengel, R.W., Pascoe, D., and Shore, I. A frequency-response procedure for evaluating and selecting hearing aids for severely hearing-impaired children. *J. Speech Hear. Disord.,* 1971, *36,* 341–353.

Giolas, T.G., Owens, E., Lamb, S.H., and Schubert, E.D. Hearing performance inventory. *J. Speech Hear. Disord.* 1979, *44,* 169–195.

Harford, E.R. A microphone in the ear canal to measure hearing aid performance. *Hear. Instruments, 31,* 14–32, 1980a.

Harford, E.R. The use of a miniature microphone in the ear canal for verification of hearing aid performance. *Ear Hear., 1,* 329–337, 1980b.

Hedgcock, L.D. Prediction of the efficiency of hearing aids from audiograms. Unpublished Ph.D. dissertation, University of Wisconsin, 1949.

High, W.S., Fairbanks, G., and Glorig, A. Scale of self-assessment of hearing handicap. *J. Speech Hear. Disord.,* 1964, *29,* 215–230.

Hodgson, W. Hearing-aid counseling and orientation. In J. Katz (ed.), *Handbook of Clinical Audiology,* ed. 2. Baltimore: Williams & Wilkins, 1978.

Jerger, J., and Hayes, D. Hearing aid evaluation. *Arch. Otolaryngol.,* 1976, 102.

Johnson, D. Assessment of communication characteristics of a young deaf adult population: techniques for evaluating their communication skills. *Am. Ann. Deaf,* 1976, *121,* 409–424.

Kasten, R. The hearing aid as related to rehabilitation. In J. Alpiner (ed.), *Handbook of Adult Rehabilitative Audiology.* Baltimore: Williams & Wilkins, 1978.

Kasten, R., and Warren, M. Learning to use the hearing aid. In W. Hodgson, and D. Skinner (eds.), *Hearing Aid Assessment and Use in Audiologic Habilitation.* Baltimore: Williams & Wilkins, 1977.

Killion, M.C. Earmold options for wideband hearing

aids. *J. Speech Hear. Disord..*, 1981, *46*, 10–20.

Killion M.C., and Monser E.L. CORFIG: Coupler response for flat insertion gain. In G. A. Studebaker and I. Hochberg (eds.), *Acoustical Factors Affecting Hearing Aid Performance.* Baltimore: University Park Press, 1980.

Kricos, P. Vibrotactile discrimination of speech sounds by normal, hearing-impaired, and visually-impaired individuals. *J. Acad. Rehabil. Audiol.*, 1977, *10*, 25–33.

Lamb, S. H. Speech discrimination assessment scale—a preliminary report. Paper presented at the Monte Corona Conference Center, California, as part of the symposium: Amplification for Sensorineural Hearing Loss, 1971.

Leveitt, H., and Collins, M.J. An experimental protocol for the prescriptive fittings of a wearable master hearing aid. In G.A. Studebaker and I. Hochberg (eds.), *Acoustical Factors Affecting Hearing Aid Performance.* Baltimore: University Park Press, 1980.

Lickie, D., and Ling, D. Audibility with hearing aids having low frequency characteristics. *Volta Rev.*, 1968, *70*, 83–86.

Ling, D. Implications of hearing aid amplification below 300 cps. *Volta Rev.*, 1964, *66*, 723–729.

Ling, D. Speech discrimination by profoundly deaf children using linear and coding amplifiers. *IEEE Trans. Aud. Electroacoust. Au-27*, 1969, 298–303.

McCandless, G.A. High frequency hearing loss and hearing aid selection. Paper presented at the International Hearing Aid Seminar, San Diego, 1974.

Medical Research Council 1947. Committee on Electro-Acoustics. Hearing aids and Audiometers. MCR Special Report Series No. 261, HM Stationery Office, London, 1947.

Millin, J.P. Speech discrimination as a function of hearing aid gain: implications in hearing aid evaluation. Masters thesis, Western Reserve University, 1965.

Millin, J.P. Practical and philosophical considerations. In M. Pollack (ed.), *Amplification for the Hearing Impaired.* New York: Grune & Stratton, 1975.

Nabelek, I., and Robinette, L.N. A comparison of hearing aids with amplitude compression. Mimeographed paper, University of Tennessee, 1975.

Noble, W.G., and Atherley, G.R.C. The hearing measurement scale. *J. Aud. Res.*, 1970, *10*, 229–250.

Nober, E.H. Vibrotactile sensitivity of deaf children to high intensity sound. *Laryngoscope*, 1967, *77*, 2128–2146.

Nothern, J.L., and Downs, M.P. *Hearing in Children.* Baltimore: Williams & Wilkins, 1974.

Owens, E., and Fujikawa, S. The hearing performance inventory and hearing aid use in profound hearing loss. *J. Speech Hear. Res.*, 1980, *23*, 471–479.

Pascoe, D. Frequency responses of hearing aids and their effects on the speech perception of hearing-impaired subjects. *Ann. Otorhinolaryngol.*, 1975, 84.

Peterson, P.M. Further studies of perception of amplitude-compressed speech by impaired listeners. Masters thesis, M.I.T., February 1980.

Pickett, J. Tactual communication of speech sounds to the deaf: comparison with lipreading. *J. Speech Hear. Disord.*, 1963, *28*, 315–330.

Pollack, D. *Educational Audiology for the Limited Hearing Infant.* Springfield, Ill.: Charles C Thomas, 1970.

Punch, J.L., and Beck, E.L. Low frequency response of hearing aids and judgements of aided speech quality. *J. Speech Hear. Disord.*, 1980, *45*, 3.

Randolph, K.J. Subjective accuracy versus objective performance in a word discrimination task. Paper presented at the annual ASHA convention, Houston, Tex., 1976.

Resnick, D.M., and Becker, M. Hearing aid evaluation—a new approach. *A.H.S.A.*, 1963, *5*, 695–699.

Ross, M. Hearing aid evaluation. In J. Katz (ed.), *Handbook of Clinical Audiology.* Baltimore: Williams & Wilkins, 1972.

Ross, M. Hearing aid selection for preverbal hearing-impaired children. In M. Pollack (ed.), *Amplification for the Hearing Impaired.* New York: Grune & Stratton, 1975.

Ross, M., and Lerman, J. *Word Intelligibility by Picture Identification.* Pittsburgh: Stanwix House, 1971.

Rupp, R.R. An approach to the communicative needs of the very young hearing impaired child. *J. Acad. Rehabil. Audiol.*, 1971, 4, 11–22.

Schein, J.D., Gentile, A., and Haase, K.W. Development and evaluation of an expanded hearing loss scale questionnaire. In *Vital and Health Statistics.* PHS Pub. 1000-series 12, Public Health Service. Washington, D.C.: U.S. Government Printing Office, 1965.

Shambaugh, G. *Surgery of the Ear.* Philadelphia: W. B. Saunders, 1967.

Shore, I., Bilger, R.C., and Hirsh, I.J. Hearing aid evaluation: Reliability of repeated measurements. *J. Speech Hear. Disord.*, 1960, *25*, 152–170.

Simmons, F.B. Diagnosis and rehabilitation of deaf newborns: Part II. *A.H.S.A.*, 1980, *22*, 475–479.

Sims, D.G., Gottermeier, L., and Walter, G.G. Factors contributing to the development of intelligible speech among prelingually deaf persons. *Am. Ann. Deaf*, 1980, *125*, 374–381.

Smith, C. Residual hearing and speech production in deaf. Doctoral dissertation, City University of New York, 1972.

Thomas, I.B., and Sparks, D.W. Discrimination of filtered/clipped speech by hearing impaired subjects. *J. Acoust. Soc. Am.*, 1971, *49*, 1181.

Vargo, S. Intelligibility of amplitude compressed speech in quiet: normal and pathological hearing groups. *Audiol. Hear. Educ.*, 1977, *3*, 2, 16–17.

Villchur, E. Signal processing to improve speech intelligibility in perceptive deafness. *J. Acoust. Soc. Am.*, 1973, *53*, 1646–1657.

Villchur, E. A critical survey of research on amplitude compression. In C. Ludvigsen and J. Barford (eds.), Sensorineural Hearing Impairment and Hearing Aids. *Scand. Audiol. Suppl.*, 1978a, *6*, 305–314.

Villchur, E. Signal processing. In M. Ross and T. Giolas (eds.), *Auditory Management of Hearing-Impaired Children.* Baltimore: University Park Press, 1978b.

Villchur, E. Amplitude compression as an aid to the intelligibility for the hearing impaired: conflicting results on different experiments. Paper presented at the 64th AES Convention, New York City, 1979.

Walter, G.G., and Sims, D.G. The effect of prolonged hearing aid use on the communication skills of young deaf adults. *Am. Ann. Deaf*, 1978, *123*, 548–554.

Watson, N.A., and Knudsen, V.D. Selective amplification in hearing aids. *J. Acoust. Soc. Am.*, 1940, *11*, 406–419.

Webster, J.C., and O'Shea, N.P. Current developments in auditory speech discrimination tests for the profoundly deaf at NTID. *Am. Ann. Deaf*, 1980, *125*, 350–359.

Yanick, P. Improvement in speech discrimination with compression versus linear amplification. *J. Aud. Res.*, 1973, *13*, 333–338.

Yanick, P. Effects of signal processing on intelligibility of speech in noise for persons with sensorineural hearing loss. *J. Am. Audiol. Soc.*, 1976a, *1*, 229–239.

Yanick, P. Signal processing to improve intelligibility in the presence of noise for persons with ski-slope sensorineural hearing impairment. *J. Audiol. Eng. Soc.*, May 1976b.

Yanick, P. New concepts in signal processing and hearing habilitation. Paper presented at the Second Symposium on the Application of Signal Processing Concepts to Hearing Aids, The Pennsylvania State University, March 1979.

Young, L.L., Goodman, J.T., and Carhart, R. The intelligibility of whitened and amplitude compressed speech in a multitalker background. *J. Speech Hear. Res.*, 1980, *23*, 393–404.

Zerlin, A. A new approach to hearing-aid selection. *J. Speech Hear. Res.*, 1962, *5*, 370–376.

Zink, G.D. Hearing aids children wear: a longitudinal study of performance. *Volta Rev.*, 1972, *74*, 41–52.

Chapter 21

The Cochlear (Implant) Prosthesis: Theoretical and Practical Considerations

CHARLES W. PARKINS, PH.D.
ROBERT A. HOUDE, PH.D.

One of the new developments in aids for the deaf is the "cochlear implant" or, more appropriately, the cochlear prosthesis. This is an attempt to help those patients whose hearing loss is too severe for amplification and who, because of their sensory neural etiology, have not been affected by the innovations and progress made in middle ear surgery for conductive deafness. The first attempts at electrical stimulation of hearing can be traced back to Volta in 1790. Although the field is really still in its infancy, significant progress has been made since the early attempts of Djourno and Eyries (1957) to electrically stimulate an exposed eighth nerve in a patient whose cochlea had been destroyed by a cholesteatoma.

RATIONALE

The rationale for a cochlear implant may be illustrated by comparing the input stages of the auditory system (the cochlea and eighth nerve) to the mechanical system shown in Figure 21.1. A ribbon-like structure representing the basilar membrane of the cochlea is displaced in space by the incoming sound wave and this displacement is detected and quantified by the mechanical to electrical transducers of this mechanical system, representing the hair cells of the organ of Corti. To each transducer is connected a number of output lines, usually about 10, relaying this displacement information to higher decoding centers. The input signal to the transducer is an analogue signal (continuously varying). The output signal on each of the transmission lines is a digital signal (sequence of pulses) whose rate is proportional to the displacement of the transducer. This pulse rate code is probabilistic. Although the average rate functions of each of the transmission lines connected to one transducer will be similar, the actual timing of the pulses will differ

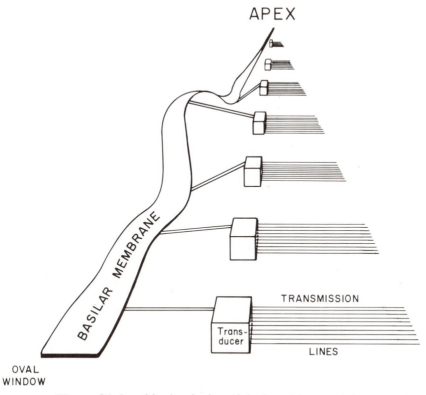

Figure 21.1.   Mechanical model of cochlear activity.

randomly for each transmission line. In this analogy, sensory deafness can be considered to be a loss of the transducer function of the model with the conduction lines remaining intact. The rationale for the cochlear prosthesis, therefore, is to bypass these damaged transducers and directly stimulate the transmission lines in a specific manner that will produce the same digital code in each of these transmission lines that would have been produced through normal transducer function. This approach makes several very basic assumptions that may or may not be true. First, it assumes that in the mixed bag of pathologies categorized as sensorineural deafness, a significant number of patients have their main defect at the sensory (hair cell) level with a significant number of surviving and functional auditory nerve neurons available at the cochlear level for stimulation. Studies of human temporal bones from patients with sensorineural deafness of varying etiologies show a spectrum ranging from total hair cell and total neuronal loss through conditions in which there is total hair cell loss and partial neuronal loss to conditions of mild sensorineural loss such as in presbycusis in which there is partial loss of both sensory and neural elements with a large number of surviving neurons. The basic unanswered question is how many neurons over what frequency distribution are necessary to provide the input which will result in speech discrimination. The second assumption is that with a full complement of normal neurons, a scheme for electrically stimulating these neurons can be devised to produce response patterns in these neurons that can be interpreted by higher order decoding centers in the auditory neurological system as intelligible speech.

FIRST GENERATION IMPLANTS

Despite these and many other unanswered questions regarding the physiology of the auditory system, work on clinical cochlear implants has continued and progressed. In 1961, William House, a pioneering otological surgeon from Los Angeles, attempted electrical stimulation of the cochlea by means of a single wire electrode placed on the promontory and on the round window during middle ear surgery. He was encouraged by these results and the earlier work by Djourno and Eyries (1957) and began work on a single channel monopolar cochlear implant electrode to be placed in the scala tympani through the round window. Some of these early attempts at electrical stimulation of the promontory or round window in patients with mixed hearing loss probably resulted in electrophonic stimulation instead of true electroneural stimulation. In electrophonic stimulation, the electrical field set up by the electrode actually produces movement of the basilar membrane of the cochlea. This movement is propagated along the basilar membrane in a normal fashion with appropriate frequency-place decoding. If there are a significant number of surviving hair cells, the patient may hear in the normal physiological manner providing both good pitch perception and speech discrimination. In true electroneural stimulation, however, the hair cells are not functioning and the electrical stimulation must directly produce responses in individual auditory nerve neurons. Therefore, some of these unusually good results with electrical stimulation of patients with mixed losses were probably due to the electrophonic mechanism rather than true electroneural hearing.

The first generation implants have in general been single channel devices. Although William House attempted several implants with four or five monopolar channels, he was unable to demonstrate an advantage for these more complex electrode systems over a single wire electrode placed in the first turn of the scala tympani of the cochlea with an indifferent electrode placed on the promontory or in the temporalis muscle (House, 1976). There were problems with insulation in a number of these early multichannel implants, resulting in shorts between channels producing, in essence, a single channel device. The multichannel electrodes required that a plug be brought out through the skin to provide individual connections to drive each channel with a different stimulus. The single channel device could be driven with an inductance coil buried just beneath the skin, which in turn is driven by similar inductance coil held in place on the exterior surface of the skin.

This eliminated the necessity for a transcutaneous plug which invariably became infected or extruded by the patient. The electrical stimulating scheme was developed by working with a very motivated patient who was fairly sophisticated in signal processing, having previously been a ham radio operator prior to the onset of his drug-induced sensorineural deafness. They worked many hours trying different stimulating schemes before finally arriving at a 16,000-Hz carrier wave which was modulated by the analogue signal representing the acoustic stimulus. This resulted in a more "natural" sounding stimulus than applying the acoustic analogue signal directly to the electrode. This still did not produce true speech discrimination.

Also in the early 1960's Robin Michelson developed a single channel cochlear implant which was also placed in the scala tympani through the round window (Michelson, 1971). It differed from the House implant in several ways. First of all, it was a bipolar implant with both electrodes placed within the cochlea. These electrodes were placed side by side and held up against the basilar membrane by means of a silicone rubber (Silastic) carrier molded to the shape of the scala tympani's first half turn. The electrical stimulus applied to the implanted electrode was simply the analogue signal representing the acoustic stimulus. Michelson also used an inductance transcutaneous system eliminating the need for percutaneous plugs.

SINGLE CHANNEL RESULTS

Because of the controversy and misunderstandings regarding the results produced by the single channel devices, the National Institute of Health commissioned Robert Bilger to study the then available single channel implanted patients. This consisted mostly of patients implanted by the House group and two implanted by Michelson. This study (Bilger et al., 1977) documented a number of real benefits produced by the single channel implants in keeping with the theoretical potential of a single channel device. First of all, they provided an auditory monitor of the environment allowing the implanted patient to discriminate certain environmental sounds. The implanted patient could now hear the knock on his door, the ring of the telephone, and the warning of a car's horn even though the information he received was mainly low frequency and rhythm. Secondly, these devices were found to be a significant aid to speech(lip)reading. Speechreading provides significant information regarding the place of articulation, but relatively little information on the rhythm of speech or the differentiation of voiced and unvoiced segments. The implant, however, was most effective in providing voiced versus nonvoiced and rhythm information, including the intensity envelope and fine timing of speech. Bilger also demonstrated that the patient's own voice quality improved when wearing the implant. The implant allowed him to monitor the intensity of his own voice and adjust it appropriately. Last, but not least, was the psychological advantage to the postlingually deaf patient. The study documented fairly good frequency discrimination below 200 Hz for all of the implanted patients. A few patients could even discriminate frequencies up to a 1000 Hz. All of these patients had a compressed dynamic range for intensity which was at least partially compensated for by the implant electronics. None demonstrated speech discrimination above a chance level on speech discrimination tests. Owen Black, part of Bilger's evaluation team, demonstrated a potential problem with the implanted patient. He demonstrated some increase in instability when the patient had his cochlear implant turned on when tested on the postulography platform. This device detects the swaying motion of the patient and the corrective maneuvers automatically taken to maintain balance. The patients themselves, however, did not complain of any instability or vertigo while using their implants.

Two of the patients implanted by House have since died of unrelated causes. The histopathological evaluation of the cochleas has been published by Johnsson et al. (1979) with some rather surprising results. The sections of the cochlea demonstrate that the implanted wire actually violated the scala media at one point. The electrode itself was encased in a sleeve of connected tissue which may explain some of the impedence changes noted in the implanted electrodes during the first 6 weeks or so of implantation. Most surprising, however, was the fact that there were almost no neurons left in this cochlea. Although no functional results for the implanted patient were published in this article, it was stated that the patient was using and gaining benefits from his implant as recently as 6 months prior to his demise.

Cochlear prosthesis work in England has centered around direct stimulation of the auditory nerve by means of a middle ear promontory electrode avoiding invasion of the cochlea itself and therefore minimizing the chance of damage to surviving neurons. The electrode is placed in the middle ear on the boney bulge (promontory) produced by the basilar turn of the cochlea. Results of this system are claimed to be similar to the results found above by Bilger with single channel devices invading the cochlea (Fourcin et al., 1979).

Critics of the single channel cochlear implants have pointed out that these devices do not take advantage of or reproduce the frequency specific (tonotopic) arrangement of the auditory neurological system. The mechanical properties of the basilar membrane of the cochlea create in essence an orderly arrangement of band pass filters with the high frequencies located at the base of the cochlea near the round and oval windows and the low frequencies located at the apex (opposite end of the basilar membrane). Each consecutive location on the basilar membrane from base to apex is therefore most sensitive to a specific frequency component of the incoming complex auditory stimulus, ranging from high frequency to low frequency as diagrammed in Figure 21.2. This is very roughly analogous to the keys on a piano. The majority of the eighth nerve neurons attach to only one inner hair cell. Each such neuron represents the motion of only one point on the basilar membrane and is therefore frequency specific. This orderly arrangement of fibers within the auditory (eighth) nerve can be observed by microelectrode auditory nerve recordings. This orderly tonotopic arrangement of frequencies has also been documented at each successive level of the auditory neurological system from the cochlear nucleus to the temporal lobe of the cerebral cortex. The arrangement, however, becomes increasingly complex at higher

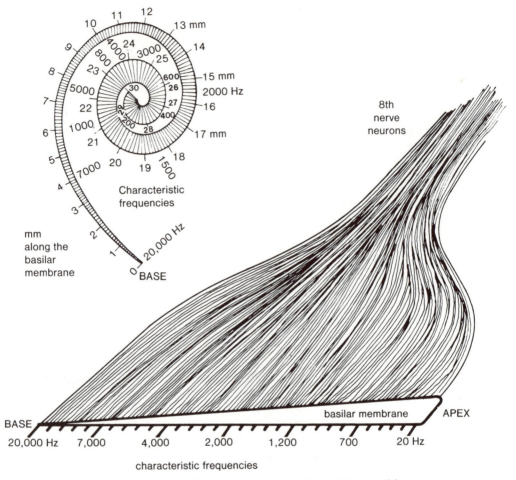

Figure 21.2. Tonotopic organization of the cochlea.

levels. In designing a cochlear prosthesis, the stimulating electrode should consist of a number of discrete channels designed to stimulate small discrete groups of auditory nerve fibers so that this frequency specific arrangement may be utilized to the greatest advantage.

Pitch perception itself, however, is not solely a tonotopic phenomenon. A second theory for pitch perception comes into play for low frequency acoustic stimuli below approximately 500 Hz. This theory is known as the volley theory and proposes a neural timing mechanism which can establish the timing interval between waves or peaks of the acoustic stimulus thereby determining the period of the stimulus which can then be interpreted as pitch. Single eighth nerve neuron studies have documented the presence of this volley

information in neurons responding to low frequency stimulation up to 1000 Hz. Between 1000 Hz and 4000 Hz there is a progressive loss of this volley information. A well-designed cochlear implant system should, therefore, be able to transmit both the volley information as well as the place or tonotopic information to the appropriate frequency specific regions of the auditory nerve. This will require a multichannel system.

The monopolar/bipolar configurations for single channel cochlear prosthesis are straightforward. In monopolar stimulation the active electrode is either within the cochlea or on the promontory. A return or common electrode is placed elsewhere in the body, usually in the region of the temporalis muscle or sometimes in the eustachian tube region of the middle ear. This creates a fairly large electrical field with a large amount of shunting of the current through the relatively low resistance of the perilymph fluid of the cochlea resulting in the stimulation of a fairly large number of neurons as they enter the cochlea. Black and Clark (1980) have demonstrated that the current which is most closely correlated to the neural response is that current which leaves the scala tympani, presumably through the habenula perforata through which the individual nerve fibers enter the cochlea. The bipolar system places both the active and the return electrode within the scala tympani as diagrammed in Figure 21.3. This produces a much smaller electrical field than monopolar stimulation and, therefore, has the advantage of stimulating a smaller, more discreet population of eighth nerve neurons. Bipolar stimulation, however, has the disadvantage of requiring higher stimulating currents because a fair amount of current passes directly between the

two electrodes and only a small amount of the current actually passes through the habenula perforata where the neurons are stimulable. In monopolar stimulation, all of the current leaves the cochlea presumably mainly by the habenula perforata route. Multielectrode systems can be much more complex as seen in Figure 21.4. The monopolar configuration is the simplest (Fig. 21.4A). Multiple electrodes are placed at specific distances along the basilar membrane. The electrical stimulus (stimulating one of these electrodes at a time) produces an electrical field between the active electrode within the scala tympani and the common electrode outside the cochlea. The discreteness of the responding population of neurons is determined by the amount of electrical spread within the scala tympani which has a lower electrical resistance than the pathway through the habenula perforata. In cases in which more than one of the electrodes within the scala tympani are stimulated simultaneously at different volt-

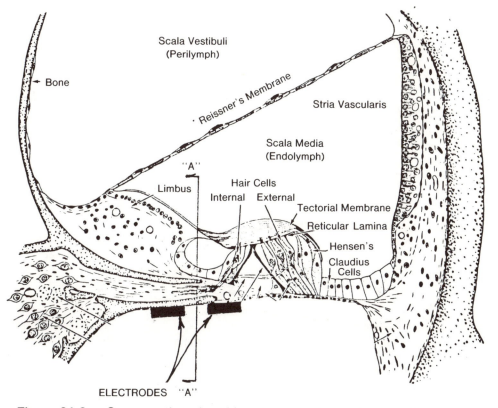

Figure 21.3.   Cross section of cochlea showing bipolar electrode placement.

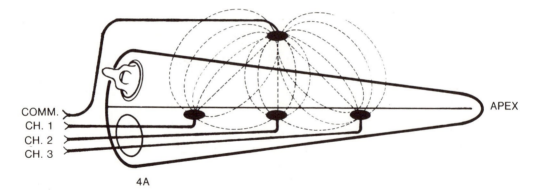

4A

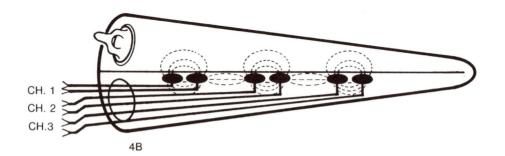

4B

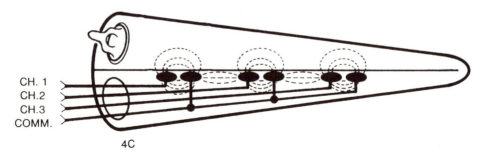

4C

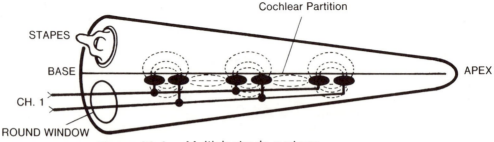

Figure 21.4. Multielectrode systems.

ages, a significant amount of shunting of current between electrodes can take place. In the bipolar configuration (Fig. 21.4B), each channel consists of a pair of electrodes within the scala tympani. The theoretical result to stimulation with one electrode pair produces a fairly discrete responding population of neurons. Each electrode pair represents a specific frequency region. In simultaneous stimulation, there again can be a fair amount of shunting of current between adjacent channels, depending on the ratio of the spacing of bipolar pairs to the spacing of adjacent channels. The pseudo-bipolar configuration (Fig. 21.4C) is a compromise between monopolar and bipolar configurations and represents an attempt to minimize the number of conductors which must be placed within the cochlea and still retain some of the discreteness of the bipolar stimulation pattern. There is a bipolar pair of electrodes for each stimulus channel; however, only the active electrode for each channel has its own discrete conductor. The return electrodes are all tied together in one common return. This allows a moderate amount of shunting of the return pathway but keeps it within the cochlea, producing a discrete electrical field which is larger than the true bipolar field, but smaller than a true monopolar stimulation scheme. Finally, there is a multielectrode single channel stimulation scheme (Fig. 21.4D) as currently in use by Michelson. In this case, all of the active electrodes are tied together and all the return electrodes are tied together. This theoretically produces the same response from all responding neurons.

SECOND GENERATION IMPLANTS

In the early 1960's while House was working on his single channel cochlear implant, Blair Simmons was working on a 4–5 channel rigid electrode to be implanted directly into the auditory nerve by means of a surgical approach into the modiolus through the round window niche (a middle ear surgical approach). Simmons (1966) presented a very detailed report of his findings with implanted patients and their perceptive experience. Although there were different qualities and pitches perceived with different electrode placements, these placements were not reproducible from patient to patient. Each implanted patient required preliminary mapping of his electrode system for its specific sensations prior to attempting a coding scheme for speech. The modiolar implant system has not to date resulted in speech discrimination. The advantages of the modiolar system are: (1) it places the electrode

surfaces in direct contact with the neurons to be stimulated, thereby requiring the lowest currents for stimulation; and (2) direct placement of the electrode into the eighth nerve bundle which potentially contains neurons representing the entire speech frequency range avoids the mechanical problems associated with reaching the low frequency neurons with a scala tympani electrode. There are a number of disadvantages to the modiolar implant: (1) the frequency representation of neurons within the eighth nerve at this point is roughly a spiral arrangement with high frequencies on the outside and low frequencies toward the inside of the nerve trunk. This is not a truly spiral arrangement and clumping of frequencies does exist. This produces, however, a very close proximity of neurons of all frequencies. It is, therefore, very difficult to discretely stimulate small populations of frequency specific neurons without stimulating neurons of vastly differing frequency representation. (2) Placing the electrode directly into the auditory nerve probably produces significant damage to a number of neurons just from the process of the implantation; and (3) this approach theoretically provides for a more direct access of infection to the central nervous system by producing a potential direct communication between the middle ear space and the internal auditory canal.

In France, Chouard has developed a different approach to the multichannel problem. He implants between 7 and 12 electrodes directly into the cochlea by means of individual burr holes in the outer wall of the cochlea. This entails a dual surgical approach both through the middle ear and through a middle cranial fossa craniotomy, elevating the temporal lobe for direct access to the backside of the first and second turns of the cochlea to reach the speech frequency regions. He uses monopolar electrodes with small pieces of silicone rubber placed on each side of the electrode within the cochlea to block longitudinal spread of current within the cochlea. Not much has been written about his coding system, but intensity is apparently coded as the pulse rate of the stimulus to each electrode. Chouard claims up to 100% discrimination for his patients on learned word lists. The main advantage of this approach is that it produces direct access to the frequency-specific regions of the cochlea, especially those of low frequency. There are several disadvantages to this approach. The middle cranial fossa approach requires intracranial surgery in which the temporal lobe is elevated extradurally. The middle fossa craniotomy has a certain incidence of complications, including meningitis and temporal lobe epilepsy, although these complications are very rare. This approach traumatizes the cochlea in a number of locations. At the current time, there is no documentation of the degree of cochlear or neural damage produced by this approach. It has been demonstrated by Schindler and Merzenich (1974) that damage to the osseous spiral lamina or basilar membrane produces significant neural degeneration. The transcutaneous plugs used in Chouard's patients to connect the multiple electrodes to their drivers became infected and had to be removed. Although a transcutaneous stimulating system has been defined, it is very expensive and results with this system are not available to this author at this time. No independent investigator has evaluated these implanted patients to confirm their actual speech discrimination.

The remaining second generation multichannel systems have all utilized the round window/scala tympani approach. Eddington et al. (1978) published a detailed study of the sensations produced by changes in electrode position and in stimulus parameters for multichannel cochlear implants. They studied patients previously implanted by House and also patients implanted by Brackman with up to 7 channels, including one patient with a unilateral sensorineural deafness. They found that stimulus rate when stimulating with either a square wave or a sinusoidal stimulus at rates of 80 Hz to 800 Hz were interpreted as variation in pitch. Below about 80 Hz, perception was that of a "flutter." There is also a pitch sensation attributed to the position of the electrode within the cochlea with the more apical electrodes perceived as lower pitches and the more basal electrodes. They also demonstrated an interaction between electrode position and stimulus frequency. When an apical (low frequency) electrode was stimulated with a high frequency stimulus, it was perceived as a higher pitch than a more basal electrode (high frequency) stimulated with a low frequency stimulus. They therefore confirmed both the volley and the place codes for pitch as well as an interaction between the two parameters. Both threshold and subjective loudness appeared to be related to the charge per phase delivered by an electrical stimulus between the frequencies of 100 and 1000 Hz. Using sinusoidal stimuli in which the charge per phase delivered with low frequency stimulation is greater than the charge per phase for high frequency stimulation both thresholds were lower and subjective loudness greater for the lower frequency stimulation. When using square wave (constant current) stimulation in which the duration of the biphasic square wave was kept constant and, therefore, the charge per phase kept constant and only the repetition rate (frequency) varied, there was minimal change in threshold and subjective loudness when changing this repetition rate. Although most of these studies were performed in a monopolar mode, some bipolar stimulation was used with similar results. The bipolar stimulation was perceived as a more pure pitch sensation than monopolar stimulation.

Graham Clark's group from Australia (Clark et al., 1981) have designed a multichannel electrode consisting of consecutive platinum foil rings wrapped around a silicone rubber cylinder with the conductors to the rings carried within the center of the cylinder. Every other ring is connected to a common return producing a pseudo-bipolar configuration with a total of 10 channels (20 rings). In this case the current fields are produced between the active electrode and the ground return on either side of the active electrode (Fig. 21.5). Studies of patients implanted with this electrode system produced findings similar to Eddington's demonstrating both the volley and place codes for pitch. Clark, however, found that the differences in electrode placement had a certain speech formant quality and therefore has used electrode position to represent formant frequency. His processing consists of extracting the fundamental frequency and energy of the voicing source and representing this as the electrical stimulus frequency and intensity. He then determines the dominant spectral content of speech in the mid-frequency range (second formant)

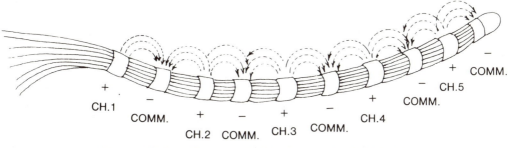

Figure 21.5. The pseudo-bipolar electrode (Clark).

and selects the electrode to be stimulated based on this dominant spectral peak. He has found in two implanted patients that this stimulus scheme provides a 10% isolated word recognition and a 20% phoneme in isolated word recognition. He found that this device is most useful as an aid to lipreading.

Burian's group in Vienna, Austria, has developed a multichannel electrode system consisting of eight bipolar channels which may be stimulated either in a bipolar or pseudo-bipolar manner (Burian et al., 1979). This electrode consists of a bundle of wires molded into a thin silicone rubber carrier with electrode surfaces consisting of small platinum balls located on opposite sides of the carrier in a staggered fashion. This provides for maximum separation of electrode pairs and, according to Hochmair, minimizes the effect of changes in the electrical field produced by rotation of the electrode within the scala tympani. The stimulation scheme is not documented in the currently available articles, but in part consists of a pulse code generated on zero crossings of the analogue (or filtered analogue) wave form. A speech discrimination as high as 50% has been claimed by this group. These results have not been confirmed or refuted by an independent evaluation team.

Michelson's group in San Francisco has also developed a multichannel bipolar electrode consisting of a bundle of wires with mushroom-shaped tips in a silicone rubber carrier molded slightly smaller than the diameter of the scala tympani. The electrode positioning is different from the Hochmair electrode. The electrode surfaces are placed radially at 90° from each other and aligned so that one electrode resides under the basilar membrane and the second electrode adjacent to the modiolus. The electrode is designed to retain this orientation during insertion. There has been difficulty, however, retaining this orientation in the most apical electrodes. The electrodes consist of eight bipolar channels and have been tested in both a multichannel and a single channel configuration (the same signal is simultaneously delivered to each electrode pair). At this time, the multichannel configuration requires a percutaneous plug, but the single channel configuration utilizes inductance coupling, avoiding the need for the plug and its associated problems. Several patients have been implanted with this system, yielding some interesting results. The differences between single channel and multichannel configurations were not as great as would be anticipated. The stimulus used is an analogue signal with dynamic compression representing (1) the acoustic signal for the single channel configuration, or (2) a band pass filtered speech signal passed at a frequency representing the electrode placement for each channel in the multichannel configuration. The tonal quality produced by the multichannel configuration was more "pure tone like" than the single channel configuration (stimulating all the channels simultaneously). Speech discrimination did not differ significantly between the two modalities. Speech discrimination of words in sentences approximated 50% in both modality. Disconnecting any of the channels in either modality produced a significant decrease in speech discrimination. This was especially true for the more apical (low frequency) channels. Rhyme tests demonstrated that these patients had most difficulty recognizing speech sounds with the same first formant but differing second formants. The patient with the better discrimination had actually lost his hearing slowly over a period of years, losing the high frequencies first and progressing down to the low frequencies. One can, therefore, speculate that this patient had indeed learned to function with only rhythm and low frequency (first formant) type of information and carried this learned speech recognition pattern over to his implant stimulation. These results, however, are significantly better than they obtained with their earlier bipolar single channel device or any of the single channel devices evaluated by Bilger.

At this time, it is advantageous to further define the problem in terms of the physical parameters of the speech signal, the psychoacoustics of speech perception, and the response patterns of single eighth nerve neurons to speech stimulation.

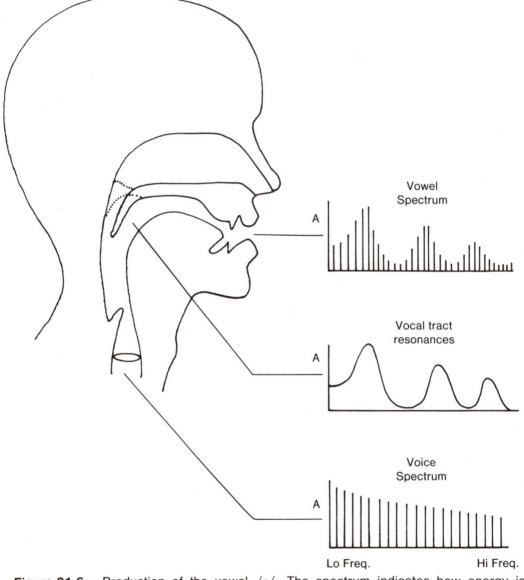

Figure 21.6. Production of the vowel /ɛ/. The spectrum indicates how energy is distributed in frequency.

THE SPEECH SIGNAL

The objective of speech activity is to produce meaningful groups and sequences of acoustic signals or sounds—meaningful because they conform to a pre-agreed upon common code—the language.

A speaker produces the speech sounds by regulating the airstream as it passes from the lungs to the atmosphere. This regulation is accomplished by movements of the various parts of the vocal mechanism: lips, jaw, tongue, soft palate, pharynx, vocal folds, and lungs. This degree of flexibility in the vocal mechanism permits the production of quite a wide range of sounds which differ significantly. Speakers of English generally have the ability to produce some 40 different phonemes (sounds which can effect a change in meaning).

The sounds of speech can be categorized into two major classes—the continuants, sounds which can be sustained and can be produced by a nonchanging vocal tract, and the noncontinuants, sounds which are produced by the vocal tract changing in certain specified manners.

Continuants might be voiced (airstream modulated by the oscillation of the vocal folds or glottis) or voiceless (airstream forced through a narrow constriction or over an edge so as to produce turbulent airflow (heard as frication or noise). Figure 21.6 shows the production of a voiced continuant—the vowel /e/ as in "bed." The airstream from the lungs is chopped into repetitive pulses by the oscillatory action of the vocal folds producing a sound with a fundamental frequency (vocal pitch) and rich in harmonics. This signal is then further modified by the vocal tract which exhibits certain resonances corresponding to its particular shape. The vocal tract shape acts as a filter and is best understood by comparing the spectrum of the sound at the vocal fold source to the spectrum of the output sound at the lips. The difference between the source spectrum and the output spectrum is the vocal tract transfer function, or spectral envelope. The prominences in the spectral envelope correspond to the principal resonances or formants of the vocal tract. We note that the output speech sound can be satisfactorily described in terms of the characteristics of the source (vocal frequency or pitch, and intensity) and the characteristics of the spectral envelope (formant frequencies). The same vowel sound /e/ is shown in Figure 21.7 in spectrographic form. The prominences or formants in the spectrum in Figure 21.6 appear as dark bands in the spectrogram of Figure 21.7.

Voiceless continuant sounds are produced by the vocal tract filtering a voiceless sound source. The voiceless sound source is usually produced by forcing air through a small constriction in the tract, which results in turbu-

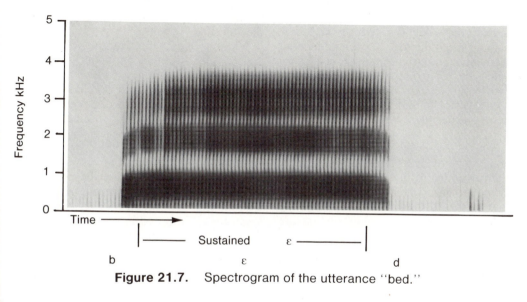

Figure 21.7. Spectrogram of the utterance "bed."

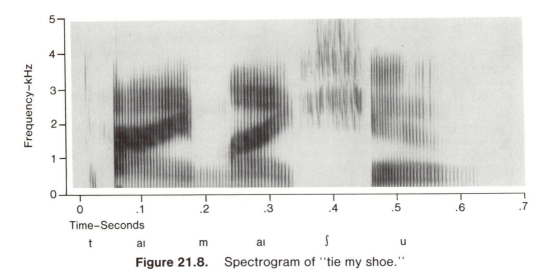

Figure 21.8. Spectrogram of "tie my shoe."

lent air flow and a noisy, fricative sound. Some examples of voiceless continuants are /h/ as in "hay" in which a turbulent fricative source is created at the glottis (sometimes called aspiration), /ʃ/ as in "shoe" in which the frication is produced at the alveolar ridge just behind the upper incisors, and /f/ as in "fee" in which the turbulent source occurs at the constriction formed by the lower lip and upper incisors.

Noncontinuant sounds, such as most of the consonants, are distinguished by the manner in which the vocal tract configuration is changed. These speech sounds differ on the basis of the timing of events and the rate at which changes take place. The basic notion of representing a sound in terms of its source signal and spectral envelope can still be used to characterize noncontinuant sounds if we consider the changing sound to be represented by a sequence of short-term spectra, i.e., the spectra of short intervals of sound rather than spectra of long continuous intervals.

Figure 21.8 shows the spectrogram of the utterance "tie my shoe" illustrating a number of the perceptual distinctions which have to be made to "hear" the correct message. The release of the /t/ tongue tip closure at the alveolar ridge results in a burst of pressure which appears as a sharp line across almost all frequencies. Following this burst, low intensity frication at the glottis (aspiration) takes place while the tongue moves toward the position appropriate for the next vowel. Voicing begins at the time 0.047 second. If the voice onset time (from burst to onset of voicing) were significantly less, the sound would be perceived as the voiced plosive /d/ rather than the voiceless plosive /t/. The formants are then seen to change in frequency during the production of the diphthong /ai/. They change sharply as the labial closure of /m/ is formed and then released to produce the second diphthong /ai/ in "my." Finally, voicing stops and air is forced through a constriction formed by the tongue at the alveolar ridge to produce the fricative /ʃ/, and then voicing begins again as the tongue moves to the appropriate position for the vowel /u/ in "shoe."

We note that in this example, which consists principally of noncontinuant sounds, the aspects of the speech signal which are important to perception are again the characteristics of the source signal (voiced/voiceless/both) and the spectrum, changing in time.

Speech Perception

With what resolution or precision must the spectrum and the source signal be represented to provide satisfactory speech perception? The question of precision in representing a spectrum is illustrated in Figure 21.9. Figure 21.9a shows the spectrum to be represented. In Figure 21.9b the spectrum is represented by a single value (the amplitude of a single full-band channel). In Figure 21.9c the spec-

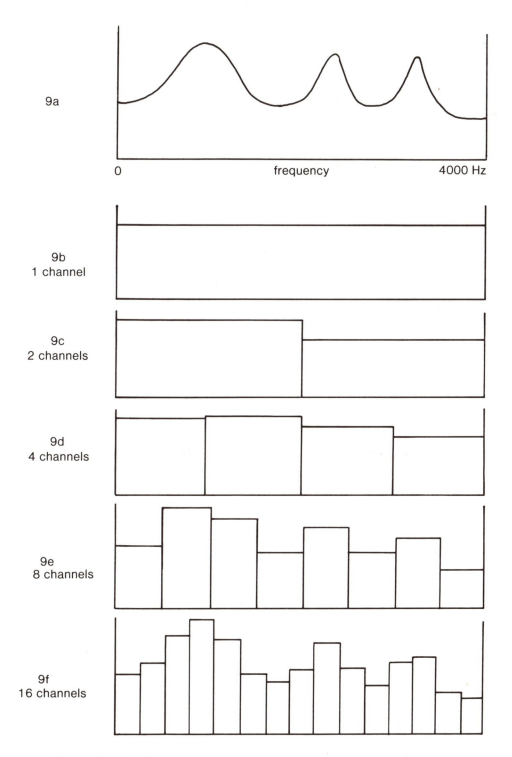

9a

9b
1 channel

9c
2 channels

9d
4 channels

9e
8 channels

9f
16 channels

0   frequency   4000 Hz

Figure 21.9.   Spectrum represented by varying number of channels.

trum is represented by two values (the amplitudes of the two half-band channels). As the number of channels is increased the representation becomes more similar to the original spectrum, the precision—or number of spectrum channels required to adequately represent the spectrum—is provided by the results of research in the design of channel vocoders (Schroeder, 1964). The channel vocoder analyzes and reproduces speech in terms of a source signal and a number of spectrum channels. Vocoder studies found that a very satisfactory speech signal could be provided (intelligibility of 95%) by representing the spectrum in terms of 15 channel amplitudes, at a rate of 50 spectra/sec. Fewer channels, or a slower spectrum rate, resulted in significant reductions in intelligibility (Flanagan et al., 1979).

The precision with which the source signal must be reproduced for satisfactory preservation of speech information is illustrated in Figure 21.10. Figure 21.10*A* is the speech signal resulting from the utterance "pie mice." The basic information in the source signal which is important to perception is the identification of the source signal type as voiced or voiceless, the periodicity or vocal pitch of the voiced portions, and the intensity. This information may be retained in a speech envelope representation of the signal. A speech envelope of "pie mice" is shown in Figure 21.10*B*. The speech envelope is the rectified and smoothed version of the speech pressure waveform. The degree of smoothing (the time resolution) which is imposed on the envelope is an important factor in determining how much of the source information is retained. In the case of Figure 21.10*B*, little smoothing is present, the time resolution is fine enough to follow the periodicity of the waveform, clearly indicating pitch and distinguishing voiced portions from nonvoiced portions. Figure 21.10*C* shows a speech envelope signal in which the time resolution is not as fine, the pressure waveform is more smoothed, and it is difficult to distinguish voiced from unvoiced portions of the signal.

From these considerations we are able to make a statement concerning the precision with which the source signal should be represented for satisfactory speech perception. The precision can be stated either in terms of a smoothing time constant (the time that a

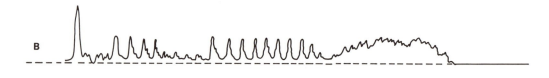

Figure 21.10. Speech signal from "pie mice" (*A*); speech envelope with short time constant (*B*); speech envelope with long time constant (*C*).

system, responding to an amplitude step, takes to reach 63% of that step) or in terms of the rate at which independent samples of the high resolution speech envelope must be taken. A smoothing time constant of 2 msec, or independent samples of the speech envelope taken every 2 msec, is sufficient to preserve the source information necessary for satisfactory perception.

Thus we have concluded that in order to provide adequate speech perception, a speech signal may be represented in short time spectrum and source signal form, with the follow-

ing precision:

> *Short-time spectrum precision*
>
> Frequency range: 0–8 kHz
> Analysis interval: 20 msec
> Number of frequency channels: 15 (not uniformly distributed in frequency)
>
> *Source signal (speech envelope) precision*
>
> Smoothing time constant: 2 msec
> Sampling rate: 50 samples/sec

It is of interest to relate these requirements to the physiology of the cochlea. Figure 21.11

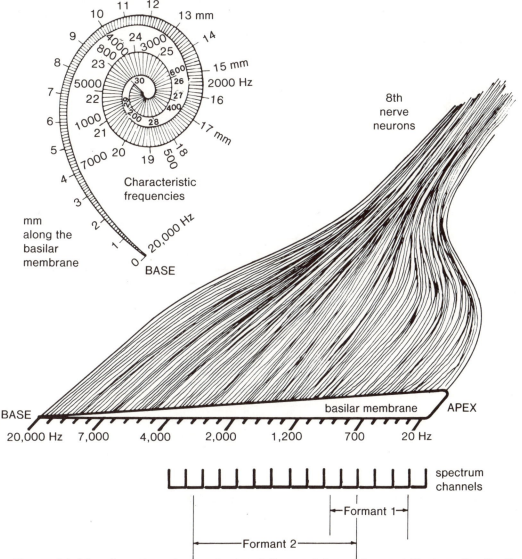

Figure 21.11. Location of speech signal (formant 1 and formant 2) along the basilar membrane.

shows the tonotopic frequency map of the cochlea with the speech frequency range and 15 spectrum channels superimposed. Note that the speech perception region of the cochlea lies along the more apical portion of the basilar membrane and not the basal portion which is more accessible from the round window. It should also be noted that the normal cochlear process provides more than adequate time resolution to represent either 50 short time spectra/sec or 500 amplitude samples/sec of the speech envelope.

Neural Responses

Many studies have been published since Kiang's original monograph of 1965 (Kiang et al., 1965) studying the responses of single auditory nerve neurons to acoustic stimulation. One of the early criticisms of the cochlear implant endeavors has been that the cochlear implants have frequently not taken advantage of the known coding as demonstrated in these single auditory neuron responses. Since the discharge patterns of a single neuron is probabilistic in nature and since its response during stimulation is frequently difficult to separate from the probabilistic spontaneous discharge pattern, a basic statistical technique called the post-stimulus-time (PST) histogram has been developed to demonstrate the response as shown in Figure 21.12. This figure demonstrates a 538-Hz neuron's response to a tone burst at its characteristic frequency (CF); i.e., the frequency to which the neuron responds at its lowest threshold. The top trace is the analogue signal (a continuously varying signal) representing the acoustic stimulus. The next 16 traces represent the single auditory neuron's response to each of 16 consecutive repetitions of the stimulus. In this digital response, the only information delivered is whether or not a response has occurred at a specific point in

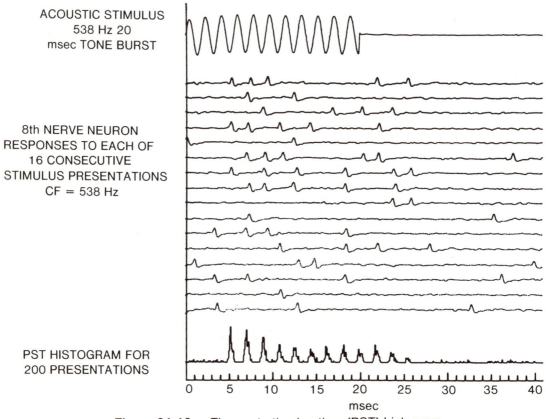

ACOUSTIC STIMULUS
538 Hz 20
msec TONE BURST

8th NERVE NEURON
RESPONSES TO EACH OF
16 CONSECUTIVE
STIMULUS PRESENTATIONS
CF = 538 Hz

PST HISTOGRAM FOR
200 PRESENTATIONS

Figure 21.12. The post-stimulus-time (PST) histogram.

time. The amplitude and shape of the individual response is unimportant. This also illustrates the probabilistic nature of the response where the probability of a response occurring at any one instant is roughly proportional to the analogue signal at that instant. The basic procedure for constructing the PST histogram is to repeat the stimulus a large number of times (200 in this case) and carefully record in very fine time gradations when the neural response occurred in relationship to the stimulus. The responses that are not related to the stimulus are distributed randomly in time while those responses directly due to the stimulus add in time as shown in the bottom trace of this figure. In comparing the response to the stimulus, there is a time lag in the response due largely to the time it takes the displacement wave to travel along the basilar membrane to reach the location of the neuron. There are also more responses at the onset of the stimulus

than at the end, even though the stimulus is of constant amplitude. This is the well-documented adaptation effect (Smith, 1979).

Each single neuron responds only to acoustic stimuli with frequencies within its own specific frequency range. This frequency range can be plotted as the stimulus intensity threshold for each frequency and is called the neuron's frequency threshold curve or tuning curve. This frequency threshold curve can be approximated by a band pass filter with adjustable attenuation slopes for modeling purposes as demonstrated in Figure 21.13. Some of the standard features of frequency threshold curves are: (1) a very sharply tuned tip at the neuron's CF and (2) the high frequency skirt is usually much steeper than the low frequency skirt or tail of the tuning curve. This is especially true for the more high frequency neurons and less so for low frequency neurons.

Based on the large volume of eighth nerve

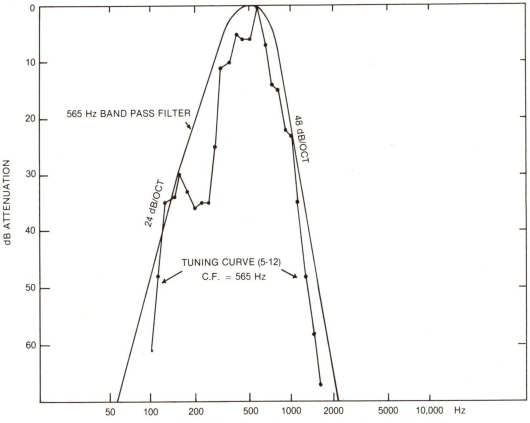

Figure 21.13. Approximation of the filter characteristics of a single auditory neuron.

single neuron data available in the literature, a number of models have been proposed to relate the acoustic signal input to the neural output. The model we have proposed (Parkins, 1979) is shown in Figure 21.14. The incoming signal I_t is separated into its frequency components by the mechanical filter of the basilar membrane and its interaction with the hair cell. The traveling wave and filter function produce a phase lag between F_t and I_t greatest at the low frequency end of the spectrum. The band pass signal (F_t) is half wave rectified by the hair cell's stimulatory displacement phase and low pass filtered by the 1-msec refractory period of the hair cell or hair cell neuron transmission. The final hair cell processing stage may be considered to be an adaptation processor. The resulting signal (H_t) represents the probability

of the neural response. H_t is input into a number of individual neuron spike generators which are probabilistic with their discharge rates being both proportional to the amplitude of the probability signal (H_t) and also to the time since the last neural response.

The results of each of these processing stages are compared to real data from a 538-Hz characteristic frequency eighth nerve neuron in Figure 21.15. The first trace is the acoustic stimulus, a sharp rise/fall time tone burst at the neuron's characteristic frequency. The second trace F_t demonstrates the result of the band pass filter shaped to the neuron's frequency threshold curve (tuning curve). The filter and basilar membrane latency shifts account for the latency of the neuron's response. The filter effect also produces a more gradual rise/fall time with some post-

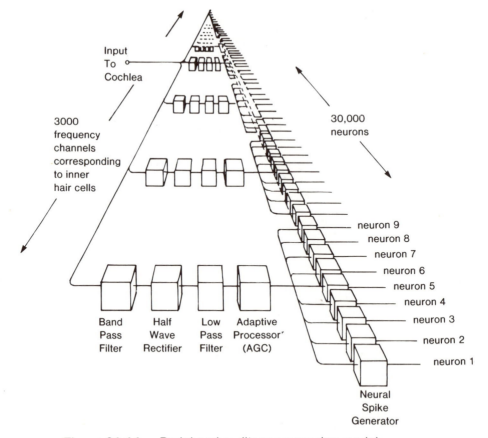

Figure 21.14.   Peripheral auditory processing model.

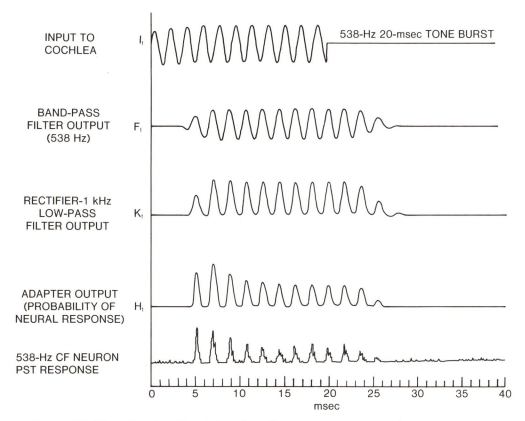

Figure 21.15. Results of peripheral auditory processing model (low frequency).

stimulus ringing. The 1-kHz low pass filter has little effect on this 538-Hz waveform in K_t. The adaptation effect seen in H_t emphasizes the onset of the tone burst and improves the fit of the processed analogue signal with the last trace which is the neuron's actual response to the stimulus plotted as a PST histogram. This processing model also predicts the responses of high frequency neurons as seen in Figure 21.16 illustrating a neuron with a characteristic frequency of 3045 Hz. Here the low pass filter has a much more prominent effect seen in the third trace (K_t) because the characteristic frequency is higher than the low pass filter cutoff frequency (1 kHz). The output of the low pass filter shows a change in level, following the envelope of the original signal, but very little of the 3045-Hz high frequency component. The closer the high frequency component is to the cutoff frequency of the low pass filter, the greater

the amplitude of the high frequency component. Again, the adaptation effect is necessary to match the processed signal to the neuron's PST response.

Figure 21.17 demonstrates the affect of this processing scheme on a more complex stimulus, speech. The top trace is the first 70 msec of the word "boot." The importance of the adaptation effect is seen in the difference between the third and fourth traces. The adaptation effect strongly emphasizes the burst of the "B" and the timing of the onset of voicing at the beginning of the "U." The emphasis of this timing is also seen in the PST histogram in the bottom trace. This timing is very important in the differentiation between voiced and nonvoiced consonants in speech, and may be very important in the design of the cochlear implant processor.

The PST histogram technique for demonstrating the relationship between the neural

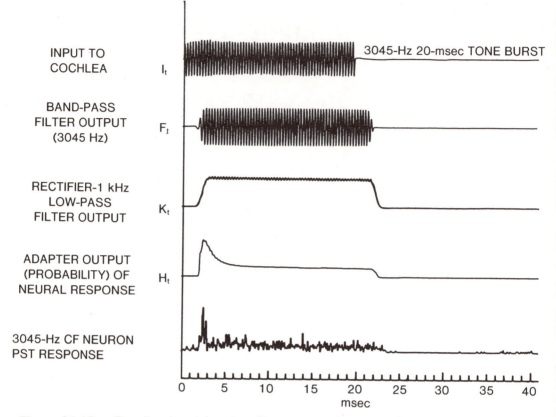

INPUT TO
COCHLEA I_t

BAND-PASS
FILTER OUTPUT
(3045 Hz) F_t

RECTIFIER-1 kHz
LOW-PASS
FILTER OUTPUT K_t

ADAPTER OUTPUT
(PROBABILITY) OF H_t
NEURAL RESPONSE

3045-Hz CF NEURON
PST RESPONSE

3045-Hz 20-msec TONE BURST

Figure 21.16.   Results of peripheral auditory processing model (high frequency).

response and the stimulus entails adding the responses of one neuron to many repetitions of the same stimulus resulting in the PST histogram shown in Figure 21.12. The auditory neurological system obviously does not function in this fashion since it must decode one isolated presentation of the stimulus. Because of the probabilistic nature of the neural response and because adjacent neurons vary little in frequency selectivity and latency, one can assume that sampling the responses of 100 adjacent neurons to one stimulus presentation will produce a histogram which will be very similar to one produced by 100 responses from one neuron. It would, however, be a "simultaneous" or "instantaneous" histogram rather than the usual "sequential" PST histogram. One could, therefore, consider each of the individual eighth nerve responses shown in Figure 21.12 to have been recorded from 16 adjacent individual neurons. This would be more pertinent to the topic of au-

ditory coding since it is much more likely that the central auditory system "listens" to the "simultaneous histogram" from a population group rather than perform a lengthy temporal integration necessary for a sequential analysis of individual neurons (although the temporal integration of loudness over a 200-msec period is a well-documented phenomenon). The goal for electrical stimulation, therefore, should be to produce an instantaneous responding neural fiber sum which is proportional to the output of the signal processing model H_t at any point in time.

Kiang and Moxon (1972) have demonstrated that single auditory neurons respond to electrical stimulation with an all or none response as do axons elsewhere in the neurological system. They have also demonstrated that the pulse rate of any specific neuron exhibits a very narrow dynamic range in response to electrical stimulation. Based on this information, it is safe to assume that none

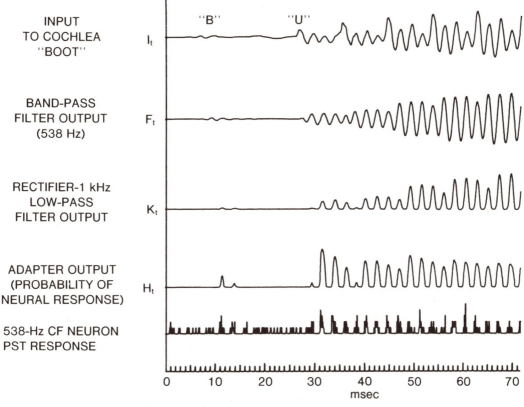

Figure 21.17.   Peripheral auditory processing model response to speech.

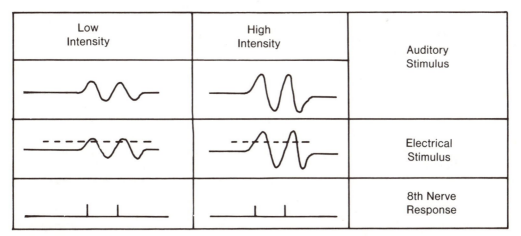

Figure 21.18.   Theoretical neural response to electrical stimulation using the acoustic waveform.

of the cochlear implant stimulating systems described above have resulted in the type of neural fiber modulation proposed in the previous paragraph. Most of the stimulus schemes use an analogue stimulus. Systems using the acoustic signal, such as Michelson's, theoretically produce one synchronous discharge from all of the neurons that are within

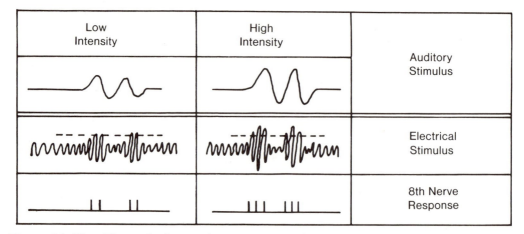

Low Intensity	High Intensity	
		Auditory Stimulus
		Electrical Stimulus
		8th Nerve Response

Figure 21.19. Theoretical neural response to electrical stimulation with a high frequency carrier modulated by the acoustic waveform.

the threshold region of the stimulation electrode when the analogue signal reaches the neuron's current threshold level. For stimuli under 1000 Hz, and especially for the fundamental frequency in speech, each neuron within threshold of the stimulating channel should respond at a specific point on the rising phase of the stimulus (Fig. 21.18). Even considering that some neurons will have higher thresholds than others, one can still hypothesize that the responding neurons will discharge only during the rising phase of the stimulus. This synchronous response of neurons is in distinct contrast to the PST histogram responses to both pure tone and speech stimulation as shown in Figures 21.15 and 21.17. Neurons responding to acoustical stimulation tend to fire during the complete "on" half cycle of the stimulus. The House technique of using a 16-kHz carrier wave should produce a response that more closely approaches the physiological response to acoustic stimulation (Fig. 21.19). This will produce more neural responses during the "on" phase of the stimulus for low frequency stimulus components. This system does not take into consideration the refractory period (1 msec) of a neuron to electrical stimulation or attempt to modulate the population of neurons. The population response pattern will be quite unpredictable and again will occur mostly on the rising phase of the stimulus wave form. Much more attention needs to be given at this time to the coding for the electrical stimulus.

COCHLEAR IMPLANTATION: A CLINICAL SOLUTION?

The fundamental questions are, "Has the cochlear implant reached the stage in its development where its benefits outweigh its potential problems? Should the cochlear implant be used now as a clinical treatment modality for patients with sensorineural deafness?" Several cochlear implants by several investigators in Europe are currently being used to treat patients with sensorineural deafness. In the United States, the main force for clinical implant treatment has been from the House Ear Institute in Los Angeles. Their single channel monopolar prosthesis has been made available to a limited number of clinicians (coinvestigators) around the country for implantation into profoundly deaf patients who fit the following strict criteria: (1) The patient must not have any useful speech discrimination in either ear even when aided with the most powerful hearing aid available. (2) The patient must be postlingually deaf and be highly motivated with no psychological problems as evaluated by psychological testing. (3) Hearing loss in the better ear must be at least 90 dB at 500 Hz and 100 dB at 1 and 2 kHz. (4) There must be no response to acoustical stimulation as measured by electrocochleography (indicating a sensory loss). (5) Transtympanic stimulation of the promontory using a transtympanic electrode under local anesthesia must produce an auditory sensation suggesting a surviving population of neurons (House et al., 1979). Each implanted patient undergoes approximately 80 hours of rehabilitation over a 4-month period following implantation. This rehabilitation is designed to help the patient understand the sounds that he hears and help him use this information as cues in lip(speech)reading. The results of these single channel implants have been well documented by Bilger (1977). Although single channel wire implants have been removed from the cochlea and replaced without apparent change in the results of the electrical stimulation, the question of whether implantation of a cochlea causes enough neural damage to make it unfit for reimplantation with a better multichannel device remains unanswered. The proponents of implantation now state that since the implant is only placed in one ear, and in most cases, the worse ear, there is still one ear left for future implantation of a better device. The decision on whether the advantages of the single channel device outweigh the disadvantages must be made by the patient and the physician involved. The multielectrode Michelson prosthesis is currently being implanted only at San Francisco. At the present time, it should be considered as still in the clinical research stage, although it too may be available shortly as a treatment modality.

A number of nontrivial problems must be solved before a cochlear prosthesis with consistently good speech discrimination will be available. First there are the mechanical problems of the electrode itself. A multichannel electrode 30 mm long which can consistently reach the second turn of the cochlea atraumatically to stimulate the 300-Hz region has not yet been designed. It must position the electrode surfaces in a manner that will produce the lowest possible threshold for nearby neurons and be very specific in the population stimulated. The problem of determining the number of necessary channels has not been totally solved nor has the problem of placing the large number of conductors required by these channels through the small diameter of the round window and scala tympani. Sixteen wires has been the maximum limit in most of the current generation of implants. Thirty conductors would be required by a 15 channel bipolar system. There are also basic problems involving the materials themselves. An adequate insulation is

needed which provides the necessary electrical insulation, does not break down over time, and is biocompatible. Although several methods of transmitting the complex multichannel signals fom an external source to the implanted electrodes have been proposed, this problem is far from being solved. A simple induction system as used for the single channel device does not have the data rate necessary for multichannel stimulation. The percutaneous plug, although it may be used temporarily during attempts to solve the coding problems, is not a long-term biocompatible device and is not acceptable for a clinical treatment modality. A most important problem is the necessary code for electrical stimulation. This coding must recognize and take advantage of the appropriate cues in the speech signal as well as make use of the current knowledge of the digital coding of the acoustic signal at the neurological level. This requires some rather complex analogue to digital processing. One may conclude then that the day of the cochlear implant has not yet arrived. It is, however, highly likely that this day will come in the very near future and that the "bionic ear" will be a reality.

References

Bilger, R.C. Evaluation of subjects presently fitted with implanted auditory prothesis. *Ann. Otol. Rhinol. Laryngol. Suppl. 38*, 1977, 86.

Black, R.C., and Clark, G.M. Differential electrical excitation of the auditory nerve. *J. Acoust. Soc. Am.*, 1980, *67*, 868–874.

Burian, K., Hochmair, E., Hochmair-Desoyer, I., and Lessel, M.R. Designing of and experience with multichannel cochlear implants. *Acta Otolaryngol.*, 1979, *87*, 190–195.

Clark, G.M., Tong, Y.C., Martin, L.F.A., and Busby, P.A. A multiple channel cochlear implant: An evaluation using an open-set word test. *Acta Otolaryngol.*, 1981, *91*, 173–175.

Djourno, A., and Eyries, C. Prothese auditive par excitation electrique a distance du nerf sensoriel a l'aide d'un bobinage inclus a demeure. *Presse Med.*, 1957, *35*, 14–17.

Eddington, D.K., Dobelle, W.H., Brackmann, D.E., Mladejovsky, M.G., and Parkin, J.L. Auditory prosthesis research with multiple channel intracochlear stimulation in man. *Ann. Otol. Rhinol. Laryngol.*, 1978, *87*, Part 2, 1–39.

Flanagan, J.L., Schroeder, M.R., Atal, B.S., Crochiere, R.E., Jayant, N.S., and Tribolet, J.M. Speech coding. *IEEE Trans. Commun.*, 1979, *Com-17*, No. 4, 710–737.

Fourcin, A.J., Rosen, S.M., Moore, B.C., Douek, E.E., et al. External electrical stimulation of the cochlea: Clinical, psychophysical, speech-perceptual and histological findings. *Br. J. Audiol.*, 1979, *13*, 3, 85–107.

House, W.F. Cochlear implants. *Ann. Otol. Rhinol. Laryngol. Suppl. 27,* 1976, *85.*

House, W.F., Berlinger, K.I., and Eisenberg, L.S. Present status and future directions of the ear research institute cochlear implant program. *Acta Otolaryngol.,* 1979, *87,* 176–184.

Johnsson, L.G., House, W.F., and Linthicum, F.H. Bilateral cochlear implants: Histological findings in a pair of temporal bones. *Laryngoscope,* 1979, *89,* 759–762.

Kiang, N., and Moxon, E. Physiological considerations in artificial stimulation of the inner ear. *Ann. Otol.,* 1972, *81,* 714–730.

Kiang, N.Y.S., Watanabe, T., Thomas, E.C., et al. *Discharge Patterns of Single Fibers in the Cat's Auditory Nerve.* Cambridge, Mass.: MIT Press, 1965.

Michelson, R.P. The results of electrical stimulation of the cochlea in human sensory deafness. *Ann. Otol.,* 1971, *80,* 914–919.

Parkins, C.W. Single eighth nerve neuron responses to speech as a model for a cochlear prosthesis. In D.L. McPherson (ed.), *Advances in Prosthetic Devices for the Deaf: A Technical Workshop.* Rochester, N.Y.: National Technical Institute for the Deaf, 1979, 291–301.

Schindler, R.A., and Merzenich, M.D. Chronic intracochlear electrode implantation: Cochlear pathology and acoustic nerve survival. *Ann. Otol.,* 1974, *83,* 202–216.

Schroeder, M.R. Vocoders: analysis and synthesis of speech. *Proc. IEEE,* 1964, *54,* No. 5, 720–734.

Simmons, F.B. Electrical stimulation of the auditory nerve in man. *Arch. Otolaryngol.,* 1966, *84,* 2–54.

Smith, R.L. Adaptation, saturation, and physiological masking in single auditory nerve fibers. *J. Acoust. Soc. Am.,* 1979, *65,* 166–178.

Part VII

English Training

Chapter 22

English Training for the Primary and Secondary Level Deaf Student

ROBERT HOFFMEISTER, PH.D.
ALINDA M. DRURY, PH.D.

SIGN SYSTEMS AND INSTRUCTION

A LEARNING MODEL
    PREREQUISITES FOR THE MODEL
    LEVELS OF THE MODEL
    ASSESSING LINGUISTIC COMPETENCE

APPLICATION OF THE MODEL
    LEXICON BUILDING
    SYNTAX AND SEMANTICS
    PRAGMATICS

Since the first educational programs for the deaf were established in the United States over 150 years ago, teachers have been faced with an academic dilemma. They have wanted and needed to teach both English language skills and traditional academic subjects, such as science, math, and geography. Since academic subjects have required English as a mode of instruction, the greater instructional emphasis has always been placed on teaching English. As a result, deaf children have had less exposure to the amount and quality of school subjects than have their English-speaking peers. It is not surprising, then, that deaf students score low on academic achievement tests (Goetzinger and Rousey, 1959; Gentile and DiFrancesca, 1969; Furth, 1973; Moores, 1978). The fourth-grade achievement levels exhibited by the average deaf high-school graduate could be considered a result of both English deficits and a lack of knowledge and information about the world.

However, it is important to keep in mind that deficits in English and lack of knowledge of school subjects do *not* automatically imply deficits either in communicative competence or functional knowledge. Deaf individuals live successfully in the adult world, hold jobs, buy homes, pay taxes, and socialize among their friends. Low scores on tests which are standardized on hearing students completing regular public school programs may reflect, in addition to lack of facility in English, a more general cultural difference.

Nevertheless, we are left with the fact that English is the language of the larger society, and, therefore, important for a number of reasons. Skill in English may affect the standard of living of deaf individuals and their relative social position within the deaf community. Respect within the deaf community is garnered by many factors, including facility in communicating with both deaf and hearing individuals. And while communication within the deaf community may be accomplished through American Sign Language (ASL), communication with the hearing community depends on speaking, writing, and/or Manually Coded English (MCE) skills, all of which require a solid foundation in English.

It is also important to recognize that deaf

adults, who may have had great difficulty learning English, still consider English to be one of the most important skills to master even after having completed their formal education (Maestas y Moores, 1980). Meath-Lang (1978) has pointed out that deaf adults appreciate the need to understand English in order to read, both for everyday survival and pleasure. Again, while knowledge of English affects the communicative competence between deaf and hearing people, it does not necessarily affect the success of communication among members of the deaf community. It is important to maintain a perspective that English is not synonomous with communicative competence.

American Sign Language has been used by the majority of deaf adults since the early 1800's (Moores, 1978; Padden and Marcowicz, 1976), and Signed English systems have been part of the education of the deaf since 1965 (Gustafson et al., 1972; Anthony, 1977; Wampler, 1971). The rapid changeover in educational programs to signed systems has not been associated with a parallel changeover in how and what we teach deaf children. Now that very young deaf children have access to a communication system and the concomitant wealth of information such a system provides, they should be arriving at the primary level of instruction with a great deal more than deaf children of past generations (Moores et al., 1974; Schlesinger, 1978). Teachers must be prepared to deal with this situation. The fact that these deaf children will have more and easier access to information about the world does not imply that they will know English. Teaching English still remains a problem.

In the past, teaching English and teaching language have been the same thing. However, language for a deaf student must be more than their knowledge of English. Contemporary teachers of the deaf must be equipped with a model that accounts for the language behavior of the deaf child. If language is considered to be a consistent rule-governed form of communication, the consistency and set of rules must be acknowledged in description beyond the deaf child's use of English. Signed systems (including ASL) have their own sets of rules and their own internal and external requirements for consistency. It is

imperative that teachers know and use this information to teach English more effectively.

The problem of teaching English to deaf children is compounded by the fact that teachers are attempting to teach English while *using* English. It is further compounded by the fact that signed English systems used by many teachers may not be presented to deaf children in a consistent manner (Marmor and Petitto, 1979). Children cannot be expected to learn the system of English rules if the input they receive is inconsistent. Such inconsistency may tend to confuse the child as to what rules govern which utterances. The purpose of this chapter is to discuss why deaf children have problems in English and to propose possible steps for the remediation of some of the problems.

SIGN SYSTEMS AND INSTRUCTION

The introduction of sign systems into American classes for the deaf has only recently received general acceptance. There were a number of motivations for this change. One was the recognition of the need for an efficient system of communication in order to teach the academic content areas. A second reason comes from the last two decades of child language research. This body of research provides evidence for the overwhelming importance of early, consistent language input for overall development and academic success (Menyuk, 1980). A third motivation comes from a body of research showing the academic advantages of deaf children who have early exposure to manual communication (Moores et al., 1974; Moores, 1978; Meadow, 1966).

The shift to the use of sign systems has been substantial. Jordan, Gustafson, and Rosen (1979) report that of 551 programs serving deaf children, only 9 have remained committed to using an approach other than total communication (TC). While this change is fundamental, it cannot be expected to solve the complexities of teaching English to deaf children and brings with it a number of problems. First of all, there is no single, standard sign system being used by a majority of programs. This lack contributes to teacher training problems and possible problems for teachers who may transfer from one program to another.

A second problem lies in the fact that, to date, there is no evidence that *any* sign system which is a visual-manual mode of communication can faithfully represent the oral-aural aspects of English. Certainly, there is no doubt that Manually Coded English (MCE) systems may be used effectively for communication (Cokely, 1979). It is also true that the developers of these sign systems (Gustafson et al., 1972; Bornstein, 1973; Anthony, 1977) have made sincere attempts to represent English by including signs for various English morphemes. However, MCE is a way of representing English, as writing is, and may not include all of the information of spoken English. While it is theoretically possible to consistently represent English on the hands, recent studies indicate that in practice it is extremely difficult. Marmor and Petitto (1979) and Kluwin (1981) report that even teachers with training in Signed English and extensive experience signing with deaf children do not sign in English, morpheme for morpheme.

A third problem concomitant with the use of a signed system, or total communication, is that it is often, and inappropriately, thought of as a method. A signed system is not a method in the same sense that phonics is a method of teaching reading. A method is used to structure and teach the relationship of one piece of information to another in order to teach it more effectively. A phonics approach is used to teach the relationship between the sounds of English and their corresponding printed representations. Total communication, on the other hand, is a mode used to deliver information. It is a means of transmitting information. The signs are not used in an analytic sense to provide access to sign information, but rather are used to actually transmit information.

All of these problems should not be taken to mean that a signed system should not be used for teaching English to deaf children. On the contrary, as stated earlier, a signed system can provide a means of easy, consistent communication between teacher and child. In their haste to provide deaf children with an appropriate education, programs have adopted sign systems without fully considering the implications, while expecting far too much from the system itself. The simple addition of a signed system to the classroom has not, and cannot be expected to, automatically increase English skills in a substantial way. It can increase the amounts of general information presented in class and provide an opportunity for increasing facility with English.

A LEARNING MODEL

In order to provide effective instruction, teachers must have an in-depth understanding of what is to be taught and how learning occurs. These are simplistic statements about complex processes and require a grasp of the difference between structure and function. *Teaching* involves the presentation of information to a student who must then process the information. In order to optimize learning, input must be organized, logical, and matched to the capabilities of the student. *Learning* is the process by which the input from teaching is perceived, decoded, encoded, and then stored by the student. This is not the place to present a detailed explanation regarding information processing models. However, educators must recognize that for students to operate efficiently, the input must be planned to fit the cognitive structures of the students. Hence, the student's functioning level must be coordinated with the level of the input.

It is not enough just to know the parts of what is taught; teachers must know how the parts work together. Models can support such understanding and provide a way of organizing parts into a whole. A model can be thought of as a framework, or a flow chart, showing starting points, end points, and relationships among parts. If a teacher has a model of what is to be taught, teaching is likely to be consistent and orderly, thereby promoting efficient learning.

Learning is developmental. Prior information is used to discover new information to make predictions about how new information fits with the prior information. Since a model is a way of organizing information, it can also be used as a guide for matching teaching to learning. A model enables us to make judgments about particular students. More specifically, a model is necessary to establish (1) where the child is in relation to the model, (2) where the child is in relation to peers, (3) where the child is to proceed next in the developmental progression, and (4) what is necessary in order that the child can arrive at the next step in the model. While the above applies to all aspects of education, this chapter is particularly concerned with models of teaching languages—especially English. It must be understood that English is only one way of representing language. Language is knowing what to say (sign) and how to say (sign) it. The specific rules of how one delivers what one wants to say are found in any language (see Chapter 1). Children learn language from the input they receive, and what they produce linguistically is a reflection of that input (Brown, 1973; DeVilliers and DeVilliers, 1978). How is it that children make sense of the input?

Prerequisites for the Model

In order for children to systematically comprehend the input, they must have appropriate prerequisite cognitive capabilities (Slobin, 1973). There are strong interdependencies between cognitive and linguistic abilities that must be established. For young children acquiring a first language in typical circumstances, the establishment of organizational abilities underlies linguistic development.

Children are born with the ability and the need to make sense of the world. This inherent tendency plus appropriate stimuli and feedback from the environment provide the child an opportunity to begin to organize the world into meaningful categories. Assigning objects perceived in the world to categories depends on the ability to note meaningful differences among things. Not all differences are meaningful—they are meaningful only if we need them to be. Many differences are culturally specified. For example, in English, we choose to divide the color spectrum into seven basic color names, while other cultures and languages may have fewer or more names.

Differences, to the child, may be established in a variety of ways. Eve Clark (1973) proposes that differences are feature-bound and that as the child becomes aware of more and more features, more differences are noted, and therefore, the opportunity is there to establish more "finely tuned" categories.

This process can be seen in the young child who initially calls all 4-legged furry animals "dog," but with more experience with various kinds of 4-legged furry animals, learns to differentiate them into categories of dog, cat, horse, guinea pig, cow, etc.

As more and more differences are noted, one strategy for organizing the input, as implied above, is to attach symbols to the differences. These symbols may be at the general level for a prototypical instance of an object (e.g., dog), at a superordinate level for establishing a class of object members based on some common functional or physical properties (in this case, animal), or at a subordinate level for referring to a specific item within a class of objects (golden retriever). When children are able to attach symbols (i.e., words or signs) to these perceptual or functional categories, they have the means with which to organize, separate, store, and recall information that helps them understand the differences.

Hearing-impaired children, when presented with a signed system, have a means with which they are able to develop classification strategies for the organization, storage, and recall of information. The problem for the classroom teacher is to differentiate which strategies the child is *capable* of using (cognitive ability to separate objects into common physical and functional groups) from the linguistic skills necessary to *express* the strategy. In other words, teachers must be aware of children's cognitive abilities and be prepared to provide the appropriate linguistic input.

The next step is to develop a set of rules with which the symbolic units for classes of objects and events may be combined for delivering a more complex message. Abstracting systematic linguistic rules from a consistent language model is an ability assumed to be inherent in all normally hearing and deaf children (Lenneberg, 1967; Hoffmeister and Moores, 1979). However, the ability to abstract rules does not imply that the child is consciously aware of which strategies are necessary and sufficient for the acquisition of language. It is here that consistent input be maintained in order that the child may establish a system separating important pieces of information from unimportant pieces of information. A model which matches input with the abilities of the child will always be using the child's capabilities for advancing within the model.

Levels of the Model

Having established the cognitive prerequisites for the learning of a language, a model of language is necessary to aid in the development of a plan to consistently present the language. Again, when teaching language to deaf children, it is imperative to remember that language and English are not the same thing. All languages can be considered to share these four basic systems:

Delivery level—the system used to actually produce the message.
Syntactic level—the system used to structure the message into a specific language.
Semantic level—the system used to make the message meaningful.
Pragmatic level—the system used to modify the message depending on the social-cultural context.

Each level must be independently focused upon when teaching a language to deaf children. It is imperative that how the message is delivered be separated from the information itself. In the past it was difficult to separate the two because both content and form were taught through form alone. That is, teachers were attempting to teach information *about* the delivery system (English) while using the same delivery system (English). There were few other avenues to explain the differences.

The problem of using a system to teach information *about* that same system is particularly apparent when correction and evaluation techniques are implemented in the classroom. When the teaching of "language" is integrated into the classroom content areas, students are forced to develop strategies to learn content, "language," and classroom rules.

In developing strategies to learn content, the student's language and other cognitive capabilities interact to receive, decode, and encode information. It may be assumed from prior research that the cognitive capabilities of deaf students are basically equivalent to those of nondeaf students (Furth, 1966, 1973; Vernon, 1967). Therefore, information to be

learned will depend on the deaf student's capabilities in some language system (not necessarily English).

At the same time, the student is expected by the teacher to learn substantive issues from the content being delivered. The student must establish an organizational scheme for maintaining the information. If the input were to be absorbed and organized by a fluent user of English, the problem would only have to do with the level of sophistication of the content and how well that matched the capabilities of the students. Given that the students are knowledgeable and prepared in areas related to the content, learning the information should pose no problems.

In typical classrooms for the deaf there is an implied expectation in the attempt to "integrate language" within the classroom. This typically means that in addition to content information, some instruction in using correct grammatical expressions of the content is also given. The problem is that in content discussions the "correction and evaluation" by the teacher may not effectively separate content and form for the student. The student is then responsible to deduce which particular information set was intended, the content or the form.

For example, in the following exchange the process of teaching content becomes confounded when integrated with the teaching of English:

(1) Teacher: The Indians were sent to reservations by the white man.
(2) Student response: The Indians sent to reservation the white man.
(3) Teacher correction: "Let's say it again"—repeats sentence (1).

Note that the deaf student may or may not be sure whether the correction is for the content of the utterance or for the form of the utterance. Since this is "not" a language lesson, the teacher is not planning a lesson on passivization and does not make this distinction.

(4) Teacher repeats: The white man sent the Indians to the reservations.

In attempting to clarify sentence (1), the teacher repeats the content but in a new form.

This new information may now result in further confusion for the deaf student (especially at junior-high level). This confusion is in how to process English passives which are rearrangements of the English ordering subject-verb-object (S-V-O). Quigley et al. (1978) have shown that deaf students process the passive as S-V-O which in the above example would result in a contradiction of sentence (1) and sentence (4) in *content*. The fact that the form has been altered by the teacher to preserve content may not even be deduced. Students then become insecure about what the "correction" procedure was intended to do, and as Quigley et al. (1978) point out, they develop rigid strategies for decoding information presented in English. When this process has been encountered for a long period of time, other strategies must be developed in an attempt to gain as much information as possible and decrease the error rate in classroom behavior, forcing students to develop classroom rules.

With the recent acceptance of signed systems in the education of the deaf, the separation of the form and content may be accomplished more readily in the classroom, hopefully reducing the need for students to develop rigid rules. Teaching English may be enhanced when signed systems and English are viewed as sharing language components that may have certain similarities and differences. The teaching of English as a language system based upon auditory-vocal rules must be separated from the use of a signed system based upon visual-manual rules. It is then even more important to separate the teaching of either of these forms from the content required in the substantive academic areas of the classroom.

Understanding the separation of these systems permits the implementation of clear evaluation techniques which establish the linguistic base known by the deaf child who has been exposed to English and a signed system. Let us assume that the child is more fluent in the signed system than in English.

The fluency developed by the explicit input of a signed system is the basis of language one (L_1) for the deaf student. This knowledge can be used to map L_1 onto language two (L_2)—English. Explicit and implicit knowledge of L_1 can be used to teach L_2. To do this, teachers must have a clear understanding of the four levels of both L_1 and L_2. The levels and concomitant rules of signed languages, including American Sign Language, must be known by teachers if they are to effectively teach English to deaf students using a signed language. Knowing these rules and their levels of application will increase the teacher's understanding of how well L_1 and L_2 are known and what aspects of each still need to be learned.

Assessing Linguistic Competence

The basic linguistic competence of the deaf child, whether in a total communication classroom or an auditory-oral setting, must be assessed using a framework in which auditory-vocal knowledge is separated from gestural-sign production knowledge. In the past ten years we have seen an increase in the amount of information about the structure of American Sign Language (ASL), the acquisition of ASL and Signed English, and the development of speech in deaf children (Klima and Bellugi, 1980; Hoffmeister, 1977; Hoffmeister and Goodhart, 1978; Hoffmeister and Wilbur, 1980; Ling, 1976; Moores, 1978; Maestas y Moores, 1980; Goldin-Meadow, 1981). This information has provided detailed descriptions from which deaf children may be taught and assessed.

In order to appreciate the child's linguistic functioning, the teacher must also know how the child functions in other domains. Assessment, therefore, should be conducted within at least six areas. The reason for assessing overall communicative competence is to explore and describe what the deaf child *is able* to produce and comprehend. Beginning from a *positive* assessment automatically builds in successful experiences for deaf children.

The deaf child's abilities should be investigated in all of the following areas in order that the child's linguistic functioning can be viewed within a total framework.

Cognitive Functioning. Is the child able to organize the environment, make predictions given basic information from the environment (generalizations), establish order within the environment in terms of spatial and temporal events?
Linguistic Functioning. Is the child able to map various environmental events onto a system for delivering information both within and outside the occurrence of the events? Is the child able to

manipulate the communication system in a systematic way?

Social Functioning. Is the child able to initiate and maintain contact with peers? Is the child able to make his needs and wants known?

Perceptual Functioning. Is the child able to discriminate objects and events within the environment, especially visually? Is the child able to comprehend who the initiators and recipients are in familiar and unfamiliar events?

Academic Functioning. Is the child able to learn basic skills? Is the child able to apply knowledge about signs and/or English to printed English?

Behavioral Functioning. Is the child able to maintain high levels of attention and low levels of frustration? Is the child able to maintain emotional stability?

Perceptual, visual-motor skill, and linguistic functioning are highly correlated (Hanson et al., 1969). However, this does not imply cause and effect; it simply suggests that these are highly related functioning areas and a problem in one may create a problem in another (Menyuk, 1980).

Each child should be assessed for those skills in the cognitive, perceptual, and behavioral areas that are specifically related to linguistic functioning. The ability to attend to visual tasks, discriminate and reproduce environmental shapes, organize different environmental objects across more than one related category are all correlated with linguistic functioning. Developmental skills, such as sequencing, memory, recall, and storage, which are not dependent on vocal language but basic to language in general, must be specifically assessed.

After assessing the basic cognitive, perceptual, and behavioral functioning, linguistic functioning can be evaluated in detail. The purpose of the assessment is to discover the rules known by the child. To what extent can s/he manipulate the language systems?

The fact that language is a rule-governed behavior implies that to learn language one must learn a set of rules that, when operating efficiently and together, provide a system through which one may "know" a language. Assessment of linguistic functioning must occur within the child's knowledge base; new information cannot be introduced during evaluation. Thorough assessment must include a description of both comprehension and production at the delivery, syntactic, semantic, and pragmatic levels.

Evaluations for deaf students must be a comparison of how well each student functions within each level of both printed and spoken English, Signed English, Pidgin Sign English (see Woodward, 1973, and Reilly and McIntire, 1980, for discussions of PSE), and American Sign Language (ASL). Each student must be evaluated as to the possibility of having varying skills within each language system and within each level. For example, young deaf children should be evaluated as to their knowledge of sentence level variation—are they able to recognize and produce a question, a passive, a negative from a simple active declarative base sentence? Older deaf children must be evaluated as to whether they are able to recognize and produce different types of embedded sentences—subject relativization, object relativization, complementation, and other combinations of less complex sentences. Each language system has different rules for deriving nouns from verbs and verbs from nouns for establishing compounds, and when to use superordinate categories. A judgment regarding the "language" of a deaf student cannot be made without the teacher's awareness of this kind of information.

Assessing the linguistic behavior of a deaf student, whether the child is in a primary or a secondary program, involves the separation of the different delivery systems—printed English, spoken English, Signed English, and ASL—and their separate analyses. Linguistic functioning is only one aspect of a student's abilities; it must be considered along with perceptual, cognitive, social, academic, and behavioral functioning. Developing a comprehensive profile will provide a solid foundation from which instruction about English language, ASL, Signed English, reading, and writing may be implemented. Such assessment procedures provide a great deal of information about what the deaf child is capable of performing rather than what he is *not* able to do. As a result, instruction can proceed positively.

APPLICATION OF THE MODEL

Teachers using a Signed English system are not necessarily producing English in another mode. Differences can exist between English and sign at any of the four levels of the model. Such differences can create an inconsistent message.

Recognizing that there are differences between the linguistic systems will help teachers be sensitive to the processes children must use in order to decode the information as it is presented. Comprehending a message presented in sign and speech requires a decoding and encoding system that permits a cross-matching of units and levels to occur. At each level of a language, a match must be established between the incoming information and the rules of the receiver. When Signed English is used as a communication mode, the user has to know its rules. In addition, when written English is used, a mapping must occur between the knowledge of Signed English and written English. As more and more information is gained about Signed English and how it affects the language knowledge of deaf children, educators will be better prepared for teaching English as a second language through Signed English. Deaf children of hearing parents who are receiving a consistent sign language from their parents appear to modify their production based on the efficiency mechanisms of the visual channel (Hoffmeister and Goodhart, 1978; Goodhart, 1978; Schlesinger, 1978; Hoffmeister et al., 1978). Where sign production may make better use of space, as in pronominals, verb modulations for direct object, and verb modulations for location, deaf children reduce the extended sign input presented by Signed English (Goodhart, 1978). Even deaf children with limited input from hearing mothers appear to develop efficient visual-spatial communication systems to convey *and* receive information (Goldin-Meadow and Feldman, 1975; Feldman et al., 1977; Goldin-Meadow, 1981). This information validates the importance for educators to understand fully the need to establish models of language for the teaching of English.

Since deaf children develop some form of communication which compensates either partially or completely for the lack of vocal fluency, teachers must be prepared to skillfully assess these skills. If a consistent set of rules can be established for the communication produced, it can be considered as language one (L_1) for that child. Having an extensive language evaluation coupled with a detailed model of language will enable the teacher to clearly aid the child in developing strategies with L_1 as a base. L_1 structures and rules may then be used to map information onto language two (L_2) structures and rules. Each language system may have limitations at any level—delivery, syntactic, semantic, pragmatic—and mismatching between languages can occur at any level. For example, think of the deaf child learning a signed system who must later map that system onto English. In order to decode information, rules must be established to separate one sign from another and one word from another. Obviously, the rules will differ.

Decoding strategies will also occur at the syntactic/morphological level where rules must be established to determine the minimal units of meaning. For example, bound and free morphemes must be separated in L_1 (Signed English) and then mapped onto rules for L_2 (spoken-written English). In the signed system, the child may understand the past tense morpheme in the sign BEFORE, but may not associate this with the past tense morphemes in English (-ed, -t, and the irregular forms). This example makes clear that the mapping from L_1 to L_2 may not be an obvious one-to-one correspondence; these associations may have to be explicitly taught.

Similarly, at the semantic level, a specific set of mapping skills need to be established between signs and English words, in order that the signed system can be used to teach English. For example, the sign CAR and the English word CAR may have the same referent but are not necessarily equivalent in the extension of the underlying semantic application. That is, the sign CAR may also include trucks, tractors, and buses which have different representations in English. In addition, in Signed English, maintaining the same movement and place of production but with a change in handshape from a "C" to a "D" changes the sign CAR, a noun, to the sign DRIVE, a verb. This is not the equivalent of changing the English noun *car* to the English verb *drive*.

There are rule variations at each level between language systems. Using derivational information in one system or channel does not necessarily mean that it is easily transferred to another system *without explicit teaching*. A model of each language system is necessary not only to match linguistic information from one system to another but also to enable the user to make good guesses about new information. For example, when new lexical items enter into communication via conversation or written exchanges, having knowledge of the underlying rules of the language allows the receiver to predict the form class of the new word, predict its sentential usage, and decode its meaning. With knowledge of some of the rules of each level in L_1, comprehension of new linguistic information is much easier in L_2 (Poplack, 1981; Lavendera, 1981).

Rules for producing new signs are at the phonological and morphological levels, rules for determining how signs are ordered are at the syntactic and semantic levels, and rules for the individual and combinatorial meanings of signs are at the semantic level. In addition, there are rules for how we maintain a theme in a conversation. Discourse rules take into account how the information is related to one theme, how utterances that follow each other are related to each other, how time (past or present) is maintained across the theme, how one reduces redundancy by using pronominal processes, and how turn-taking is indicated at the end of a statement or at the conclusion of a theme. Finally, there are a set of rules which determine what type of syntactic structure is called for within the context of the conversational dyad. Statements, questions, negatives, ellipses, imperatives, and so forth are established within the contextual framework of a conversation. All bilingual children need to be armed with explicit strategies for how to match these structures in various systems.

The previous section presented a plan by which a child's knowledge base may be integrated into a model of linguistic development. A developmental model requires some assumptions. It does not matter what the child *"doesn't"* know but what s/he *does* know. For example, given that the child knows how to comprehend an S-V-O type of sentence in English by being able to identify the agent, patient, and action implies that such categories as agent, patient, and action are not only known by the student but also that the student has the ability to indicate that *John*

kissed Mary is different from *Mary kissed John*.

Such information permits the instructor to use basic S-V-O, agent-action-patient relationships to teach new lexical items overtly, while covertly teaching their cognitive-semantic relationships within sentential contexts.

At this point in our discussion, it should be clear that knowledge of linguistic rules for producing Signed Engish are just as important as knowledge of the linguistic rules of English. Establishing a common model for both linguistic systems enables the teaching of strategies for mapping one system to another. Using the model aids the teacher in predicting where within each language system the deaf child may be placed.

Table 22.1 presents a general schemata for comparing language skills within the language model we have presented. It has already been pointed out that there are different skills basic to language, including strategies for decoding, encoding, organizing, storing, and retrieving information. If the delivery level is to require separate strategies for English, Signed English, and ASL, then instruction about these three language systems must be separated. From the assessment of the deaf student the teacher will have an extensive description of what is known about the child's languages. It is important to use the language which is best known by the student both to teach more about the best known language and to learn more about the other languages.

Initially, instruction about language should concentrate on the cognitive skills of perception, organization, and memory. Cognitive strategies need to be enhanced to help the student separate important from nonimportant information. That is, deaf students need to attend to differences and similarities, things that are able to stand alone (free) and things that must be attached to other things (bound). Lexical items learned from other parts of the day (old information) should be incorporated in discussions about language. Information considered during this part of the school day will focus on strategies and rules regarding either English, Signed English, or ASL, *not* about policemen, nuclear energy, algebra, or other content areas.

Table 22.1

Components for Comparing Language Systems

1. Delivery System
   A. Establish appropriate rules for combinations of minimal units to deliver message.
   B. Establish minimal units of the language systems.
   C. Map combinations of minimal units to appropriate lexical choices.
2. Semantic System
   A. Establish appropriate rules for symbols and categorization.
   B. Map event to appropriate lexical representation.
   C. Develop strategies for organizing lexical system into the following categories:
      1. Animate-inanimate symbols
      2. Action-stative symbols
      3. Inflectional (bound vs. free) symbols
      4. Spatial indicators (bound vs. free)
         a. Stationary
         b. Transitory
      5. Descriptors
         a. Quantitative
         b. Qualitative
   D. Establish strategies for appropriate semantic relationships within sentential units (agents related to action, experiencers related to stative, patient related to recipient, etc.).
3. Syntactic System
   A. Establish appropriate sequence of representatives that reflect the purpose of the utterance.
   B. Establish appropriate sentential categories of allowable utterances (NP = subject).
   C. Map semantic categories within sentential units (subject = agent, patient, etc.).
   D. Establish allowable variations in basic sequence.
   E. Establish appropriate rules for marking allowable variations, and map these to appropriate sentential unit.
4. Pragmatic System
   A. Establish strategies for choosing appropriate sentence sequence within conversation.
   B. Establish appropriate strategies for introducing, maintaining, and ending conversation.

Lexicon Building

There are a number of processes used to increased the size of the lexicon. One of these is the distinction between basic object categories and their subordinate and superordi-

nate levels. There are basic rules in English, Signed English, and ASL for creating subordinate and superordinate categories from the basic object level category.

In English the basic level *CAR* may be more specifically a *Pontiac*, and the same is true of ASL. However, the superordinate *vehicle* in English is not translatable into the classifier VEHICLE in ASL. That is, although both have noun-like uses, the ASL classifier has much more extended use within the language.

Another lexical process that teachers need to understand is compounding. Procedures for developing compounds can be found in ASL, English, and Signed English, and these can be taught as information to be learned *about* the language.

Other morphological processes include constructing plurals and possessives. It is important for the student to recognize that plural and possessive indicators in all three systems are bound morphemes and must be attached to a base. When knowledge of the plural is acquired in one system, that knowledge can be used to teach the same process in the other systems.

Learning any one of these processes or others (e.g., noun, verb, or adjective derivations discussed earlier) may occur faster in the signed system and can then be used to teach the analoguous process in English. This morphological/lexical knowledge can then be integrated with information about the syntax and semantics of each language system.

Syntax and Semantics

Instruction about syntax and semantics will be concerned with how noun phrases function as agents and experiencers, how verb complexes represent actions or stative events, and how noun phrases within the verb complex function as patients and locatives. For example, learning about checking accounts and banks is separate from learning that they are nouns. Information the student has learned about the subject matter can be used to teach about language. After teaching a lesson on checking accounts, that same information can be used to teach that nouns like bank, deposit, and balance can also be used as verbs—banking, depositing, and balancing.

Within the syntactic level, the three systems again have similarities and differences, and rules must be developed to indicate the potential manipulation of subject, verb, and object; strategies need to be taught to decode and encode word orders allowed in all three systems. Noun phrases may occur in various places within the sentence. However, linguistic constraints require that if the noun is not to be in its expected place, the movement be identified by some means. Markers are used in all three systems. For example, in English, *by* is used to indicate the subject in the passive, *to* for the beneficiary in indirect object sentences. In ASL, only movement of specific sentence units is allowed, depending on the capability of marking the verb. If a directional verb is used (e.g., GIVE), it may mark subject and object; if a locational verb is chosen, it may mark object or location. The flexibility of sentential movement may be explicitly compared across language systems so that deaf students will be able to develop their own strategies for comparing how the systems differ or are similar.

All languages include some sort of redundancy rules. These rules may be within syntax, as in the above marker systems, or within discourse, as in the use of pronominals or particular sentence types that highlight the subject. These processes may be taught to aid deaf students in learning about the operation of redundancy in the three language systems.

Knowledge of how semantic information is reflected in the surface structure of the language will aid the teacher in instruction, particularly when the teacher needs to correct a student's utterance. It is important to recognize that English and ASL have different surface structures, and that even *within* one language, the same semantic information can be expressed via different surface structures. This information enables the teacher to focus correction on the appropriate level.

The following example illustrates how the teacher would take a student's utterance and explicitly teach the ASL and/or English structures used to convey the student's intent. This would also provide a good opportunity for the teacher to point out the importance of word order in English as opposed to ASL.

Student (in sign):	POINT CROOK SHOOT POINT MAN.
Teacher (ASL):	The information is correct. The verb should be directed toward the space or object indicated by the pointing. This helps to remember who shot whom.
Teacher (English):	POINT CROOK and POINT MAN is produced by using *the crook* and *the man.* In English, the verb, if past, is SHOT. SHOOT is present. The order of subject-verb-object is correct in English.

Although this is a simplistic example of correction in detail, the student is given the correct information *about* the language based on his/her sentence. It is not mentioned that the student produced a *wrong* utterance, merely that these are the procedures for producing grammatically correct sentences in English or ASL. This becomes more clear if a student produces the passive in English incorrectly. For example, the teacher provides the active sentence, "The girl kissed the boy," and asks the student to produce the passive form.

Student: The girl was kissed by the boy.

Even though the sentence is a correct passive, the teacher has the opportunity to correct the student on both the semantic and syntactic levels. A *semantic* correction would point out to the student that the girl is the agent in the original sentence and that this information is contradicted in the student's sentence. A *syntactic* correction would point out that in order to transform an active sentence into a passive, the order of the agent and recipient must be reversed, the auxiliary *was* added, and the preposition *by* inserted.

Pragmatics

Pragmatic issues in each of the systems may be discussed by initially setting up situations which require different types of sentences by the speaker. This insures that *syntactic* sentence types interact with context, and context specifies the semantic intent of the utterance. The focus of the utterance is the choice of the speaker and occupies a pivotal point in the sentence. It may be set off by using a variety of strategies involving processes of topic and comment in all three language systems. Discourse processes may be capitalized upon in conversation and then compared with written English. Strategies involving this area of language must be used to aid students in choosing sentence types to maintain the theme and continuity of the conversation/message.

SUMMARY

The purpose of this chapter has been to orient the reader to a particular viewpoint regarding English instruction for the hearing-impaired school child. We have attempted to outline a theoretical approach from which specific instructional techniques can be inferred.

The major point of the chapter is that language instruction cannot occur in a vacuum for the teacher or the student. The teacher must have a theory/model about how languages work, how children learn languages, and how children learn in general. And the student requires consistent, clear input from which to extrapolate both information about the world and the rules of the language.

The model we have presented views the child as an active learner capable of constructing the rules of the language. In order to be able to do this, the language, and information about it, presented to the child must be consistent. This issue of consistency is not a problem for hearing children, who are surrounded by hearing adults who know and speak the language fluently. However, for deaf children, for whom the auditory message is incomplete and/or modality differences exist, more attention must be given to conscientiously providing a good model. In order to do this, it is incumbent upon teachers to become familiar with how languages work.

We have outlined here a simplistic model of the various levels of language systems. Familiarity with these components of language and how they work will enable the good teacher to provide, in addition to proper linguistic input, appropriate instruction and feedback to the child.

We have also emphasized the importance of a thorough assessment of the child's comprehension and production in English, Signed English, and ASL. This information can then be used to design appropriate instructional techniques. It can also be used to remind the teacher that the student may have varying abilities across languages and that the stronger language can be used to teach the newer one.

Finally, we hope we have provided a framework for teachers from which English skills can be taught and developed. We return to our original concern about teaching English and teaching the content areas. Hopefully, with extended information about languages and how they work, teachers will be better equipped to separate language instruction from academic instruction.

References

Anthony, D. *Seeing Essential English*, vols. 1 and 2. Anaheim, CA: Educational Services Division, Anaheim Union School District, 1977.

Bornstein, H. A description of some current sign systems designed to represent English. *Am. Ann. Deaf*, 1973, *3*, 454–463.

Brown, R. *A First Language*. Cambridge, Massachusetts: Harvard University Press, 1973.

Clark, E. How children describe time and order. In C. Ferguson and D. Slobin (eds.), *Studies in Child Language Development*. New York: Holt, 1973.

Cokely, D. *Guidelines for Manual Communication*. Washington, D.C.: Pre-College Programs, Gallaudet College, 1979.

DeVilliers, J., and Devilliers, P. *Language Acquisition*. Cambridge, Massachusetts: Harvard University Press, 1978.

Feldman, H., Goldin-Meadow, B., and Gleitman, L. Beyond the creation of language by linguistically deprived deaf children. In A. Lock (ed.), *Action, Gesture and Symbol: The Emergence of Language*. New York: Academic Press, 1977.

Furth, H. *Thinking without Language*. New York: The Free Press, 1966.

Furth, H. *Deafness and Learning: A Psychosocial Approach*. Belmont, California: Wadsworth Publishing, 1973.

Gentile, A., and DiFrancesca, S. *Academic Achievement Test Performance of Hearing Impaired Students, United States, Spring 1969*. Washington, D.C.: Gallaudet College, Office of Demographic Studies, 1969.

Goetzinger, C, and Rousey, E. Educational achievement of deaf children. *Am. Ann. Deaf*, 1959, *104*, 221–231.

Goldin-Meadow, S. Language development without a language model. Paper presented at Society for Research in Child Development Biennial Meeting, Boston, 1981.

Goldin-Meadow, S., and Feldman, H. The creation of a communication system: A study of deaf children of hearing parents. *Sign Lang. Stud.*, 1975, *8*, 225–234.

Goodhart, W. The development of sign language behavior of a deaf child of hearing parents. Unpublished manuscript, Boston University, 1978.

Gustason, G., Pfetzinger, D., and Zawolkow, E. *Signing Exact English*. Rossmoor, California: Modern Signs Press, 1972.

Hanson, G., Hancock, B., and Kopra, L. *Relationships among Audiological Status, Linguistic Skills, Visual-Motor Perception, and Academic Achievement of Deaf Children*. Austin, Texas: University of Texas, Final Report, BEH Grant #4-7002353-2051, 1969.

Hoffmeister, R. The influential point. Paper presented at the National Symposium on Sign Language Research and Training, Chicago, June 1977.

Hoffmeister, R., and Goodhart, W. The semantic and syntactic analysis of the sign language behavior of a deaf child of hearing parents. Paper presented at the M.I.T. Conference on the Linguistic Aspects of American Sign Language, Cambridge, Massachusetts, April 1978.

Hoffmeister, R., Goodhart, W., and Dworski, S. Symbolic gestural behavior in deaf and hearing children. Mini-seminar presented at American Speech and Hearing Association Annual Convention, San Francisco, November 1978.

Hoffmeister, R., and Moores, D. Predicting the abstract linguistic abilities of deaf children. Paper presented at Convention of American Instructors of the Deaf, Austin, Texas, 1979.

Hoffmeister, R., and Wilbur, R. The acquisition of sign language. In H. Lane and F. Grosjean (eds.), *Recent Perspectives on American Sign Language*. Hillsdale, New Jersey: Lawrence Erlbaum Asssociates, 1980.

Jordan, I., Gustason, G., and Rosen, R. An update on communication trends at programs for the deaf. *Am. Ann. Deaf*, 1979, *124*, 350–357.

Klima, E., and Bellugi, U. *The Signs of Language*. Cambridge, Massachusetts: Harvard University Press, 1980.

Kluwin, T. A preliminary description of the control of interaction in classrooms using manual communication. *Am. Ann. Deaf*, 1981, *126*, 510–514.

Lavendera, B. LoQuebramos: But Only Performance. In R. Duran (ed.), *Latino Language and Communicative Behavior*. Norwood, New Jersey: Ablex Press, 1981.

Lenneberg, E. *The Biological Foundations of Language*. New York: John Wiley & Sons, 1967.

Ling, D. *Speech and the Hearing-Impaired Child: Theory and Practice*. Washington, DC: A. G. Bell Press, 1976.

Maestas y Moores, J. Early linguistic environments: Interactions of deaf parents with their infants. *Sign Lang. Stud.*, 1980, *26*, 1–13.

Marmor, G., and Petitto, L. Simultaneous communication in the classroom: How well is English grammar represented? *Sign Lang. Stud.*, 1979, *23*, 99–136.

Meadow, K. The effect of early manual communication and family climate on deaf child's development. Unpublished doctoral dissertation, University of California, Berkeley, 1966.

Meath-Lang, B. A comparative study of experienced and non-experienced groups of deaf college students: Their attitudes toward language learning. *Teaching English Deaf*, 1978, *5*, 9–14.

Menyuk, P. Nonlinguistic and linguistic processing in normally developing and language disordered children. In *Speech and Language: Advances in Basic Research and Practice*, vol. 4. New York: Academic Press, 1980.

Moores, D. *Educating the Deaf: Psychology, Principles, and Practices*. Boston: Houghton Mifflin, 1978.

Moores, D., Weiss, K., and Goodwin, M. *Evaluation of programs for Hearing-Impaired Children: Report of 1972–1973*. Minneapolis: University of Minnesota Research, Development and Demonstration Center in Education of Handicapped Children, Research Report No. 81, 1974.

Padden, C., and Marcowicz, M. Cultural conflicts between hearing and deaf communities. In A. Crammatte and F. Crammatte (eds.), *Proceedings of the Seventh World Congress of the World Federation of the Deaf*. Silver Spring, Maryland: Association of the Deaf, 1976.

Poplack, S. Syntactic structure and social function of code switching. In R. Duran (ed.), *Latino Language and Communicative Behavior*. Norwood, New Jersey: Albex Press, 1981.

Quigley, S., Wilbur, R., Power D., Montanelli, D., and Steinkamp, M. *Syntactic Structures in the Language of Deaf Children*. Urbana-Champaign, Illinois: Institute for Child Behavior and Development, University of Illinois at Urbana-Champaign, 1978.

Reilly, J., and McIntire, M. American Sign Language and Pidgin Sign English: What's the difference? *Sign Lang. Stud.*, 1980, *27*, 151–192.

Schlesinger, H.S. The acquisition of bimodal language. In I.M. Schlesinger (ed.), *Sign Language of the Deaf: Psychological, Linguistic and Sociological Perspectives*. New York: Academic Press, 1978.

Slobin, D. Cognitive prerequisites for the development of grammar. In C. Ferguson and D. Slobin (eds.), *Studies of Child Language Development*. New York: Holt, 1973.

Vernon, M. Relationship of language to the thinking process. *Arch. Genet. Psychiatry*, 1967, *16*, 325–333.

Wampler, D. *Linguistics of Visual English*. Santa Rosa, California: Early Childhood Education Department, Aurally Handicapped, Santa Rosa City Schools, 1971.

Woodward, J. Some characteristics of Pidgin Sign English. *Sign Lang. Stud.*, 1973, *3*, 39–46.

Chapter 23

Reading and Writing Instruction for Deaf Young Adults

KATHLEEN EILERS CRANDALL, PH.D.

This chapter is devoted to the deaf adolescent and young adult and his or her needs with respect to reading and writing instruction. The information is directed to English language specialists, reading and writing specialists, and language pathologists who work with deaf students in secondary and postsecondary environments. The author assumes that these educators realize the need for a background in linguistics and psycholinguistics and are seeking to apply knowledge from these disciplines to teach deaf adolescents and young adults to read and write more effectively. The literature (Wrightstone et al., 1962; Trybus et al., 1973) comparing deaf students' reading performance with that of their hearing counterparts should be familiar to readers of this chapter. These data indicate that we have not succeeded in teaching the vast majority of deaf people to read at a level that will permit them access to academic and professional activities available to their hearing peers. Furthermore, we have not determined why deaf students encounter significant difficulty in learning to read and write. This pervasive and complex problem calls for input from a variety of disciplines to answer questions such as:

1. What are the necessary skills for successful reading and writing?
2. With which reading and writing skills do deaf students have difficulties?
3. Which reading and writing skills do deaf students need to learn and why?
4. How might deaf students best learn those reading and writing skills that are determined important?

This chapter is organized around each of these questions. While there are few definitive answers available, it is hoped that this information will enable instructors, researchers, and material developers to more critically analyze how students' needs can best be addressed.

SKILLS NECESSARY FOR SUCCESSFUL READING AND WRITING

In a general sense, reading can be defined as obtaining meaning through the printed word and writing as conveying information through the printed word (Gibson and Levin, 1975). After reviewing approximately 1500 post-secondary deaf students' reading and writing skills over several years through the use of the California Reading Test (Tiegs and Clark, 1963) and the NTID Written Language Test (Crandall, 1980b), it is apparent that reading and writing scores are significantly correlated (r = 0.58). However, a reading score cannot accurately predict a students' writing score, and vice versa. For example, of the 317 students who entered NTID in the summer of 1980, 10 achieved reading comprehension scores at a 12.0 grade level equivalent (GLE); their writing scores ranged from 8.9 points (writing characterized by occasional inflectional morphological errors and spelling and punctuation errors) to 10.0 points (a writing sample free from any written English anomalies). Their mean writing score was 9.51 (S.D. = 0.40). Of these same 317 students, 7 obtained a writing score of 10.0 points; their reading comprehension scores ranged from 7.9 GLE to 12.0 GLE. This group of students had a mean reading GLE of 10.5 (S.D. = 1.30). These data indicate that reading and writing skills require separate assessment and suggest that different skills are being activated during performance in these two general areas.

Skills Necessary for Reading

A fundamental question is whether reading comprehension involves a unitary competence or a number of skills. Lennon (1962) and Farr (1969) after extensively reviewing research on reading comprehension found little agreement regarding the specific factors or the number of factors involved in reading comprehension. In fact, Goodman (1969), who defines reading as a kind of information processing that occurs when the reader decodes print, claims a division of this complex process into distinct components is artificial. It is not even clear at what point in the reading process, reading comprehension should be considered; Harrison and Dolan (1979) suggest that reading comprehension could be considered in the context of cognitive skills employed following initial decoding of print.

Both Goodman and Harrison and Dolan

suggest that when a person reads, first the print is decoded and then meaning is assigned. If this is correct, the reader must have some system for decoding printed symbols and some system for assigning meaning. Since the printed symbols in modern written language systems are mediators of language, not direct mediators of ideas (Gelb, 1963; Bollinger, 1975), in order for decoding to occur an individual must know the language system upon which the print is based and also employ various cognitive skills or strategies to successfully comprehend reading materials. Written English is based on spoken English and thus is an auditory-based system, not a visual-based system. Hearing children learning to read English have already established a sense of phonemes, morphemes, words, phrases, clauses, and longer discourse units. To be successful at reading then, we might hypothesize that deaf people, too, need to have this linguistic knowledge. As pointed out by Bochner and others (in this volume), deaf individuals have not mastered the English linguistic system and do not seem to have sufficient input currently available to them in either the auditory, speechread, manually coded, or printed forms to successfully acquire it in the vast majority of cases.

The exact manner in which an individual applies linguistic skills during the reading process is not understood. Two competing theories are described by Wolfram et al. (1979). In the *dependent* theory, it is claimed that print must be transferred into an inner representation of the sounds of the language and then the reader uses processing strategies similar to those used in processing spoken language. The *parallel* theorists claim that good readers typically do not start their reading process by changing print to sound, but process the syntactic and semantic units directly. Regardless of which of these theories is actually correct, linguistic knowledge of at least the syntactic and semantic components of the language system is necessary for reading. The difference between the two theories is whether or not knowledge of the phonological component and its relationship to writing is critical for the reader in getting to the semantic and syntactic components.

Perhaps these two theories are both appropriate but at different stages in learning to read. Coady (1979) claims that beginning readers rely more on letter-sound correspondences and syllable-morpheme information while the more experienced reader relies more on semantic, syntactic, and discourse cues. We do not know, however, if it is mandatory that an individual learn to use letter-sound correspondences and syllable-morpheme information in the beginning learning stages of reading in order to progress to more advanced stages.

For the purpose of this chapter, and in view of the reading difficulties manifested by the deaf population, it seems reasonable to address each of the probable skills involved in reading from the point at which print is encountered to the point at which interpretation is derived. This entire process would involve both linguistic and other cognitive skills. A brief description of these skills as they relate to reading follows.

LINGUISTIC SKILLS FOR READING

According to Goodman's (1973) model, a reader must make use of linguistic cues at the word, sentence, and discourse levels. At the word level, these cues can include: (1) relationships between graphemes and phonemes, (2) relationships between spelling patterns and morphemes, and (3) relationships between the entire printed word and the spoken form. To make use of these cues, it is essential for the reader to have a sense of phomenes, morphemes, and words.

Cues at the word level, according to Goodman (1973), assist the reader in recoding printed language into spoken language. Allen (1972) and Baron (1973) argue that the use of spelling patterns to determine morphological components need not result in recoding into spoken forms; the reader may be able to go directly from the printed morpheme to meaning. For example, if the reader recognizes the printed word *resign* but is unfamiliar with the printed word *resignation* and its morphophonemic rules for pronunciation, the correct meaning may still be derived if the derivational morpheme *-ation* is detected and understood. However, when these word level cues do result in a recoding into spoken forms, then decoding for meaning occurs via internal speech.

Internal speech is defined by Conrad (1979) as the silent manipulation of spoken words to achieve some cognitive goal. There is objective evidence that internal speech is present during reading. This evidence comes from three different approaches to detecting the presence of internal speech—electromyography (EMG) studies, memory confusions, and letter detections. The most direct evidence is based on EMG findings.

Significant electrical activity has been recorded from the muscles involved in speech production while subjects are silently reading. Edfeldt (1960) found the level of electrical activity increased with the difficulty level of the read passage. Locke and Fehr (1970) reported a correlation between the speech muscles involved and the type of sounds represented by the letters in printed words during silent reading; an increase in EMG activity from the lip muscles was recorded when subjects read words with labial consonants. McGuigan (1970) and McGuigan and Winstead (1974) established that this increased level of activity from the speech muscles during reading was not attributable to an overall increase in covert muscular activity from a resting state. They were unable to obtain an increase in EMG response from nonspeech muscles. EMG techniques have not been employed for the investigation of the presence of internal speech in deaf individuals during silent reading. The above evidence leading us to deduce the presence of internal speech during reading comes entirely from hearing individuals. Without such additional evidence we cannot conclude that internal speech is or is not present when deaf people read, nor that another internal recoding strategy could not be effectively used.

Short-term memory studies also indicate the type of internal coding system being used. It is hypothesized that the type of features causing the most difficulty in a memory task reflect the type of code being used (Conrad, 1972b; LaBerge, 1972; Locke, 1971; Norman, 1972; Sachs, 1974; Hanson, 1981; Mark et al., 1977). When subjects have more difficulty recalling phonetically similar words, they are thought to be relying on a coding strategy that is phonetically based. When more difficulty is observed for the recall of visually similar words, a visually based coding system is implied.

Conrad (1979) reviewed a variety of short-term memory tasks used with hearing and deaf subjects as well as problems associated with various research designs. Locke and Locke (1971) analyzed children's errors in a graphemic recall task. They found error responses of hearing children tended to be phonetically similar to the target letter; error responses of deaf children with unintelligible speech tended to be dactylically similar to the target; and error responses of deaf children with intelligible speech were between the two above groups. Conrad (1972a) presented two sets of letters to hearing and deaf children. One set contained letters phonetically similar; the other set contained letters with similar shapes. He learned that the hearing children experienced less difficulty with the set having similar shapes and the deaf children with the set having similar phonetic properties. These types of studies indicate that when hearing individuals memorize items, phonetic information is the predominant cue for remembering. This finding is taken as further supporting evidence that hearing people are using some form of speech coding for mediation. We cannot arrive at a similar conclusion for deaf individuals because they do not behave homogeneously on these recall tasks. Conrad (1979) matched deaf students on IQ, degree of hearing loss, and cause of deafness and found that those students who used a visual imagery code demonstrated memory for visually distinctive words comparable to what those who used a phonetic code demonstrated for phonetically distinctive words.

Conrad (1979) also looked at the relationship between the level of reading comprehension obtained by deaf children and the use of internal speech as indicated by recall tasks. He found the use of internal speech was a major significant factor along with intelligence and degree of hearing loss in determining reading comprehension ability. However, even after controlling for the effects of intelligence and hearing loss, children using internal speech read about 2 years above those not using internal speech. Caution must be exercised in drawing conclusions. The children in Conrad's studies were educated in Britain and thus had been educated orally. We can presume that teachers used instructional strategies that stressed mediation by speech codes, not visual codes. We, therefore, cannot conclude that a visual coding strategy could not also effectively support the reading process.

In addition to EMG and memory studies, researchers have also used letter detection tasks to infer the presence of internal speech. Locke (1978), Chen (1976), and Corcoran (1966) asked individuals to strike out all occurrences of the letter *e* in passages of prose. Corcoran found hearing subjects did not detect silent *es* as well as nonsilent *es*. Chen and Locke found deaf subjects detected silent and nonsilent *es* with equal facility.

The above cited studies provide evidence that hearing people are using internal speech for making use of at least word level cues in reading. But we do not know where in the reading process an inability to use internal speech mediation will have the greatest impact, nor if a visual coding strategy can be used effectively in lieu of internal speech.

Another source of linguistic cues is found at the sentence level. These cues deal with the syntactic, morphological, semantic, and prosodic relationships between words and word clusters. Weber (1970) postulates that beginning readers can rely on their knowledge of spoken language to facilitate the decoding of units larger than syllables or words. However, printed language does not indicate relationships between words in the same way as speech. In speech, sounds and words are not discrete units like letters and words in print. Furthermore, the suprasegmental cues of stress, juncture, and intonational contour are more or less absent in print. Thus, the reader has to get the information these cues convey through other means.

Evidence that syntactic cues at the sentence level are being used in reading comes from eye-voice span and eye movement research. Other evidence is found in studies investigating the effect of various syntactic structures and semantic units on reading comprehension.

Levin (1979) defines the eye-voice span (EVS) as the distance that the eye is ahead of the voice in reading aloud. In his book, he presents a thorough history and review of EVS research. EVS, although studied for over 80 years, has during the past 15 years been of interest because of the light it sheds on the process of reading. The typical procedure used in measuring the EVS is to have a person read aloud; when the person's utterances reach some predefined word, the text is removed from view. The person is then asked to report the words seen beyond the last word said aloud when the text was removed. Simultaneous recordings of the reader's eye movements and voice may also be made.

Levin and Kaplan (1968) determined that the EVS is not only a guess about the text beyond the word actually uttered; they found that correct guesses occur for about one word per thousand when a reader is unable to view forthcoming text while reading. And when such text is available, there is a direct relationship between the EVS and the grammatical constraints present in the text (Levin and Kaplan, 1968; Resnick, 1970; Vasquez et al., 1977–1978). The probability of reading to a grammatical boundary increases according to the number of grammatical constraints available to the reader when the text is removed. EVSs are the longest where constraints are the highest. This phenomenon has been best demonstrated in comparing EVSs in right- and left-embedded sentences. Levin et al. (1972) using college students determined through cloze procedures (the subject supplies words that have been systematically deleted from the text by the investigator) that right-embedded sentences were more constrained than left-embedded sentences and then in EVS experimentation with the same subjects and sentences found that EVSs were longer for right-embedded sentences.

The EVSs of second graders already tend to stop at grammatical boundaries (Levin and Turner, 1968). But, the size of EVSs rises sharply at the fourth grade and slowly thereafter (Rode, 1974–1975). The EVSs of fourth graders frequently stop at clause boundaries while those of third graders stop more often at phrase boundaries. Rode claims that third graders are using syntax to the same degree but are limited by memory capabilities.

The EVS is also sensitive to semantic and prosodic features. Vasquez et al. (1977–1978) found more semantically meaningful phrases yielded longer EVSs for college students than less semantically meaningful phrases. Zolinger (1974) found that children at the fourth, fifth, and sixth grades demonstrated different EVSs according to stress placement in answers to questions. Their EVSs were longest when they read sentences that required stress to be placed on the final lexical item in a sentence and shortest when required on the subject.

With one exception (Cooley, 1981), EVS has not been studied in deaf individuals. Since an individual's EVS varies according to the degree of grammatical constraints in a text, it could be used with deaf students to determine what grammatical constraints were significant for them. Cooley (1981) investigated the EVSs of 25 deaf college students in right- and left-embedded sentences. Her deaf students were all born deaf and had pure tone averages greater than 90 dB. Their speech intelligibility (Subtelny et al., 1981) was rated at 4.0 or better, indicating speech which is intelligible with the exception of a few words or phrases (4.0) to completely intelligible (5.0). The deaf students obtained reading grade equivalent scores ranging from 7.1 to 12.0 (mean = 9.44) on the reading comprehension subtest of the California Reading Test, Junior High Level (Tiegs and Clark, 1963). Cooley also included 28 hearing college students in her experiment. Both the hearing and the deaf students demonstrated longer EVSs for the more grammatically constrained right-embedded sentences confirming the Levin et al. (1972) findings. For both sentence types, hearing students had significantly longer EVSs than deaf students. EVSs that ended at English grammatical boundaries were observed significantly more often for hearing students. However, the deaf students with higher reading levels (grade equivalent scores of 10.6 to 12.0) had EVSs similar to the hearing students for both sentence types and their EVSs ended at English grammatical boundaries significantly more often than those of deaf students with lower reading levels. This study showed that EVS is a promising area for investigating how deaf students use sentence level cues in reading.

Research in the area of eye movements has also yielded information on the importance of sentence level cues for reading. Wanat (1971) reported adult readers demonstrated fewer forward fixations and spent less time on forward fixations while reading right-embedded sentences than while reading left-embedded sentences. Regressive eye movements did not differ for these two sentence types. Wanat also found fewer and shorter forward fixations for active sentences than for passive sentences; however, more regressions occurred and more time was spent on regressions in passive than in active sentences. We find a course of development similar to that of the EVS for the distance between fixations (saccade length). There is a fairly rapid growth until fourth grade, a plateau until about the middle of high school, and then another smaller increase in saccade length (Levin, 1979). Eye movement patterns of deaf individuals during reading have not been reported.

Evidence that sentence cues are critical for reading comprehension also comes from research on the effect of different sentence types on comprehension. Quigley has done the most extensive research to date on deaf students in this area for the development of the *Test of Syntactic Abilities* (Quigley et al., 1978). Drury (1980) studied the effects of varying syntactic and vocabulary difficulty on the reading comprehension of deaf college students using a cloze procedure. She found that the variation of these two parameters exerted a differential effect on students' cloze scores. Good readers, indicated by their grade equivalent scores on the California Reading Test, Junior High Level, reading comprehension subtest, were less affected by the variation of one of these parameters than were poor readers.

The use of linguistic cues at the discourse level for reading has received far less attention than word and sentence level cues. The linguistic principles underlying relationships between sentences and between paragraphs have not been adequately defined to investigate how they affect reading efficiency. Discourse level cues include linguistic devices signaling beginnings and ends of passages, changes in perspective, comparisons between viewpoints, as well as writing styles differentiating fiction from nonfiction, poetry from prose, or scientific writing from speculation. Clark and Clark (1977) and Kretschmer and Kretschmer (1978) discuss the discourse level information used in spoken conversations as part of pragmatics. We cannot assume that the same devices are used in print. Differences between the two modes exist because a reader is not as easily able to verify understanding with the author as the listener is with the speaker in conversations.

To summarize the areas of research that have provided information about linguistic skills needed for reading, Table 23.1 provides a breakdown of the levels of linguistic skills thought to be involved and the types of research available to substantiate the use of these skills in reading by hearing and deaf individuals.

OTHER COGNITIVE SKILLS FOR READING

In Goodman's (1973) model, reading also requires the use of contextual references, the use of past experiences, and the conceptual attainments of the reader.

The reader is faced with fewer nonlinguistic contextual cues to assist him or her in deriving the appropriate meaning from a message than is the listener in a conversation. Just as the effective listener makes use of environmental cues to understand spoken conversations, the effective reader must use cues available in texts such as formats, headings, charts, graphs, tables of contents, indexes, and pictures. A reader also learns to vary reading strategies according to his or her purpose for reading and learns to identify the author's intended purpose by the format and style present.

Readers learn to read carefully for details, to skim when they need general ideas from the text, and to scan in order to quickly locate specific information. The existence of such strategies has been verified. Levin and Cohn (1968) found that EVS was responsive to intentions of readers already at the second grade. Children in the second, fourth, ninth, and eleventh grades were asked to read passages under three conditions: (1) reading out loud to a teacher or friend—the normal condition, (2) reading all the details because someone would ask them questions—the careful condition, and (3) reading without paying attention to each detail because no questions would be asked and they just needed to get the general idea of the story—the skimming condition. At each of the four grades, the "careful" instructions yielded the shortest EVS, the "normal" instructions resulted in a longer EVS, and the "skimming" instructions in the longest EVS. In the earlier

Table 23.1

Types of Research Currently Available Related to Linguistic Skills Used in Reading by Hearing and Deaf Readers

Population	Levels of Linguistic Skills Used in Reading[a]		
	Word level	Sentence level	Discourse level
Hearing	EMG Memory confusion Letter detection	EVS Eye movement Syntactic/semantic complexity effects	Story schema
Deaf	Memory confusion Letter detection	EVS Syntactic/semantic complexity effects	

[a] EMG, electromyography; EVS, eye-voice span.

grades, the children demonstrated EVSs for the normal condition close to those for the careful condition. However, at the high school grades, the EVSs obtained for the normal condition were closer to those for the skimming condition. From these data, Levin and Cohn conclude that normal reading for beginners involves processes they typically use for detailed reading. Younger, less experienced readers normally use strategies requiring close attention to each word and little forward scanning. Older, more experienced readers usually read for general ideas, so that strategy is similar to the normal for them. We do not have comparable information for deaf readers and, thus, cannot say whether they have learned to vary their reading strategies according to their purpose for reading.

Readers also rely on their prior knowledge of the content to determine effective reading strategies (Allen, 1972). Drury (1980) hypothesizes that deaf readers' comprehension of passages will be affected by the degree of prior knowledge they have on topics to be read when syntax and vocabulary parameters are held constant and only prior knowledge is varied. Additionally, we can ask whether deaf students have learned to vary their reading strategies depending on their own familiarity with a topic when the purpose for reading is held constant.

Along with some prior knowlege on the topic to be read, a reader needs to have prior experience with the style or format used by the author for effective reading to occur. Stein and Glenn (1977) have investigated the rules used by children for recalling stories. They found children were using a schematic representation of stories to guide them in reading. The sophistication and utility of this schema is most likely developed through prior experience with written stories. Adult readers have probably constructed a variety of schematic frameworks that are accessed not only for the reading of stories, but also for the reading of scientific reports, technical manuals, text books, historical reports, opinion papers, recipes, etc. It is reasonable to hypothesize that the ability to comprehend the information contained in these formats relates directly to the individual's prior experience with such forms and his or her construction of the appropriate schematic representation.

Skills Necessary for Writing

Far less objective information is available on the processes required for writing compared to those required for reading. Simplistically, we can consider writing as the reverse of reading. The reader needs to determine the meaning intended by the writer; whereas, the writer must determine what he or she intends to communicate to the reader and then express it according to the convention of the system being used.

To write effectively, the author must have knowledge of the topic, knowledge of the context in which the message will be used, and an awareness of the background and needs of the intended readers. Also the writer must have an understanding of the formats typically used to achieve the intended purpose. For example, when writing directions, we typically present them in the order they are to be performed; when writing a research paper, we do not discuss the results of our statistical tests before describing the subjects and the procedures used to obtain our data; when writing a biography, we typically follow a chronological pattern; etc. The above are some of the cognitive skills required for effective writing.

Appropriate linguistic skills are also needed for writing to be effective. Writers, like readers, need to be familiar with rules for forming coherent discourse units. They need to understand how to begin and end a written message, how to inform the reader of the topic(s) being written about, how to change topics and show relationships between topics, how to form sections and paragraphs, and how to change from one sentence to the next.

Writers, like readers, also need to be familiar with the syntactic and semantic rules for forming written sentences, and with the morphographemic rules for writing words in their language system.

Little research is available on the development of writing skills by hearing individuals. Bissex (1980) presents a case study of her son's learning to write in which he progressed from a relatively simple and undifferentiated form of writing at age 5 with no spaces between words and largely a linking of letters to sound of words to a more conventional system by age 7 with word segmentation, punctuation, and a morphophonemic spelling system. Initially, he spoke the words aloud as he wrote them; later he wrote silently and judged spellings more by sight than sound. Even his earliest writings at 5 years were sentence forms, not only individual words. He communicated full propositions through writing, but Bissex does not compare the syntax in her son's spoken and written language forms.

In a study investigating the grammatical structures used by hearing children in grades 3 through 8, Crandall (1978a) found that the overall percent of main clauses compared to embedded clauses decreased as the children's grade placement increased and the percent of embedded clauses increased as grade placement increased. The greatest increase in frequency of use of embedded adverbial and adjectival clauses occurred between the

fourth and fifth grades, while the greatest increase in frequency of use of embedded nominal clauses occurred between the fifth and sixth grades. At the third grade only three types of embedded clauses were used by at least 15% of the children, while at the eighth grade seven types of embedded clauses were used by at least 15% of the children. There were no second level embeddings (embedded clauses within embedded clauses) used by at least 15% of the third or fourth graders; at the fifth grade only full adverbial clauses were found to be embedded at the second level by at least 15% of the children; and at the eighth grade second level embeddings used by at least 15% of the children included full adverbial, infinitive, and relative clauses.

Deaf children usually do not come to the learning of written language with a rich spoken language base. However, some deaf children come with a rich base in signed language. We do not understand how these children relate their language system to written English nor if a conventional written language system can be learned as a first language.

If the main purpose of writing is to communicate ideas, it is important to determine the effect of nonconventional written language on reader intelligibility (or comprehensibility). Burt and Kiparsky (1974) have investigated comprehensibility of English sentences produced by foreign students learning English as a second language. Crandall (1976) has investigated the intelligibility of deaf college students' written English.

Burt and Kiparsky collected a number of English syntax mistakes made by foreign students from a variety of countries in both their oral and written English used in and out of class and attempted to find a hierarchy of errors which a teacher could use to determine what is most important to correct. Their hierarchy was designed to provide teachers with information on how the violation of specific rules affected comprehensibility. They concluded that students' mistakes fell into two major categories: (1) global mistakes—the violation of rules involving the overall structure of a sentence, relations across constituent clauses, or across major constituents of simple sentences; and (2) local mistakes—violations of rules within a constituent, or within the clause of a complex sentence. They determined that global mistakes affect comprehensibility more than local mistakes. The relationship of this finding to teaching is discussed later in this chapter.

Crandall (1976) collected written language samples from deaf college students. All of the samples were written by the students in response to a short linguistic-free cartoon film. First the samples were sorted into five performance categories by teachers knowledgeable about written language problems of deaf students. The five categories were: (1) the reader is unable to understand the written message, (2) the reader is able to understand clearly little of the written message, (3) the reader is able to understand clearly about one half of the written message, (4) the reader is able to understand clearly most of the written message, and (5) the reader is able to understand clearly the entire written message. The results of this initial sorting indicated that readers did distinguish among these general performance guidelines and found compositions written by deaf college students varied as to their intelligibility. A Pearson (product-moment) correlation coefficient was calcu-

lated for a sample of 57 compositions each independently rated on the 1 to 5 performance scale by two judges (r = 0.58, $p < 0.01$). Each of the five categories of compositions were next studied to determine the types of English grammatical violations they contained. Compositions receiving a rating of 5 typically contained either no violations or spelling and punctuation errors only. Those receiving a 4 contained frequent English inflectional and derivational morphological errors; those with a 3 rating contained function word and contentive word errors. The compositions with ratings of 2 contained English structural errors involving the omission or ordering of major constituents. Compositions with a rating of 1 were rare for this group of deaf college students and were characterized by multiple major constituent omission and ordering errors. Based on this analysis a scoring procedure was developed. Scores, categories, and descriptors are given in Table 23.2. Each sentence received a score signifying the most severe error in the sentence. Sentence scores for the first 10 sentences in a composition were averaged to obtain an overall composition score. Experienced teachers were trained to use this scoring system and

Table 23.2

Scores, Categories, and Descriptors Used in Determining Written Language Intelligibility

Score	Category	Description
10	Acceptable	Free of mechanical and linguistic anomalies
9	Mechanical	Punctuation errors, spelling errors, word division errors, contiguous repetition of word within a sentence
8	Inflection	Bound inflectional morphemes, articles, phrase and clause *and* omission
7	Derivation	Bound derivational morphemes within nouns, verbs, and modifiers
6	Functor	Free functors including prepositions, verb particles, selected modifiers, conjunctions, infinitive *to*, pronouns, auxiliaries, modals, determiners, and negatives
5	Contentive	Contentive stem substitutions and additions
4	Structural	Major constituent omission and word order involving obligatory subject, verb, object
3	Multiple structural	Two or more 4-type anomalies within one *t*-unit
2	Unconnected	Listing of single words or naming of substantives
1	Unrecognizable	Unrecognizable words in lists, letter lists, scribble, only pictures

those who were able to obtain a correlation coefficient of 0.90 or more on overall composition scores and a correlation coefficient of 0.80 or more on a sentence-by-sentence score for a preselected sample of compositions were asked to score the original 57 compositions. These scores were then evaluated for interrater reliability ($r = 0.81$; $p < 0.001$), and these objective scores were compared with the initial subjective scores to determine construct validity for the use of grammatical correctness as a predictor of reader intelligibility; the validity coefficient that was obtained, $r = 0.59$; $p < 0.01$, was interpreted to support the hypothesis that grammatical correctness assessed by this scoring system reflected written language intelligibility.

The writing samples collected from the hearing children in grades 3 through 8 (Crandall, 1978a) were subjected to this intelligibility analysis. Each clause written by the children was assigned an intelligibility score. A significant effect of grade placement upon intelligibility was found. Clauses were written more intelligibly as grade placement increased. No interaction between grade placement and intelligibility by clause types was found. Within a given grade children wrote all clauses they attempted at similar intelligibility levels. It may be that native speakers have intuitive knowledge about what constitutes intelligibility in writing and avoid those structures that they think they cannot write intelligibly. Such a hypothesis merits investigation and would have significant implications for instruction.

The Burt and Kiparsky findings on comprehensibility and the Crandall findings on intelligibility in written language are pertinent to instruction in writing. The underlying assertion in both these studies is that successful writing is comprehensible writing.

READING AND WRITING DIFFICULTIES OF DEAF STUDENTS

In the previous section, research providing evidence for the validity of the use of linguistic cues at the word, sentence, and discourse levels in reading and writing was presented as well as a discussion of other cognitive skills thought to be required for successful reading

and writing. In this section, now that some bases for the existence of these behaviors have been established, deaf students' difficulties in the use of these skills is briefly reviewed.

Although there is considerable documentation showing that deaf adolescents' and adults' reading and writing skills are considerably below those of their hearing peers, there is less information on the exact nature of their difficulties. The majority of the difficulties in reading and writing have been attributed to a lack of mastery of the English language. An extensive review of English in the deaf population is presented by Bochner in this volume. The focus in education of the deaf has been on improving English language skills hoping that will in turn improve reading and writing skills. The teaching of English may proceed through auditory-vocal channels using spoken English, through visual-manual channels using signed English, through visual-written channels using printed English, or through some combination of the above. We have little objective data to support the use of one or another of these approaches to teaching English to the deaf and even less on how these approaches affect the learning of reading and writing.

There is little available research on the actual abilities and motivation of deaf adolescents and adults to learn reading and writing. The deaf adolescent has had years of direct instructional intervention designed to teach reading and writing. He or she cannot be considered a naive learner and has established definite impressions about the purpose of learning English, the type of instruction received, and has specific motivations for continuing the pursuit of learning English (Meath-Lang, 1980). Nonetheless, demographic studies indicate that deaf students demonstrate little growth in reading achievement between the ages of 13 and 20 years and only about 10% of deaf young adults read at or above the eighth-grade level (Trybus and Karchmer, 1977). However, there is indication that deaf adults can improve their reading and writing skills at a rate better than that reported in demographic studies (Hammermeister, 1971; Crandall, 1978b and 1980a). Hammermeister studied 60 deaf adults who had completed their education at a residential school for the deaf 7–13 years prior to her investigation. Ten of these adults had attended college. She found that their reading vocabulary skills as measured by the Stanford Achievement Test, word meaning subtest, had significantly increased after completing high school; the subjects obtained a mean GLE score of 5.08 upon completing high school and as adults a score of 5.72. Their reading comprehension skills as measured by the paragraph meaning subtest did not show a significant increase; a mean GLE of 5.57 was obtained in high school compared to a mean GLE of 5.68 as adults. These findings in vocabulary are in agreement with Lenneberg's (1966) claims that vocabulary is an aspect of language that continues to grow into adulthood. Crandall (1980a) reported that deaf college students enrolled in special courses designed to teach reading and writing skills significantly improved both their vocabulary and reading comprehension skills as measured by the California Reading Test. After 40 weeks of instruction, the 265 students in the study had increased their vocabulary GLE scores from 7.38 to 8.52 and their reading comprehension GLE scores from 8.46 to 9.44. These results are similar to the 10 college subjects in Hammermeister's study who increased their vocabulary scores from 6.77 to 8.54 and their comprehension scores from 8.61 to 9.60. The reasons for the lack of growth in reading comprehension by noncollege students is not readily apparent. Perhaps the direct instruction provided at college produced this growth, or perhaps a minimum achievement level is necessary for growth in reading comprehension to occur in adulthood. To capitalize on this apparent ability to increase vocabulary and reading comprehension skills in adolescense and adulthood, we must have more specific information on the nature of the task difficulties. Hammermeister's results indicate that an increase in English vocabulary knowledge does not necessarily have observable effects on reading comprehension. This coupled with Drury's (1980) findings that vocabulary complexity causes fewer problems in reading comprehension than syntactic complexity for deaf college students leads to the hypothesis that deaf adults do not increase their knowledge of English syntax without direct instruction and

that improved knowledge of syntax will not follow solely from additional exposure to print in the environment. If the latter occurred, we should see far greater growth in reading skills during adolescence and adulthood than are now obtained.

Krashen (1975) investigated the effects of exposure versus the effects of instruction on the English proficiency of adults learning English. His findings support the above hypothesis that deaf adolescents and adults require instruction, not only exposure to demonstrate greater growth in reading. He correlated English placement examination scores with students' reports of the number of years they had spent in English-speaking countries and the number of years they had received formal instruction. He found that formal instruction was a better predictor of English proficiency than years in the environment and suggests that the isolation of rules and the feedback for error correction received during instruction are necessary for adult language learning. If this is true, it becomes critical for us to know which rules need isolation and which errors should be corrected if we are to have a greater impact on the learning of reading and writing by deaf adolescents and adults.

Quigley et al. (1976) have provided thus far the most detailed information on deaf students' knowledge of English syntax. Their data provide information on which English syntactic structures have been learned and their order of difficulty. Their research resulted in the *Test of Syntactic Abilities* (TSA) (Quigley et al., 1978). Both a screening test and a diagnostic test are available. Test responses yield individual data on nine English structures—negation, conjunction, determiners, question formation, verb processes, pronominalization, relativization, complementation, and nominalization. Group data are reported for deaf students in the United States from the ages of 10–19 years, hearing students in the United States from the ages of 8–16 years, deaf students in Australia from the ages of 10–15 years, deaf students in Canada from the ages of 8–18 years, and deaf college students in the United States. Quigley and King (1980) compared the performance of the above groups as well as a group of hearing college students studying English as a second language. They present some of the strategies and distinctive syntactic constructions used by these groups and conclude that there is support for the hypothesis that English is developed in similar ways by deaf students and hearing students learning English as a first or second language. They base their support on the presence of similar error patterns, strategies, and orders of difficulty on the TSA. Quigley and King, however, caution that "similar orders of difficulty do not imply similar orders of acquisition." Thus, their conclusion of similar development should be considered tenuous until we have information on order of acquisition. Nonetheless, the diagnostic information available from the TSA can be useful in determining which structures to isolate and provide feedback on when instructing deaf students.

We have no comparable measure to determine what specific lexical difficulties are encountered by deaf readers and writers. Walter (1978) hypothesized that frequency of occurrence in print was a good predictor of deaf students' vocabulary knowledge and devised a test to investigate his hypothesis. His results indicated that frequency of occurrence in print as calculated by Carroll et al. (1971) was related to vocabulary acquisition. Deaf students ranging in age from 10 years to college age knew those words with high frequencies of occurrence better than those with low frequencies. His investigation dealt with content words and their most commonly used meanings only. Walter's work along with that of Silverman-Dresner and Guilfoyle (1972) gives us some information on which words deaf students are likely to know at various ages, but little information as to the specific difficulties deaf students encounter in vocabulary acquisition.

In the area of discourse level linguistic skills and other cognitive skills for reading, there is less information available on deaf students' specific difficulties. Discourse level processing is an important component in making inferences in reading (Athey, 1980). Stein and Glenn (1977) found that hearing first graders were already making inferences when information in stories was missing. Marshall (1970) studied 9-year-old hearing children who obtained 4.0–4.9 GLE reading comprehension scores and deaf 16-year-olds

who also obtained 4.0–4.9 GLE reading comprehension scores. He found that although both the deaf and hearing students were able to make use of discourse level cues on a cloze task using third-grade reading materials, the hearing students consistently surpassed the deaf students. Walter (1975) found that deaf college students experienced significantly more difficulty on inference questions than on direct factual or literal questions on the California Reading Test.

Difficulty in making inferences seriously impedes reading comprehension because in the process of making inferences, new information is assimilated to known information and one's experential base is modified. We do not know whether these apparent problems in making inferences are due to inabilities to use linguistic cues in reading materials, use of inappropriate cognitive strategies, or a lack of content knowledge brought to the reading task. Without such information, areas of focus in the teaching of inference skills are largely guesswork.

READING AND WRITING SKILLS NEEDED BY DEAF ADOLESCENTS AND ADULTS

To capitalize on the potential abilities of deaf adolescents and adults, attention must be paid to their individual needs. Thus, a program of realistic diagnostic assessment of needs, instruction focusing on specific needs, assessment of skill growth, and evaluation of instruction are necessary. Few diagnostic tools are available for investigating specific reading and writing behaviors of deaf adolescents and adults. Because severe learning problems occur in these areas and because our teaching has not been extremely successful to date, diagnostic instruments are essential. (See Walter in this volume for assessment techniques.) For the majority of these students, only a few years of education are still available. It is essential to define precisely what the student is currently doing, what he or she needs to know and how it is best taught and learned.

There is considerable debate as to whether prelingually deaf persons acquire the English language using processes and strategies similar to those of hearing persons acquiring English (Gromley and Franzen, 1978; Scholes et al., 1978; Bochner, 1978; Quigley and King, 1980). This debate cannot be settled by studying which words, structures, or cognitive skills have been learned at different ages by deaf and hearing people; we will need to investigate the strategies used by the deaf in processing written English. If it is learned that deaf people are acquiring the language in the same way but at a slower rate than hearing people, diagnostic insight regarding their linguistic system is not critical. However, if they are using different strategies to learn and process written English, diagnostic assessment of deaf people's reading and writing skills will need to be based on models other than those of hearing people learning English.

Diagnostic evaluation of discrete linguistic components thought to be involved in reading and writing, such as syntax, morphology, lexicon, or phonology, need to be approached cautiously even if they are based on the correct model. They may not provide the appropriate instructional guidance if we do not understand the interrelations among these components as they contribute to reading and writing behavior and their relationship to paralinguistic and extralinguistic factors on an individual basis. Bever (1970) states that the presence and structure of language cannot be studied as a "composite function of various descriptively isolable language behaviors."

Affective variables may also influence deaf students' reading and writing needs. By the time adolescence is reached, a deaf student has completed about 10 years of English language instruction and is typically aware of his or her reading and writing difficulties. We might hypothesize that one of the reasons for very little progress in reading and writing occurring during adolescence and adulthood is due to a lack of any real motivation in these areas. This does not appear to be the case, however. Costello (1977) and Donnels (1976) report deaf adults rank English language training a high priority and consider improvement of written English critical for success. Meath-Lang (1978) found that deaf college students with at least 1 year of full-time employment were significantly more positive toward continued English language instruction than those without such experi-

ence. Crandall (1978b) replicated Meath-Lang's study with high-school deaf students and found that students with employment experiences again demonstrated more positive attitudes toward English language instruction. Both of these findings imply that deaf students need contact with the environment outside of the school, i.e., experience with the environment education is preparing them for, in order to develop positive attitudes regarding reading and writing.

We cannot determine the skills a reader or writer must learn without first establishing the goals of instruction. Crandall (1978b) argues that programs for deaf students can have two interrelated goals: (1) to establish proficiency in the target language symbol system, or (2) to acquire strategies to reduce negative effects of less than proficient competency. Success with the first goal will result in accomplishment of the second; but the converse is not true. Traditionally the teaching of reading and writing skills has been designed with the first goal in mind; but we have not experienced the needed success to also accomplish the second goal. This condition leaves the deaf adult in an unfortunate position. He or she experiences negative reactions in situations where reading or writing cannot be avoided because written information is misinterpreted and the resultant behavior inappropriate. Instructional programs designed to achieve goal 1 above will begin by determining which reading and writing skills the individual does not possess and then attempt to teach those skills. The program designed to achieve goal 2 will examine the skills already known by the individual and seek to capitalize upon those strengths. However, to work toward goal 2, we need an individual who has, in fact, acquired at least a minimum set of skills.

By adolescence or young adulthood in spite of low reading test scores, it is reasonable to expect that some reading and writing skills have been learned. For example, even though many deaf people are unable to obtain reading scores above the fourth-grade level, reading has been found to be their most efficient and effective means of receiving information (Gates, 1970; Norwood, 1976; North and Stevenson, 1975). This finding suggests either that deaf people have acquired some successful reading strategies that are not reflected in grade equivalent scores or that deaf individuals have been more successful in acquiring reading skills than other receptive communication skills. Because our teaching programs have usually focused their efforts on instruction of reading and writing skill components not already possessed by a deaf student but thought to be necessary for English linguistic proficiency, we might conclude that deaf students have acquired some successful strategies to avoid negative effects in spite of our teaching. At this point, the reader is referred back to the discussion of writing samples obtained from hearing children and the hypothesis that these native speakers had some intuitive knowledge about what constituted intelligibility in writing and avoided structures they thought they could not write intelligibly. Again, it is unlikely that these hearing children learned this strategy in school. We can hypothesize that deaf adolescents and adults would benefit from instruction specifically directed at the reduction of negative effects associated with weak reading and writing skills.

INSTRUCTION OF NEEDED READING AND WRITING SKILLS

It is reasonable to expect that many reading materials deaf people encounter outside of the English classroom will not be written at an easily comprehensible level. Materials will typically contain lexical items, syntactic structures, and discourse organization units that are outside the individual's English linguistic competency level. In fact, most deaf students are unable to read the books often used to teach reading. Quigley et al. (1976) analyzed the syntactic structures present in a series of reading textbooks frequently used with deaf children. They compared the frequency of occurrence of syntactic structures in these books with children's performance on the *Test of Syntactic Abilities* (Quigley et al., 1978) and found a significant discrepancy between occurrence and understanding. For example, 18-year-old deaf students obtained a mean of 59% correct in understanding relative clause embeddings and these structures appeared in 12 out of 100 sentences in a sixth-grade reading text; these same students re-

ceived a mean score of 63% correct in understanding infinitive and gerundive complements and these structures appeared in 32 out of 100 sentences in a sixth-grade reading text.

Written language data obtained from deaf college students indicated that at entry to college the written language of the average student was approximately 70% intelligible (Crandall and Albertini, 1980). The written language generated by the average deaf high-school student was found to be approximately 60% intelligible (Johnson and Kadunc, 1980). These data indicate a reader will encounter significant difficulty in comprehending these students' written communication.

In both the reading and writing measures above, the variance of scores around the mean is large. Thus, a reading or writing program must be planned on an individual basis. If our goal is to reduce negative effects directed toward the deaf adolescent and adult because of the misunderstandings resulting from his or her reading, an analysis of what the individual can and cannot understand must be undertaken. We will need to determine which type of lexical items, which syntactic structures, and which discourse arrangements can be understood as well as which combinations of these variables are comprehensible to the individual. This information will need to be evaluated as the individual's purpose for reading varies—e.g., reading for general information, for detailed information, or to locate specific items—and as the assumptions of the author vary regarding the prior content knowledge possessed by the reader.

Knowledge of these skills on an individual basis will enable us to design instructional programs focused on strengths. The objectives of instruction would be to increase the student's awareness of which reading materials can be comprehended under which conditions, to enable the student to predict when different reading rates are appropriate, and to increase independent learning skills in locating and using resources when specific reading difficulties arise. These resources may include (1) the use of an appropriate dictionary, (2) the use of an appropriate grammar text, (3) the location and use of relevant context cues in the text to clarify potential misunderstandings, (4) the location of background content information on the subject being read, (5) the use of organization schema to detect interrelations between propositions or (6) the use of input other than print to obtain the information.

This type of instructional program would be teaching primarily reading strategies and deemphasizing the direct teaching of English linguistic components. Materials for this program would need to be designed to gradually enable the student to use these strategies successfully with increasingly difficult reading materials both linguistically and cognitively. Currently, this type of program does not exist in the fields of reading education, deaf education, or in the field of teaching English to speakers of other languages. However, some of the components of such a program are in existence. Spache (1976) reviewed research conducted on hearing individual's use of context cues and presents an outline for a training program to promote greater skill in that area. Ekwall (1977) provides a procedure for diagnosing students' knowledge of context cues and procedures for instruction. Both Spache's and Ekwall's materials are meant for hearing speakers of English. From the field of teaching English as a second language, there is the *Longman Dictionary of Contemporary English* (Procter, 1978). The dictionary is designed for adults not proficient with English. Examples and definitions in the dictionary use controlled syntactic structure and vocabularly; only 2000 words are used and are listed at the back of the dictionary. The dictionary, therefore, contains definitions that are simpler than the words being used. Difficult definitions found in most dictionaries discourage many deaf students from using them. A sample sentence follows each definition and each of the 55,000 entries is coded as to its grammatical function within sentences. A teacher's guide and a student workbook accompany the dictionary. Several English instructors of deaf college students have found this dictionary useful (Haggerty, in progress). Another component available and originally developed for hearing readers, but currently being used in advanced English courses for deaf college students, is designed to provide organization schema to assist the reader in comprehending interrelationships among ideas in prose (Long et al., 1978). Reading and writing materials related to students' major areas of study are helpful for teaching students the role and use of background information. Such materials also contain the linguistic units students have experienced or will experience in their other courses. Teachers and researchers in a subfield of English as a second language, English for special purposes, have developed a body of literature addressing theories and procedures for using materials from a variety of technical and scientific areas for teaching English (Mackay and Mountford, 1978).

As previously stated, the majority of reading programs for deaf children are English language programs and stress acquisition of the target language symbol system. Although it is important for teachers to be cognizant of what has and is being practiced and what is available, it is not the purpose of this chapter to redescribe these programs. The reader is referred to Kretschmer and Kretschmer (1978, Chapter 6) for an extensive review of educational procedures.

In the teaching of writing, instruction could also be approached with the goal of reducing negative effects. To accomplish this, information is needed related to which types of words, structures, organizational units, topics, and purposes the deaf adolescent or adult can already write successfully. Studies of writing behavior have primarily looked at the types of problems encountered by deaf writers (Cohen, 1967; Odom et al., 1967; Myklebust, 1965; Kretschmer, 1972), and not at the effect of these problems on comprehensibility. Crandall (1976) and Burt and Kiparsky (1974) have addressed written language problems as they relate to comprehensibility. Analysis of the syntactic environments in which deaf adults' written language errors occur shows that some structures are written more intelligibly than others (Crandall, in progress). This finding suggests a writing program could be designed in which the student acquired a sensitivity regarding how to control his or her writing to better ensure its being intelligible. Fortunately in writing, the writer has control over how something is stated; whereas in reading, this power is not available. As with the design of reading programs, individual rather than group data would be necessary to plan a program.

The above recommendations should not be interpreted to imply that we should stop teaching specific English linguistic components to deaf adolescents and adults or that these students cannot increase their knowledge of the English language. It is a change in emphasis that is being advocated.

We have not been extremely successful in teaching reading and writing to deaf students by concentrating almost entirely on linguistic components. Until we have more precise information on how deaf students process these components while reading and writing, we will probably be unable to make significant strides. Many deaf adolescents and most deaf adults already possess a useful language system (Wilbur, 1979). They are asked to learn to read and write in a language based on an auditory system. Our goal in reading and writing instruction is that deaf individuals' reading and writing behavior should not result in their being denied educational, career, or recreational opportunities available to their hearing peers.

Very few investigations exist in which techniques or procedures used in the teaching of reading and writing to deaf people are evaluated. The studies which do exist have typically looked at the effects of oral and total communication environments on reading or writing (Moores, 1978) or the effects of socioeconomic level, degree of hearing loss, intelligence, and age of entry to school (Jensema, 1975; Trybus and Karchmer, 1977).

Recently a program of research to determine the effect of a variety of instructional variables on the improvement of reading and writing skills has been undertaken at NTID. In the below studies, reading comprehension was measured with the California Reading Test (Tiegs and Clark, 1963) and written language intelligibility with the NTID Written Language Test (Crandall, 1980a). The program of reading and writing instruction offered at NTID is described by Walter (1976) and Crandall (1978b). Crandall and Albertini (1980) investigated the effects of nine instructional variables on rate of reading and writing skill development: (1) hours of instruction per week, (2) amount of instructional hour used for teaching, (3) presentation design, (4) quantity of teacher utterances, (5) degree of approximation to English of teacher utterances, (6) degree of student involvement, (7) quantity of student utterances, (8) degree of approximation to English of student utterances, and (9) students' prior work experience. Even though significant gains in reading and writing were demonstrated by each of the 16 classes studied, only 4 of the 9 variables had a significant effect on the rate of written language skill development; none significantly affected the rate of reading comprehension gains. All of the variables related to intensity of teaching—1, 2, and 4 above—were significant. The authors advise that an increase in hours of instruction will not be efficient unless maximum use of the allotted time and quantity of teacher utterances also receive attention. There is probably a point at which too great a quantity of utterances on the part of the teacher will result in students not having sufficient interaction in the classroom. These findings related to intensity of teaching are supported in the English as a second language literature (Strevens, 1977; Krashen, 1975). The additional variable found to be significant by Crandall and Albertini was presentation design. Students in classes using an instructional design in which grammatical structures and vocabulary were isolated and taught in a logical sequence made the greatest gains. In this design, the students knew which items were being taught and these items were presented with critical features that distinguished them from other items. In most of these classes teachers sought to improve students' knowledge of the linguistic items involved in reading and writing and also provided advice to students regarding which of these items they could reasonably control in their writing.

Malcolm et al. (1980) hypothesized that it would be beneficial to provide reading and writing instruction to deaf college students at an intermediate English level, using strategies designed to capitalize on their strengths in aural-oral communication. They selected students for their experimental group who had speech intelligibility scores of 3.6 or more (Subtelny et al., 1981) and hearing discrimination scores of 15% or more (Johnson, 1976). These students were grouped together for reading and writing instruction offered by an English specialist together with a speech pathologist and an audiologist. A control group with equivalent reading, writing, speech, and hearing discrimination scores was given reading and writing instruction together with other students having equivalent reading and writing scores but various speaking and listening abilities. The control group was taught by the English specialist alone. They found the experimental group demonstrated significantly greater gains in reading comprehension than the control group. Forman and Spector (1980) describe the rationale and some procedures for providing multidisciplinary English language instruction in reading, writing, speaking, and listening skills to deaf students. An experiment similar to the Malcolm et al. (1980) study, was conducted by Keach (1981) with deaf college students at a beginning English level and the same results were obtained. Students grouped together with good aural-oral skills made significantly greater reading comprehension gains than when they received instruction grouped only by English level. Currently we do not know if a similar positive effect on reading and writing gains would be realized if students who had good American Sign Language skills were grouped together for English instruction and instruction were designed to capitalize on their strengths in sign language.

Additional information is needed for us to be able to explain why the above results were obtained. Perhaps the students with good aural-oral skills were using an internal speech code for decoding printed materials and the instruction promoted its use. Such a conclusion cannot be made without objective evidence that this was happening. Furthermore, we need to determine why these students made significantly greater gains in reading but not in writing when this approach was used. Also we need to have reasons for the finding that teaching intensity and the presentation designs thus far investigated affected writing more positively than reading.

Before we can significantly alter the success patterns deaf students demonstrate in learning to read and write, we will need to (1) understand the processes deaf readers and writers are using, (2) determine how these processes relate to reading and writing success, and (3) determine the reading and writing strategies deaf adolescents and adults can use to compensate for a lack of proficiency with the English language.

References

Allen, P. What teachers of reading should know about the writing system. In R. Hodges and E. Rudorf (eds.), *Language and Learning to Read.* New York: Houghton & Mifflin, 1972, 87–99.

Athey, I. Language, reading and the deaf. In N.N. Reynolds and C.M. Williams (eds.), *Proceedings of the Gallaudet Conference on Reading in Relation to Deafness.* Washington, D.C.: Gallaudet College, 1980, 260–297.

Baron, J. Phonemic stage not necessary for reading. *Q. J. Exp. Psychol.*, 1973, *25*, 241–246.

Bever, T.G. The cognitive basis for linguistic structures. In J. Hayes (ed.), *Cognition and the Development of Language.* New York: John Wiley, 1970, 279–362.

Bissex, G.L. *Gyns at Work: A Child Learns to Write and Read.* Cambridge, Mass.: Harvard University Press, 1980.

Bochner, J.H. Error, anomaly, and variation in the English of deaf individuals. *Lang. Speech*, 1978, *21*, 174–189.

Bollinger, D. *Aspects of Language*, Ed. 2. New York: Harcourt-Brace-Jovanovich, 1975.

Burt, M., and Kiparsky, E. Global and local mistakes. In J. Schumann and N. Stenson (eds.), *New Frontiers in Second Language Learning.* Rowley, Mass.: Newbury House Publishers, 1974.

Carroll, J.B., Davies, P., and Richman, B. *Word Frequency Book.* New York: American Heritage Publishing, 1971.

Chen, K. Acoustic image in visual detection for deaf and hearing college students. *J. Gen. Psychol.*, 1976, *94*, 243–246.

Clark, H., and Clark, E. *Psychology and Language.* New York: Harcourt-Brace-Jovanovich, 1977.

Coady, J. A psycholinguistic model of the ESL reader. In R. Mackay, B. Barkman, and R. Jordan (eds.), *Reading in a Second Language.* Rowley, Mass.: Newbury House Publishers, 1979, 5–12.

Cohen, S. Predictability of deaf and hearing story paraphrasing. *J. Verb. Learn. Verb. Behav.*, 1967, *6*, 916–921.

Conrad, R. Short-term memory in the deaf: a test for speech coding. *Br. J. Psychol.*, 1972a, *67*, 173–180.

Conrad, R. Speech and reading. In J.F. Kavanaugh and I. Mattingly (eds.), *Language by Ear and by Eye: The Relationships between Speech and Reading.* Cambridge, Mass.: MIT Press, 1972b.

Conrad, R. *The Deaf School Child: Language and Cognitive Function.* London: Harper & Row, 1979.

Cooley, J.D. *Use of Grammatical Constraint in Reading by Young Deaf Adults as Reflected in Eye-Voice Span.* Rochester, N.Y.: NTID, 1981.

Corcoran, D.W.J. An acoustic factor in letter cancellation. *Nature*, 1966, *210*, 658.

Costello, E. Continuing education for deaf adults: a national needs assessment. *Am. Ann. Deaf*, 1977, *122*, 26–32.

Crandall, K.E. The NTID written language test: procedures and reliability. Paper presented at the Annual Convention of the American Speech and Hearing Association, Houston, November 1976.

Crandall, K.E. Development of clausal complexity and grammatical acceptability in written language. Paper presented at the Annual Convention of the American

Speech and Hearing Association, San Francisco, November 1978a.

Crandall, K.E. Reading and writing skills and the deaf adolescent. *Volta Rev.*, 1978b, *80,* 319–332.

Crandall, K.E. English proficiency and progress made by NTID students. *Am. Ann. Deaf,* 1980a, *125,* 417–426.

Crandall, K.E. *Written Language Scoring Procedures for Grammatical Correctness According to Reader Intelligibility.* Rochester, N.Y.: NTID, 1980b.

Crandall, K.E. Clausal complexity and intelligibility in deaf students' writing. Rochester, N.Y.: NTID, in progress.

Crandall, K.E., and Albertini, J.A. An investigation of variables of instruction and their relation to rate of English language learning. *Am. Ann. Deaf,* 1980, *125,* 427–434.

Donnels, L. Adult basic education program for deaf people. In *Proceedings of the 47th Meeting of the Convention of American Instructors of the Deaf.* Washington, D.C.: U.S. Government Printing Office, 1976, 480–483.

Drury, A.M. Syntactic complexity, vocabulary difficulty, and readability for deaf college students. Doctoral dissertation, University of Rochester, Rochester, N.Y., 1980.

Edfeldt, A.W. *Silent Speech and Silent Reading.* Chicago: University of Chicago Press, 1960.

Ekwall, E.E. *Teacher's Handbook on Diagnosis and Remedation in Reading.* Boston: Allyn & Bacon, 1977.

Farr, R. *Reading: What Can Be Measured?* International Reading Assoc., Research Fund Monograph for the ERIC/CRIER Reading Review Series, 1969.

Forman, J.D., and Spector, P.B. A multi-disciplinary approach to teaching English. *Am. Ann. Deaf,* 1980, *125,* 400–405.

Gates, R.R. The reception of verbal information by deaf students through a television medium—a comparison of speechreading, manual communication and reading. In *Proceedings of the 44th Convention of the American Instructors of the Deaf,* 1970, 513–522.

Gelb, I.J. *A Study of Writing,* Rev. Ed. Chicago: University of Chicago Press, 1963.

Gibson, E.J., and Levin, J. *The Psychology of Reading.* Cambridge, Mass.: MIT Press, 1975.

Goodman, K. Analysis of oral reading miscues: applied psycholinguistics. *Reading Res. Q.,* 1969, *5,* 9–30.

Goodman, K. The psycholinguistic nature of the reading process. In K. Goodman (ed.), *The Psycholinguistic Nature of the Reading Process.* Detroit: Wayne State University, 1973, 13–26.

Gromley, K., and Franzen, A. Why can't the deaf read? Comments on asking the wrong question. *Am. Ann. Deaf,* 1978, *123,* 542–547.

Haggerty, P. Use of the *Longman Dictionary* by deaf students. Rochester, N.Y.: NTID, in progress.

Hammermeister, F.K. Reading achievement in deaf adults. *Am. Ann. Deaf,* 1971, *116,* 25–28.

Hanson, V. Processing of written and spoken words: evidence for common coding. *Memory Cognit.,* 1981, *9,* 93–100.

Harrison, C. and Dolan, T. Reading comprehension—a psychological viewpoint. In R. Mackay, B. Barkman, and R. Jordan (eds.), *Reading in a Second Language,* Rowley, Mass.: Newbury House Publishers, 1979, 13–23.

Jensema, C. *The Relationship between Academic Achievement and the Demographic Characteristics of Hearing Impaired Children and Youth.* Series R, Number 2. Washington, D.C.: Office of Demographic Studies, Gallaudet College, 1975.

Johnson, D.D. Communication characteristics of a young deaf adult population: techniques for evaluating their communication skills. *Am. Ann. Deaf,* 1976, *121,* 409–424.

Johnson, D.D., and Kadunc, N.J. Usefulness of the NTID communication profile with secondary-level students. *Am. Ann. Deaf,* 1980, *125,* 337–349.

Keach, R.B. *Effects of Concurrent and Complementary Training in Spoken, Read, and Written English: Reading Comprehension and Written Language.* Rochester, N.Y.: NTID, 1981.

Krashen, S.D. The critical period for language acquisition and its possible bases. In D. Aaronson and R.W. Rieber (eds.), *Developmental Psycholinguistics and Communication Disorders.* New York: New York Academy of Sciences, 1975, 211–224.

Kretschmer, R.R. Jr. Transformational linguistic analysis of the written language of hearing impaired and normal hearing students. Doctoral dissertation, Columbia University, New York City, 1972.

Kretschmer, R.R., Jr., and Kretschmer, L.W. *Language Development and Intervention with the Hearing Impaired.* Baltimore: University Park Press, 1978.

LaBerge, D. Beyond auditory coding. In J.F. Kavanaugh and I. Mattingly (eds.), *Language by Ear and by Eye: The Relationships between Speech and Reading.* Cambridge, Mass.: MIT Press, 1972.

Lenneberg, E.H. The natural history of language. In F. Smith and G.A. Miller (eds.), *The Genesis of Language.* Cambridge, Mass.: MIT Press, 1966.

Lennon, R.T. What can be measured? *Reading Teacher,* 1962, *15,* 326–337.

Levin, H. *The Eye-Voice Span.* Cambridge, Mass.: MIT Press, 1979.

Levin, H., and Cohn, J.A. Studies of oral reading: The effects of instruction on the eye-voice span. In H. Levin, E.J. Givson, and J.J. Gibson (eds.), *The Analysis of Reading Skill.* Final report, Project 5-1213 from Cornell University to the U.S. Office of Education, December, 1968, 254–283.

Levin, H., and Kaplan, E.L. EVS within active and passive sentences. *Lang. Speech,* 1968, *11,* 251–258.

Levin, H., and Turner, E.A. Sentence structure and the eye-voice span. In H. Levin, E.J. Gibson, and J.J. Gibson (eds.), *The Analysis of Reading Skill.* Final report, Project 5-1213 from Cornell University to the U.S. Office of Education, December, 1968, 196–220.

Levin, J., Grossman, J., Kaplan, E., and Yang, R. Constraints in the EVS in right and left embedded sentences. *Lang. Speech,* 1972, *15,* 30–39.

Locke, J.L. Phonemic processing in silent reading. *Percept. Mot. Skills,* 1971, *32,* 905–906.

Locke, J.L. Phonemic effects in the silent reading of hearing and deaf children. *Cognition,* 1978, *6,* 175–187.

Locke, J.L., and Fehr, F.S. Young children's use of the speech code in learning. *J. Exp. Child Psychol.,* 1970, *10,* 367–373.

Locke, J.L., and Locke, V.W. Deaf children's phonetic, visual, and dactylic coding in a graphemic recall task. *J. Exp. Psychol.,* 1971, *89,* 142–146.

Long, G., Hein, R., and Coggiola, D. *Networking: A Semantic-based Learning Strategy for Improving Prose Comprehension*. Rochester, N.Y.: NTID, 1978.

Mackay, R., and Mountford, A. *English for Specific Purposes*. London: Longman, 1978.

Malcolm, A., Albertini, J.A., Burke, M.E., and Humphrey, B.K. A comparison of English language skill improvement between interdisciplinary and non-interdisciplinary English classes. *Am. Ann. Deaf*, 1980, *125*, 435–438.

Mark, L.S., Shankweiler, D., Liberman, I.Y., and Fowler, C.A. Phonetic recoding and reading difficulty in beginning readers. *Memory Cognit.*, 1977, *5*, 623–629.

Marshall, W.A. Contextual constraint on deaf and hearing children. *Am. Ann. Deaf*, 1970, *115*, 682–689.

McGuigan, F.J. Convert oral behavior during the silent performance of language tasks. *Psychol. Bull.*, 1970, *74*, 309–326.

McGuigan, F.J., and Winstead, C.L., Jr. Discriminative relationship between covert oral behavior and the phonemic system in internal information processing. *J. Exp. Psychol.*, 1974, *103*, 885–890.

Meath-Lang, B. A comparative study of experienced and non-experienced groups of deaf college students: their attitudes toward language learning. *Teach. Engl. Deaf*, 1978, *5*, 9–14.

Meath-Lang, B. Deaf students' perceptions of their English language learning: Rationale for an experienced-based curriculum model. Doctoral dissertation. University of Rochester, Rochester, N.Y., 1980.

Moores, D.F. *Educating the Deaf: Psychology, Principles, and Practices*. Boston: Houghton Mifflin, 1978.

Myklebust, H.R. *Development and Disorders of Written Language,* Vol. 1, *Picture Story Language Test*. New York: Grune & Stratton, 1965.

Norman, D. The role of memory in the understanding of language. In J.F. Kavanaugh and I. Mattingly (eds.), *Language by Ear and Eye: The Relationships between Speech and Reading*. Cambridge, Mass.: MIT Press, 1972.

North, A., and Stevenson, V. The effects of total communication, manual communication, oral communication, and reading on the factual information in residential school deaf children. *Am. Ann. Deaf*, 1975, *120*, 48–57.

Norwood, M. Comparison of an interpreted and captioned newscast among deaf college graduates. Doctoral dissertation, University of Maryland, 1976.

Odom, R., Blanton, R., and Nunnally, J. Some "cloze" technique studies of language capability in the deaf. *J. Speech Hear. Res.*, 1967, *10*, 816–827.

Proctor, P. *Longman Dictionary of Contemporary English*. London: Longman, 1978.

Quigley, S.P., and King, C.M. Syntactic performance of hearing impaired and normal hearing individuals. *Appl. Psycholinguist.*, 1980, *1*, 329–356.

Quigley, S.P., Wilbur, R.B., Power, D.J., Montanelli, D.S., and Steinkamp, M. *Syntactic Structures in the Language of Deaf Children*. Urbana, Ill.: Institute for Child Behavior and Development, 1976.

Quigley, S.P., Steinkamp, M.W., Power, D.J., and Jones, B.W. *Test of Syntactic Abilities*. Beaverton, Ore.: Dormac, 1978.

Resnick, L.B. Relations between perceptual and syntactic control in oral reading. *J. Educ. Psychol.*, 1970, *61*, 382–385.

Rode, S. Development of phrase and clause boundary reading in children. *Reading Res. Q.*, 1974–1975, *10*, 124–142.

Sachs, J.S. Memory in reading and listening to discourse. *Memory Cognit.*, 1974, *2*, 95–100.

Scholes, R., Cohen, M., and Brumfield, S. Some possible causes of syntactic deficits in the congenital deaf English user. *Am. Ann. Deaf*, 1978, *123*, 528–535.

Silverman-Dresner, T., and Guilfoyle, G. *Vocabulary Norms for Deaf Children*. Washington, D.C.: Alexander Graham Bell Association for the Deaf, 1972.

Spache, G.D. *Diagnosing and Correcting Reading Disabilities*. Boston: Allyn & Bacon, 1976.

Stein, N.L., and Glenn, C.G. A developmental study of children's construction of stories. Paper presented at the Conference of the Society for Research in Child Development, New Orleans, March 1977.

Strevens, P. Causes of failure and conditions for success in the learning and teaching of foreign languages. In H.E. Brown, C.A. Yorio, and R. J. Crymes (eds.), *On TESOL '77 Teaching and Learning English as a Second Language: Trends in Research and Practice*. Washington, D.C.: TESOL, 1977, 266–277.

Subtelny, J.D., Orlando, N.A., and Whitehead, R.L. *Speech and Voice Characteristics of the Deaf*. Washington, D.C.: Alexander Graham Bell Association for the Deaf, 1981.

Tiegs, E.W., and Clark, W.W. *California Reading Test, Junior High Level, WXYZ Series*. Monterey, Calif.: California Test Bureau, 1963.

Trybus, R., and Karchmer, M. School achievement scores of hearing-impaired children: National data on achievement status and growth patterns. *Am. Ann. Deaf*, 1977, *122*, 62–69.

Trybus, R., Buchanan, C., and DiFrancesca, S. *Studies in Achievement Testing, Hearing Impaired Students, United States, Spring 1971*. Series D, No. 11. Washington, D.C.: Office of Demographic Studies, Gallaudet College, 1973.

Vasquez, C.A., Glucksberg, S., and Danks, J.H. Intergration of clauses in oral reading: the effects of syntactic and semantic constraints on the eye-voice span. *Reading Res. Q.*, 1977–1978, *13*, 174–187.

Walter, G.G. *Evaluation of the California Reading Test for Use with Post-Secondary Deaf Students*. Rochester, N.Y.: NTID, 1975.

Walter, G.G. English skills assessment and program planning for NTID students. *Proceedings of the 47th Meeting of the Convention of American Instructors of the Deaf*. Washington, D.C.: U.S. Government Printing Office, 1976, 592–602.

Walter, G.G. Relationship of word knowledge to word frequency in young adult deaf students. *J. Commun. Disord.*, 1978, *11*, 137–148.

Wanat, S.F. *Linguistic Structure and Visual Attention in Reading*. Newark, Del.: International Reading Association Research Reports, 1971.

Weber, R.M. First graders' use of grammatical context in reading. In H. Levin and J.P. Williams (eds.), *Basic Studies on Reading*. New York: Basic Books, 1970,

147–163.

Wilbur, R. *American Sign Language and Sign Systems.* Baltimore: University Park Press, 1979.

Wolfram, W., Potter, L., Yanofsky, N., and Shuy, R. *Reading and Dialect Differences.* Arlington, Va.: Center for Applied Linguistics, 1979.

Wrightstone, J.W., Aronow, M.S., and Moskowitz, S. Developing reading test norms for deaf children. In *Test Service Bulletin, No. 98.* New York: Harcourt, Brace and World, 1962.

Zolinger, R.H. The psychological reality of information focus for the reader. Doctoral dissertation, Case Western Reserve University, Cleveland, Ohio, 1974.

Part VIII

Classroom Communication

Chapter 24

Preparation and Use of Educational Interpreters

ANNA WITTER-MERITHEW
RICHARD DIRST, M.S.

The past decade has introduced many new concepts into the educational process. Many of these new concepts are the result of legislative actions, such as PL 94-142 and Section 504 of the Vocational Rehabilitation Act of 1973. In an effort to implement these laws, school administrators have been confronted with the need for new and different types of personnel to assist in the education of handicapped children. One such personnel type is the interpreter for the hearing-impaired student.

The purpose of the educational interpreter is to extend communication between individuals who may not share a common communication mode or who in some circumstances are unable to share direct communication.

The interpreter, therefore, extends or represents ideas, moods, thoughts and words in the language modes the individuals use. This process and the technical skills associated with it are complex.

Interpreting is one method of facilitating communication between hearing-impaired individuals and hearing persons. The interpreter is able to transform the spoken words of a hearing person into a form of communication understood by the hearing-impaired person or transmit vocally the words or ideas of the hearing-impaired person to the hearing person. Such interpreting can be done by using either sign language or oral communication techniques. Interpreting also combines the use of both sign language and oral communication in a process known as simultaneous interpreting.

The communication barriers created by a hearing impairment have a cumulative effect and can often result in significant experiential deprivation. The hearing-impaired individual is frequently isolated within the family, denied meaningful relationships and can often feel like a foreigner within their own land. These barriers may affect social life, vocational life, education, recreation and the psychological/emotional development of the hearing-impaired individual. In other words, the entire sphere of human relationships can be affected by a hearing impairment. The interpreter, as a facilitator of communication, provides a medium to reduce the communication barriers faced by hearing-impaired individuals in a hearing society.

Any successful educational process requires a team effort. Ideally the teacher and student should function together as a team with common goals. Often the teacher employs the assistance of parents, aides, librarians, resource teachers and other professionals as a part of this "team effort." When an interpreter becomes part of the educational process, s/he too should become an integral part of this team.

The purpose of this chapter is to provide some insights into the roles and responsibilities of interpreters within the educational process. Additionally, the chapter will provide an historical perspective on interpreting and interpreter training, describe the various types of interpreting, the hierarchy of skill development associated with interpreting, sample coursework, and information for consumers of interpreting services.

HISTORY OF INTERPRETING

The first "interpreters" were hearing children of deaf parents, religious workers, and educators of the hearing-impaired. These individuals often concern themselves charitably, sympathetically, authoritatively, or paternalistically with the well being of hearing-impaired individuals. These first interpreters often "helped" the hearing-impaired individual at the expense of the individual's independence. While philanthropic in nature,

these interpreters often harmed the process more than helped.

During the late 1950's, there was an emerging recognition of the importance of interpreting services and the limited number of competent interpreters became evident. By the mid-1960's, this recognition was manifested by reports and several pieces of federal legislation. The Babbidge Report in 1965 and the National Conference on the Education of the Deaf in 1967 recommended that the full range of postsecondary and adult education programs available to the general public *also* be made accessible to the hearing-impaired population. In 1965, Public Law 89-333, the Vocational Rehabilitation Act, authorized interpreting services as a vocational rehabilitation (VR) case service for deaf clients. In June 1964, the Rehabilitation Services Administration sponsored a meeting of communication "helpers" at Ball State Teachers College. From this meeting the National Registry of Professional Interpreters and Translators for the Deaf was established. In 1965, at a second meeting in Washington, D.C., the name of the organization was changed to the Registry of Interpreters for the Deaf (RID).

From the mid-1960's until the mid-1970's, the profession of interpreting grew dramatically. A code of ethics to ensure the professionalism of interpreters was developed and accepted by the membership. In 1972 the RID initiated a system of evaluations and certifications of interpreters to determine the competency level of an interpreter based on skill performance. Interpreters began to receive payment for services instead of a strictly volunteer service.

Presently the RID offers certification in three areas: sign language interpreting, oral interpreting and specialized certificates in legal interpreting and performing arts interpreting. Certificates are awarded to interpreters taking a performance evaluation based on the interpreter's proficiency and competence at various levels of skill and knowledge of the interpreting profession. Since 1972, over 3000 certificates have been issued by the RID to interpreters throughout the country.

The RID currently has a national membership of 5000 members with affiliated RID chapters in 48 states. In addition to providing a national evaluation/certification system, the RID serves as the professional organization for interpreters and distributes information to prospective interpreters and consumers of interpreting services.

Federal legislation in the 1970's legitimized interpreting as a right of the hearing-impaired individual. The Vocational Rehabilitation Act of 1973 (PL 93–112) emphasized that interpreting was a legitimate case service for deaf persons. Section 504 of the Act provided equal access of all services for handicapped individuals, including the elimination of communication barriers for the hearing impaired. This was followed by the Education for All Handicapped Children Act of 1974 (PL 94-142) which mandated greater integration of handicapped children, including deaf children, into the public school system. In 1978, the Vocational Rehabilitation Amendments (PL 95-602) not only placed the interpreter in the mainstream of the habilitation and rehabilitation process, but further guaranteed the deaf individual full access to services through interpreting.

PL 94-142 and Section 504 of the Rehabilitation Act are the primary basis for providing interpreters in educational settings from elementary school through postsecondary and adult education programs. Both of these pieces of legislation and their pursuant regulations require equal accessibility of all programs to handicapped students, which includes interpreting services for hearing-impaired students through the use of either sign language interpretation or oral communication interpretation.

INTERPRETER PREPARATION

Prior to the establishment of the National Registry of Interpreters for the Deaf, there were no defined expectations of individuals performing the interpreting task. Additionally, there were no programs offering formal interpreter preparation.

Earlier in this chapter, the impact of legislation on the interpreting profession was discussed. Likewise, legislation had an impact on the efforts to prepare interpreters. During the decade of the 1960's, several postsecond-

ary programs for hearing-impaired persons were established. These were: California State University at Northridge (CSUN) in 1964, National Technical Institute for the Deaf (NTID) in 1967, and three regional technical/vocational programs established in 1969: Delgado Community College, St. Paul Technical Vocational Institute, and Seattle Community College. Prior to this time, Gallaudet College, established in 1864, served as the major environment for postsecondary liberal arts education for hearing-impaired students.

Hearing-impaired students attending these newly established programs were often mainstreamed into classes with hearing students. The mainstreaming resulted in the need for various support services, inclusive of interpreting. The need for interpreters exceeded the supply, and the institutions began efforts to formally train interpreters. Many of the initial efforts were designed to fulfill an immediate need. The programs provided a large number of individuals, with an introduction to the interpreting profession, followed by on-going practicum and skill development through in-service training and supervision. This concept of "mass production" provided an increase in the *quantity* of services, but frequently the *quality* of services was lacking.

In 1973, individuals affiliated with the Deafness Research and Training Center at New York University wrote a proposal to regionalize efforts to train interpreters. This proposal was funded by the Rehabilitation Services Administration (RSA) and established the National Interpreter Training Consortium (NITC). This consortium consisted of six institutions across the United States. The implementation of this grant, which was completed in 1979, served a vital function in establishing curriculum guidelines, preparing trainers of interpreters, and increasing consumer awareness about interpreting needs.

All of these initial programs were complimented by the establishment of over 30 additional interpreter training programs. Also, Public Law 95-602 authorized the establishment of federally funded regional training programs across the United States. The Congress appropriated monies in 1981 to fund 10 such programs. The selection and establishment of these programs continues the important effort initiated by the NITC.

Most known interpreter training programs are described in a text entitled *A Resource Guide to Interpreter Training for the Deaf Programs* (Witter-Merithew et al., 1980). This guide provides a description of each program, student population, application procedures, and other related information.

In 1978 the RID established a set of accreditation guidelines (referred to in other sections of this chapter) for interpreter training programs. These guidelines are designed to insure quality preparation of interpreters graduating from programs which receive the RID professional accreditation. These guidelines are presently being reviewed and modified for implementation. During this same year the National Academy, associated with Gallaudet College, sponsored a conference to discuss the State of the Art of Interpreter Training. The result of this conference was a document entitled, *Interpreter Training: State of the Art* (Yoken, 1979), and is available through the Gallaudet College National Academy. It describes various materials, resources and curriculums related to interpreter training.

Through the combined efforts of NTID and St. Paul Technical Vocational Institute, interpreter trainers from all over the United States came together in 1979 to organize themselves into a group called the Conference of Interpreter Trainers. The purpose of this collective effort is the sharing of materials and resources, professional growth opportunities for trainers and to upgrade the teaching standards within the profession.

The future trends in interpreter training are likely to be influenced by several factors: continued implementation of current legislation, strides of the Conference of Interpreter Trainers, implementation of the RID Accreditation Guidelines, and the changing needs/expectations of the consumers of interpreting services.

HIERARCHY OF SKILL DEVELOPMENT

In order to determine the necessary skills an educational interpreter should possess, it is helpful to analyze the tasks that are associated with interpreting. A review of the section about the roles/responsibilities of the educational interpreter and interpreting terminology provides an initial job analysis. The RID has additionally listed a series of competencies which students graduating from an interpreter training program should possess. These competencies, abstracted from the *RID Proposed Accreditation Guidelines* (RID, 1978) are categorized into the areas of skill, knowledge, and attitudes. Graduates of interpreter training programs should possess the following skills, attitudes, and knowledge.

Skills

1. All certificate graduates from programs for training simultaneous and/or oral interpreters will demonstrate the following competencies:
   a. An ability to arrange appropriate interpersonal environmental conditions (e.g., lighting, seating, and mechanics) in response to one-to-one or group situations;
   b. An ability to effectively transmit the style, mood, and intent of the communicators;
   c. An ability to apply appropriate auditory and visual memory techniques as they apply to interpreting and translating;
   d. An ability to use appropriate signing and/or public speaking techniques as they apply to interpreting and translating;
   e. An ability to use the existing variety of telecommunication devices;
   f. An ability to select the appropriate language and/or communication system for given situations (*note*: for oral interpreters this would include the ability to select a level of English syntax and vocabulary which is appropriate for the skill level of the speechreader);
2. All certificate graduates from a program designed to train oral interpreters will also demonstrate an ability to rephrase sentences, retaining their original meaning, for higher visibility in speechreading;
3. All certificate graduates from a program designed to train simultaneous interpreters

will also demonstrate the following competencies:

a. An ability to use conversational ASL;
b. An ability to use conversational Manually Coded English;
c. An ability to translate a message from one mode (spoken/manual) to another (manual/spoken or spoken/spoken) in a quasisimultaneous manner;
d. An ability to interpret from one language (ASL or English) to another (English or ASL) consecutively;
e. An ability to select the appropriate level of English syntax and vocabulary as it applies to interpreting for deaf children, deaf youth, or deaf adults.

Attitudes

1. All certificate graduates from programs for training simultaneous and/or oral interpreters will demonstrate the following attitudes:
   a. A continuing interest in and evidence of developing and upgrading their professional competencies;
   b. An interest in and evidence of performing their functions in accordance with national, state, and local guidelines, regulations, and ethics;
   c. A recognition of their personal performance strengths, weaknesses and limitations;
   d. An interest in and evidence of fostering healthy interpersonal relationships.
2. All certifiable graduates from a program designed to train oral interpreters will also demonstrate the following attitudes:
   a. A strong support to pertinent professional organizations with special interest in promoting speech, speechreading and use of residual hearing;
   b. A high interest in and evidence of relating to hearing-impaired individuals of various ages and interests in the community who rely on speechreading, with or without the supplement of hearing, as their primary mode of communication;
   c. A strong willingness to work with speechreaders manifesting a variety of levels of competency.
3. All certifiable graduates from a program

designed to train simultaneous interpreters will also demonstrate the following attitudes:
   a. A strong support to pertinent professional organizations related to deafness, interpreting, sign language, or oralism;
   b. A strong interest in and involvement with the national and local deaf communities;
   c. A strong willingness to work with a variety of sign language or other communicative strategies such as gestures and the oral method.

Knowledge

1. All certifiable graduates from programs for training simultaneous and/or oral interpreters will know about the following:
   a. The principles of communicative and interpersonal dynamics;
   b. The principles of interpreting and translating;
   c. The respective roles of interpreters and translators;
   d. The psychosocial aspects of issues related to deafness;
   e. Situational processes and protocol;
   f. Professional organizational activities, certificates, publications and educational and work environments related to hearing-impaired (deaf and hard of hearing) children, youth, and adults;
   g. Hearing aids and their usage;
   h. Audiology, speech pathology, and various etiologies of deafness;
   i. The variety of telecommunications devices;
   j. Current trends and issues in education of the hearing-impaired (deaf and hard of hearing).
2. All certifiable graduates from a program designed to train oral interpreters will also know about the following:
   a. Existing formal systems of lipreading (speechreading) instruction;
   b. Homophemes (look-alike words) and words with low visibility and how to rephrase for added comprehension;
   c. The broad range of responsive behavior among individuals with hearing loss of varying degrees;

d. Integration of hearing-impaired children in regular classes, theory and practice, and integration and assimilation as processes.
3. All certifiable graduates from a program designed to train simultaneous interpreters will also know about the following:
   a. The linguistics of ASL and English;
   b. The history of the development of manual/visual language.

Most interpreters function within a simultaneous interpreting mode. This mode combines skills associated with oral interpreting and sign language interpreting. The chart in Table 24.1 gives an example of the sequence in the hierarchy of interpreting skill development.

This chart addresses only the technical or psychomotor skills of interpreting. While developing and mastering these skills, students would additionally be introduced to coursework related to the knowledge and attitudinal learning associated with interpreting.

The chart demonstrates that, as one example, the mastery of memory retention skills is a prerequisite to the mastery of actual interpreting skills. Additionally, mastery of oral interpreting skills precedes the mastery of simultaneous interpreting skills.

The four major content areas of interpreter preparation are:

Knowledge of Deafness. Coursework associated with various aspects and issues related to the social, academic, psychological and personal development of hearing-impaired persons and the implications of a hearing loss.

Interpreting Skills. Coursework associated with the hierarchy of skill development and mastery of interpreting skills. This mastery often requires 2–4 years of learning and practice.

Theory and Practice of Interpreting. Coursework related to the practices and rule learning associated with interpreting. Linguistical considerations, technical considerations, and interpreting terminology are learned.

The Professional Interpreter. Coursework related to professional standards and expectations, organizations, job opportunities, resume writing, career potential and certification.

These content areas may be distributed among a variety of courses and cover a 2–4-year time period. Coursework should be complimented with on-going practicum and critique.

ROLES AND RESPONSIBILITIES

Interpreting Process

An interpreter for the hearing-impaired is a facilitator of communication between a hearing-impaired individual(s) and a hearing person(s). The interpreter will convey the spoken message of a hearing person through the use of sign language and/or lip movements and convey in voice the message of the hearing-impaired person. The interpreter conveys the message between the individuals, but does not enter the dialogue as a contributing member of the communication.

During the interpreting process there are at least three individuals involved: a hearing person, a hearing-impaired person, and an interpreter. Clear delineation and understanding of the roles, responsibilities, and rights of the individuals involved in the process will facilitate a successful communication event.

Interpreting services are appropriate in educational settings when a student is unable to participate fully in the classroom and/or extracurricular activities due to communication difficulties (the inability to receive spoken

Table 24.1

Heirarchy of Interpreting Skill Development

1. Memory retention skills
2. Adequate facial expression and body language
3. Comprehension of the spoken/signed message of a hearing impaired person
4. Ability to orally interpret and translate
5. Mastery of sign vocabulary and language structure
6. Ability to communicate in sign language
7. Ability to simultaneously interpret and translate
8. Mastery of specialized vocabularies in English and sign language
9. Mastery of simultaneous interpreting and translating

communication and/or express himself/herself intelligibly through speech). Depending on the needs of the individual student and the program prescribed by the student's individual educational plan (IEP), interpreting may include conveying a spoken message to the hearing-impaired student through the use of sign language and/or lip movement. It might also include conveying the hearing-impaired student's signed or spoken message to others through speech. The interpreter hired to meet these individual needs may be either a sign language interpreter or an oral interpreter.

Interpreting Terminology

Interpreters who provide services to hearing-impaired persons and hearing persons generally use one of three methods of interpreting.

Oral Interpreting. The interpreter presents the speaker's remarks by mouthing the words without use of voice. This process also employs the use of facial/body expression and natural gesturing to convey the mood, intent, and feelings of the speaker. The interpreter may change some of the speaker's words to words that are easier to speechread.

Sign Language/Manual Interpreting. The interpreter presents the spoken remarks of a speaker by using signs and fingerspelling. This process also employs the use of facial/body expression to convey the mood, intent, and feelings of the speaker. The interpreter may mouth words but not necessarily every word.

Voice Interpreting. The interpreter will represent the signed message of a hearing-impaired person by using spoken English. This term also applies to the interpreter's spoken representation of a hearing-impaired person's spoken message. Since some people are often unfamiliar with the speech patterns of a hearing-impaired person, an interpreter may be used to present the information in more intelligible speech.

Not all interpreters are skilled in all three methods of interpreting. The persons responsible for hiring the interpreter will need to make sure that the interpreter's skills and qualifications are in fact compatible with a student's needs.

Interpreters using any of these general methods may interpret or they may transliterate. These two terms deal with language structure and comprehension and require some definition.

Interpret. The incidental or substantial rewording or rephrasing of a speaker's remarks. Generally this term refers to changing the language of the sender's communication to another language; e.g., English to American Sign Language and vice versa.

Transliterate. Changing the mode of the communication within the same language; e.g., English speech into a signed or manual code for English, or English speech represented in a more visible, speech-readable form, as in oral interpreting.

An interpreter will also follow one of two formats while interpreting: consecutive or simultaneous.

Consecutive. The interpreting format where the interpreter receives small amounts of information from a speaker, then pauses to represent the information into the other language. Then the process continues in this alternating until completed. This is the most appropriate format when ASL and English are being used, but because it is time-consuming, it is usually reserved for one-to-one situations.

Simultaneous. The interpreting format where the interpreter is interpreting at the same time the speaker is talking or signing. The interpreter will lag behind only a few words or a sentence. This format is the expected norm for interpreters and works well when interpreting from one form of English to another.

Most public schools prefer the use of Signed English or a manual code for English with nonvocalized lip movements since these systems represent the spoken message in English; however, there are some instances when American Sign Language may be the preferred and appropriate mode of communication.

Role of the Educational Interpreter

In an elementary or secondary school setting, the educational interpreter serves as one member of the hearing-impaired student's educational team. Generally, this team will include the student's classroom teacher(s), specially trained resource or supplemental teacher(s), tutors, notetakers, educational interpreter, and other ancillary personnel.

The educational interpreter's primary role is to be a facilitator of communication in the classroom. The interpreter interprets all communication from the instructors and students in class, instructional materials such as films, and so forth. Depending on student need, the interpreter may also interpret comments, recitations, reports, and verbal test responses of the hearing-impaired student to the teacher and classmates.

Another important role of the interpreter is to encourage increased independence on the part of the hearing-impaired student. As part of the general function of encouraging increased independence, the interpreter should, on a daily basis, be indirectly teaching the student how to use an interpreter appropriately and effectively. Additionally, the interpreter, or the interpreter supervisor, should teach the hearing-impaired student his/her own role and responsibility in the use of an interpreter.

By the time a student enters high school s/he should assume full responsibility for his/her own success or failure on meeting course requirements. In addition to increased self-confidence, the hearing-impaired student should have developed communication strategies allowing him to interact with others in his environment. Many hearing-impaired students in high school are able to work individually or in small group settings without an interpreter. Depending on the nature of the activity and the needs of the individual student, the classroom teacher may choose to dismiss the interpreter for that period.

The interpreter, as a member of the educational team, can serve an important role in the development and implementation of the hearing-impaired student's IEP. The interpreter very often possesses a working knowledge of the student's ability to function in a regular classroom setting. The interpreter can describe each student's mode of communication. The interpreter would also be able to describe other behaviors which the student may exhibit, such as attention span, motivation, peer interactions, and comprehension of various parts of the classroom activities.

The information which the interpreter has acquired will assist the student, teachers, and parents as they design and implement an appropriate educational program. The IEP should include an indication of the desired mode of communication for classroom interpreting; that is, whether the interpreters should use American Sign Language, Manually Coded English, Signed English, or oral interpreting. While the background and experience of individual interpreters may vary, the training of interpreters does not automatically include any formal preparation to determine appropriate educational options.

Most classroom teachers have had no experience working with an interpreter. They are generally unfamiliar with how the interpreter can assist them as they work with the hearing-impaired students in the classroom. Sometimes, the teacher may feel threatened by the presence of another adult in the room or there may be a tendency to add inappropriate functions to the interpreter's role. A formal in-service program for teachers would provide information about interpreting and assist the interpreter and classroom teacher in establishing an effective and productive relationship. For example, the interpreter has the responsibility to ensure the student understands the sign for a particular word or concept, but teaching the concept is the responsibility of the teacher. The interpreter and teacher should discuss new vocabulary in advance.

Since the interpreter has not been hired as a teacher, it would generally be inappropriate for the interpreter to assume any of the instructional responsibilities in the classroom, such as executing a test, assisting in grading papers, modifying curriculum, counseling, or disciplining students. The interpreter should not make educational decisions in lieu of the classroom teacher, respond for the student, or respond for the teacher. If the interpreter is doing things other than interpreting, the job title of interpreter would be inappropriate, and the job description should clearly outline the job responsibilities for the individual.

Administration and Supervision of Interpreters

In public schools which operate a special department for hearing-impaired students, the interpreter will generally report to the coordinator of services for hearing-impaired students. The coordinator is responsible for hiring, evaluations, and any other administrative or supervisory responsibilities as dictated by school policy. The coordinator should assure the procedures are in place to provide both teachers and interpreters the opportunity to resolve role conflicts, or other problems which might arise. In this setting, it is the responsibility of the coordinator to develop and clarify the communication philosophy of the program and to assist the interpreter in developing the skills necessary to function consistently with program goals.

In schools with no on-site coordinator services for hearing-impaired students, the building principal becomes the interpreter's chief administrator. As such, the principal must develop procedures to guarantee that the interpreter is hired and evaluated by a qualified person.

When developing an interpreter's schedule, it is important to remember that interpreting is physically exhausting. It is best to arrange the interpreter's schedule so that lecture and nonlecture classes are mixed whenever possible. The interpreter should not be completely scheduled from early morning to late afternoon. Periodic breaks need to be arranged throughout the day to maintain maximum efficiency.

Procedures should be established so that any special activities, such as field trips, assemblies, etc., will be covered by an interpreter when necessary. This may be easily accomplished through minor revisions in the forms used by the school to schedule the events. Extracurricular and after school activities must also be considered.

Dual Role Assignments

There are times when a school system cannot employ an educational interpreter on a full-time basis, and may wish to assign additional responsibilities to the interpreter. This creates a dual role situation; i.e. interpreter/tutor, interpreter/aide, interpreter/sign language instructor. Although this type of employment is generally discouraged, the reality of the situation often dictates the necessity.

If a dual role position is created, it must be clearly understood by the interpreter and others involved on the educational team what the responsibilities include. These additional responsibilities should also be clearly defined in the job description. It is also advisable to delineate percentages of time the interpreter will spend in each responsibility. The school system will need to be assured that the interpreter has the skills required for the additional role and responsibilities.

General Responsibilities

The educational interpreter serves as a member of the educational support team for hearing-impaired students. The interpreter's main responsibility is to serve as a facilitator of communication between the hearing-impaired student(s) and hearing individuals (i.e., instructional staff, other students). The following are specific responsibilities of an educational interpreter.

1. Transliterating and/or interpreting in educational classrooms, as assigned;
2. Transliterating and/or interpreting for other activities, conferences, telephone calls, workshops, as assigned;
3. Completing paper work as it relates to the interpreting tasks;
4. Preparing for interpreting assignments by studying content area, lesson plans, outlines, etc.;
5. Establishing physical setting in conjunction with the classroom teacher to optimize communication interaction;
6. Meeting with classroom teacher on a regular basis in regard to communication needs of the students;
7. Providing information to the classroom teacher, students (particularly the deaf students), and other staff, on how to maximize benefit from interpreting services;
8. Serving as a member of the IEP team as it relates to the communication needs of the hearing-impaired student;
9. Acting as a resource person for others about interpreting;
10. Participating in professional improvement activities;
11. Interpreting for extracurricular activities when possible.

There are additional functions which an educational interpreter may serve in a school system if they are qualified. The system needs to be aware that all interpreters do not have the qualifications to conduct these additional functions. If any of these additional functions are assigned to the interpreter, they should be included in the job description and clearly understood by the interpreter at the time of employment: (1) sign language instruction; (2) consumer education workshops; (3) deafness workshops; (4) supervision of other interpreters; (5) scheduling of interpreting services; (6) evaluating/critiquing other interpreters; (7) sign collection and recording; (8) transcribe written materials for educationally related materials, e.g., play scripts, audio tapes; (9) set up resource section in library; and (10) clerical duties.

School administrators should realize that there are certain areas which place the interpreter in a conflicting role with the basic responsibilities of an interpreter. One such responsibility is a counseling role. Since the hearing-impaired student may often relate to the interpreter due to the ease of communication, the hearing-impaired student may often request advice and counsel of the interpreter. The interpreter has not been trained to be a counselor and should not be placed in this position, but should refer the student to a counselor. The interpreter may function as a facilitator of communication between the counselor and the hearing-impaired student, but not as counselor unless s/he has the training and was hired to perform such responsibilities.

The following are responsibilities which may cause conflict with the role of the interpreter: (1) disciplining; (2) counseling; (3) notetaking; (4) rewriting of instructional materials; (5) advisor for youth groups; (6) liaison with families—social work; (7) teacher (language modification, etc.); (8) job placement; (9) speech therapy; (10) evaluator; (11) teacher aide; (12) provide transportation; (13) media specialist; and (14) language assessment.

CONSUMER EDUCATION

In order to make use of an interpreter as part of the educational process an effective and successful experience, it is important that the consumers, both hearing and hearing-impaired, understand their responsibilities in the interpreting process.

Some techniques that the teacher can employ to make the interpreting process as effective as possible are:

1. Taking time at the onset of the class to discuss with the interpreter and the students the interpreter's role in the classroom setting. This procedure allows all participants associated with the interpreting process to have a clear understanding of their individual responsibilities, needs and expectations;
2. Discuss class format with the interpreter. It is much easier for the interpreter to follow the instructors' "line of thinking" if they are attuned to the objectives and format of each class section;
3. Minimize movement when possible. Opportunities for direct communication between the hearing-impaired students and the teacher are enhanced when the teacher is in "full view." This allows the student to receive associational cues from the teacher, such as facial expression and body language. The nonverbal information often has a major impact on how a message is received;
4. Be sensitive to the "time lag" factor associated with the interpreting process. The interpreter lags behind a few words to insure their understanding of the message so there can be an appropriate representation to the hearing-impaired student. This lag time allows the interpreter to properly identify who is speaking in a group discussion or to direct attention to a demonstration or activity. When using media or some form of visual aide, it is important for the student to have time to look at the visual and absorb information before returning their attention to the interpreter. Since the hearing-impaired student processes most information visually, it is not possible to view the media and interpreter simultaneously;
5. Check periodically with the hearing-impaired student and the interpreter to make sure they are comfortable with the process;
6. Minimize the use of idiomatic phrases and language abstraction. Since some hearing-impaired students are unfamiliar with English idioms, it is difficult for them to conceptualize through an interpreter;

7. Emphasize new and technical vocabulary. Since vocabulary and technical terms may appear on exams or have an important influence on the learning process, it is helpful if the interpreter and student are alerted to new vocabulary and technical terms prior to their introduction in the classroom;
8. The pace of the teacher's speech affects the interpreting process. If the teacher speaks too rapidly, it makes it difficult for the interpreter to process the information effectively.

The use of these techniques can assist the teacher in managing the classroom process more appropriately while maximizing the effectiveness of the interpreter as part of the educational process.

The hearing-impaired student, as is true with any student, has certain responsibilities within the educational process. The student can assist in making the interpreted process successful by adapting a few simple practices. The student should:

1. Inform the interpreter and teacher when they are having difficulty understanding the message, keeping up with the speed, or when clarification is needed;
2. Review technical and new vocabulary before each class period;
3. Actively assist with resolving problems as they arise;
4. Be sensitive to the needs of the teacher and interpreter and clearly state their needs. The interpreting process requires equal cooperation if it is to be successful;
5. Provide the interpreter with an outline or script before formal presentations (such as a book report) are made to the class or instructor. This practice maximizes the interpreter's ability to represent the hearing-impaired student accurately.

The interpreter's responsibilities during the process are centered around three basic professional concepts: integrity, impartiality and confidentiality. The interpreter is responsible for maintaining the integrity and intent of what the teacher and student communicate. The interpreter also remains impartial— not interjecting personal opinion or counsel, which in some cases could be in direct conflict with the teacher or student. The interpreter must keep all information that is conveyed during the interpreting process confidential. This confidentiality protects both the hearing-impaired student and the teacher, particularly if sensitive information is transmitted during an interpreting assignment.

Other students in the class, who are non-hearing-impaired, might also find some general knowledge about the interpreter and his role helpful. This knowledge can assist them in their direct and interpreted interactions with the hearing-impaired students.

Communication is a shared responsibility. When all members of the process have a clear understanding of their roles and responsibilities within the process, the potential success is maximized.

SUMMARY

The educational interpreter has become an important member of the educational team for hearing-impaired students in elementary, secondary, and postsecondary programs during the past decade. Federal legislation, particularly PL 94-142 and Section 504 of the Rehabilitation Act, has provided the impetus for the "mainstreaming" of the hearing-impaired students in public schools and colleges and universities with the addition of interpreting services.

The addition of the interpreter in classrooms has been a new experience for most public school teachers and college instructors. It has also been a new experience for interpreters and hearing-impaired students. Information on the roles and responsibilities of each of those involved in the interpreting in the classroom setting has not been available until very recently. This type of information will assist all those involved to better provide successful communication.

The training of educational interpreters has also developed over the past few years. This training was begun as the need for additional interpreters became evident. The development of the hierarchy of skills required for educational interpreters and the curriculum development for training educational interpreters will help prepare skilled and effective interpreters to serve as members of the educational team.

References

Babbidge, H.S. *Education of the Deaf.* A report to the secretary of H.E.W. by his advisory committee on the Education of the Deaf. Washington, D.C.: U.S. Government Printing Office, 0-765-119, 1965.

Dirst, R., and Caccamise, F. History of interpreting. In *Introduction to Interpreting.* Washington, D.C.: Registry of Interpreters for the Deaf, Inc., 1980.

Education of the Deaf, the Challenge and the Charge: A Report of the National Conference on Education of the Deaf, Colorado Springs, April, 1967. Washington, D.C.: U.S. Government Printing Office, 1967.

Hurwitz, T.A., and Witter-Merithew, A. Principles of interpreting in an educational environment. In M.E. Bishop (ed.), *Mainstreaming: Practical Ideas for Educating Hearing-Impaired Students.* Washington, D.C.: Alexander Graham Bell Association for the Deaf, 1979.

RID Proposed Accreditation Guidelines. RID, Inc., 1978

Witter-Merithew, A., and Braddock, A. Effective use of the educational interpreter in the RIT classroom. *Teaching Institute Newsletter,* 1978 No. 4. *The Most Feasible Use of Interpreters as Support Personnel for Successful Mainstreaming of Deaf Students into Regular Technical Vocational and Other School Settings.* Conference Proceedings, Carlson, B., et al., St. Paul, Minn., 1979.

Witter-Merithew, A., Siple, L., Carlson, B., and Dirst, R. *A Resource Guide for Interpreter Training for the Deaf Programs.* Washington, D.C.: U.S. Government Office for Handicapped Individuals, 1980.

Yoken, C. *Interpreter Training: the State of the Art.* Washington, D.C.: The National Academy of Gallaudet College, 1979.

Chapter 25

Tutoring and Notetaking as Classroom Support Services for the Deaf Student

JIMMIE JOAN WILSON, M.A.

REQUIREMENTS FOR TUTOR/NOTETAKERS
    QUALIFICATIONS FOR TUTOR/NOTETAKERS

TRAINING OF TUTOR/NOTETAKERS
    PSYCHOSOCIAL IMPACT OF A SEVERE HEARING LOSS
    TUTOR TRAINING
    NOTETAKER TRAINING
    ADVANTAGES FOR TEACHERS

MANAGEMENT OF A TUTOR/NOTETAKER PROGRAM
    MANAGER QUALIFICATIONS AND DUTIES

Experience has indicated, and research has validated, the vital and paramount importance of tutoring and notetaking as support services for hearing-impaired young people in educational settings. Nonetheless, these vital services are the ones most resisted by school administrators, who fear their cost (while not, apparently fearing the costs of interpreting services), and militated against by faculty, who usually argue that the hearing-impaired children should "do it for themselves." The purpose of this chapter is to demonstrate the essential nature of notetaking and tutoring and to meet the objections usually raised in hopes that these services will be made more widely available to hearing-impaired students and their teachers.

The Education for All Handicapped Children Act, PL 94-142, has encouraged more parents of hearing-impaired children to seek educational placement for their children in local elementary and secondary schools rather than in traditional segregated educational institutions for the hearing-impaired. In addition, hearing-impaired students are seeking out postsecondary training in increasing numbers. Each year approximately 1500 deaf students enter postsecondary programs. Many of these students attend the National Technical Institute for the Deaf and Gallaudet College, or otherwise participate in established college-level programs for the hearing-impaired. Also, numerous deaf students will select a program having no special supports, then, as with their earlier education, may request support services to which they believe they are entitled.

Such educational mainstreaming is doomed to failure if appropriate support services are not made available to students *and* to their teachers. Mainstreaming without support services has been compared with child abuse (Bishop and Hurwitz, 1980) and could be considered "teacher abuse" as well. Without support services such as interpreting, tutoring and notetaking, hearing-impaired students are unable to have equal access to the classroom. For these students barriers are communicative, not architectural. They need access to the classroom presentations and materials, not merely entry into the room.

Support service for deaf students in classes with normally hearing students traditionally has meant a sign-language interpreter. However, an interpreter is not enough to meet all the needs of students, because not all deaf students *know* manual communication, and some prefer not to learn sign language. With only an interpreter, a hearing-impaired person must *look* at a teacher or interpreter constantly for understanding by speechreading and/or the use of manual communication. As a result, most hearing-impaired students have great difficulty in taking meaningful notes for themselves, though this should be encouraged whenever possible. Many students see notes as their primary source of study material, and would prefer a notetaker to an interpreter if forced to make a choice.

It would seem that notetaking and tutoring support services are needed for several reasons: (1) for *clarification* of classroom procedures and materials, (2) for *reinforcement* of concepts gained from reading and studying, (3) to provide *information* about daily classroom proceedings for the teacher or parents, (4) to *begin* the development of skills necessary for maximum use of support services in later school years, (5) to *guarantee* equal access to classroom materials, and (6) to provide an *in-class source* of information for the teacher about hearing loss and support services. It is obvious that a tutoring and notetaking program serves more purposes than merely reviewing material or reteaching for the student.

It is realistic to assume that at the second-grade level or earlier if students have adequate reading skills, notetaking and tutoring support are important, vital support services for the hearing-impaired person. For students in kindergarten and first grade, notes provide information for the teacher of the deaf or for parents who function as tutors even when students themselves are unable to read the notes. The notes also set the stage for assisting students to visualize the written word as their primary mode of study and learning in the future. This is a crucial skill for any student, but is particularly true for the hearing-impaired. Students must learn how to use support services advantageously, and the earlier this skill is developed, the more effective will be the program.

Experience has shown that junior high hearing-impaired students begin to experience a substantial information deficit. This is a result of several factors: (1) teachers make assumptions that students have understood instructions, (2) classes are larger, (3) public address systems are often used for information transmission, (4) students are expected to be more independent, and (5) great emphasis on gaining information through lectures and reading. Both notetaking and tutoring services provide students with a "home base" of information to help overcome the information deficit.

Further, in junior high school there are more discussion groups and noisy lab situations making it difficult for hearing-impaired students, who depend on residual hearing and speechreading, to see or hear as much as they did in earlier grades. Classes proceed at a more rapid pace, vocabulary is more technical and students are expected to read and understand much more on their own. Teachers present material through lectures and students are expected to listen and retain what they hear or see after only one presentation. These situations are compounded at the high school and college levels.

At all levels, hearing-impaired students have recounted painful memories about the examination they missed because of not knowing about it, the activity that was changed, the "F" they received because an assignment was done incorrectly. Such information was missed because of an announcement on the PA system or because of teachers who have the unfortunate habit of talking to the blackboard. The hearing-impaired student did not see to speechread or did not even know anything was being said. With a few experiences such as this, students develop a constant anxiety that they are missing something important.

For a hearing-impaired student, whose language is usually below grade level, all the situations identified above can interact to create a stressful and counter-productive learning environment. The students experience anxiety because they are afraid of missing something. Behavior problems may occur in younger children because the students can feel more in control of the situation when they are the center of attention.

Since our educational system, at all levels, is geared toward the lecture method, hearing-impaired students are often put into an unfavorable situation. They cannot look at the book or paper on the desk and at the same time maintain vigilance to see if anyone is speaking. A trained tutor/notetaker can solve many of these problems. A notetaker sitting nearby can cue the hearing-impaired student if necessary, or write down what is being said when the student is unable to watch.

If the tutor/notetaker is a member of the class, though this can present some difficulties, s/he is probably taking some kind of notes anyway, and could be quickly trained to work efficiently as a notetaker. It is possible for one notetaker to make as many as three or four good copies of the notes at the same time using pressure-sensitive, carbonless paper. This provides a copy for the teacher, the notetaker, one for the hearing-impaired student, and one for the tutor, if tutoring is done by another person.

Some classes may need only minimal notetaking—specific details about homework, reading to be done, points to be covered on the next test, dates of tests, etc., other classes require a detailed transcript of the class proceedings. By working with the classroom teacher, and taking into account the specific needs of each student, the notetaker and the manager of the notetaker service can decide on the level of notetaking required.

The purpose of this chapter is to describe the development of a tutoring and notetaking program in an educational setting. As we mentioned earlier, interpreting may also be an important part of any support services provided to hearing-impaired students in a mainstreamed environment if the student can utilize an interpreter effectively. In some instances, a tutor/notetaker may be the only appropriate support service. For details of developing an interpreting program, the reader is referred to Chapter 24 of this book.

REQUIREMENTS FOR TUTOR/NOTETAKERS

Tutoring/notetaking can be provided by a wide range of individuals: volunteers, peers, paraprofessionals, or professionals. As shown in Table 25.1 the decision on who does the notetaking must be based on several factors. Student or peer notetakers will cost no money for salaries, but turnover will be high and notes may be of lesser quality. On the other hand, students as notetakers can have a positive effect on social interaction between normally hearing and hearing-impaired students. This can be an especially positive result of mainstreaming. A hearing-impaired student acting as a tutor can also be an effective way to enhance the social interaction and reduce the dependent stance of the hearing-impaired students.

On the high school or junior high school level, normally hearing students can be notetakers (after appropriate training), reporting to the resource room teacher, classroom teacher or teacher for the hearing-impaired. These student notetakers can be "paid" with academic credit for independent study or community service activities. Other payments could be a page in the yearbook, an awards ceremony or a party. Upperclassmen taking notes for younger students also provide excellent role models, and the pride this gives to the tutor or notetaker can also be a form of payment in satisfaction.

Qualifications for Tutor/Notetakers

Regardless of whether a program director decides to use professionals, paraprofessionals, or volunteers, the following qualifications must be considered as basic for anyone taking notes or providing tutoring.

Background in the Subject Matter. A tutor or notetaker should have experience in the area for which they are providing services. This presents difficulties if students are used in these roles. Experience has shown that it is difficult to both be enrolled in the class for credit and be a tutor/notetaker at the same time. The roles can be mutually exclusive. For example, how can one participate in class discussion and take notes at the same time? This should be kept in mind and carefully

Table 25.1
Advantages and Disadvantages for Providers of Tutor/Notetaking Services[a]

Provider	Advantages	Disadvantages

Volunteers	Availability
	Low cost
		High turnover
		Undependable
		Little control over
		  quality
		Poor communication
		  skills

Paraprofessionals	Availability
	Moderate cost
	Control quality
	Fair communication
	  skills
	Dependable
		High turnover
		Require moderate
		  management

Professionals	Control quality Dependable Good communication skills Low turnover Management skills	Availability High cost

[a] From Osguthorpe et al. (1980).

monitored when it is necessary to have students responsible for taking notes for deaf students in their own classes.

Outstanding Academic Achievement. If students are to be the notetakers, they should have some recognized academic qualifications. One good source for recruiting at the secondary level is the local National Honor Society chapter or other organizations reflecting and recognizing academic excellence. Teachers can be contacted for recommendations of former outstanding students, or students themselves can recommend their peers.

Awareness of the Handicapping Effects of Hearing Loss. Everyone dealing with academic support services to the hearing-impaired should have a good orientation to hearing loss and problem engendered by the loss. Empathy, not sympathy, is vital. An understanding of the reasons some hearing-impaired students may exhibit unusual social and academic behaviors, the language levels of the students, specific learning problems, etc., are all necessary to write an appropriate set of notes or to provide information to the classroom teacher concerning specific students. It is also necessary to write notes to meet the specific needs of individual students

whose educational handicaps can vary widely.

Self-Assurance in Working with Teachers. It is natural for teachers to be hesitant about having hearing-impaired students or other handicapped students in class. These students can present problems the teachers are not prepared to handle. The teacher may not have had any previous experiences with anyone who is handicapped, much less have such a student in class. The tutor/notetaker can help the teacher in alleviating such fears by providing basic information, and acting as a liaison to others in the school or elsewhere who can be of support to the teacher's needs. The tutor/notetaker can be a resource to the teacher as well as the handicapped students.

Comfort in Accepting Criticism or Dealing with Hostility. It is also normal for anyone working in a support service function to be criticized—fairly or unfairly—and a tutor or notetaker must see the difference and react appropriately. Our experience has been that many times the hostility or criticisms from teachers are symptoms of real fear of deafness or lack of confidence in their own ability to meet the student's needs. The tutor/notetaker can calm these fears.

Ability to Accept Supervision. A tutor or notetaker must be prepared to work independently in the classroom, dealing with students and teachers, and at the same time be ready to accept guidance or supervision from others who may be more knowledgeable or who are in authority. Supervisors need to be kept informed of day-to-day happenings, particularly if a potential problem exists. These factors underline the need for good communication relationships.

TRAINING OF TUTOR/ NOTETAKERS

Notetaking, while it looks like a simple process on the surface, is *extremely* difficult. The notetaker must first of all understand what is being said, then consolidate and summarize the material, organize it meaningfully and write it down while listening to new information from the class proceedings. In some ways, it is more difficult than sign language interpreting because the notetaker is open to criticism by everyone who has access to the notes. For these reasons, the person who works as a notetaker should be well-trained and well-managed, and also well-rewarded, whether monetarily or with credit and recognition.

As a result, a well-developed program for training tutor/notetakers should be developed. Procedures for managing and developing a program for tutor/notetakers is well described in *The Tutor/Notetaker: Providing Academic Support to Mainstreamed Deaf Students* (Osguthorpe, 1980) and in *Manager's Guide to the Tutor/Notetaker: Providing Academic Support to Mainstreamed Deaf Students* (Osguthorpe et al., 1980).

A tutor/notetaker training program should be divided into three distinct sections: (1) training in the psychosocial impact of severe hearing loss, (2) training in tutoring, and (3) training in the techniques and functions of notetaking. The first area is most vital: information about hearing loss or deafness.

Psychosocial Impact of a Severe Hearing Loss

The typical student/candidate for a tutor/ notetaker should also be familiar with the psychosocial impact of deafness. Such a program should give particular attention to sensitizing new tutor/notetakers to this fact, and helping them deal first with their own attitudes, then with the attitudes of others with whom they must work. Because of their communication differences, whether it is using manual communication, or speaking with obvious difficulty, hearing-impaired persons are often ridiculed or ostracized. Even in college, teachers often show the same attitudes that hearing-impaired persons meet in other places. Educational society is not superior because it may be better-educated.

Nix (1976) and others have compared the problems of deafness with the problems of racial minorities, and the new legislation concerning the rights of the handicapped with civil rights laws. Education of the hearing-impaired brings with it all the hostilities and misconceptions that our culture has toward anyone who is different, whether that person is from a particular ethnic or racial group, is physically handicapped, or has a different accent or whatever—different often equals unwanted.

Tutor Training

Probably the greatest difference between teaching and tutoring is that good tutoring should be nonthreatening and individualized. No evaluation or grading is involved. Attention is given to the communication needs of the students, on *building trust and rapport*, and allowing the student to set the agenda and direction of tutoring sessions.

In training sessions, both preservice and inservice, experienced tutor/notetakers can be excellent as trainers. Role-playing, particularly, is a good training technique and the experienced tutor/notetakers are excellent for this type of activity. The experienced tutor/ notetakers can act as mentors for new peers and also for training hearing-impaired students in using tutoring/notetaking services, and for assistance in management.

A tutor/notetaker should be trained for the following eventualities:

Clarification of Procedures. Procedures clarification is a straightforward explanation of information on the procedures of the class, such as when assignments are due, what it should contain, and when examinations are scheduled, etc.

Preparation for Examination. In preparing a student for an examination, a tutor might work with the student on writing tests for practice by working on the specific topics and giving help on the specific skills necessary for test-taking.

Supplementing Course Content. This activity results in an in-depth, and perhaps remedial look at the course content. The tutor brings in supplementary materials, helps the student in defining vocabulary, outlines chapters in the textbook, or reworks class notes. This activity can actually be a form of re-teaching, and requires approaching the subject from an alternative direction. For this reason, adequate teaching skills are required on the part of the tutor. The teacher can also be involved in directing tutoring sessions, particularly on the elementary or secondary level where peer tutors would not be skilled in adapting materials or devising alternative approaches.

Special Project Development. Students are often confused and insecure about an independent assignment, or need help in choosing a topic and then going about doing the necessary work. The tutor can suggest several alternatives, then go through the process of topic selection with the student. This activity should not mean actually doing the work for students, but is like a "guided tour" helping them develop the skills necessary for independent work.

In each of the activities listed above, the role of the tutor should be that of striving to increase the independence and self-confidence of the student. Nothing is really achieved if the tutor forgets this fact. All support service personnel should probably be trying to decrease students' needs for support. The tutor can and should give the student the skills necessary to achieve independent learning rather than foster dependence. The tutor must become empathetic, supportive, non-punitive and encouraging

Notetaker Training

A training program for notetakers should include ample time for the potential notetakers to practice taking notes, then for evaluating them, discussing the experience, and discussing or comparing them with others. Dur-

ing the first 2 or 3 weeks after a notetaker begins work, the manager should give daily feedback to the notetaker. This attention can gradually be decreased, but should not be totally eliminated. Such monitoring will prevent the development of bad habits and help notetakers feel more secure in the quality of their own notes.

The duties and responsibilities of notetaking, summarized from *The Tutor/Notetaker* (Osguthorpe, 1980) are:

Be on Time to Class. Notetakers cannot have complete notes if they miss the beginning of class. Often dates for examinations are set, and assignments or other information are announced in the beginning of a class. The notetaker should also be unobtrusive in the class and coming in late is not a way to achieve this!

Get Feedback from Teachers and Students. Notetakers must establish an attitude of openness that will facilitate communication about problems and ensure that appropriate criticisms and suggestions are communicated. Evaluation must be a constant activity so feedback is essential.

Determine Your Role in Class. The teacher, the notetaker, and the students must know exactly what to expect from each other. Should the notetaker ask questions in class, for example, when something is not understood, or wait until after the class? Does the teacher want a copy of the notes each day? What kind of interaction between notetaker and teacher is most appropriate? Again, this is communication that must be established and maintained to prevent misunderstanding and foster a team spirit.

Be Unbiased. The opinions, beliefs, or attitudes of the notetaker should not be reflected in the notes, but a clear, objective restatement of the classroom proceedings and information should be written.

A sample page of notes, shown in Figure 25.1, illustrates some of the most crucial principles of effective notetaking. For example, look at the margins (white space), the organization, and the clarification of vocabulary in the notes. The teacher did not explain the vocabularly, such as "revolution," "evolution," expecting the students to know the words. The tutor/notetaker had personal knowledge of the hearing-impaired students' language difficulties, and explained the con-

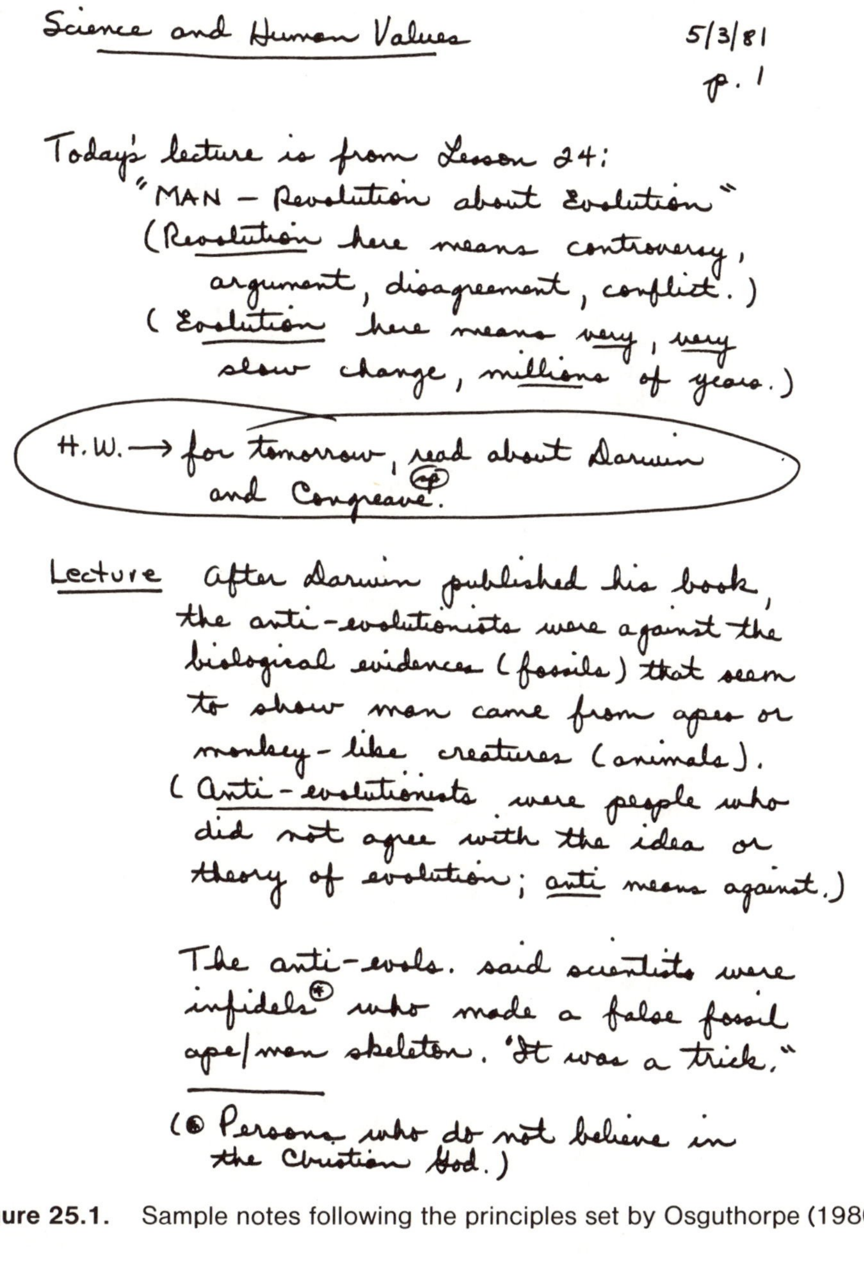

Science and Human Values   5/3/81

                                                    p. 1

Today's lecture is from Lesson 24:
    "MAN – Revolution about Evolution"
    (Revolution here means controversy,
        argument, disagreement, conflict.)
    (Evolution here means very, very
        slow change, millions of years.)

H.W. → for tomorrow, read about Darwin
        and Congreave.(sp)

Lecture   After Darwin published his book,
        the anti-evolutionists were against the
        biological evidences (fossils) that seem
        to show man came from apes or
        monkey-like creatures (animals).
        (Anti-evolutionists were people who
        did not agree with the idea or
        theory of evolution; anti means against.)

        The anti-evols. said scientists were
        infidels⊕ who made a false fossil
        ape/man skeleton. "It was a trick."

        _____

        (⊕ Persons who do not believe in
            the Christian God.)

Figure 25.1. Sample notes following the principles set by Osguthorpe (1980).

cepts with simple definitions or synonyms which can be amplified later in tutoring sessions. The notetaker was not sure about the spelling of Congreave, and indicated that by "Sp." Homework (H-W) is set off by a box, and the fact that the lecture is beginning is indicated. The notetaker also went back later and added a definition of the word "infidel." This was easy to do because enough space was routinely left at the bottom of the page.

For a more detailed description of the note-taking process, the reader is referred to *The Tutor/Notetaker* (Osguthorpe, 1980).

Advantages for Teachers

It is often surprising to classroom teachers to realize that the presence of support service personnel in their class is as much for the teacher's benefit as for the handicapped students. When the teacher and the support personnel begin to think of each other as part of a team, everyone benefits.

Dr. Fred L. Wilson, a veteran teacher at the Rochester Institute of Technology who regularly teaches classes including hearing-impaired and normally hearing students and uses support services, writes (Wilson, 1980):

> One of our faculty was suddenly taken ill and it was necessary for me to take over his course. The excellent set of notes on file for his course enabled me to take up exactly where he left off, continue as he planned, and remain faithful to his concept and expectations. We didn't plan for such emergencies but notes provided me a real asset when it did happen.

I mentioned before that support personnel must be diagnostic of student limitations. With my student load I cannot give deaf students all the attention they may require: how to use the library, how to write a research paper, how to present a class presentation, how to pick a topic for a project—all skills a college student is expected to bring to campus. The tutor/notetaker can assist students to become aware of their own limitations and to be specific about what they do not understand. This may be one of the most important qualities for success in college work.

Thus, the notes and tutoring are a valuable resource available to the teacher, enabling him or her to feel secure in that many of the special needs of the hearing-impaired student are being met without his encountering unreasonable demands. On the elementary and secondary level the notes also enable parents to have a good picture of what happens in class, knowledgeable to be in discussions with the teacher, and to support their children in homework and other class-related activities. If support personnel work toward helping teachers see benefits for themselves, all aspects of the program may be enhanced.

MANAGEMENT OF A TUTOR/ NOTETAKER PROGRAM

In addition to training, consistent, knowledgeable management of tutor/notetaking services provides a vital component to the success of the program. Depending on the setting, management can be done by a variety of persons. In public schools, some possibilities are the classroom teacher, the resource room teacher, the teacher of the deaf, the speech pathologist, the educational audiolo-

gist, the interpreter (if the interpreter also has credentials in education), or someone within the school administration. In college programs, a counselor or office of special services director can provide management.

Manager Qualifications and Duties

The manager should be familiar with the principles of tutoring and notetaking as well as be knowledgeable about the school environment and the principles of mainstreaming. The manager should be sensitive to the organization and to the needs of its various personnel, and make every effort to work within the organizational framework. For example, every organization has formal and informal communication networks, both of which are important for providing good support services.

Ideally, a manager should have background, training and experience in the educational problems of deafness and some practicum experience as a *provider* and *trainer* of persons in tutoring or notetaking services. It is difficult to evaluate a tutor/notetaker's work if the evaluator has no experience in providing the services, or has not been involved in training.

One major responsibility of a manager is recruiting and training of tutor/notetakers. Detailed information and suggestions on these procedures are included in *The Manager's Guide* (Osguthorpe et al., 1980). Although these manuals and materials were based on research done on the college level, field-testing in other settings has shown that the basic principles are valid at all educational levels.

The manager should keep in close contact with tutor/notetakers and with teachers in whose classes the tutor/notetakers are working. Regularly, at least once each term, the manager should make sure that everyone involved in the process—the teachers, tutor/notetakers, and hearing-impaired students—has, in writing, a description of the total program. The persons involved and their responsibilities should be included in an information packet. Students and teachers need an orientation or training session, with regular follow-up so that each is clear about the process. On the elementary level, and probably through high school, parents should also be included in this information sharing through the IEP process.

No assumptions of understanding should be made without consistent efforts at communication with everyone involved. Clear lines of communication should be established in the beginning and carefully maintained, so that appropriate and regular feedback and evaluation of the program can be assured.

SUMMARY

Notetaking and tutoring, particularly notetaking, have been found to be necessary support services for mainstreamed hearing-impaired students. These services can be provided by peers, older students, paraprofessionals, adults, volunteers or professionals. The key factors for a successful program are training and management. Notes are useful for students, teachers, parents, and resource personnel and can meet a variety of needs presented by most special needs students.

Though not as much research attention has been given to peer notetaking as to peer tutoring, it is logical to assume that the act of notetaking, paying close attention to classroom representations, etc., enhances the notetaker's listening skills and therefore has a positive effect on academic achievement in the same manner as peer tutoring (Hartley, 1977; Houser, 1974). When the pressure of tests, homework, and evaluation are taken away, notetakers can devote their attention fully to the material and seem to feel positive about their own learning in the situation. At least one professor who has had students before and after notetaking/tutoring training and experience reports a marked growth in hearing students' maturity and class achievement.

The resulting interaction between the students and tutor/notetakers should be positive. The hearing-impaired students are assured of equal access to classroom materials and teachers are freed from some of the extra attention that is necessary for handicapped students in a mainstreamed classroom.

The results are positive and costs can be low. The provision of tutoring and notetaking, as support services to hearing-impaired students, should be seen as a necessity and relatively simple to provide. These support services are now being provided in a wide variety of educational institutions, such as the Technical Vocational Institute, St. Paul, Minnesota; Seattle Central Community College, Seattle, Washington, and public schools in Chicago, and Rochester, New York. Hearing-impaired students are being given the support services that enable them to reach their potential and to participate more fully in their world.

References

Bishop, M., and Hurwitz, A.T. (eds.) Teaching hearing-impaired students in a mainstreamed environment. A checklist published at the Rochester, New York Institute of Technology, 1980.

Hartley, S. Meta-analysis of the effects of individually paced instruction in mathematics. Unpublished doctoral dissertation, University of Colorado, Boulder, Col., 1977.

Houser, V. Effects of student-aide experience on tutors' self-concept and reading skills. Unpublished doctoral dissertation, Brigham Young University, Provo, Utah, 1974.

Nix, G. *Mainstream Education for Hearing-Impaired Children and Youth.* New York: Grune & Stratton, 1976.

Osguthorpe, R. *The Tutor/Notetaker: Providing Academic Support to Mainstreamed Deaf Students.* Washington, D.C.: Alexander Graham Bell Association for the Deaf, 1980.

Osguthorpe, R., Wilson, J., Goldmann, W., and Panara, J. *Manager's Guide to the Tutor/Notetaker: Providing Academic Support to Mainstreamed Deaf Students.* Washington, D.C.: Alexander Graham Bell Association for the Deaf, 1980.

Wilson, F. The tutor/notetaker as a support service for deaf students: Viewpoint of a classroom teacher. Paper presented at the meeting of the Association on Handicapped Student Services Programs in Post Secondary Education, and published in the *Proceedings* of the conference, May 1980, Denver, Colorado.

Chapter 26

Amplification in the Classroom for the Deaf Student

MARY E. CAMPBELL, PH.D.

One of the most valuable resources available to teachers of hearing-impaired children is the maximum utilization of each student's residual hearing. However, to make optimal use of this potential avenue of learning, the careful fitting, monitoring and maintenance of amplification equipment must be practiced. Ling and Ling (1978, p. 86) state hearing aids have become the most important tool for optimally utilizing residual hearing. The importance of education and training in hearing aid use cannot be overemphasized. However, the students' and parents' attitude, the amount of effort devoted to training, and the type and location of the educational program or environment in which the student is expected to learn must also be taken into consideration. Further, it is critical to have persons available who have expertise in audiology and education of hearing-impaired students. Finally, it is necessary to carefully plan and provide for additional amplification equipment, such as extra hearing aids and hearing aid parts, to be used in the event of equipment failure. This chapter will explore some of these needs in the following sections.

EDUCATIONAL SETTINGS

A variety of educational settings are utilized for students who are hearing-impaired. Each setting may well have its advantages and disadvantages as an educational placement for hearing-impaired students. However, this chapter will attempt to examine these settings only as they relate to the utilization of a student's residual hearing.

Self-Contained Classrooms

A classroom which is designed exclusively for hearing-impaired students should have advantages over all other settings in providing a low noise environment. Such a classroom should be placed in a relatively quiet location within the school and should be designed to maintain a relatively low level of interfering noise generated both from within and outside the room. The following considerations are important for controlling the acoustic environment:

1. Controlling interference of outside noises, e.g., airplanes, trains, traffic, playground activity, hall traffic, noise from band or gymnasium activities;
2. Providing acoustical treatment of the classroom itself, e.g., acoustic tiles, absorbent cork boards or bulletin boards, carpeting and drapes;
3. Controlling interference from electrical equipment e.g., fluorescent lights, overhead projectors, air conditioners and heat-

ing systems free of excessive background noises.

All of the above-mentioned potential noise interference sources are important to control in *any* environment in which hearing-impaired students are educated, but to fail to attend to these features when designing rooms specifically for hearing-impaired students would be inexcusable. Self-contained classrooms may be located in schools for the deaf, in clinics, or in regular schools designed for nonhandicapped students. The ease of management of amplification may vary with location but the quality of the classroom acoustic environment should be equally easy to establish and maintain regardless of the specific type of facility housing the class. Further reading on classroom design and/or modification to specifications for deaf students is provided by Borrild (1978), and Bess and McConnell (1981).

Resource Rooms

Resource rooms are usually located in regular school settings. Some of these rooms are designed exclusively for hearing-impaired students. Other rooms may accommodate other types of handicapped students as well. Because this classroom may be designed for serving other types of handicapped students who may well be in the majority, one or two hearing-impaired students may not command the attention necessary to provide for optimal conditions in which to use their residual hearing. This type of situation must be carefully monitored. Even students with mild to moderate losses need training and monitoring in order to learn to utilize their residual hearing to advantage. All of the aforementioned issues related to providing a relatively noise free acoustic environment are equally important when locating, designing or equipping resource rooms within a school building.

Regular Classroom

The acoustics in classrooms for regular education standards vary considerably. Some are in relatively new buildings with quiet lighting and acoustically treated walls and ceilings. Other classes occupy rooms in old buildings with reverberating surfaces throughout and high untreated ceilings. Regardless of location, few rooms have carpeting and may have lighting, heating, and cooling systems which may produce considerable background noise. Administrators who are responsible for the placement of hearing-impaired students should consider the classrooms available and choose the setting carefully.

Special Purpose Learning Environments

Not all education occurs in the traditional setting of a regular classroom. Hearing-impaired students take classes in school shops, gymnasiums, and even out of doors. Each learning situation presents unique challenges for the student who needs to utilize information through a less-than-perfect auditory system. On-the-job training can also call for the utilization of specific types of amplification systems, such as an FM system which enables the hearing-impaired student to function most effectively.

AUDIOLOGICAL MANAGEMENT FACTORS

Personnel

It is important to examine the educational setting in which the student is expected to work, but it is also necessary to look at some less obvious factors such as geographical location, the size of the district, the availability of equipment, and the facilities and personnel to train students and to monitor the performance of the amplification equipment used. If the hearing-impaired student is located in a centralized program with many other hearing-impaired students, it is more likely that an educational audiologist will be available for monitoring equipment and for providing in-service training for teachers. If such a person is not a member of the staff, arrangements for such services may be made through contractual agreements with another school district, a hospital, or a university. School districts can work cooperatively and hire such a person on a shared-time basis. Small districts may contract with larger districts for this type of support help. Regardless of how it is obtained, it is strongly recommended that such a person should be available to assist teachers, parents, and students. This service is needed

no matter where the child is educated. The amount of time an audiologist works in a district will vary greatly and should be related to the size of the district, the number of students, and the amount of amplification equipment which needs to be monitored.

Repair Service

Another important service to establish is an in-house, amplification repair service, and/or a consulting company which will provide fast, quality service on every piece of auditory equipment used for hearing-impaired students in the school system. A staff member in the school system should be responsible for checking all malfunctioning equipment and sending the equipment in for repairs as needed. This person may be an audiologist, an administrator, or a teacher. However, a technician, a teacher aide, or a secretary may be assigned the responsibility of checking the equipment, if s/he has been trained to do so. Careful records should be kept of the equipment which is sent in and the specific problem it exhibits. Patterns of specific complaints should be noted in case that (1) practices which may tend to cause equipment to malfunction may be modified, and (2) equipment which is not durable will not be purchased in the future. Also, checking equipment which has been "repaired" and noting manufacturers' repair records, warranty problems, and length of service time are important. Money should be budgeted so that equipment can be kept in optimal working condition.

Hearing Aid Evaluations

The availability of clinics where hearing aid evaluations may be done is essential. Establishing good communication between school personnel and persons working in these clinics allows for cooperative planning and exchange of information concerning the effectiveness of specific hearing aids for a student both in the ideal setting of a sound-treated chamber and in the school environment. Otologists may also work closely with the schools regarding referrals and follow-up.

Hearing aid dealers may also be helpful and should be contacted when questions arise concerning a specific hearing aid which the dealer has sold to particular students. File cards containing specific information about each student's hearing aid are extremely useful to school personnel. Such records should contain the make, model, recommended setting, and dealer's name and telephone number. The battery type recommended and other pertinent information should also be listed. If students are using Crippled Children or other assistance programs, their number and date of expiration are important to note. Often parents appreciate a reminder of expiration dates so that they can renew their application early enough to avoid a lapse in coverage.

Consultants

Consultants from hospitals, universities, and knowledgeable state department personnel can be a valuable resource to programs for hearing-impaired. The closer these personnel work with the local programs the more understanding and mutual respect they will have for each other.

AMPLIFICATION EQUIPMENT

It is critical that a person who is knowledgeable of the type of program each student attends and who is familiar with the types of hearing aids and auditory training systems available should be involved in determining what amplification equipment should be worn by a hearing-impaired student in the various school settings. This person could be a teacher of hearing-impaired, a knowledgeable administrator, or an audiologist. No matter which person makes the decision, it is essential that they be familiar with:

1. The student's hearing loss and ability to utilize auditory information;
2. The type of classroom setting in which the student will be functioning;
3. The teacher's primary teaching style of instruction, i.e., class discussion, lecture, programmed instruction;
4. The amount of student-to-student communication necessary;
5. The noise level in which the instruction is given;
6. The availability of replacement units and

prompt repair in case of breakage of auditory equipment;
7. The willingness of the teacher to utilize and monitor equipment;
8. The cost of the equipment;
9. The versatility of the equipment;
10. The durability of the equipment.

There is an abundance of manufacturers of hearing aids and other amplification equipment which could be used by students within an educational setting. However, for purposes of this chapter, it is useful to put them into groups according to their method of transmission and reception.

Hard Wire Systems

The utilization of group amplifying systems in classrooms for hearing-impaired children has been practiced in many schools for the deaf since the early 1930's. The students are connected to a master unit through individual earphone control boxes, headset cords, and headsets or button type receivers. The teacher wears a microphone and may utilize a nondirectional microphone which hangs from the ceiling or is placed on the table. Directional table microphones are also commonly used.

Some of these units are still utilized today and can be very effective in certain situations (Johnson and Castle, 1976). The main limitation is the constraining nature of the cords, connecting headsets, and microphone. However, in tutoring situations these units work very well. The quality can be excellent when the units are maintained in good working order.

FM Systems

The most versatile and most widely used group amplifying equipment today are FM systems. These systems work by transmission and reception of the radiofrequency bands 72 through 75 megahertz. The teacher wears a unit which broadcasts to the students. Each student wears a unit which picks up the teacher's signal. The students may set their units so that they can hear each other through environmental hearing aid microphones contained within their individual units. The major advantage of this system is the freedom from restraining cords for the student and the teacher. They are both free to move about the room, building, or to work out of doors. The teacher can be heard clearly in any setting through the teacher's microphone when the student is trained to use the unit appropriately. Noise levels in a classroom could necessitate turning off the students' environmental microphones in order to obtain the clearest signal desired from the teacher.

One manufacturer makes an FM system in which each student unit broadcasts to the teacher's unit; and the teacher unit then rebroadcasts back to every other student unit. This system provides excellent quality of not only the teacher's messages but that of each student as well. Experience with this particular type of equipment has proved to be excellent for self-contained classrooms for hearing-impaired students.

Infrared Systems

This classroom system works like FM systems, except that it transmits true stereo with infrared light as the carrier signal. It has excellent fidelity, and is free of radio and adjacent classroom interference problems (direct sunlight from windows can interfere, however). The teacher's and students' speech is picked up by two environmental, hard wire microphones. The classroom system is not portable and component parts are expensive.

Loop Systems

Modern loop systems operate within a classroom or area which is surrounded by a wire or loop. The students wear their own hearing aids which receive a signal from the teacher or other students through inductance pick up on their hearing aid when set on the "Telephone" (T) position. The teacher wears a microphone and the student may use table, directional microphones or hear each other from nondirectional microphones placed in the classroom. They may also utilize the environmental microphones in each student's individual aid. Many of these units are still in use. However, the unsightliness of the loop wire, the problems with adjacent classroom interference, the hard wire connections limiting the mobility of the teacher, and the introduction of the FM auditory training systems have made most of these systems obsolete for classroom use. They may, however, be the most economical system for auditoriums and theaters. Installation of the loop must be carefully done to avoid dead spots in the inductive field which limit reception.

Combination Systems

There is at least one FM "miniloop" system which utilizes the child's personal hearing aid(s). This combination enables the student to wear the hearing aid as part of the amplification equipment used in the classroom. It allows the student to hear the teacher with minimum background noise through a teacher-worn FM transmitting microphone. A student FM unit picks up the teacher's signal and drives a small loop attached to the student unit. The student's own hearing aid set on the telephone position picks up the "miniloop" signal from the student unit. The classroom discussion is heard through the student's hearing aid microphone. Some personal hearing aids seem to operate much better than others with this system. Care must be taken to evaluate the quality of reception with each specific aid.

An excellent reference for more detailed information on all types of amplification equipment is Bess and McConnell's recent book, *Audiology, Education, and the Hearing-Impaired Child* (1981).

Individual Hearing Aids

The utilization of personal hearing aids is very common within the school environment. Even if other types of equipment are used within the classroom, many students should wear their personal hearing aids in other school situations, such as during class projects or discussions, on the playground, in study halls, or at lunch. An audiologist might recommend a body aid, a behind-the-ear aid, or in the case of mild losses, even an in-the-ear aid. Hopefully, two hearing aids are recommended when such is appropriate for the student. The hearing aids are fitted to each student's particular hearing loss. This personalized fitting should enable the student to utilize his/her residual hearing to advantage in many school settings. The advantage to students wearing their personally fitted hearing aids is just that! They are selected for each student because of how well that particular student profits with *that* particular hearing aid.

Monaural and Binaural Individual Hearing Aids

It has been my experience that fitting the student with two hearing aids generally improves the reception of speech and language. Also, the student can better localize the speaker or sound source. However, if the audiometric pattern of the hearing loss is very difficult between ears or if one ear distorts the signal so that it drastically interferes with the better ear, the audiologist will recommend the utilization of one hearing aid. If such is the case, the school personnel should be certain to utilize any group amplification on only *one* ear.

SET UP OF AMPLIFICATION EQUIPMENT

Most of the units in use today have a method of controlling the amount of sound received by each ear. Probably the control settings most easily understood by the child as well as the teacher are those on hard wire units. Usually these units have control boxes with a left and a right ear volume control knob.

The individual units for FM systems usually have adjustments which are relatively child-proof and must be set by an audiologist or by a teacher of the hearing-impaired who is familiar with the equipment. Some of the group units are binaural in that they have two separate microphones, located a few inches apart. The manufacturer claims that the units improve sound localization and true binaural amplification just as two behind-the-ear aids would. However, it is important to note that all signals received from a teacher who is utilizing a microphone is a nondirectional monaural signal. Only when the students are using environment microphones on their units are there any true binaural signals received.

This is true also of signals received directly from equipment such as movie projectors, tape, records, etc. If the auditory trainer is worn strictly for the reception of the teacher, in most cases the monaural units balanced

for both ears should do equally well as the more expensive binaural ones. If a student is only to utilize amplification in one ear, such a student should do well with a monaural unit also. The importance of knowing each child's amplification needs and having them utilize only the type of equipment which is necessary for them to obtain maximum benefit should be obvious. The most expensive equipment is not always best or necessary for a specific student in a given situation. School administrators should examine the situation carefully. It is often more important to have a supply of back-up units than it is to have only enough of what is perceived to be "the best" equipment available.

Individual Settings of Group Amplifying Equipment

Problems may occur if the unit is sent in for repair. Usually the unit is set on maximum and the volume is equalized for both right and left ears by the repairman. It is then returned to school with the test adjustments and not the settings which were set for the particular student. If the unit is returned to the student without being reset, the student will not be receiving the proper benefit from the unit. Careful records are necessary to insure the availability of information which is necessary to reset the unit after repair.

Microphone Placement

The proper utilization of microphones is critical when utilizing group auditory training equipment. If the sensitivity control for the microphone is set to amplify more than is necessary, it may pick up a great deal of background interference and distort the teacher's message. The teacher should adjust the microphone level only to the level necessary for the student to consistently hear clearly and with enough volume. This lower sensitivity helps to reduce interfering background noise which may be occurring in the environment. Each student can adjust his/her volume control to a comfortable listening level.

Another important aspect of using directional microphones is the need to speak relatively closely to the microphone. The directional microphone is designed to pick up only the sound source close to it. Therefore, putting it on a table or hanging it somewhere will not provide quality amplification. The manufacturers usually suggest the proper distance from the mouth for their product. The teachers should also experiment with the microphone to determine the best distance, remembering that the greater the distance between the teacher's mouth and the microphone, the greater the amount of noise which will mix and interfere with the teacher's speech. Head-mounted microphones similar to what telephone operators use have been found to be useful in higher background noise situations.

RULES FOR THE CLASSROOM TEACHER

One cannot help a student to maximize his/her residual hearing if that person is not completely familiar with the student's hearing loss and the hearing aids and equipment used by them. Teachers need to perfect their skills to detect even small variations in a student's ability to respond to auditory information. The teacher must set appropriate expectations for each student. This involves knowing how to interpret and apply good audiological information about that student, having familiarity with and checking for possible problems with equipment, and knowing what can be expected to be accomplished with it.

Answer These Questions

Obtain good otological/audiological data and make sure all of it is utilized to the student's advantage. Be able to answer the following questions:

1. Are there any problems which should be corrected medically? Is there evidence of an ear infection or other conductive hearing loss?
2. Is the equipment (hearing aids—auditory training unit) delivering both the quality and amount of volume for which it is set?
3. What should the student be expected to understand given the particular configuration of the hearing loss? Is it critical that goals be realistic but *not* constraining?
4. What does the student usually do given specific auditory tasks? Do you note any

changes from what would be expected? How do you account for these changes?
5. Are both ears receiving the type of amplification which is needed? If binaural amplification is not recommended, why not?
6. Are there special concerns such as emotional disturbance or loudness tolerance problems which make the utilization of residual hearing more difficult? What has been recommended to relieve the situation?

Match Equipment Set Up to the Classroom Activity

When choosing the appropriate amplification equipment for the student to use in a given situation, the following questions should be carefully considered.

1. To whom or to what is the student expected to be listening? Will the audio source change frequently?
2. How much interfering noise will be present within the environment?

If one person is doing the majority of the talking and if the background is noisy, the use of a directional microphone worn by the speaker may be especially effective. Controlling the use of environmental microphones used by the student receiver will also add to clearer reception. Environmental or nondirectional microphones always add interference if they are turned on when they are not being used. The "environmental microphone" can be an internal microphone within the receiver units, table microphones, or stationary nondirectional microphones. It is important to plan the proper use of these nondirectional microphones or not to use them at all when a clear (low background noise) signal from the speaker is desired. For example, if the student is using an FM system in a regular classroom s/he should be instructed to turn off the environmental microphone for that period of time when only the teacher is speaking. A much clearer signal will be received.

If the student wears a binaurally fitted hearing aid during group discussion rather than a group auditory training unit, s/he may receive more accurate auditory information as well as improve the ability to localize the speaker.

These are only a few examples of equipment usage considerations which should be studied. One should be encouraged to experiment with several variations in the set up of the system in order to match the particular needs of the situation. Do *not* accept a recommendation that "this system is best" when it comes from some other classroom situation. Be a critical observer and come to your own conclusions knowing the reasons for your decisions.

Train Students to Use Their Residual Hearing

Training in the use of a student's residual hearing is essential and should be part of every activity during the school day. There are some auditory training programs available (see Chapters 17–19) which can be used for the more structured lessons, but the utilization of a student's residual hearing must be part of *every* activity. Different expectations for each student may be necessary, but nearly all students are capable of developing skills in analyzing information through the use of their residual hearing. Provide them with this opportunity and the experience which is necessary to establish it as an avenue for learning.

Monitor Amplification Equipment

The most critical area in the utilization of residual hearing is providing consistent, quality amplification. It is an absolute crime to teach a student how to utilize auditory information to advantage and then to deprive him of it part of the time. This situation must be avoided at all costs! The following list of conditions will help.

1. Identify the person responsible for responding quickly to teachers who have located faulty amplification equipment. This person must have a replacement system available for the student or class.
2. Monitor auditory systems while in use. It is the teacher's responsibility to check both the students' receiver units and personal aids. Depending upon the age of the student, this checking should be done as often as is necessary to insure quality amplification for the student. It is highly recommended that electroacoustic hearing aid checking equipment be available to assist in monitoring equipment rather than re-

lying totally upon the sometimes faulty listening evaluation.

Teachers should have the following equipment:

1. A personal earmold, a monitor receiver, and stethoscope for listening checks of hearing aids and amplification equipment;
2. A battery tester which has a dial to show the strength of the hearing aid battery;
3. Extra batteries for each piece of equipment which may need them;
4. Extra parts (cords, headsets, microphone cords, etc.) at a nearby location;
5. Extra units or loaner stock of hearing aids available immediately upon request if a breakdown occurs.

The careful monitoring of the auditory systems should be seen as a prerequisite to beginning the teaching day.

SUMMARY

This chapter has described the types of amplification equipment available and how they may be used to best suit classroom activities. To do less than apply the very most effective method of providing each and every student with the opportunity to utilize his/her residual hearing to the fullest extent possible is to make the hearing-impaired child less resourceful than is necessary. It is up to us to "give him a break."

References

Bess, F., and McConnell, F. *Audiology, Education, and the Hearing-Impaired Child.* St. Louis: C.V. Mosby, 1981.

Borrild, K. Classroom acoustics. In M. Ross and T. Giolas (eds.) *Auditory Management of Hearing-Impaired Children.* Baltimore: University Park Press, 1978.

Freeman, B.A., Stephen, S.J., and Riggs, D.F. Classroom amplification: Considerations for systems selections. *Hear. Instruments,* June 1981, 16–17.

Gaeth, J.H., and Lounsbury, E. Hearing aids and children in elementary schools. *J. Speech Hear. Disord.,* 1966, 289–293.

Johnson, D., and Castle, W. *Info Series II: Equipment Designed to Improve the Communication Skills of the Deaf.* Rochester, N.Y.: National Technical Institute for the Deaf, 1976.

Ling, D., and Ling, A. *Aural Habilitation.* Washington, D.C.: Alexander Graham Bell Association for the Deaf, 1978.

Ling, D. *Speech and the Hearing Impaired Child: Theory and Practice.* Washington, D.C.: Alexander Graham Bell Association for the Deaf, 1976.

Index

Subject Index